The Rinehart Handbook for Writers

About the Title of This Book

Stanley M. Rinehart, Jr. (1897–1969), was a distinguished book publisher. In 1929, he, his brother Frederick, and editor John Farrar founded the publishing house of Farrar & Rinehart, which later became (in 1946) Rinehart & Company, and then (in 1960) Holt, Rinehart and Winston. As president of Rinehart & Company, Stanley Rinehart published such works as Norman Mailer's *The Naked and the Dead,* the "Nero Wolfe" detective novels of Rex Stout, and Rinehart Editions, a series of quality paperback editions of classic literature. The firm began its college department in 1934 and soon became a major publisher in the field, specializing in the humanities and social sciences. Today, Harcourt Brace College Publishers carries on this same tradition of publishing excellence through such noteworthy volumes as *The Rinehart Handbook for Writers, The Rinehart Guide to Grammar and Style,* and *The Rinehart Reader.*

The Rinehart Handbook for Writers

Fourth Edition

Bonnie Carter

Craig Skates

formerly of

The University of Southern Mississippi

Harcourt Brace College Publishers

Fort Worth Philadelphia San Diego

New York Orlando Austin San Antonio

Toronto Montreal London Sydney Tokyo

Publisher Christopher P. Klein
Executive Editor Michael Rosenberg
Developmental Editor Michell Phifer
Senior Project Editor Cliff Crouch
Project Editor Deanna Johnson
Senior Production Manager Tad Gaither
Production Manager Jane Tyndall Ponceti
Senior Art Director Don Fujimoto

Book design adapted from original text design by Caliber Design Planning and cover design by Albert D'Agostino

International Standard Book Number: 0-15-501984-8

Acknowledgments/Permissions

Dorothy Sayers. From "Are Women Human?" by Dorothy L. Sayers. First appeared in *Unpopular Opinions.* Reprinted by permission of David Higham Associates, Ltd. London.
Ann Sexton. "Cinderella," from *Transformations.* Copyright © 1971 by Anne Sexton. Reprinted by permission of Houghton Mifflin Co. All rights reserved.

Address for editorial correspondence: Harcourt Brace College Publishers, 301 Commerce Street, Suite 3700, Fort Worth, Texas 76102

Address for orders: Harcourt Brace, Inc., 6277 Sea Harbor Drive, Orlando, Florida, 32887

Phone: 800/782-4479, or (in Florida only) 800/433-0001

Printed in the United States of America

6 7 8 9 0 1 2 3 4 5 016 9 8 7 6 5 4 3 2

To the Instructor

Each composition class is unique. The abilities and attitudes of students vary from class to class, and the teaching styles of instructors change as their experience, priorities, and students change. Because of this special environment, *The Rinehart Handbook for Writers,* Fourth Edition, is comprehensive and flexible. It suits a variety of teaching methods and a broad spectrum of course content. For a given class, instructors can choose either a single strategy or a combination of strategies from the following options.

Language Study

Instructors who wish to focus on language can begin with Part I (Review of the Basics), which describes the traditional system of word classes, and can then move to Parts II (Structural and Grammatical Problems) and III (Punctuation and Mechanics), which emphasize clarity and correctness. Part IV (Style) concentrates on techniques for manipulating material and appealing to audiences through word choice and sentence structure. Language is also the focus of Section 39e (Evaluation of Evidence), which treats such subjective topics as emotional appeals and diversions, imprecision, equivocation, and logical fallacies. Appendices A and B contain information on spelling and English as a second language. The Glossary of Usage demonstrates that preferred usage depends sometimes on clarity and logic and other times on fashion and the choices made by influential writers. The Glossary of Terms supplies quick answers to questions about meaning and locates detailed explanations within the text.

Traditional Composition

Instructors who prefer to teach a traditional course in composition will find that Part V (The Writing Process) explains how to develop a paper—from choosing a subject through revising the final draft. "Argument and Critical Thinking" (Chapter 39) leads students through the stages of an argumentative paper—developing the subject and the conflict, framing a thesis, gathering evidence, examining logic, and choosing a structure. This chapter also emphasizes the critical thinking required in any writing project.

Research Paper Writing

Instructors who wish to teach the research paper will find a complete guide in Chapters 40 and 41. In fact, there is ample material for an entire course on research writing. "Research Papers in Progress" and "Research Papers and Documentation" make up a comprehensive and practical manual for researching, writing, incorporating sources, documenting, and typing. These chapters explain two styles of documentation (MLA and APA) and include three student models (one on Mark Twain's desertion from the military, one on discrimination in Japanese business, and one on Anne Sexton's modern version of "Cinderella"). In addition, Chapter 39 (Argument and Critical Thinking) features material on gathering information, finding a thesis, and evaluating evidence. This chapter also includes a documented research paper.

Writing across the Curriculum

The Rinehart Handbook provides many varied writing projects appropriate for students taking courses in the liberal arts, science, business, and many other disciplines. In Part V (The Writing Process), sample subjects and paragraphs illustrate prose from disciplines such as archaeology, sociology, film, history, sports, language, biology, zoology, law, literature, ecology, aviation, chemistry, computer science, recreation, and technology. This mix, which extends throughout the handbook, stresses the importance of writing outside the composition classroom.

Word Processing

Material on word processing appears throughout the text wherever it is pertinent to the tasks that students are undertaking. Highlighted boxes labelled *The Computer Connection,* which appear frequently throughout Part V (The Writing Process), help students use computers to find a subject, organize the paper, draft the paragraphs, revise, and edit the final work. These *Computer Connection* boxes also provide detailed information explaining how to use computerized spell checkers, thesauruses, library references, and indexes. In addition, the Glossary of Terms contains a handy list of computer terminology.

Whatever the focus, students will benefit from developing their skills and transforming their prose into a satisfactory product. They will, we hope, learn to view this handbook as a reference tool for use inside and outside the composition classroom.

The Teaching and Learning Package

For the Instructor

Exercises to accompany The Rinehart Handbook for Writers, Fourth Edition. The exercises are plentiful and apply to all sections of the text, including the appendices on spelling and English as a second language. Many of the exercises are passages for editing, which instructors can assign for practice or for tests. The *Exercises* can be purchased alone or packaged with *The Rinehart Handbook* for a slight additional charge.

Instructor's Manual with Answer Key to accompany The Rinehart Handbook for Writers, Fourth Edition. The manual includes general advice for beginning instructors as well as suggestions for teaching each major section of the text. Instructors can request that both the exercises and the answer key be packaged with *The Rinehart Handbook for Writers,* Fourth Edition.

For the Student

Writing in the Disciplines, Third Edition. With comprehensive coverage of the recently updated MLA and APA styles and CBE documentation, this guide helps students write research papers in the humanities, social sciences, sciences, and business. Ten sample student papers across the disciplines are included.

Preparing for the TASP® provides students with two complete grammar and essay sections based on the Texas state exam. Writing prompts give sample topics, and student essays illustrate levels of competency for the essay portion of the test. The answer key briefly explains each correct response and cross-references the *Rinehart Handbook* for further clarification.

Preparing for the CLAST® also provides two grammar and essay sections based on the Florida state exam. Essay-writing tips and sample writings help students prepare for the essay competency test. The answer key again briefly explains each correct response. Cross-references to the *Rinehart Handbook* give users the location of appropriate material.

Webster's Collegiate Dictionary, Tenth Edition, in either hard or soft cover, may be purchased together with *The Rinehart Handbook* at a substantially reduced price.

Software

For the Instructor

ExaMaster. A computerized test bank available for DOS, Windows, and Macintosh operating systems, *ExaMaster* includes 800 questions for skill testing and diagnostic evaluation. These questions will include chapter references to the *Handbook,* allowing instructors to direct students to particular sections for clarification and further study. Questions appear in two different formats: multiple choice and error identification. Instructors can utilize this versatility by choosing questions by type, by chapter, or at random; they can even write their own. *ExaMaster* is available with a Scantron interface.

For the Student

Writing Tutor IV. This individualized software tutorial program provides additional instruction and practice on topics that range from commas to paragraph development. The program offers a variety of exercise formats (highlighting, completion, sentence and paragraph writing) and encourages students to make several attempts at correct answers. The program provides an explanation for both correct and incorrect responses and maintains students' scores. It is available for DOS, Windows, and Macintosh operating systems.

Rinehart On-Line. As an on-line handbook, *Rinehart On-Line* works with any word processing program to give students ready access to handbook references while composing. It is a valuable ancillary for any English department with a computer writing lab that uses either Macintosh, Windows, or DOS operating systems.

For complimentary copies of these teaching and learning aids, please contact your local sales representative, or write to: English Marketing Manager, Harcourt Brace College Publishers, 301 Commerce, Suite 3700, Fort Worth, Texas 76102.

Acknowledgments

We thank the following colleagues for the comments and advice on previous editions: Steve Adams, Northeast Louisiana University; Joy Allameh, Eastern Kentucky University; Kristine Anderson, Southern Technical Institute; Bruce Appleby, Southern Illinois University; Tracey Baker, University of Alabama—Birmingham; Conrad Bayley, Glendale Community College; Jane Bouterse, Texarkana College; Henry Brown, Midwestern State University; Alma Bryant, Fort Valley State College; Rebecca Butler, Dalton College; James Bynum, Georgia Tech; Joe Christopher, Tarleton State University; Peggy Cole, Arapahoe Community College; Deborah Core, Eastern Kentucky University; James Creel, Alvin Community College; Joseph Davis, Memphis State University; Ralph Dille, University of Southern Colorado; Charles Dodson, University of North Carolina; Linda Doran, Volunteer State Community College; Joseph Dunne, St. Louis Community College at Meramec; Elizabeth Fifer, Lehigh College; Eleanor Garner, George Washington University; Jan Goodrich, Embry-Riddle Aeronautical University; George Haich, University of North Carolina—Wilmington; Charles Hall, Memphis State University; June Hankins, Southwest Texas State University; Stephen Hathway, Wichita State University; David Higgins, Cameron University; Gertrude Hopkins, Harford Community College; Peggy Jolly, University of Alabama—Birmingham; Edwina Jordan, Illinois Central College; Edward Kline, University of Notre Dame; Cheryl Koski, Louisiana State University; Ruth Laux, Arkansas Technical University; Jane E. Lewis, University of Southern Mississippi; Russell Long, Tarleton State University; Andrea Lunsford, University of British Columbia; Robert Lynch, New Jersey Institute of Technology; Lisa McClure, Southern Illinois University—Carbondale; Beverly McKay, Lenoir Community College; Louis Molina, Miami-Dade Community College South; Sam Phillips, Gaston College; Kenneth Rainey, Memphis State University; Sally Reagan, University of Missouri—St. Louis; Edward Reilly, St. Joseph's College; John Reuter, Florida Southern College; Michael Rossi, Merrimack College; Cheryl Ruggiero, Virginia Polytechnic Institute and State University; Gary Simmers, Dalton College; Mike Slaughter, Illinois Central College; Joyce Smoot, Virginia Polytechnic Institute and State University; Charles Sphar, Delmar College; Jo Tarvers, University of North Carolina—Chapel Hill; John Taylor, South Dakota State University; Elizabeth Thomas, University of New Orleans—Lake Front; George Trail, University of Houston; Daryl Troyer, El Paso Community College; Gloria Tubb, Jones County Junior College; Richard Vandeweghe, University of Colorado at Denver; Harold Veeser, Wichita State University; Art Wagner, Macomb Community College; Laura Weaver, University of Evansville; Betty Wells, Central Virginia Community College; Jack White, Mississippi State University; Marie Wolf, Bergen Community College; Peter Zoller, Wichita State University; Carolyn Drakeford, Benedict College; Chick White, West Texas State University; Noel Mawer, Edward Waters College; Patricia Phillips, Detroit College of Business; Donald Anderson, Marist College; David Rosenwasser, Muhlenberg College; Virginia Polanski, Stonehill College; Richard Kleinman, Cumberland College; Charlotte Perlin, University of Miami; Chris Baker, Lamar University; and Albert Wilhelm, Tennessee Technical University.

Thanks also go to these colleagues for their comments and advice on the fourth edition: George Crandell, Auburn University; Edward Palm, Glenville State College; Donna Smith, Odessa College; Mary Sauer, Indiana University—Purdue University at Indianapolis; Margaret Arnold, Baker College—Flint; Lennet Daigle, North Georgia College; Judith Bentley, South Seattle Community College; Michael Kleeberg, Ball State University; Harry Papagan, Lord Fairfax Community College; and David Miller, Fayetteville Technical Community College.

In addition, we are indebted to Penny Stewart for her work on Appendix B: English as a Second Language; to Michael Salda for his expertise in documenting electronic sources; and to Robert Dornsife and David Roberts for their material updating the Computer Connections. Their contributions eased our burdens and improved the book.

Many thanks to the staff at Harcourt Brace who made the fourth edition possible. Thanks to Michell Phifer, our developmental editor, for keeping us on track. Thanks to Michael Rosenberg, our executive editor, for his innovative ideas and unfailing good nature. Finally, we owe a very special debt to Clifford Crouch, our senior project editor, who tackled all problems with patience and solved them with skill.

B.C.
C.S.

To the Student

A handbook should be handy. In other words, you should have no difficulty finding in it the material you need. If you are using *The Rinehart Handbook for Writers,* Fourth Edition, in a composition class, your instructor can help you learn how to locate information. Remember, however, that you will not always have an instructor to guide you. Therefore, you should become familiar with the organization so that you can find information quickly and easily.

Look carefully at the table of contents to determine what material is available and where it appears. Learn to use the index and glossaries. Make sure you understand the correction symbols and the numbering system of the book. Pay close attention to cross-references; they direct you to related sections of the text. Also, if you use a word processor for writing, consult the highlighted boxes labelled *The Computer Connection.* These boxes appear throughout the text to offer advice for using a word processor creatively and efficiently.

The Rinehart Handbook for Writers contains all the information you need for writing in the classroom and most of what you need for writing in a professional setting. If you use the book effectively, you may be surprised at how much your writing skills improve—and with them your confidence in yourself and your future.

The Computer Connection

Throughout this handbook, you will find highlighted boxes that are labelled *The Computer Connection.* Each box contains advice on how to use word processing for specific writing tasks; each relates directly to the material immediately preceding the box. In addition, words and phrases common to word processing appear in the Glossary of Terms.

Although it may take some getting used to, the computer can make writing much easier. Mistakes can be eliminated in an instant; retyping entire papers is never necessary; material can be easily moved; and aids such as spelling checkers and graphics programs are available. If you have little experience writing with a computer, look over the list below. It offers practical advice about common pitfalls.

Suggestions for the Computer Novice

- Save your work after every paragraph or so to avoid losing data if there is a power loss or other computer failure.
- Set the automatic save command of the word processor to save your file at least every ten minutes.
- Make backup copies of your files. Keep at least two computer disks. Label one "work disk" and the other "backup disk." Make backups of the work disk every time you change a file.
- Store computer disks at room temperature. Extremely cold temperatures can make the magnetized plastic brittle and also more susceptible to static electricity. Extremely high temperatures and direct sunlight can warp disks and make them unreadable.
- Keep disks away from electronic devices such as radios and television sets. Avoid dust, dirt, and moisture.
- Do not touch the plastic media inside the disk cover. Never open the shutter that covers the plastic media.
- On IBM-compatible machines, insert and remove disks from drives only after the drive light has gone off, indicating that the drive has stopped spinning.
- Use a program such as Disinfectant (freeware) or McAfee's Virus Scan to check your disks for viruses—computer programs designed to destroy or alter data on a disk.
- Be cautious about letting others put their disks into your computer. Make sure their disks have been previously scanned for viruses.

Contents

To the Instructor v
To the Student xi

Part I

A Review of the Basics 1

1 Nouns 2
1a Proper and Common Nouns 3
1b Singular and Plural Nouns 4
1c Possessive Nouns 5

2 Pronouns 6
2a Personal Pronouns 7
2b Demonstrative Pronouns 8
2c Relative Pronouns 9
2d Interrogative Pronouns 10
2e Indefinite Pronouns 10

3 Adjectives and Adverbs 12
3a Adjectives 12
3b Adverbs 13
3c Adjective and Adverb Forms 15

4 Verbs and Verb Phrases 17
4a Basic Forms 17
4b Auxiliaries and Verb Phrases 18
4c Tense 20
4d Progressive Forms 22
4e Voice 23
4f Mood 24

5 Verbals and Verbal Phrases 28

5a Infinitives and Infinitive Phrases 28
5b Participles and Participial Phrases 29
5c Gerunds and Gerund Phrases 30
5d Absolute Verbal Phrases 30

6 Function Words 32

6a Prepositions and Prepositional Phrases 32
6b Conjunctions 33
6c Determiners 37
6d Expletives 38

7 Clauses and Sentences 40

7a Clause Patterns 40
7b Independent Clauses 45
7c Dependent Clauses 45
7d Elliptical Clauses 50
7e Kinds of Sentences 50

Part II

Structural and Grammatical Problems 53

8 Sentence Fragments 54

8a Dependent Clause Fragments 55
8b Phrase Fragments 56

9 Comma Splices and Fused Sentences 54

9a Revision with a Comma and a Coordinating Conjunction 58
9b Revision with a Semicolon 58
9c Revision with a Colon 60
9d Revision by Creating Two Sentences 60
9e Revision with a Dependent Clause or Phrase 60

10 Subject-Verb Agreement 62

10a Intervening Words between Subject and Verb 64
10b Subjects Joined by *And* 64

10c Subjects Joined by *Or/Nor* 65
10d Indefinite Pronouns As Subjects 65
10e Relative Pronouns As Subjects 67
10f Subjects of Linking Verbs 67
10g Subjects That Follow Verbs 67
10h Collective Nouns and Amounts As Subjects 68
10i Titles As Subjects 69
10j Foreign Nouns As Subjects 69
10k Subjects Ending in *-ics* 69
10l "Words" As Subjects 70

11 Nonstandard Verb Forms 71
11a Nonstandard Principal Parts 71
11b Dropped *-s/-es* and *d/-ed* Verb Endings 72
11c Verbs Confused with Similar Words 73

12 Pronoun Reference 74
12a Implied Reference 74
12b Broad Reference 75
12c Indefinite *You, They,* and *It* 76
12d Ambiguous Reference 77
12e Mixed Uses of *It* 77
12f Remote Reference 78
12g Titles and Headings As Antecedents 78

13 Pronoun-Antecedent Agreement 80
13a Antecedents Joined by *And* 81
13b Antecedents Joined by *Or/Nor* 81
13c Indefinite Pronouns and Sexist Language 82
13d Generic Nouns and Sexist Language 83
13e Collective Nouns As Antecedents 83

14 Case of Nouns and Pronouns 85
14a Case in Compound Constructions 86
14b Pronoun Case after *Be* 87
14c *Who/Whom* and *Whoever/Whomever* 88
14d Case in Elliptical Clauses 89
14e Possessive Case with Gerunds 89

15 **Nonstandard Adjective and Adverb Forms 91**
15a Confusion of Adjectives and Adverbs 91
15b Inappropriate Comparative and Superlative Forms 92
15c Inappropriate Demonstratives 94

16 **Dangling and Misplaced Modifiers 95**
16a Dangling Modifiers 96
16b Misplaced Modifiers 99

17 **Shifts 102**
17a Shifts in Tense Sequence 102
17b Shifts in Infinitives and Participles 105
17c Shifts in Mood 107
17d Shifts in Voice 107
17e Shifts in Number 108
17f Shifts in Person 108
17g Shifts between Direct and Indirect Discourse 109
17h Mixed Constructions or Faulty Predications 109

18 **Split Constructions 112**
18a Split Subjects and Verbs 112
18b Split Verbs and Complements 113
18c Split Verbs 113
18d Split Infinitives 114

19 **Incomplete Constructions 116**
19a Omissions in Compound Constructions 117
19b Omitted *That* 117
19c Incomplete Comparisons 118

20 **Parallelism 120**
20a Parallelism in Compound Structures 121
20b Parallelism in Series, Lists, and Outlines 123

Part III

Punctuation and Mechanics 127

21 Commas 128

21a Commas between Independent Clauses Joined by Coordinating Conjunctions 128
21b Commas after Introductory Prepositional Phrases, Verbals, and Dependent Clauses 129
21c Commas to Set Off Nonrestrictive Elements 132
21d Commas between Items in a Series and between Coordinate Adjectives 135
21e Commas in Place of Omitted Words 137
21f Commas to Set Off Parenthetical, Transitional, and Contrastive Elements 137
21g Commas to Set Off Interjections, Words in Direct Address, and Tag Questions 139
21h Commas in Special Contexts: in Dates, Places, Addresses; in Numbers; with Titles of Individuals; with Quotation Marks 140
21i Commas to Ensure Intended Reading 142
21j Inappropriate Commas 142

22 Semicolons 145

22a Semicolons between Independent Clauses Not Joined by Coordinating Conjunctions 145
22b Semicolons between Independent Clauses Joined by Transitional Expressions 146
22c Semicolons between Independent Clauses Joined by Coordinating Conjunctions 147
22d Semicolons between Items in a Series with Internal Punctuation 148
22e Inappropriate Semicolons 149

23 Colons 150

23a Colons before Lists 150
23b Colons before Appositives That End Sentences 151
23c Colons between Independent Clauses 151

23d Colons before Grammatically Independent Quotations 152
23e Colons between Titles and Subtitles 152
23f Colons in Correspondence 152
23g Colons with Numerical Elements 153
23h Inappropriate Colons 153

24 Dashes, Parentheses, and Brackets 155
Dashes 155
24a Dashes to Set Off Appositives Containing Commas 155
24b Dashes to Set Off Nonrestrictive Modifiers Containing Commas 156
24c Dashes to Emphasize Sentence Elements 156
24d Dashes with Interrupters 157
Parentheses 157
24e Parentheses to Enclose Interrupters 157
24f Parentheses for References to Pages, Figures, Tables, and Chapters 158
Brackets 158
24g Brackets around Insertions in Direct Quotations 158
24h Brackets for Parentheses inside Parentheses 159

25 Periods, Question Marks, and Exclamation Points 160
Periods 161
25a Periods as End Punctuation 161
25b Periods in Outlines and Displayed Lists 161
25c Inappropriate Periods 162
Question Marks 162
25d Question Marks as End Punctuation 162
25e Question Marks within Sentences 163
Exclamation Points 164
25f Exclamation Points in Dialogue 164
25g Exclamation Points with Interjections 164
25h Exclamation Points for Emphasis 164

26 Apostrophes 166
26a Apostrophes to Indicate Possession 166
26b Apostrophes to Create Contractions 168

26c Apostrophes to Indicate Plurals of Letters and Words Used as Words 168
26d Inappropriate Apostrophes 169

27 **Quotation Marks and Ellipsis Marks 171**
Quotation Marks 171
27a Quotation Marks to Enclose Direct Quotations 171
27b Quotation Marks with Other Punctuation Marks 173
27c Quotation Marks in Dialogue 175
27d Quotation Marks in Titles 175
27e Quotation Marks around Words Used in Special Ways 176
27f Inappropriate Quotation Marks 176
Ellipsis Marks 177
27g Ellipsis Marks to Show Omissions 177
27h Ellipsis Marks to Show Interruption in Dialogue 180

28 **Italics/Underlining 181**
28a Italics/Underlining in Titles 181
28b Italics/Underlining for Words, Numbers, and Letters Used as Such 184
28c Italics/Underlining for Sounds 185
28d Italics/Underlining for Foreign Words 185
28e Italics/Underlining for Vehicles Designated by Proper Names 185
28f Italics/Underlining for Emphasis 186

29 **Hyphens and Slashes 187**
Hyphens 187
29a Hyphens in Compound Nouns and Verbs 187
29b Hyphens in Compound Modifiers 188
29c Hyphens with Some Prefixes 189
29d Hyphens in Numbers 190
29e Hyphens for Word Divisions at the Ends of Lines 191
Slashes 191
29f Slashes between Alternatives 191
29g Slashes for Making Combinations 192
29h Slashes between Lines of Poetry 192
29i Slashes for Fractions 192

30 **Abbreviations and Numbers** 193

Abbreviations 193

30a Abbreviations vs. Full Words 193

30b Punctuation and Capitalization in Abbreviations 196

Numbers 197

30c Numbers Expressed in Numerals 197

30d Numbers Expressed in Words 198

30e Mixed Numerals and Words 199

31 **Capital Letters** 200

31a Capitalization of First Words 200

31b Capitalization of Proper Names and Proper Adjectives 202

31c Capitalization of Titles of Honor or Rank 204

31d Capitalization of Academic and Professional Degrees 205

31e Capitalization in Titles of Written Material and Artistic Works 206

31f Capitalization in Some Abbreviations 207

31g Capitalization of *I* and *O* 207

31h Inappropriate Capitals 207

Part IV

Style 211

32 **Word Choice** 212

32a Levels of Formality 212

32b Precise Prose 214

32c Vigorous Prose 217

32d Cluttered Prose 221

32e Discriminatory Language 226

33 **Sentence Style** 230

33a Variety 230

33b Emphasis 242

33c Streamlining 246

33d Figures of Speech 254

33e Sound and Rhythm 255

Part V

The Writing Process 259

34 The Search for Ideas 260
34a Journals 260
34b Meditation 261
34c Brainstorming 262
34d Clustering 263
34e Freewriting 264
34f Ladders 265
34g Question 266
34h Classical Topics 269
34i Reading and Listening 270

35 Decisions 273
35a Purpose 273
35b Audience 274
35c Voice 276
35d Thesis 279
35e Patterns 284
35f Outlines 291

36 Paragraphs 296
36a Body Paragraphs 297
36b Introductory Paragraphs 308
36c Concluding Paragraphs 315

37 Revision 322
37a Unity 323
36b Development 326
37c Coherence 328
37d Style 336
37e Grammar, Punctuation, and Mechanics 339
37f Titles 343
37g The Finished Paper 344

38 Composition in Progress 350

Part VI

Special Writing Projects 361

39 Argument and Critical Thinking 362
39a Subject 363
39b Conflict 364
39c Thesis 367
39d Kinds of Evidence 368
39e Evaluation of Evidence 371
39f Structure 381
39g Sample Argument 387

40 Research Papers in Progress 394
40a Subject 394
40b Purpose 398
40c Preliminary Library Research 403
40d Working Bibliography 417
40e Locating Material 418
40f Working Outline 419
40g Note-taking 421
40h Plagiarism 422
40i Using Sources 426
40j Drafting the Paper 428

41 Research Papers and Documentation 433
41a MLA Documentation 434
41b Sample Research Paper Using MLA Style—Answering a Question 447
41c Sample Research Paper Using MLA Style—Interpreting Literature 457
41d APA Documentation 469
41e Sample Research Paper Using APA Style—Presenting an Argument 478

Appendix A Spelling 487
SPa Tips for Improving Spelling 488
SPb Spelling Patterns 490
SPc Lists of Frequently Misspelled Words 495

Appendix B English as a Second Language 498

ESLa The Noun Phrase 499
ESLb Head Nouns 499
ESLc Determiners 500
ESLd Pre-Determiners 504
ESLe Pre-Noun Modifiers 505
ESLf Post-Noun Modifiers 507
ESLg The Active-Voice Verb Phrase 508
ESLh Tense 510
ESLi Modal Auxiliaries 511
ESLj Auxiliaries *Have* and *Be* 512
ESLk Passive-Voice Verb Phrase 512
ESLl *Do* Auxiliary 513
ESLm Chains of Verbs 514
ESLn Questions 517
ESLo Negative Sentences 518
ESLp Tag Questions to Identify Sentences 519

Glossary of Usage 522

Glossary of Terms 550

Index 589

PART

I

A REVIEW OF THE BASICS

The grammar of a language is a system of predictable patterns: words fit together to form phrases; phrases join to form clauses; clauses create sentences. If you can recognize the system's components, you can understand descriptions of acceptable or effective constructions, and you can look up information in an index or glossary. In short, recognition underlies improvement of your writing skills.

1 Nouns
2 Pronouns
3 Adjectives and Adverbs
4 Verbs and Verb Phrases
5 Verbals and Verbal Phrases
6 Function Words
7 Clauses and Sentences

CHAPTER

1

NOUNS

Nouns are commonly defined as "words that name persons, places, or things." Although this definition is rather limited, it does contain a key word—*name.* Anything in the physical and mental worlds can be named with a noun.

PEOPLE:	Susan, doctor, singer, family
PLACES:	ocean, Canada, home, campus
THINGS:	popsicle, shoe, fingernail, crater
QUANTITIES:	pound, quart, inch, dollar
SENSES:	sound, smell, taste, feel
FEELINGS:	hope, disappointment, anxiety, peace
OCCURRENCES:	earthquake, wedding, party, contest
ACTIONS:	handshake, smile, leap, wink

You can usually recognize a noun by its function, that is, the position it fills in a phrase or a sentence.

- Nouns follow the articles *a, an,* and *the.*

a field   the light

an apple   the car

- Nouns appear in phrases after descriptive words known as modifiers.

a muddy field	the bright light
a red apple	the new car

- Nouns join with prepositions to form prepositional phrases.

through a field	behind the light
in an apple	under the car

- Nouns join with other nouns to form compounds and phrases.

field house	light bulb
apple pie	car wreck

- Nouns join with verbs to form sentences.

A field lay between the house and the lake.

Pat gave the teacher an apple.

The light was brilliant.

My most pressing problem was my car.

1a PROPER AND COMMON NOUNS

Proper nouns are official names, such as names of people, organizations, geographical locations, holidays, languages, and historical events. You can easily recognize proper nouns in prose because they begin with capital letters. **Common nouns,** all other nouns, are usually not capitalized unless they appear as the first word in a sentence. (See Chapter 31.)

Proper Nouns	Common Nouns
Muhammad Ali	athlete
United Kingdom	country
Saks	store

Okefenokee	swamp
English	language

1b SINGULAR AND PLURAL NOUNS

Nouns have **number**—that is, they are either **singular** or **plural.** Singular nouns refer to one person, place, or thing; plural nouns to more than one. Disregarding number can lead to errors in agreement of subject and verb. (See Chapter 10.)

(1) Simple nouns

Most nouns form plurals with the addition of *-s* or *-es,* sometimes with a slight adjustment in spelling, such as changing *y* to *i* or doubling a consonant.

SINGULAR	PLURAL
week	weeks
box	boxes
quiz	quizzes
destiny	destinies
hero	heroes

Some nouns form plurals in unpredictable ways.

SINGULAR	PLURAL
leaf	leaves
foot	feet
mouse	mice
child	children
salmon	salmon
criterion	criteria

(2) Compound nouns

A compound noun is made up of two or more words functioning as a single noun. The forms of compounds are somewhat unpredictable. In some, the words are separated (*half dollar*); in others, hyphenated (*man-of-war*); and in others, written together (*holdup*).

In addition, the plurals of compounds are formed in different ways. Regularly, the last word in the compound is plural (*gentlemen, backlogs, pocket knives*). But sometimes, the first word is plural (*sisters-in-law, leaves of absence*). And occasionally, either way is acceptable (*attorney generals* or *attorneys general*). Consult a dictionary for the correct forms of compound nouns. If no plural appears, then consider the noun regular and pluralize the last word.

1c POSSESSIVE NOUNS

Nouns have **possessive forms,** which indicate a variety of meanings.

OWNERSHIP:	my sister's house (house belonging to my sister)
AUTHORSHIP:	Ibsen's plays (plays by Ibsen)
SOURCE:	the mayor's permission (permission from the mayor)
MEASUREMENT:	a year's leave (leave of a year)
DESCRIPTION:	men's dormitory (dormitory for men)

You can recognize possessive nouns in prose because they contain apostrophes. Some possessive nouns are formed by the addition of an apostrophe and an *s;* others, by just an apostrophe after a final *s: institution's, James's, doctors', Raiders'.*

For a more detailed discussion of the forms and uses of possessive nouns, see 26a.

CHAPTER

2

PRONOUNS

The word **pronoun** means literally "for a noun," and pronouns do, in fact, occur in most of the same positions as nouns and noun phrases.

NOUN:	Students can have identification cards made at the sports arena.
PRONOUN:	You can have identification cards made at the sports arena.
NOUN PHRASE:	I left your coat with the attendant at the door.
PRONOUN:	I left your coat with someone at the door.
NOUN PHRASE:	The collie ate the whole turkey.
PRONOUN:	The collie ate what?

Often, pronouns substitute for previously stated nouns or noun phrases, called **antecedents.**

Voters did not turn out today. They were deterred by the weather.

The curry was so hot that few people could eat it.

A taxpayer whose returns are audited should hire an accountant.

Although they make up a relatively small class of words, pronouns are in constant use. Notice that of the two passages that follow, the one without pronouns sounds unnatural.

WITHOUT PRONOUNS

Emily Dickinson is regarded as a great American poet. Even though Emily Dickinson lived in seclusion, Dickinson's poems have universal significance: Dickinson's poems concern the relationship between the inner self and the outer world. Dickinson regarded the relationship between the inner self and the outer world as tragic. Dickinson examined the relationship between the inner self and the outer world with irony and wit.

WITH PRONOUNS

Emily Dickinson is regarded as a great American poet. Even though she lived in seclusion, her poems have universal significance: they concern the relationship between the inner self and the outer world. She examined this relationship, which she regarded as tragic, with irony and wit.

2a PERSONAL PRONOUNS

The seven **personal pronouns** have different forms for different functions.

I, me, my, mine

you, your, yours

he, him, his

she, her, hers

it, its

we, us, our, ours

they, them, their, theirs

These personal pronouns can be described by four characteristics: number, person, gender, and case.

- **Number** is either singular (*I, you, he, she, it*) or plural (*we, you, they*).
- **Person** identifies whether the pronoun is speaking, spoken to, or spoken about.

FIRST PERSON SINGULAR: *I* [speaker] hear the phone.

FIRST PERSON PLURAL: *We* [speaker and others] demand a recount.

SECOND PERSON: *You* [person spoken to] must apply before June 1.

THIRD PERSON: *She* [person spoken about] is a new client.

- **Gender** is the sex represented by third-person singular pronouns:

  masculine (*he*), feminine (*she*), neuter (*it*)

- **Case** involves the various forms a pronoun takes according to its use in a sentence. (Case forms and their uses are discussed in Chapter 14.)

  They [subject form] are my friends.

  Don't call *them* [object form].

  Their [possessive form] house is on Main Street.

The *-self/-selves* personal pronouns

In addition to case forms, personal pronouns also have compound forms, made by adding the suffixes (endings) *-self* or *-selves: myself, yourself, himself* (not *hisself*), *herself, itself, ourselves, yourselves, themselves* (not *theirselves*). These forms are used in two ways.

- As **reflexives,** the *-self/-selves* pronouns function as objects that rename the subjects of sentences (*we enjoyed ourselves*).
- As **emphatics,** the *-self/-selves* pronouns repeat, for emphasis, the words and phrases they refer to (*she races the boat herself*).

2b DEMONSTRATIVE PRONOUNS

The only **demonstrative pronouns** are *this* and *that,* along with their corresponding plurals, *these* and *those.* A demonstrative can be used alone to point out that something is relatively near to or far from the speaker.

This certainly has been a better year than that. [*This* year is the present year; *that* is past.]

I prefer these to those. [*These* are closer to the speaker than *those.*]

A demonstrative pronoun usually precedes a noun and functions like the determiner *the* to indicate that something has been previously mentioned.

Dieters should avoid beef, pork, and lamb when dining out, since these meats are high in both calories and fat. [*These meats* refers to beef, pork, and lamb.]

In the last game of the season, the coach threw a chair at the referee; that tantrum cost him his job. [*That tantrum* refers to the coach's behavior.]

2c RELATIVE PRONOUNS

The **relative pronouns** are as follows.

who,* whom* (referring to people)

which, what (referring to things)

that, whose* (referring to either people or things)

Since their function is to introduce adjective clauses (7c.2) and noun clauses (7c.3), you can use relative pronouns to combine sentences and eliminate choppy prose.

CHOPPY: I voted for the candidate. He promised the least.

IMPROVED: I voted for the candidate who promised the least.

CHOPPY: Julia arrived in a limousine. She had rented it at great expense.

IMPROVED: Julia arrived in a limousine, which she had rented at great expense.

*These forms represent different cases: subjective (*who*), objective (*whom*), and possessive (*whose*). See Chapter 14.

CHOPPY: Only one creature recognized Ulysses. It was his dog.

IMPROVED: The only creature that recognized Ulysses was his dog.

The relatives *who, which,* and *what* sometimes appear with the suffix *-ever* in noun clauses.

Whoever raises the most money wins the trip.

Discuss first whichever question seems easiest to you.

He said whatever came to his mind.

2d INTERROGATIVE PRONOUNS

The **interrogative pronouns** (*who, whom, whose, which,* and *what*) introduce questions that ask for information, rather than a yes or no answer. (For the distinction between *who* and *whom,* see 14c.)

Who painted the ceiling of the Sistine Chapel?

Whose idea was it to tell stories on the way to Canterbury?

Which house was Liberace's?

What did Arthur call his sword?

2e INDEFINITE PRONOUNS

Most **indefinite pronouns** need not refer to specific people or things and can be completely general, such as those in the following two sentences.

Anyone can raise tropical fish.

To an adolescent, everything seems a crisis.

However, indefinites can also refer to something definite—a noun or noun phrase already named or about to be named.

Numerous needleleaf trees grow in the Southeast, but few are as graceful as the loblolly pine.

Many of the North American totems depict birds and fish.

Many indefinite pronouns can serve as determiners, modifying nouns. (See 6c.)

Neither apartment had enough closet space.

We expected some support from the local media.

Indefinite Pronouns		
all	everyone	no one
another	everything	nothing
any	few	one
anybody	many	other
anyone	more	others
anything	most	several
both	much	some
each	neither	somebody
either	nobody	someone
everybody	none	something

Two indefinites, called **reciprocal pronouns,** require antecedents. *Each other* refers to two persons or things; *one another,* to more than two.

The two participants debated each other for an hour.

The four directors communicate with one another by telephone.

CHAPTER

3

ADJECTIVES AND ADVERBS

Adjectives and **adverbs** are modifiers—that is, they describe, limit, or qualify some other word or words. Most modifiers flesh out basic sentence structure but do not change it. For example, if the underlined modifiers were deleted, the structure of the following sentence would be unaltered.

> Suddenly I came over a steep rise and saw a panoramic sweep of brilliantly blue water and alabaster sand.

On the other hand, some modifiers are not merely descriptive additions but part of the basic sentence structure. For example, if the underlined words in the following sentences were deleted, the structures would be unfinished.

> The water is cold.
>
> Grady seemed angry.
>
> The court declared the law unconstitutional.
>
> The auditor is here.

3a ADJECTIVES

Adjectives modify nouns and a few pronouns to express attributes such as quality, quantity, or type. You can usually identify adjectives by their characteristic positions, or functions.

- Before nouns (and occasionally pronouns)

  rusty scissors

  flexible plastic

  new one

- After *very*

  very rusty

  very flexible

  very new

- After forms of the verb *be*

  The scissors are rusty.

  This plastic is flexible.

  That one is new.

3b ADVERBS

Adverbs modify adjectives, other adverbs, verbs, and whole clauses. Consequently, you will find adverbs in a variety of forms and positions.

- Most adverbs are made by the addition of *-ly* to adjectives: *boldly, smoothly, actively, gracefully, suddenly.* These adverbs can usually be moved about in sentences.

  Suddenly, all the lights went out.

  All the lights suddenly went out.

  All the lights went out suddenly.

- A small but widely used group of adverbs includes *now, then, soon, still, last, here, there, always, never, once*—expressions of time, place, distance, and frequency. These adverbs, too, can often be moved about in sentences.

  Now we hope to buy a condominium.

  We now hope to buy a condominium.

  We hope to buy a condominium now.

- Also movable are the conjunctive adverbs: *furthermore, however, therefore, also, thus, instead, consequently,* and so forth. Sometimes called transitional expressions, the conjunctive adverbs modify whole clauses and provide transition between sentences and paragraphs. (See *Transitional Expression* in the Glossary of Terms.)

  The commercial is extremely annoying; also, it is insulting to women.

  The commercial is extremely annoying; it is also insulting to women.

- Another type of movable adverb is produced by the combination of *some, any, every,* and *no* with words like *how, place, where,* and *way: somehow, someplace, anywhere, anyway, everywhere, nowhere.*

  Somehow we managed to get the canoe righted.

  We somehow managed to get the canoe righted.

  We managed somehow to get the canoe righted.

  We managed to get the canoe righted somehow.

- The suffixes *-ward* and *-wise* produce adverbs like *backward, southward, lengthwise,* and *clockwise.* These adverbs usually occur after a verb or its object.

  The man was walking backward.

  Cut the board lengthwise.

- Some adverbs, the qualifiers, restrict or intensify adjectives and other adverbs: *very, quite, really, rather, hardly, somewhat,* and so forth. The qualifiers appear immediately before the words they modify.

  The boat was hardly visible from shore.

  He turned down my request very cheerfully.

- When not coupled with nouns, some prepositions can also function as adverbs: *in, out, up, down, over, under, inside, outside,* and so forth. These adverbs usually express place or direction and appear with verbs.

We were locked inside.

Don't look down.

- Adverbs that function as interrogatives—*when, where, why,* and *how*—normally appear at the beginning of a clause or before an infinitive.

  Where is the next meeting?

  We don't know when the funds will be available.

  The first chapter explains how to string a guitar.

3c ADJECTIVE AND ADVERB FORMS

Most adjectives and adverbs have three forms, sometimes called **degrees.** The **positive** form is the simple form of a modifier (*a new building*). The **comparative** form makes a comparison between two people or things (*the newer of the two buildings*) and between a person or thing and other individual members of a group (*a building newer than any other in town*). The **superlative** form compares three or more people or things (*the newest of the three buildings*) and describes the position of a person or thing within its group (*the newest building in town*).

Most one-syllable and some two-syllable adjectives and adverbs show degree with *-er/-est* forms (*short, shorter, shortest; funny, funnier, funniest; near, nearer, nearest*).

Adjective

POSITIVE: The lake is large.

COMPARATIVE: Sardis is the larger of the two lakes.

SUPERLATIVE: Superior is the largest of the Great Lakes.

Adverb

POSITIVE: I arrived early for the dinner party.

COMPARATIVE: I arrived earlier than anyone else.

SUPERLATIVE: Of all the guests, I arrived earliest.

Some adjectives and adverbs have irregular comparative and superlative forms, for example, *good, better, best; many, more, most; badly, worse, worst.*

POSITIVE:	In light years, Mercury is not far from the sun.
COMPARATIVE:	Saturn is farther from the sun than Jupiter.
SUPERLATIVE:	Pluto is farthest from the sun.

Adjectives and adverbs without *-er/-est* forms show degree with *more* and *most* or *less* and *least.* These adjectives and adverbs have at least two but usually three or more syllables (*careful, more careful, most careful; important, less important, least important; fully, more fully, most fully; suddenly, less suddenly, least suddenly*).

Adjective

POSITIVE:	The kitchen was spacious.
COMPARATIVE:	The kitchen was more spacious than the den.
SUPERLATIVE:	The kitchen was the most spacious room in the house.

Adverb

POSITIVE:	The campaign was carefully planned.
COMPARATIVE:	This year's campaign was less carefully planned than last year's.
SUPERLATIVE:	This year's campaign was the least carefully planned of the three.

You can be sure that any word with degree is either an adjective or an adverb. For a discussion of the appropriate use of comparatives and superlatives, see 15b.

CHAPTER

4

VERBS AND VERB PHRASES

Verbs and **verb phrases** make up the most versatile word class in the language. They state action, occurrence, and existence. In addition, their various forms and functions can express an enormous range of meaning and subtle distinctions. Without doubt, the effective use of English requires mastering the verb system.

4a BASIC FORMS

All verbs and verb phrases include one of the basic forms. Three of these forms—base, past, and past participle—are often called the three **principal parts.** As the charts illustrate, regular verbs make their past forms and past participles by adding *-d* or *-ed* to the base; irregular verbs do not follow this predictable pattern.

In addition to the three principal parts, two other forms exist for all verbs, both regular and irregular: the *-s* form, made by adding *-s* or *-es* to the base, and the present participle, made by adding *-ing* to the base. Thus, all verbs (except *be,* which is treated separately) can be said to have a total of five possible forms.

Examples of Regular Verbs				
Base	-s *Form*	*Past*	*Past Participle*	*Present Participle*
assume	assumes	assumed	assumed	assuming
drag	drags	dragged	dragged	dragging
dry	dries	dried	dried	drying
enjoy	enjoys	enjoyed	enjoyed	enjoying
fix	fixes	fixed	fixed	fixing

Examples of Irregular Verbs				
Base	-s *Form*	*Past*	*Past Participle*	*Present Participle*
begin	begins	began	begun	beginning
cut	cuts	cut	cut	cutting
draw	draws	drew	drawn	drawing
eat	eats	ate	eaten	eating
leave	leaves	left	left	leaving
think	thinks	thought	thought	thinking

You will find a complete list of irregular verbs and their principal parts under *Irregular Verb* in the Glossary of Terms. Also, for information about correct use of verb forms, see Chapter 11.

The verb *be* does not follow the patterns of other verbs; it has eight forms, including three for the *-s* form and two for the past form.

Forms of *Be*				
Base	-s *Form*	*Past*	*Past Participle*	*Present Participle*
be	am	was	been	being
	is	were		
	are			

4b AUXILIARIES AND VERB PHRASES

Frequently, the verb in a sentence is not a single word but a phrase. In the phrase, the last verb is the **main verb,** and all preceding verbs are **auxiliaries.**

Intense heat does not affect the paint.

The orchestra has been rehearsing.

The wallet might have been stolen.

There are four categories of auxiliaries that combine with one another and with main verbs to create a variety of structures and subtle shades of meaning: auxiliaries that use *be, have,* or *do* and modal auxiliaries.

(1) *Be* auxiliary

The *be* auxiliary appears in one of eight forms (*am, is, are, was, were, be, being, been*) and is always followed by the present or past participle.

AUXILIARY + PRESENT PARTICIPLE OF *LEAVE:*	He is leaving.
AUXILIARY + PAST PARTICIPLE OF *FIRE:*	I was fired today.

(2) *Have* auxiliary

The *have* auxiliary appears in one of four forms (*have, has, had, having*) and is always followed by a past participle.

AUXILIARY + PAST PARTICIPLE OF *FORGET:*	I have forgotten the combination.
AUXILIARY + PAST PARTICIPLE OF *BREAK:*	The quarterback had broken his ankle.

(3) Modal auxiliaries

The modal auxiliaries influence the "mood" of verbs by expressing ideas such as ability, obligation, necessity, and possibility. For example, the verb *complete* takes on slightly different meanings when accompanied by different modal auxiliaries.

ABILITY:	The crew can complete the job in one week.
OBLIGATION:	You should complete the investigation before you begin the report.
NECESSITY:	We must complete the remodeling by June.
POSSIBILITY:	I may complete the course in time for graduation.

The common modal auxiliaries are *will, would, can, could, shall, should, may, might,* and *must.* These auxiliaries are followed by the base form of either the main verb, the *be* auxiliary, or the *have* auxiliary.

AUXILIARY + BASE FORM OF *ARRANGE:*	The director will arrange a meeting.
AUXILIARY + BASE FORM OF *BE* AUXILIARY:	She might be living in Paris.
AUXILIARY + BASE FORM OF *HAVE* AUXILIARY:	I could have taken three courses this summer.

(4) *Do* auxiliary

The *do* auxiliary appears in one of three forms (*do, does, did*) and is always followed by the base form of the main verb. This auxiliary is unique in that it cannot combine with other auxiliaries.

AUXILIARY + BASE FORM OF *REVEAL:*	The studies do reveal current trends.
AUXILIARY + BASE FORM OF *BLOOM:*	The tree did not bloom this year.

4c TENSE

Tense places the verb in a time frame. For example, past tense can express an action already completed, and present perfect tense can express an action begun in the past but not yet completed. Nevertheless, tense is not always equivalent to time, and the uses of tenses can overlap. Present and future tense, for instance, often convey the same idea.

PRESENT TENSE: Intense heat causes the surface to crack.

FUTURE TENSE: Intense heat will cause the surface to crack.

The following charts show the range of meanings that can be expressed by the three simple tenses (present, past, and future) and the three perfect tenses (present perfect, past perfect, and future perfect).

Simple Tenses

Formation	*Uses*	*Examples*
Present		
-s form in third-person singular; base form everywhere else	present time with certain verbs, especially referring to senses	I hear a car in the driveway.
	statements of fact	The Amazon empties into the Atlantic.
	repetitive action	She walks to school.
	references to works of art and literature	In the *Mona Lisa,* the woman smiles enigmatically.
	future time	The races start tomorrow.
Past		
past form	past occurrences	The Rams won the game.
Future		
will + base form and sometimes *shall* + base form*	future time	The store will open in May.
	results of conditions	If suddenly heated, air will expand violently.

*In current usage, *shall* and *will* often suggest different meanings. *Shall we go?* is an invitation meaning "Would you like to go?" *Will we go?* asks "Are we going?" *Shall* also occurs in set expressions (*we shall overcome*), in laws and resolutions (*the court shall set the fine*), and in heightened prose (*we shall never surrender*).

Perfect Tenses		
Formation	*Uses*	*Examples*
Present Perfect *have/has* + past participle	occurrences completed at an unspecified time in the past	He has sung at the Met.
	action begun in the past and continuing to the present	We have always gone to Vermont in June.
Past Perfect *had* + past participle	past action occurring before some other past action	The troops had reached the river when the message arrived.
Future Perfect *will* + *have* + past participle	action that will occur before or by the time of another future action	We will have left by the time he arrives.

4d PROGRESSIVE FORMS

The six tenses have **progressive forms** that indicate actions in progress. A progressive verb is made with a form of the verb *be* followed by a present participle (an *-ing* form of the verb). The following charts explain the progressive forms and their uses.

Simple Progressive Forms		
Formation	*Uses*	*Examples*
Present Progressive *am/is/are* + present participle	action currently in progress	Crowds are lining the streets.
	future time	He is sailing Monday.
Past Progressive *was/were* + present participle	past action in progress	I was sleeping when he called.
Future Progressive *will be* + present participle	future action in progress	Kathy will be traveling next month.
	future action that is not continuous	She will be arriving at noon.

Perfect Progressive Forms		
Formation	*Uses*	*Examples*
Present Perfect Progressive		
have/has + *been* + present participle	continuous past actions still occurring or occurring until recently	The committee has been considering the issue all week.
Past Perfect Progressive		
had + *been* + present participle	past action in progress until another past action occurred	He had been lifting weights daily before his doctor advised restraint.
Future Perfect Progressive		
will + *have* + *been* + present participle	continuous future action that will be complete at some other future time	He will have been pitching for fifteen years by the time the season ends.

4e VOICE

Some verbs can be expressed in both active and passive voice. In **active voice,** the subject acts or in some way controls the action of the verb, and the object receives the action. Active-voice sentences have this pattern:

ACTOR	VERB	RECEIVER
An auditor	has checked	the figures.
Snow	covers	the mountains.
My dog	ate	my lunch.
Disney	is filming	the movie.

In **passive voice,** the subject receives the action. The actor or agent, if named, appears in a prepositional phrase beginning with *by* or *with.* It is easy to recognize passive-voice verbs: they always contain a form of *be* plus the past participle. Sentences with passive-voice verbs have this pattern:

Receiver	Form of *Be*	Past Participle	*By* or *With*	Actor
The figures	have been	checked	by	an auditor.
The mountains	are	covered	with	snow.
My lunch	was	eaten	by	my dog.
The movie	is being	filmed	by	Disney.

Often in passive voice, the agent is not named: the *by* or *with* phrase is omitted.

ACTIVE: The horse threw the rider over the fence.

PASSIVE: The rider was thrown over the fence by the horse.

PASSIVE: The rider was thrown over the fence.

ACTIVE: Trash littered the streets.

PASSIVE: The streets were littered with trash.

PASSIVE: The streets were littered.

For a discussion of when to avoid and when to use the passive voice, see 33c.2.

4f MOOD

The **mood** of a verb indicates whether the idea expressed is a fact (indicative mood), a command (imperative mood), or a matter of desire or possibility (subjunctive). The three moods are expressed through special verb forms.

(1) Indicative mood

The **indicative mood** is used to make statements and ask questions.

She paints murals.

Squirrels ate the birdseed.

Who is your senator?

Has the mail arrived?

This mood has six tenses, explained by the charts in 4c and 4d.

(2) Imperative mood

The **imperative mood** is used to give commands. The omitted but understood subject of all imperative verbs is the singular or plural *you.* In addition, for all verbs except *be,* the imperative is the form used with *you* in the present tense.

POSITIVE	NEGATIVE
Answer the memo.	Do not/Don't answer the memo.
Order the sirloin.	Do not/Don't order the sirloin.

The imperative of the verb *be* is always *be* for positive commands and *do not/don't be* for negative commands.

POSITIVE	NEGATIVE
Be serious.	Do not/Don't be serious.
Be an observer.	Do not/Don't be an observer.

(3) Subjunctive mood

The forms of **subjunctive** verbs (other than *be*) are the same as the forms of the indicative except in one respect: the *-s* is not added in the third-person singular present tense.

SUBJUNCTIVE: Heaven forbid.

INDICATIVE: Heaven forbids.

With *be,* the present-tense subjunctive is always *be;* the past-tense subjunctive is always *were.*

SUBJUNCTIVE: We demand that the accused be tried in a court of law.

INDICATIVE: The accused is tried in a court of law.

SUBJUNCTIVE: Even if the movie were free, I would not see it.

INDICATIVE: The movie was free, but I did not see it.

In current English, the subjunctive mood has limited use, appearing only in three special contexts.

- The subjunctive is present in a few traditional expressions, such as farewells and blessings.

SUBJUNCTIVE: Peace be with you.

INDICATIVE: Peace is with you.

SUBJUNCTIVE: Long live the queen.

INDICATIVE: The queen lives long.

- The subjunctive is used in clauses introduced by conjunctions such as *if, as if,* and *as though* to express hypothetical situations or conditions contrary to fact.

SUBJUNCTIVE: If a left turn signal were installed, traffic flow would improve.

INDICATIVE: When a left turn signal was installed, traffic flow improved.

SUBJUNCTIVE: If I were you, I would not smoke.

INDICATIVE: I am not you, but I don't think you should smoke.

- The subjunctive occurs in *that* clauses naming demands, recommendations, wishes, and needs.

SUBJUNCTIVE: We demand that the terms of the contract be met.

INDICATIVE: The demands of the contract are met.

SUBJUNCTIVE: The committee recommended <u>that</u> he <u>submit</u> a proposal.

INDICATIVE: He <u>submits</u> a proposal.

SUBJUNCTIVE: I wish I <u>were</u> good at math. [*That* is understood after *wish.*]

INDICATIVE: I <u>am</u> good at math.

SUBJUNCTIVE: It is urgent <u>that</u> the police department <u>enforce</u> zoning regulations.

INDICATIVE: The police department <u>enforces</u> zoning regulations.

CHAPTER

5

VERBALS AND VERBAL PHRASES

A **verbal** is a present participle (*winning*), a past participle (*won*), or an infinitive (*to win*) functioning in a sentence as something other than a verb. A verbal may function as a noun, an adjective, or an adverb.

> Winning was all that mattered to him.
>
> Teams are rated by the number of games won.
>
> We were surprised to win.

A **verbal phrase** is a verbal plus any words that complete its meaning.

> Winning the game was all that mattered to him.
>
> Teams are rated by the number of games won within the conference.
>
> We were surprised to win so easily.

5a INFINITIVES AND INFINITIVE PHRASES

Infinitives begin with *to,* followed by a verb (*to go, to think, to seem*). These verbals appear alone or in phrases and can function as adverbs, adjectives, and nouns.

- As adverbs

The audience rose to cheer the performance. [modifying *rose*]

This exercise machine is difficult to use. [modifying *difficult*]

The river flows too slowly to do much damage. [modifying *slowly*]

To return to my question, is the government interfering in another country's affairs? [modifying the rest of the sentence]

- As adjectives

Many writers have a tendency to use too many commas. [modifying *tendency*]

A poison to kill fire ants is now available. [modifying *poison*]

- As nouns

To invest successfully in oil requires the instincts of a good gambler. [subject of *requires*]

Darwin believed natural selection to be important in the origin of plants and animals. [object of *believed*]

The delegates argued about how to cast the votes. [object of *about*]

The "sign" of the infinitive, *to,* is omitted after certain verbs like *let, help, make, hear, see,* and *feel.*

Let the record show that only four people were present.

We saw her steal the necklace.

5b PARTICIPLES AND PARTICIPIAL PHRASES

Participles exist in two forms: the present participle and the past participle. You can always identify a present participle by its *-ing* ending—for example, *walking, thinking, singing.* The past participle is the form that can follow *have* in a verb phrase—for example, *walked, thought, sung.* Participles, alone or in phrases, can act as adjectives to modify nouns or pronouns.

The missing passengers apparently drowned after the ferry capsized. [present participle modifying *passengers*]

The passengers, missing after the ferry capsized, apparently drowned. [present participial phrase modifying *passengers*]

The frightened people panicked and fled the hostile "Martians." [past participle modifying *people*]

Frightened by the broadcast, people panicked and fled the hostile "Martians." [past participial phrase modifying *people*]

5c GERUNDS AND GERUND PHRASES

Gerunds are present participles (*walking, believing, feeling*) functioning as nouns. Like other verbals, gerunds can appear alone or in phrases.

Selling beer without a license is illegal. [subject of *is*]

The patient had lost his hearing because of a childhood illness. [object of *had lost*]

Mendel devoted his time to studying genetics. [object of *to*]

5d ABSOLUTE VERBAL PHRASES

An **absolute phrase** does not modify any one element in a sentence but instead modifies the rest of the sentence. Thus, the absolute phrase seems rather loosely connected. There are two types of absolute verbal phrases.

- The first is a familiar expression containing a participle or an infinitive.

  Speaking of friends, Susan let me use her credit card when I was broke.

  To tell the truth, my vacation was more work than my job.

- The second is the nominative absolute—a phrase beginning with a noun or pronoun that acts as the subject of the verbal. The nominative absolute is somewhat formal and usually explains causes or adds details to sentences.

  His fortune squandered on cards and horses, he went to work as a valet.

The seas being rough, we put into harbor.

The estate will be liquidated, everything to be sold at auction.

The gunfighter of Hollywood westerns was casually sinister—guns slung low on his hips, hat cocked rakishly over one eye, steps measured and slow.

CHAPTER

6

FUNCTION WORDS

Nouns, verbs, adjectives, and adverbs make up the greater part of our vocabulary and convey most of the semantic meaning of sentences. However, meaning also depends on **functions words:** prepositions, conjunctions, determiners, and expletives. These words create structure. If the function words are removed from a sentence, all that remains is a list of unrelated vocabulary items.

WITH FUNCTION WORDS:	Under the canopy sat a man and a woman waiting for the bus.
WITHOUT FUNCTION WORDS:	canopy sat man woman waiting bus

You might think of the vocabulary items as bricks and of the function words as the mortar that holds them together: both are necessary to build meaning.

6a PREPOSITIONS AND PREPOSITIONAL PHRASES

A **prepositional phrase** contains a preposition and its object, usually a noun, noun phrase, or pronoun. The following list includes some of the most common prepositions. Those made up of two and three words are called **phrasal prepositions.**

above	during	onto
across	except	out
after	except for	outside of
against	for	over
around	from	past
as	in	since
at	in front of	through
away from	in spite of	toward
because of	into	under
before	like	until
beneath	near	up
between	of	with
by	off	within
by means of	on	without
down		

As the following examples demonstrate, prepositional phrases can modify a variety of elements.

boats in the harbor [modifying a noun]

a rusty bicycle without wheels [modifying a noun phrase]

everything on the back porch [modifying a pronoun]

ran through the alley [modifying a verb]

performing at Christmas [modifying a verbal]

optimistic about the future [modifying an adjective]

In addition to their use as modifiers, prepositional phrases can also function like nouns, usually as objects but occasionally as subjects.

The creature emerged from behind the snow bank. [object of *from*]

After Thursday will be too late. [subject of sentence]

6b CONJUNCTIONS

Conjunctions are grammatical connectors that link sentence elements and express relationships between ideas. For instance, conjunctions attribute causes and effects; signal time sequences; indicate alternatives, parallels, or contrasts. As you can see from reading the following passage, prose without conjunctions can be disjointed.

WITHOUT CONJUNCTIONS

We rarely think in terms of meters/liters. We are accustomed to inches/pounds. There has been an effort to change to the metric system. The changeover has met strong opposition. We are familiar with a foot. We can estimate length fairly accurately in feet. We can easily stride off a distance to measure it in yards.

The addition of conjunctions makes clear the relationships of the ideas.

WITH CONJUNCTIONS

We rarely think in terms of meters and liters because we are accustomed to inches and pounds. Although there has been an effort to change to the metric system, the changeover has met strong opposition. We are so familiar with a foot that we can estimate length in feet fairly accurately, and we can easily stride off a distance to measure it in yards.

(1) Coordinating conjunctions

Coordinating conjunctions connect words, phrases, and clauses to grammatically coordinate, or equal, structures. Five coordinators—*and, but, or, nor,* and *yet*—can join any structures that are grammatically equal.

NOUNS:	I always order fish or chicken.
VERBS:	We did not eat nor sleep for five days.
ADJECTIVES:	The singer was loud but off-key.
PREPOSITIONAL PHRASES:	The road runs through the valley and up the mountains.
CLAUSES:	He was a stern man, yet he was patient.

Two coordinators—*for* and *so*—connect only independent clauses.

INDEPENDENT CLAUSES:	The conductor stopped, for the cellist had begun to snore.

INDEPENDENT CLAUSES: English has only a few inflections, so it does not have a very flexible word order.

(2) Correlative conjunctions

A special type of coordinating conjunction, the **correlative,** has two parts that connect elements of equal grammatical structure—two nouns, two verbs, two adjectives, two dependent clauses, two independent clauses, and so forth. The correlatives *both . . . and* and *not . . . but* connect elements within clauses.

ADJECTIVES: The program includes both isometric and aerobic exercise.

NOUNS: The problem is not the hardware but the software.

Three sets of correlatives—*not only . . . but also, either . . . or, neither . . . nor*—can connect two independent clauses as well as elements within independent clauses.

ADJECTIVES: The stove is not only compact but also fuel efficient.

PREPOSITIONAL PHRASES: Paper is made either by a mechanical process or by a chemical process.

NOUNS: Neither Melville nor Hawthorne is as popular with students as Poe is.

CLAUSES: Not only did the Egyptians distinguish between planets and stars, but also they devised a 365-day calendar.

(3) Subordinating conjunctions

Subordinating conjunctions introduce dependent clauses (7c) and express relationships such as cause, contrast, condition, manner, place, and time. Some commonly used subordinators are listed here.

after	except that	than
although	if	that

as	in case	unless
as if	in that	until
as though	now that	when
because	once	whenever
before	since	where
even though	so that	while

The following examples suggest the versatility of subordinate clauses, but for a more complete discussion, see 7c.1.

MODIFYING A VERB:	You should act as though you are accustomed to such elegance.
MODIFYING AN ADJECTIVE:	I am sure that he has forgotten the appointment.
MODIFYING A CLAUSE:	When the movie began, the theater was empty.

(4) Comparative conjunctions

A special type of subordinating conjunction has two parts—for example, *so . . . that* and *as . . . as.* These conjunctions usually introduce clauses of measurement or degree; that is, they introduce ideas that express how much or to what extent. The following are the most common **comparatives.**

- *as . . . as*

  She is not as clever as I thought she was.

- *so . . . that*

  Paul was so scared that he was shaking.

- *such . . . that*

  He is such a nice man that people take advantage of him.

- A comparative form of an adjective or adverb . . . *than*

  The river is cleaner than it was last year.

  This pump works more efficiently than the old one did.

- A superlative form of an adjective . . . *that*

  His Thunderbird was the fanciest car that I had ever seen.

  The game is the most complicated that the company has designed.

6c DETERMINERS

Determiners signal that a noun will follow, if not immediately, then shortly. Some words are always determiners.

- The articles—*a, an, the*

  A new theory about dinosaurs has been proposed.

  Where did you hide the chocolate chip cookies?

- Some possessive pronouns—*my, her, its, our, your, their, whose*

  Her German accent sounds authentic.

  Whose music did they play?

- An indefinite pronoun—*every*

  Every item was marked down 50 percent.

In addition, some nouns and pronouns frequently function as determiners.

- Possessives: *his, everyone's, Kathy's, today's,* and so on

  DETERMINER: Leading the discussion is his responsibility.

  PRONOUN: The responsibility is his.

- Demonstrative pronouns: *this, that, these, those*

  DETERMINER: You must pack these provisions for the trip.

  PRONOUN: The necessary provisions are these: food, water, and first-aid equipment.

- Indefinite pronouns: *each, either, neither, all, some, many, much, any, few, more, less,* and so on

DETERMINER: Few inventors achieve success.

PRONOUN: Of the thousands of inventors, few achieve success.

- Interrogative pronouns: *which, what*

DETERMINER: We could not determine which virus was present.

PRONOUN: A virus was present, but we could not determine which.

- Cardinal numbers—*one, two, three,* and so on

DETERMINER: The terrorists showed pictures of four hostages.

NOUN: There were six hostages, but the terrorists showed pictures of only four.

6d EXPLETIVES

The two **expletives,** *it* and *there,* are "filler words" that introduce clauses and allow the real subjects to be delayed until after the verbs or verb auxiliaries. *There* usually introduces a clause with a noun or noun phrase as the subject.

SUBJECT FIRST: A phone is ringing.

SUBJECT DELAYED: There is a phone ringing.

SUBJECT FIRST: A notice from the bank is on your desk.

SUBJECT DELAYED: There is a notice from the bank on your desk.

When the real subject of a clause is an infinitive or a *that* clause, beginning with the expletive *it* sounds more natural than beginning with the subject.

SUBJECT FIRST: To call is important.

SUBJECT DELAYED: It is important to call.

SUBJECT FIRST: That the dam will break is unlikely.

SUBJECT DELAYED: It is unlikely that the dam will break.

The expletive *it* has an additional function—to introduce constructions that have no real subject.

It is raining.

It is noisy in here.

CAUTION: The words *it* and *there* are not always expletives. *There* can function as an adverb; *it* is frequently a pronoun. Compare the following pairs of sentences:

EXPLETIVE: There are three horses in the paddock.

ADVERB: Three horses are there in the paddock.

EXPLETIVE: It is dangerous to jog after eating.

PRONOUN: Jogging after meals is dangerous. It should be avoided.

CHAPTER

7

CLAUSES AND SENTENCES

A **clause** is a grammatical construction with both a subject and a predicate. The simple subject consists of at least one noun (or noun equivalent); the complete subject consists of the noun and its modifiers. The predicate consists of at least one verb and its modifiers. In addition, the predicate may include one or more complements, that is, words necessary to complete the meaning of the verb. As the following examples show, the predicate makes an assertion about its subject.

SUBJECT	PREDICATE
Travis	defended the Alamo.
Everyone in the elevator	panicked.
The convention	will be in Des Moines next year.

An independent, or main, clause expresses a complete idea and can occur by itself as a **sentence** (see 7b). A dependent, or subordinate, clause must occur as part of a sentence. Both independent and dependent clauses have the same structural patterns.

7a CLAUSE PATTERNS

In all clause patterns, the subject is a noun (or noun equivalent) and any modifiers. What distinguishes the patterns from one another is the predicate structure, which is determined by the type of verb it contains—intransitive, transitive, or linking.

(1) Intransitive verb pattern

Technically, an **intransitive verb** is complete by itself and is the only element needed in the predicate structure.

SUBJECT +	INTRANSITIVE VERB
The doctor	smiled.
The prisoner	has escaped.
They	were leaving.

Frequently, however, the pattern is fleshed out by an adverbial modifier following the verb.

The doctor smiled <u>sheepishly</u>.

The prisoner has escaped <u>through a tunnel</u>.

They were leaving <u>before the party was over</u>.

(2) Transitive verb patterns

A **transitive verb** in the active voice requires a direct object, a complement that receives the action. Notice that without the direct objects, the verbs in the following sentences do not seem complete. In addition, some transitive verbs allow indirect objects, and some allow object complements. As a result, there are three transitive verb patterns.

- In one pattern, the subject performs the verb's action, and the direct object receives or is affected by the verb's action.

SUBJECT +	TRANSITIVE VERB +	DIRECT OBJECT
The FBI	investigated	him.
A local press	has published	her memoirs.
Energy shortages	would change	our lifestyles.

One way that you can test this pattern is to convert it to the passive voice (see 4e). In this conversion, you move the direct object to the subject position, where it still receives the verb's action.

He was investigated by the FBI.

Her memoirs have been published by a local press.

Our lifestyles would be changed by energy shortages.

- Another kind of complement, the indirect object, is common with a few transitive verbs—including *give, make, tell, show, bring, send, sell,* and *offer.* This object appears between the verb and the direct object; like the direct object, it completes the verb's meaning.

SUBJECT	TRANSITIVE VERB	INDIRECT OBJECT	DIRECT OBJECT
Our courts	cannot deny	a felon	due process.
My uncle	knitted	me	a wool sweater.
The professor	asked	us	only one question.

You can identify an indirect object by converting it to a prepositional phrase (with *to, for,* or occasionally *of*) and shifting it to follow the direct object.

Our courts cannot deny due process <u>to a felon</u>.

My uncle knitted a wool sweater <u>for me</u>.

The professor asked only one question <u>of us</u>.

- Still another kind of complement, the object complement, can occur with a few transitive verbs—including *make, consider, call, elect, appoint, declare, name,* and *choose.* In this pattern, the complement is an adjective or a noun that follows the direct object and refers to it. Without the complement, the verb often means something a bit different or makes no sense. For instance, try reading the following examples with and then without the object complement.

SUBJECT	TRANSITIVE VERB	DIRECT OBJECT	OBJECT COMPLEMENT
The fog	will make	travel	dangerous.
The reporter	called	the senator	devious.
I	kept	the letter	a secret.
Most people	consider	the tomato	a vegetable.

You can identify an object complement by making a kind of equation between it and the direct object: *Travel is dangerous. The senator is devious. The letter is a secret. The tomato is a vegetable.*

(3) Linking verb patterns

A **linking verb** requires a subject complement, which completes the meaning of the verb and refers to the subject.

- An adjective can fill the position of subject complement with almost all linking verbs—*be;* verbs with meanings similar to *be* (including *seem, appear, become, grow, remain*); and verbs that refer to the senses (*look, taste, smell, sound,* and *feel*).

SUBJECT +	LINKING VERB +	ADJECTIVE SUBJECT COMPLEMENT
Most of the guests	were	obnoxious.
The surface	feels	rough.
The crowd	grew	restless.
The witness	seemed	hostile.

Notice that you can test the pattern by making a noun phrase with the subject and subject complement: *obnoxious guests, rough surface, restless crowd, hostile witness.*

- Sometimes the subject complement is a *predicate nominative*—a noun or pronoun that names or refers to the subject. The most common verbs in this pattern are *be, become, remain, seem,* and *appear.*

Subject +	Linking Verb +	Noun or Pronoun Subject Complement
The main problem	is	you.
Stacy	became	a jockey.
All the cousins	remained	friends.

You can test the pattern by making an equation of the subject and the subject complement: *problem = you; Stacy = jockey; cousins = friends.*

- With *be* and *become,* the subject complement can be a possessive:

Subject +	Linking Verb +	Possessive Subject Complement
That Jaguar	is	Karen's.
The responsibility	became	mine.
The loss	would be	everyone's.

Notice that the subject and complement make a noun phrase: *Karen's Jaguar; my responsibility; everyone's loss.*

- Finally, with *be* only, the complement can be an adverb or an adverb phrase that locates the subject in time or space.

Subject +	Linking Verb +	Adverb Subject Complement
A police officer	is	outside.
The meeting	will be	tomorrow.
The game	was	at 7:30.

In this pattern, the subject and subject complement can combine to form a noun phrase. The complement, however, follows the subject: *police officer outside; meeting tomorrow; game at 7:30.*

7b INDEPENDENT CLAUSES

Independent clauses (sometimes called *main clauses*) may stand by themselves as sentences.

SUBJECT	PREDICATE
The book	examines human cruelty.
The ideas	are not pessimistic.
A hostile crowd	had gathered.
Serbian assassins	waited.

In addition, independent clauses can be joined to produce compound sentences.

The book examines human cruelty, but the ideas are not pessimistic.

A hostile crowd had gathered; the Serbian assassins waited.

7c DEPENDENT CLAUSES

Like independent clauses, **dependent clauses** (also called *subordinate clauses*) have subjects and predicates. Unlike independent clauses, they cannot stand alone as sentences, and they usually begin with an introductory word that signals dependence.

INTRODUCTORY WORD	SUBJECT	PREDICATE
because	it	causes tarnishing
that	we	call Baalbeck
if	their tires	are underinflated

Because they are not complete in themselves, dependent clauses must be attached to independent clauses:

Pewter articles no longer contain lead because it causes tarnishing.

The town that we call Baalbeck was known to the Greeks as Heliopolis.

Drivers waste gasoline if their tires are underinflated.

Dependent clauses function in sentences as modifiers or as nouns and are generally classified as adverb clauses, adjective clauses, and noun clauses.

(1) Adverb clauses

The most versatile of dependent clauses is the **adverb clause,** which can modify verbs, adjectives, adverbs, and whole clauses. In fact, any dependent clause that does not act as a noun or modify a noun can safely be called an adverb clause.

Adverb clauses are introduced by subordinating conjunctions to express relationships such as time, cause, purpose, condition, contrast, comparison, place, and manner. Most of the subordinating conjunctions can be grouped according to these relationships.

- **Time:** *when, whenever, while, after, before, as, just as, as soon as, until, since, ever since, once, as long as*

  The British blockaded Germany when World War II broke out.

  As soon as a dolphin is born, the mother pushes it to the water's surface for its first breath of air.

- **Cause:** *because, since, now that, once, as, in case*

  Because some years produce better wines, experts often judge quality by the vintage year.

  In Nebraska, most farmers must install irrigation systems in case rainfall is under 10 inches a year.

- **Purpose:** *so that, in order that*

  So that his arrival would be noticed, the star hired teenagers to mob the airport.

  Place bluebird houses facing south in order that the birds can avoid the north wind.

- **Condition:** *if, unless, once, provided that, whatever, whoever, whichever, whether or not, no matter how (which, what, when, who, were), assuming that*

  Please check the color-coded map if you do not know the correct subway line.

No matter how much he eats, he never gains weight.

- **Contrast:** *although, even though, even if, though, except (that), whereas*

  Even though the superhighways have made travel faster, they have also made it less scenic.

  The Aztec capital was as large as a European city, although the Indians neither domesticated animals nor used wheels.

- **Comparison:** *as . . . as, so . . . as, so . . . that, more . . . than, most . . . that, than*

  The Royal Canadian Mounted Police are as effective in reality as they are in legend.

  The Imperial Hotel in Tokyo was so well built that it survived the destructive 1923 earthquake.

- **Place:** *where, wherever*

  We saw nothing but litter where the fair had been.

  The migrant workers went wherever jobs were available.

- **Manner:** *as, as if, as though, just as, just as if*

  She walked with her shoulders squared and head erect as though life were her adversary.

  The Celtics played as if the championship were at stake.

(2) Adjective clauses

Adjective clauses modify nouns and pronouns. These clauses are often called *relative clauses* because they are introduced by relative pronouns (*who/whom/whose, which, that*) or relative adverbs (*when, where, why*). Unlike a subordinating conjunction, which merely connects an adverb clause to a main clause, a relative introducer functions within an adjective clause as a noun or an adverb. Also, the relative introducer follows and refers to the word or phrase being modified.

One-fifth of the water that runs off the Earth's surface is carried by the Amazon.

Afghanistan is a landlocked country whose strategic location has affected its history.

Ellen Terry, who played all of Shakespeare's heroines, was a celebrated actress for almost fifty years.

A tax on tea brought about the Boston Tea Party, which triggered the Revolutionary War.

In Connecticut, November is the month when the wild animals and insects retreat to shelter.

Sometimes an adjective clause appears without a relative introducer. In such cases, the introducer is understood to be *that.*

The playwright [that] he emulates is Tennessee Williams.

The robots [that] they manufacture are installed in chemical plants.

The adjective clause is sometimes set off with commas and sometimes not, depending on its relationship to the noun it modifies. For a discussion of how to punctuate adjective clauses, see 21c. For a discussion of when to use *who/whom* and *whoever/whomever,* see 14c.

(3) Noun clauses

Noun clauses function in the same ways that all nouns do—as subjects, objects, and complements. These clauses are introduced with a variety of words, most of which begin with *wh-*.

that, who, whom, whose, which, what

whoever, whomever, whatever, whichever, however

whether, where, when, how, if

- **Noun clauses as subjects**
  A noun clause functioning as a subject can appear at the beginning of a sentence.

Whatever you decide is acceptable to me.

This pattern, however, is not very common. More often, the expletive *it* begins the sentence, and the subject clause is moved to the end. (See 6d.)

That a need will arise is unlikely.

It is unlikely that a need will arise.

What you study doesn't matter.

It doesn't matter what you study.

- **Noun clauses as direct objects**
  Noun clauses probably appear most frequently as direct objects after verbs like *say, believe, think, decide, propose, hope,* and *prove*—usually verbs that name some sort of mental activity.

The scientist calculated that a million black holes exist in our galaxy.

The group proposed that San Francisco ban the building of more skyscrapers downtown.

Sometimes the subordinator *that* is left out, although it is understood by a reader.

Ecologists hope [that] the whooping crane can be saved.

Buddhists believe [that] monks should live a life of poverty.

- **Noun clauses as objects of prepositions**
  When the noun clause appears as the object of a preposition, the clause usually begins with *whether, how, what, whatever, whoever,* or some other interrogative word.

After improving the telephone, Edison turned his attention to how one might permanently record sound.

When he received his "visions," Edgar Cayce was totally unconscious of what went on around him.

- **Noun clauses as subject complements**
  Sometimes, after the verb *be,* noun clauses function as subject complements (predicate nominatives) to rename the subject.

The problem was that Edward the Confessor died without an heir.

The candidate will be whoever can afford to run.

7d ELLIPTICAL CLAUSES

In an **elliptical clause**, one or more words that can be readily understood by the reader are dropped from the complete structure. The most common omissions in elliptical clauses are a relative pronoun (*that* or *whom*), the subject and a form of *be*, or a previously stated verb or predicate.

Most economists believe [that] the bond market is improving.

Dylan Thomas died at age thirty-nine while [he was] on an American tour.

The Appalachian National Scenic Trail is longer than any other hiking trail in the country [is long].

As a rule, private colleges charge more tuition than public colleges [charge].

Bats of some species roost in colonies of millions; others [roost], in solitude.

7e KINDS OF SENTENCES

Independent clauses appear alone or in combinations—with other independent clauses or with dependent clauses. One method of classifying sentences is based on the number and kinds of clauses in a single construction. According to this classification system, there are four categories of sentences: simple, compound, complex, and compound-complex.

(1) Simple sentence

A **simple sentence** is made up of only one independent clause. The sentence may contain modifiers and compound elements (for example, compound subjects and verbs), but it may not contain more than one subject-predicate structure.

Cigarette smoke contains carbon monoxide.

For most college students, computers and calculators have become essential.

The Rhone flows south through France and then empties into the Mediterranean.

(2) Compound sentence

A **compound sentence** is made up of two or more independent clauses. The primary ways to coordinate independent clauses are with commas and coordinating conjunctions (*and, but, or, for, nor, so, yet*) and with semicolons.

For centuries, Brittany was an independent state, but now the area is part of France.

The restaurant was dark, the air was filled with smoke, and the music was deafening.

Socrates wrote nothing; his thoughts are known only through the works of Plato and Xenophon.

(3) Complex sentence

A **complex sentence** is made up of one independent clause and one or more dependent clauses—adverb, adjective, or noun.

Although most rifle experts have 20/20 vision, pistol experts are often very nearsighted.

The game involves three contestants who spin a roulette wheel.

Whoever could solve the riddle of the Sphinx would be spared her wrath.

(4) Compound-complex sentence

A **compound-complex sentence** is made up of two or more independent clauses and one or more dependent clauses.

London's Great Exhibition, which opened in 1851, was designed to show human progress; it brought together in the "Crystal Palace" industrial displays remarkable for their day.

Alchemists believed that they could change lesser metals into gold, and although they failed, they helped establish the science of chemistry.

The fathom once was the distance that a Viking could encompass in a hug; a gauge was the distance that lay between the wheels of a Roman chariot; an acre was an area that could be plowed in one day by a team of two oxen.

PART

II

STRUCTURAL AND GRAMMATICAL PROBLEMS

When you write, you must concentrate on matters such as content, organization, purpose, and audience. Naturally, incorrect constructions are likely to appear in early drafts of a composition. Therefore, before you complete a final draft, read your work carefully and revise any sentences that contain structural or grammatical problems. Careful revision will ensure clear and logical prose.

8 Sentence Fragments
9 Comma Splices and Fused Sentences
10 Subject-Verb Agreement
11 Nonstandard Verb Forms
12 Pronoun Reference
13 Pronoun-Antecedent Agreement
14 Case of Nouns and Pronouns
15 Nonstandard Adjective and Adverb Forms
16 Dangling and Misplaced Modifiers
17 Shifts
18 Split Constructions
19 Incomplete Constructions
20 Parallelism

CHAPTER

8

SENTENCE FRAGMENTS

A **sentence fragment** is an incomplete structure punctuated as a complete sentence but lacking the necessary independent clause. The following passage shows how confusing sentence fragments can be.

> Humans accept death as their certain destiny. In nature, however, everything does not die. The hydra, a freshwater, tube-shaped creature. The hydra's body cells regenerate every two weeks. Giving it an unlimited life expectancy. Except for predators and diseases, some fish might never die. Because they never stop growing. In a sense, the amoeba doesn't die. It simply divides. And thus not only survives but also multiplies.

The six complete sentences in the passage express complete thoughts, even out of context.

> Humans accept death as their certain destiny.
>
> In nature, however, everything does not die.
>
> The hydra's body cells regenerate every two weeks.
>
> Except for predators and diseases, some fish might never die.
>
> In a sense, the amoeba doesn't die.
>
> It simply divides.

In contrast, the four fragments seem meaningless.

The hydra, a freshwater, tube-shaped creature.

Giving it an unlimited life expectancy.

Because they never stop growing.

And thus not only survives but also multiplies.

In a few special instances, fragments do not handicap communication.

- **Dialogue:** "Now," thought William. "Now."
- **Deliberate sylistic effects:** The play catches everyone and everything in its swirl. Rather like a tornado.
- **Questions and answers:** When? Only ten years from now.
- **Interjections:** Oh! Well.
- **Advertising:** The best hardware for your best software.
- **Idioms:** The sooner the better. So much for that.

As a general rule, however, you should avoid fragments. If you do find a fragment while revising your prose, you can either attach it to a complete sentence or convert it to a complete sentence.

8a DEPENDENT CLAUSE FRAGMENTS

A dependent clause contains a subject and a predicate and begins with a subordinating word such as *since, if, because, although, who, which, that* (see 7c). When punctuated as a complete sentence, a dependent clause is considered a fragment.

FRAGMENT: Registration was a nightmare. Although I did get the courses I wanted.

REVISED: Registration was a nightmare, although I did get the courses I wanted.

REVISED: Registration was a nightmare. I did, however, get the courses I wanted.

FRAGMENT: At age twenty-six, Jefferson began Monticello. Which he did not complete until he was sixty-eight.

REVISED: At age twenty-six, Jefferson began Monticello, which he did not complete until he was sixty-eight.

REVISED: At age twenty-six, Jefferson began Monticello, but he did not finish it until he was sixty-eight.

8b PHRASE FRAGMENTS

A phrase is a construction without a subject and a predicate. Ordinarily, a phrase should not appear alone, punctuated as though it were a complete sentence.

FRAGMENT: Manufacturers will hold a trade fair in St. Louis next month. The fair to promote new sports equipment.

REVISED: Manufacturers will hold a trade fair in St. Louis next month to promote new sports equipment.

REVISED: Manufacturers will hold a trade fair in St. Louis next month. The event will promote new sports equipment.

FRAGMENT: The department's bloodhound has trailed 165 missing people. And has found 85 percent of them.

REVISED: The department's bloodhound has trailed 165 missing people and has found 85 percent of them.

REVISED: The department's bloodhound has trailed 165 missing people; she has found 85 percent of them.

FRAGMENT: Spider Man's strength and climbing ability came from a remarkable source. The bite of a radioactive spider.

REVISED: Spider Man's strength and climbing ability came from a remarkable source: the bite of a radioactive spider.

REVISED: Spider Man's strength and climbing ability came from a remarkable source. He was bitten by a radioactive spider.

FRAGMENT: She quit smoking last Christmas. Because of a chronic cough.

REVISED: She quit smoking last Christmas because of a chronic cough.

REVISED: She quit smoking last Christmas. At that time, her cough had become chronic.

CHAPTER

9

COMMA SPLICES AND FUSED SENTENCES

Two independent clauses joined with only a comma create a **comma splice,** so called because the clauses are "spliced" together. Two clauses run together without a conjunction or proper punctuation create a **fused sentence,** also called a *run-on* or *run-together sentence.*

COMMA SPLICE:	Pickpockets have become a serious problem, tourists should be especially alert in crowded areas.
FUSED SENTENCE:	Pickpockets have become a serious problem tourists should be especially alert in crowded areas.

Neither of these constructions is acceptable in standard written English. If you find a comma splice or a fused sentence in your rough drafts, you can revise it in one of five ways.

- Use a comma and a coordinating conjunction.
- Use a semicolon.
- Use a colon.
- Create two sentences.
- Create a dependent structure.

9a REVISION WITH A COMMA AND A COORDINATING CONJUNCTION

Comma splices and fused sentences can often be revised by connecting the clauses with both a comma and a coordinating conjunction (*and, but, or, nor, for, so, yet*). This option works well when the sentence does not contain much internal punctuation and one of the conjunctions expresses the proper relationship between the two clauses.

COMMA SPLICE: Winter lasts six months in Wyoming, life gets hard at 20 to 40 degrees below zero.

FUSED SENTENCE: Winter lasts six months in Wyoming life gets hard at 20 to 40 degrees below zero.

REVISED: Winter lasts six months in Wyoming, and life gets hard at 20 to 40 degrees below zero.

COMMA SPLICE: My dormitory room is supposed to house two people comfortably, actually it has only enough space for a six-year-old child.

FUSED SENTENCE: My dormitory room is supposed to house two people comfortably actually it has only enough space for a six-year-old child.

REVISED: My dormitory room is supposed to house two people comfortably, but actually it has only enough space for a six-year-old child.

9b REVISION WITH A SEMICOLON

A semicolon works well when the clauses in a comma splice or fused sentence do not have a relationship easily expressed by one of the coordinating conjunctions.

COMMA SPLICE: The novel is remarkable, Mr. Wright has written over 50,000 words without once using the letter *e*.

FUSED SENTENCE: The novel is remarkable Mr. Wright has written over 50,000 words without once using the letter *e*.

REVISED: The novel is remarkable; Mr. Wright has written over 50,000 words without once using the letter *e.*

The semicolon can also be used in addition to a coordinating conjunction when the first clause has internal punctuation.

COMMA SPLICE: Standing on the pier, her blond hair blowing in the breeze, she looked frail, innocent, and vulnerable, she was actually planning a robbery.

REVISED: Standing on the pier, her blond hair blowing in the breeze, she looked frail, innocent, and vulnerable; yet she was actually planning a robbery.

The semicolon is especially appropriate when the second independent clause begins with a transitional expression (or conjunctive adverb) such as *therefore, consequently, finally, for example, nevertheless, however, then.* (For a more complete list of these expressions, see *Transitional Expression* in the Glossary of Terms.)

Be careful not to confuse coordinating conjunctions and transitional expressions. A conjunction actually links clauses grammatically and cannot move from its position between the two.

POSSIBLE: They discovered that the library ceiling contained asbestos, but the school could not afford to have the material removed.

IMPOSSIBLE: They discovered that the library ceiling contained asbestos; the school could not, but, afford to have the material removed.

A transitional expression, on the other hand, is not a conjunction but an adverb and can move about in its clause.

POSSIBLE: They discovered that the library ceiling contained asbestos; however, the school could not afford to have the material removed.

POSSIBLE: They discovered that the library ceiling contained asbestos; the school could not, however, afford to have the material removed.

An easy way to distinguish between the two types of words is to remember that all the coordinating conjunctions have only two or three letters, whereas all the transitional expressions have four or more.

9c REVISION WITH A COLON

Occasionally, one independent clause is followed by another that explains or amplifies it. In this very special case, you can join the two clauses with a colon.

COMMA SPLICE: The economics of the country caused the 1848 revolution, harvests and commerce were at a low.

REVISED: The economics of the country caused the 1848 revolution: harvests and commerce were at a low.

9d REVISION BY CREATING TWO SENTENCES

You can effectively revise many comma splices and fused sentences by creating two separate sentences—particularly when you want a major break between the clauses. This revision is especially useful when the two clauses are long or when you want to emphasize each clause.

COMMA SPLICE: Unlike most of my friends, I cannot abide watching those silly, mindless situation comedies, for one thing, I resent having the laugh track tell me when to be entertained.

REVISED: Unlike most of my friends, I cannot abide watching those silly, mindless situation comedies. For one thing, I resent having the laugh track tell me when to be entertained.

9e REVISION WITH A DEPENDENT CLAUSE OR PHRASE

Often you can correct a comma splice or fused sentence by changing one of the independent clauses to a dependent clause or phrase.

This correction is a good solution when you want to indicate a special relationship—a relationship such as time, place, condition/result, cause/effect, contrast, and so forth.

FUSED SENTENCE:	Sometimes I craved fried foods floating in grease then I ate in the school cafeteria.
REVISED WITH A DEPENDENT CLAUSE:	When I craved fried foods floating in grease, I ate in the school cafeteria.
REVISED WITH A PHRASE:	Craving fried foods floating in grease, I ate in the school cafeteria.

This correction also works well when the two independent clauses have a noun or noun phrase in common.

COMMA SPLICE:	We desperately need zoning laws, the construction of unsightly commercial buildings could be prevented by zoning laws.
REVISED WITH A DEPENDENT CLAUSE:	We desperately need zoning laws, which could prevent the construction of unsightly commercial buildings.
REVISED WITH A PHRASE:	We desperately need zoning laws to prevent the construction of unsightly commercial buildings.

s/v agr 10

CHAPTER

10

SUBJECT-VERB AGREEMENT

Standard English requires **subject-verb agreement**—that is, a verb form appropriate for the subject. In general, agreement depends on three factors: person, number, and tense.

- **Person** refers to whether the subject is speaking, spoken to, or spoken about.

FIRST PERSON:	The subject is *I* or *we*.
SECOND PERSON:	The subject is *you*.
THIRD PERSON:	The subject is any noun or pronoun except *I*, *we*, or *you*.

- **Number** refers to singular (one) and plural (more than one).
- **Tense** is the verb feature that indicates time (see 4c). All verbs require agreement in the third person of the present tense and the present perfect tense. Notice the *-s* form of the verb (4a) appears in the singular of these tenses but not in the plural.

Present Tense

PERSON	SINGULAR	PLURAL
FIRST:	I upset him.	We upset him.
SECOND:	You upset him.	You upset him.
THIRD:	Anything upsets him.	All things upset him.

Present Perfect Tense

PERSON	SINGULAR	PLURAL
FIRST:	I have upset him.	We have upset him.
SECOND:	You have upset him.	You have upset him.
THIRD:	Something has upset him.	Several things have upset him.

The verb *be* requires agreement in more instances than other verbs. Notice in the following examples that the singular and plural forms differ in the first and third persons of the present tense, in the first and third persons of the past tense, and in the third person of the present perfect tense.

Present Tense

PERSON	SINGULAR	PLURAL
FIRST:	I am a student.	We are students.
SECOND:	You are a student.	You are students.
THIRD:	She is a student.	They are students.

Past Tense

PERSON	SINGULAR	PLURAL
FIRST:	I was a student.	We were students.
SECOND:	You were a student.	You were students.
THIRD:	Amy was a student.	Amy and Jake were students.

Present Perfect Tense

PERSON	SINGULAR	PLURAL
FIRST:	I have been a student.	We have been students.
SECOND:	You have been a student.	You have been students.
THIRD:	The professor has been a student.	Professors have been students.

When the subject of a sentence is simple and appears next to its verb, subject-verb agreement usually presents no problems. But some subjects are tricky. As you edit your writing, watch for constructions such as the following that can cause agreement problems.

10a INTERVENING WORDS BETWEEN SUBJECT AND VERB

Often the subject of a sentence is followed by a phrase or clause that contains a noun. Be sure that the verb agrees with the true subject and not with a noun that follows the subject.

> Emission that pours from the smokestacks has polluted the area.
>
> The instructions outlined in the manual were not clear.
>
> A collection of glass animals was arranged on the table.
>
> The development of new techniques leads to increasingly accurate test results.

10b SUBJECTS JOINED BY *AND*

In general, when a sentence has two or more subjects joined by *and,* use a plural verb.

> The governor and the attorney general drive limousines.
>
> Sun and wind cause skin burn.
>
> McDonald's, Wendy's, and Burger King have been waging commercial warfare.

CAUTION: This convention does not apply to subjects joined by phrases such as *as well as, together with, in addition to.*

> The governor, as well as the attorney general, drives a limousine.
>
> Hot sun, together with strong wind, causes severe skin burn.
>
> McDonald's, in addition to Wendy's and Burger King, has been waging commercial warfare.

EXCEPTIONS: Use a singular verb in two instances.

- When *each* or *every* precedes subjects joined by *and*

> Each governor and each attorney general was assigned a limousine.
>
> Every hamburger chain and every fried chicken franchise has been engaged in commercial warfare.

- When the subjects joined by *and* refer to a single person, thing, or idea

Red beans and rice is a popular Cajun dish.

My best friend and confidant has betrayed me.

10c SUBJECTS JOINED BY *OR/NOR*

When the subjects of a sentence are joined by *or* or *nor* (or *either . . . or, neither . . . nor*), make the verb agree with the subject closer to it. If the closer subject is singular, the verb is singular; if the closer subject is plural, the verb is plural.

Neither the boxwood nor the roses have survived the ice storm.

Neither the roses nor the boxwood has survived the ice storm.

CAUTION: This practice can cause awkward constructions, particularly with the verb *be* when the subjects are in different persons: *Either Steve or I am in charge.* Although this sentence is technically correct, you may want to avoid awkwardness by using two clauses instead of one: *Either Steve is in charge, or I am.*

10d INDEFINITE PRONOUNS AS SUBJECTS

Some indefinite pronouns are always singular, some are always plural, and some can be either.

- Singular verbs are required with the following indefinite pronouns used as subjects.

another	everybody	nothing
anybody	everyone	one
anyone	everything	other
anything	neither	somebody
each	nobody	someone
either	no one	something

Neither is acceptable.

Each was published in 1989.

Everyone comments on the vivid colors.

s/v agr 10d

When phrases and clauses follow these indefinite pronouns, be careful not to mistake an intervening noun for the subject of the verb.

Neither of these essays is acceptable.

Each of the studies was published in 1989.

Everyone who sees the paintings comments on the vivid colors.

- Plural verbs are required with the following indefinite pronouns used as subjects.

both	few	several
many	others	

Both have graduated with honors.

Many claim to have seen UFOs.

- When the following indefinite pronouns are used as subjects, meaning determines whether the verb is singular or plural.

all	more	none
any	most	some

If the indefinite pronoun refers to a noncountable noun (*confusion, laughter, art*), use a singular verb. If the indefinite pronoun refers to a plural, countable noun (*residents, pages, machines*), use a plural verb.

NONCOUNT/SINGULAR:	Most of the confusion was over.
COUNT/PLURAL:	Most of the residents were elderly.
NONCOUNT/SINGULAR:	Some of the laughter was dying.
COUNT/PLURAL:	Some of the pages were missing.

Some writers always use a singular verb with *none,* even when it refers to a plural, countable noun.

None of the players was fined.

Nevertheless, most contemporary writers prefer a plural verb when the reference is plural.

None of the players were fined.

10e RELATIVE PRONOUNS AS SUBJECTS

When a relative pronoun (*that, which, who*) is the subject of a clause, make the verb agree with the pronoun's antecedent—the word or phrase that the pronoun stands for.

The Phantom is powered by engines that deliver 17,900 pounds of thrust. [engines deliver]

Her celebrated collection of photographs, which documents Christmas in rural America, is on display during December. [collection documents]

When the relative pronoun is preceded by *one of those* . . . or *one of the* . . . make the verb plural.

He is one of those students who always study early. [students study]

When the relative pronoun is preceded by *the only one of* . . ., make the verb singular.

He is the only one of the students who always studies early. [one studies]

10f SUBJECTS OF LINKING VERBS

A linking verb may connect a singular subject with a plural complement or a plural subject with a singular complement. (See 7a.3.) Regardless of the number of the complement, the verb agrees with its subject.

My chief entertainment was the old movies on television.

The old movies on television were my chief entertainment.

10g SUBJECTS THAT FOLLOW VERBS

Verbs agree with their subjects even when normal sentence order is inverted and the subjects are delayed.

There are three reasons for the mistake.

There is a good reason for the mistake.

Covering the wall were dozens of ancestral portraits.

Covering the wall was a medieval tapestry.

10h COLLECTIVE NOUNS AND AMOUNTS AS SUBJECTS

A collective noun refers to a group that forms some sort of unit, for example, *team, class, audience, enemy, orchestra, panel, crew, family, club.* When these nouns refer to the group as a whole, use a singular verb; when they refer to the individual members of the group, use a plural verb.

Parliament sits in majestic houses along the Thames. [*Parliament* refers to the governing body as a unit.]

Parliament disagree on the tax issue. [*Parliament* refers to the individuals within the group since a unit cannot disagree with itself.]

The team is on the court. [*Team* refers to the group as a unit.]

The team are taking their practice shots. [*Team* refers to the individuals within the group since each team member must take practice shots by himself or herself.]

A plural verb with a collective noun (*team are*) sounds peculiar to most people and is therefore uncommon. Instead, writers usually prefer to pair a plural verb with a subject that is obviously plural.

The members of Parliament disagree on the tax issue.

The players are taking their practice shots.

When the subject refers to a unit amount, a kind of lump sum, use a singular verb. When the subject refers to several units, use a plural verb.

Four days seems a reasonable time.

Four days were marked off on the calendar.

With some amounts, either a singular or a plural verb is appropriate.

Three truckloads of gravel was (or were) needed to fill the hole.

When the word *number* is the subject and is preceded by *the,* use a singular verb. When *number* is preceded by *a,* use a plural verb.

The number of students taking workshops has increased.

A number of students have signed up for the workshop.

10i TITLES AS SUBJECTS

Titles are considered singular, regardless of whether the words in them are singular or plural.

African Kingdoms is assigned reading.

Gulliver's Travels satirizes human nature.

10j FOREIGN NOUNS AS SUBJECTS

Some nouns borrowed from foreign languages have retained their foreign plurals and do not "look" plural to an English speaker. If you are not sure about the number of a foreign noun, consult an up-to-date, standard dictionary. There you will find, for example, that *genera* is the plural form of *genus; stimuli,* the plural of *stimulus,* and *media,* the plural of *medium.*

Data is probably the most commonly used of these foreign nouns because it occurs frequently in technical literature. Traditionally, *datum* is the singular form and *data* is the plural.

The data were gathered over a six-month period.

Increasingly, however, *data* is treated as a noncountable noun (such as *information*) and is used with a singular verb.

The data was gathered over a period of six months.

10k SUBJECTS ENDING IN *-ICS*

A number of words in English end in *-ics: linguistics, physics, mathematics, economics, ceramics, statistics, ballistics, athletics, aerobics, gymnastics, calisthenics, acoustics, politics, ethics,* and so on.

s/v
agr
101

When referring to a body of knowledge or a field of study, a noun ending in *-ics* requires a singular verb. When referring to activities, the same noun requires a plural verb.

> Politics is one of the major industries in this country.
>
> His politics make me nervous.
>
> Calisthenics is required in the qualification trials.
>
> Calisthenics are simple gymnastic exercises.

101 "WORDS" AS SUBJECTS

A word cited as the word itself is marked in one of three ways: enclosed in quotation marks, underlined, or italicized. Whether singular or plural, the word cited requires a singular verb.

> "Fiddlesticks" was my grandmother's favorite expression.
>
> In law, *person* means either a human being or an organization with legal rights.
>
> People is a plural noun.

CHAPTER

11

NONSTANDARD VERB FORMS

Nonstandard verb forms occur most commonly for three reasons.

1. A writer does not know the correct principal parts of irregular verbs and thus writes a verb such as *had went* for *had gone.*
2. A writer transfers the sounds of speech to writing and drops a letter, producing a verb such as *use to* for *used to.*
3. A writer confuses a verb with a word that closely resembles it, using *loose,* for example, instead of *lose.*

The wrong verb form may not always obscure meaning. If you make the errors just described, a reader will possibly understand what you mean but will judge you uneducated—or at the very least, careless. Therefore, when revising your prose, make sure you have used verbs and their forms correctly.

11a NONSTANDARD PRINCIPAL PARTS

The principal parts of verbs include three forms—the base, or infinitive form; the past-tense form; and the past participle. (See 4a.) Ordinarily, problems do not arise with regular verbs because the past form and the past participle are identical (*cure, cured, cured; look, looked, looked*). Irregular verbs, however, have unpredictable forms for the past tense and the past participle (*do, did, done; break, broke, broken*). Furthermore, the forms have different uses. The past form expresses a past occurrence and is used alone—without auxiliaries. The past participle is used after forms of *have* to express the perfect tenses and after forms of *be* to express the passive voice.

PAST: The axle broke for the third time.

PRESENT PERFECT: The axle has broken for the third time.

PASSIVE VOICE: The axle was broken by the impact.

The wrong form of an irregular verb is considered nonstandard English. If you are ever unsure of the principal parts of a verb, check the forms in a dictionary or in the Glossary of Terms under the heading *Irregular Verbs.*

NONSTANDARD: The letter come Monday.

STANDARD: The letter came Monday.

STANDARD: The letter had come Monday.

NONSTANDARD: Someone had stole my tennis racquet.

STANDARD: Someone had stolen my tennis racquet.

STANDARD: Someone stole my tennis racquet.

11b DROPPED *-S/-ES* AND *-D/-ED* VERB ENDINGS

Two important verb endings are *-s/-es* and *-d/-ed.* The *-s/-es* occurs with all verbs in the present-tense singular, except those whose subjects are *I, we,* and *you.* The *-d/-ed* occurs with regular verbs to form the past tense and past participle. In conversation, speakers sometimes drop these endings, producing verb forms such as the ones in the following sentences.

-s DROPPED: He exist on potato chips and sodas.

-d DROPPED: We use to go to New Orleans every year.

-ed DROPPED: They box the equipment yesterday.

In writing, however, you must retain the *-s/-es* and *-d/-ed,* regardless of whether you would pronounce them. Dropping these important endings will result in nonstandard verb forms:

NONSTANDARD: That reporter always ask personal questions.

STANDARD: That reporter always asks personal questions.

NONSTANDARD: The players are suppose to practice every day.

STANDARD: The players are supposed to practice every day.

NONSTANDARD: You cannot successfully reheat bake potatoes.

STANDARD: You cannot successfully reheat baked potatoes.

11c VERBS CONFUSED WITH SIMILAR WORDS

Writers sometimes confuse verbs with words that are similar in spelling, pronunciation, or meaning—for example, *affect/effect, lie/lay, imply/infer.* Regardless of the source of confusion, you can solve the problem by looking up a troublesome verb in a dictionary. There you will find the principal parts, the meaning, and sometimes notes on usage. Furthermore, the following pairs of words are discussed in the Glossary of Usage.

accept, except
advice, advise
affect, effect
aggravate, irritate
bring, take
burst, bust
censor, censure
complement, compliment
comprise, compose
convince, persuade
device, devise
emigrate, immigrate
ensure, insure
hanged, hung
imply, infer
lay, lie
lend, loan
lose, loose
orient, orientate
precede, proceed
prosecute, persecute
raise, rise
set, sit
use, utilize

CHAPTER

12

PRONOUN REFERENCE

A pronoun's antecedent is the person, thing, or idea to which the pronoun refers. Normally, a pronoun takes its meaning from its antecedent.

> The French flag is called the "Tricolor" because it has three vertical bands of different colors. [The pronoun *it* stands for the antecedent *the French flag.*]

> Nathaniel Currier issued his first two prints in 1835. [The pronoun *his* stands for the antecedent *Nathaniel Currier.*]

When you revise, make sure that the antecedent of each pronoun is absolutely clear. The following discussion covers the common problems of **pronoun reference.**

12a IMPLIED REFERENCE

A pronoun's antecedent must be stated, not merely implied. In the following sentence, the appropriate antecedent of *one* is *horse,* but *horse* does not appear.

IMPLIED REFERENCE: At first, horseback riding scared me because I had never been on one.

To avoid implied reference, you can provide a clear antecedent or remove the pronoun.

CLEAR ANTECEDENT: At first, I was scared to ride a horse because I had never been on one.

REMOVAL OF PRONOUN: At first, horseback riding scared me because I had never ridden before.

In the next sentence, the possessive *Homer's* is functioning as a modifier, not as a noun, and therefore cannot serve as the antecedent of *he.*

IMPLIED REFERENCE: In Homer's poems, he recounts the events of the Trojan War.

The antecedent *Homer* can be provided, or *he* can be eliminated.

CLEAR ANTECEDENT: In his poems, Homer recounts the events of the Trojan War.

REMOVAL OF PRONOUN: Homer's poems recount the events of the Trojan War.

12b BROAD REFERENCE

In broad reference, a pronoun has no antecedent and stands instead for an idea or ideas expressed in the preceding discussion. Although readers can sometimes understand broad reference, it is usually not clear and should be avoided. For example, in the following passage, a reader cannot be sure what the writer means by the pronoun *this.*

BROAD: The space above the spout of a boiling kettle of water is filled with an invisible gas called "water vapor," or "steam." The visible cloud above this space is not steam but droplets of water formed when the gas cools. This is called "condensation."

To avoid this kind of broad reference, you can supply a noun or noun phrase that describes the idea referred to.

REVISED: The space above the spout of a boiling kettle of water is filled with an invisible gas called "water vapor," or "steam." The visible cloud above this space is not steam but droplets of water formed when the gas cools. This droplet formation is called "condensation."

Another kind of broad reference involves a dependent clause that begins with *which.*

BROAD: Next semester, personal computers can be connected to the university system, which will reduce the amount of equipment students will need to work at home.

The pronoun *which* seems to refer to *university system* but, in fact, refers to the entire idea expressed by the preceding clause: "Next semester, personal computers can be connected to the university system." The sentence should be revised to provide a clear antecedent for *which* or to remove the pronoun.

CLEAR ANTECEDENT: Next semester, personal computers can be connected to the university system—an arrangement which will reduce the amount of equipment students will need to work at home.

REMOVAL OF PRONOUN: Next semester, personal computers can be connected to the university system, reducing the amount of equipment students will need to work at home.

12c INDEFINITE *YOU, THEY,* AND *IT*

In conversation, speakers frequently use *you, they,* and *it* indefinitely—that is, to refer to people or things in general. This kind of reference, however, is not acceptable in formal writing.

INDEFINITE *YOU:* You can inherit certain diseases.

REVISED: People can inherit certain diseases.

INDEFINITE *THEY:* In Houston they have thousands of acres of parks.

REVISED: Houston has thousands of acres of parks.

INDEFINITE *IT:* It states in the Declaration of Independence that everyone is created equal.

REVISED: The Declaration of Independence states that everyone is created equal.

12d AMBIGUOUS REFERENCE

A pronoun should refer unmistakably to one antecedent. If a pronoun seems to refer to more than one, the meaning is ambiguous. Consequently, readers cannot immediately identify which possible antecedent is meant. For example, in the following sentence, *they* can refer to *fire fighters,* to *city council members,* or to both.

AMBIGUOUS REFERENCE: When the fire fighters met with the city council members, they outlined the problems.

The sentence must be revised to eliminate the ambiguity.

REVISED: The fire fighters, who outlined the problems, met with the city council members.

REVISED: The fire fighters met with the city council members, who outlined the problems.

REVISED: At the meeting, the fire fighters and the council members outlined the problems.

12e MIXED USES OF *IT*

The word *it* can be used as a personal pronoun, an expletive, or a predicate substitute.

> I wanted the Corvette as soon as I saw it. [The pronoun *it* refers to the noun phrase, *the Corvette.*]
>
> It is dangerous to sleep in the sun. [The expletive *it* begins the sentence and delays the subject, *to sleep in the sun.*]
>
> If you really want to major in music, you should do it. [*Do it* substitutes for part of the predicate, *major in music.*]

When *it* is used in different ways in the same sentence or sequential sentences, the result can be confusing and awkward. In the following passage, for example, *it* appears first as a pronoun, second as an expletive, and third as a predicate substitute.

Mixed Use

Our financial adviser suggests that we sell our house since it has become a drain on our budget. It is hard, however, to let go of a place with beautiful memories; and we really don't want to do it.

For clarity's sake, the passage should be rewritten to eliminate mixed use of *it.* In the following revised version, *it* is used twice as a personal pronoun, referring to *house.*

Revised

Our financial adviser suggests that we sell our house since it has become a drain on our budget. The house is so full of beautiful memories, however, that we don't want to give it up.

12f REMOTE REFERENCE

A pronoun must be close enough to its antecedent to make the reference instantly clear. For example, in the following passage, a sentence intervenes between the pronoun *they* and its antecedent, *fairies.*

Remote Antecedent

Fairies—small, magical creatures—appear in most of the folklore of the Middle Ages. During that time, belief in magic exerted a strong influence on human behavior. They might be mischievous, helpful, or fearsome; but always they interfered in the daily lives of the folk.

The pronouns are so remote from their antecedent that the reference is unclear. Repeating the noun antecedent solves the problem.

Revised

Fairies—small, magical creatures—appear in most of the folklore of the Middle Ages. During that time, belief in magic exerted a strong influence on human behavior. Fairies might be mischievous, helpful, or fearsome; but always they interfered in the daily lives of the folk.

12g TITLES AND HEADINGS AS ANTECEDENTS

Titles of papers and headings in the text cannot be the antecedents of pronouns.

No Antecedent

Glaciers

They are rivers of ice, with movement measured in inches per day instead of miles per hour. . . .

Revised

Glaciers

Glaciers are rivers of ice, with movement measured in inches per day instead of miles per hour. . . .

CHAPTER

13

PRONOUN-ANTECEDENT AGREEMENT

A pronoun must agree in number with its antecedent—that is, the noun or noun phrase to which the pronoun refers. A singular antecedent requires a singular pronoun; a plural antecedent, a plural pronoun.

SINGULAR ANTECEDENT/SINGULAR PRONOUN: The amethyst is usually purple or bluish-violet; it is a semiprecious stone made from a variety of quartz.

PLURAL ANTECEDENT/PLURAL PRONOUN: Amethysts are usually purple or bluish-violet; they are semiprecious stones made from a variety of quartz.

When revising, be sure of **pronoun-antecedent agreement.** In most cases, you simply find the antecedent and check to see whether it matches the pronoun in number. If the number of an antecedent is not obvious, the following guidelines will help you choose the appropriate pronoun.

13a ANTECEDENTS JOINED BY *AND*

Usually, antecedents joined by *and* require a plural pronoun.

PLURAL PRONOUN: The wombat and the bandicoot carry their young in pouches.

In two instances, however, antecedents joined by *and* require a singular pronoun.

- When the antecedents refer to a single person, place, thing, or idea

SINGULAR PRONOUN: The judge and executioner eyes his victim impassively.

SINGULAR PRONOUN: The candidate loudly supports law and order—as though it were debatable.

- When *each* or *every* precedes the compound

SINGULAR PRONOUN: Each hot spell and each rainstorm took its toll on my dwindling vegetable garden.

SINGULAR PRONOUN: Every retired bronc rider and calf roper in the Southwest had paid his entry fee.

13b ANTECEDENTS JOINED BY *OR/NOR*

When singular antecedents are joined by *or/nor,* use a singular pronoun. When plural antecedents are joined by *or/nor,* use a plural pronoun.

SINGULAR PRONOUN: The field judge or the back judge blew his whistle.

PLURAL PRONOUN: Neither the Russians nor the Chinese sent their delegations.

When one antecedent is singular and the other plural, the pronoun agrees with the nearer antecedent. To avoid an awkward sentence, place the plural antecedent nearer the pronoun.

AWKWARD: Neither my grandparents nor my mother would sign her name to the petition.

REVISED: Neither my mother nor my grandparents would sign their names to the petition.

13c INDEFINITE PRONOUNS AND SEXIST LANGUAGE

A common problem in pronoun-antecedent agreement occurs with indefinite pronouns that can refer to people: *anybody, anyone, each, either, everybody, everyone, neither, nobody, no one,* and *none.* In casual conversation, speakers often use the plural pronoun *their* with these indefinites:

INFORMAL: Everyone in the auto-repair clinic provides their own tools.

This construction, however, is not acceptable in formal prose. *Everyone* is singular and requires not only a singular verb but also a singular pronoun. In the past, writers used *he, him,* or *his* to refer to both males and females.

OUTDATED: Everyone in the auto-repair clinic provides his own tools.

Today, the use of a masculine pronoun for both men and women is often considered sexist language and should be avoided if feasible. (See 32e.) One alternative is to change the antecedent, the verb, and the pronoun to the plural.

PLURAL CONSTRUCTION: Participants in the auto-repair clinic provide their own tools.

Another alternative is to use both a masculine and a feminine pronoun.

SINGULAR CONSTRUCTION: Everyone in the auto-repair clinic provides his or her own tools.

Remember, however, that frequent use of both masculine and feminine pronouns is awkward and wearisome. If you do not want to switch to the plural, you should eliminate pronouns where possible.

AWKWARD: Everyone in the auto-repair clinic provides his or her tools so that he or she can work individually with instructors. The clinic, however, furnishes the vehicles needed by everyone for his or her hands-on training.

REVISED: Everyone in the auto-repair clinic provides the tools for working individually with instructors. The clinic, however, furnishes the vehicles needed for hands-on training.

13d GENERIC NOUNS AND SEXIST LANGUAGE

Sexist language can be a problem when nouns are used generically to refer to all members of a group—*the astronaut* can refer to all astronauts, *the writer* to all writers, *the swimmer* to all swimmers, *the police officer* to all police officers. Even though these generic nouns refer to more than one person, they require singular pronouns. Formerly, writers used *he, him, his,* which were supposed to refer to both sexes. Today, the use of masculine pronouns to refer to both males and females is often thought unacceptable. (See 32e.)

OUTDATED: The astronaut must begin his training long before a flight.

You can make such a sentence acceptable by including both the feminine and the masculine pronoun or by rewriting the sentence with plural nouns and pronouns. Or you can eliminate the pronoun altogether.

SINGULAR PRONOUNS: The astronaut must begin his or her training long before a flight.

PLURAL PRONOUN: Astronauts must begin their training long before flights.

NO PRONOUN: The astronaut must begin training long before a flight.

13e COLLECTIVE NOUNS AS ANTECEDENTS

Collective nouns—such as *audience, jury, orchestra, committee, family*—are singular when they refer to a group as a unit and plural

pn
agr
13e

when they refer to the individual members in the group. Therefore, depending on their meanings, collective nouns may require singular or plural pronouns.

GROUP AS A UNIT: The family incorporated itself for tax purposes.

INDIVIDUAL MEMBERS: The family are squabbling over their grandfather's estate.

If *the family are* sounds peculiar to you—as it does to many people—you can always supply a subject that is clearly plural.

PLURAL SUBJECT: The members of the family are squabbling over their grandfather's estate.

CHAPTER

14

CASE OF NOUNS AND PRONOUNS

Nouns and pronouns have **case,** that is, different forms for different functions. Most pronouns and all nouns change form only in the possessive—the case that expresses such ideas as ownership (*your phone*), authorship (*Ann's poetry*), measurement (*week's pay*), and source (*president's power*). A few pronouns have three cases.

Subjective	*Objective*	*Possessive*
I	me	my/mine
he	him	his
she	her	her/hers
we	us	our/ours
they	them	their/theirs
who	whom	whose
whoever	whomever	

The subjective forms of these pronouns are used as subjects and subject complements, sometimes called *predicate nominatives.*

> We fed the animals a high-protein diet. [subject]

> The first guest to arrive was she. [subject complement]

The objective forms are used as objects and as subjects and objects of infinitives.

> The voters will never elect him. [direct object]

> The new hospital gave them hope. [indirect object]

I felt the painting looking at me. [object of preposition]

My manager wanted me to hire them. [subject and object of infinitive]

In addition to case, some pronouns have forms made with the suffixes *-self* and *-selves: myself, yourself, himself, herself, itself, ourselves, yourselves, themselves.* These forms are used in two ways.

- As reflexives: objects that rename subjects

  She corrected herself.

  The winners congratulated themselves.

  I was ashamed of myself.

- As emphatics: pronouns that repeat, for emphasis, the nouns or pronouns they refer to

  The owner himself waited on tables.

  You must write the letter yourself.

  They catered the party themselves.

Although use of incorrect pronoun case does not ordinarily mislead the reader, it is considered nonstandard. Therefore, when you revise your papers, check the case of pronouns carefully. The following guidelines should help you choose the appropriate forms.

14a CASE IN COMPOUND CONSTRUCTIONS

Compounding in no way affects the case of a pronoun. When in doubt about which case is appropriate, simply drop all other elements in the compound construction. Then you can readily determine the correct form.

The Senator hired Mary and (I or me). [You would write *The Senator hired me,* not *The Senator hired I.* Thus, the correct sentence is *The Senator hired Mary and me.*]

Both his brother and (he or him) attended Yale. [You would write *He attended Yale,* not *Him attended Yale.* Thus, the correct sentence is *Both his brother and he attended Yale.*]

In a compound appositive, pronoun case depends on the use of the word that the appositive renames. An appositive renaming a subject or subject complement is in the subjective case; an appositive renaming an object or object complement is in the objective case.

> The centers, Hackett and he, were benched for fighting. [*Hackett and he* renames the subject, *centers.* Thus, the pronoun is in the subjective case.]

> The cabin was built by three people—Craig, Ray, and me. [*Craig, Ray, and me* renames *people,* the object of the preposition *by.* Thus, the pronoun is in the objective case.]

Compounds that often cause mistakes contain pronouns in the first-person singular. Always use *me* as the object of any preposition, regardless of the context.

NONSTANDARD: Just between you and I, the credit union is in financial trouble.

CORRECT: Just between you and me, the credit union is in financial trouble.

Use the pronoun *myself* only as a reflexive or an emphatic. Never use *myself* when the subjective or objective case is called for.

NONSTANDARD: Brett and myself had dinner at Antoine's.

CORRECT: Brett and I had dinner at Antoine's.

NONSTANDARD: The coach saw Lee and myself at the party.

CORRECT: The coach saw Lee and me at the party.

14b PRONOUN CASE AFTER *BE*

In conversational English, most people use pronouns in the objective case as complements of *be.*

INFORMAL: It's me.

INFORMAL: That's him.

Although the objective case is appropriate in conversation, the subjective case is required in formal writing.

FORMAL: The first dignitary presented at state occasions was always he.

FORMAL: The only medical doctor in the county was she.

14c *WHO/WHOM* AND *WHOEVER/WHOMEVER*

Although the form *whom* is not common in conversation, you should observe the case distinctions between *who/whoever* (subjective case) and *whom/whomever* (objective case) when you write or speak in formal English.

To use the forms correctly, you must determine the pronoun's use in its own clause—whether independent or dependent. You can make this determination by the following method.

1. Isolate the pronoun's clause, and ignore the rest of the sentence.
2. Put the parts of the isolated clause in normal sentence order (subject + verb + other elements).
3. Substitute pronouns to see which fits. If you would normally use *he, she,* or *they,* choose *who* or *whoever.* If you would normally use *him, her,* or *them,* choose, *whom* or *whomever.*

A few sample sentences will illustrate the method.

(Who/whom) did you contact?

You did contact who/whom?

You did contact him.

Whom did you contact?

These are the recruits (who/whom) we think will go to OCS.

Who/whom will go to OCS?

They will go to OCS.

These are the recruits who we think will go to OCS.

The newspaper always attacks (whoever/whomever) the governor appoints.

The governor appoints whoever/whomever.

The governor appoints her.

The newspaper always attacks whomever the governor appoints.

14d CASE IN ELLIPTICAL CLAUSES

Dependent clauses introduced by *than* or *as* are often elliptical—that is, some parts are not stated but understood (7d). When an elliptical clause contains a pronoun, you might have to fill in the missing parts to determine the pronoun's case. For example, suppose you were trying to decide which pronoun to use in the following sentence: *Her parents seemed younger than (she/her.)* Completing the sentence will reveal the correct form.

ELLIPTICAL: Her parents seemed younger than she.

COMPLETE: Her parents seemed younger than she seemed.

In some elliptical clauses, either subjective or objective case is possible. Be sure to choose the pronoun form that conveys the intended meaning.

ELLIPTICAL: The skiing lessons helped Joan more than I.

COMPLETE: The skiing lessons helped Joan more than I helped Joan.

ELLIPTICAL: The skiing lessons helped Joan more than me.

COMPLETE: The skiing lessons helped Joan more than they helped me.

ELLIPTICAL: Her friends annoy me as much as she.

COMPLETE: Her friends annoy me as much as she annoys me.

ELLIPTICAL: Her friends annoy me as much as her.

COMPLETE: Her friends annoy me as much as they annoy her.

14e POSSESSIVE CASE WITH GERUNDS

A gerund is the *-ing* form of a verb functioning as a noun (5c). In formal prose, nouns and pronouns acting as determiners for gerunds

case 14e

must be in the possessive case: *my singing, Frank's passing, their whispering.* In conversation, you might say, "I don't mind him spending the money." But you should write, "The public objected to his spending money on state dinners"—because it is the spending that the public objects to, not him. *His* identifies whose spending it was.

INFORMAL: The listeners quickly tired of the candidate evading the issue.

FORMAL: The listeners quickly tired of the candidate's evading the issue.

INFORMAL: The security office objected to them parking in the fire lanes.

FORMAL: The security office objected to their parking in the fire lanes.

CHAPTER

15 NONSTANDARD ADJECTIVE AND ADVERB FORMS

Adjectives and adverbs are modifiers—that is, they describe and qualify other elements of sentences. Adjectives modify nouns and pronouns. Adverbs modify verbs, adjectives, other adverbs, and whole clauses. (See Chapter 3.) Many adjectives and adverbs have characteristic forms. Confusion or misuse will produce **nonstandard adjective and adverb forms.**

15a CONFUSION OF ADJECTIVES AND ADVERBS

Be careful not to substitute adjectives for adverbs. A few adjectives and adverbs (such as *fast, early, late*) share identical forms. However, the adjective and adverb forms of most modifiers are different. In fact, many adverbs are formed by adding *-ly* to adjectives. For example, *serious* and *perfect* are adjectives; *seriously* and *perfectly* are adverbs.

ADJECTIVE SUBSTITUTED FOR ADVERB:	We talked serious about our future.
REVISED:	We talked seriously about our future. [adverb modifying *talked*]

REVISED: We had a serious conversation about our future. [adjective modifying *conversation*]

ADJECTIVE SUBSTITUTED FOR ADVERB: He recited the speech perfect.

REVISED: He recited the speech perfectly. [adverb modifying *recited*]

REVISED: His speech was perfect. [adjective modifying *speech*]

You probably have little difficulty with modifiers such as *serious/seriously* and *perfect/perfectly.* However, because of a conflict between conversational and written English, a few pairs of modifiers are particularly troublesome.

awful/awfully	most/almost
bad/badly	real/really
good/well	

The adjective forms of these modifiers should be used after linking verbs such as *feel, taste, sound,* and *smell.* (See 7a.3.)

ADVERB SUBSTITUTED FOR ADJECTIVE: I feel badly.

REVISED: I feel bad.

If you have problems with any of these troublesome modifiers, look them up in the Glossary of Usage at the end of this book. There they are defined, and their appropriate uses are discussed and illustrated.

15b INAPPROPRIATE COMPARATIVE AND SUPERLATIVE FORMS

Most adjectives and adverbs have three forms, or degrees. The positive form is the simple form of the modifier. The comparative form (expressed by *-er, more,* or *less*) is used to compare two items. The superlative form (expressed by *-est, most,* or *least*) is used to compare more than two items. (See 3c for discussion and examples.)

Do not use the comparative form to refer to more than two items or the superlative to refer to only two.

INAPPROPRIATE COMPARATIVE: Jones is the more interesting of all the lecturers.

REVISED: Jones is the most interesting of all the lecturers.

INAPPROPRIATE SUPERLATIVE: We should buy the fastest of the two printers.

REVISED: We should buy the faster of the two printers.

Avoid double comparisons—the use of *more* or *most* with another comparative or superlative modifier. Sentences containing double comparisons are nonstandard.

DOUBLE COMPARISON: This summer is more hotter than the last.

REVISED: This summer is hotter than the last.

DOUBLE COMPARISON: The most unusualest piece in the collection was an ebony necklace.

REVISED: The most unusual piece in the collection was an ebony necklace.

Some adjectives, called ***absolutes,*** cannot logically express degree. For example, one thing cannot be more first than another nor more infinite: something is either first or not, either finite or infinite. About other adjectives, however, there is disagreement. Some people claim that perfection, uniqueness, and correctness can be approximated. Thus, one thing can be more perfect, more unique, or more correct than another. Other people apply strict logic: something is either perfect or imperfect, unique or not unique, correct or incorrect.

Because many readers disapprove of the comparison of absolutes, you can always insert *more nearly* before the adjective.

QUESTIONABLE COMPARISON: The second portrait is a more perfect likeness than the first.

REVISED: The second portrait is a more nearly perfect likeness than the first.

15c INAPPROPRIATE DEMONSTRATIVES

The demonstratives (*this, that, these,* and *those*) can function not only as pronouns but also as determiners—*this concept, that tablet, these entries, those mistakes.* Only two problems are usually associated with these modifiers.

- The use of *them* in place of *these* or *those*

NONSTANDARD: Them shoes were half price.

REVISED: Those shoes were half price.

- The use of *these* instead of *this* before a singular noun like *kind, sort,* or *type*

NONSTANDARD: These kind of flowers bloom twice a year.

REVISED: This kind of flower blooms twice a year.

REVISED: These kinds of flowers bloom twice a year.

CHAPTER

16

DANGLING AND MISPLACED MODIFIERS

The function of modifiers is to describe other words—to qualify, limit, intensify, or explain them. Thus, modifiers and the words they describe form a close relationship, which must be immediately clear to readers. When a modifier is not clearly related to any other word in its sentence, it is called **dangling.**

DANGLING PHRASE: To have a successful camping trip, the right equipment must be packed.

REVISED: To have a successful trip, campers must pack the right equipment.

DANGLING CLAUSE: When covered with a fine white ash, the chicken should be placed on the grill.

REVISED: When the coals are covered with a fine white ash, the chicken should be placed on the grill.

When a modifier seems to relate to the wrong element in a sentence, it is called **misplaced.**

MISPLACED PHRASE: He led me to a corner table with a sneer.

REVISED: With a sneer, he led me to a corner table.

MISPLACED CLAUSE: We cooked fresh vegetables on an old wood stove that we had picked that morning.

REVISED: On an old wood stove, we cooked fresh vegetables that we had picked that morning.

Both types of faulty modification can create awkward and confusing constructions. Therefore, when you revise your writing be sure to eliminate dangling and misplaced modifiers.

16a DANGLING MODIFIERS

Although any modifier can dangle, the problem occurs most commonly with verbal phrases and elliptical clauses. (See Chapter 5 and 7d.)

(1) Dangling verbals: participles, infinitives, and gerunds

When a verbal phrase modifier begins a sentence, the verbal should refer to the subject of the following clause. Without this logical connection between the verbal and the subject, the modifier dangles. To revise an introductory dangling verbal, you can make the logical connection between verbal and subject, or you can eliminate the verbal.

DANGLING PARTICIPLE: Scoring a touchdown in the last seconds, the game was won 6–0.

REVISED: Scoring a touchdown in the last seconds, the team won the game 6–0.

REVISED: The team won the game 6–0 with a touchdown in the last four seconds.

DANGLING INFINITIVE: To restore the damaged wood, a special chemical was used.

REVISED: To restore the damaged wood, they used a special chemical.

REVISED: A special chemical restored the damaged wood.

DANGLING GERUND: In deciding the case, illegally obtained evidence was used.

REVISED: In deciding the case, the judge used illegally obtained evidence.

REVISED: The judge's decision was based partially on illegally obtained evidence.

Less common is a dangling modifier in the middle or at the end of a sentence. If the relationship between actor and action is not immediately clear, the sentence will be weak or confusing. To revise this kind of dangling structure, you can make a clear connection between the verbal and a preceding noun or pronoun, or you can eliminate the verbal.

DANGLING GERUND: My dexterity improved by practicing the piano.

REVISED: I improved my dexterity by practicing the piano.

REVISED: Piano practice improved my dexterity.

DANGLING PARTICIPLE: The evidence showed an increase in the water-pollution level, concluding that the habitat might endanger waterfowl.

REVISED: The evidence showed an increase in the water-pollution level, suggesting that the habitat might endanger waterfowl.

REVISED: Because the evidence showed an increase in the water-pollution level, researchers concluded that the habitat might endanger waterfowl.

A few verbals do not dangle, even though they do not modify a specific noun. These include nominative absolutes (5d) as well as common expressions that modify whole sentences (*considering, assuming, to conclude, to tell the truth,* and so forth).

NOMINATIVE ABSOLUTE: The swing set finally assembled, Father lay down in complete exhaustion.

COMMON EXPRESSION: Considering the expense, the trip isn't worth it.

COMMON EXPRESSION: To tell the truth, an independent candidate would have a good chance.

(2) Dangling elliptical clauses

In an elliptical clause (7d), the subject and a form of the verb *be* are sometimes omitted. If an elliptical dependent clause is correctly constructed, its omitted subject is the same as the subject of the main clause.

ELLIPTICAL: While attending Radcliffe, she began her autobiography. [*She was* is omitted after *while.*]

ELLIPTICAL: Although responsible for the crash, the air controller refuses to accept any blame. [*The air controller is* is omitted after *although.*]

An elliptical clause dangles when the omitted subject is not the same as the subject of the main clause. To correct a dangling clause, you can make the subject of the main clause the same as the omitted subject of the elliptical clause. Or you can rewrite the sentence to avoid the ellipsis.

DANGLING CLAUSE: While living in Tahiti, rich, tropical settings were painted by Gauguin.

REVISED: While living in Tahiti, Gauguin painted rich, tropical settings.

REVISED: In Tahiti, Gauguin painted rich, tropical settings.

DANGLING CLAUSE: If dissatisfied with a product, a complaint should be made.

REVISED: If dissatisfied with a product, the consumer should complain.

REVISED: The consumer who is dissatisfied with a product should complain.

16b MISPLACED MODIFIERS

A modifier can be positioned so that it seems to modify the wrong word or phrase. It is possible to misplace any sort of modifier—a word, a phrase, or a clause.

(1) Misplaced words

The most commonly misplaced words are "qualifiers" such as *only, nearly, simply, almost, even,* and *just.* In speech, these words usually occur before the verb, regardless of what they modify. In written English, however, you should place qualifiers immediately before (or as near as possible to) the words they modify.

MISPLACED: He only died yesterday.

REVISED: He died only yesterday.

MISPLACED: The students just pay one-third of the cost.

REVISED: The students pay just one-third of the cost.

Misplacement of words other than qualifiers often leads to ambiguity.

AMBIGUOUS: Follow the instructions for installing the antenna carefully. [*Carefully* can modify either *follow* or *installing.*]

REVISED: Follow carefully the instructions for installing the antenna. [*Carefully* modifies *follow.*]

REVISED: Follow the instructions for carefully installing the antenna. [*Carefully* modifies *installing.*]

(2) Misplaced prepositional phrases

You should place prepositional phrases as near as possible to the words or elements they modify because placement affects the meaning of sentences.

The researchers studied aggressive behavior in Washington. [*In Washington* modifies *behavior.*]

The researchers in Washington studied aggressive behavior. [*In Washington* modifies *researchers*.]

Misplacing a prepositional phrase can produce a sentence that is unclear or even silly.

MISPLACED: The computer contained the voting statistics we had collected on the hard disk.

REVISED: On the hard disk, the computer contained the voting statistics we had collected.

MISPLACED: Heinrich planned to conquer France on his deathbed.

REVISED: On his deathbed, Heinrich planned to conquer France.

(3) Misplaced clauses

Dependent clauses should refer clearly and logically to the words that they modify. In some sentences, you can move misplaced dependent clauses near the words they modify. In other sentences, you may have to rewrite to eliminate the misplaced clauses.

MISPLACED: The archeologists found at the site a ceramic pot they had been digging in for two years. [Clause modifies *pot*.]

CLAUSE MOVED: The archeologists found a ceramic pot at the site they had been digging in for two years. [Clause modifies *site*.]

MISPLACED: Because of his allergies, he could not drive a tractor in a hayfield that was not air-conditioned. [Clause modifies *hayfield*.]

CLAUSE ELIMINATED: Because of his allergies, he could not drive an un-air-conditioned tractor in a hayfield. [*Un-air-conditioned* modifies *tractor*.]

(4) Squinting modifiers

"Squinting" modifiers are misplaced in such a way that they can modify either the preceding or the following elements.

SQUINTING: The courses he teaches frequently have been cancelled. [*Frequently* modifies either *teaches* or *have been cancelled.*]

REVISED: The courses he frequently teaches have been cancelled. [*Frequently* modifies *teaches.*]

REVISED: The courses he teaches have been cancelled frequently. [*Frequently* modifies *have been cancelled.*]

SQUINTING: They told him after the meeting to submit a proposal. [*After the meeting* can modify *told* or *to submit.*]

REVISED: After the meeting, they told him to submit a proposal. [*After the meeting* modifies *told.*]

REVISED: They told him to submit a proposal after the meeting. [*After the meeting* modifies *to submit.*]

CHAPTER

17

SHIFTS

A **shift** is any unnecessary change from one pattern to another. In all writing, readers anticipate certain patterns. For example, in a single sentence, they expect a verb to follow a subject and an object to follow a transitive verb. In a passage, they are puzzled if past time shifts to the present without a reason or if the same noun shifts from singular to plural.

An illogical shift hampers communication; it moves the readers' attention away from your message. Therefore, while revising, watch for shifts. They are easy to make in early drafts when you are concentrating on ideas rather than on grammatical structure.

17a SHIFTS IN TENSE SEQUENCE

In a passage of prose and even within a single sentence, the verb forms should follow a consistent and logical pattern—usually called tense sequence. This sequence involves not only the verb tenses but also very often the modal auxiliaries *can, could, will,* and *would.* (For a more complete discussion of tense and modal auxiliaries, see 4b, 4c, and 4d.)

(1) Simple tenses

Tense establishes the time frame of a verb. The simple present usually indicates that an activity always or normally happens, while the simple present progressive indicates that an activity is currently happening. The simple past indicates that an activity is already complete, while the simple past progressive indicates a past activity in progress. Obviously, when the time frame changes from present to past or past to present, so do the verb forms. On the other hand, when the time does not change, neither should the verb forms.

PRESENT TIME: Convertibles always sell [present] best in the spring when the weather is [present] warm.

PRESENT TIME: Convertibles are selling [present progressive] well this spring because the weather is [present] unusually warm.

PAST TIME: Convertibles sold [past] well last spring after interest rates fell [past].

PAST TIME: Convertibles sold [past] well last spring when interest rates were falling [past progressive].

(2) Perfect tenses

The perfect tenses can indicate a "layering" of time; that is, they establish a relationship between one time and another. The present perfect (*have/has* + past participle) can say that an activity began in the past and continues into the present. The past perfect (*had* + past participle) can say that one past activity was completed before another specified time in the past. In general, follow these guidelines for sequencing the perfect tenses:

- Use present perfect with present tense or time.
- Use past perfect with past tense or time.

PRESENT TIME: I take [present] scuba diving from a woman who has taught [present perfect] for ten years.

PAST TIME: I took [past] scuba diving from a woman who had taught [past perfect] for ten years.

(3) Modal auxiliaries

Modal auxiliaries are words like *can, could, will, would, should, might, must.* (See 4b.3.) Instead of time, these words express ideas

shft 17a

like ability, possibility, recommendation, and requirement. When sequencing verbs, pay special attention to *can/could* and *will/would.* Conversational English allows a rather careless and unsystematic use of these four modals. In written English, however, the conventions are stricter.

- Use *can* with *will* and *could* with *would.*
- Use *can* and *will* with present tense and time.
- Use *could* and *would* with past tense and time.

Illogical shifts in verb sequence will result from mismatching modals, tenses, and times. So, remember to observe the conventions not only within single sentences but also throughout passages.

SHIFTED: If you can predict market trends, you would make a fortune.

SHIFTED: If you could predict market trends, you will make a fortune.

CONSISTENT: If you can predict market trends, you will make a fortune.

CONSISTENT: If you could predict market trends, you would make a fortune.

SHIFTED: She thought she can sell real estate.

SHIFTED: She thinks she could sell real estate.

CONSISTENT: She thinks she can sell real estate.

CONSISTENT: She thought she could sell real estate.

SHIFTED: The gym is spacious and well arranged. For example, the free weights are in a large, mirrored room by themselves. Therefore, you can concentrate on your form, and you would not bump into people who were using the Nautilus machines.

CONSISTENT PRESENT: The gym is spacious and well arranged. For example, the free weights are in a large, mirrored room by themselves. Therefore, you can concentrate on your form, and you will not bump into people who are using the Nautilus machines.

CONSISTENT PAST: The gym was spacious and well arranged. For example, the free weights were in a large, mirrored room by themselves. Therefore, you could concentrate on your form, and you would not bump into people who were using the Nautilus machines.

(4) Historical present

When discussing literature, use the "historical present." In other words, no matter when the work is set, describe the action as though it were currently taking place. For example, Sinclair Lewis's novel *Main Street* takes place in the first half of the twentieth century, but you use present time to report the activities of the characters.

> The conflict in *Main Street* is between Carol and the town. The citizens of Gopher Prairie are self-satisfied; Carol is bored and bewildered by their complacency.

When you want to show layers of time, you can use the perfect verb forms. The present perfect indicates that one action began before another and still continues. For example, the following sentence shows two different time frames: first Carol *marries* and later she *realizes,* but she is still married.

> Carol realizes that she has married a man who shares their complacency.

The past perfect indicates than one action occurred before another and no longer continues. For example, the next sentence shows these two time frames: first Carol *dreams* and later she *proves,* but she no longer dreams.

> In college, she had dreamed of doing something important: "I'll get my hands on one of those prairie towns and make it beautiful." But once in a real prairie town, Carol proves to be an ineffectual reformer.

17b SHIFTS IN INFINITIVES AND PARTICIPLES

In addition to main verbs and auxiliaries, prose usually contains infinitives and participles, often called *verbals* (see Chapter 5).

Although verbals function as nouns and modifiers, they are still verb forms and therefore must be consistent with the time frame of a sentence or passage.

(1) Infinitives

The choice of infinitive form depends upon the main verb in the clause. In general, follow these guidelines.

- To express a time the same as the main verb or later than the main verb, use the present infinitive (*to* + base form).

  They are trying to repair the old bridge. [Both times are present.]

  They tried to repair the old bridge. [Both times are past.]

  The university plans to host the conference. [Hosting comes later than planning.]

- To express a time earlier than the main verb, use the perfect infinitive (*to* + *have* + past participle).

  I would like to have completed my course work before this year. [Completing comes earlier than liking.]

(2) Participles

As with infinitives, the choice of participle form depends upon the main verb in the clause. In general, follow these guidelines.

- To express a time the same as the main verb or later than the main verb, use the present participle (*looking, going*).

  By thinning the trees, we ensure better growth. [Both times are present.]

  Bolting out of the gate, the horse threw its jockey. [Both times are past.]

- To express a time earlier than the main verb, use the past participle (*looked, gone*) or the perfect participle (*having looked, having gone*).

Tired of the silly argument, Scott left the meeting. [Tiring came earlier than leaving.]

Having tired of the silly argument, Scott left the meeting. [Tiring came earlier than leaving.]

17c SHIFTS IN MOOD

The indicative is the verb mood most common in prose. But sometimes, for special meanings, you use the imperative or the subjunctive mood. (See 4f.) You can mix moods when the logic of a passage demands the shift, but an unnecessary or illogical shift results in awkward prose.

SHIFTED: If I were [subjunctive] an honor student and I was [indicative] ready to graduate, I would apply to a medical school.

CONSISTENT: If I were [subjunctive] an honor student and I were [subjunctive] ready to graduate, I would apply to a medical school.

SHIFTED: In one day, eat [imperative] no more than 30 milligrams of cholesterol, and you should drink [indicative] no more than 4 ounces of alcohol.

CONSISTENT: In one day, eat [imperative] no more than 30 milligrams of cholesterol, and drink [imperative] no more than 4 ounces of alcohol.

CONSISTENT: In one day, you should eat [indicative] no more than 30 milligrams of cholesterol, and you should drink [indicative] no more than 4 ounces of alcohol.

17d SHIFTS IN VOICE

The term *voice* refers to whether the subject of a sentence performs the action (active voice) or receives the action (passive voice). (See 4e.) You should not shift, without good reason, between active and passive voice—particularly within a sentence. A shift in voice usually results in an awkward and cumbersome sentence.

SHIFTED: In the eighteenth century, Noah Webster set out [active] to make American English independent from British English; and through his books, great influence was exerted [passive] on the language.

CONSISTENT: In the eighteenth century, Noah Webster set out to make American English independent from British English; and through his books, he exerted great influence on the language.

17e SHIFTS IN NUMBER

The term *number* refers to singular (one) and plural (more than one). You should not shift carelessly between singular and plural nouns that should have the same number.

SHIFTED: Beekeepers wear protective veils over their face.

REVISED: Beekeepers wear protective veils over their faces.

SHIFTED: Frequently, a person exercises to relieve stress. As a result, people sometimes become psychologically dependent on excessive exercising.

REVISED: Frequently, people exercise to relieve stress and, as a result, sometimes become psychologically dependent on excessive exercising.

17f SHIFTS IN PERSON

The term *person* refers to first person (*I, we*), second person (*you*), and third person (all other pronouns and all nouns). Shifts in person usually involve *you* and a noun. If you are directly addressing your reader, you can revise these shifts by using *you* consistently. However, if you are referring to a group of people in general, revising in the third person is the better solution.

SHIFTED: Off-campus students should use the bus system because you get frustrated trying to park every day.

REVISED IN SECOND PERSON: If you live off campus, you should use the bus system because you will get frustrated trying to park every day.

REVISED IN THIRD PERSON: Off-campus students should use the but system because they get frustrated trying to park every day.

17g SHIFTS BETWEEN DIRECT AND INDIRECT DISCOURSE

In direct discourse, the exact words of a speaker or writer appear in quotation marks: *Truman said, "If you can't convince them, confuse them."* In indirect discourse, the words of the speaker or writer are not reported exactly, and the quotation marks are omitted: *Truman said that if you can't convince people, you should try to confuse them.* A shift from one type of discourse to the other can create an awkward, unbalanced sentence.

SHIFTED: The reporter said, "I would rather write about steeplechases than football games," but that his editor would not approve.

The reporter's words should be stated in either direct or indirect discourse.

DIRECT DISCOURSE: The reporter said, "I would rather write about steeplechases than football games, but my editor wouldn't approve."

INDIRECT DISCOURSE: The reporter said that he preferred to write about steeplechases rather than football games but that his editor would not approve.

17h MIXED CONSTRUCTIONS OR FAULTY PREDICATIONS

When the structure of a sentence shifts so that the elements in the subject and predicate do not fit together, the result is a mixed construction, also called a *faulty predication*. The various ways that structures can be mismatched are not entirely predictable;

nevertheless, the problem lies either in the grammar of the sentence or in the logic.

(1) Ungrammatical shifts

One common ungrammatical shift occurs when a writer tries to express a reason or a definition with a pattern such as *the reason is because, something is when, a place is where.* When *be* is the main verb in a sentence expressing a reason or definition, the structure of the sentence should be *noun = noun.* In other words, the subject is a noun (or noun equivalent); therefore, the complement in the predicate should also be a noun (or noun equivalent). The conjunctions *because, when,* and *where* introduce adverb clauses, which are not noun equivalents. In the following revisions, the complements are changed from adverb constructions to noun constructions.

SHIFTED: The reason tuition increased was because enrollment dropped. [adverb clause introduced with *because*]

REVISED: The reason tuition increased was that enrollment dropped. [noun clause introduced with *that*]

SHIFTED: A malapropism is when a person humorously misuses a word. [adverb clause introduced with *when*]

REVISED: A malapropism is the humorous misuse of a word. [noun phrase]

SHIFTED: Farm teams are where players train for the major leagues. [adverb clause introduced by *where*]

REVISED: Farm teams are training grounds for the major leagues. [noun phrase]

Another way to remove a shift from noun to adverb complement is to rewrite the sentence without using *be.*

REVISED: Tuition increased because enrollment dropped. [adverb clause modifying *increased*]

REVISED: A malapropism results when a person humorously misuses a word. [adverb clause modifying *results*]

REVISED: At farm clubs, players train for the major leagues. [adverb phrase modifying *train*]

(2) Illogical shifts

In another kind of mixed construction, the subject and predicate do not fit together logically. For example, in the following shifted sentences, the subjects cannot perform the action of the verbs. The revised sentences make a logical connection between the parts.

SHIFTED: The use of some plastics can melt in microwave ovens. [The use cannot melt.]

REVISED: Some plastics can melt in microwave ovens. [Some plastics can melt.]

SHIFTED: Tanning lotions have changed their sales efforts to appeal to our fear of skin cancer. [Lotions cannot change sales efforts.]

REVISED: Manufacturers of tanning lotions have changed their sales efforts to appeal to our fear of skin cancer. [Manufacturers can change sales efforts.]

SHIFTED: The desk clerk's attitude was filled with arrogance and indifference. [An attitude cannot be filled.]

REVISED: The desk clerk was arrogant and indifferent. [A clerk can be arrogant.]

CHAPTER

18 SPLIT CONSTRUCTIONS

A grammatical construction consists of closely related items—for example, subject and predicate, auxiliary verb and main verb, verb and object. In a **split construction,** the items are separated by an interruptive element, such as a modifier or parenthetical remark. No rule forbids the splitting of a construction, but you should be cautious. Some splits blur meaning and sound awkward.

18a SPLIT SUBJECTS AND VERBS

Subjects and verbs do not always appear next to each other; modifiers or other elements may interrupt the construction. Be sure, however, that the interruption is not so long that it distracts a reader or creates a cumbersome structure. You can often revise a sentence with a split subject and predicate by moving the intervening element.

SPLIT: The language, with a simple sound system of only five vowels and seven consonants, is easy to learn.

REVISED: With a simple sound system of only five vowels and seven consonants, the language is easy to learn.

In some cases, you can restructure the sentence to position the subject and verb closer together. In the following sentence, for example, the long interruptive element can be rewritten as the predicate.

SPLIT: Our campus newspaper, which caricatures such groups as graduate students, athletes, sorority and fraternity members, and independents, is edited by two promising comedy writers.

REVISED: Our campus newspaper, edited by two promising comedy writers, caricatures such groups as graduate students, athletes, sorority and fraternity members, and independents.

Another possible solution is to divide a cumbersome construction into two separate sentences.

SPLIT: Shopping malls, which have grown from clusters of shops to elaborate structures with fountains, exotic plants, restaurants, and theaters, have led the American consumer to associate buying with entertainment.

REVISED: Shopping malls have grown from clusters of shops to elaborate structures with fountains, exotic plants, theaters, and restaurants. These extravagant centers have led the American consumer to associate buying with entertainment.

18b SPLIT VERBS AND COMPLEMENTS

Sometimes a modifier separates a verb from its direct object or subject complement—elements that complete the verb's meaning. When a verb and its completer are separated unnecessarily, the interruptive element should be moved to another place in the sentence.

SPLIT: The marathoner injured, during the last race, his left foot.

REVISED: The marathoner injured his foot during the last race.

SPLIT: No one knows, although some historians estimate about 5,000, exactly how many soldiers the Germans lost on D-Day.

REVISED: Although some historians estimate about 5,000, no one knows exactly how many soldiers the Germans lost on D-Day.

18c SPLIT VERBS

The verbs in many sentences are not single words but phrases: *would improve, will be moving, has been profiteering, could have been defined.* Frequently adverbs occur between the parts of a verb phrase. In fact, sometimes the natural place for an adverb seems to be within, rather than before or after, a verb phrase.

The issue was hotly debated.

Experts are now predicting a rise in prices.

The new drug will not produce any side effects.

Nevertheless, you should not split a verb phrase awkwardly with a long modifier, especially a prepositional phrase or a clause.

SPLIT: The insurance company is, regardless of the number of people involved in an accident, required to pay each one.

REVISED: Regardless of the number of people involved in an accident, the insurance company is required to pay each one.

SPLIT: A conversion will, when the plates are in metric measurement, give the needed dimensions.

REVISED: A conversion will give the needed dimensions when the plates are in metric measurement.

18d SPLIT INFINITIVES

An infinitive is the *to* form of a verb: *to go, to understand, to be.* In a split infinitive, the *to* is separated from the verb itself: *to sometimes go, to not so clearly understand, to soon be.* In general, you should avoid splitting infinitives—particularly with long modifiers—since the split can create awkward constructions.

SPLIT INFINITIVE: The robot's three-pronged finger arrangement allows it to with a great deal of accuracy pick up objects.

REVISED: The robot's three-pronged finger arrangement allows it to pick up objects with a great deal of accuracy.

Even splitting an infinitive with a short modifier can sometimes create an awkward rhythm.

SPLIT INFINITIVE: Don Knotts' portrayal of Deputy Barney Fife seems to never lose popularity.

REVISED: Don Knotts' portrayal of Deputy Barney Fife seems never to lose popularity.

Of course, you cannot always avoid splitting an infinitive because of the normal patterns of the language. In the following sentence, for example, *more than* cannot be moved.

NORMAL SPLIT: We expect our profits to more than double next year.

Other times, you may want to split an infinitive to ensure your intended meaning or to avoid an awkward sentence rhythm. For instance, the following split infinitive is acceptable.

ACCEPTABLE SPLIT: The task force met to quickly assess the extent of the oil spill.

If you try to avoid the split by placing *quickly* in front of *to,* you change the meaning of the sentence.

CHANGED MEANING: The task force met quickly to assess the extent of the oil spill.

If you place *quickly* after *assess,* you create an awkward structure.

AWKWARD STRUCTURE: The task force met to assess quickly the extent of the oil spill.

inc
19

CHAPTER

19

INCOMPLETE CONSTRUCTIONS

In some sentences, a word or words needed for grammatical completeness may not appear. The omission does not always detract from the meaning. For example, the following sentences would be perfectly clear even if the words in brackets were omitted.

> Did you think [that] we weren't coming?
>
> The police made the arrest while [they were] on a routine inspection.
>
> Zombies have always frightened me more than werewolves [have frightened me].

Sometimes, however, an omission makes a sentence confusing.

CONFUSING:	She writes more often to her representative than you.
POSSIBLE MEANING:	She writes more often to her representative than you do.
POSSIBLE MEANING:	She writes more often to her representative than she does to you.

When a reader doesn't know exactly what the writer has left out, the construction is not acceptable. You can easily correct **incomplete constructions** by adding the necessary words.

19a OMISSIONS IN COMPOUND CONSTRUCTIONS

Make sure that the omission of a necessary part of a compound expression does not obscure structure or meaning.

OMISSION OF DETERMINER:	My teacher and counselor advised me to study physics. [*My teacher and counselor* could refer to one person or two.]
REVISED TO MEAN ONE PERSON:	My teacher counseled me to study physics.
REVISED TO MEAN TWO PEOPLE:	My teacher and my counselor advised me to study physics.
OMISSION OF PART OF VERB:	I have never and will never be interested in the stock market. [*Been* must follow *have.*]
REVISED:	I have never been and will never be interested in the stock market.
OMISSION OF PART OF IDIOM:	The bright lights detract and ruin the effect of the display. [*From* must follow *detract.*]
REVISED:	The bright lights detract from and ruin the effect of the display.

19b OMITTED *THAT*

Frequently, the word *that* can be omitted from the beginning of a noun clause without any loss of meaning.

> The players believed [that] they would win.

In some sentences, however, the omission will cause the main clause and the noun clause to fuse. Readers cannot tell where one clause ends and the other begins. For instance, in the following sentence, the subject of the second clause looks like the object of the first clause.

Omission of *That:*	He noticed the mistake worried me.
Revised:	He noticed that the mistake worried me.

19c INCOMPLETE COMPARISONS

Omissions frequently occur in comparisons, and usually a reader can fill in the missing word or words with no difficulty.

This route is as long as that one [is long].

The copies from this machine are darker than those [copies are dark].

The weather is hotter this week than [it was] last [week].

In some comparative constructions, however, the omissions cause the comparison to be incomplete. For example, in clauses beginning with *than* or *as,* an omission can create ambiguity. A reader cannot with certainty fill in the missing word or words.

Incomplete:	Stray dogs are friendlier to me than my roommate.
Possible Meaning:	Stray dogs are friendlier to me than my roommate is.
Possible Meaning:	Stray dogs are friendlier to me than they are to my roommate.

Also, in *than* or *as* clauses, the omission of *other* may cause something to be illogically compared to itself. For example, in the following sentence, the omission suggests that Texas is not a state.

Incomplete:	Texas produces more oil than any state.
Revised:	Texas produces more oil than any other state.

A double comparison requires the three conjunctions *as . . . as . . . than*—for example, "The pig is *as* smart *as,* if not smarter *than,* the dog." The omission of the second *as* makes the first comparison incomplete.

Incomplete:	Aiken's autobiography is as successful, if not more successful than, Adam's.

REVISED: Aiken's autobiography is as successful as, if not more successful than, Adam's.

Incomplete comparisons may also result from unexplained modifiers. Modifiers like *best, worst, cutest,* or *sweetest* should be completed.

INCOMPLETE: *Gone with the Wind* is the best movie.

POSSIBLE MEANING: *Gone with the Wind* is the best movie ever made.

POSSIBLE MEANING: *Gone with the Wind* is the best movie I have ever seen.

In informal conversation, a speaker sometimes uses *so, such,* or *too* as an intensifier without explaining results—*so nice, too hard.* In formal English, however, these modifiers signal comparisons or measurements, and the omitted explanation leaves the idea incomplete. A writer, therefore, must either complete the comparison or use a true intensifier like *very* or *extremely.*

INCOMPLETE: The noise of the plane was so loud.

REVISED: The noise of the plane was so loud that we could not hear what was said.

REVISED: The noise of the plane was extremely loud.

In addition, an omission may cause the illogical comparison of two different classes of entities. For example, in the following sentence, the writer has compared a technique to a contender.

INCOMPLETE: His technique for throwing the discus is unlike any other contender.

REVISED: His technique for throwing the discus is unlike any other contender's.

REVISED: His technique for throwing the discus is unlike that of any other contender.

//
20

CHAPTER

20

PARALLELISM

Sentences frequently contain lists of two or more items. Such items in a sequence must be parallel; that is, they must have the same grammatical structure. The following examples illustrate parallel sequence.

2 NOUN PHRASES:	The best beer has both natural ingredients and natural fermentation.
3 PREPOSITIONAL PHRASES:	The Shakespeare company has traveled not only to city theaters and to college campuses but also to small communities.
4 VERB FORMS:	"Uncooperative" computers have been riddled with bullets, burned up with gasoline, stabbed with screwdrivers, and hammered with shoes.
3 NOUN CLAUSES:	We now know that sleep has at least four depths, that dreaming is most intense in the period of rapid eye movement, and that sleep deprivation is dangerous.

Be sure to make items parallel in a compound structure, a series, a list, or an outline. A mixture of grammatical structures lacks logic and symmetry.

20a PARALLELISM IN COMPOUND STRUCTURES

The two items in a compound structure must be grammatically the same: *pencil* and *paper, working* and *playing, to search* and *to find, when they read* and *when they listen.* Although the two items are most often linked by *and,* there are several other ways to connect them.

(1) Compounding with coordinating conjunctions *(and, but, or, nor, yet)*

The elements on either side of a coordinating conjunction must be the same grammatical construction.

NOT PARALLEL: The heat wave will increase the demand for electricity and causing power outages. [*And* joins a verb phrase to a participial phrase.]

REVISED WITH 2 VERB PHRASES: The heat wave will increase the demand for electricity and will cause power outages.

NOT PARALLEL: The bicycle path should be located along Route 234 or to follow the Pendleton River. [*Or* joins a prepositional phrase to an infinitive phrase.]

REVISED WITH 2 PREPOSITIONAL PHRASES: The bicycle path should be located along Route 234 or beside the Pendleton River.

(2) Compounding with correlative conjunctions *(not only . . . but also, not . . . but, either . . . or, neither . . . nor, both . . . and)*

Whatever grammatical element follows the first part of a correlative conjunction must also follow the second part.

NOT PARALLEL: I will either leave from National Airport or from Dulles. [*Either* is followed by a verb; *or* is followed by a prepositional phrase.]

REVISED WITH 2 PREPOSITIONAL PHRASES: I will leave either from National Airport or from Dulles.

NOT PARALLEL: The reporter wondered both what the lawyer had meant and the need for reporting the remark. [*Both* is followed by a noun clause; *and* is followed by a noun phrase.]

REVISED WITH 2 NOUN CLAUSES: The reporter wondered both what the lawyer had meant and whether the remark should be reported.

NOT PARALLEL: We not only want to visit the Corcoran Gallery but also the Hirshhorn Museum. [*Not only* is followed by a verb; *but also* is followed by a noun.]

REVISED WITH 2 NOUN PHRASES: We want to visit not only the Corcoran Gallery but also the Hirshhorn Museum.

(3) Compounding with other connecting words *(not, as well as, rather than, less than, more than, from . . . to, instead of)*

Some words and phrases create compound structures in the same manner as the coordinating conjunctions: they must join elements with the same grammatical structure.

NOT PARALLEL: We should advertise the car wash rather than to be overlooked by potential customers. [*Rather than* joins a verb phrase to an infinitive phrase.]

REVISED WITH 2 VERB PHRASES: We should advertise the car wash rather than be overlooked by potential customers.

NOT PARALLEL: The reporter has covered the trial from the swearing in of the jury to when the judge sentenced the murderer. [*From . . . to* joins a noun phrase to a subordinate clause.]

REVISED WITH 2 NOUN PHRASES: The reporter has covered the trial from the swearing in of the jury to the sentencing by the judge.

NOT PARALLEL: My history t/eacher is guilty of telling about past events instead of an explanation of them. [*Instead of* joins a gerund phrase and a noun phrase.]

REVISED WITH 2 GERUND PHRASES: My history teacher is guilty of telling about past events instead of explaining them.

20b PARALLELISM IN SERIES, LISTS, AND OUTLINES

A sequence of more than two items may appear within a sentence or in a list with one item under the other. All the items, no matter how many, must have the same grammatical structure.

NOT PARALLEL: The students go to the clinic to get vitamins for anemia, for aspirins for headaches, or just counseling. [The series contains an infinitive phrase, a prepositional phrase, and a noun phrase.]

REVISED WITH 3 NOUN PHRASES: The students go to the clinic to get vitamins for anemia, aspirins for headaches, or counseling for their emotional problems.

NOT PARALLEL: I asked the curator whether the museum was well funded, about the style of paintings it featured, and to supply the names of its patrons. [The series contains a noun clause, a prepositional phrase, and an infinitive phrase.]

REVISED WITH 3 CLAUSES: I asked the curator whether the museum was well funded, what style of paintings it featured, and if he would supply the names of its patrons.

NOT PARALLEL: The members decided to fulfill these responsibilities:

1. Meet with parents and guardians
2. Meet with interested citizens
3. Answers to questions from the media
4. A record of responses to telephone calls

[The list contains two verb phrases and two noun phrases.]

REVISED WITH 4 VERB PHRASES: The members decided to fulfill these responsibilities:

1. Meet with parents and guardians
2. Meet with interested citizens
3. Answer questions from the media
4. Record responses to telephone calls

NOT PARALLEL:

Slang: Its Useful Purposes

I. Slang used to identify social groups
II. To enliven language
III. Slang gives us new names
IV. Euphemisms for things that are unpleasant or offensive

[The outline contains a noun phrase, an infinitive phrase, an independent clause, and a noun phrase.]

REVISED WITH 4 SENTENCES:

Slang's Useful Purposes

I. Social groups use slang as a sign of identification.
II. Slang develops to enliven language, to eliminate monotony.
III. Slang gives us names for new things, such as physical objects or social movements.
IV. Slang supplies euphemisms for unpleasant or offensive actions and places.

REVISED WITH SERIES OF NOUNS:

The Usefulness of Slang

I. In-group identification
II. Variety
III. Names for new things
IV. Euphemisms

PART

III

PUNCTUATION AND MECHANICS

Punctuation and mechanics are signals that work together with words and structures to create meaning. With the aid of these signals, readers anticipate, link, separate, stress, de-emphasize, and characterize ideas according to a writer's wishes. In fact, readers rely so heavily on these marks that their misuse can distort or obscure intended meaning. Therefore, to communicate clearly, you must use punctuation marks and mechanics according to standard practice.

21 Commas
22 Semicolons
23 Colons
24 Dashes, Parentheses, and Brackets
25 Periods, Question Marks, and Exclamation Points
26 Apostrophes
27 Quotation Marks and Ellipsis Marks
28 Italics/Underlining
29 Hyphens and Slashes
30 Abbreviations and Numbers
31 Capital Letters

CHAPTER

21 COMMAS

The most versatile of all punctuation marks, **commas** enclose, separate, and set off information. Because commas indicate sentence structure and meaning, their use is essential to clear writing.

21a COMMAS BETWEEN INDEPENDENT CLAUSES JOINED BY COORDINATING CONJUNCTIONS

One way to join two independent clauses is with a comma and a coordinating conjunction (*and, but, or, nor, for, so,* and *yet*).

> The Vice President will arrive at 9:30, and the commissioning of the battleship will begin at 10:00.

> The regular edition of the dictionary is twelve volumes, but the compact edition is only two.

> I have to maintain a C average, or my parents will make me pay for my own courses.

> All the dormitories were full, so we were housed temporarily in local motels and hotels.

You may omit the comma when the independent clauses are very short and parallel in structure and when the conjunction is *and, but, or,* or *nor.*

The lights are off and the door is locked.

You should, however, always include the comma when the conjunction is *for, so,* and *yet.* Because these conjunctions can function as other parts of speech, the comma prevents misreading. For example, in the first sentence of the following pair, *for* seems to be a preposition; in the second, the comma makes clear that *for* is a conjunction.

MISLEADING: They went back home for their roots were there.

CLEAR: They went back home, for their roots were there.

In the first sentence of the next pair, *yet* seems to be an adverb of time; in the second, *yet* is clearly a conjunction.

MISLEADING: We didn't want to go yet we thought it was our duty.

CLEAR: We didn't want to go, yet we thought it was our duty.

NOTE: When independent clauses are long or contain internal punctuation, you may prefer to join them with a semicolon and a coordinating conjunction to show the major break in the sentence. (See 22c.)

If you approach the colt slowly, talking in a calm voice, you can gain his confidence; but if you move abruptly or speak sharply, he will bolt.

21b COMMAS AFTER INTRODUCTORY PREPOSITIONAL PHRASES, VERBALS, AND DEPENDENT CLAUSES

An introductory or dependent clause appears at the beginning of a sentence or another clause—either independent or dependent. For a discussion of verbals, dependent clauses, and independent clauses, see Chapter 5 and Chapter 7.

(1) Introductory prepositional phrases

A comma usually follows a long introductory prepositional phrase (a preposition and its object) or a combination of phrases.

INTRODUCING A SENTENCE:	At yesterday's press conference, the coach denied the NCAA charges of recruiting violations.
INTRODUCING A DEPENDENT CLAUSE:	The local television station announced that as a result of a recent campaign, the city government had agreed to improve the public bus service.
INTRODUCING A SENTENCE:	After a bizarre wedding ceremony in the health spa, the couple jogged off into the sunset.
INTRODUCING A SECOND INDEPENDENT CLAUSE:	The well-known *couturiers* once catered to the idle rich, but with so many women now in the business world, designers are taking a more practical approach to fashion.

If a prepositional phrase is short and does not interfere with ease of reading, you can omit the comma.

By 1862 the pony express no longer existed.

At twilight we always heard the whippoorwill.

(2) Introductory verbals and verbal phrases

You should place a comma after an introductory verbal (participle, infinitive, or gerund) or verbal phrase, regardless of its length. (See Chapter 5.)

PARTICIPIAL PHRASE INTRODUCING A SENTENCE:	Built in 1752, Connecticut Hall is the oldest building on the Yale campus.
PARTICIPIAL PHRASE INTRODUCING A SECOND INDEPENDENT CLAUSE:	He swung the door open; then realizing his error, he stammered and backed from the room.
INFINITIVE PHRASE INTRODUCING A SENTENCE:	To avoid the crowds, I did my Christmas shopping in September.

GERUND PHRASE INTRODUCING A SENTENCE:	By encroaching on the dense woods, we have greatly reduced the wild turkey population.

Use a comma even after a single introductory participle or infinitive.

PARTICIPLE INTRODUCING A SENTENCE:	Exhausted, she fell asleep on the chair.
INFINITIVES INTRODUCING A FIRST AND SECOND INDEPENDENT CLAUSE:	To jitterbug, you must tense your arm muscles, but to waltz, you must relax them.

(3) Introductory adverb clauses

Most introductory clauses are adverb clauses, introduced by subordinate conjunctions such as *after, although, as soon as, because, before, even though, if, once, since, unless, when, where, while.* (See 7c.1.) Usually, a comma should separate an introductory adverb clause from the rest of the sentence.

> Although hypnosis now has a recognized place in medicine, the technique has its opponents.
>
> Unless the student newspaper can generate more advertising, readers will have to pay fifty cents per issue.
>
> When a tuning fork is struck, the tone remains always the same.

A comma should also follow an adverb clause that introduces a subsequent clause in a sentence.

> A baby is born with the language center in the left side of the brain, but if he or she suffers brain injury very early in infancy, the language center can shift to the right side.
>
> The power went out because when I plugged in the coffeepot, I overloaded the circuit.

After a short introductory clause that does not interfere with ease of reading, you can omit the comma. Nevertheless, the comma is always appropriate.

CORRECT: When it snows I get depressed.

CORRECT: When it snows, I get depressed.

(4) Introductory noun clauses

Normally, a noun clause used as an object or complement follows the verb and should not be separated from the rest of the sentence with a comma. (See 7c.3.)

COMPLEMENT: People can be whatever they want to be.

DIRECT OBJECT: The group automatically oppose whomever labor supports.

When the normal order is reversed and the noun clause is introductory, it should be followed by a comma.

INTRODUCTORY COMPLEMENT: Whatever people want to be, they can be.

INTRODUCTORY OBJECT: Whomever labor supports, the group automatically opposes.

NOTE: A noun clause that functions as the subject of a sentence should not be followed by a comma.

Whatever you prefer is acceptable to me.

21c COMMAS TO SET OFF NONRESTRICTIVE ELEMENTS

The terms *nonrestrictive* and *restrictive* usually refer to adjective clauses, verbals and verbal phrases, and appositives (words and phrases that rename or restate). A nonrestrictive element is not essential to the meaning of its sentence. In other words, readers do not need the element to identify the word or phrase it follows. By setting off a nonrestrictive element with commas, you point to its nonessential role in the construction.

NONRESTRICTIVE CLAUSE: A widely cultivated fruit is the strawberry, which belongs to the rose family.

NONRESTRICTIVE VERBAL PHRASE: Pompeii, covered by volcanic ash, was sealed for almost 1,700 years.

NONRESTRICTIVE APPOSITIVE: Lister, a physician at Glasgow University, founded antiseptic surgery.

In contrast, a restrictive element is essential to the meaning of its sentence. Readers use the element to identify the word or phrase it follows. The absence of commas around a restrictive element points to its essential role in the construction.

RESTRICTIVE CLAUSE: The rose that I prefer is the edible strawberry.

RESTRICTIVE VERBAL PHRASE: The volcanic ash covering Pompeii sealed the city for almost 1,700 years.

RESTRICTIVE APPOSITIVE: Antiseptic surgery was founded by the physician Lister.

Several techniques will help you determine whether an element is restrictive or nonrestrictive.

- **Look for the introductory words in clauses.**

  A clause that begins with *that* is restrictive.

  The Warren Report summarizes the events that relate to John F. Kennedy's assassination.

  Athletes should eat foods that are high in complex carbohydrates.

  A clause with no introductory word is restrictive.

  The lands Alexander conquered stretched from Greece to northwestern India. [*That* is understood before *Alexander.*]

  The artists we admire usually startle or amuse us. [*Whom* or *that* is understood before *we.*]

  A clause that begins with *which* is usually nonrestrictive.

  The area is famous for its pink grapefruit, which is unusually sweet.

  Her hobbies, which included rock climbing and camping, led to her career as a forest ranger.

- **Look for proper nouns.**

  An element following a proper noun is usually nonrestrictive.

One of Europe's most effective monarchs was Elizabeth I, who successfully overcame religious strife, a bankrupt treasury, war with France, and the Spanish Armada.

The Dalmatian, also called the coach dog, closely resembles a pointer.

The best known American clown was probably Emmett Kelly, the forlorn tramp.

- **Look for elements that can refer to only one possible person, place, or thing.**

  Elements with only one possible referent are nonrestrictive.

  My family hero is my mother's mother, who once rode a horse from Dallas to San Francisco.

  His first car, purchased from a neighbor for $300, was a '58 Pontiac.

  I was craving my favorite cold-weather food, vegetable soup.

- **Look for appositives introduced by *or*.**

  Appositives introduced by *or* are nonrestrictive because they explain or define the nouns they follow. Without commas, the appositives will seem to be alternatives in *either/or* compounds. In the following sentence, for instance, *body language* defines *kinesis.* Were the comma removed, the sentence would erroneously suggest alternatives, *either body language or kinesis.*

  The company trains all its personnel in kinesis, or body language.

- **Check intended meaning.**

  Occasionally, an element can be either nonrestrictive or restrictive, depending on the writer's intent. In these cases, punctuation must indicate the meaning. For example, the first sentence below, with commas, means "All politicians sacrifice integrity for power, and all are dangerous." In contrast, the second sentence, without commas, means "Some politicians sacrifice integrity for power, and those particular politicians are dangerous."

NONRESTRICTIVE: Politicians, who sacrifice integrity for power, are dangerous.

RESTRICTIVE: Politicians who sacrifice integrity for power are dangerous.

Similarly, different punctuation in the next two sentences produces different meanings. The writer of the first sentence has only one daughter; the writer of the second, more than one daughter.

NONRESTRICTIVE: I spent Christmas with my daughter, who lives in Miami.

RESTRICTIVE: I spent Christmas with my daughter who lives in Miami.

21d COMMAS BETWEEN ITEMS IN A SERIES AND BETWEEN COORDINATE ADJECTIVES

Without commas, parallel items in a sentence can run together and obscure meaning. Commas separate the items and make the meaning clear.

(1) Items in a series

A series is a list of three or more parallel structures—three or more nouns, adjectives, verb phrases, prepositional phrases, dependent clauses, independent clauses, and so on. Ordinarily, you should use commas to separate items in a series. (If the series items themselves contain commas, use semicolons. See 22d.)

ADJECTIVES: We are looking for someone reliable, efficient, and versatile.

NOUN PHRASES: When in doubt about the procedure, consult the lab manual, the operational instructions, or the student assistant.

DEPENDENT CLAUSES: When I returned to my room, I found that my roommate had eaten lunch on my bed, that one of his friends had spilled coffee on my history notes, and that another friend had borrowed my sports jacket.

INDEPENDENT CLAUSES: The roots absorb the water from the soil, the sapwood carries the water to the leaves, and the leaves make food for the tree.

Some writers, particularly journalists, omit the comma before the conjunction and the last element in the series. However, omission of this comma can sometimes cause misreading.

UNCLEAR: The Grievance Committee met with three petitioners, two students and a faculty member.

The reader cannot know whether the committee met with six people or with three. But proper punctuation can make the meaning clear.

CLEAR: The Grievance Committee met with three petitioners, two students, and a faculty member. [six people, listed as items in a series]

CLEAR: The Grievance Committee met with three petitioners**:** two students and a faculty member. [three people, presented as an appositive following a colon]

(2) Coordinate adjectives

Coordinate adjectives can be rearranged and can be logically connected by *and.* In the absence of *and,* commas should separate coordinate adjectives.

COORDINATE: He liked to play tennis on a shady, secluded court.

REARRANGED: He liked to play tennis on a secluded, shady court.

CONNECTED WITH *AND:* He liked to play tennis on a shady and secluded court.

Noncoordinate adjectives, which can be neither rearranged nor connected with *and,* should not be separated by commas.

NONCOORDINATE: He liked to play tennis on an old clay court.

IMPOSSIBLE: He like to play tennis on a clay old court.

IMPOSSIBLE: He liked to play tennis on an old and clay court.

When an adjective phrase contains both coordinate and non-coordinate adjectives, the same principle applies: commas should appear in positions where *and* could be inserted.

COORDINATE AND NONCOORDINATE: I was met at the door by two large, shaggy, playful Irish setters.

POSSIBLE: I was met at the door by two large and shaggy and playful Irish setters.

IMPOSSIBLE: I was met at the door by two and large and shaggy and playful and Irish setters.

21e COMMAS IN PLACE OF OMITTED WORDS

When consecutive clauses have parallel structure and common vocabulary, a comma can replace the verb or part of the predicate.

Rankin received 312 votes; Jenkins, 117. [The comma replaces *received.*]

The older sister wanted to be an actress, and the younger sister, a doctor. [The comma replaces *wanted to be.*]

The first question was on the prose of the eighteenth century; the second, on the poetry; and the third, on the drama. [The commas replace *was.*]

21f COMMAS TO SET OFF PARENTHETICAL, TRANSITIONAL, AND CONTRASTIVE ELEMENTS

Commas set off parenthetical, transitional, and contrastive elements to show that these structures are added to an otherwise complete sentence.

, 21f

(1) Parenthetical elements

A parenthetical element is a structure that could be enclosed in parentheses without changing the meaning of the sentence. The element can occur within a sentence and interrupt the structure abruptly, or it can appear at the end of a sentence and serve as a concluding remark. In either case, use a comma or commas to set off the element from the rest of the sentence.

INTERRUPTING THE SUBJECT AND VERB:	The coach, according to informed sources, intends to leave after this season.
INTERRUPTING THE VERB AND OBJECT:	The bank officers said, believe it or not, that they had accurately reported the assets.
INTERRUPTING THE VERB PHRASE:	She was not, strictly speaking, managing the estate.
CONCLUDING REMARK:	Salaries have not improved at all during the past three years, at least not as far as the clerical staff is concerned.

(2) Transitional expressions

Transitional expressions, or conjunctive adverbs, are words and phrases such as *however, therefore, for example, in conclusion, accordingly, nevertheless, in addition,* and so on. (For a complete list, see *Transitional Expression* in the Glossary of Terms.) You should set off these expressions with commas.

> Houseplants available at nurseries can be expensive and, in addition, difficult to grow. Therefore, people without green thumbs are often reluctant to spend money to watch their purchases wither and die. There is, however, a solution for people who want to grow plants with little expense or effort—the avocado.
>
> The seed of a well-ripened avocado planted in porous soil will sprout and produce a good-sized plant in a few weeks. An avocado plant grown in the house will not, of course, flower or bear fruit.

Nevertheless, it will provide inexpensive, luxurious, and trouble-free greenery.

(3) Contrastive elements

Elements that contrast with whatever has preceded usually begin with words like *not, never, but, unlike,* and *rather than.* Normally, you should set these elements off with commas.

It was the beginning, not the end, of the social upheaval.

Our codes of conduct in those days were dictated by our peers, never by our parents.

You may omit the commas when the contrastive elements are not abrupt. To emphasize the elements, however, always include the commas.

NOT EMPHATIC: The speech was informative but tedious.

EMPHATIC: The speech was informative, but tedious.

21g COMMAS TO SET OFF INTERJECTIONS, WORDS IN DIRECT ADDRESS, AND TAG QUESTIONS

Interjections, words in direct address, and tag questions are all elements loosely connected to a basic clause. Use commas to set off these elements from the rest of the sentence.

(1) Interjections

An interjection is an exclamation with no grammatical connection to the rest of the sentence. You may punctuate an interjection as a separate sentence with a period or an exclamation point. Or you may punctuate it as part of another sentence by setting it off with a comma or commas.

Well, the time has finally come to act.

His costume was, no kidding, a shower curtain.

(2) Words in direct address

You should always set off words in direct address, which name whomever or whatever is spoken to.

Excuse me, sir, is this the plane to Denver?

Sit and beg, Butch.

(3) Tag questions

Tag questions appear at the end of statements and ask for verification. Always set these questions off with commas.

The budget was balanced, wasn't it?

She did not ask for a second opinion, did she?

21h COMMAS IN SPECIAL CONTEXTS: IN DATES, PLACES, ADDRESSES; IN NUMBERS; WITH TITLES OF INDIVIDUALS; WITH QUOTATION MARKS

When you position commas in special constructions such as dates and addresses, you should follow current conventions and practices.

(1) Dates, places, and addresses

The commas in dates, places, and addresses serve to isolate each item for the reader.

- Pattern: Month day, year,

  She graduated on May 22, 1986, from Loyola University. [commas before and after the year when the day is given]

- Pattern: Day month year

  She graduated 22 May 1986 from Loyola University. [no commas when the day precedes the month]

- Pattern: Month year

  She graduated in May 1986 from Loyola University. [no commas when the day is unspecified]

- Pattern: City, state,

  We surveyed the voters in St. Louis, Missouri, two weeks before the election. [commas before and after the names of states]

- Pattern: Street address, city, state zip code,

  Ship the package to 1110 East Marina Road, Dallas, TX 75201, within ten days. [comma between street address and city; comma between city and state; no comma between state and zip code; comma between zip code and material that follows]

(2) Numbers expressing amounts

Commas indicate thousands and millions in numbers of five or more digits. Many people also prefer commas in four-digit numbers.

> Last year the company sold 2,165 records; this year they sold 1,926,021.

(3) Titles of individuals

A title following a name should be set off with commas.

> Applications for the summer co-op program should be sent to Kathryn McLeod, travel director, or to Carl Jenkins, personnel director.

Usually, *Jr.* or *Sr.* following a name is set off with commas. Some people, however, prefer to omit the commas, and you should honor that preference.

> Mr. and Mrs. James W. Marcott, Jr., hosted the reception.

> James Hillery Godbold Sr. donated the funds.

(4) Direct quotations

Commas should set off a grammatically independent quotation from the words that identify its source. When a comma and a closing quotation mark occur together, the comma comes first.

"You can't expect to hit the jackpot," said Flip Wilson, "if you don't put a few nickels in the machine."

"The results of the tests are insignificant," according to Dr. Landrum.

"It was a perfect title," Dixon thought, "in that it crystallized the article's niggling mindlessness, its funereal parade of yawn-enforcing facts, the pseudo-light it threw upon non-problems." (Kingsley Amis)

A comma is not appropriate when a quotation is an integral part of the sentence structure.

Ayn Rand defined civilization as "the progress toward a society of privacy."

Who said that for every credibility gap, there is a "gullibility fill"?

21i COMMAS TO ENSURE INTENDED READING

In some instances, commas are necessary simply to prevent misreading. For example, in the following sentence, the comma indicates that *can try* is not a unit.

CONFUSING: Employees who can try to carpool twice a week.

CLEAR: Employees who can, try to carpool twice a week.

In other instances, commas create stylistic effects. For example, the commas in the next two sentences are not grammatically necessary; instead, they indicate pauses and create a reading different from the usual.

"There is no safety in numbers, or in anything else." (James Thurber)

The child had never had a guardian, and never had a friend.

21j INAPPROPRIATE COMMAS

Commas are inappropriate in the following situations, except when necessary to ensure proper reading.

- Between major sentence elements—such as subject and predicate, verb and object, items in a verb phrase

INAPPROPRIATE: Several people on horseback, suddenly appeared at the bridge. [separation of subject and predicate]

REVISED: Several people on horseback suddenly appeared at the bridge.

INAPPROPRIATE: Conner realized, that he wanted to go home. [separation of verb and object]

REVISED: Conner realized that he wanted to go home.

- Between two items joined by a coordinating conjunction or correlative conjunctions unless those items are independent clauses

INAPPROPRIATE: The road began at the edge of the field, and ended abruptly in the middle. [separation of two verbs]

REVISED: The road began at the edge of the field and ended abruptly in the middle.

INAPPROPRIATE: We hoped the commission would prohibit not only channelization, but also the planting of kudzu. [separation of two objects]

REVISED: We hoped the commission would prohibit not only channelization but also the planting of kudzu.

INAPPROPRIATE: Most critics agreed that the plot relied too heavily on coincidence, and the director relied too heavily on special effects. [separation of two dependent clauses, with *that* understood after *and*]

REVISED: Most critics agreed that the plot relied too heavily on coincidence and the director relied too heavily on special effects.

- After the final adjective in a series

INAPPROPRIATE: He wore a cheap, shabby, and ill-fitting, suit.

REVISED: He wore a cheap, shabby, and ill-fitting suit.

- After a coordinating or a subordinating conjunction

INAPPROPRIATE: We ate at a terrible restaurant that featured waffles and, fried seafood.

REVISED: We ate at a terrible restaurant that featured waffles and fried seafood.

INAPPROPRIATE: Nothing grows in that section of the yard because, there is too much lime in the soil.

REVISED: Nothing grows in that section of the yard because there is too much lime in the soil.

- Between an indirect quotation and the rest of the sentence

INAPPROPRIATE: The author said, that the historical data had been carefully researched.

REVISED: The author said that the historical data had been carefully researched.

CHAPTER

22

SEMICOLONS

; 22

Semicolons are marks of punctuation weaker than periods but stronger than commas. Basically, there are two positions for semicolons: between independent clauses and between items in a series that contain commas. In each position, the semicolon occurs between coordinate elements—that is, elements of the same grammatical construction.

22a SEMICOLONS BETWEEN INDEPENDENT CLAUSES NOT JOINED BY COORDINATING CONJUNCTIONS

Independent clauses can be joined in a variety of ways, depending on the ideas expressed. (See 33a.1.) The semicolon is a logical choice when the ideas in each clause seem fairly equal and balanced. For example, in the three sentences that follow, the semicolon functions like the conjunction *and.*

> The left brain controls the right side of the body; the right brain controls the left side.
>
> Shakespeare's vocabulary included about 20,000 words; Milton's included about 11,000.
>
> Lights went out; elevators stopped; traffic stood still.

The semicolon is also an option when none of the coordinating conjunctions (*and, but, or, for, nor, so, yet*) seems to express the appropriate relationship.

> The bus was a bizarre sight; it lurched, swayed, and heaved itself forward like a drunk.
>
> Their motive was not money; it was something far more interesting than that.
>
> Benjamin Franklin carried out a number of experiments with lightning; in one of them, he passed an electric current through a chain of six men.

Semicolons should not be overused within a single passage. They are more noticeable than commas and thus should be used sparingly, lest they lose their effect.

OVERUSED: Bluegrass is an old-timey sound from Virginia, Tennessee, and Kentucky; it is the most traditional form of country music. Now the bluegrass festival has become a popular entertainment; families pack picnic lunches to spend the day listening to professionals and amateurs play. Some fans listen to the performances on the stage; others wander about enjoying the impromptu sessions on the grounds.

REVISED: An old-timey sound from Virginia, Tennessee, and Kentucky, bluegrass is the most traditional form of country music. Now the bluegrass festival has become a popular entertainment. Families pack picnic lunches to spend the day listening to professionals and amateurs play. Some fans listen to the performances on the stage; others wander about enjoying the impromptu sessions on the grounds.

22b SEMICOLONS BETWEEN INDEPENDENT CLAUSES JOINED BY TRANSITIONAL EXPRESSIONS

When two independent clauses are joined, their relationship is often signalled by a transitional expression, such as *however, therefore, also, nevertheless, for example, consequently,* or *instead.* (For a more complete list, see *Transitional Expression* in the Glossary of Terms.) These expressions are not grammatical conjunctions but adverbs modifying the entire clause. Thus, in the absence of a true conjunction, the semicolon joins the clauses.

> People under stress report long, complex dreams; however, people with placid lives report dreams that are uneventful and usually uninteresting.

> Each year the group publishes a list of words and phrases that should be banned from the language; for example, one year it listed "at this point in time" and "have a nice day."

The difference between a transitional expression and a conjunction can be illustrated very simply: a transitional expression can be moved about in a clause; a conjunction cannot.

POSSIBLE: We feared that computers would increase unemployment; instead, they have created more jobs.

POSSIBLE: We feared that computers would increase unemployment; they have, instead, created more jobs.

POSSIBLE: We feared that computers would increase unemployment, but they have created more jobs.

IMPOSSIBLE: We feared that computers would increase unemployment, they have, but, created more jobs.

22c SEMICOLONS BETWEEN INDEPENDENT CLAUSES JOINED BY COORDINATING CONJUNCTIONS

Ordinarily a comma appears between two independent clauses joined by a coordinating conjunction (*and, but, or, nor, for, so, yet*). However, when the first independent clause contains commas, a semicolon clarifies the structure.

UNCLEAR: Of the 11,000 men who encamped at Valley Forge, only 8,000 came with shoes, and only 8,000 survived.

REVISED: Of the 11,000 men who encamped at Valley Forge, only 8,000 came with shoes; and only 8,000 survived.

UNCLEAR: The books effectively deal with systems and languages such as UNIX, BASIC, PASCAL, C, COBOL, but these books cost approximately twenty dollars each.

REVISED: The books effectively deal with systems and languages such as UNIX, BASIC, PASCAL, C, COBOL; but these books cost approximately twenty dollars each.

When only one comma occurs in the first independent clause, you can use a comma or a semicolon with the conjunction. Either of the following versions is appropriate.

By purchasing a month-long pass for the train, travelers can save five dollars; but a year-long pass will save ninety dollars.

By purchasing a month-long pass for the train, travelers can save five dollars, but a year-long pass will save ninety dollars.

22d SEMICOLONS BETWEEN ITEMS IN A SERIES WITH INTERNAL PUNCTUATION

Ordinarily commas separate items in a series.

We subscribe to *Time, Newsweek,* and *Harper's.*

If, however, the items themselves contain commas, semicolons are required to mark the separation.

UNCLEAR: The train stops in Birmingham, Alabama, Atlanta, Georgia, Charlotte, North Carolina, and Charlottesville, Virginia.

REVISED: The train stops in Birmingham, Alabama; Atlanta, Georgia; Charlotte, North Carolina; and Charlottesville, Virginia.

UNCLEAR: The most significant dates of the Civil War were April 12, 1861, July 3, 1863, and April 9, 1865.

REVISED: The most significant dates of the Civil War were April 12, 1861; July 3, 1863; and April 9, 1865.

UNCLEAR: The participants in the exhibit are Judi Parker, who paints in watercolor, Simon Rogers, who is a potter, and Peter Mondavian, who sculpts in transparent plastic.

REVISED: The participants in the exhibit are Judi Parker, who paints in watercolor; Simon Rogers, who is a potter; and Peter Mondavian, who sculpts in transparent plastic.

22e INAPPROPRIATE SEMICOLONS

Avoid semicolons in these positions:

- Between elements that are not coordinate

INAPPROPRIATE: Only 7 plays by Sophocles now exist; even though he supposedly wrote 124.

REVISED: Only 7 plays by Sophocles now exist, even though he supposedly wrote 124.

- Before a list

INAPPROPRIATE: I have checked the following sources; encyclopedias, almanacs, indexes, and abstracts.

REVISED: I have checked the following sources: encyclopedias, almanacs, indexes, and abstracts.

REVISED: I have checked the following sources—encyclopedias, almanacs, indexes, and abstracts.

: 23

CHAPTER

23

COLONS

Although the **colon** is used in diverse constructions, it has only two basic purposes: to point ahead and to separate. No matter what its purpose, the colon has a formal and official tone.

23a COLONS BEFORE LISTS

A colon sometimes announces that a list will follow. Usually, the list is written not as a tabulation but as a continuation of the sentence. However, in scientific, technical, and business writing, the list is often separated from the sentence and itemized down the page.

NONTECHNICAL WRITING: Several American writers have died young without completing work they had started**:** F. Scott Fitzgerald, Nathanael West, and James Agee.

TECHNICAL WRITING: According to sports psychologists, athletes can improve their performances by several techniques**:**

1. goal setting
2. mental practice
3. relaxation

Most experts agree that a complete sentence should precede a colon. In fact, writers often precede a list with an expression like *the following* or *as follows* in order to avoid splitting elements, such as a verb or preposition from its object.

SPLIT: We visited: Athens, Kusadasi, Rhodes, and Heraklion.

REVISED: We visited the following places: Athens, Kusadasi, Rhodes, and Heraklion.

SPLIT: The root *carn* appears in: *incarnation, carnage,* and *carnival.*

REVISED: The root *carn* appears in the following words: *incarnation, carnage,* and *carnival.*

23b COLONS BEFORE APPOSITIVES THAT END SENTENCES

An appositive renames and identifies another sentence element, as *pitcher* renames *Satchel Paige* in the following example.

> Satchel Paige, a great pitcher, entered the major leagues at the age of 42.

When an appositive appears at the end of a sentence, an introductory colon creates drama or emphasis.

> Seventy years after the hoax of the Piltdown Man, a surprising new suspect has been found: Sir Arthur Conan Doyle.

> All the evidence points to the same conclusion: that a vast source of oil exists in the area.

23c COLONS BETWEEN INDEPENDENT CLAUSES

Usually, two independent clauses are joined with a comma and a coordinating conjunction or with a semicolon. On occasion, however, the second clause explains or illustrates the first clause or some part of it. A colon between the two clauses can indicate this special relationship. If the second clause is a formal statement or principle, you may capitalize the first word.

Galileo discovered that Copernicus was correct: Earth was not the center of the universe.

The most exciting shot in volleyball is the spike: one team tries to drive the ball across the net at up to 110 miles an hour.

23d COLONS BEFORE GRAMMATICALLY INDEPENDENT QUOTATIONS

A grammatically independent quotation is a complete sentence or several complete sentences. Ordinarily a comma separates the quotation from the rest of the sentence, but when the quotation is especially long and when the tone is formal, a colon may separate the two.

In a radio address on April 7, 1932, Roosevelt made a statement that still seems modern: "These unhappy times call for the building of plans . . . that build from the bottom up and not from the top down, that put their faith once more in the forgotten man at the bottom of the economic pyramid."

In 1945 Einstein wrote optimistically: "I do not believe that civilization will be wiped out in a war fought with the atomic bomb. Perhaps two-thirds of the people of the Earth might be killed, but enough men capable of thinking, and enough books, would be left to start again, and civilization could be restored."

23e COLONS BETWEEN TITLES AND SUBTITLES

A colon separates a title from a subtitle.

The Masks of God: Creative Mythology

Famine on the Wind: Plant Diseases and Human History

"Boomerang: The Stick That Returns"

"*Timon of Athens*: A Reconsideration"

23f COLONS IN CORRESPONDENCE

Several elements in business correspondence contain colons.

- Salutation

  Dear Ms. Plavin:

- Attention or subject line

  Attention: Dr. Grace Fortune

  Subject: Reassignment of Duties

- Headings in memoranda

  To: Part-Time Employees

  From: Milton Greenberg, Personnel Director

  Date: May 3, 1993

23g COLONS WITH NUMERICAL ELEMENTS

In several types of numerical sequences, colons separate the parts—hours from minutes, chapters from verses, and numbers in ratios.

5:30 P.M.	Psalms 29:2
10:00 A.M.	4:3

23h INAPPROPRIATE COLONS

Do not use a colon between the following elements.

- An independent and a dependent clause or phrase

INAPPROPRIATE: I have received only one response to my letters: although I wrote to twenty companies.

REVISED: I have received only one response to my letters, although I wrote to twenty companies.

- The parts of a phrase—for example, a verb and its complement, a preposition and its object, or *to* and the rest of the infinitive

INAPPROPRIATE: Is acid rain ruining: our gardens, our lakes, our farms?

REVISED: Is acid rain ruining our gardens, our lakes, our farms?

INAPPROPRIATE: Please send catalogues to: Carolyn Hacker and Stephen Hastings.

REVISED: Please send catalogues to Carolyn Hacker and Stephen Hastings.

INAPPROPRIATE: They are planning to: secure funds and send out a request for bids.

REVISED: They are planning to secure funds and send out a request for bids.

CHAPTER

24

DASHES, PARENTHESES, AND BRACKETS

- 24

Dashes, parentheses, and **brackets** primarily enclose information, isolating it from the rest of a sentence. But the effect of these three marks of punctuation is somewhat different. Dashes emphasize the elements they enclose. Parentheses de-emphasize interrupters and nonessential elements. Brackets usually enclose clarifications, especially in direct quotations.

DASHES

24a DASHES TO SET OFF APPOSITIVES CONTAINING COMMAS

An appositive is a word or phrase that renames or restates. Dashes set off an appositive containing commas so that a reader can see where it begins and ends. As the examples show, an appositive may appear in the middle of a sentence, at the end, or at the beginning.

CONFUSING: A number of the Founding Fathers, Jefferson, Madison, Adams, Hamilton, were extremely intellectual.

REVISED: A number of the Founding Fathers—Jefferson, Madison, Adams, Hamilton—were extremely intellectual.

CONFUSING: The pitcher can throw a variety of breaking pitches, curves, screwballs, and knuckleballs.

REVISED: The pitcher can throw a variety of breaking pitches—curves, screwballs, and knuckleballs.

CONFUSING: A poet, dramatist, novelist, essayist, historian, Voltaire has been an influential figure in the history of thought.

REVISED: A poet, dramatist, novelist, essayist, historian—Voltaire has been an influential figure in the history of thought.

24b DASHES TO SET OFF NONRESTRICTIVE MODIFIERS CONTAINING COMMAS

Ordinarily commas set off a nonrestrictive modifier, whether a clause or a phrase. (See 21c.) When the modifier itself contains commas, however, dashes can make its boundaries clear.

> Jules Feiffer—who has produced cartoons, novels, plays, and screenplays—uses humor to reflect human folly.

> By the eighteenth century, riddles—written, at least—were becoming less suggestive and vulgar.

24c DASHES TO EMPHASIZE SENTENCE ELEMENTS

Dashes can emphasize any kind of construction (a word, a phrase, or a clause) that can be set off or separated from the rest of the sentence.

> We have noticed a persistent quality in the lives of famous people—confidence.

They were stealing—via computer—hundreds of thousands of dollars in goods and services.

In *Walden,* Thoreau tells how he built his cabin—down to the cost of the nails.

Most people who read food magazines never cook anything by the recipes—they're too difficult.

24d DASHES WITH INTERRUPTERS

Dashes effectively set off an element that interrupts the continuity of prose, separates the essential parts of a sentence pattern, or breaks a piece of dialogue.

The author was sitting—slouching, really—on the sofa.

"I never knew—well, I don't suppose it matters now."

"But not—I really wouldn't call the move a mistake."

PARENTHESES

24e PARENTHESES TO ENCLOSE INTERRUPTERS

Parentheses isolate and de-emphasize elements that interrupt a sentence or passage. Interrupters may be explanations, illustrations, or clarifications. They may be single words, phrases, or even whole sentences.

Since 1603, the royal arms of Britain have been supported by the English lion (dexter) and the Scottish unicorn (sinister).

KYB CHG (Keyboard Change) allows an operator to change the keyboard arrangement.

Monticello (pronounced *Montichel'lo* in the Italian way) was built on a Virginia hilltop Jefferson's father had left him.

When one whole sentence interrupts another, the interrupter neither begins with a capital letter nor ends with a period.

> After the Civil War, gangs of homeless burglars (they called themselves "yeggs") rode the freight trains, robbing and stealing along the way.

When a whole sentence is inserted between sentences, the interrupter begins with a capital letter and ends with a period. The final parenthesis follows the period.

> In his early youth Wordsworth was an enthusiast for the French Revolution. (He had been influenced by the ideas of Rousseau.) But as he grew older, he became increasingly conservative.

24f PARENTHESES FOR REFERENCES TO PAGES, FIGURES, TABLES, AND CHAPTERS

Parentheses can enclose references to specific pages, to relevant figures or tables, or to different chapters. The following examples illustrate the two ways to make these references: inside a sentence or as a separate sentence.

> A map of the river shows where each aquatic plant still grows (45).

> James McNeill Whistler is considered the forerunner of abstract art. (See pp. 52–76.)

> The inertial reel makes seat belts lock up automatically (see the accompanying diagram).

> Safes fall into two types: fire-resistant safes for records and burglar-resistant safes for money. (See figs., p. 167.)

BRACKETS

24g BRACKETS AROUND INSERTIONS IN DIRECT QUOTATIONS

Exact quotations taken out of context often contain pronouns without clear references, terms needing explanation, or names without identification. In such situations, you can insert clarifications in brackets after the unclear word or phrase. Or you may replace the unclear word or phrase with the bracketed clarification.

> De Tocqueville wrote, "They [the Americans] have all a lively faith in the perfectibility of man."
>
> or
>
> De Tocqueville wrote, "[The Americans] have all a lively faith in the perfectibility of man."

> The author points out, "The Countess of Lovelace [Byron's daughter] met Babbage and soon became the first computer programmer."
>
> or
>
> The author points out, "[Byron's daughter] met Babbage and soon became the first computer programmer."

You may also use brackets to insert corrections in direct quotations.

> Harry Truman wrote a letter to his daughter on March 19, 1956, saying, "If you don't trust the people you love . . . you'll be the unhappiest and [most] frustrated person alive."

Instead of adding a correction, a writer can insert *sic* in brackets following the error to show that it appeared "thus" in the source.

> From Hyeres, Fitzgerald wrote Thomas Boyd: "The moon is an absolutely *au fait* Mediteraenean [sic] moon with a blurred silver linnen [sic] cap . . . we're both a little tight and very happily drunk."

To emphasize an element in the source being quoted, you may italicize (or underline) the element and insert an explanation in brackets.

> According to the article, "As a society, we need to grapple with the *real* problem—which is the lack of consensus—not about public education, but over what public education should be about [italics mine]."

24h BRACKETS FOR PARENTHESES INSIDE PARENTHESES

On the very rare occasions when parentheses are required inside parentheses, brackets replace the inner set.

> Most psychologists believe that phobias are stress related. (But a recent study [1994] suggests that agoraphobia may have biological origins.)

CHAPTER

25

PERIODS, QUESTION MARKS, AND EXCLAMATION POINTS

Periods, question marks, and **exclamation points** are called end (or terminal) marks because they appear primarily at the ends of complete sentences. The period most commonly occurs after sentences and abbreviations. The question mark occurs mainly after a direct question. Exclamation points are common only after statements in advertising copy, warnings in instructions, and emotional speeches in dialogue.

PERIODS

25a PERIODS AS END PUNCTUATION

Periods follow several types of complete sentences.

STATEMENTS:	Mardi Gras is the last day before Lent.
COMMANDS:	Use linseed oil on saddles and bridles.
INDIRECT QUESTIONS:	He asked whether we had a reservation.

After polite requests, usually in correspondence, you may use either a period or a question mark.

Would you please send me your brochure on wildflowers.

Would you please send me your brochure on wildflowers?

To set off a mild interjection, you may use either a period or a comma (21g.1).

Well. Hindsight is always 20-20.

Well, hindsight is always 20-20.

25b PERIODS IN OUTLINES AND DISPLAYED LISTS

Periods follow numbers and letters in displayed lists, unless the numbers and letters are enclosed in parentheses.

Cathedrals

I. Types of Cathedrals
   A. Palace Churches
   B. Abbeys
II. Famous Cathedrals
   A. French Cathedrals
   B. English Cathedrals
   C. Italian Cathedrals

The report should include the following:

1. Abstract
2. Introduction

3. Procedure
4. Discussion
5. Conclusions and recommendations

25c INAPPROPRIATE PERIODS

Do not use periods in the following situations.

- After a period marking the end of an abbreviation

INAPPROPRIATE: The ceremony began at 3:00 P.M..

REVISED: The ceremony began at 3:00 P.M.

- After words and phrases in displayed lists

INAPPROPRIATE
Improperly canned foods can spoil for four reasons:
1. growth of yeasts and molds.
2. growth of bacteria.
3. presence of enzymes.
4. process of oxidation.

REVISED
Improperly canned foods can spoil for four reasons:
1. growth of yeasts and molds
2. growth of bacteria
3. presence of enzymes
4. process of oxidation

QUESTION MARKS

25d QUESTION MARKS AS END PUNCTUATION

The question mark is used as end punctuation in several different constructions.

- After direct questions

  When is the off-season in Florida?

- After sentences with tag questions

  September is unusually hot, isn't it?

- After elliptical questions in a series

  Should politicians be required to reveal all the details of their private lives? Why? And to whom?

25e QUESTION MARKS WITHIN SENTENCES

Direct questions usually appear alone.

> What will be won?

On rare occasions a direct question appears, not alone, but as the subject of a sentence.

> What will be won? was on their minds.

In this case, the question mark emphasizes the question. Be careful, however, to avoid using a question mark if the question is indirect and cannot appear separately.

INAPPROPRIATE: What we can gain by further negotiation? is the first question.

REVISED: What we can gain by further negotiation is the first question.

REVISED: What can we gain by further negotiation? is the first question.

A question mark can also express doubt about a fact such as a date, a place, a statistic, and the like.

> The first edition of the novel (1918?) was banned in the United States.

> The most famous of the Cleopatras (VII?) lived from 69 to 30 B.C.

EXCLAMATION POINTS

25f EXCLAMATION POINTS IN DIALOGUE

An exclamation point is used in dialogue to indicate that the speaker is shouting or expressing intense feelings.

"Stop!" the engineer shouted. "There is a unicorn on the tracks!"

"Shut up!" she said between clenched teeth. "Just shut up!"

25g EXCLAMATION POINTS WITH INTERJECTIONS

Interjections are expressions of emotion, such as *well, goodness, oh,* and *whew.* You can punctuate a mild interjection with a period or a comma.

Well. I suppose we could reconsider the matter.

Oh, he does not understand.

When the interjection expresses strong emotion, however, you can use an exclamation point.

Well! You've said quite enough.

Whew! That car barely missed me!

25h EXCLAMATION POINTS FOR EMPHASIS

Exclamation points are often used in warnings to catch the reader's attention and help prevent accidents.

WARNING! DO NOT USE NEAR OPEN FLAME!

In prose, exclamation points can emphasize something astonishing or ironic.

New pesticides arrive at the rate of five hundred a year!

If we are lucky, we will have to battle only mosquitoes and ignorance!

You should, however, use exclamation points for emphasis very, very sparingly. When overused, they lose their dramatic effect.

Inexperienced writers sometimes try to convey enthusiasm by using exclamation points and vague words such as *great, wonderful, marvelous,* and *perfect.* Specific details, however, are more convincing than exclamation points, as the following two passages illustrate.

INEFFECTIVE: My favorite place to visit in winter is Rancho Mirage in the California desert. The scenery is marvelous! And the weather is great!

REVISED: My favorite place to visit in winter is Rancho Mirage in the California desert. The town is set in a lush oasis surrounded by a stark desert and rugged mountains. The temperature gets up to about 80 degrees during the day and down to about 60 degrees at night.

Another ineffective use of the exclamation point is to stress the importance of an idea. A better technique is to use words and phrases that express more specifically the degree of the idea's importance. Compare these sentences.

VAGUE: We must revise the nursing curriculum!

REVISED: One of our major goals should be to revise the nursing curriculum.

REVISED: Our primary concern should be the revision of the nursing curriculum.

REVISED: Until we revise the nursing curriculum, we can make no progress at all.

26a

CHAPTER

26

APOSTROPHES

Apostrophes have three functions to form possessives, to allow contractions, and in a few contexts to precede *s* in plurals. By far the most common of the three, however, is to indicate possession.

26a APOSTROPHES TO INDICATE POSSESSION

The grammatical term *possession* refers to such relationships as ownership, origin, and measurement *Claudia s house, the professor s approval, a week s vacation.* Some pronouns have special possessive forms: *my/mine, our/ours, your/yours, his, her/hers, its, their/theirs, whose.* Nouns and all other pronouns are made possessive by the addition of an apostrophe plus *s* or simply an apostrophe.

The general rules for showing possession with apostrophes follow.

- Add *s* to most singular nouns and to singular indefinite pronouns.

  doctor → doctor's diagnosis

  novel → novel's plot

  Don Quixote → Don Quixote's quest

  Ross → Ross's boat

Ms. Jones → Ms. Jones's office

everybody → everybody's responsibility

someone → someone's parking space

neither → neither's fault

- Add ' to singular proper names when the addition of another *-s* would make pronunciation peculiar or difficult.

  Jesus → Jesus' teachings

  Moses → Moses' leadership

  Aristophanes → Aristophanes' plays

  Xerxes → Xerxes' conquests

- Add ' to plural nouns that end in *s.*

  teachers → teachers' pay

  divers → divers' training school

  six months → six months' pay

  trees → trees' roots

- Add ***'s*** to plural nouns that do not end in *s.*

  oxen → oxen's yokes

  children → children's art

  bacteria → bacteria's behavior

  alumni → alumni's involvement

  sheep → sheep's pasture

- Add ***'s*** or ' to the last word of a compound noun or pronoun.

  editor in chief → editor in chief's opinion

  attorney generals → attorney generals' decisions

  no one else → no one else's business

- Add ***'s*** or ' to the last name only to indicate joint possession.

  Lebanon and Syria → Lebanon and Syria's disagreement

Crick and Watson → Crick and Watson's discovery

juniors and misses → juniors and misses' department

- Add **'s** or ' to each name to indicate individual possession of more than one noun.

the mayor and governor → the mayor's and governor's policies

the Falcons and Saints → the Falcons' and Saints' schedules

26b APOSTROPHES TO CREATE CONTRACTIONS

In contractions, the apostrophe takes the place of omitted letters, numbers, or words.

it's = it is, it has	goin' (dialect) = going
who's = who is, who has	don't = do not
they're = they are	won't = will not
I'll = I will	would've = would have
'65 = 1965	we'd = we would
rock'n'roll = rock and roll	o'clock = of the clock

Remember that *till, though,* and *round* are all words, not contractions. Do not write *'till, 'though,* and *'round.*

26c APOSTROPHES TO INDICATE PLURALS OF LETTERS AND WORDS USED AS WORDS

Whenever possible, form the plurals of letters or words used as such in the usual way—by adding an *s.* Sometimes, however, the *s* alone is not clear; then you should add an apostrophe plus the *s.* The apostrophe prevents the *s* from looking like a part of a letter or word.

UNCLEAR PLURAL: She writes her *m*s and *n*s alike.

CLEAR PLURAL:	She writes her *m*'s and *n*'s alike.
UNCLEAR PLURAL:	You have used too many *and*s.
CLEAR PLURAL:	You have used too many *and*'s.

Notice that the problem occurs only with lowercase letters, not with capitals (*GIs, YMCAs, CEOs*).

26d INAPPROPRIATE APOSTROPHES

Do not use apostrophes in the following situations.

- Within a word, even though the word itself ends in *s*

NONSTANDARD	REVISED
Charle's	Charles's
Jone's	Jones's
the Raider's	the Raiders'

- In the plural of an ordinary word

NONSTANDARD	REVISED
tomato's	tomatoes
price's	prices

- In the plural form of numerals. Although once considered standard, the apostrophes are no longer necessary.

NOT CURRENT	REVISED
5's	5s
10's and 1,000's	10s and 1,000s
1960's	1960s

- In the possessive forms of personal pronouns and in the possessive form of *who.* All personal pronouns and the pronoun *who* form possessives without the apostrophe.

NONSTANDARD	REVISED
it's/its'	its
her's/hers'	hers
your's/yours'	yours
our's/ours'	ours
their's/theirs'	theirs
who's	whose

NOTE: Readers are especially confused by the incorrect use of *it's* and *who's* as possessives. Remember that *it's* and *who's* are contractions for *it is* or *it has* and *who is* or *who has;* they are never possessives.

NONSTANDARD: Do not buy the album; it's lyrics are not worth hearing more than once.

REVISED: Do not buy the album; its lyrics are not worth hearing more than once.

NONSTANDARD: They discussed Planet 10, who's existence has been suggested by irregularities in the orbits of Uranus and Neptune.

REVISED: They discussed Planet 10, whose existence has been suggested by irregularities in the orbits of Uranus and Neptune.

CHAPTER

27

QUOTATION MARKS AND ELLIPSIS MARKS

Although quotation marks and ellipsis marks have several uses, these marks appear most often in quotations, reproductions of someone s exact words. **Quotation marks** show the beginning and end of the citation. **Ellipsis marks** indicate where a part or parts of the original statement have been deleted.

QUOTATION MARKS

27a QUOTATION MARKS TO ENCLOSE DIRECT QUOTATIONS

Direct quotations of a few sentences or lines should be enclosed in quotation marks. The identifying expressions, such as *the source said* or *according to the source,* appear at the beginning, middle, or end of the quotation and should not be enclosed inside the quotation marks.

> According to George Marshall, “The refusal of the British and Russian peoples to accept what appeared to be inevitable defeat was the great factor in the salvage of our civilization.”
>
> “The refusal of the British and Russian peoples to accept what appeared to be inevitable defeat was,” George Marshall maintained, “the great factor in the salvage of our civilization.”
>
> “The refusal of the British and Russian peoples to accept what appeared to be inevitable defeat was the great factor in the salvage of our civilization,” George Marshall reported in 1945.

Quotation marks also should enclose a part of a quoted statement.

> George Marshall reported that Britain’s and Russia’s refusal to accept defeat in World War II was “the great factor in the salvage of our civilization.”
>
> George Marshall pointed out that Britain’s and Russia’s refusal to accept “inevitable defeat” in World War II saved civilization.

You should not use quotation marks when a quoted passage is long, that is, more than four typed lines or more than forty words. Instead, you should set up the passage as a “block,” separate from the text, with each line indented.

Also, do not use quotation marks with an indirect quotation, one in which the source is paraphrased.

> George Marshall pointed out that in World War II Britain and Russia saved civilization by refusing to give up.

On some occasions, a quoted passage may itself contain a quotation. If a quoted passage already contains quotation marks, double marks (“. . .”) surround the whole passage, and single marks (‘. . .’) surround the inside quotation. On a keyboard, make the single quotation marks with the apostrophe key.

ORIGINAL: His situation reminds one of a line, a plea really, from Maurice Sendak’s harrowing slapstick fantasy *Higglety Pigglety Pop!:* “There must be more to life than having everything.” (Leonard Marcus)

QUOTATION: Marcus points out that the child’s situation reminds him of a “plea . . . from Maurice Sendak’s harrowing slapstick fantasy *Higglety Pigglety Pop!:* ‘There must be more to life than having everything!’”

27b QUOTATION MARKS WITH OTHER PUNCTUATION MARKS

When closing quotation marks appear with other marks of punctuation, strict conventions govern the order.

(1) Quotation marks with the period and the comma

A closing quotation mark should follow a period or comma. This rule applies even when closing quotation marks are both single and double.

> The judge who handled the case referred to the problem that "most defendants are indigents without easy access to assistance."
>
> "I've never seen a 3-D movie," she insisted.
>
> After finishing "The Headless Cupid," he read "The Famous Stanley Kidnapping Case."
>
> The book pointed out that "Japan is creating enormous research and industrial centers called 'technopolises.'"

EXCEPTION: When a parenthetical citation intervenes, the quotation mark should precede the citation, and the period should follow.

> Stendhal conducts "the rites of initiation into the nineteenth century" (Levin 149).

(2) Quotation marks with the semicolon and the colon

A closing quotation mark should always precede a semicolon or colon.

> Many people in business and government use jargon and "acronymese"; in fact, they often leave ordinary people totally in the dark.
>
> He said, "The work must be finished on time"; and he meant it.

The sign listed the scheduled performances of "Mostly Mozart": July 19, July 27, and August 2.

According to the report, "Japan is shifting to a basic research phase": no longer will Japan be dependent on borrowed findings.

(3) Quotation marks with the question mark, exclamation point, and dash

The quotation mark should follow a question mark, exclamation point, or dash that punctuates the quoted material.

The advertisement asked, "Why give the common, when you can give the preferred?"

At the end of the game, the happy fan shouted, "Time to celebrate, man!"

He said, "No—" and was immediately interrupted.

A closing quotation mark should precede a question mark, exclamation point, or dash that punctuates the unquoted part of the sentence.

Which character says, "I am a feather for each wind that blows"?

Don't ever write an antiquated expression like "heretofore"!

"These"—he pointed to a tray of snails—"are delicious."

Sometimes both the quoted and unquoted material in a sentence are questions. In these cases, the closing quotation mark should follow the question mark.

What poem asks, "And by what way shall I go back?"

Did you ask, "Was H. L. Mencken from Baltimore?"

On rare occasions, a sequence may include a single quotation mark, a double quotation mark, and a question mark.

The professor asked the class, "Who wrote 'Ozymandias'?"

In this example, the single quotation mark should go first because the title it encloses is not a question; the question mark should go next because the quoted material, not the unquoted, is the question; and the double quotation mark should go last to conclude the quote.

27c QUOTATION MARKS IN DIALOGUE

When a dialogue with two or more speakers is represented on paper, the exact words of the speakers are placed inside quotation marks. Ordinarily the spoken words are interrupted with comments that set the scenes, identify the speakers, and create the tone. You must separate these comments from the spoken dialogue, as in the following excerpt from Joseph Conrad's "An Outpost of Progress."

> "Is this your revolver?" asked Makola, getting up.
>
> "Yes," said Kayerts; then he added very quickly, "He ran after me to shoot me—you saw!"
>
> "Yes, I saw," said Makola. "There is only one revolver; where's his?"
>
> "Don't know," whispered Kayerts in a voice that had become suddenly very faint.

You indicate every change of speaker by a new paragraph with quotation marks before and after the speech. To show that one speaker continues for more than one paragraph, place a quotation mark before each paragraph, but place the closing quotation mark only after the last paragraph. The following example includes two paragraphs containing the words of one speaker. Notice the omission of the quotation mark at the end of the first paragraph.

> The professor gave us instructions before we began to dig for dinosaur remains: "In digging for bones, you will excavate in one small area, moving earth bit by bit with an ice pick. If you are not careful, you could accidentally sweep away bones.
>
> "Always remember that dinosaurs deserve this care. They roamed the earth for 140 million years. Humans have so far only survived 4 million."

27d QUOTATION MARKS IN TITLES

Ordinarily, the way a title is marked tells a reader whether the title refers to a whole work or to only part of a larger work. Titles of collections and long works, such as anthologies and novels, appear in italics (or underlining). Titles of short works, such as short stories and poems, appear in quotation marks. In general, italicize titles found on the covers of published works, and enclose in quotation marks titles found within the covers. (For a complete discussion of italics, see 28a.)

SHORT STORY:	"Her Sweet Jerome," from *In Love and Trouble*
SHORT POEM:	"Terrence, This Is Stupid Stuff," from *A Shropshire Lad*
ESSAY:	"Sootfall and Fallout," from *Essays of E. B. White*
ARTICLE:	"The Mystery of Tears," from *Smithsonian*
EDITORIAL:	"Facts and Figures for the President," from the *Fort Wayne News-Sentinel*
CHAPTER:	"Velikovsky in Collision," from *Ever Since Darwin*
TV EPISODE:	"A Sound of Dolphins," from *The Undersea World of Jacques Cousteau*
SONG:	"It Ain't Necessarily So," from *Porgy and Bess*

27e QUOTATION MARKS AROUND WORDS USED IN SPECIAL WAYS

Quotation marks can show that words have been used in a special sense—for an ironic effect, with a twist of meaning, or as words. Make sure, however, that an enclosed word is indeed used in a special way. If it is not, the quotation marks will mislead readers.

> She insisted that the graduates from "her" school would never do such a thing.
>
> The report contained the "facts" of the case.
>
> When people talk about the movie, they use words like "strange," "haunting," and "weird."

27f INAPPROPRIATE QUOTATION MARKS

Avoid quotation marks in the following instances.

- Around the title of a composition when it appears on a title page or on the first page of a manuscript

INAPPROPRIATE: "A Hero for Today"

REVISED: A Hero for Today

- Around a nickname used in place of a name

INAPPROPRIATE: In the 1950s, "Fats" Domino was one of the big names in rock and roll.

REVISED: In the 1950s, Fats Domino was one of the big names in rock and roll.

- Around a slang or a trite expression used for lack of a more effective one

INAPPROPRIATE: "Last but not least," we must consider the endangered species.

REVISED: Finally, we must consider the endangered species.

- Around *yes* and *no* unless you are writing dialogue

INAPPROPRIATE: Answer "yes" or "no."

REVISED: Answer yes or no.

ELLIPSIS MARKS

27g ELLIPSIS MARKS TO SHOW OMISSIONS

Ellipsis marks are a sequence of spaced periods that indicate an omission in a direct quotation. The number of periods you use depends on what has been omitted.

(1) Omission within a single sentence

To show an omission within a single sentence, use three periods with a space before, between, and after each period.

ORIGINAL QUOTATION

"For the root of genius is in the unconscious, not the conscious, mind." (Dorothea Brande, *Becoming a Writer*)

QUOTATION WITH ELLIPSIS MARKS

Dorothea Brande wrote, "For the root of genius is in the unconscious . . . mind."

(2) Omission at the end of a sentence

To show an omission at the end of a sentence, use a sentence period followed by three spaced periods.

ORIGINAL QUOTATION

"Most people who bother with the matter at all would admit that the English language is in a bad way, but it is generally assumed that we cannot by conscious action do anything about it." (George Orwell, "Politics and the English Language")

QUOTATION WITH ELLIPSIS MARKS

According to Orwell, "Most people who bother with the matter at all would admit that the English language is in a bad way. . . ."

NOTE: When the quotation is obviously a fragment of the whole, you do not use ellipsis marks at the end.

QUOTATION WITHOUT ELLIPSIS MARKS

Orwell comments that most people concerned about English think it's "in a bad way."

(3) Omission of a whole sentence or several sentences

If an omission involves a whole sentence or several sentences, use four periods—the period of the last sentence quoted plus the three spaced periods showing ellipsis.

ORIGINAL QUOTATION
"Children are a relatively modern invention. Until a few hundred years ago they did not exist. In medieval and Renaissance painting you see pint-size men and women, wearing grown-up clothes and grown-up expressions, performing grown-up tasks." (Shana Alexander, "Kid's Country")

QUOTATION WITH ELLIPSIS MARKS

As Shana Alexander points out, "Children are a relatively modern invention. . . . In medieval and Renaissance painting you see pint-size men and women, wearing grown-up clothes and grown-up expressions, performing grown-up tasks."

(4) Omission at the beginning of a quotation

Do not use ellipsis marks to show an omission at the beginning of a quotation; instead, work the quoted words into your own syntax. The absence of an initial capital letter shows that the whole passage is not included. Also, when the quotation is obviously a fragment of the whole, you do not use ellipsis marks at the end.

ORIGINAL QUOTATION
"America's group of republics is merged in one, in the eyes of the world; and, for some purposes, in reality: but this involves no obligation to make them all alike in their produce and occupations." (Harriet Martineau, *Society in America*)

QUOTATION WITHOUT ELLIPSIS MARKS
Martineau wrote in 1834 that the merging of America's republics "involves no obligation to make them all alike."

(5) Omission of a line or lines of poetry

Use a line of spaced periods to show the omission of one or more lines of poetry. Remember that when you quote several lines of a poem, you should show them indented and formatted as in the original, without quotation marks.

ORIGINAL QUOTATION

Power, like a desolating pestilence,
Pollutes whate'er it touches; and obedience,
Bane of all genius, virtue, freedome, truth,
Makes slaves of men, and, of the human frame
A mechanized automaton.

QUOTATION WITH ELLIPSIS MARKS

Shelley writes in “Queen Mab”:

Power, like a desolating pestilence,
Pollutes whate'er it touches; and obedience,
. . . .
Makes slaves of men, and, of the human frame
A mechanized automaton.

27h ELLIPSIS MARKS TO SHOW INTERRUPTION IN DIALOGUE

In dialogue, ellipsis marks can show interruption of a thought or statement.

> “Well, Judge, I don't know . . .” and whatever he meant to say trailed off into silence.

> “That car costs forty thousand . . . uh . . . forget it.”

CHAPTER

28

ITALICS/ UNDERLINING

Italic type is a slanted typeface used in printing and word processing to distinguish titles, foreign words, and words used in other special ways. When italic type is not available, **underlining** is the appropriate substitute. In fact, most style guides (including those of the Modern Language Association and the American Psychological Association) require underlining for manuscripts, even though italics will appear in typeset copy.

28a ITALICS/UNDERLINING IN TITLES

Titles are marked either with quotation marks (27d) or with italics. As a general rule, italics are used for complete works; quotation marks, for parts of works. If you underline to represent italics, do not break the line. An unbroken line displays the title as a single unit and facilitates reading.

Although publishers do not always agree about when to use italics and when to use quotation marks, it is common practice to italicize the following kinds of titles.

- Books and book-length poems

  The Red Badge of Courage

  The Short Stories of Saki

Four Screen Plays of Ingmar Bergman

Don Juan

- Plays and movies

ital 28a

Othello

Crimes of the Heart

Dr. Strangelove

- Reports and long pamphlets

Handbook of Utilization of Aquatic Plants

A Nation at Risk: The Imperative for Educational Reform

- Newspapers, magazines, and journals

Predominant practice is not to italicize *the* beginning a title.

the Washington Post

the New Republic

Art in America

Journal of Dental Research

- Operas, ballets, albums

Verdi's Rigoletto

Bach's Well-Tempered Clavier

Horowitz at the Met

Paul Simon's There Goes Rhymin' Simon

- Television and radio series

The Shadow

The Jack Benny Show

Star Trek

Masterpiece Theatre

- Paintings and sculpture

  Absinthe Drinkers by Degas

  Guernica by Picasso

  Sky Cathedral by Louise Nevelson

  Three Way Piece No. 2 by Henry Moore

NOTE: Remember to consider the punctuation following a title.

Italicize or underline punctuation that is part of a title.

> They are acting in Who's Afraid of Virginia Woolf?

Do not italicize or underline sentence punctuation following a title.

> Have you ever read Babbitt?

Do not italicize an apostrophe or an apostrophe plus an *s* that is added to a title.

> The Counterfeiters' plot
>
> Time's editorial

EXCEPTIONS: Do not italicize the following titles.

- Names of standard dictionaries and encyclopedias unless referred to by their formal names

  Webster's Dictionary (Webster's Third New International Dictionary)

  Random House Dictionary (The Random House Dictionary of the English Language)

  Americana (Encyclopedia Americana)

- Names of standard religious books

  Bible

  Koran

  Talmud

- Directories and catalogs

  Atlanta Telephone Directory

  JC Penney Catalog

- The title of a composition when it appears on a title page or at the top of the first page of a manuscript

  The Trouble with Television

  The Unforgettable Miss Sternberger

28b ITALICS/UNDERLINING FOR WORDS, NUMBERS, AND LETTERS USED AS SUCH

When a word, letter, or number refers to itself rather than to its usual meaning, italics alert readers to this special use. Compare, for example, the following two sentences. In the first, *dog* has its usual meaning of canine animal; in the second, it refers to the word *dog*.

> The dog barked.
>
> *Dog* comes from Anglo-Saxon.

Compare the use of *225* in the next two sentences. In the first, *225* refers to a quantity; in the second, it refers to the number itself.

> We planted 225 tulip bulbs in front of the courthouse.
>
> Someone had written *225* in the wet cement.

Often this special use is signalled by the insertion of "the word," "the letter," "the number," or some other appropriate description.

> In a legal document, the word *said* refers to something or someone previously mentioned.
>
> His shirts are monogrammed with the letters *HCC*.

Even when the signal is not present, it can be easily supplied.

> He says *you know* after every sentence.
>
> He says [the words] *you know* after every sentence.
>
> Southerners sometimes drop a final *r*.
>
> Southerners sometimes drop a final *r* [sound].
>
> The British put two *e*'s in *judgment*.
>
> The British put two [letter] *e*'s in [the word] *judgment*.

NOTE: Words that refer to themselves can appear in quotation marks instead of italics. (See 27e.)

28c ITALICS/UNDERLINING FOR SOUNDS

Italicize sounds that are represented by words or combinations of letters.

> The music had a recurrent ta ta ta tum refrain.

> With a woosh-thump, the golf club sent the white ball over the fair-way.

28d ITALICS/UNDERLINING FOR FOREIGN WORDS

Italicize foreign names of the scientific genus and species of animals and plants.

> The new threat to the marsh is Hydrilla verticillata, which can choke out all other life.

Italicize foreign words that are not considered part of the vocabulary of English.

> People assume that movies with gladiators, casts of thousands, and elaborate costumes must ipso facto be bad.

> On the ship we ate in the tourist-class salle à manger.

Some foreign words are in such common use that they are now considered English. For example, words such as *ex officio, ballet, connoisseur,* and *debut,* though originally Latin and French, no longer need italicizing. When you are sure a word of foreign origin is familiar to your audience, you need not italicize it.

28e ITALICS/UNDERLINING FOR VEHICLES DESIGNATED BY PROPER NAMES

Italicize the proper names of ships, aircraft, and spacecraft.

> U.S.S. Iowa

> Challenger

28f ITALICS/UNDERLINING FOR EMPHASIS

You can italicize words for emphasis, but you should use this device in moderation. Overuse negates its impact.

The department's expenditures are edging toward the 300-billion-dollar mark.

She works all day as a secretary, and she still likes to type.

CHAPTER

29

HYPHENS AND SLASHES

Unlike other punctuation marks such as commas and semicolons, **hyphens** and **slashes** never signal sentence structure. Instead they function on the word level hyphens to create compound words and slashes to show alternatives and make combinations.

HYPHENS

29a HYPHENS IN COMPOUND NOUNS AND VERBS

Compound nouns and verbs appear in three forms. Some are separated (*safe house*); others are hyphenated (*safe-conduct*); and still others are written together (*safeguard*). Often the hyphens distinguish between a noun and verb form, but even so, you cannot be sure which form contains the hyphen.

has-been (noun)	has been (verb)
send-off (noun)	send off (verb)
single-space (verb)	single space (noun)
black-market (verb)	black market (noun)

There is one fairly consistent tradition: hyphenated nouns can show the dual nature of jobs and roles.

actor-director	secretary-treasurer
player-coach	city-state
clerk-typist	restaurant-lounge

Otherwise, your only guide for hyphenating nouns and verbs is an up-to-date dictionary. Although all dictionaries do not agree, they at least provide authority for whatever practice you follow.

29b HYPHENS IN COMPOUND MODIFIERS

You should hyphenate a compound modifier preceding a noun so that readers will immediately understand that the modifier forms a single unit and a single concept. For example, *30-gallon cans* refers to cans that hold 30 gallons, whereas *30 gallon cans* refers to 30 cans that hold one gallon. Compare the meanings of the following pairs.

four-glass sets	four glass sets
man-eating clams	man eating clams
above-mentioned facts	above mentioned facts
long-remembered story	long remembered story

If a compound modifier does not appear before a noun, omit the hyphen or hyphens.

HYPHENATED:	Fire destroyed the sixteenth-century building.
NOT HYPHENATED:	The architecture was sixteenth century.
HYPHENATED:	The machine registers only low-frequency sounds.
NOT HYPHENATED:	The sounds should be low frequency.
HYPHENATED:	I own a one-and-a-half-year-old beagle.
NOT HYPHENATED:	The beagle is one and a half years old.

A few compound modifiers preceding nouns are exceptions to this practice. You should not hyphenate a modifier made of an *-ly* adverb plus another word.

carefully written paper

highly successful restaurant

badly designed building

Also, do not use hyphens when a compound modifier is obviously a unit, as in the case of a modifier made from a proper noun, a foreign expression, or a standard compound noun.

Red Cross office

prima facie evidence

child welfare payment

When two compound modifiers have a word in common (*three-column and five-column charts*), the common word need not appear but once (*three- and five-column charts*). Notice, however, that you should retain the hyphen in each piece of the compound.

whole- or half-year lease

forty- or fifty-thousand dollars

10-, 12-, and 15-pitch typefaces

American-bred, -owned, and -trained colt

29c HYPHENS WITH SOME PREFIXES

Most prefixes are attached directly to the base word, but *self-* and *ex-* are attached with hyphens.

self-defense	ex-champion
self-education	ex-clerk
self-conscious	ex-husband

Use a hyphen when a prefix is attached to a proper noun (easily identified by its capital letter).

non-European	pre-Columbian
mid-Atlantic	anti-Communist
neo-Platonic	un-American

Sometimes a hyphen is necessary to distinguish words that would otherwise be identical.

recover	re-cover	reform	re-form
prejudicial	pre-judicial	extraordinary	extra-ordinary

When reading is complicated by a repeated letter or by two vowels in a row, use a hyphen to separate the prefix from the base.

non-nuclear	pro-union
anti-inflation	semi-independent

Many words with repeated letters that were once hyphenated are now written solid—for example, *preempt* and *reentry.* A current dictionary will usually illustrate acceptable spelling.

29d HYPHENS IN NUMBERS

Use a hyphen with the following numbers.

- Spelled-out numbers from twenty-one to ninety-nine, whether they appear alone or as part of a larger number

  Alexander the Great died when he was only thirty-two.

  Thirty-two hundred of the automobiles were recalled.

- Spelled-out fractions, unless either the numerator or denominator already contains a hyphen

  One-fourth of those surveyed had voted.

  The arrow missed by two thirty-seconds of an inch.

- A range of numbers

  During the years 1975–1981, the building served as the library.

  See pages 25–96.

29e HYPHENS FOR WORD DIVISIONS AT THE ENDS OF LINES

Writers sometimes hyphenate words at the ends of lines in order to align the right margin. Words split between two lines, however, usually distract readers and slow down their reading pace. In addition, frequent hyphenation makes a paper look messy. If you must hyphenate, follow these guidelines.

- Divide words only between syllables. If you are not sure of the divisions, either do not divide the word, or look for the correct syllabication in the main entry of a dictionary.
- Consider pronunciation. *Chemotherapy* makes more sense divided *chemo·therapy* than *chem·otherapy; fra·ternity* seems preferable to *frater·nity.*
- Do not leave one letter on a line by itself. For example, *a·like* and *tax·i* should not be divided.
- Do not divide the last word on a page. It is inconvenient to turn the page to find the rest of the word.

SLASHES

29f SLASHES BETWEEN ALTERNATIVES

A slash between words can show alternatives—*and/or, he/she, pass/fail.* The mark replaces the *or* that would otherwise be needed to separate the alternatives.

radio/television

A.M./P.M.

animal/vegetable

In informal or technical papers, the slash is acceptable; in formal or nontechnical papers, the *or* is preferred.

29g SLASHES FOR MAKING COMBINATIONS

Combinations of words or numbers in compounds and sequences sometimes contain slashes.

Dallas/Fort Worth

The MacNeil/Lehrer News Hour

20/20 vision

4/21/81

1984/85

poet/critic/scholar

29h SLASHES BETWEEN LINES OF POETRY

Two or three lines of poetry can be quoted in their original form or in prose form (incorporated into a sentence, from margin to margin). When the prose form is used, slashes show the poetic line divisions.

> Byron writes in *Don Juan,* "'Tis strange, but true; for truth is always strange;/ Stranger than fiction: if it could be told,/ How much would novels gain by the exchange!"

29i SLASHES FOR FRACTIONS

When a fraction is written in numerals, a slash separates the numerator from the denominator: *1/3, 3/5, 5/12.*

CHAPTER

30 ABBREVIATIONS AND NUMBERS

abbr 30

The appropriate use of **abbreviations** and **numbers** depends in large part on their context. Abbreviations are appropriate in some circumstances; full words, in others. Sometimes, numbers should be expressed in words: other times, numerals are required. The following discussion outlines the conventions and describes the contexts that govern them.

ABBREVIATIONS

30a ABBREVIATIONS VS. FULL WORDS

Some abbreviations are so standard that the full form almost never appears. Others, however, may be used only in certain instances.

- Titles and ranks

  Use the abbreviations *Mr., Mrs.,* and *Ms.* when they appear before names. (*Miss* is not an abbreviation and is not followed by a period.)

  Use the abbreviations *Jr.* and *Sr.* when they appear as part of a name: *Joseph W. Alsop, Jr.* The full words are appropriate only on formal invitations.

You may abbreviate *doctor* when the title appears before a name: *Dr. Williams.*

You may abbreviate civil and military titles when they appear before a full name but not before a last name alone.

ACCEPTABLE: Lt. Gov. John Bird, Col. Betty Morden

ACCEPTABLE: Lieutenant Governor Bird, Colonel Morden

UNACCEPTABLE: Lt. Gov. Bird, Col. Morden

You may abbreviate *Reverend* and *Honorable* when they precede a full name and do not follow *the.* Do not, however, abbreviate these titles when they precede a last name alone or when they follow *the.*

ACCEPTABLE: Rev. Donald Yanella, Hon. Ann Lott

ACCEPTABLE: Reverend Yanella, the Honorable Ann Lott

UNACCEPTABLE: Rev. Yanella, the Hon. Lott

- Degrees and certifications

  You may abbreviate scholarly degrees (*B.A., M.S., Ph.D.*). Remember that when a degree follows a name, no other title should precede the name.

  ACCEPTABLE: Alice M. Cotton, Ph.D.

  UNACCEPTABLE: Dr. Alice M. Cotton, Ph.D.

- Time, days, and months

  Abbreviate time designations, such as *A.M., P.M., EST, CDT, A.D., B.C.* Remember that *A.D.* precedes a year and *B.C.* follows.

  ACCEPTABLE: The Han dynasty lasted from 202 B.C. to A.D. 220.

  UNACCEPTABLE: The Han dynasty lasted from 202 B.C. to 220 A.D.

  In prose, always write out the names of days and months.

ACCEPTABLE:	The ship sails on Friday, January 13.
UNACCEPTABLE:	The ship sails on Fri., Jan. 13.

- Latin Expressions

  Except in extremely formal papers, use abbreviations for Latin expressions such as *i.e., e.g., vs.,* and so forth.

- Acronyms and familiar initials

  The full forms of initials pronounced as words (acronyms) are almost never written out: *sonar, ZIP, COBOL, Alcoa, NASA, snafu.* Neither are the full forms of many familiar initials: *UFO, ESP, IQ, ID, R.S.V.P., IBM, FBI, NBC.*

- Reference notations

  Abbreviate words such as *page(s), figure, edition,* and *volume* when they appear in bibliographies and documentation: *pp. 13-26, fig. 4, 3rd ed., Vol. 1.*

- Geographical Locations

  In general, do not abbreviate geographical locations except in addresses. In any context, however, you may write *Washington, D.C.,* or *U.S.* when it is used as an adjective but not as a noun.

ACCEPTABLE:	U.S. currency
ACCEPTABLE:	currency in the United States
UNACCEPTABLE:	currency in the U.S.

- Addresses

  In formal letters, do not abbreviate words such as *street, avenue, road,* and *building.* Also, when a compass direction precedes a street name, it is part of the name and not abbreviated: *49 Northwest Farris Street.* When a compass direction follows a street name, it indicates a city's section and is abbreviated: *49 Farris Street, NW.*

  You have the option of abbreviating names of states and territories with the two-letter codes used by the U.S. Postal Service.

Alabama	AL	Florida	FL
Alaska	AK	Georgia	GA
Arizona	AZ	Guam	GU

Arkansas	AR	Hawaii	HI
California	CA	Idaho	ID
Canal Zone	CZ	Illinois	IL
Colorado	CO	Indiana	IN
Connecticut	CT	Iowa	IA
Delaware	DE	Kansas	KS
District		Kentucky	KY
of Columbia	DC	Louisiana	LA
Maine	ME	Oklahoma	OK
Maryland	MD	Oregon	OR
Massachusetts	MA	Pennsylvania	PA
Michigan	MI	Puerto Rico	PR
Minnesota	MN	Rhode Island	RI
Mississippi	MS	South Carolina	SC
Missouri	MO	South Dakota	SD
Montana	MT	Tennessee	TN
Nebraska	NE	Texas	TX
Nevada	NV	Utah	UT
New Hampshire	NH	Vermont	VT
New Jersey	NJ	Virgin Islands	VI
New Mexico	NM	Virginia	VA
New York	NY	Washington	WA
North Carolina	NC	West Virginia	WV
North Dakota	ND	Wisconsin	WI
Ohio	OH	Wyoming	WY

30b PUNCTUATION AND CAPITALIZATION IN ABBREVIATIONS

Because the use of periods with abbreviations changes from time to time, you should check current practice in an up-to-date dictionary. There you will find that some abbreviations contain periods (*Dist. Atty., Sept., R.S.V.P.*), some have optional periods (*ft.* or *ft, lb.* or *lb, E.S.T.* or *EST*), and some have none.

Chemical symbols: Cu, N, Zn, Au

Acronyms: NATO, UNESCO, CORE

Military terms: POW, USA, GI

Points of the compass: NE, NW, SE

States in Postal Service abbreviations: HI, OH, AZ, OK

In general, the capitalization of an abbreviation reflects that of the full word: *GOP (Grand Old Party)*, *Ph.D. (Doctor of Philosophy)*, *hwy. (highway)*, *Btu (British thermal unit)*. But capitalization of a few abbreviations cannot be predicted by the capitalization in the full words: *eV (electron volt)*, *a.m.* or *A.M. (ante meridiem)*, *A.D. (anno Domini)*, *n.d.* or *N.D. (no date)*. When you are unsure of capitalization, check a recent dictionary.

NUMBERS

30c NUMBERS EXPRESSED IN NUMERALS

In any type of paper, use numerals for the following. (See 30d for the appropriate use of numbers expressed in words.)

- Numbers in dates and addresses

  On June 31, 1989, the couple moved to 520 State Street.

- Exact amounts of money

  Each participant is charged $7.50.

  The starting salary is $21,000.

- Sections of books and page numbers

  Chapter 2 ends on page 9.

- Numbers that accompany abbreviations and symbols

  The temperature was 8° F at 6:30 a.m.

  Less than 5% of the group successfully quit smoking.

- Measurements and statistics

  Only 6 percent of the applicants qualified for aid.

  This soup contains 9 grams of fat per serving.

- Fractions, decimals, ratios, and mathematical functions

  They had restored about 4/5 of the Indian mound.

  Multiply the result by 5.

For other numbers, non-technical and technical writers generally follow different systems and use numerals for the following.

- In non-technical papers, most numbers that require more than two words (Hyphenated numbers such as *thirty-eight* are counted as one word.)

  In the OED, the meanings are illustrated by more than 83,000 quotations.

  The twenty stories were selected from more than 350 publications.

- In technical papers, all numbers 10 and above

  From a low of 21 in 1944, the whooping crane population topped 200 in the late 1980s.

  The four barrier islands have a total of 51 miles of beach.

30d NUMBERS EXPRESSED IN WORDS

Words are appropriate for the following numbers.

- In non-technical papers, numbers that can be stated in one or two words (The numbers in dates, addresses, measurements, etc., are always numerals, 30c.)

  About four hundred years ago, Christopher Marlowe, at the age of twenty-nine, was murdered in a bar fight.

  Supposedly, the Cult of Isis has over fifteen thousand followers in fifty countries.

- In technical papers, numbers from one to nine

  Only three red-cockaded woodpeckers have been seen in the area in the last eight years.

  The mutual fund's return for the last six months was 11.95%.

- EXCEPTION: In parallel structures, the numbers should be all numerals or all words depending on the clearest presentation and the style used in the rest of the paper.

  The garden contains two hundred varieties of bulbs and thirty shrubs.

  The museum has expanded its presentation from 85 paintings to 125. [clearer than *eighty-five* and *one hundred and twenty-five*]

  According to the responses, 5 people had never voted; 25 had voted occasionally; and 17 had voted in every election.

- In both non-technical and technical papers, numbers that begin sentences.

  One hundred and twenty-five pages into the book, readers finally learn the narrator's identity.

  Forty-five copies of the questionnaire were distributed, and 32 were returned.

30e MIXED NUMERALS AND WORDS

For clarity and ease of reading, use a combination of words and figures in two circumstances.

- Adjacent modifiers

  When two separate numbers make up adjacent modifiers, express one number in numerals and one in words.

  We need ten 12-foot planks.

  They bought 5,000 thirteen-cent stamps.

- Large rounded numbers

  Because *million* and *billion* require so many zeros when expressed in numerals, readers find it easier to comprehend a combination of numerals and words.

  We cannot expect a city government to accommodate 8 million people.

  The debt was an awesome 5 billion dollars.

cap 31

CHAPTER

31 CAPITAL LETTERS

Primarily, **capital letters** signal the beginnings of sentences and designate proper names and official titles. The practice of capitalizing the first word of a sentence is simple and stable. But the practice of capitalizing proper names and titles is more complex; authorities disagree, and conventions change. Furthermore, a word may be capitalized in one situation but not in another. The solution to most problems of capitalization, however, can be found in a standard up-to-date dictionary or a handbook like this one.

31a CAPITALIZATION OF FIRST WORDS

By capitalizing the first word in an element, you can alert readers to the start of something new for example, a complete sentence, a quotation, a line of poetry, or an item in a list. In some cases, capitalization is required; in other cases, it is optional.

(1) Required capitals

- The first word in a complete sentence

  Students broke the security of the computer system.

  Does Assateague Island have nude beaches?

EXCEPTION: You should not capitalize a sentence's first letter when the sentence appears inside parentheses within another sentence.

The school's decision surprised everyone (he was, after all, a star player).

- The first word in a quotation that begins a new sentence

Macbeth asks, "Will all great Neptune's ocean wash this blood clean from my hand?"

NOTE: When the quoted sentence is split, only the first word begins with a capital letter.

"In a real dark night of the soul," Fitzgerald writes, "it is always three o'clock in the morning."

If the quotation does not begin a new sentence, the first word is not capitalized.

Mussolini believed that only war put "the stamp of nobility upon the peoples who have the courage to face it."

- The first word in each line of a traditional poem

But words are things and a small drop of ink,
Falling like dew upon a thought, produces
That which makes thousands, perhaps millions, think.

From Byron's *Don Juan*

- The first word in each entry of an outline

Japanese Military Operations in Indochina
I. Military reasons for the operations
II. Entry of the Japanese
  A. Occupation of Laos
  B. Occupation of Vietnam
  C. Occupation of Cambodia
III. Japanese wartime bases
IV. Surrender to the Allied forces

- The first word of a salutation and complimentary close

My dear Sir:	Yours truly,
To whom it may concern:	Sincerely yours,

(2) Optional capitals

- The first word in an elliptical question

  Does an office this small really need a copier? Two word processors? A switchboard?

  Is the book a novel? an autobiography? a travelogue?

- The first word in a formal statement after a colon

  The lesson we learned was this: Work helps keep juveniles out of trouble.

  Orson Welles' reputation is a mystery: he is considered a genius on the basis of one work—*Citizen Kane.*

- The first word of each item in a list

  The benefits include:

Life and medical insurance	Investment programs
Accident insurance	Retirement program

  The test determined the car's

(1) reliability	(3) performance
(2) comfort	(4) economy

31b CAPITALIZATION OF PROPER NAMES AND PROPER ADJECTIVES

Proper nouns are the names of specific persons, places, and things. In general, you should capitalize these nouns and the adjectives derived from them.

France	French culture
Colombia	Colombian coffee
Jefferson	Jeffersonian ideals
Henry James	Jamesian story

The following categories illustrate the kinds of words considered proper nouns and adjectives.

NAMES OF PEOPLE AND ANIMALS:	Gerry Wieland, Jean Kindelberger, Tom Sawyer, Trigger, Gargantua
PLACE NAMES:	Venus, Africa, Potomac River, Montpelier, Union Station, Statue of Liberty
ORGANIZATIONS:	Department of State, Committee for Economic Development, Milwaukee Chamber of Commerce, National Council of Churches
HISTORICAL NAMES:	Elizabethan Age, Tonkin Resolution, Truman Doctrine, Battle of Wounded Knee, Renaissance
RELIGIOUS TERMS:	God; He, His, Him [referring to God in a religious context]; Buddhism; Shinto; Palm Sunday, Ramadan
NAMES IN EDUCATION:	California Polytechnic State University, Basic Wiring II, World History 101, Rhodes Scholarship, Scholastic Aptitude Test
AWARDS:	National Book Award, Pulitzer Prize, Good Conduct Medal, Medal of Honor
CALENDAR TERMS:	Monday, August, Veterans Day, Bastille Day
PRODUCT NAMES:	Renault Alliance, Ford Mustang, Soyuz T-5, Frigidaire, Ivory soap [The common term of a product's name is usually not capitalized.]
ETHNIC TERMS:	English, Japanese, Serbian, Sioux, Indo-European
BIOLOGICAL TERMS:	*Equidae, Bovidae, Canis rufus, Alligator mississippiensis* [Species are not capitalized.]

CHEMICAL ABBREVIATIONS: O [oxygen], Au [gold]

Also, you capitalize nicknames or substitutes for proper names.

OFFICIAL NAMES	SUBSTITUTES
New York City	Big Apple
Missouri	Show Me State
Earl Hines	Fatha Hines
William Warren	Grandfather (but *my grandfather*)
Mayor Stone	Mayor

Some words derived from proper nouns, however, are no longer capitalized; others are capitalized at times. For example, the word *maverick* (derived from the name of Senator Samuel A. Maverick of Texas) is not capitalized; the word *draconian* (derived from the Athenean lawgiver Draco) is sometimes capitalized and sometimes not. Check current practice in an up-to-date dictionary.

NO LONGER CAPITALIZED

boycott (after C. C. Boycott)

bourbon (after Bourbon County, Kentucky)

quixotic (after Don Quixote)

SOMETIMES CAPITALIZED, SOMETIMES LOWERCASE

Platonic/platonic (after Plato)

Scotch/scotch (after Scotland)

Herculean/herculean (after Hercules)

31c CAPITALIZATION OF TITLES OF HONOR OR RANK

Always capitalize titles of honor or rank—governmental, military, ecclesiastical, royal, or professional—when they precede names. When these titles do not precede names, you usually do not capitalize them.

CAPITAL: In Texas, Governor Miriam A. "Ma" Ferguson served from 1925–27 and from 1933–35.

NO CAPITAL: Miriam A. "Ma" Ferguson of Texas served as governor of Texas after her husband was impeached.

CAPITAL: In 1863, General William S. Rosecrans fought at Chickamauga.

NO CAPITAL: William S. Rosecrans, a general with the Union army, fought at Chickamauga.

CAPITAL: After retiring, Professor Deutsch went into politics.

NO CAPITAL: After retiring, Dr. Deutsch, a professor of American history, went into politics.

You may, however, capitalize a few titles even when they do not precede names: President, Vice President, and the titles of other important members of the government. Either capital or lowercase letters are correct, but be consistent throughout a composition.

Taft, the largest man ever to serve as President (or president), weighed over 300 pounds.

Elihu Root, Secretary of State (or secretary of state) under Theodore Roosevelt, won the 1912 Nobel peace prize.

Margaret Chase Smith, the Senator (or senator) from Maine, campaigned for the Republican presidential nomination in 1964.

31d CAPITALIZATION OF ACADEMIC AND PROFESSIONAL DEGREES

Capitalize academic and professional degrees only when they appear immediately after a name or when they are abbreviated.

CAPITALS: George Pratt, Doctor of Laws, died last year.

CAPITALS: George Pratt, LL.D., died last year.

NO CAPITALS: George Pratt earned his doctor of laws degree in 1932.

CAPITALS: Doris Leigh completed her B.A. degree in 1912.

NO CAPITALS: Doris Leigh completed her bachelor of arts degree in 1912.

CAPITALS: Lee Wallerstein, CPA, made the audit.

NO CAPITALS: An independent certified public accountant made the audit.

31e CAPITALIZATION IN TITLES OF WRITTEN MATERIAL AND ARTISTIC WORKS

Although there are various styles for capitalization within titles, the Modern Language Association (MLA) calls for capitalizing these words:

- The first word [When *the* is the first word of a periodical, it is dropped from the title, e.g., *Washington Post,* not *The Washington Post.*]
- The last word
- Every noun, pronoun, verb, adjective, adverb, and subordinating conjunction
- Any word that follows a colon, dash, or question mark

The following words are not capitalized unless they are the first or last words of a title.

- Articles [*a, an, the*]
- Coordinating conjunctions and prepositions
- The infinitive marker [*to*]

When you use the MLA system, you must determine the part of speech of each word in a title. In the following examples, notice especially that *or* is a coordinating conjunction, *if* is a subordinating conjunction, *to* is an infinitive marker, and *with* is a preposition.

> "Tall Talk: Half-Truth or Half-Lie"
>
> "Well, If I Called the Wrong Number, Why Did You Answer the Phone?"

A World to Win

Still Life with Clay Pipe

A frequent variation of the MLA system is to capitalize subordinating conjunctions and prepositions that have four or more letters. If you prefer this variation, you would capitalize, for example, the subordinating conjunctions *when, unless,* and *because,* but not *if.* You would capitalize the prepositions *with, between,* and *toward,* but not *in, out,* and *of.*

31f CAPITALIZATION IN SOME ABBREVIATIONS

Times of day are written A.M. and P.M. or a.m. and p.m. In print, these abbreviations are usually in small capitals. A few other abbreviations are capitalized even though the terms they replace are not, for example *T.V.* or *TV* (for *television*), *B.A.* (for *bachelor of arts*), *R.R.* or *RR* (for *railroad*), *POW* (for *prisoner of war*), *NE* (for *northeast*), *O* (for *oxygen*), A.D. (for *anno Domini*).

31g CAPITALIZATION OF *I* AND *O*

The pronoun *I* is always capitalized, even when it is a part of a contraction—*I'm* or *I've.* The expression *O* is capitalized, except when spelled *oh.*

31h INAPPROPRIATE CAPITALS

You should not capitalize the following words.

- Common nouns, even when they appear in phrases that contain capitals

American history	Maxwell House coffee
Epson computer	French poodle

- Words referring to areas of study, unless they are titles of specific courses

Capitals	No Capitals
Economics 302	economics
Algebra II	algebra
Studies in British Literature	literature
Introduction to Computing	computer science

NOTE: The names of languages are proper and are always capitalized: *French, English grammar, Chinese literature.*

- Words expressing family relationships, like *mother, father, aunt, uncle, grandmother,* and *grandfather,* unless they precede or substitute for names

CAPITAL: We learned to garden by helping Uncle Will.

NO CAPITAL: We learned to garden by helping our uncle.

CAPITAL: When she was sixty-five, Grandmother bought a Porsche.

NO CAPITAL: When she was sixty-five, my grandmother bought a Porsche.

- The words *north, south, southwest,* and so on when they refer to compass directions [These words are capitalized when they refer to regions.]

CAPITAL: The North won the Civil War.

NO CAPITAL: Drive north.

CAPITAL: The first Europeans to explore the Southwest were the Spaniards.

NO CAPITAL: The area lies southwest of here.

- Seasons, unless they are personified

CAPITAL: "Come, gentle Spring! ethereal Mildness! come."

NO CAPITAL: You plant the seeds in the spring.

- *Earth, moon,* and *sun* except when these words are used in connection with named planets (and without *the*)

CAPITAL:	Mercury and Venus are closer to the sun than Earth is.
NO CAPITAL:	The earth is the fifth largest planet.
CAPITAL:	The distance of Earth from Moon is 238,857 miles.
NO CAPITAL:	In an eclipse, the moon is too small to hide the sun.

PART

IV

STYLE

A writing style results from a number of details: vocabulary, sentence length, sentence patterns, figures of speech, sound and rhythm. Often these details are spontaneous choices—a reflection of the writer's personality, education, and experience. But reliance on spontaneous decisions will not always produce effective writing. Developing a good prose style requires thoughtful choices of words and sentence structures.

32 Word Choice
33 Sentence Style

CHAPTER

32

WORD CHOICE

wd
style
32

The English language has borrowed extensively from other languages. The result is an enormous vocabulary of some million words, many with similar meanings. *Roget's Thesaurus,* for example, lists almost 100 synonyms for *insane* and over 150 synonyms for *destroy.* From this abundance, writers choose the words that best fit intended meaning and individual styles.

32a LEVELS OF FORMALITY

Each time you write, you should decide whether to use a formal or an informal voice. The decision depends on your purpose and your audience. A formal voice is appropriate for business correspondence, reports, research papers, and articles in scholarly journals—documents in which writers distance themselves personally from readers. On the other hand, an informal voice is appropriate for purposes such as humorous writing, advertising, and articles in popular magazines—material in which writers try to establish a personal relationship with readers. Thus, you should use a formal style to establish a polite, professional relationship with a reader and an informal style to establish a friendly, conversational relationship.

The degree of formality or informality is established in large part by vocabulary. Words derived from Anglo-Saxon (Old English) seem more informal and conversational than words derived or borrowed from other languages. For example, the Anglo-Saxon derivatives *lucky, get, buy,* and *crazy* seem less formal than their synonyms derived from Greek and Latin: *fortunate, obtain, purchase,* and *demented.* Likewise, the English words *therefore* and *masterpiece* are less formal than their Latin counterparts *ergo* and *magnum opus.*

Clipped forms are more informal than full forms. For example, *pro, ad,* and *deli* are more informal than *professional, advertisement,* and *delicatessen.* Likewise, contractions (*can't, isn't, it's*) are more informal than uncontracted forms (*cannot, is not, it is*).

First person (*I, we*) and second person (*you*) are less formal than third (*one, the writer, the student*). If you are writing about yourself, *I* certainly seems more natural than *one* or *this writer.* If you are addressing the reader personally, *you* seems natural. Avoid, however, using *you* to mean people in general. (See 12c.)

Slang is informal—sometimes, very informal—and its appearance in formal documents can reduce them to the absurd. Imagine, for example, coming upon this sentence in a university bulletin: *Students with wheels should boogie on over to the security office and get a decal.* On the other hand, a carefully chosen slang expression can make prose more interesting, vivid, or efficient. *Razzmatazz* is more interesting than *a flashy display. Bug a telephone* is more vivid than *equip a telephone with a microphone. Computer nerd* is certainly more efficient than *a person who forgets the social amenities in an obsession for computers.* Remember, however, that an abundance of slang will make prose seem silly. Furthermore, the meanings of slang expressions are frequently unstable, changing unpredictably from time to time and audience to audience.

Choosing a formal or informal voice is often arbitrary; in many circumstances, readers will accept either. But whichever you choose, you should maintain it consistently throughout a composition. Notice how the voice in the following passage seems to shift from formal to informal and back to formal. As a result, the reader gets mixed signals about the writer's attitude.

SHIFTED

If a person has no computer experience, shopping for a personal computer is very frustrating—primarily because the novice and the sales personnel do not use the same vocabulary. A salesperson will toss off a lot of stuff about memory, hard disks, and menus. And the novice will stand by nodding wisely but without a clue. This problem could be overcome if sales personnel were taught to explain in non-technical terms the capabilities of the equipment they sell.

A consistent voice—either informal or formal—makes clear the writer's attitude.

INFORMAL

If you have no computer experience, shopping for a personal computer is a nightmare—primarily because the computer-impaired and the salespeople don't speak the same language. A salesperson will toss off a lot of stuff about memory, hard disks, and menus. And you will stand there nodding like an idiot but without a clue. This problem could be overcome if salespeople were taught to talk in plain English.

FORMAL

If a person has no computer experience, shopping for a personal computer is very frustrating—primarily because the novice and the sales personnel do not use the same vocabulary. A salesperson will casually discuss memory, hard disks, and menus. And the novice will stand by nodding wisely but understanding nothing. This problem could be overcome if sales personnel were taught to explain in non-technical terms the capabilities of the equipment they sell.

Remember that when you adopt a voice, you should maintain it consistently throughout a composition. Otherwise, your reader will not know how to react.

32b PRECISE PROSE

In conversation, you can be somewhat relaxed about the words you choose because a listener can stop you and ask for clarification. Furthermore, you can watch the listener for signs of confusion, and you can restate or clarify as you go along. But in writing, you have no such opportunities. Your language should be as precise as possible to ensure that your reader understands exactly what you mean. This precision rests primarily on vocabulary. To control the meaning of your prose, you should carefully consider the meanings of words—both their denotation and connotation. And you should try to strike the right balance between the general and the specific, between the abstract and the concrete.

(1) Denotation and connotation

The denotation of a word is the dictionary definition, the word's meaning devoid of any emotional association. The word *penguin* denotes a flightless marine bird; the word *piano* denotes a familiar keyboard instrument. If you want to use a word recently acquired or found in a thesaurus, make sure you know the word's denotation. Archie Bunker got laughs by saying, "You're invading the issue"; and Dizzy Dean was famous for remarks like "The players went back to their respectable bases." Except for an intentional comic effect, however, such mistakes (malapropisms) will ruin your credibility.

In addition to denotation, you should consider whether a word has connotation—that is, whether it evokes an emotional response. For example, to most readers, *home* seems more personal and secure than *house.* When we think of a house, we usually envision a building. But we think of home as more than a building: It is family, childhood memories, friends, and even an entire community. Consider the word *spy.* It evokes the image of an unsavory character, probably a traitor. But *secret agent* calls up James Bond, the dashing hero, using wit and muscle to overcome evil. The denotation of *suave* is "smoothly gracious or polite; polished." The connotation suggests a man—one who is perhaps continental. On the other hand, *sophisticated* suggests either a man or a woman—worldly wise and refined. *Peril* seems more serious and more imminent than *danger; zealot,* more fanatical than *enthusiast; naked,* more stark than *nude.*

Keep in mind that many words have emotional associations, and try to choose vocabulary that will convey exactly the meaning you intend.

(2) General and specific words

General words refer to classes or categories (*magazine*); specific words refer to particular members of a class or category (*Newsweek*). Whether a word is general or specific is sometimes relative. For example, *media* is more general than *magazine,* and *last week's Newsweek* is more specific than *Newsweek.* The following lists illustrate a gradual progression from general to specific.

sports	food	clothes
↓	↓	↓
baseball	Italian food	pants
↓	↓	↓
the White Sox	pasta	blue jeans
↓	↓	↓
the White Sox game Friday	fettuccini	Levis

When you write, you should try to balance the general with the specific because both are inherent in the way we think. In other words, we sometimes reason by induction—moving from specific instances to find a generalization. For example, a person who sneezes every time a cat appears will conclude that he or she is allergic to cats. At other times, we reason by deduction—applying a general principle to a specific instance. A person who has an established allergy to cats and who suddenly begins sneezing will deduce that there is a cat in the area.

As we think and reason, we move back and forth from induction to deduction, from specifics to generalities. If you use both general and specific words when you write, readers are more likely to follow your reasoning process and thus more readily grasp your meaning. Suppose, for example, that you want to make the point that children learn valuable social skills in kindergarten. Relying exclusively on either general or specific words will obscure the point.

TOO GENERAL: Kindergartens benefit children by allowing interaction in a social environment. In kindergarten, children lose some of their egocentric perspective and learn to tolerate the needs and feelings of others.

TOO SPECIFIC: In kindergartens, children must share blocks, desks, and coloring books. Therefore, children learn not to snatch a toy that someone else is playing with. They also learn to say "please" and "thank you."

A mixture of general and specific words can convey the general idea and clarify it with details.

MIXED USE: Kindergartens benefit children by teaching them valuable social skills. For example, they learn to share desks, toys, and the teacher's attention. They learn that saying "please"

> and "thank you" is more pleasant and productive behavior than fighting and crying.

When you write, use general words for summing up and explaining; use specific words for supporting and detailing. This way, readers will understand not only what your conclusions are but also how you arrived at them.

(3) Abstract and concrete words

Abstract words denote ideas, qualities, feelings—anything that has no physical existence. Concrete words denote specific realities—anything that can be seen, touched, heard, smelled, or tasted. Although both kinds of words appear in most prose, an overreliance on abstract terms can mask meaning and bore readers. For example, suppose you were defining the abstract concept of frustration. You could clarify the concept and enliven the discussion with a description of frustrating incidents—a traffic jam, a computer that refuses to compute, a test unrelated to lectures or reading assignments.

A good way to see the difference between abstract and concrete terms is to pair the two in sentences like the following.

> Happiness is a cancelled 8:00 class on a cold, rainy morning.
>
> Luxury is the smell of leather upholstery in a new Ferrari.
>
> Panic is realizing that next Wednesday's test is this Wednesday.

In each of these sentences, the quality of the abstract word is made real by the concrete and familiar example.

If your prose seems impersonal and vague, try adding concrete facts, instances, and examples that will enliven, enrich, and clarify your meaning.

32c VIGOROUS PROSE

To put some vigor and energy into your writing, you must think honestly about your subject. Otherwise, you may be tempted to rely on tired expressions repeated so often that they have become meaningless. You may also be tempted to avoid speaking directly about an unpleasant or controversial subject and thus create dull and lifeless prose. You do not have to be a professional writer to express yourself with energy and directness. But you do have to think honestly and speak honestly.

(1) Clichés

wd style 32c

Clichés are expressions, perhaps once vivid but now stale from overuse. A cliché conveys a superficial thought—if indeed it conveys any thought at all. In fact, it usually detracts from the point. To recognize clichés, question the effectiveness of overly familiar expressions, and look for certain clues. One clue is that clichés often contain repeated sounds.

tried and true	takes the cake
black and blue	no great shakes
worse for wear	rhyme or reason
betwixt and between	rise and shine
super duper	wishy-washy
hit the hay	eager beaver
fit and trim	

Another clue is that clichés are frequently comparisons, such as metaphors and similes. (See 33d.) But instead of being fresh and interesting, these comparisons have become overly familiar and boring.

out in left field	avoid like the plague
chip on his shoulder	open a can of worms
dropped like a hot potato	make no bones about it
as cool as a cucumber	pretty as a picture
like a bolt from the blue	busy as a beaver
right in there pitching	

Some clichés neither contain repeated sounds nor express comparisons. They are merely combinations that for some reason catch on and then are repeated again and again.

as luck would have it	crushing blow
last but not least	stifling heat
sick and tired	hardened criminal
make a long story short	not half bad
stark raving mad	cruel fate
better late than never	a bang-up job
sigh of relief	one in a million
more easily said than done	rude awakening
agonizing defeat	agree wholeheartedly

If you do not think honestly about a subject, you may find yourself relying on clichés. Consider, for example, this passage on holiday stress.

> To me, the Christmas holidays are stressful because I always wind up rushing around at the last minute trying to find the perfect gifts for friends and relatives. Between shopping, cooking, cleaning, and going to parties, I never find the time for rest and relaxation before I have to return to the hectic pace of school.

The writer has not really thought about the subject but has merely strung clichés together (*wind up, rushing around at the last minute, the perfect gifts, rest and relaxation, hectic pace*). As a result, the passage is lifeless. Avoiding the clichés would encourage the writer to say something more interesting and vigorous.

> I would like to go home for Christmas to a quiet house where I could recover from the constant pressure of school deadlines. Instead, I go home to chaos. I plunge into department stores crowded with tired, irritable shoppers and search for gifts among the overpriced junk. I spend hours helping my parents to cook rich, fatty foods and to clean greasy, gunk-encrusted pans. I try to find rest in a house filled with breakable decorations and visiting children. No wonder the holidays cause stress.

You can, of course, use a cliché that has exactly the right meaning. But you would be wise to follow the lead of William L. Shirer and let the reader know you are not using the expression naively. In his autobiography, *Twentieth Century Journey,* Shirer remarks of his adventures as a foreign correspondent, "To say that 'there is no substitute for experience' may be indulging in a stale cliché, but it has much truth in it."

wd style 32c

(2) Euphemisms

The etymology of *euphemism* points to its meaning; in Greek *eu* means "good" and *pheme* means "speech." Thus, a euphemism is the substitution of a polite or inoffensive term for one that might be considered coarse or unpleasant. For example, you would probably be more comfortable writing *senior citizen* rather than *old person* or writing *disabled* rather than *crippled.* Many euphemisms like these result from a natural and well-intentioned motive—to make reality seem less harsh and cruel. But when euphemisms distort or glorify the ordinary, they can be dishonest and pretentious. A government that supports assassination might call it "neutralization"; a jeweler who sells rhinestones might advertise "faux diamonds"; a person who deals in pornography might describe the books and movies as "adult."

Dependence on euphemisms creates a weak style that evades the reality of its subject. For example, in the following passage, the subject is hidden behind indirect euphemisms (*peer pressure, experiment with artificial stimulants, social isolation, mental and physical disorders*).

> Students are constantly under peer pressure to experiment with artificial stimulants. Those who resist the pressure will often suffer social isolation. Those who succumb to the pressure, however, can suffer serious physical and mental disorders.

The euphemisms in the passage weaken the urgency of the problem. Without the euphemisms, the dangers become real, and the real has impact and vigor.

> Students are constantly pressured by their classmates to drink and take drugs. Those who resist the pressure will often lose friends and

invitations. Those who do not resist, however, can lose their minds or even their lives.

Whenever possible, avoid dishonest and evasive language. Use, instead, direct and vigorous expressions. The list that follows suggests possible substitutions for some common euphemisms.

Euphemisms	Direct Expressions
correctional facility	prison
previously owned cars	used cars
depopulate	kill
revenue enhancements	taxes
mobile manor	trailer park
interred	buried
nonpassing grade	failing grade
preneed arrangements	funeral arrangements
sanitary engineer	garbage collector
horticultural surgeon	tree trimmer

32d CLUTTERED PROSE

If you have ever tried to make sense out of tax instructions or an insurance policy, you know how frustrating cluttered prose can be. Readers should not have to sort through unnecessary words and confusing phrases, searching for meaning. Good writing is clear; the meaning comes through readily. So when you revise, remember to clear out the clutter that results from gobbledygook, surplus words, and dense noun phrases.

(1) Gobbledygook

There is a widespread movement in government and business to eliminate gobbledygook, also called *jargon, bureaucratic language, double-talk, officialese, federalese,* and *doublespeak*. This language is full of abstractions, indirect words, and convoluted constructions; it is devoid of humanity and sensitivity. You can recognize gobbledygook by its pomposity and wordiness.

GOBBLEDYGOOK: The committee must implement the operationalizing of those mechanisms and modes of activity and strategies necessary to maintain the viability of the institution's fiscal management operations.

REVISED: The committee must take measures to ensure the institution's financial security.

The success rate of the "plain English" movement is not impressive, probably because the causes of gobbledygook have not been eliminated (and possibly cannot be). Gobbledygook flourishes for a variety of reasons: its writers have nothing substantive to say; they do not fully understand their subjects; they try to protect themselves from criticism of their ideas; they do not really want anyone to understand what they say; they believe, rightly or wrongly, that the inflated prose impresses readers.

Some of the words and phrases popular in gobbledygook follow. You should avoid them and use instead their "plain" counterparts.

GOBBLEDYGOOK	PLAIN ENGLISH
initiate	begin
terminate	end
utilize	use
transmit	send
administrate	administer
notate	note
orientate	orient
summarization	summary
origination	origin
routinization	routine
pursuant to	according to

cognizant of	aware of
conversant with	familiar with
inoperative	broken
at this point in time	now
prior to	before
subsequent to	after
a majority of	most
a number of	many, some
of considerable magnitude	large
as a means of	for
as a result	so
at the rate of	at
due to the fact that	because
for the purpose of	for
in connection with	about
in the interest of	for
in such a manner as to	to
in the neighborhood of	about

When readers must struggle to glean sense from a passage, the consequences of gobbledygook are always annoyance and frustration. But when the struggle takes place in documents relating to business, medicine, insurance, and taxes, the consequences can endanger the economy and the public well-being. As William Zinsser comments in *On Writing Well,*

> What people want is plain talk. It's what the stockholder wants from his corporation, what the customer wants from his bank, what the widow wants from the Government office that is handling her Social Security. There is a yearning for human contact and a resentment of bombast. Any institution that won't take the trouble to be clear and personal will lose friends, customers and money.

(2) Surplus words, or redundancies

Surplus words congest prose with redundancies and meaningless clutter. Without thinking, people often use phrases like these: *past history, blue in color, playground area.* Yet, some of the words in these phrases are unnecessary. History is always in the past; blue is a color; and a playground is an area. As the following passage demonstrates, surplus words add nothing to prose except flab.

SURPLUS WORDS: Our future plans are to add workshops in the areas of accounting, the method of maintaining automobiles, and the process of organic gardening. Instructors will begin with the basic fundamentals and then advance forward at a rate acceptable to individual persons enrolled. The end result will be a kind of class-directed learning technique.

Cutting the surplus away allows the ideas to emerge from the flab.

REVISED: We plan to add workshops in accounting, automobile maintenance, and organic gardening. Instructors will begin with the fundamentals and advance at a rate acceptable to the individuals enrolled. The result will be class-directed learning.

Listed are some familiar redundancies.

any and all	4:00 P.M. in the afternoon
basic fundamentals	free gift
completely finished	full and complete
consensus of opinion	future plans
crisis situation	important essentials
different individuals	in actual fact
each and every	modern world of today
educational process	personal friend

end result	reduce down
final outcome	true facts

(3) Dense noun phrases

The compounding of nouns has long been a tendency in English. The language is full of such noun combinations as *tennis court, china cup, lawn mower,* and *garden party.* These compounds are more economic and sound more like English than *court for tennis, cup made of china, mower for lawns,* and *party in a garden.*

Three or more nouns, however, may produce a compound so "dense" that the reader has trouble deciding what modifies what. For example, consider the noun phrase *campus sorority standards board.* A reader must guess at the meaning: A standards board for campus sororities? A sorority standards board located on campus? A standards board made up of members of campus sororities? Adding an adjective even further confounds readers: *new campus sorority standards board.* What is new? The campus? The sorority? The standards? The board?

You can sometimes clarify a dense phrase by the use of hyphens. Also, you can always rewrite part of the structure as a modifying phrase. The following examples demonstrate the two techniques.

DENSE PHRASE:	new employee investment policy
CLARIFIED WITH HYPHEN:	new employee-investment policy
CLARIFIED WITH HYPHEN:	new-employee investment policy
DENSE PHRASE:	government industry regulations
CLARIFIED BY REWRITING:	government regulations for industries
CLARIFIED BY REWRITING:	regulations for government industries
DENSE PHRASE:	Nevada historical artifacts conference
CLARIFIED BY REWRITING:	conference in Nevada on historical artifacts
CLARIFIED BY REWRITING:	conference on historical artifacts found in Nevada

32e DISCRIMINATORY LANGUAGE

When editing your work, watch for discriminatory language, that is, language showing bias against any group. The appearance of ethnic, racial, sexual, or other biased terms will not only offend readers but also undermine your credibility and authority.

Of course, most writers do not deliberately choose to offend. Sometimes, however, discriminatory language is subtle and easily overlooked. The following guidelines can help ensure that you have not inadvertently included language that seems thoughtless or insensitive.

(1) Observing current usage

Try to use the terms currently preferred by the group you are discussing. Avoiding negative designations is usually easy; most people know which words demean or degrade deliberately. At times, however, the preferred terms are difficult to discover because preferences change. *Lunatic asylum,* for instance, gave way to *insane asylum,* in turn replaced by *mental hospital; slow students* became *students with a learning disability.* You may have to look to the news media, language authorities, or, when appropriate, the groups themselves for current designations.

(2) Avoiding irrelevant information

In general, avoid pointing out a person's race, age, gender, religion, ethnic background, or appearance, unless it is pertinent to the subject being discussed. For example, in an analysis of a skater's form and technique, a reference to the person's race or religion would ordinarily be out of place. In a discussion of a mayoral election, describing a candidate's hairstyle may make your opinions seem frivolous.

(3) Avoiding stereotypes

Stereotyping has no place in thoughtful writing. Informed, perceptive writers do not assume that certain groups of people have inherent characteristics—that some groups are arrogant, some deferential, some lazy, some industrious, some smart, some stupid.

In general, try to avoid typecasting: the absent-minded professor; the jolly fat man; the prissy spinster librarian; the backward South; the bland and boring Midwest; prudish New Englanders; brusque Germans. These are not merely types; they are clichés. So even if you do not insult your readers with a stereotype, you will certainly bore them.

(4) Avoiding sexist categories

Unless you are writing specifically about male and female roles or characteristics, you are wise not to generalize about these subjects.

- Avoid assumptions about professions. For example, executives, pilots, and doctors are not necessarily male; secretaries, flight attendants, and nurses are not necessarily female. As a rule, you should not point out the gender of a professional person: *a lady executive*, *a female pilot*, *a male nurse*, *a man secretary*.
- In the interest of fairness, use the same kind of language for the same characteristics in males and females. For example, do not call a male *angry*, and a female *upset* or a male *commanding* and a female with the same personality *bossy*. On the other hand, do not belittle a male's ego and praise a female's self-esteem.
- Use parallel terms to refer to males and females. *Man* is a parallel to *woman*, *boy* to *girl*, and *gentleman* to *lady*. A *man and his wife* is not parallel; *a husband and wife* or *a couple* is preferable. A man's given name and a woman's married name are not parallel. Instead of writing *Dan Blake and Mrs. Richard Mullins*, write *Dan Blake and Amy Mullins*.

(5) Using neutral terms

Nouns and pronouns that do not refer to gender are called "neutral." In current usage, these words are preferred for groups that include women as well as men. For example, *fire fighters* has replaced *firemen*. You need not go to the extreme of writing *huperson* for *human* or *freshperson* for *freshman*. Nevertheless, if a reasonable, neutral term exists for a mixed-gender group, you should use it.

- As the following list indicates, many masculine nouns have neutral substitutes.

EXAMPLE	NEUTRAL
manpower	personnel
policeman	police officer
mailman	mail carrier *or* postal worker
early man	early humans
Congressmen	members of Congress

- Unless you are sure you are writing to a man, do not use *Dear Sir* as the salutation of a business letter. Instead, write *Dear Sir or Madam*, use a personalized greeting, or write a simplified letter with no salutation and no complimentary close. The *Dear Sir* salutation reflects a male-dominated business world and could easily offend the very person being asked for a favor.

- Referring to males and females with the pronouns *he*, *him*, and *his* is viewed today as outdated. Often, you can substitute compounds like *he or she* and *her or him*, but repeated use of these compounds in a passage sounds unnatural. The following techniques can help you avoid awkward repetition.

  Make the noun anteccedent and the pronouns plural.

  EXAMPLE: Each student must bring his own blue book.

  NEUTRAL: All students must bring their own blue book.

  Change the masculine pronoun to an article (*a, an, the*).

  EXAMPLE: Everyone was struggling with his assignment.

  NEUTRAL: Everyone was struggling with the assignment.

  Change clauses to phrases.

  EXAMPLE: When each contestant arrives, he will be given the rules.

  NEUTRAL: After arriving, each contestant will be given the rules.

- Some writers prefer to avoid any mention of gender, even suffixes such as *-man* and *-ess*. As a result, *chair* or *chairperson* has become a substitute for *chairman*; *waitperson* or *waitron* for *waitress*; and so on. Many people, however, find this practice artificial. In fact, the U. S. Air Force decided to retain the term *airman*, since all substitutes sounded overly contrived.

If you object to a slavish search for unisex language, you can use more traditional terms. But remember your audience. When addressing women, for example, you may want to use the suffix *-woman* (as in *chairwoman* or *councilwoman*). In most instances, however, suffixes designating a female are unnecessary; the neutral words *aviator*, *executor*, and *poet* are preferable to the outdated words *aviatrix*, *executrix*, and *poetess*.

(6) Maintaining objectivity

Try to maintain an objective view of all persons and groups. As a writer, you will probably address audiences that include white males; Anglo-Saxon protestants; and people with some degree of money, power, and social advantages. Therefore, avoid blanket assumptions about such groups as sorority and fraternity members, people who attend private schools, or men in civic organizations. Prejudice is unfair and offensive—even when directed against those felt to be privileged or powerful.

Avoiding discriminatory language is important. Just as important, however, is avoiding a witch hunt. Taken to extremes, "political correctness" will weaken your writing. *Middleman*, for example, is a perfectly legitimate term, widely understood. There is no point in confusing readers by substituting *distributional intermediary* merely to avoid the suffix *-man*. Little is gained by referring to a stripper as an *ecdysiast* when most readers will not recognize the euphemism. And no one is going to take seriously a writer who calls short people *vertically challenged*. Remember, the point of considerate language is to be fair and polite, not to be obscure or silly.

CHAPTER

33

SENTENCE STYLE

sent style 33

A good prose style is smooth, clear, and interesting. These qualities rarely appear in a rough draft. Instead, they result from thoughtful revising from deliberate polishing of sentence structure to achieve variety, emphasis, and clarity; from heightening the effect with sound, rhythm, and figures of speech. In other words, good style requires finding clear and interesting structures to replace those that may be confusing or monotonous. The sections that follow offer some suggestions to help you revise prose by choosing structures that effectively express your ideas. Because many of the techniques require you to be familiar with phrase and clause structure, you may wish to review Chapter 5 and Chapter 7.

33a VARIETY

Although the number of possible sentences in English is infinite, the number of possible clause patterns is limited. (See 7a.) In fact, most sentences have the underlying pattern *subject* + *verb* + *object* or *complement.* If nothing is added to these basic patterns, the result is monotonous, choppy prose one short, simple sentence after another. In the following passage, for example, all the sentences are short and simple. To make things worse, they all begin in the same way, with the subject followed immediately by a verb.

CHOPPY: Wilson was born an aristocrat. He was brought up in a conservative family. He was trained as a Hamiltonian. He became the greatest leader of the plain people since Lincoln.

The original version, in Morison and Commager's *The Growth of the American Republic,* is vastly superior.

ORIGINAL: Born an aristocrat, bred a conservative, trained a Hamiltonian, he became the greatest leader of the plain people since Lincoln.

The basic pattern of this sentence is very simple: *he became leader* (subject + verb + complement). But the three introductory modifiers give the sentence an interesting structure and sound not found in the choppy passage.

Even a series of fairly long sentences can be as monotonous as choppy prose if the structures never vary. The following passage, for example, consists only of independent clauses joined by *and* or *but.* In addition, each clause begins with the subject and verb.

MONOTONOUS: George Pratt compared the horses' footfalls, and made an interesting discovery. The two horses seemed to run at the same speed, but Secretariat covered more distance per stride. Secretariat covered 23.8 feet per stride, and Riva Ridge covered 23.2 feet.

Variations can eliminate the monotony. Notice that in the revised version, not only the structures but also the beginnings of the sentences are varied.

REVISED: By comparing the horses' footfalls, George Pratt made an interesting discovery. Although the two horses seemed to run at the same speed, Secretariat covered more distance per stride than Riva Ridge—23.8 feet versus 23.2 feet.

Variety in sentence structure, however, does not guarantee good writing. Even when sentence structure is varied, prose can sound monotonous if each sentence begins with the subject and verb of the main clause.

MONOTONOUS: Science recognizes a number of differences between men and women. Men are physically stronger, for example, whereas women have more physical stamina. Men have more genetic defects and weaker immune systems although women are more prone to phobias and depression. Neither sex should feel superior or inferior. The differences fit together like the pieces of a jigsaw puzzle, and they create the whole picture of human beings.

The monotony can be eliminated by beginning some of the sentences with modifiers.

REVISED: Science recognizes a number of differences between men and women. For example, whereas men are physically stronger, women have more physical stamina. Although men have more genetic defects and weaker immune systems, women are more prone to phobias and depression. But neither sex should feel superior or inferior. Like the pieces of a jigsaw puzzle, the differences fit together to create the whole picture of human beings.

Coordination and subordination are two techniques for combining ideas and structures. Practicing these techniques will help you learn to manipulate—and thus to vary—sentence structure and sentence beginnings. With a knowledge of how to combine ideas in different ways, you can avoid simplistic and repetitious expression of thought.

(1) Combine independent clauses through coordination.

The most effective way to join two independent clauses depends on the relationship between the ideas expressed in the clauses. If the ideas have a kind of equality, you can simply connect one clause to the other with a comma and the conjunction *and* or with a semicolon.

SEPARATED: In the early 1900s, cocaine was used in many patent medicines. It was even present in the original formula of Coca-Cola.

COMBINED: In the early 1900s, cocaine was used in many patent medicines, and it was even present in the original formula of Coca-Cola.

COMBINED: In the early 1900s, cocaine was used in many patent medicines; it was even present in the original formula of Coca-Cola.

Another way to show equality of ideas is to use the semicolon and a transitional expression such as *also, furthermore, in addition,* or *moreover.* The transitional expression can appear immediately after the semicolon or at some other appropriate place in the second clause.

SEPARATED: Pesticides have contaminated much of our groundwater. They have left residues on much of the food we eat.

COMBINED: Pesticides have contaminated much of our groundwater; in addition, they have left residues on much of the food we eat.

COMBINED: Pesticides have contaminated much of our groundwater; they have, in addition, left residues on much of the food we eat.

When clauses have a cause/effect relationship, they can be joined with a comma and the coordinating conjunction *so* or *for* or with a semicolon and a transitional expression such as *therefore, consequently, as a result,* or *thus.*

SEPARATED: His two interests were medicine and children. He became a pediatrician.

COMBINED: His two interests were medicine and children, so he became a pediatrician.

COMBINED: His two interests were medicine and children; consequently, he became a pediatrician.

Contrasting clauses can be joined with a comma and a coordinating conjunction *but, or, nor,* or *yet* or with a semicolon and a transitional expression such as *however, nevertheless,* or *on the other hand.*

SEPARATED: Augustus gave the Senate control of the peaceful provinces. He kept under his authority the unstable provinces of the frontier.

COMBINED: Augustus gave the Senate control of the peaceful provinces, but he kept under his authority the unstable provinces of the frontier.

COMBINED: Augustus gave the Senate control of the peaceful provinces; he kept under his authority, however, the unstable provinces of the frontier.

Other transitional expressions such as *for example, then,* and *in fact* link clauses. When clauses are joined with semicolons, these words can establish the relationship of the second clause to the first.

SEPARATED: An otherwise rational person often performs superstitious rituals. A baseball player may refuse to pitch without his favorite hat.

SECOND CLAUSE AS EXAMPLE: An otherwise rational person often performs superstitious rituals; a baseball player, for example, may refuse to pitch without his favorite hat.

SEPARATED: Her apartment was full of all sorts of animals. It seemed more like a pet store than a place to live.

SECOND CLAUSE AS REINFORCEMENT: Her apartment was full of all sorts of animals; in fact, it seemed more like a pet store than a place to live.

SEPARATED: To make the rock garden, cover the area with heavy plastic to keep out weeds. Add a layer of pea gravel for the base.

SECOND CLAUSE AS SECOND STEP: To make the rock garden, cover the area with heavy plastic to keep out weeds; then, add a layer of pea gravel for the base.

Alternatives can be emphasized by the correlative conjunctions *either . . . or* or *neither . . . nor.*

SEPARATED: The movies are getting sillier. Or I am getting more cynical.

COMBINED: Either the movies are getting sillier, or I am getting more cynical.

As the examples show, independent clauses are usually joined with conjunctions or with semicolons. Two less common devices are the colon and the dash. The colon indicates that the second clause explains or illustrates the first.

SEPARATED: The river was deceptively tranquil. Beneath the smooth, gently flowing surface were treacherous undertows.

SECOND CLAUSE AS EXPLANATION: The river was deceptively tranquil: beneath the smooth, gently flowing surface were treacherous undertows.

SEPARATED: The heat wave created a picnic atmosphere. Children played in the park fountains, while barefooted adults drank lemonade beneath shade trees.

SECOND CLAUSE AS ILLUSTRATION: The heat wave created a picnic atmosphere: children played in park fountains, while barefooted adults drank lemonade beneath shade trees.

Like the colon, the dash signals that the second clause explains the first or serves as an afterthought or addition to the first. Between independent clauses, the dash is a dramatic mark of punctuation, so you should use it sparingly. Overuse defeats the purpose.

SEPARATED: Cheerleaders are the most useless addition to football games. Their frantic efforts are almost totally ignored by the fans.

SECOND CLAUSE AS EXPLANATION: Cheerleaders are the most useless addition to football games—their frantic efforts are almost totally ignored by the fans.

SEPARATED: Ice cream doesn't taste as good as it did when I was a child. Spinach doesn't taste as bad either.

SECOND CLAUSE AS AFTERTHOUGHT: Ice cream doesn't taste as good as it did when I was a child—spinach doesn't taste as bad either.

The different techniques available for joining independent clauses allow you to clarify a relationship between ideas as well as to vary sentence structure. In choosing a technique, consider not only the need to avoid monotony but also the relationship you want to express.

(2) Combine shared elements through coordination.

When two or more sentences share elements—such as subjects, predicates, or parts of predicates—you can avoid repetition and simplistic prose by compounding the common elements with simple coordinators like *and, but,* and *or;* with correlative coordinators like *not only . . . but also, either . . . or, both . . . and;* and with expressions like *in addition to, as well as, but not.*

SEPARATED: Garlic contains natural antibiotics. Onions also contain these substances.

COMBINED SUBJECTS: Garlic and onions contain natural antibiotics.

SEPARATED: The players didn't seem to understand what had happened. And the referees didn't either.

COMBINED SUBJECTS: Neither the players nor the referees seemed to understand what had happened.

SEPARATED: The Great Wall of China was built entirely by hand. It took hundreds of years to complete.

COMBINED PREDICATES: The Great Wall of China was built entirely by hand and took hundreds of years to complete.

SEPARATED: Leafy trees add beauty to your landscape. They also help lower your energy bill in the summertime.

COMBINED PREDICATES: Leafy trees not only add beauty to your landscape but also help lower your energy bill in the summertime.

SEPARATED: Your body requires the macronutrients (fats, carbohydrates, and proteins). It also requires the micronutrients (vitamins and minerals).

COMBINED DIRECT OBJECTS: Your body requires the macronutrients (fats, carbohydrates, and proteins) as well as the micronutrients (vitamins and minerals).

SEPARATED: He was willing to assume the privileges of the office. He was not, however, willing to assume the responsibilities.

COMBINED OBJECTS OF INFINITIVES: He was willing to assume the privileges of the office but not the responsibilities.

SEPARATED: She was a well-known jazz singer. She was also a well-respected portrait artist.

COMBINED COMPLEMENTS: She was both a well-known jazz singer and a well-respected portrait artist.

(3) Subordinate with adverb clauses.

One structure very useful for combining ideas is the adverb clause, which expresses time, place, cause, purpose, condition, manner, and contrast. The nature of the information in the adverb clause is clearly signaled through the use of an introductory subordinating conjunction such as *when, until, where, because, so that, if, as though, although,* and the like. (See 6b.3 and 7c.1.) Thus, adverb clauses can improve clarity in prose by flatly stating, through the subordinating conjunction, how one idea relates to another. In addition, since most adverb clauses can introduce sentences, they provide a way to vary sentence beginnings.

SEPARATED: Billie Jean King won nineteen tournaments in 1971. She became the first woman tennis player ever to earn $100,000 a year.

COMBINED: When Billie Jean King won nineteen tournaments in 1971, she became the first woman tennis player ever to earn $100,000 a year.

SEPARATED: Our school system offers almost no instruction in financial planning. Few of us learn to handle our finances in an intelligent manner.

COMBINED: Since our school system offers almost no instruction in financial planning, few of us learn to handle our finances in an intelligent manner.

SEPARATED: Mid-afternoon drowsiness is often called the "post-lunch dip." It occurs regardless of when, or if, we eat.

COMBINED: Although mid-afternoon drowsiness is often called the "post-lunch dip," it occurs regardless of when, or if, we eat.

(4) Subordinate with adjective clauses.

The adjective clause can help eliminate the choppy prose that results from too much repetition of nouns and personal pronouns. In this structure, ideas are joined with relative words like *which, who/whom/whose, when,* and *where.* (See 2c and 7c.2.)

SEPARATED: The last stop on the tour was King's Tavern. This tavern was originally a hostel at the end of the Natchez Trace.

COMBINED: The last stop on the tour was King's Tavern, which was originally a hostel at the end of the Natchez Trace.

SEPARATED: Hamlin Garland spent his youth on farms in Wisconsin, Iowa, and South Dakota. He learned firsthand about grim pioneer life on these farms.

COMBINED: Hamlin Garland spent his youth on farms in Wisconsin, Iowa, and South Dakota, where he learned firsthand about grim pioneer life.

SEPARATED: I was forced to go to my first dance with Father's nephew, Talbot. His hair was longer than mine. And he danced like a trained bear.

COMBINED: I was forced to go to my first dance with Father's nephew, Talbot, whose hair was longer than mine and who danced like a trained bear.

(5) Subordinate with verbal phrases.

The essential element in a verbal phrase is a verbal—a verb form (*to see, seeing, seen*) functioning as a noun, an adjective, or an adverb. In addition, a verbal phrase contains one or more of the following: a subject, object, complement, or modifiers. (See Chapter 5.) Subordinating with verbal phrases can eliminate repetition of nouns and personal pronouns and provide a source for varying sentence beginnings.

SEPARATED: The wedding date was already set. She felt compelled to go through with the marriage.

COMBINED: Having already set the wedding date, she felt compelled to go through with the marriage.

SEPARATED: You can dust the face lightly with a white, frosted powder. This procedure will produce a faint glow.

COMBINED: To produce a faint glow, you can dust the face lightly with a white, frosted powder.

SEPARATED: Vines covered the entire house. They almost concealed it from the casual observer.

SEPARATED: Vines covered the entire house, almost concealing it from the casual observer.

(6) Subordinate with appositives.

The appositive, one of the most versatile structures in prose, restates or renames a word or phrase. When immediately following the word or phrase it renames, the appositive adds information. When introducing a sentence, it serves as a descriptive lead-in to the subject and an unusual beginning for a sentence. And if postponed until the end of a sentence, it lends a bit of drama and suspense. The following examples demonstrate how the appositive works to make prose more efficient and structure more interesting.

SEPARATED: This automobile is an up-to-date mechanical achievement. It has a permanently engaged, all-wheel drive system.

APPOSITIVE INSIDE: This automobile, an up-to-date mechanical achievement, has a permanently engaged, all-wheel drive system.

SEPARATED: The Anchor Pub is the last survivor of the many Southwark taverns. It was built on the site of the Globe Theatre.

APPOSITIVE AT BEGINNING: The last survivor of the many Southwark taverns, the Anchor Pub was built on the site of the Globe Theatre.

SEPARATED: For the ten years of her imprisonment, Marie concentrated on revenge. It was the only thing that kept her alive.

APPOSITIVE AT END: Only one thing kept Marie alive for the ten years of her imprisonment: the thought of revenge.

Writers frequently use appositives to add ideas after an independent clause. Appositives like these can prevent short, repetitious sentences and vague pronoun references. One way to employ the technique is to repeat a word or words in the preceding structure.

SEPARATED: Chaucer tells us of a pilgrimage to the shrine of a saint. The pilgrimage is more social than religious.

COMBINED: Chaucer tells us of a pilgrimage to the shrine of a saint, a pilgrimage more social than religious.

SEPARATED: Our climate is precariously balanced. This means that a tiny variation in the earth's orbit could cause another ice age.

COMBINED: Our climate is precariously balanced—so precariously that a tiny variation in the earth's orbit could cause another ice age.

Another way to use the technique is to begin the appositive with a word or phrase that summarizes the preceding idea or ideas.

VAGUE PRONOUN: Health experts recommend that we decrease fat and increase fiber in our diets. This may lower our risk of cancer.

COMBINED: Health experts recommend that we decrease fat and increase fiber in our diets, two steps that may lower our risk of cancer.

VAGUE PRONOUN: Because so much of the business world now provides information rather than goods, many adults must return to school for retraining. This will change the recruiting tactics of universities.

COMBINED: Because so much of the business world now provides information rather than goods, many adults must return to school for retraining—a trend that will change the recruiting tactics of universities.

33b EMPHASIS

Most of the sentences in a composition should be direct and unadorned with stylistic flourish. They should not have parts that are unusually long or artfully balanced. They should not call out to a reader for special notice. Sometimes, however, an idea warrants such notice. You can then create a dramatic structure by rearranging the parts of an ordinary sentence, by expanding a part beyond the reader's expectations, by building to a climactic conclusion, or by noticeably balancing the parts. These kinds of dramatic structures should appear sparingly because too many will make prose seem artificial and contrived. Used occasionally, however, and in the right situations, dramatic sentences will strengthen prose.

(1) Periodic sentences

The most common kind of sentence is the "loose" construction, which begins with the main idea in an independent clause, followed by less-important details. This order is considered normal because English speakers seem naturally to progress from subject to verb to complement, with additions and modifiers tacked on. In the periodic sentence, the normal order is reversed, and the main idea is postponed until the end. A periodic order seems to hang the reader in suspension—anticipating the outcome.

LOOSE: This house was the last of the century-old buildings we had tried in vain to protect.

PERIODIC: Of the century-old buildings we had tried in vain to protect, this house was the last.

LOOSE: Don't order spaghetti when you go to an important business lunch, where you must present a neat, efficient, controlled image.

PERIODIC: When you go to an important business lunch, where you must present a neat, efficient, controlled image, don't order spaghetti.

When exaggerated, a periodic sentence calls attention not only to the idea at the end but also to the structure itself. In the following example, the writer begins with a long, detailed modifier, postponing the main idea until a final short clause, *the realities emerged.* The result is a fairly dramatic sentence that a reader will notice and enjoy.

> Through the motes of cracker dust, corn meal dust, the Gold Dust of the Gold Dust Twins that the floor had been swept out with, the realities emerged. (Eudora Welty)

In the next example, an introductory adverb clause and the parenthetical *you may ask* delay the point and thus add to the humor of the question—when it finally comes.

> If Man has benefited immeasurably by his association with the dog, what, you may ask, has the dog got out of it? (James Thurber)

In the following passage, two consecutive periodic sentences heighten the intensity of the writer's main idea: *the only difference between music and Musak is the spelling* and *it's all the same to me.*

> First off, I want to say that as far as I am concerned, in instances where I have not personally and deliberately sought it out, the only difference between music and Muzak is the spelling. Pablo Casals practicing across the hall with the door open—being trapped in an elevator, the ceiling of which is broadcasting "Parsley, Sage, Rosemary, and Thyme"—it's all the same to me. (Fran Lebowitz)

(2) Cumulative sentences

The cumulative sentence is an exaggerated loose structure that piles up—or accumulates—structures at the end. One type of exaggeration is a long series of modifiers, like the *who* clauses in the following sentence.

> Grant was one of a body of men who owed reverence and obeisance to no one, who were self-reliant to a fault, who cared hardly anything for the past but who had a sharp eye for the future. (Bruce Catton)

A series of phrases at the end of a sentence can also produce a cumulative effect.

> This time the sorrel mare was in the lot before he heard it at all, the rider collarless and even bareheaded, trembling, speaking in a shaking voice as the woman in the house had done, his father merely looking up once before stooping again to the horse he was buckling, so that the man on the mare spoke to his stooping back. (William Faulkner)

In the next sentence, the writer begins with two main clauses and then tacks on a series of examples after the word *say.* The length of the structure and the number of details creates an attention-getting sentence.

> Summer will be admitted to our breakfast table as usual, and in the space of a half a cup of coffee I will be able to discover, say, that Ferguson Jenkins went eight innings in Montreal and won his fourth game of the season while giving up five hits, that Al Kaline was horse-collared by Fritz Peterson at the stadium, that Tony Oliva hit a single off Mickey Lolich in Detroit, that Juan Marichal was bombed by the Reds in the top of the sixth at Candlestick Park, and that similar disasters and triumphs befell a couple of dozen-odd of the other ballplayers—favorites and knaves—whose fortunes I follow from April to October. (Roger Angell)

(3) Climactic sentences

Another strategy for achieving emphasis is the climactic sentence, in which multiple ideas move up a scale—from less important to more important, from simple to complex, from the ordinary to the extraordinary. The climactic sentence can also build to a point, then shift suddenly from the literal to the ironic or from the normal to the unexpected. The effect is that the last idea expressed receives the most emphasis.

> The letter, written in pencil, expressed intense admiration, confessed regrets about the past, revealed deep sorrows—and was never mailed.

> Like us, stars have a cycle of life from birth, through youth and maturity, to decline and death.

> He fidgeted, took practice swings, spit, adjusted his clothes, kissed his bat, stepped into the batter's box, and struck out.

When the content lends itself to drama, the climactic sentence can be particularly effective, as the following sentence illustrates.

> Thus it is that the mouse seems always to dangle so languidly from the jaws, lies there so quietly when dropped, dies of his injuries without a struggle. (Lewis Thomas)

(4) Balanced sentences

A balanced sentence creates a symmetry—a noticeable and deliberate symmetry—achieved with parallel structure and often with repetition of key vocabulary. The "echo" of structure and words emphasizes the comparison or contrast of ideas.

> You cannot get a job without experience, and you cannot get experience without a job.

> From afar, the island looked like a tropical paradise of white sand and sparkling blue sea; up close, the island looked like a garbage dump of trash and polluted water.

When the structure and vocabulary of a sentence are perfectly balanced, the result can be quite dramatic. For example, the second sentence in the following passage has perfectly balanced independent clauses, with the subject and complement of the first clause (*seamen, gentlemen*) reversed in the second clause (*gentlemen, seamen*.)

> There were gentlemen and there were seamen in the Navy of Charles II. But the seamen were not gentlemen, and the gentlemen were not seamen. (Lord Macaulay)

Consecutive sentences can also be balanced; that is, a structure can be repeated and vocabulary carried over for two or more sentences in a row. In the next passage, the echo effect is created by the repetition of *when* clauses with *power* as the subject, followed by independent clauses with *poetry* as the subject.

> When power leads man toward arrogance, poetry reminds him of his limitations. When power narrows the areas of man's concern, poetry

reminds him of the richness and diversity of his existence. When power corrupts, poetry cleanses, for art establishes the basic human truths which must serve as the touchstone of our judgment. (John Kennedy)

A balanced structure can highlight an idea or keep prose from sounding monotonous. Remember, however, that if overused, this kind of structure, especially when exaggerated, will seem pretentious and will rapidly wear on a reader's nerves.

33c STREAMLINING

Effective writing is easy to read. It allows a reader to move smoothly through sentences without laboring to discover structure and meaning. If your pose seems cumbersome and hard to read, you may be obscuring the meaning by packing too much into single sentences, by including too many empty or passive verbs, or by clouding the connection between subjects and verbs. Practicing the following techniques can help you streamline your writing and produce crisp, clear sentences that throw no obstacles in a reader's path.

(1) Empty verbs and nominalizations

Empty verbs, such as *be, have,* and *make,* have little or no meaning themselves and must absorb meaning from their contexts. Since these verbs do not express action, they are frequently accompanied by a nominalization, that is, an expression of action in noun form. Using unnecessary nominalizations can result in cumbersome structures, as the following sentence illustrates.

> Rescue teams are making attempts to uncover the mine shaft, but authorities have no expectations of success.

Expressing the action in verbs rather than nouns tightens and streamlines the structure.

> Rescue teams are attempting to uncover the mine shaft, but authorities do not expect success.

In revising, you should keep an eye out for nominalizations that weaken structure and pad your prose. The following pairs of sentences demonstrate how easily you can eliminate unnecessary nominalizations. Often the solution is simply to express the action in a strong verb or verbal. Notice that the revised versions are shorter and crisper.

ORIGINAL: We had hopes that the students would vote for the abolition of the curfews.

REVISED: We hoped that the students would vote to abolish the curfews.

ORIGINAL: The basis of the achievement of your goal is the development of a positive attitude.

REVISED: To achieve your goal, you must develop a positive attitude.

ORIGINAL: To make a discovery about how many people felt a necessity for longer lab hours, I made use of a simple questionnaire.

REVISED: To discover how many people needed longer lab hours, I used a simple questionnaire.

(2) Weak passives

In an active sentence, the agent of the action appears in the subject position, and the receiver of the action appears as the direct object. In a passive sentence, this order is reversed. The receiver of the action appears in the subject position but still receives the action. The agent of the action can appear as an object of the preposition *by*.

ACTIVE: Locusts ruined their crops.

PASSIVE: Their crops were ruined by the locusts.

A passive sentence can be useful in certain situations. For example, a writer can choose the passive to emphasize the receiver of the action. The following pair of sentences illustrates the different emphasis found in active and passive constructions.

ACTIVE: The Etruscans and the Greeks influenced the earliest Roman sculpture.

PASSIVE: The earliest Roman sculpture was influenced by the Etruscans and the Greeks.

The active sentence focuses attention on the agents (*the Etruscans and the Greeks*), whereas the passive sentence focuses attention on the receiver of the action (*earliest Roman sculpture*).

Also, a writer can choose the passive because the agent is unknown or unimportant in the context. In such cases, the phrase containing *by* or *with* and the agent is usually left out.

PASSIVE: The telephone lines were cut.

PASSIVE: Equity courts in the United States are called Courts of Chancery.

The passive may be preferable in some situations, but in others, it may be unnecessarily weak and wordy, especially when a *by* phrase supplies the agent. Active versions tend to be more concise, emphatic, and lively than their passive counterparts because the subject acts and the verb does not require the *be* auxiliary. Also, when the agent of the action figures significantly in the content, the active focuses a reader's attention on the right words.

WEAK PASSIVE: Booster cables should never be connected to a frozen battery <u>by you</u>.

ACTIVE: You should never connect booster cables to a frozen battery.

WEAK PASSIVE: The investors were swindled out of 10 million dollars <u>by Arnold and Slack</u>.

ACTIVE: Arnold and Slack swindled the investors out of 10 million dollars.

Compare the following two passages. The passive version obscures the important role of the host, calling attention instead of the result of his actions.

WEAK PASSIVE

Before a Japanese tea ceremony, the tea room and surrounding gardens were cleaned by the host. Then a fire is made in the hearth and the water is put on to boil. When the guests arrive, the tea bowl, tea caddy, utensils for tending the fire, incense burner, and other necessary tools are carried in by the host. After the tea is prepared in a historical ritual, each guest is served. Finally, all utensils having been removed, the guests are bowed to, the signal that the ceremony has been completed.

In contrast, the active version is livelier and emphasizes the importance of the agent (the host) in the action (the ceremony).

ACTIVE

Before a Japanese tea ceremony, the host cleans the tea room and surrounding gardens. Then he makes a fire in the hearth and puts the water on to boil. When the guests arrive, he carries in the tea bowl, tea caddy, utensils for tending the fire, incense burner, and other necessary tools. After preparing the tea in a historical ritual, the host serves each guest. Finally, he removes all utensils and bows to guests, the signal that the ceremony is over.

(3) Unnecessary *that, who,* and *which* clauses

When revising prose, look for adjective clauses that begin with *that, who,* or *which* followed by a form of the verb *be* (*that is, who are, which were,* etc.). Frequently, these are empty words that can be deleted. The deletion converts this kind of clause to a word or phrase—a more efficient structure.

UNNECESSARY CLAUSE: The teacher had a smile that was skeptical.

REVISED: The teacher had a skeptical smile.

UNNECESSARY CLAUSE: W. C. Fields often played swindlers who were dedicated to the rule "never give a sucker an even break."

REVISED: W. C. Fields often played swindlers dedicated to the rule "never give a sucker an even break."

UNNECESSARY CLAUSE: Radon, which is a radioactive gas that forms naturally underground, can seep into buildings.

REVISED: Radon, a radioactive gas that forms naturally underground, can seep into buildings.

(4) Excessive verb forms

If a sentence seems congested and difficult to follow, check it to see whether it contains too many verb forms. Any verb form—main verb, infinitive, or participle—is the potential basis for a sentence. As a result, the addition of each verb form to a sentence complicates the structure. Consider, for instance, the following sentence with four verb forms.

> Residents who reveal in the city's tradition of eccentricity expect 25,000 visitors to join in the dancing under the palm trees.

Embedded are four potential sentences.

> Residents reveal in the city's tradition of eccentricity.
>
> Residents expect 25,000 visitors.
>
> The visitors will join in.
>
> The visitors will dance under the palm trees.

Because there are only four verbs, the sentence is not unduly complicated. But when too many verb forms are packed into a sentence, the structure will groan and collapse under its own weight, as in this sentence from a government document.

> Excessive Verb Forms
>
> After conducting surveys concerning public opinion toward automated highway systems, the department decided to abandon plans to allocate funds for studying such systems and is investigating mass transit systems that might help to alleviate congestion on highways leading into metropolitan areas.

Asking a reader to plow through eleven ideas in one sentence is simply asking too much. The solution is to split the sentence into smaller units and to eliminate some of the empty verbs that contribute nothing to the meaning. For example, *conducting surveys* can be expressed as *surveying; to allocate funds for studying* can be expressed as *to fund studies.* And because *decide to* and *help to* do not contribute information or clarity, they can be eliminated.

> Revised
>
> After surveying public opinion toward automated highway systems, the department abandoned plans to fund studies of such

systems. Instead, the department is investigating mass transit systems that might alleviate congestion on highways leading into metropolitan areas.

Now the first sentence has four verb forms, and the second has three. The result is a more streamlined passage that is easier to read.

(5) A clear connection between subject and verb

To understand a sentence readily, a reader must make a swift connection between the subject and its verb. If too many words intervene between the two, the vital connection is obscured, and the reader must grope for the sense. In the following example, 14 words intervene between the subject (*Second City*) and the verb (*has launched*).

OBSCURE CONNECTION: Second City, originally a group of University of Chicago students who formed an improvisational repertory company, has launched an astonishing number of our best comic actors.

Since most sentences can be revised in several ways, the revision you choose depends on the meaning you want to convey. For instance, to emphasize *Second City,* the subject of the preceding example, you should probably leave it at the beginning—a place of emphasis. In this case, a possibility is to split the sentence. The original subject plus the intervening words could be made into a complete sentence. Adding a little transition between the two sentences would make their relationship clear.

CLEAR CONNECTION: Second City was originally a group of University of Chicago students who formed an improvisational repertory company. Since its origin, the group has launched an astonishing number of our best comic actors.

To emphasize *comic actors* instead of *Second City,* you could shift to a passive sentence. In this version, the original subject and intervening words move to the end, and the new subject *an astonishing number of our best comic actors* is now closer to its verb.

CLEAR CONNECTION: An astonishing number of our best comic actors have been launched by Second City, originally a group of University of Chicago students who formed an improvisational repertory company.

In the next example, 29 words separate the subject (*police officers*) from its verb (*are*).

OBSCURE CONNECTION: Police officers, who are apparently the only members of our society with legitimate excuses to use an assortment of deadly weapons and to drive fast with lights flashing and sirens blaring, are the favorite subjects of television writers.

Because the subject and the subject complement (*favorite subjects*) are interchangeable, switching the two elements can clarify the sentence.

CLEAR CONNECTION: The favorite subjects of television writers are police officers, who are apparently the only members of our society with legitimate excuses to use an assortment of deadly weapons and to drive fast with lights flashing and sirens blaring.

If this solution seems unappealing, an alternative is to rewrite the original intervening words as an adverb clause and move it to the beginning of the sentence. Thus, you bring together the subject and verb.

CLEAR CONNECTION: Because they are apparently the only members of society with legitimate excuses to drive fast, blare sirens, flash lights, and knock heads, police officers are the favorite subjects of television writers.

A compound subject, especially one containing modifiers, can be so cumbersome that the subject-verb connection is obscured.

OBSCURE CONNECTION: Osteoclasts, dismantling cells that destroy old bone, and osteoblasts, construction cells that help form new bone, combine to create a continuous remodeling process.

The complete subject contains the simple subjects (*osteoclasts, osteoblasts*) as well as the appositives (*dismantling cells, construction cells*) and adjective clauses (*that destroy . . . , that help . . .*). This lengthy construction overwhelms the verb (*combine*). One way to solve the problem is to move the shorter noun phrase from the end to the subject position.

CLEAR CONNECTION: A continuous remodeling process results from a combination of osteoclasts, dismantling cells that destroy old bone, and osteoblasts, construction cells that help form new bone.

Another way to clarify the connection between subject and verb is visual: parentheses can help the reader isolate the subjects and "read around" the appositives. Also, this solution eliminates four commas.

CLEAR CONNECTION: Osteoclasts (dismantling cells that destroy old bone) and osteoblasts (construction cells that help form new bone) combine to create a continuous remodeling process.

If the sentence still sounds cumbersome, it can be split, expanding the original subject to one sentence and the original predicate to another. Again, enclosing the appositives in parentheses reduces commas.

CLEAR CONNECTION: Dismantling cells (osteoclasts) destroy old bone, whereas construction cells (osteoblasts) help form new bone. This combination creates a continuous remodeling process.

As the examples demonstrate, the problem with long sentences is frequently not the length itself but rather the distance between the subject and the verb. Thus, when you revise your writing, pay attention to the subject-verb connection; make sure it is immediately clear. In the process, you will also streamline your prose, making it easier to read.

33d FIGURES OF SPEECH

Figures of speech communicate through comparison or association rather than through literal meaning. For example, the familiar expression *shed light on the matter* is not literal, but figurative. No reader would think of light in its actual sense of electromagnetic radiation. Instead readers make this association: *light* makes things clearer, more visible; therefore *shed light* means *make clear.* The concreteness and vividness of effective figures of speech can often communicate more directly and more intensely than abstractions and generalizations.

Probably the most common figures of speech are metaphor, simile, personification, and hyperbole. In a metaphor, two dissimilar things are said or implied to be the same. Thus, one thing (usually unfamiliar or abstract) becomes clearer because of its similarity with the other thing (usually familiar or concrete). For example, Churchill uses the concrete *tossing sea* and *firm ground* to contrast two abstract ideas.

> I pass with relief from the tossing sea of Cause and Theory to the firm ground of Result and Fact. (Winston Churchill, *The Malakand Field Force*)

In some metaphors the abstract ideas are not expressed but suggested. For example, Canby uses the concrete *fabric* to suggest the abstract idea of structure—something holding writing together. He uses *jelly* to suggest the idea of a formless mass—something without shape or structure.

> Without the support of reasoned thought the fabric of writing may collapse into a jelly of words. (Henry Seidel Canby, *Better Writing*)

Like the metaphor, the simile compares two dissimilar actions or things. Unlike the metaphor, the simile must include the comparative word *like* or *as.*

SIMILE WITH *LIKE:* Like a monster of the sea, the nuclear-powered research submarine NR-1 prowls the twilit depth of the Bahamas during a practice dive. (Emory Kristof, "NR-1, The Navy's Inner-Space Shuttle," *National Geographic*)

SIMILE WITH *AS:* Humor can be dissected, as a frog can, but the thing dies in the process and the innards are discouraging to any but the pure scientist. (E. B. White, "Some Remarks on Humor," *The Second Tree from the Corner*)

A personification is a special type of metaphor in which something not human (animal, object, place, idea) is given some human characteristic: *patient forest, marriage of flavors, eloquence of the museum, heart of the atom, sister continent.* In the following quotation, the writer personifies the winds:

> I'm alone here for much of the summer, these hot winds my only dancing partner. (Gretel Ehrlich, "A Season of Portraits")

A hyperbole is an exaggeration. For example, instead of being literal (*they spend too much money*), a writer can intensify the reader's awareness of size by writing a hyperbole (*the national defense budget couldn't pay their bills for one month*).

Although figures of speech are common in poetry and fiction, they should be used only sparingly in nonfiction. If you do use occasional figures of speech, try to avoid those that seem inappropriately exaggerated ("the fraternity system is a cancer, malignant and festering, which must be excised") or trite ("he is a stubborn as a mule"). Instead, try to choose those that help to clarify and enliven your writing.

33e SOUND AND RHYTHM

All human beings respond to the sounds of words and phrases. Children in the process of learning language constantly engage in sound play. They chant in games: *Red Rover, Red Rover, send Rachel right over; Cinderella, dressed in yellow, went upstairs to kiss her fellow.* They experiment with tongue twisters: *Peter Piper picked a peck of pickled peppers.* They show off with Pig Latin: *An-cay ou-yay eak-spay is-thay?* They delight in spoonerisms: *Mardon me padam; this pie is occupewed. Allow me to sew you to another sheet.*

Most adults rarely indulge in sound play just for fun, but they do respond to the music of the language. Television advertising, for instance, relies heavily on sound gimmicks to sell products and ensure that consumers remember brand names and slogans. Politicians use sounds and rhythmic patterns to capture the emotions of audiences. And of course, sound and rhythm help separate poetry from prose.

English speakers seem to respond to certain sounds in rather predictable ways. For example, /j/ and /ch/ often suggest noise (*jabber, jingle, chime, chirp*). Short words that end in /p/, /t/, and /k/ have a crisp, staccato effect (*pop, tap, pat, whack*). Repetition of /l/ can produce a liquid effect (*lily, lullaby, lyrical*). The sequence of /uh/ or /ih/ plus an /f/ and a /y/ can make a word seem as light as air (*fluffy, puffy, whiffy*).

In addition to individual sounds, the language also has phrasal rhythms that can wed sound to ideas. For example, phrases with lots of unstressed syllables seem to move fast: *It's funny how rapidly phrases go running along on the page.* Phrases made up mostly of stressed syllables seem to move much slower: *Like gunmen at high noon, some words walk slow.*

In the following excerpt from *An Essay on Criticism,* Alexander Pope admirably demonstrates how sound can reinforce sense. The first two lines state Pope's thesis—that a writer must deliberately make use of sound symbolism.

(1) 'Tis not enough no harshness gives offense,

(2) The sound must seem an echo to the sense:

(3) Soft is the strain when Zephyr gently blows,

(4) And the smooth stream in smoother numbers flows;

(5) But when loud surges lash the sounding shore,

(6) The hoarse, rough verse should like a torrent roar:

(7) When Ajax strives some rock's vast weight to throw,

(8) The line too labors, and the words move slow;

(9) Not so when swift Camilla scours the plain,

(10) Flies o'er the unbending corn, and skims along the main.

In the third line of the excerpt, the repetition of /s/ suggests the sighing of the wind. In the fourth, the /sm/ and /st/ make silk-like sounds, and the long vowels in *smooth, stream, smoother,* and *flows* make the line flow slowly. The /g/, /sh/, and /r/ sounds in lines (5) and (6) echo the noise of the surf pounding the shore. Lines (7) and (8) have many more stressed than unstressed syllables and so seem to have *vast weight* and to *move slow.* In lines (9) and (10), the predominance of unstressed syllables makes words *skim along.* Thus Pope makes the sound *an echo to the sense.*

Another technique writers use for rhythmic effect is repetition of words and phrases. Consider Winston Churchill's famous "Dunkirk" speech before the House of Commons during World War II. The repetition of *we shall* and *we shall fight* sets up a cadence, culminating in the bold line *we shall never surrender.*

> We shall not flag or fail. We shall go on to the end. We shall fight in France, we shall fight on the seas and oceans, we shall fight with growing confidence and growing strength in the air, we shall defend our island, whatever the cost may be, we shall fight on the beaches, we shall fight on the landing grounds, we shall fight in the fields and in the streets, we shall fight in the hills; we shall never surrender.

In the next example, Adlai Stevenson not only repeats the words *rule* and *law* but also repeats a structure: compound nouns joined by *and.*

> As citizens of this democracy, you are the rulers and the ruled, the law givers and the law-abiding, the beginning and the end.

To achieve this moving passage about the carrying of the Olympic flame across the country in 1984, Lance Morrow uses sound to complement sense.

> The flame came fluttering out of the darkness into an early morning light. Americans in bathrobes would sometimes stand by the sides of two-lane roads, and as a runner carried the Olympic torch toward them, they would signal thumbs up and break the country silence with a soft, startling cheer. Their faces would glow with a complex light—a patriotism both palpable and chastened, a kind of reawakened warmth, something fetched from a long way back.

The passage begins with the repetition of /f/ sounds, suggesting softness, the way the flame must have looked in the *early morning light.* In the second sentence, Morrow uses a number of /s/ sounds, again suggesting softness. He ends the sentence with *a soft, startling cheer,* startling the reader with an unusual idea—that something soft can also be startling. The rhythm of the last sentence is made interesting by the three appositives after the dash, which have a chantlike quality. Also the choice of the verb *fetched* is perfect. It is a crisp word, a no-nonsense word; and it is an old-fashioned word, appropriate for something from a long way back. The passage ends with three, single-syllable words to slow the movement, *long way back.* And the final word ends with the crack of a /k/.

As the examples indicate, effective writing is not merely clear and correct. It also sounds good. You may not be able to manipulate the sounds of the language with the expertise of the writers quoted here. You should, nevertheless, practice listening to what you write. Read it aloud. Try several versions. Pick the one that sounds the best, the one that is "an echo to the sense."

PART

V

THE WRITING PROCESS

No matter what the writing project, the process is essentially the same: thinking about a subject, finding an organization, producing a draft, revising until the final paper is satisfactory. This process, however, is not necessarily linear, with each stage completed before the next one begins. For instance, some writers think a subject through and then write an entire rough draft before revising. More commonly, writers think a while, write a while, think some more, revise parts of their work, think again, write again, and so on. Regardless of the sequence, it is important to work through the whole process.

34 The Search for Ideas
35 Decisions
36 Paragraphs
37 Revision
38 Composition in Progress

CHAPTER

34

THE SEARCH FOR IDEAS

search 34

The universal lament of students in composition classes is, of course, "I can't think of anything to write about." Most students (even most professional writers) have at times found themselves staring into space with eyes glazed and mind blank, waiting for inspiration that will not come. And searching for ideas week after week, semester after semester, can be tiresome indeed.

Nevertheless, whenever you need an idea for a composition, you can make the search much easier if you do not wait passively for inspiration but instead learn the productive techniques discussed in this chapter. Some people use free association to generate ideas at random, and others prefer to channel ideas in specific directions.

Probably you will not like all the techniques suggested; every method will not suit every personality or subject. Remember, however, that if a technique is not productive in one instance, it might be in another—when you are in a different mood or have a different subject.

34a JOURNALS

Keeping a journal does not mean keeping a record of your daily activities. Rather it means writing regularly about things that happen to you; things that puzzle, excite, anger, or depress you; things that make you laugh; things that interest you.

Whether for your eyes alone or for others', a journal can help your writing in several ways. First, you can structure your entries in any way you choose. You can try out techniques for getting ideas, write impressions, record anecdotes, or practice answering essay tests. Also, journal keeping helps you get used to putting words on paper and allows you to write without stress or fear of censure. Finally, a journal can function as a source of subjects for writing. You can record observations, immediate reactions, goals, frustrations, any of which might eventually be useful in a paper.

Although a journal may include any material you choose, journal keeping does require a certain discipline. For a journal to be useful, you must write in it regularly, preferably every day. So get a notebook that is portable and sturdy enough to hold up with lots of use. Many writers try to write at the same time each day, in the same place, for the same amount of time—say one hour. You may prefer, however, to write at different times of the day for different lengths of time.

Besides writing in your journal, you should read it regularly. You may find there some patterns that are revealing and productive. For example, if a certain person turns up again and again in your journal, perhaps you should consider that person's role in your life and write about it. If a certain problem keeps reappearing, perhaps you should write about its cause or its solution. In this way, your journal can be a source of specific subjects for writing assignments. Consider, for example, this journal entry, which led the student to write a paper on the most common types of phobias.

> I was on an elevator today when a girl next to me had some kind of attack. She got faint and couldn't breathe — or ~~felt~~ like she couldn't. They said that she ~~hyppen~~ hyperventilated — couldn't get enough oxygen — or maybe she got too much, I forget which. She was OK. They said she had an anxiety attack caused by claustrophobia.

34b MEDITATION

As a tactic for generating ideas, meditation involves concentrated reflection. Some writers recommend sitting or lying down facing a blank wall so that nothing visual can interrupt the flow of thought. Such a drastic measure, however, may not be necessary for everyone. Some people can concentrate in busy environments, and many people do their best thinking while driving or jogging alone. So choose whatever place allows you to concentrate on your innermost thoughts.

If you have a subject, focus on that. If you do not have a subject, begin by picking a person, a place, an object, an incident, or an idea. Then let your mind move spontaneously from that initial point. Concentrate on what you are thinking, but do not try to direct your thoughts. If you come to some particularly interesting idea, focus on it and expand it.

Meditating has the advantage of being much faster than other techniques for getting ideas, simply because you do not have to write your thoughts down. But it has the disadvantage that you may forget some of your best material. A compromise is to talk into a tape recorder. This practice will slow you down only a bit and will preserve every strand of thought. Then you can listen to the meditation several times to find in it the most interesting or fruitful ideas, which you can record in your journal.

34c BRAINSTORMING

Brainstorming, a free-association technique, has proved successful in business, where members of a group get together to explore a topic or solve a problem—each person spontaneously contributing ideas that can stimulate other ideas.

Whether done in a group or alone, brainstorming should be completely unstructured. The theory is that structuring impedes the creative flow of ideas, whereas brainstorming allows the subconscious to release blocked ideas, no matter how irrelevant or silly they seem to be. If you try brainstorming, remember that you cannot predict which ideas will be useful. Consequently, you should jot down the ideas in words, phrases, sentences, doodles—anything that comes to you. After about ten minutes of brainstorming, go back through what you have written. Eliminate the extraneous, link related ideas, and think further about anything that strikes you as interesting.

Looking over the brainstorming notes below, the writer noticed two related patterns: that the biology curriculum is difficult and that biology majors are a strange breed. From those two ideas, she wrote a character sketch of a typical biology major.

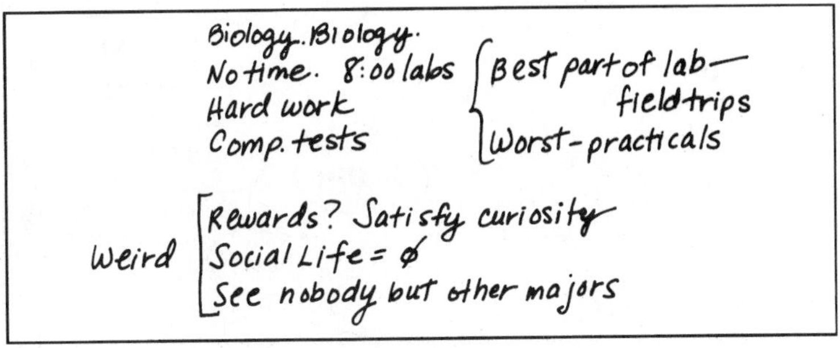
Biology. Biology.
No time. 8:00 labs
Hard work
Comp. tests
Best part of lab—
fieldtrips
Worst-practicals
Weird
Rewards? Satisfy curiosity
Social Life = ø
See nobody but other majors

Sometimes brainstorming leads to a potential idea, but not to a fully realized one. In those cases, you can start over, using that idea to initiate another brainstorming exercise. You can repeat the process any number of times, each time exploring an idea in more depth or from a different perspective.

34d CLUSTERING

In a variation of brainstorming, called clustering, ideas are linked through a graphic system of circles and arrows. To use this technique, start out by writing a topic, or "nucleus" word, in the middle of a blank page. Then, radiating out from the nucleus, write words that are suggested to you by the topic. Continue to write associations, circling each and linking it with an arrow to a related word, as shown on the following page.

The point of clustering is to release the creative element of the mind. Usually, the system will, at some point, produce a subject for writing. For instance, in the preceding example, the writer saw in the clustering the possible subject of how the Corvette has changed over the years—suggested to him by the word *Corvette* and his nucleus word, *time.*

One advantage of clustering is that the jottings are not completely unstructured; the arrows show the directions of thought and ideas appear in related groups, any of which might be developed into a composition. Also, if a subject needs further development, it can become the nucleus of another clustering exercise.

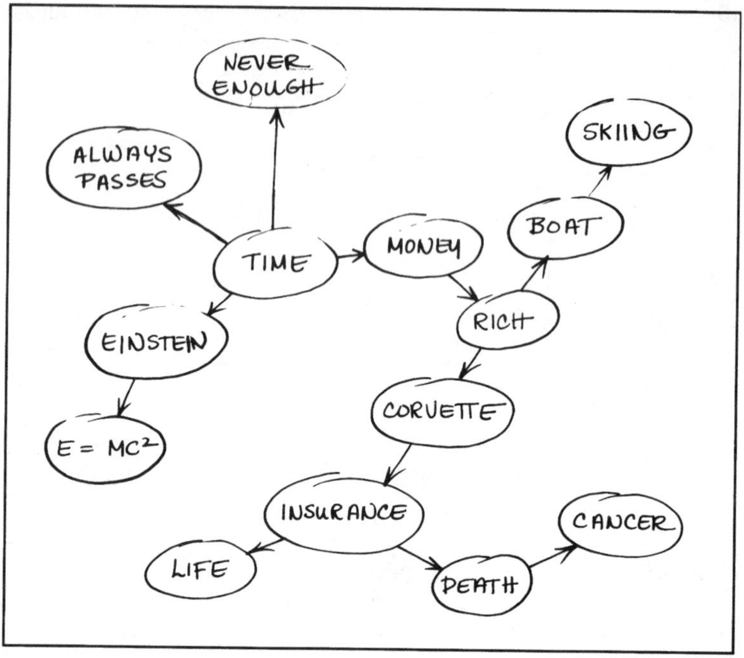

34e FREEWRITING

Freewriting is much like "talking on paper"—simply writing whatever thoughts occur, no matter how random or unimportant they may seem. Unlike brainstorming, which employs random jottings, freewriting is done in sentences or, at least, in constructions that express complete ideas. The technique serves several purposes. First, the very act of writing stimulates thinking. And many writers say that freewriting is like limbering up, like the finger exercises a pianist does before playing. Second, freewriting can turn vague ideas into visible words, thus indicating the potential of a subject.

While reading over some freewriting notes (see facing page), a student writer found that she was interested in her second idea—that her computer science teachers discouraged working in groups, contrary to the actual practice of teamwork in the business world. She ultimately produced a paper arguing that the necessity for grades creates an artificial learning environment.

> More and more projects are assigned for computer lab. a lot of people work on programs together—in groups. But most teachers would rather you didn't. I can't understand why because companies expect you to work in teams mostly. What I hate about lab is people laughing and acting stupid and silly at the next terminal to the one I'm using. Some people wear Walkman's to the lab to shut out the noise.

To use the technique, you should set some time or length limit on the process. When the limit is up, read what you have produced. If something interests you, you can use it as a starting point for another freewriting, or you can develop it with another method for getting ideas. Although freewriting may not produce polished prose, it can produce a number of ideas and occasionally a usable first draft.

34f LADDERS

Subjects like *cities, baseball,* or *movies* are too broad for a good paper, and ideas such as *friendship, warfare,* or *pollution* are too abstract. If you are struggling with unmanageable subjects such as these, you might want to construct ladders—graduated scales of words or ideas, beginning with the abstract or general and moving toward the concrete or specific.

By constructing ladders, you can discover concrete ways to talk about subjects. For example, the subject *cities* is entirely too general and unfocused. But if you think of *cities* as being on the top rung of a ladder, you can place a more specific subject on the next rung and continue down the ladder until a topic strikes you as a good one for a paper. Perhaps you move from *cities* to *New York* to *New York delis* and then end with the promising topic *New York-style hero sandwiches.* With this topic you could, for example, classify the kinds of heroes, compare the New York hero with the New Orleans po'boy, or describe the process of assembling the ideal sandwich.

Notice how the ideas in the following sample ladders progress downward toward manageable topics.

FRIENDS
↓
CHILDHOOD FRIENDS
↓
JAMES AND DAVID
↓
A DISAGREEMENT THAT LED TO A FIGHT

BASEBALL
↓
YANKEES
↓
CASEY STENGEL
↓
CASEY STENGEL'S HUMOR

ADVERTISING
↓
TELEVISION ADVERTISING
↓
BEER COMMERCIALS
↓
STEREOTYPES IN BEER COMMERCIALS

MOVIES
↓
OLD MOVIES ON T.V.
↓
MUSICALS FROM THE 50's
↓
PRODUCTION NUMBERS IN 50's MUSICALS

34g QUESTIONS

Because asking questions is one of the most natural mental processes, you may find it a comfortable and productive technique. Questions that naturally come to mind can get you started brainstorming, freewriting, or clustering. You can even keep a section in your journal for questions as they occur to you. At times questions may lead productively to a written composition.

Who is my most peculiar relative?
What kind of car would I like to own?
Where would I go on an ideal vacation?
When should a student decide on a major?
How does an ATM work?

If questions don't come immediately to mind, you can use the "journalistic questions." Reporters once claimed that the opening of a news story had to answer Who? What? When? Where? Why? How?

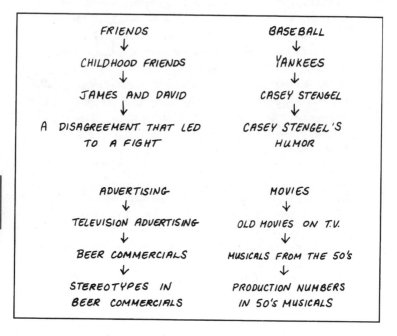

These six questions, however, if answered superficially, may produce no more than a sentence.

> On November 8, 1995, the star basketball player at our school was indicted for betting on games in order to get money for drugs.

The sentence answers all six questions, but it does not establish a direction for a composition. A more productive use of the questions is to concentrate on one or two for a given subject. For example, the subject of corruption in college athletics might be explored with *why:* Why does a player risk a career by betting on a game? Or with *how:* How does a basketball player "throw" a game?

Questions can help you explore any type of subject—to find out how much you know about it or to narrow your focus sufficiently to deal with it in a concrete way. The following lists illustrate the kinds of questions that develop naturally from a general subject.

An Object or Device (e.g., a sea shell, a videotape machine)

What are its parts?

How is it used?

Are there categories of it?

What are people's opinions of it?

How did it originate?

A Process (e.g., running a marathon, enlarging a photograph)

What are its steps or stages?

Is it difficult or easy?

Does it happen naturally?

What causes it?

What are its consequences?

A Person (e.g., a relative, a typical school principal)

What does he/she do?

What does he/she look like?

What are his/her ambitions? Values?

How is he/she typical or unusual?

What do people think about him/her?

A Place (e.g., the Vietnam War Memorial, a mountain lake)

What are its characteristics?

What places is it similar to or different from?

Why would someone want to go there or live there?

How is this place unusual? Special?

An Event (e.g., the Chicago fire, a soccer match)

What caused it?

What did it cause?

How is it like over events?

Is it part of a trend or an isolated event?

What is its significance?

How could it have been avoided?

How did people respond to it?

An Idea or Abstraction (e.g., homesickness, fascism)

What is its definition?

What is its significance?

What is it similar to or different from?

What is its history?

How has it affected society?

A Problem (e.g., immigration, drugs)

What caused or causes it?

Who or what does it affect?

Where does it occur?

Is it social, political, financial, personal, or practical?

What is a possible solution?

What are the obstacles to a solution?

What would life be like without the problem?

A Judgment or Opinion (e.g., "People who refuse to work should not be allowed to vote." "Public transportation should be free.")

How are the key words in it defined?

Is it logical?

Can it be proved?

What kind of evidence can prove or disprove it?

What are its consequences?

What are counterarguments?

What testimony can support it?

34h CLASSICAL TOPICS

In ancient Greece, rhetoricians and orators used the classical topics to help them develop lines of argument for persuasive speaking. In fact, the word *topic* comes from the Greek *topos,* which means "place"; thus, the classical topics were places to find arguments. Although used by the Greeks primarily for argument, the topics can effectively stimulate thought since they represent the way the mind works naturally to consider a subject.

definition	saying what something is
comparison	saying what a subject is like or unlike
relationship	looking at causes and effects, antecedents and consequences
circumstance	exploring possibility or impossibility, past or future fact
testimony	discovering what is known, thought, and said about a subject

Consider the subject "physical fitness." The topic *definition* suggests a look at its components (good muscle tone, low percentage of body fat, endurance, and so forth) or its types (fitness for the average person and fitness for an athlete in training). *Comparison* suggests an analogy to emotional and mental fitness or a contrast between a physically fit person and someone who is not. Comparison might also extend to comparing and contrasting degrees of physical fitness.

Relationship might lead to the causes of fitness or its effects. *Circumstance* can raise the question of the possible and impossible: what level of fitness is or is not possible for, say, a person who works every day in an office. It can also suggest a look at the past or the future, thus generating a question such as, "Were Americans more fit years ago?" or "Are we likely to be less fit in the future?"

The last classical topic, *testimony,* directs attention to research and data about the subject. It suggests finding out what authorities say about fitness, conducting an opinion poll on fitness, examining statistics to discover facts about the fitness of the general public or a certain group of people, or soliciting accounts of personal experiences with fitness. Finally, these data-gathering techniques might be combined for a fairly extensive investigation.

The classical topics probably will not help you find a subject, but once you have one, they will help you narrow the subject into something manageable and interesting.

34i READING AND LISTENING

When you are just getting started on a paper, your research is not structured library work but casual exploring—looking through newspapers and magazines, conducting informal interviews, listening to radio and television news and talk shows. A discussion with a student who is also a mother might lead to a paper comparing her problems with those of other students. A television discussion of prison conditions might lead to an argument for better vocational training for inmates. A look at classified advertisements could suggest a paper on selecting a good used car or managing a garage sale. A radio story on an animal shelter's use of dogs for medical experimentation could lead to an argument against this practice or one vindicating the need for it.

The advantage of finding a subject through reading and listening is that in the process you also get a head start collecting usable details. Suppose, for example, you read in a magazine that only one-fourth of the electorate regularly vote. You might try to find out why this is so. You could begin by interviewing voters in your age group to discover what motivates them to vote or not to vote. You could look for a government document describing the voting trends for different age groups, economic groups, regional groups, or religious groups. If you decide to write on why students lack motivation to vote, you will have already collected some information from the interviews or from your reading.

The Computer Connection

Like pens, pencils, and typewriters, computers are tools to help writers turn thoughts into words. In fact, many writers believe that the computer may be the most flexible, adaptable writing tool ever invented. It is the easiest way we have for getting on paper the fragmented ideas and mental hopscotch that make up the writing process. With a computer, you can freely type your thoughts and ideas at random. You don't have to worry about their order or significance because with the touch of a few command keys, you can later add material, move sentences and paragraphs around, and type over errors. You can save anything useful and get rid of the rest. You can even throw material into a "wastebasket" file and retrieve it later if you change your mind.

search 34i

Suggestions for Getting Ideas

- Keep a journal in a separate file or on a separate disk, and add to it regularly. A computer journal has several advantages over a notebook. For instance, it saves time and storage space. In addition, a computer journal, because it is in a file, is more private than a notebook: nosy people cannot easily rummage through your personal thoughts without your consent.
- Try freewriting on the computer as a way to generate ideas for a paper. You can turn down the contrast on the screen so that you can't see what you're typing. This way, you won't be distracted from the flow of your ideas. After ten minutes, turn up the screen contrast and read through the results. If you find something that interests you, delete everything else, and freewrite again from that starting point.
- Anytime you get an idea for a paper, add it to an "idea" file. When it's time to begin a writing assignment, review your idea file for a suitable subject.
- Look for information to help you with a writing project through computer bulletin boards or electronic networks such as the Internet. A growing number of writers are using networks to communicate about writing projects.

CHAPTER

35 DECISIONS

After finding a subject and generating ideas about it, you are likely to have a jumble of facts and thoughts meaningful to you but to no one else. To make the jumble meaningful to a reader, you must go beyond the subject itself and consider your purpose, audience, and voice. Furthermore, you must narrow your subject to a thesis, or controlling idea, that can bring a composition into focus; and you must choose a pattern for structuring the composition. Of course, if the first thesis or pattern does not work, you can always change to another. But you should make tentative decisions. Planning helps you develop the composition and locate any gaps that must be filled by further thought or research.

35a PURPOSE

Purpose is an important consideration in writing, one that is closely tied to audience. Occasionally you might write for your own eyes alone. Normally, however, you write to an audience for a purpose. One simple but effective classification system divides purpose into four categories: *impression, information, argument,* and *entertainment.*

Of course, the purposes frequently are mixed; for example, an impression is often entertaining, and an argument must contain information. Nevertheless, most writing does have an overriding or dominant purpose, and that purpose helps to unify the writing. If your purpose is primarily to convey an impression, you reconstruct an emotional or physical experience from a subjective point of view. If you intend to inform, you communicate objective knowledge of such things as appearances, processes, or procedures. In argument, you use facts and reason to persuade your reader to agree with your opinion or to act as you have directed. To entertain your reader, you write to amuse, to excite, or to divert attention from weighty and serious matters.

Most often your purpose is predetermined. When your journal entries express your thoughts and feelings, then your purpose is impression. If you must write up a laboratory experiment or describe a field trip, your purpose is to convey information. The purpose of a proposal or a letter to a newspaper is usually to argue a point. Often in creative writing or in a journalistic feature story, you seek to entertain.

But sometimes your assignment is open-ended, and you can choose a purpose. Your choice controls, at least to some extent, the handling of the subject. Suppose, for instance, that you have decided to write about the parking problem on your campus. You could create an impression by describing the morning traffic snarl and the feelings of frustration and anger it produces in you. You could inform readers about the causes of the problem or argue that parking should be confined to off-campus lots, with shuttle buses provided for drivers. You could entertain your readers by describing the various strategies that drivers use to grab parking places.

Through your purpose, you transmit a message. If you have no clear purpose in mind, readers may not know whether you want them to laugh, to sympathize, to learn something, to be convinced, or to share an experience with you. If, however, your purpose is clear to you and you keep it in mind while you write, readers stand a good chance of getting the message.

35b AUDIENCE

When you choose a purpose, you answer the question *Why am I writing?* Next, you should give some thought to the question *Who will read what I write?* In other words, you must now envision your readers, commonly called the *audience.* Obviously, the more you know about your readers, the better you can communicate with them. You can begin your audience analysis with general questions such as these:

- Is my audience one reader, several, or many?
- What is the age, education, and background of the audience?
- Do I know my audience well, slightly, or not at all?
- Does my audience have any particular mind-set or prejudices?
- How much does the audience already know about my subject?
- How much background information does my audience need?

Next, you can consider why your readers will read your work or how they will use the information you supply. In other words, *what are the readers' expectations?* Asking questions such as the following will make the audience profile more specific.

- Does my audience need the information? Have they requested it?
- Does my audience want to be informed? Entertained? Both?
- Will readers use my work to make a decision?
- Will readers carry out my instructions step by step?

Analyzing your audience and considering their expectations will help you achieve your purpose and determine the content of your paper. Suppose, for example, you are writing an article for the school newspaper on recreational camping. You know generally that your readers are fellow college students. Nevertheless, to write a good article, you must probe a little further. Do you want to address people who have never camped? Or will you address experienced campers? Furthermore, how will your readers use the information? Will they get helpful but general tips? Detailed instructions on supplies, equipment, and procedure? An overview of the pleasures and pitfalls? Or an entertaining look at why an urban dweller should not date people who like to camp? Answering these questions will help you get a grip not only on the audience but also on the purpose and content of your paper.

One audience that particularly confuses student writers is the teacher. In college classes, you normally write in response to a teacher's assignment. Usually, however, you should not write directly to your teacher—particularly in a composition class. Papers in a composition class serve as practice for the writing you will do beyond the classroom; thus, you should learn to address varied and realistic audiences. Therefore, with most school compositions, you pretend to have an audience other than your teacher.

With essay examinations, on the other hand, you have a somewhat different situation. Naturally, your teacher is the audience, one with a great deal of knowledge about your subject. In this case, you are not informing your audience; you are trying to demonstrate your own knowledge or skills. To be successful, you must consider the teacher's expectations, because examination questions can be designed for different purposes. Does the teacher expect you merely to supply certain facts, such as what causes earthquakes and how their intensity can be predicted? Or does the teacher expect you to demonstrate critical thinking—say, to point out weaknesses in an economic theory, compare the domestic policies of two different presidents, or interpret a novel not discussed in class? In any examination, you must meet the teacher's expectations by showing that you have mastered the required information or skills.

No matter who your readers are, however, and no matter what they expect, you should express your views honestly. Do not become so timid about audience that you lose confidence in your own ideas. Do not, for example, pepper your prose with expressions such as *in my opinion* or *other people may not agree with me.* If you have a view that may differ from the reader's, express it without qualifications. Good writing is honest writing.

Finally, respect your audience enough to abide by the standard conventions of sentence construction, punctuation, usage, and spelling. Remember that unlike listeners, readers cannot observe your facial expressions, your gestures, and your tone of voice. Therefore, you must make a special effort to be clear and correct. If you want to get your message across, you should pay attention to the audience receiving it.

35c VOICE

As a writer, you must adopt an effective and appropriate voice through which you speak to the audience. If you are writing fiction, you can invent a voice—for example, that of an all-knowing creator or of a specific character in the fiction itself. But if you are writing nonfiction, the voices available to you are projections of your own different roles or personality traits. Depending on the occasion, you might speak as a friend, an impersonal observer, a concerned citizen, an antagonist, or an enthusiastic fan. Also, your voice may reflect traits or moods—serious, light-hearted, neutral, detached, energetic, or emotional.

For a formal paper, such as a research paper, you should write in the third person—that is, without using the first person (*I, we*) or second person (*you*). A third-person voice helps establish a serious tone and a polite distance between writer and reader. For an informal paper, you can write in the first person, referring to yourself as *I.* A first-person voice helps you establish a personal relationship with readers and seems more natural than calling yourself *one* or *this writer.*

SERIOUS, FORMAL VOICE IN THIRD PERSON

One problem that plagues many students is burnout. This emotional state is usually associated with stress on the job, but it can also occur in school. Its most common symptoms are emotional exhaustion and negative attitudes. In addition, burnout can lead to depression, weight loss or gain, and physical illness.

LIGHT-HEARTED, INFORMAL VOICE IN FIRST PERSON

I've read a good bit lately about burnout, an emotional state usually associated with stress on the job. But it seems that this problem can also occur in school, because I am certainly burned out. Have you ever considered how stressful it can be trying to dress appropriately for class, football games, volleyball games, pizza parties, cookouts, and formal dances? Just the sheer pressure of trying to find people to borrow clothes from has left me depressed. Also, the food I have eaten at all these outings has made me overweight. Both symptoms are sure signs of burnout.

The use of second person *you* is acceptable in informal papers if you are speaking directly to your reader, giving advice or instructions or sharing experiences. You must, however, be consistent. Notice how the voice changes from third to second person in the following passage.

MIXED THIRD AND SECOND PERSON

Moving out of an apartment is always more trouble than the mover expects. He or she begins in a methodical manner, packing items neatly in sturdy boxes and labeling the boxes. After a day or so, you realize that you seem to have just as many unpacked items as you had to begin with. At this point, the mover panics and begins throwing items at random into garbage bags and pillowcases.

To use the second person in this case, you would need to establish the reader as someone who has moved or might likely move in the future. Then, you could speak directly to him or her.

CONSISTENT SECOND PERSON

If you have ever moved out of an apartment, you know that the process is always more trouble than you expect. You begin in a methodical manner, packing items neatly in sturdy boxes and labeling the boxes. After a day or so, you realize that you seem to have just as many unpacked items as you had to begin with. At this point, you panic and begin throwing items at random into garbage bags and pillowcases.

Second person is tricky, and you should use it with caution. Be sure not to use it to place readers in a group to which they cannot belong. Consider this sentence, for instance.

As a baseball pitcher, you must prepare yourself for a game not only physically but also mentally.

If the reader is not a baseball pitcher, the sentence is not logical.

A writer's voice (sometimes called a *role, mask, stance,* or *persona*) must sound sincere. For example, if you fake the voice of a person more sophisticated than you really are, you risk sounding phony or even silly. And by all means, avoid grafting onto your prose unfamiliar synonyms found in a dictionary or thesaurus. Although some synonyms can be used interchangeably, many cannot. You can substitute *parcel* for *package* without any change of meaning. You cannot, however, substitute *incapable* for *incompetent* even though the two words appear as synonyms in many dictionaries. *Incapable* means lacking ability or power; *incompetent* means unfit or unqualified for a job. Thus, while *He was incompetent on the job* makes sense, *He was incapable on the job* does not. Therefore, do not be satisfied merely to find synonyms. Look also for a word's full meaning and proper context. Certainly, you should add new words to your vocabulary, but you should not use them inappropriately to "elevate" your voice.

Whatever voice you choose must be consistent throughout an entire paper; one voice should not intrude on another. If you assume a distant and dignified voice in the beginning, do not insert a casual or personal remark. A technical paper, for example, is no place for a joke. Slang is inappropriate in a letter of application. Likewise, if you start out in a conversational voice, you should not suddenly become formal. For example, if you begin by calling yourself *I,* do not switch to *this writer.* Or, if you have been using a humorous tone, do not suddenly become solemn.

Although various voices are possible, the choice you make is rarely arbitrary. A composition about possible nuclear war will not be written with the same voice as a composition about computer nerds. A letter to a newspaper requires a voice different from that of a letter to a friend. A reminiscence will not have the same voice as a theoretical argument. Your voice must fit its context—that is, the subject, the purpose, and the audience.

35d THESIS

By this time in the writing process, you have probably found a subject, perhaps through freewriting, brainstorming, asking questions, or one of the other techniques for getting ideas. Your subject may be very general (*fast food*) or somewhat specific (*a dieter's guide to fast food*). It may be a feeling (*frustration, grief,* or *satisfaction*). Or it may be an opinion (*the quarter system is better than the semester system*). Whatever your subject, you should refine it into a workable thesis—a specific statement that can control and direct a paper.

A thesis clarifies your subject and helps you make some initial decisions about the material you will include or exclude. Even though you are quite likely to revise your thesis or change it altogether as the paper progresses, you should not neglect this important step. The five questions that follow will help you test a thesis to make sure it is promising.

(1) Is the thesis a complete idea?

Because the thesis states the point of your paper, it should be a complete idea. Otherwise, you will not know what direction you wish to take. Thus, a good first step for finding a thesis is to write a complete sentence about your subject. For example, *a degree in business* could become *A business degree is effective preparation for law school.*

(2) Is your thesis compatible with your purpose?

If you want to convey an impression, your thesis should allow vivid description—for example, *The first time I saw a John Wayne movie, I found my childhood hero.* If you want to entertain with a humorous paper, your thesis should be one that promises a light-hearted approach, such as *One of the funniest old movies on television is "The Conqueror," starring John Wayne as Genghis Khan.* If you intend to inform, you should summarize the information that you mean to explain—*Although people associate John Wayne with heroes, he played a few memorable villains.*

If your purpose is to argue, your thesis must state a debatable opinion or a judgment. For example, you cannot argue a fact, such as *John Wayne was a popular movie star.* Wayne was indeed a popular star, and a counterview is impossible. Also, there is little point in arguing a generally accepted idea, such as *John Wayne was a popular actor because the role of the two-fisted hero appealed to the American public.* On the other hand, an unexpected viewpoint can produce an interesting argument: *Much of John Wayne's popularity as an actor resulted from his outspoken patriotism in real life.*

(3) Is the thesis clear and specific?

A vague thesis cannot control material much more effectively than a simple topic. For example, consider this thesis: *Studying a foreign language is a good idea.* It does not indicate who is studying what language. Furthermore, since the word *good* can have any number of meanings, the sentence is not much more specific than *studying a foreign language.* A better thesis is a specific statement such as *Taking French helped me understand the grammar of English.* This thesis can control the subject and thus the choice of materials. When you formulate a thesis, make a specific statement and avoid vague words such as *good, bad, excellent, terrible,* and *nice.* Unless a thesis can exert control, it is of very little use.

(4) Will the thesis lead to a paper of an appropriate length?

Suppose that you are assigned a paper of approximately 500 words and that you choose the thesis *In recent years, advertising has be-*

come more and more suggestive. This statement is much too broad. It indicates that you will look at all forms of advertising over a period of time. A more specific statement could narrow the subject to one particular type of current advertising: *Magazine advertisements for men's cologne rely on suggestive images to sell the product.* This thesis could be adequately supported in 500 words.

It is also possible to narrow a subject too much. For example, you would not get very far with the thesis *The parking problem on campus is caused by a shortage of spaces.* Once you establish that the number of available parking spaces exceeds the number of cars, you have proved your point. But with an expanded thesis like *The parking problem could be alleviated by a more efficient use of space,* you could use the figures on available spaces and cars to help support your recommendations.

(5) Is your thesis supportable?

Sometimes a thesis that sounds reasonable initially will turn out to be insupportable for one reason or another. Perhaps the thesis is not logical—for instance, *Good eating habits will prolong life.* A person can eat properly and still die very young from a disease or an accident. A more supportable thesis is *Good eating habits will increase mental and physical stamina.* Or perhaps the thesis is simply too dogmatic—for instance, *There are three causes of depression.* Scientists who have researched depression for years are uncertain about all of its causes; therefore, this idea cannot be supported. A more reasonable thesis is *Depression can be caused by stress, loneliness, or poor health.* This thesis does not rule out other causes; it simply addresses three.

After you have settled on a possible thesis, you can start assembling material to support it. If you have used some of the techniques for finding something to write about (Chapter 34), you can sort through your collection of notes and select those that are pertinent. Or, if you have already written a first rough draft, you can rewrite it with your thesis in mind. Further, if you plan to write an argument, you can list evidence for and against your thesis. The result will be a kernel that you can develop into a complete paper.

Of course, as you develop a draft, you may find that your thesis does not work very well. Perhaps you do not have enough material to support the idea. Perhaps the thesis is too broad to control material or too narrow to produce more than a paragraph or two. Or perhaps you change your opinion while writing the paper. Instead of struggling with an unsatisfactory thesis, revise it to suit the material you want to include. Or abandon the thesis altogether and find another. In fact, you may have to try several times to find something that works, but the search will be worthwhile in the long run. With a good thesis, one you can effectively support, you are much more likely to write a good paper. Notice that in the composition in progress (Chapter 38), the student writer changed and refined the thesis several times throughout the drafts of the paper. The thesis does not appear in its final form until the fourth and last draft.

The examples that follow show how several student writers moved from a topic to a thesis specific enough to control the content of a paper.

1. The student first narrowed the general topic *detective novels* to *the settings of detective novels.* In her first attempt at a thesis, she wrote *In detective novels, the setting is usually important.* This thesis, however, was too broad for the length of the paper assigned. She narrowed the thesis to *In Elmore Leonard's "La Brava," the setting is very interesting.* Since the word *interesting* did not offer much direction, she tried again and produced the workable thesis *In Elmore Leonard's "La Brava," readers learn about the Miami that tourists never see.*

2. The student wanted to discuss *the advantages of word processing over typing* and began with the sentence *Word processing is better than typing.* He then rejected this vague thesis and wrote *Because a word processor encourages revision, its use can improve composition grades dramatically.* When he tried to write a rough draft, however, he found that he had little to say, since revision naturally improves papers and thus grades. The thesis was too narrow. He then wrote *Using a word processor can improve grades.* In his paper, he was able to discuss the advantages of revising compositions, typing lecture notes, and producing attractive out-of-class assignments.

3. The student wanted to write on *fly fishing* and first formulated the vague thesis *Fly fishing is a good sport,* which offered no direction for the paper. She then tried *Fly fishing requires more skill than any other type of fishing.* This idea proved unsatisfactory not only because it was too broad but also because it would be very hard to support. Next, she formulated the supportable thesis *Fly*

fishing is a difficult sport. And finally, she revised the sentence to give direction to the paper: *Fly fishing is a difficult sport because it requires physical skill, concentration, and practice.*

4. Disgusted with his roommate for watching television constantly, the student writer chose the subject *couch potatoes.* In his irritation, he tried the thesis *Couch potatoes are lazy* and then *Couch potatoes are stupid.* Since neither statement was supportable, he tried *Most television programming is so boring that a couch potato must have a problem very much like a drug addiction.* He realized, however, that he did not know enough about drug addiction to support the position. At this point, he reconsidered his subject. Primarily, the irritating roommate watched situation comedies. The writer then abandoned his original idea and found a productive thesis: *The plots of current family-comedy shows are essentially "Leave It to Beaver Revisited."*

5. The writer began with the subject *the importance of studying computer science* and then changed it to *the advantages of studying computer science.* She first tried the thesis *Students who understand computers have more career options than those who do not.* In writing a first draft, however, she found that she had not fully considered what she meant by "understand computers." The draft moved from students with expertise in theory and design, to students with programming skills, to students with computer literacy. She revised her thesis to state *Computer literacy is an advantage in almost any profession.* She was then able to define "computer literacy" and discuss its advantages to people in fields such as accounting, law, marketing, and office management.

These experiences show the importance of finding a suitable thesis. If the student writers had spent less time looking for a productive thesis statement, they would have had much more trouble producing a satisfactory paper.

The Computer Connection

A computer helps you not only to get thoughts down on paper but also to make decisions. How should you handle your raw material? What should you keep or cut? How should you organize? What should you emphasize? Because adding, deleting, and rearranging is easy, you can experiment with different purposes, voices, and thesis statements to see which best suit your material. You can then print a hard copy of the different versions and compare them.

Continued on next page

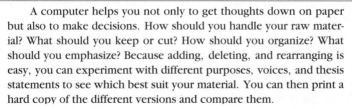

Continued from previous page

Suggestions for Making Decisions

- Type an idea for a subject and then brainstorm to find a thesis statement that might lead to a rough draft.
- Write a rough draft with a definite purpose in mind—impression, information, argument, or entertainment. If your purpose doesn't seem to fit the subject, switch to another purpose and redraft.
- Use computer bulletin boards and e-mail to analyze audience response. Pay close attention to occasions when you feel your writing was clearly understood or misunderstood.
- Try out different voices on the bulletin boards and e-mail. Vary between serious and lighthearted, formal and informal, neutral and partisan, energetic and passive. Which seem most effective?
- If you use a computer program with multiple windows, you can keep notes or old versions in one window while at the same time composing in another.

35e PATTERNS

Sometimes the best pattern for a paper is implicit in the thesis. *There are only three types of bartenders* leads naturally into classification. *I survived rush week* suggests a narrative that outlines events. *The campus parking problem could be solved by increased rates for permits* could take the form of problem/solution. A comparison/contrast pattern is an obvious plan for *Solar energy is more practical in the southern United States than in New England.* Enumeration of evidence is the likely development for *Air travel has its inconveniences.*

When a method of development is not implicit in the thesis, you must consider among possible patterns. For example, suppose your thesis were *Ulysses S. Grant was a weak president.* You could contrast Grant to strong presidents. You could treat his policies in a cause/effect pattern or illustrate his character with one detailed narrative. Or you might classify Grant's failings into two categories: his failure to stand up to radicals in Congress and his failure to police corruption among his associates. You could then enumerate examples under each category.

Each of the patterns can serve to shape an entire paper or one section of a paper. At times, the patterns seem to overlap rather obviously. However, they are presented not as pure forms but only as methods to help you frame and direct ideas.

(1) Description

Description is the presentation of details that create a verbal picture of what something is or appears to be. Many of the papers you write in a composition class are likely to require some description. Obviously, you should not include all the details possible. Instead, you should select those details that best characterize what you are describing. Also try to strike a good balance; too few details will communicate little to the reader, and too many will obscure the picture.

Once you have decided which details to include, you must find some way to arrange them. One possibility is to organize spatially, from top to bottom, left to right, far away to close up—so that the reader sees the picture as though a video camera were ranging over the scene. Spatial arrangement works well for descriptions of buildings, bridges, parks, works of art, and scenes in nature. You can also move from positive to negative features or negative to positive. For example, you might present a favorite old car by first describing its good points and then its bad or vice versa. Or you can arrange details from the more obvious to the less obvious, describing your grandfather, let us say, first with those details obvious to anyone and then with subtle traits known only to people close to him.

Often your subject and the point you want to make about it will guide your choice. Often more than one option will seem logical. Whatever the arrangement, the details should be organized, not presented merely at random.

(2) Narration

Narration tells a story, recounts events, or outlines the stages of a process. The arrangement of the actions can be strictly chronological, without interruptions, in the order in which they occurred or do occur. The arrangement can also be predominantly chronological, interrupted with flashbacks to previous actions. Or it can be episodic, with actions grouped into incidents not necessarily sequential.

Narration is a good scheme for recounting an experience or relating an anecdote, such as an uncomfortable job interview or a trip that turned into a comedy of errors. Narration is also a logical pattern for explaining a process, such as how a chemistry experiment works or how to rappel down a mountainside. When you choose narration to structure a paper, take special care to include only the details that advance the story or the account of the procedure. Extra information causes the reader to ask the deadly question, "So what?"

(3) Enumeration

In enumeration, details are listed to support the thesis of a whole paper or the topic sentence of a paragraph. The details may be anything appropriate to the subject—facts, statistics, examples, precedents, or testimony. Suppose, for example, you have the thesis *Vigorous exercise can help reduce stress.* You could enumerate statistics from studies that support your position and testimony from people who have overcome stress by exercise. Or consider this idea: *Art and theater majors dress differently from other students on campus.* You could enumerate the types of clothes that will prove your point.

Writers disagree about the best order for enumeration. Some prefer the order of increasing importance, in which the most important items come last. Others, arguing that readers remember best what they read first, position items in order of diminishing importance. In any case, all agree that the most important items should not be put in the middle.

(4) Comparison/contrast

Comparison/contrast shows how things are similar or different. This technique is appropriate for a thesis such as *"Gone With the Wind" and "So Red the Rose" deal similarly with the destruction of the planter class after the Civil War.* With this thesis, the paper would probably minimize differences and highlight similarities. On the other hand, a paper with the thesis *The parent-child relationship in single-parent families differs radically from that in two-parent families* would emphasize differences.

Comparison/contrast is an obvious pattern for presenting a conflict—for example, the feud between farmers and cattle owners in the American West, conflicting arguments about the theme of *Macbeth,* or the ideology of the Republican Party as opposed to that of the Democratic Party. When the purpose is to argue, the paper supports one side of the conflict. When the purpose is to inform, the paper describes the conflict without taking sides.

The two most common arrangements for a comparison/contrast pattern are *block* and *alternating.* Suppose, for example, you were comparing an article in *Reader's Digest* with the original to determine how an article can be simplified and shortened in a digested version. In the block arrangement, you would first discuss one version of the article, including each point of comparison and contrast, and then move to the other version, discussing the same points. In the alternating arrangement, you would organize the paper according to the points of comparison, with the two versions under each point. The following outlines help clarify the difference between the methods.

BLOCK ARRANGEMENT

1. Original version of magazine article
    1.1. Length
        a. The whole article
        b. Paragraphs and sentences
    1.2. Vocabulary
    1.3. Effect
2. *Reader's Digest* version of magazine article
    2.1. Length
        a. The whole article
        b. Paragraphs and sentences
    2.2. Vocabulary
    2.3. Effect

ALTERNATING ARRANGEMENT

1. Length
    1.1. The whole article
        a. Original version
        b. *Reader's Digest* version

1.2. Paragraphs and sentences
  a. Original version
  b. *Reader's Digest* version
2. Vocabulary
  2.1. Original version
  2.2. *Reader's Digest* version
3. Effect
  3.1. Original version
  3.2. Reader's Digest version

For most subjects, the alternating arrangement works best. It allows you to bring the similarities and differences close together so that a reader need not think back to another part of the paper to make mental connections. The block arrangement, on the other hand, works well when the comparison is very simple and does not depend on details.

(5) Classification

In classification, items from a general category are grouped into smaller categories on the basis of selected principles. As the following list suggests, any number of subjects can be classified.

Melville's novels might be classified by their subject matter—those primarily autobiographical and those allegorical.

Comic strips might be classified by type of satire—social or political or both.

Sports commentators might be classified according to attitude—the ex-jock, the statistician, and the fan.

Sleeping bags might be classified by their fill—those containing down, Dacron, or polyurethane foam.

Watches might be classified by the image they produce—professional, trendy, ostentatious, macho.

The structure of a classification paper grows naturally out of the subject matter. Each class constitutes a section (a paragraph or more) of the final composition.

(6) Illustration

An illustration is an example that makes a generality specific or an abstraction concrete. The illustration may be a narrative, a description, a fact, or anything that makes an idea graphic or real.

An entire paper built on one extended illustration usually takes a narrative form. For example, an argument that criminals should work to compensate their victims might narrate one incident, from the commission of a crime through a successful program of compensating the victim to the criminal's rehabilitation.

On the other hand, a paper built on a series of illustrations usually has an enumeration pattern. A writer could enumerate the examples of Muhammad Ali, Joe Louis, and Sonny Liston to support the thesis *Boxing should be outlawed because of the brain damage suffered by participants.*

(7) Definition

A word can be defined with a synonym (*probity* means "honesty") or with a formal explanation that puts the item defined into a general class, or genus, and then differentiates it from other members of that class: "A *misanthrope* is a person [general class] who hates humanity [differentiation]." Obviously, when an entire paper is devoted to definition, the subject must be expanded with other structures. For example, "What is a soap opera?" might be answered by a variety of methods.

CLASSIFICATION:	the types of soap operas
COMPARISON/CONTRAST:	the ways in which soaps differ from other television forms
ILLUSTRATION:	the use of one popular soap opera or several to exemplify the form

(8) Analysis

Since analysis involves breaking a whole into component parts, a number of rhetorical patterns could be considered analytical. In narration, events are broken into time segments; in classification, subjects are partitioned into categories; in comparison/contrast, subjects are divided into similarities and differences.

As a separate pattern of development, however, analysis refers to an orderly examination of components. Writers frequently have the task of analyzing a poem, a play, a mechanism, a system, a process, or collected data. The purpose of such an analysis is to bring a systematic understanding to a subject. For example, an analysis of a poem could examine the theme, the voice, the figurative language, and the sound pattern. An analysis of an insect might include these components: physical description, life history, habitat, enemies. An analysis of the process for tracing an ancestor might include interviewing relatives, checking local records, and reading genealogical collections.

(9) Problem/solution

The logic and simplicity of the problem/solution pattern make it easy to design: identification of a problem and presentation of a solution. A paper with this pattern can either emphasize the problem or the solution or give equal time to both.

A problem/solution pattern is common in arguments, where the thesis often includes both problem and solution. *The overpopulation of cats and dogs should be controlled by law,* for instance, contains the problem (overpopulation of cats and dogs) as well as the solution (control by law). Both the problem (traffic flow and automobile accidents) and a solution (a bridge over an intersection) are stated in the thesis: *A footbridge should be built over the Moncrief Avenue–Carpenter Street intersection to facilitate traffic flow and reduce accident risk for pedestrians.*

(10) Cause/effect

The cause/effect pattern is a versatile structure. A paper can begin with a cause and lead up to the effect, begin with effect and then explain cause, or shift back and forth between the two. This pattern is an obvious structure for papers on historical events but is by no means limited to discussions of the past. The structure is effective for discussions of conditions and results (if certain conditions are present, certain results can be expected) and speculations about the future (if certain trends continue, certain events are likely to occur).

The following titles suggest the range of subjects that can be organized in a cause/effect pattern as well as the emphasis a writer can impose on a subject.

The Common Causes of High Blood Pressure

The Effects of Custer's Recklessness on the Disaster at Little Big Horn

Tactics for Getting a Raise

The Future of Mount St. Helens

Telling the Truth Got Me into Trouble

You, Too, Can Have a Well-Behaved Dog

Too Many Hours in Front of a TV

If you decide to use the cause/effect pattern, be sure that your logic is sound. In other words, a preceding event does not necessarily cause the one that follows. Furthermore, many events and trends have multiple and complex causes. For advice on examining causes, see "Post Hoc Reasoning" and "Oversimplification of Cause" in Chapter 39, "Argument and Critical Thinking."

35f OUTLINES

Once you have settled on a subject and have a tentative pattern in mind, it is wise to work from some sort of plan, whether sketchy or carefully detailed. Before writing a plan, or outline, you should review any notes or material you have on hand so that you do not overlook information worthy of inclusion. Also, if at this point you need more material, you can return to techniques such as brainstorming or freewriting to refresh your memory or stimulate new thinking.

Whether you write a rough outline or a structured one depends on your personal work habits or on your assignment. Even if a structured outline is called for, most people begin with a rough outline and then refine it—usually after the paper has been completed so that changes made during the writing stage appear in the finished outline.

(1) A rough outline

A working outline need not be formal, with a system of Roman and Arabic numerals, upper- and lowercase letters, and parallel grammatical structures. Instead, it can be "rough," with the emphasis on order and content rather than form and parallelism. A rough working outline should be finished enough to reveal the omission of necessary information, the presence of superfluous material, the compatibility of the parts of the composition, and the logic of sequences. Such an outline can also help a writer to evaluate a plan.

- Is the plan one the audience can follow?
- Does the thesis require further narrowing or expanding?
- How much more material must be collected?
- Is there time to collect the material?
- Are the resources available?

For example, suppose you were structuring a paper around the thesis *The problem with dogs is mainly a problem with their owners.* You might first jot down possible segments, such as these.

barking all night	leash laws
roaming loose	strays
overpopulation	vicious
good companionship	

At this point, you should check the list for segments that should be omitted, combined, or added. The preceding list contains segments that overlap: *roaming loose* overlaps *leash laws; strays* overlaps *overpopulation. Good companionship* does not fit and should be omitted. And *disease* is a promising subject to add. Thus a working outline might look like this.

1. barking all night	4. vicious animals
2. roaming loose	5. disease
3. overpopulation	

If the rough outline has too many divisions, you may need to narrow your focus. If the outline has divisions that do not seem to go together, your thesis is probably weak, and you should change it before moving ahead. If nothing seems to work, you can go back to the techniques for getting ideas and look for new material, a new thesis, or a new subject.

(2) A structured outline

If you prefer to go beyond a rough outline to make a more structured plan before beginning a draft, you can make a topic, a sentence, or a paragraph outline. The topic outline helps ensure a logical sequence, predict paragraphing, and speed up production of a first draft. In addition, a topic outline can serve as a table of contents if the assignment requires one. A sentence outline can suggest topic sentences for paragraphs and blocks in the paper. A paragraph outline, almost a rough draft of the paper itself, is rare because few writers are prepared to develop ideas at the same time they are organizing the topic with an outline. Instead, most outlines develop gradually, progressing in detail and size as the subject is developed and the necessary information is accumulated.

Although a numbering system is not necessary for working outlines, some writers prefer to use one. A numbering system reveals the relationships between parts and the volume of material necessary to develop the subject. Two systems work well: the traditional system (Roman numerals, Arabic numerals, and letters) and the decimal system.

Traditional System

Thesis: College professors fall into four basic categories: the Students' Pal, the Scholar, the Entertainer, and the Eager Beaver.

I. The Students' Pal
  A. Youthful clothes
  B. Casual classroom presentation
    1. Informal manner
    2. Use of students' first names
    3. Tendency to give high grades
  C. Social life with students
    1. Inclusion of students in faculty activities
    2. Invitation to his/her home

        3. Teacher/student leisure activities
- II. The Scholar
    - A. Lack of attention to clothes
    - B. Serious classroom attitude
        1. Emphasis on lecturing
        2. Essay tests
        3. Preoccupation with specialized material
    - C. Lack of interest in student activities
- III. The Entertainer
    - A. Eccentric clothes
    - B. Entertaining classroom performance
        1. Lectures that resemble comedy monologues
        2. Emphasis on anecdotes and jokes
        3. Unpredictable, clever tests
    - C. View of students as audience
- IV. The Eager Beaver
    - A. Conventional clothes
    - B. Exuberant (but misguided) classroom presentation
        1. Cheerleader attitude
        2. Emphasis on class discussion and group projects
    - C. Tendency to pout if students do not respond

Decimal System

Thesis: Social problems can hurt a student's schoolwork.

1. Poverty
    - 1.1. Inadequate resources
        - 1.1.1. Lack of supplies
        - 1.1.2. Lack of equipment
        - 1.1.3. Incomplete library
    - 1.2. Poor diet
        - 1.2.1. Inability to concentrate
        - 1.2.2. Lack of stamina
        - 1.2.3. Frequent illness
    - 1.3. Necessity for part-time jobs
        - 1.3.1. Long hours
        - 1.3.2. Inadequate sleep
2. Drugs and alcohol
    - 2.1. Lack of motivation
    - 2.2. Detriment to health
    - 2.3. Influence on truancy
3. Family problems
    - 3.1. Parental divorce
        - 3.1.1. Anxiety
        - 3.1.2. Distraction from schoolwork

3.2. Parental disinterest
 3.2.1. Lack of supervision
 3.2.2. Lack of regular hours

The Computer Connection

Computers cannot write for you, but they can help you plan writing strategies and organize material. The structure of your paper will probably go through many stages, evolving as your ideas take shape. The computer makes it easy to experiment with alternatives as you look for a suitable structure.

Suggestions for Working with Structures

- Start by making a list of major topics, arguments, or incidents you want to cover. Add other topics and subtopics as they occur to you, delete items, or shift the order.
- Experiment with more than one pattern or structure for the composition. For example, you might create two outlines—one in a cause/effect pattern, another in an illustration pattern—and then see how your material adapts to each structure. Which structure seems to strengthen or enhance the material? Do you need to find better supporting material or examples? Flag sections that need work.
- Some of your best ideas for examples, titles, transition lines, or opening anecdotes may come at inconvenient moments. Don't try to work them into the material right away; instead, create a "junk" file of random material and call it up as needed.
- Don't delete early versions of outlines or other material. If you keep a record of different attempts, you can return to them to retrieve information that looks better in retrospect.
- Adopt a logical method for naming files so that you can save and easily retrieve drafts of papers. For DOS computers, use a filing system such as the following:

  paper 1.d1 (draft one of the first paper)
  paper 1.d2 (draft two of the first paper)
  paper 1.fin (final draft of the first paper)

  For Macintosh computers, use more descriptive names, but remember the 31-character limitation:

  Hamlet - draft one
  Hamlet - draft two
  Hamlet - final draft

CHAPTER

36

PARAGRAPHS

At some point in the composition process, you must move from the planning stage to the writing stage. You must get your ideas down on paper. It is at this stage that some people develop "writer's block": they stare helplessly at empty white paper—and it stares back. The mind goes completely blank or rejects every idea that surfaces.

If you should experience this inertia, two tactics may help overcome it. First, get away from the blank paper for a while and do something else. Sharpen pencils, buy new paper, clean your room, jog, or read. Second, remember that you are not trying to produce a finished product in one sitting. Instead, you are simply trying to produce a rough draft, something to work from. Try writing rapidly to keep the momentum going. Once in rough form, the first draft can be changed, supplemented, and polished.

Some writers spend most of their time on preliminaries; they think through a subject, make plans, and take notes. Then they write the entire composition and revise it. Other writers think, write, and revise intermittently—working back and forth, weaving a composition piece by piece. No single system works for every person. If you have no established pattern for the drafting process, you might want to experiment to see what works best for you. When you find something that feels comfortable and that works well, you can stick with it.

Regardless of the drafting technique you prefer, your goal is to produce a series of segments that fit together within the overall structure of the whole paper. These segments are the paragraphs, the units of information that together develop the paper's thesis. Drafting your paper paragraph by paragraph allows you to focus all your attention on developing each segment of information.

36a BODY PARAGRAPHS

The body of a composition, between the introduction and conclusion, contains the material that supports the thesis. This material must be presented in logical segments, or paragraphs. When you draft the body, think of the paragraphs as "mini-compositions" with internal structures similar to the structures of full papers. In other words, the details in a paragraph support a central idea just as the evidence of a whole paper supports its thesis.

In the drafting stage, you should not expect to produce a series of classic paragraphs, each with exemplary unity, coherence, and development. If you do, you can get bogged down, lose spontaneity, and forget where you are headed. The time to ensure each paragraph's unity, development, and coherence is during revision. You can then make sure that each paragraph is unified, that all its details relate to a single idea. You can check each paragraph's development to be sure that sufficient details cover the topic. And you can add any necessary transition to achieve coherence. (See Chapter 37, "Revision.")

(1) Paragraphs with topic sentences

A useful way to construct a paragraph is to think in terms of a topic sentence, one that states the point of the whole paragraph. The traditional paragraph begins with a general statement, or topic sentence, which is subsequently supported or developed by discussion, illustration, or examples. This organization works especially well for inexperienced writers; it improves coherence and unity because the details are all related to the stated idea. Furthermore, as the following paragraph illustrates, placing the thesis at the beginning ensures its emphasis.

TOPIC SENTENCE AT THE BEGINNING

Hypnosis can control people's vision. For example, if you were hypnotized and I told you a snake was slithering across the floor, you would not only believe me, you would actually perceive the snake as real. If I told you that there were no desk in the room, you could look right at it and not see it.

The topic sentence can occur not only at the beginning of the paragraph but also within the paragraph or at the end. These variations can relieve the monotony of a series of paragraphs, each beginning with a topic sentence.

TOPIC SENTENCE AT THE END

According to a survey, 50 percent of the prisoners convicted of murders, rapes, robberies, and assaults had been drinking before committing their crimes. Sixty percent of these prisoners had been drinking very heavily. Obviously, drinking is closely related to violence.

TOPIC SENTENCE IN THE MIDDLE

For years, whenever I tried jogging, it turned out to be a painful struggle. So I quit, tried again, quit, and on and on. But now, I have discovered the answer. I never jog alone. Jogging with others somehow makes the torture bearable. Talking gets my mind off what I'm doing, and suffering with others is better than suffering alone.

In another variation of paragraph development, writers do not state the topic sentence but rely altogether on the content to indicate the central idea. For example, the idea of the following paragraph, though not stated, is obviously that baseball fans are fickle.

TOPIC SENTENCE UNSTATED

When a baseball team is winning, fans swarm into the stadium, enthusiastic cheers fill the air, good seats go only to those who buy tickets far in advance. When a team begins to lose, the stands are half empty, the silence broken only by catcalls, boos, and moans. With homers, high batting averages, and sparkling defensive plays, the players are magnificent heroes. In a slump they turn suddenly into hopeless bums.

(2) Paragraph patterns

Like an entire composition, an effective paragraph has its own logical purpose and pattern. In fact, you can structure a paragraph with the same techniques available for whole papers—description, narration, enumeration, comparison/contrast, classification, and so forth. (See 35e.)

The point of the paragraph determines the pattern or patterns you can choose. For example, if the paragraph exists to relate an incident, the pattern will more than likely include narration, leading from one occurrence to another. If the point of the paragraph is to show similarities and differences, a comparative pattern is a logical choice. Whatever the dominant point may be, some pattern or combination of patterns can accommodate its development.

Description

You use description when you want to create an image that the reader can envision. The following paragraph, for example, paints a picture of a movie mummy that for years haunted the writer.

> It was the mid-1940s. I had just seen a movie about a mummy. I don't remember the name of it. Just the image, so powerful even still, of a man wrapped in grayish cloth around his ankles, legs, body up to the top of his head. Eyes and mouth exposed, one arm drawn up against his chest, elbow close to his side, hand clawed. The other arm dangling alongside the leg that dragged. Several strips of cloth hung loosely from that arm, swaying with each step-drag, step-drag. I don't remember where he was coming from or going to in the movie. It doesn't really matter. I knew that he was coming for me. (Frank Langella, "The Monsters in My Head," *New York Times Magazine*)

Narration

For an event, anecdote, or story, you write a narrative. A paragraph with a narrative arrangement moves from one occurrence to another, usually in chronological order. The following paragraph narrates two early electrical experiments.

> The Abbé Noilet assumed the post of "official" electrician to Louis XV and arranged the spectacle of an electric discharge passed through 180 soldiers of the guard, all of whom leapt as one man into

> the air. An even more spectacular performance was arranged by him at the Couvent de Paris. Here, he assembled 700 monks in line, each joined "electrically" to his neighbour by means of a bit of iron wire clasped in either hand. The circuit was completed by having the monks at the end joined to the prime conductor and the condenser by a similar means. At the moment of discharge, to the great joy and amusement of the king and retinue, although to the discomfort of the monks, the 700 monks, like the 180 soldiers, leapt into the air with a simultaneity of precision outrivalling the timing of the most perfect corps de ballet. (I. B. Cohen, *Benjamin Franklin's Experiments*)

Enumeration

draft 36a

Many paragraphs have an enumerative pattern. Anytime you need to present several facts or details to back up a general statement or to make a point, you use enumeration. This pattern is similar to a list, with examples itemized throughout the passage. In the following paragraph from a paper on the foolish ways people treat pets, the student writer enumerates details found in advertisements for boarding kennels.

> With family vacation plans that did not include pets, I began to search for a painless way to part company with two dogs and a cat. The Yellow Pages revealed surprising choices: a ranch, a motel, an inn, an academy, a country club, and even an animal kingdom. Our pets could luxuriate at the Pet-otel, at Paradise for Pets, at Pleasant Valley, or better yet, at Rhapsody Acres. The only ominous sounding place was the Dog House. At once of these places with "best friends" enjoying "tender loving care," the "furry four-footed companions" are provided with heated and air-conditioned accommodations, grooming, styling, and trimming. In another, they are entertained by music in "new, modern facilities with a skylighted atrium." One place transports its guests in a "pet taxi" and provides "dating." While dogs enjoy a "country atmosphere," cats step into a "jungle motif." It all sounds so appealing that my family's vacation plans paled in comparison. If it weren't for the plucking and ear tattooing, I might have considered joining the animals.

Comparison/Contrast

A paragraph can be structured around comparison (similarities) or contrast (differences) or both—whatever is appropriate or instructive. You could, for example, write about a local basketball player's skills by comparing them with the skills of a well-known player. Or you could write about a new breed of cat by contrasting the characteristics to existing breeds. In the following paragraph, the writer uses contrast to emphasize the qualities of the village of Greenwich.

> Greenwich was a Williamsburg with a difference: it wasn't dug out of the ground and rebuilt. There was another difference too: it didn't have that unnaturally genteel, sanitized look of the Virginia village that turns it into a museum. Surely, the first Williamsburg must have been a knockabout frontier town, a place of skullduggery and war, where the laundry got hung out and dogs pissed in the muddy lanes, where the scent of dung and wet horses was strong. To resurrect that town and playact the past is a good thing for Williamsburg. But it wasn't the way of Greenwich. Hidden in the tall marsh grass of the coastal lowland, the whilom seaport that once rivaled Philadelphia was remarkable. (William Least Heat Moon, *Blue Highways: A Journey Into America*)

Classification

Classification is a scheme that organizes a subject—such as people, events, or ideas—into characteristic groups on the basis of some similarity the members share. You use classification whenever you need some sort of scheme for discussing a subject composed of many items. Obviously, you cannot discuss all boats, all computers, or all Italian food. Therefore, you group the items in categories to give your subject some order. In this paragraph, the writer classifies the residents of Venice, California, into workers and nonworkers.

> The residents of Venice fall into two groups: those who work and those who don't. The latter includes senior citizens, drifters, drug addicts, would-be moviemakers, and aging hippies and surfers who have made a cult of idleness and pleasure. The other group includes lawyers, dentists, real estate brokers, accountants. Many are workaholics, attached to their jobs as they are to nothing else. They work nights and weekends, eat fast food while driving to and from their work, and live alone, longing, in the silence before falling asleep, for connection. (Sarah Davidson, "Rolling Into the Eighties," *Esquire*)

Illustration

A paragraph developed by illustration supplies evidence to back up a general statement or an abstraction. The evidence may be a narrative, a description, or enumerated examples—any information that helps to prove the truth of the paragraph's central idea. In the following passage, the student writer narrates a story to illustrate his point.

> A very sad story proves that when it comes to food, different nationalities have very different tastes. Several years ago, two French tourists, traveling with their poodle, visited Hong Kong. Despite being somewhat inconvenienced by the language barrier, they found the elegant restaurant that their guidebook had recommended. By pointing and struggling, they ordered a lavish meal. They also tried to indicate that their poodle was hungry too. The dog was led off to the kitchen by the waiter, and they began to enjoy a delicious dinner of many courses. The main course was brought in on a covered silver tray. And, you guessed it, when the dish was opened, there was their dear poodle—cooked to perfection. Needless to say, the couple flew directly home where they could enjoy such civilized delicacies as snails, tripe, and horsemeat.

Definition

A paragraph can define a key term so that readers can better understand the entire composition. You will find definition especially useful when a term is confusing or has no universally accepted meaning. Here a student writer tackles the difficult term *humanities.*

> Any course that focuses on the meaning, purpose, and values of human life is a humanities course. The humanities include primarily history, literature, philosophy, language, and anthropology. Unlike the sciences that search for facts about the concrete world, the humanities interpret life. The humanities ponder the mystery of human existence; the sciences try to remove it.

Analysis

A paragraph developed by analysis explores a subject by probing beneath its surface. The paragraph examines the units (parts, ingredients, characteristics, causes) that make up the larger whole. A machine, a person's behavior, an event, a book, a war, an idea—anything that can be divided into components can be analyzed. The student writer of the following paragraph analyzes the formula of the classic western by discussing its three components.

> A classic western of the *High Noon* school has three interlocking components. First, it has a hero of amazing purity and innocence. A

> thought inappropriate for Sunday school class has never flitted across his brain. The second necessary ingredient is an evil for the hero to battle and overcome. The evil can be represented by one person, several people, or a whole town. The third piece of the puzzle is a woman, who may or may not be a victim of the evil. Her primary purpose in the story is to beg the hero not to battle the evil and thus allow him to say, "A man's got to do what he's got to do."

Problem/Solution

Paragraphs developed with a problem/solution pattern usually begin with a statement of a problem and then move to a solution. With this structure, you can propose a solution or discuss one that already exists. Here a student writer starts with the conflict between academics and athletics and ends with a proposal for eliminating the conflict.

> In many American colleges football players fail academically. These campus heroes may perform poorly in the classroom, but no matter, just as long as they perform brilliantly on the playing field. Many people lament the unfairness, the immorality, the waste of such a system. But at most schools academic reforms have been unsuccessful and are probably impossible. The solution is to stop deceiving ourselves. These players don't always go to school to learn. Instead, they are gambling on becoming professionals. Therefore, schools should give them up as students and hire them as athletes. In that way, they could enroll in classes if they wanted to, but they would not have to. In a sense, the team would be owned as a financial and promotional investment. If we can divorce academics and athletics, we can eliminate the hypocrisy and probably improve both.

Question/Answer

A question/answer pattern generally begins with a question and moves to an answer. Clearly, this strategy for paragraphs cannot be used throughout a paper; it would become monotonous. On occasion, however, when you are supplying information, the pattern can be effective, as this paragraph illustrates.

> Why do we stand aside and let someone older or more important go through the door first? Because in early history it was sensible for the strongest man to leave the castle first, since there was always a possibility he would be met with arrows, armed opponents, or the

> rebellious peasantry waving pitchforks and scythes. Gradually, a certain honor descended upon this position. It was assumed that the most important person was also the strongest, and even if he wasn't, he could hardly deny it. Many a lord must have wished somebody else would take his place as the first man to ride out through the gates, but since honor was involved, his rank demanded that he accept it. Eventually it became, of course, purely honorific, as is the custom of offering the honor to somebody else, in the knowledge that he will refuse it. Even today men can still waste several minutes offering each other the honor of being the first to leave a meeting through a revolving door ("after you"; "no, no, after *you*"), and no doubt the same tedious politeness took place in the castle keep, with the difference that the first one out might have to fight for his life. (Michael Korda, "The Hidden Message of Manners," *Success!*)

draft 36a

Cause/Effect

Whenever your subject matter contains information that relates to a cause and an effect, you can begin with the cause and move to the effect or reverse that order. When the subject matter contains a sequence of causes and their effects, you trace the relationships, as the following paragraph does.

> Professional athletes are sometimes severely disadvantaged by trainers whose job it is to keep them in action. The more famous the athlete, the greater the risk that he or she may be subjected to extreme medical measures when injury strikes. The star baseball pitcher whose arm is sore because of a torn muscle or tissue damage may need sustained rest more than anything else. But his team is battling for a place in the World Series; so the trainer or team doctor, called upon to work his magic, reaches for a strong dose of butazolidine or other powerful pain suppressants. Presto, the pain disappears! The pitcher takes his place on the mound and does superbly. That could be the last game, however, in which he is able to throw a ball with full strength. The drugs didn't repair the torn muscle or cause the damaged tissue to heal. What they did was to mask the pain, enabling the pitcher to throw hard, further damaging the torn muscle. Little wonder that so many star athletes are cut down in their prime, more the victims of overzealous treatment of their injuries than of the injuries themselves. (Norman Cousins, "Pain Is Not the Ultimate Enemy," *Anatomy of an Illness*)

Combined Patterns

Many paragraphs involve more than one pattern. The next paragraph primarily describes the "insularity," or isolation, of the people in California's Central Valley. The writer structures the information around a topic sentence and illustrates her point with a short narrative. At the end she includes an ironic contrast of Modesto and Merced.

> U.S. 99 in fact passes through the richest and most intensely cultivated agricultural region in the world, a giant outdoor hothouse with a billion-dollar crop. It is when you remember the Valley's wealth that the monochromatic flatness of its towns takes on a curious meaning, suggests a habit of mind some would consider perverse. There is something in the Valley mind that reflects a real indifference to the stranger in his air-conditioned car, a failure to perceive even his presence, let alone his thoughts or wants. *(topic sentence)* An implacable insularity is the seal of these towns. I once met a woman in Dallas, a most charming and attractive woman accustomed to *(narrative)* the hospitality and social hypersensitivity of Texas, who told me that during the four war years her husband had been stationed in Modesto, she had never once been invited inside anyone's house. No one in Sacramento would find this story remarkable ("She probably had no relatives there," said someone to whom I told it), for the Valley towns understand one another, share a peculiar spirit. They think alike and they *(contrast)* look alike. I can tell Modesto from Merced, but I have visited there, gone to dances there; besides, there is over the main street of Modesto an arched sign which reads:
>
> WATER—WEALTH
> CONTENTMENT—HEALTH
>
> There is no such sign in Merced. (Joan Didion, "Notes from a Native Daughter," *Slouching Towards Bethlehem*)

draft 36a

(3) Order of details

A well-structured paragraph, no matter what its purpose, contains details that require a systematic arrangement. Usually, the best strategy is a progressive order—spatial, chronological, climactic, general to particular, or particular to general. An order, however, should not be so constrictive that it forces information into an artificial mold. Instead, the order should direct the flow of ideas, provide control over details, and help the reader understand how one point leads to the next.

Spatial Order

In paragraphs with a spatial order, the details of a specific space are arranged so that readers get a visual impression of it. The arrangement can follow the movement of the eye up, down, across, or around. In the following example, the writer uses spatial order to describe the photographic blowups behind the bar at Gipper's Lounge near Notre Dame University.

> This was in the Holiday Inn about three furlongs from the campus on the road to Niles, Michigan. Six days a week the Fighting Irish and other refreshments are available here in Gipper's Lounge, a shrine dedicated to the memory of George Gipp, the patron saint of football and eight-ball pool at Notre Dame. Walls of the lounge are covered with photographic blowups of football plays and players. Three dominate the decor: behind the bar stands the Gipper himself, half again larger than life, wearing the soft leather head-gear and canvas pants favored by all-America halfbacks around 1920; at his right is a huge head shot of Frank Leahy, the late, great coach; at Gipp's left, Harry Stuhldreher, Jim Crowley, Elmer Layden and Don Miller sit astride four plow horses. The riders wear football regalia with cowled woolen windbreakers, and each has a football tucked under an arm. (Red Smith, "Rum + Vodka + Irish = Fight," *The Red Smith Reader*)

Chronological Order

Chronological order presents a sequence in time, arranging events in the order in which they took place. In the following paragraph, for example, the student writer recounts the stages in a trend.

> I am one of those "reentry" students who figure prominently in education statistics these days. Many of us are women in their late forties and early fifties, divorced, with children ages fifteen to twenty-five. Most of us experienced the "women's movement" and had our "consciousness raised." We gained self-esteem, thought independent thoughts, and encouraged our children to overcome the male/female stereotyped roles. Then our husbands became successful and left us for younger women without raised consciousnesses. They also left us with children without raised consciousnesses. Worst of all, they left us with employers without raised consciousnesses, who expect women to work for less pay than men. And, so, we went back to school.

Climactic Order

One kind of climactic order moves from material of lesser importance to that of greater importance. Another kind describes small components and then moves to the whole, as does this paragraph on an ant colony.

> Still, there it is. A solitary ant, afield, cannot be considered to have much of anything on his mind; indeed, with only a few neurons strung together by fibers, he can't be imagined to have a mind at all, much less a thought. He is more like a ganglion on legs. Four ants together, or ten, encircling a dead moth on a path, begin to look more like an idea. They fumble and shove, gradually moving the food toward the Hill, but as though by blind chance. It is only when you watch the dense mass of thousands of ants, crowded together around the Hill, blackening the ground, that you begin to see the whole beast, and now you observe it thinking, planning, calculating. It is an intelligence, a kind of live computer, with crawling bits for its wits. (Lewis Thomas, "On Societies as Organisms," *Lives of a Cell*)

General-to-Particular Order

General-to-particular order begins with a general statement and moves to specific details. This order conforms to the traditional paragraph, in which the topic sentence, or general statement, appears first and is followed by support, or particular details. For example, the first sentence of the following paragraph is a very general statement. The next two sentences restrict the topic a bit, and the last sentence gives particular examples.

> Hollywood appears to be running out of new ideas. In the last few years, the number of remakes, sequels and readily-recognizable spin-offs of established winners has easily exceeded the tally of truly original concepts. Every blockbuster success inevitably spawns a host of shabby imitations. *The Exorcist* begat *Abby, The House of Exorcism, Beyond the Door* and *The Manitou; Jaws* begat *Tentacles, Tintorera the Tiger Shark, Marko—Jaws of Death, Barracuda* and *Orca; Star Wars* begat *Star Crash, Laserblast* and *Battlestar Galactica.* (Harry and Michael Medved, "The Biggest Ripoff in Hollywood History," *The Golden Turkey Awards*)

Particular-to-General Order

Particular-to-general order begins with specifics and moves to a general statement, like this passage from an essay on the evolution of behavior. This order is natural when the writer wishes to postpone the topic sentence until the end of the paragraph.

> A whale's flipper, a bat's wing and a man's arm are as different from one another in outward appearance as they are in the functions they serve. But the bones of these structures reveal an essential similarity of design. The zoologist concludes that whale, bat and man evolved from a common ancestor. Even if there were no other evidence, the comparison of the skeletons of these creatures would suffice to establish that conclusion. The similarity of skeletons shows that a basic structure may persist over geologic periods in spite of a wide divergence of function. (Konrad Z. Lorenz, "The Evolution of Behavior," *Scientific American*)

36b INTRODUCTORY PARAGRAPHS

The introduction to a paper makes a commitment to the audience by establishing the subject as well as the purpose and voice. In other words, the introduction tells the audience what to expect throughout the rest of the paper.

You can draft the introduction to a paper at any point during the writing process, depending on your preference. You may want to write it first, using it as a way to generate momentum. Or you may want to write it last, tailoring it to fit the body of the composition. Actually, you can compose the introduction any time an idea strikes. Regardless of when you write the introduction, however, remember that it is the first thing the audience reads, and it should make a favorable impression.

Often a technique for an introduction develops naturally out of the subject matter. If not, you can consult the techniques and examples that follow for ideas. Notice that some of the sample introductions are very brief and simple, whereas others are a bit more complex.

(1) Stating the thesis, or controlling idea

An introduction can state or imply the thesis that the paper will support. This technique makes the point of the paper clear to the audience from the start. In the introductory paragraph that follows, the final sentence is the thesis of the entire article.

> Some call it the Dawn of a New Computer Age. Others call it the Post-Industrial Revolution. Still others call it the Age of Knowledge. Whatever the name, computers have entered another period of change in which they will be transformed, not simply improved. During the next decade or so, computers will be constructed differently and will operate differently. Most importantly, they will begin to reason and apply logic. These developments will not merely produce a dramatic change in the role of computers worldwide; they will cause a dramatic effect on society as well. (Deb Highberger and Dan Edson, "Intelligent Computing Era Takes Off," *Computer Design*)

(2) Describing the problem

A logical introduction for a problem/solution paper is a description of the problem. The following introduction, for instance, describes the loss of the wilderness, the environmental problem that the paper addresses.

> They are best seen not on foot or from outer space but through the window of an airplane: the newly cleared lands, the expanding web of roads and settlements, the inexplicable plumes of smoke, and the shrinking enclaves of natural habitat. In a glance we are reminded that the once mighty wilderness has shriveled into timber leases and threatened nature reserves. We measure it in hectares and count the species it contains, knowing that each day something vital is slipping another notch down the ratchet, a million-year history is fading from sight. (Edward O. Wilson, "Million-Year Histories," *Wilderness*)

A statement of the problem often serves as the introduction to a literary paper. Here Bruce Morton begins with the problem: scholars agree that Fitzgerald was the model for a Hemingway character, but they do not explain why. The rest of the paper is Morton's solution—a theory that explains Hemingway's motive.

> Bruccoli, Lefcourt, and Lewis have all made credible cases for F. Scott Fitzgerald being the prototype for Francis Macomber in Hemingway's short story, "The Short Happy Life of Francis Macomber." Cumulatively, their cases based on similarities in name, character, and biography seem irrefutable. What, however, has not been heretofore established is why Hemingway chose to "go after" Fitzgerald in such a manner at that particular time. (Bruce Morton, "Hemingway's 'The Short Happy Life of Francis Macomber,'" *The Explicator*)

(3) Stating the conflict

A paper addressing a conflict often begins with a summary of both sides of the issue. In the following introduction, a student writer describes the conflicting attitudes of the farmer and the conservationist toward the coyote.

> The coyote, always a symbol of freedom and wildness on the prairie, has lately become the focus of a controversy. Ranchers are blaming the coyote for killing baby farm animals, especially lambs. These ranchers claim that the coyote is contributing greatly to their financial ruin. In the coyote's defense, members of wildlife conservation groups claim that ranchers' losses are not serious and that the ecological balance is in danger because of the poisons and traps ranchers are using to kill coyotes.

(4) Establishing a larger context

An introduction can put a subject into perspective by placing it within a larger context. In this introduction to a piece on aerial acrobatics, the student writer begins with the origins of flight and then narrows the subject to aerial acrobatics.

> When Orville Wright first flew in 1903, the problem was staying in the air; the first successful flight lasted only twelve minutes. To direct the plane right or left, he had to move his hips from side to side. Obviously, Wright's plane had little maneuverability. Early flights mainly moved straight ahead or wherever the winds blew the planes. Gradually, improved technology contributed speed, distance, and control. Finally, daredevils were inspired to try stunts. In 1913, a plane flew upside down. In 1914, a plane "looped the loop" one thousand times, did a tail spin, and flew inside a building. That was the beginning of aerial acrobatics.

(5) Sketching the background

A sketch of the subject's background can supply interesting information while focusing the audience's attention. Here the writer introduces a report on the safety of aspartame by briefly sketching the development of the sweetener.

It's one of the food industry's great success stories. A chemist working on an ulcer medicine during the 1960s casually licks the powder on his finger and finds it sweet. Nearly 20 years later the substance, aspartame, sweetens foods such as breakfast cereal, chewing gum, cocoa, instant iced tea, and whiskey sour mix. As Equal, it's a granulated sugar substitute; as NutraSweet, it sweetens Diet Coke, Diet Pepsi, and Diet Seven-Up. (William F. Allman, "Aspartame: Some Bitter with the Sweet," *Science 84*)

(6) Giving an overview

An overview tells the reader what the writer will cover and usually in what order. For example, this author leads readers to expect a paper with four major sections, outlined in the last sentence.

Freeze-dried, spray-dried, or vacuum-dried? Aluminum, plastic, or polypropylene? Wee-Pak, small pack, or six-pack? Every hiker has experienced the utter bewilderment of standing before an array of backpacking foods and trying to choose among them. The products all blend together, a jumble of colors, shapes, and sizes.

Not all commercially prepared lightweight foods are the same, however. There's a world of difference in price and content, for example, between "beef Stroganoff with noodles" and "Stroganoff sauce with beef and noodles," or between "chicken/vegetable stew" and "vegetable stew with chicken." One package will instruct you to add boiling water, while the contents of another will require some cooking. To select the items best suited to your palate, your nutritional needs, and your pocketbook, four things need to be considered: dehydrating methods, ingredient combinations, label information, and meal preparation. (Lois Snedden, "Dried and True: The Lowdown on Lightweight Foods," *Sierra*)

(7) Catching the audience by surprise

Writing meant to entertain or persuade often begins with an introduction that surprises or shocks the reader. Here Michael Arlen catches the reader's attention with his unconventional attitude in "Ode to Thanksgiving."

It is time, at last, to speak the truth about Thanksgiving, and the truth is this. Thanksgiving is really not such a terrific holiday. Consider

> the traditional symbols of the event: Dried cornhusks hanging on the door! Terrible wine! Cranberry jelly in little bowls of extremely doubtful provenance which everyone is required to handle with the greatest of care! Consider the participants, the merrymakers: men and women (also children) who have survived passably well throughout the years, mainly as a result of living at considerable distances from their dear parents and beloved siblings, who on this feast of feasts must apparently forgather (as if beckoned by an aberrant Fairy Godmother), usually by circuitous routes, through heavy traffic, at a common meeting place, where the very moods, distempers, and obtrusive personal habits that have kept them all happily apart since adulthood are then and there encouraged to slowly ferment beneath the cornhusks, and gradually rise with the aid of the terrible wine, and finally burst forth out of control under the stimulus of the cranberry jelly! (Michael Arlen, "Ode to Thanksgiving," *The Camera Age*)

(8) Identifying the source of interest

A writer's interest in a subject may spring from anywhere—from a book, an incident, a news report, a personal involvement, a casual conversation. Here, a student writer introduces a paper on "The Home Kitchen and a Happy Childhood" by summarizing a survey on carryout food.

> It looks as if people are giving up cooking, even when they eat at home. In a recent magazine survey of 5,000 people, 43 percent got carryout food primarily from fast-food restaurants, 28 percent from restaurants, and 21 percent from supermarkets. Only 8 percent of those surveyed did not purchase carryout food at all. These statistics suggest that the availability of pre-prepared food could make home kitchens obsolete. If so, childhood would be drastically altered, and for the worse.

(9) Presenting an antithesis

An argument often begins with the antithesis—the idea contrary to the thesis. This technique allows a writer to set up the opposition and then attack it. The following introduction, for example, presents a misconception about the microelectronics industry. The rest of the paper argues that the industry's traditionally clean reputation is deceiving.

When the microelectronics industry was launched about 20 years ago, it was hailed as a clean industry that would pose few health and safety problems to its workers, and even fewer to the surrounding environment. Most people assumed microelectronics would entail processes similar to those of conventional electronics. They envisioned large numbers of workers quietly soldering conductive wires onto printed circuit boards. And because the slightest bit of dust could not be permitted to contaminate the semiconductor chip, the major product of this industry, the companies' operations appeared even cleaner than anticipated. Workrooms were thoroughly ventilated with filtered air and workers wore white gowns, head coverings, and gloves. (Joseph LaDou, "The Not-So-Clean Business of Making Chips," *Technology Review*)

(10) Defining a term

You should avoid the time-worn beginning, "Webster's dictionary defines such and such as. . . ." However, you can begin by defining a key term, particularly one not fully defined in a dictionary. Here a student writer begins a composition with an original definition of *redneck.*

The name "redneck" was derived from the burned necks of farm workers. It later came to refer to poor whites in the South. Today, however, the redneck is not confined to any area of the United States or to any economic group. No, the redneck is a universal character—an insensitive and ignorant boob who is proud of the insensitivity and the ignorance.

(11) Relating an anecdote

An anecdote can lead an audience into a subject. For example, this writer uses an amusing story to introduce a discussion of the relationships between humans and animals.

A sidewalk interviewer asking people their beliefs about when human life begins, so the story goes, accosted a prosperous-looking man on his way out of a bank. "I'll tell you when life begins," the man answered. "It begins when the last kid is out of college and the dog has died."

A lot of people would argue with his second condition for life's onset, and some of them are scientists opening up a brand-new field:

human-animal relationships, specifically regarding pets, or companion animals as they came to be known in the immediately spawned jargon. This new field is of interest to me because by various avenues of accretion—most of them having to do with a collapse of willpower on my part—my house contains, at last count, 42 companion animals. This may seem excessive, but the findings of students of human-animal relationships have persuaded me that this immoderation will in fact redound to my continuing health, both physical and mental. (Jake Page, "Companion Animal Therapy," *Science 84*)

(12) Asking a question

Asking a question or two that the rest of the paper will either answer or address can stimulate the reader's curiosity. Here, a student introduces a research paper with a question that most people would like answered.

> At 10:15 P.M. on April 14, 1865, while watching a play at Ford's Theatre in Washington, D.C., Abraham Lincoln was hit by an assassin's bullet. The next morning, without regaining consciousness, Lincoln died. Almost two weeks later, his assassin, John Wilkes Booth, surrounded in a tobacco shed, was shot to death. Eight other people were implicated in the assassination, tried before a military commission, and found guilty. One of these was a woman named Mary Surratt. Ever since, a question has nagged at America's conscience. Was Mary Surratt guilty?

(13) Using a quotation

Sometimes a quotation is a natural way to introduce a paper. In fact, a statement by someone else may be the stimulant that first suggests a topic. A quotation by Samuel Johnson, for instance, led a student writer to a paper about overrated foods.

> According to Samuel Johnson, "A cucumber should be well sliced, and dressed with pepper and vinegar, and then thrown out, as good for nothing." I don't know why Johnson had such a dislike for the cucumber. Cucumber slices are delicious in salads and on sandwiches. However, there are other foods that do deserve scorn and yet for some reason are held in high esteem. Instead of cucumbers, I would like to see these foods "thrown out, as good for nothing."

(14) Using a combination of strategies

It is uncommon for writers to combine introductory techniques. In the following example, notice how the writer begins with a conflict of opinion about *The Duchess of Malfi,* then asks a question, and answers it with her thesis.

> Despite William Archer's famous diatribe against the unrealistic aspects of *The Duchess of Malfi,* the play continues to fascinate readers and playgoers alike—and to make them angry. Critical opinion on it has developed into an almost furious quarrel over the motivation of its characters, the validity of its action, the meaning of its key phrases, and the overall philosophy behind it. The Duchess herself has been described as everything from a medieval saint to a modern bitch, while the question of Ferdinand's incestuous longing has generated as much serious discussion as is usually reserved for the personality of an historical figure. Why all this controversy over what might seem like a typical Jacobean horror play? There appears to be something in Webster's dark world that lies too close to the bone for critical comfort, something as uncertain in our own minds as in the play itself. (Phoebe S. Spinrad, "Coping with Uncertainty in the *Duchess of Malfi,*" *Explorations in Renaissance Culture*)

36c CONCLUDING PARAGRAPHS

A paper should never end suddenly, as if the writer were interrupted and never returned to finish. Instead, the paper should come to some recognizable end, some logical stopping place. Papers sometimes end with the last frame in a time sequence, such as the last stage in a process or the final event in a narration. Other papers end with a concluding sentence or two. Still others end with fully developed paragraphs that contain summaries, recommendations, forecasts, or warnings. The length and formality of a conclusion depend on the length and formality of the whole composition as well as on the subject matter.

A conclusion is your last opportunity to influence the reader. Thus, you should make this segment as effective as possible. If you have trouble concluding a paper, look at the following strategies. One of them might be an appropriate choice.

(1) Returning to the thesis

Writers frequently begin with the thesis, or controlling idea, explore it in the body, and conclude by restating it. The major advantage of this structure is its clarity—a reader learns right away exactly what the point is, sees its development, and is reminded of it again in the conclusion. The following introduction and conclusion demonstrate this "envelope" pattern. Notice how the writer restates while avoiding boring repetition.

INTRODUCTION

From time to time, forgeries make the news: Hitler's diaries, George Washington's signature, a note by Shakespeare, an autobiography by Howard Hughes. Today, technology has made handwritten forgeries much easier to detect. But at the same time it has improved the techniques used by the forgers themselves.

• • •

CONCLUSION

Detecting forgeries has moved from fingerprint powder and magnifying glasses to sophisticated analyses by such devices as ultraviolet light, infrared spectroscopy, and electrostatic detection apparatus. However, in a continuing contest with criminologists, criminals also are applying the technology, especially with copying machines and computer-generated documents. The important question is whether or not the technology of detection can keep pace with the technology of making forgeries.

(2) Making a recommendation

A recommendation often serves as the conclusion for a paper comparing products, processes, or courses of action. The recommendation may be very specific or rather general. The following conclusion, for example, ends a paper that compares brands and types of sleeping bags. The recommendation here is general. It suggests a plan, rather than a particular kind of bag.

When looking at sleeping bags, draw on your personal knowledge of what has worked for you in the past. If you are inexperienced, you will need to talk with salespeople and get their recommendations. You may want to ask them what kind of sleeper they are and what kind of bag they use. Get a number of opinions before you make up your mind, and remember that every recommendation is a *guess.*

The way you sleep at home can be important. If you like to sleep in an all-pervading warmth, then you are a cold sleeper and should try to err on the warm side. If you like your skin slightly cool while you sleep, then you are a warm sleeper who can get away with a cooler and lighter bag. Sufficient warmth during sleep is a valuable commodity. So plan for the bad, and your experiences will always be good. (Mike Scherer, "Choosing Your Dream Sleeping Bag," *Sierra*)

(3) Summarizing major points

Many conclusions summarize the major points previously presented, thereby reminding readers of what they have read and reinforcing the significant ideas. This kind of conclusion works well for long, complex papers. Summaries are rarely called for in short papers, however, where readers have no trouble remembering what has been said. In the following conclusion, the writer condenses the content of her lengthy paper into three paragraphs. The phrase *in short* cues readers that a summary is about to begin.

summary of section on creation of wastes

In short, inventing and manufacturing new products has far outpaced our knowledge and ability to handle the detrimental wastes. Our scientists created new ideas that manufacturers forged into bright new products—and few had the foresight to wonder what would happen to all those ugly and poisonous wastes.

summary of section on water pollution

The brilliant technology that has produced astounding new products is now facing the problems of where to put the harmful wastes. And now all of civilization is paying the price—a growing crisis in the quality of our water.

summary of section on need for a solution

Indeed, all Americans are paying the price of living in an affluent and polluted society: a growing crisis in the quality of our water. We are finally beginning to realize that much more work, planning, and money are needed to help ensure the health of human beings, the beauty and purity of our waters, and the sanity of our nation. (Barbara Tufty, "Uses, Abuses, and Attitudes," *American Forests*)

(4) Ending with a quotation

A paper can end with a quotation—sometimes made by a famous person, sometimes by a person who has figured in the discussion. You can use this technique if the quotation is effective and appropriate, but you should not search through a book of quotations and use something only vaguely related to your point. In the following conclusion, the writer quotes a woman who is trying to save an old frontier town from destruction. In this quotation, Janaloo Hill explains what motivates her great effort to preserve a very small and remote place.

> Each year the greasewood takes root in the dry red earth and covers up just a little bit more of the rock foundations that were once Shakespeare, New Mexico. The graves of the old pioneers are threatened with obliteration now by new ditches, dug for the newly dead. Some folks in Lordsburg want the old ones moved out. "They don't know who they are, anyhow," the Hills say.
>
> But in this place 90 miles north of the Mexican border in a corner of New Mexico so remote that the only people likely to come through here are travelers en route to somewhere else, two women will continue to work toward the preservation of this lonely, historic domain.
>
> "All we're doin' here is getting out and doin' what needs to be done. A lot of people wouldn't use their own money on something like this," Janaloo admitted in a moment's acknowledgement of her rather novel existence before returning to her chores. "But you can only eat so much and drink so much . . . so why not do something that might last after you?" (Patricia Leigh Brown, "Shakespeare," *American Preservation*)

(5) Giving warning

A conclusion can serve as a vehicle to warn readers against some action or the lack of it. Here the writer warns readers against the dangers of categorizing people.

> Indeed, it is my experience that both men and women are fundamentally human, and that there is very little mystery about either sex, except the exasperating mysteriousness of human beings in general. And though for certain purposes it may still be necessary, as it undoubtedly was in the immediate past, for women to band themselves

together, as women, to secure recognition of their requirements as a sex, I am sure that the time has now come to insist more strongly on each woman's—and indeed each man's—requirements as an individual person. It used to be said that women had no *esprit de corps;* we have proved that we have—do not let us run into the opposite error of insisting that there is an aggressively feminist "point of view" about everything. To oppose one class perpetually to another—young against old, manual labour against brain-worker, rich against poor, woman against man—is to split the foundations of the State, and if the cleavage runs too deep, there remains no remedy but force and dictatorship. If you wish to preserve a free democracy, you must base it—not on classes and categories, for this will land you in the totalitarian State, where no one may act or think except as the member of a category. You must base it upon the individual Tom, Dick and Harry, on the individual Jack and Jill—in fact, upon you and me. (Dorothy Sayers, "Are Women Human?" *Unpopular Opinions*)

(6) Making a forecast

Often writers use the concluding paragraph or paragraphs to make a forecast. In this conclusion of a discussion of wine making, the writer predicts future improvements in the quality of wine.

Improvement in the quality of wine has been accelerating since the end of World War II, dramatically so within the past ten years. Today we truly live in a golden age of wine. One is tempted to wonder how wines can be improved. To answer with certainty is, of course, impossible, but it seems reasonable that new types of wines will be developed, that the quality of everyday wines will continue to improve, and that these everyday wines will become even better bargains than they are at present. Vintage wines will become even finer as the many dedicated enologists who make them find the best varieties of grapes for each microclimate and apply the appropriate sciences in their vineyards and wineries. (A. Dinsmoor Webb, "The Science of Making Wine," *American Scientist*)

(7) Calling for further study

Writers often use the conclusion to call for additional work or investigation. In this essay on the neglect of education, the student concludes by proposing a study to eliminate the problem.

The cries of alarm throughout the state about the weaknesses in the educational system should be heeded. Although the problems have resulted from many years of neglect and disinterest, we must very quickly figure out specific ways to raise educational standards. An intensive study to find remedies is essential before any improvement can occur.

(8) Showing applications

A paper that details an investigation often concludes with suggestions for possible applications of the study's findings. This report on student alcohol abuse, for instance, concludes with some practical ideas for student programs.

What seems to be needed is an early identification process that will focus on the behavioral consequences of drinking. For example, in this sample the negative consequences were in direct proportion to the severity of the drinking. By identifying problem drinkers early, based on their behavior, student personnel staff may be able to provide resources and programs for these students.

The identification process should focus on the behavioral manifestations of drinking rather than on drinking itself, because most students deny that they have a drinking problem. Programs designed for alcohol abuse should focus on students who: (a) are caught abusing alcohol; (b) while under the influence of alcohol, cause physical damage in the community or on the campus; (c) are identified as problem drinkers (e.g. through peer evaluation and referral); and (d) volunteer to participate. These programs should include a carefully designed network of components such as testing and evaluation, alcohol awareness groups, Alcoholics Anonymous meetings, and personal counseling. (T. A. Seay and Terrence D. Beck, "Alcoholism Among College Students," *Journal of College Student Personnel*)

The Computer Connection

Many people feel they must draft compositions in some special way; they can write only on a yellow legal pad, in a Big Chief tablet, with a newly sharpened Faber pencil, at a desk, on a couch. Most habits, however, are simply the result of familiarity. If you have never tried drafting on a computer, experiment with the technique. A little practice may convince you that the computer is a very comfortable way to write. Knowing that you can easily make changes lessens tension and helps keep you in an experimental frame of mind.

Suggestions for Drafting Paragraphs

- Type a topic sentence and see whether the details and explanations follow naturally. Later, if necessary, you can delete, move, or change the topic sentence; but by writing it first, you may gain momentum.
- Type each paragraph straight through so that you do not lose your train of thought. If you feel compelled to stop often to correct typographical or grammatical errors, darken your screen or avoid looking at the monitor. You can correct errors during revision.
- Print out your paragraphs frequently. If you lose momentum, you can sometimes regain it by reading a printed version of your work.
- Try printing each paragraph on a separate page. Then when you revise the composition, you can read several different arrangements to determine which sounds best.
- With a computer, you can produce paragraphs out of sequence. For example, you might compose the conclusion first, the introduction last, and the body paragraphs in any order. Then you can easily move the paragraphs around until you decide on the best arrangement.
- Do not be deceived by appearances. Because paragraphs look neat and professional on the computer screen or on a printout, writers sometimes mistake an early draft for a final version. Remember that paragraphs require frequent revision and that ideas often need clarification and rearrangement.

CHAPTER

37

REVISION

Revision is an integral part of the writing process. Too often, inexperienced writers neglect this task altogether or confuse it with proofreading for spelling and typographical errors. It is only through revising, however, that ragged drafts are transformed into a finished product.

Just for the moment, think of writing as analogous to building a house. The structure takes shape piece by piece. It begins with a plan; moves through a number of messy stages while the foundation, walls, and roof go up; and finally emerges with plaster, paint, plumbing, and doors that do not squeak. Once the process is complete, no one sees the concrete that was repoured, the windows that were rehung, or the tile that went back to the factory. A writer is at once an architect, contractor, plumber, electrician, brick mason, paperhanger, and all the other laborers. The reader is the buyer; all he or she has to do is admire the finished construction. You do not want the buyer to say, What a lot of trouble this was, but rather, What a good job this is.

Some writers correct and revise their prose as they write. Others write very fast and revise the whole work afterward. Still others revise and correct obvious problems while drafting a paper and postpone careful examination until a draft is complete. Use whatever method suits you. But if possible, take a break before attempting to revise a draft you have just completed. You should find some mental or physical activity to divert your attention from the paper.

Or if time allows, put the work aside for a day or several days. These tactics help you develop objectivity so that you can return to the manuscript as a reader rather than as the writer. Only then can you see weaknesses that you did not suspect in the composition stage. Other good editing schemes are reading your draft aloud and letting others read and critique your work. Also if possible, you should type your drafts. No matter how poor the typing, you will be able to edit a typed draft much more carefully than a handwritten draft.

Because of their speed and efficiency, computers and word processors greatly facilitate revision. Editing with a word processing program has obvious advantages over manual editing. Letters, words, lines, and paragraphs can be deleted at the punch of a button. Material can be inserted anywhere and moved effortlessly from place to place. A writer with a word processor can tinker with the text and compose in stages, letting the computer do the cutting and pasting typical in manual editing.

In addition, software programs can help locate misspellings, incorrect punctuation, and inappropriate usage. Some programs even provide statistical information about repetition of words and phrases, sentence length, passives, nominalizations, and so on. The danger, of course, is that writers may want to rely entirely on the machine to improve their weaknesses. But the machine can only offer suggestions. It is the writer who must make the decisions.

Whether your draft is handwritten, typed on a conventional typewriter, or produced on a computer, the time necessary for revising a draft depends on the individual. Nevertheless, you should devote as much effort to the revision process as time will allow. Effective revision involves several readings; few writers can concentrate on all types of problems at the same time. A methodical procedure is first to revise content, then to evaluate coherence, next to improve style, and then to check for grammatical and mechanical errors. Finally, you must proofread for typographical errors. In general, the following sections follow this procedure, guiding you through revision from larger to smaller units.

37a UNITY

In a unified paper, both the whole and each part work together to develop a single idea. The following outline and paragraph illustrate how the details of a whole composition and one of its paragraphs are related—the outline covering a number of choices faced by a novice cyclist, the paragraph covering one of the choices. No details on either level stray from the point.

THESIS: People just getting into cycling face a bewildering array of choices.

- I. Type of bike
  - A. Touring bikes
  - B. Racing bikes
- II. Number of gears
- III. Tires
  - A. Tubulars
  - B. Clinchers
- IV. Optional equipment
  - A. Helmet
  - B. Gloves
  - C. Shorts ←
  - D. Shoes

Should you buy cycling shorts? Salespeople will tell you that you certainly cannot do without the skin-tight, knee-length, Italian-style shorts. They will also point out that ordinary shorts are totally unsuitable--irritating seams, the wrong cut and fabric. Cycling shorts have no center seam to chafe the legs, and some even come lined with chamois to eliminate friction. But is all this necessary for anyone but a professional? For the ordinary rider these shorts would be like a Mets uniform for playing sandlot baseball, full pads for touch football, and spiked track shoes for a 20-minute jog. If you are not planning to enter the World Cycling Championships, you can easily forego the shorts, that is, unless your main goal is to look as though you are in training for the Championships.

When checking for unity, begin with the overall structure and then look at each separate paragraph. Unless your paper is unified around a clear thesis, there is little point in concentrating on the details that make up the paragraphs.

(1) Is the thesis clear?

Your paper should have a thesis either clearly stated or clearly implied. You should be able to find the stated thesis or formulate one from your material. In the event you cannot discover a thesis, you may have chosen a subject that doesn't interest you or that you don't know enough about. If so, return to Chapter 34, "The Search for Ideas," and begin again. This process is not as bad as it sounds. It is sometimes easier to change your subject completely than to struggle with one that is not productive.

(2) Does everything in the paper relate directly to the thesis?

One of the best ways to check the overall structure is to construct an outline from your draft or to reexamine an already existing outline. This technique can reveal places where a paper has diverged from its thesis. If you find material that is off the subject, you should remove it. You may be reluctant to delete material that you have labored to collect and struggled to write. Nevertheless, if any part of the draft might distract the reader from the thesis or is obviously irrelevant to your subject, get rid of it. Notice how the student writer of the composition in progress (Chapter 38) abandons material as the paper progresses from draft to draft.

(3) Does each paragraph have unity?

The parts of a unified paragraph should develop a single idea. A paragraph with a topic sentence that expresses the central idea is less likely to contain extraneous details than a paragraph without a stated topic sentence.

When you revise your paper on the paragraph level, you should first locate each paragraph's topic sentence or determine the central idea or purpose. Then you should delete any material that is unimportant or irrelevant.

The following paragraph begins with a clear topic sentence but shifts to another subject in the underlined sentences.

Rain forests, such as those in South America and Africa, contain more plant and animal species than does any other area in the world. For example, more bird species have been identified in a wildlife preserve in Peru than in the entire United States. If the habitat is not protected, the bird species will eventually vanish. At least 700 different tree species have been found in one forest in Borneo. That same number exists in the whole of North America. One river in Brazil contains more species of fish than all the rivers of the United States together. If nothing is done to prevent these rain forests from being cleared, untold numbers of plants and animal species will certainly become extinct.

revise 37b

The subject is clearly the abundance of species in rain forests; but in the third and last sentences, the writer strays to the subject of extinction. Fortunately, deletion of the two sentences on extinction can solve the problem without destroying the paragraph. Sometimes, however, revision requires a restructuring of the topic sentence, further research, or deletion of the entire paragraph.

37b DEVELOPMENT

Development refers to the way a whole composition or a single paragraph elaborates or builds on a thesis or topic. If an idea is developed, it is supported by a sufficient number of details, examples, illustrations, or reasons. When you revise a paper, you should check for the presence of these specifics. The length of a composition or paragraph is not always a good indication. A fairly long unit that contains nothing but general statements may still be lacking. Satisfactory development demands specifics but only logical inclusions. Do not throw in irrelevant details that distort your logic.

(1) Does the paper contain enough information to develop the thesis?

Check your introduction. Does it claim that you will discuss more than your paper delivers? If you find the information in the body insufficiently developed, you can produce more ideas with tactics such as brainstorming, clustering, and asking questions. Or you can gather additional material through research—reading, interviewing, or observing.

(2) Is each paragraph fully developed?

When you check each body paragraph, look for the topic sentence, or, if the topic sentence is not stated, think of what it would be. Then ask yourself if your reader would accept or understand the statement. If there is the least chance the reader would not, you probably should add supporting or explanatory information. A paragraph like the following lacks full development.

> "The Star-Spangled Banner," though very hard to sing, should not be replaced. Its complexity somehow makes it challenging; singers must take it seriously. Surely, every patriotic American would sorely miss the roll of the drum and the words "O'er the land of the FREE and the HOME of the BRAVE."

The cure for an underdeveloped paragraph is usually to add more details. The student who wrote the preceding paragraph improved it by explaining why the music is hard to sing and why it should not be replaced by another song.

> "The Star-Spangled Banner," through very hard to sing, should not be replaced. Who cares if singers strain their vocal chords over high notes, low notes, and extreme tonal combinations? Its complexity somehow makes it challenging; singers must take it seriously. To do away with this tradition would be like moving Washington, D.C., to Nebraska, eating spaghetti on Thanksgiving, or changing the N.Y. Mets to a soccer team. The song is history. We can share with Francis Scott Key the dramatic moment when, after the bombardment of Fort McHenry, the flag still flew. Surely every patriotic American would sorely miss the roll of the drum and the words "O'er the land of the FREE and the HOME of the BRAVE."

Brevity is not necessarily a sign that a paragraph is underdeveloped; writers sometimes include a short paragraph to add variety to prose or to emphasize material. Usually, however, material that develops one idea should be combined in one paragraph. For example, the following paragraphs are unjustifiably short. They all develop the same idea that Nancy Drew has changed since the writer s childhood reading. Combining the material will create one well-developed paragraph.

> Nancy Drew has changed a great deal since the early books. No longer is she poking around in attics hunting for clues. In current books, she taps into electronic systems, reads videotaped ransom notes, and uses cellular phones and computers.
>
> Old radio shows are now rock bands; jewel thieves are now traitors selling secrets to foreign countries. Nancy now drives a blue Mustang, wears designer jeans, and uses credit cards. She even gets involved in romances.
>
> One thing, however, has remained the same: she always solves the mystery.

37c COHERENCE

Coherence in prose refers to a smooth and logical arrangement of the parts. Sometimes coherence is spontaneous, with the flow of ideas creating a natural sequence. More often, however, this spontaneity does not occur, and you must work to interlock the pieces smoothly and logically. The task requires the effective arrangement of the paragraphs as well as adequate connection between sentences and paragraphs. Checking your draft against the following questions will help you find weaknesses and achieve coherence.

(1) Is the overall organization effective?

Even though an initial plan for organization seems sound, it may not produce a well-arranged composition, and you may have to reorganize the paragraphs. You should probably begin by taking a critical look at the overall composition. Does the body of the paper fulfill the promise of the introduction? For example, if the introduction suggests that the paper will illustrate the genre of the paperback romance with a single novel, the body should not instead classify the characters. Or if the introduction promises to analyze the novel s components, the body should not concentrate primarily on plot to the exclusion of characters, setting, and so forth.

After you look at your overall scheme, you may want to rearrange paragraphs to achieve the most logical or effective order of information. This procedure is sometimes called cutting and pasting and, in fact, is frequently accomplished in just this way. You can cut your paper into paragraphs and glue or tape them on paper in the desired order. Or you can write each paragraph on a separate page and then work out the best arrangement. And of course, if you use a computer, you can move whole blocks of the draft around with ease. If you have trouble deciding on the best order, you might try writing alternative outlines to see which seems most effective.

In the sample first draft that follows, a student summarizes information about human memory. Put together from notes taken in psychology classes and material in a psychology textbook, the draft is a hodgepodge of facts not yet arranged coherently.

DRAFT 1: NO COHERENCE

One of the most amazing abilities of the human mind is memory. In about three pounds of brain, we store all kinds of information, such as multiplication tables, the sound of a car engine, the smell of a steak cooking, and the knowledge of how to ride a bicycle.

In spite of recent discoveries and theories, no one really knows how memory works. Many researchers believe that memory is the new frontier in science. Some researchers believe that to understand memory is to understand human beings.

Short-term memory usually lasts 15 to 20 seconds and allows us to look up a telephone number and remember it long enough to dial it.

information separated from related information

Many scientists are now working on the physical nature of memory, the biochemical processes that occur in the brain when information is stored.

material to be developed or deleted

One theory about long-term memory is that our memories change as we add information. Once we make some change in a memory, the original is lost. This process is probably what happens when we revise a childhood memory with what adults tell us about the experience. We create a memory of a memory.

Two kinds of long-term memory are "declarative" and "procedural." Declarative memory involves facts, such as names, dates, places, and statistics. Procedural memory involves activities, such as doing a dance step, shooting a basketball, and tying shoes.

Our moods seem to influence what we remember. If we learn something while in a sad mood, we will remember more of the information when we are sad.

material to be developed or deleted

Some experts believe that memory is closely tied to language. We cannot remember what we cannot talk about. We cannot remember a coat we had before we knew the word coat. Other experts say "nonsense." Very small babies can remember faces, voices, movements, colors, and sounds. One explanation is that babies have procedural memory but not declarative memory. Some researchers think that declarative memory does not develop until about the age of two.

revise 37c

Our ability for long-term memory seems unlimited. The memories stored in long-term memory seem permanent.

misplaced material

Short-term memory cannot hold a great deal of information. If we hear someone list numbers or words, we very quickly lose track and can remember only a few in the right order.

misplaced material

The student writer produced a second draft of the paper by cutting and pasting the first draft, deleting some material, and rearranging the rest. The result suggests an organization: comparison and contrast of short-term and long-term memory.

DRAFT 2: OVERALL COHERENCE IMPROVED BY DELETING AND REARRANGING PARAGRAPHS

One of the most amazing abilities of the human mind is memory. In about three pounds of brain, we store all kinds of information, such as multiplication tables, the sound of a car engine, the smell of a steak cooking, and the knowledge of how to ride a bicycle.

Short-term memory usually lasts 15 to 20 seconds and allows us to look up a telephone number and remember it long enough to dial it.

material on short-term memory brought together

Short-term memory cannot hold a great deal of information. If we hear someone list numbers or words, we very quickly lose track and can remember only a few in the right order.

Our ability for long-term memory seems unlimited. The memories stored in long-term memory seem permanent.

One theory about long-term memory is that our memories change as we add information. Once we make some change in a memory, the original is lost. The process is probably what happens when we revise a childhood memory with what adults tell us about the experience. We create a memory of a memory.

Two kinds of long-term memory are "declarative" and "procedural." Declarative memory involves facts, such as names, dates, places, and statistics. Procedural memory involves activities, such as doing a dance step, shooting a basketball, and tying shoes.

material on long-term memory brought together in logical arrangement

Some experts believe that memory is closely tied to language. We cannot remember what we cannot talk about. You cannot remember a coat you had before you had the word coat. Other experts say "nonsense." Very small babies remember faces, voices, movements, colors, and sounds. One explanation is that babies have procedural memory but not declarative memory. Some researchers think that declarative memory does not develop until about the age of two.

In spite of recent discoveries and theories, no one really knows how memory works. Many researchers believe that memory is the new frontier in science. Some researchers believe that to understand memory is to understand human beings.

second paragraph of first draft moved to end

(2) Is the organization within paragraphs effective?

Once you are satisfied with the overall scheme and the ordering of the major pieces of a paper, you can turn your attention to the individual paragraphs. You can treat each piece as a mini-composition and determine whether its pattern is an effective vehicle for the information and purpose. If you are not satisfied with the patterns, you might look over the methods suggested for organizing paragraphs in Chapter 36, Paragraphs.

(3) Is there adequate connection between sentences and paragraphs?

After you have revised the arrangement of the sections, you can provide connectors, or links, to establish internal coherence. For example, you can link ideas and prevent unnecessary repetition by using pronouns such as *this, these, some, most, others, each, both, either, who,* and *which.* You can show the relationship between ideas with coordinating conjunctions: *and, but, or for, nor, so,* and *yet.* You can use subordinating conjuctions, such as *although, because, if, when,* and *where.* (Section 7c.1 lists the subordinate conjunctions and their appropriate uses.)

Another effective way to clarify the connections between ideas is to use transitional expressions such as *therefore, for example, in fact,* and *finally.* The following chart lists the common transitional expressions and their uses.

Transitional Expressions

To Express	*You Can Use*
Contrast	however, on the other hand, on the contrary, in contrast, still, nevertheless, regardless, instead
Cause/effect	therefore, thus, consequently, for this reason, as a result, otherwise, thus, then, accordingly
Time sequence	first, second, third, next, last, finally, afterward, now, then, again, soon, formerly, eventually, subsequently
Restatement	in other words, in short, in summary, that is, again

Emphasis	in fact, indeed, of course, certainly, after all, surely, actually
Addition	furthermore, moreover, likewise, also, in addition, besides
Summary	in conclusion, on the whole, all in all, in summary
Example	for example, for instance, specifically

By comparing the two paragraphs that follow, you can see how the addition of links improves coherence.

WITHOUT LINKS

My father likes to point out that he got his first car at age twenty. I got a car at age fifteen. I like to point out that his needs were very different from mine. Towns used to be organized around neighborhoods. My teen-aged father was within walking distance of almost every place he wanted to go. His high school was only four blocks from his house. After school, he could walk ten minutes to the local hamburger joint. He could find most of his friends there. To see a movie, he could walk a few blocks to pick up his best friend. They could be at the movie within a half-hour.

I need a car to get almost anywhere I want to go. My high school is seven miles from my house. Local hamburger joints in my hometown have been replaced by fast-food establishments. Fast-food establishments are usually located on frontage roads alongside superhighways. Movies are now in suburban malls. My friends and I must arrange a meeting place. We usually must drive at least a half-hour to get there.

The next time my father brings up the subject of cars, I am going to offer him a deal. I will give up my car. He will transport me. I will even pay for the gas. I suspect he and I will be very grateful for my car.

WITH LINKS

My father likes to point out that he got his first car at age twenty, yet I got a car at age fifteen. I like to point out his needs were very different from mine. Because towns used to be organized around neighborhoods, my teen-aged father was within walking distance of almost every place he wanted to go. For example, his high school was only four blocks from his house. After school, he could walk ten minutes to the local hamburger joint, where he could find most of his friends. If he wanted to see a movie, he could walk a few blocks, pick up his best friend, and be at the movie within a half-hour.

On the other hand, I need a car to get almost anywhere I want to go. My high school is seven miles from my house. Local hamburger joints in my hometown have been replaced by fast-food establishments, which are usually located on frontage roads alongside superhighways. Furthermore, movies are now in suburban malls. Consequently, my friends and I must arrange a meeting place and usually drive at least a half-hour to get there.

The next time my father brings up this subject, I am going to offer him a deal. I will give up my car if he will transport me. In fact, I will even pay for the gas. I suspect we both will be very grateful for my car.

In addition to eliminating repetition, the demonstrative pronouns (*this, these, that, those*) link repeated words and ideas and indicate phrases that summarize.

The author uses historical records to describe medieval people. She quotes these sources in the original Latin or French without offering a translation either in the text or in the notes at the end of the book. That material is consequently meaningless to readers with no knowledge of foreign languages.

Members of a single species of animals often engage in ritualized fights. This behavior has been observed in animals as diverse as wolves, iguanas, fish, snakes, and sheep. The fights serve to spread members of a species over a large territory and allow the stronger animals to mate. In general, these ritualized fights have developed to improve the quality of a species, not to reduce numbers.

If you need more information on linking words and phrases, refer to the following chart.

Linking Words and Phrases

For Information On	*Consult*
Demonstrative pronouns	2b
Relative pronouns	2c
Indefinite pronouns	2e
Conjunctions	6b, 7c(1)

In addition to words and phrases, a whole sentence can link what has gone before to what follows.

Surimi, an imitation crab product, was first developed by the Japanese. Made of fish, it is extruded into a tube shape and topped with red food coloring. The Japanese are now exporting vast quantities of surimi to the West. Americans in the fishing industry, however, are countering this market with their own tactics. They are now exporting real crabmeat to Japan. In fact, about 50 percent of U.S. crabmeat is purchased by the Japanese.

To see how internal coherence works, consider the third draft of the student paper on memory. Although the parts of the second draft were logically arranged, they did not seem to cohere. In the following version, notice how the addition of the underlined links improves coherence, tightens structure, and allows some of the paragraphs to be combined.

DRAFT 3: INTERNAL COHERENCE IMPROVED BY LINKS

One of the most amazing abilities of the human mind is memory. In about three pounds of brain, we store all kinds of information, such as multiplication tables, the sound of a car engine, the smell of a steak cooking, and the knowledge of how to ride a bicycle.

But memory involves more than just this long-term storage. Short-term memory usually lasts 15 to 20 seconds and allows us to look up a telephone number and remember it long enough to dial it. This type of memory cannot hold a great deal of information. For example, if we hear someone list numbers or words, we very quickly lose track and can remember only a few in the right order.

On the other hand, our ability for long-term memory seems unlimited, and the information stored there permanent. The permanence, however, may not be real. According to one theory, our memories change as we add information; and once we make some change in a memory, the original is lost. This process is probably what happens when we revise a childhood memory with what adults tell us about the experience. Thus, we create a memory of a memory.

Two kinds of long-term memory are "declarative" and "procedural." The first involves facts, such as names, dates, statistics. The second involves skills, such as doing a dance step, shooting a basketball, typing shoes.

This fact/skill division is at the center of a disagreement about language and memory. Some experts believe that we cannot remember what we cannot talk about. We cannot, for instance, remember a coat we had before we had the word coat. Other experts say this idea is nonsense because very small babies remember faces, voices, movements, colors, and sounds. A possible explanation for this puzzle is that babies have procedural memory but not declarative memory, which some researchers think does not develop until about the age of two.

In spite of recent discoveries and theories, no one really knows how memory works. Nevertheless, many researchers believe that memory is the new frontier in science. In fact, some believe that to understand memory is to understand human beings.

37d STYLE

To improve the style of a composition, you should look carefully at your word choice. Not only should the words you choose convey your meaning precisely, but also they should be appropriate to your purpose and audience. The trouble-shooting chart below will help you locate and revise problems with vocabulary.

Trouble-Shooting Chart for Word Choice

If You Have a Problem With	*Consult Material On*	*Section(s)*
identifying audience	audience analysis	35b
level of formality	formal and informal words	32a
	voice	35c
precise meaning	denotation and connotation	32b(1)
	general and specific words	32b(2)
	abstract and concrete words	32b(3)
dull, trite vocabulary	clich s and euphemisms	32c
bureaucratic language	gobbledygook	32d(1)
	surplus words	32d(2)
	dense noun phrases	32d(3)
discriminatory language	sexist pronoun use	13c, 13d, 32e
	stereotyping	32e

The Computer Connection

For finding synonyms, many people depend on a computer thesaurus. In fact, most word-processing programs now contain a thesaurus as a standard component. This added feature allows you to change a word that doesn t have quite the right meaning or the right sound.

Suggestions for Using a Computer Thesaurus

- If a thesaurus is not included in your word-processing program, you can add one with little cost or trouble.
- Typically, you place the cursor on the word you want to replace, and possible alternatives will appear on the screen.
- If a synonym is unfamiliar, you can call up its definition, provided that a thesaurus dictionary has been loaded. Not having a dictionary limits the value of a thesaurus; if a word is new to you, you cannot be sure it is the right one to use.
- The choice of vocabulary in a composition is yours, and the computer thesaurus will not always contain enough information to help you. Computer thesauruses are less extensive than regular dictionaries and do not always provide an acceptable substitution. For example, one computer thesaurus suggests as a synonym for the verbal *delegating,* the noun *diplomat.* To find a synonym with the right meaning, you often must use a regular thesaurus or dictionary.

In addition to word choice, good style depends on smooth, easy-flowing sentences. If parts of your composition seem choppy, labored, or awkward, the sentence structure may need revision. The following trouble-shooting chart will help you identify problem structures and improve them.

Trouble-Shooting Chart for Sentence Structure

If You Have a Problem With	*Consult Material On*	*Section(s)*
monotonous or choppy prose	varying sentence lengths, structures, or beginnings	33a
flat or unemphatic prose	dramatic structures figures of speech	33b 33d

cluttered or weak sentences	empty verbs and nominalizations	33c(1)
	weak passives	33c(2)
	unnecessary clauses	33c(3)
	excessive verb forms	33c(4)
	split subjects and verbs	33c(5)
awkward prose	sound and rhythm	33e

The Computer Connection

As William Zinsser states, the word processor is science s gift to the tinkerers and the refiners and the neatness freaks. And indeed, revision with a word-processing program has obvious advantages over the manual process. You can delete letters, words, lines, and paragraphs at the touch of a key. You can insert material and move it effortlessly from place to place without making a mess of the manuscript. You can make and unmake changes without retyping the entire page or composition.

Suggestions for Revising

- Take advantage of the ease with which you can tighten prose by pruning unnecessary words and phrases. As author Garrison Keillor notes: Word processors can be responsible for producing a great deal of flabby writing. The words come out . . . like toothpaste sometimes. There s no shortage of sheer wordage in America; more sentences are not what this country needs. The computer that helps produce flabby prose, however, can also help eliminate it.
- Create a wastebasket file to save material deleted from the text during revision. You ll feel more comfortable about making radical cuts if you know you can easily retrieve the material.
- Use a split-screen feature for calling up another file. You might, for example, display your outline on the top half of a horizontal split screen while revising a draft displayed on the bottom half. Or you might bring up an early draft of the paper on the same screen as the current version in order to compare the two.
- Print a hard copy of the text. Then revise it to correct any weaknesses in coherence, logic, or sentence structure. You can spot some weaknesses more easily on paper than you can on a screen.
- Remember that revising is not a step that occurs after you have composed your text. Experimentation should take place throughout the composing process.

37e GRAMMAR, PUNCTUATION, AND MECHANICS

Even when readers can figure out your meaning, errors in grammar, punctuation, and mechanics are distracting and undercut the merit of your composition. You will probably not locate these errors with a superficial reading. In fact, editing is very different from reading. When you read, your eyes jump from phrase to phrase; but when you edit, you must use some sort of scheme to make yourself focus on every word and structure. It is possible to slow down and control your eyes if you read the manuscript aloud or read it out of sequence, by page or by paragraph. A good plan for correcting errors in a composition is to check first for structural errors, then move to individual words, and finally look at punctuation and mechanics.

(1) Structural errors

Prose is made up to structures—phrases and clauses that are combined to express ideas. Structural errors result if the phrases and clauses are not put together correctly. To help identify and correct possible structural errors in your prose, refer to the following chart.

Trouble-Shooting Chart for Structural Errors

If You Have Difficulty Answering the Question	*Consult the Material in*
Does every sentence have at least one independent clause?	Chapter 7, Clauses and Sentences Chapter 8, Sentence Fragments
In compound sentences, are independent clauses correctly connected?	Chapter 9, Comma Splices and Fused Sentences Chapter 21, Commas, 21a Chapter 22, Semicolons Chapter 23, Colons, 23c
Do the pronouns have clear antecedents?	Chapter 12, Pronoun Reference
Do any adjective or adverb modifiers have nothing to modify or do they seem to modify the wrong element?	Chapter 16, Dangling and Misplaced Modifiers
Are any constructions split apart by an interrupter that causes awkwardness or a lack of clarity?	Chapter 18, Split Constructions

Are any constructions incomplete because of an omission?	Chapter 19, Incomplete Constructions
Are the items in sequences parallel?	Chapter 20, Parallelism

(2) Errors in the forms of words

Nouns, pronouns, adjectives, adverbs, and verbs have a variety of forms that change or add meaning. After you have read a manuscript to check the sentence construction, you should read it again to inspect the forms of the individual words. This stage of the revising process requires you to shift your attention back and forth from individual words to the larger structures in which they fit. For example, to decide on the form of a pronoun, you must determine the meaning you need and the correct case form required by the structure. Try not to hurry this stage of revising. If you go methodically through the following chart, you will be less likely to overlook errors.

Trouble-Shooting Chart for Errors in the Forms of Words

If You Have Difficulty Answering the Question	*Consult the Material In*
Are all plural noun forms correct?	Chapter 1, Nouns
Are there any nouns or pronouns (the personal pronouns or *who/whom*) with the wrong case?	Chapter 1, Nouns Chapter 2, Pronouns Chapter 14, Case of Nouns and Pronouns Chapter 26, Apostrophes, 26a
Are the comparative and superlative forms of adjectives and adverbs standard?	Chapter 3, Adjectives and Adverbs Chapter 15, Nonstandard Adjective and Adverb Forms
Is each verb in the correct form?	Chapter 11, Nonstandard Verb Forms
Is each verb in the appropriate tense?	Chapter 4, Verbals and Verbal Phrases
Do the verbs agree with their subjects in number?	Chapter 10, Subject-Verb Agreement

Do the pronouns agree with their antecedents in number?	Chapter 13, Pronoun-Antecedent Agreement
Are there unnecessary shifts from one form to another?	Chapter 17, Shifts

(3) Errors in punctuation marks and mechanics

It is not usually productive to edit for punctuation and mechanical errors until fairly late in the writing process. Structures most likely will change from draft to draft, and sentences will be deleted during revision. There is no point in correcting punctuation and mechanics until you have decided definitely on content and structure. When you reach this stage, you can survey the conventions in Chapters 21 through 31 or refer to the following chart.

Trouble-Shooting Chart for Errors in Punctuation and Mechanics

If You Have Difficulty Answering the Question	*Consult the Material in*
Are commas omitted anywhere? before a coordinate conjunction between independent clauses? after introductory elements? around nonrestrictive elements? in dates or addresses?	Chapter 21, Commas, 21a—21i
Are commas placed where they should not be?	Chapter 21, Commas, 21j
Should any commas be changed to semicolons?	Chapter 22, Semicolons, 22a—22e
Are the colons, dashes, and parentheses used correctly?	Chapter 23, Colons Chapter 24, Dashes, Parentheses, and Brackets
Are any apostrophes omitted or positioned incorrectly?	Chapter 26, Apostrophes
Are quotation marks placed correctly in relation to the other marks?	Chapter 27, Quotation Marks and Ellipsis Marks, 27b
Are hyphens used correctly in compounds?	Chapter 29, Hyphens and Slashes, 29a—29b
Are the right words capitalized?	Chapter 31, Capital Letters

(4) Spelling errors

Checking for spelling errors requires reading so slowly that your eyes fall on each individual word. A trick long used by typists is to read backward word by word, thus reading isolated words, not ideas. Another aid in detecting misspelled words is to be alert for those words that frequently cause problems—words such as *receive, occurred,* and *truly.* If you become sensitive to problem words, you can take special care to spell them correctly. Appendix A, Spelling, includes lists of problem words as well as patterns of the English spelling system.

Some writers are fortunate enough to work on a computer or word processor and to have a software program that will check documents for spelling errors. Even so, programs that check spelling will not correct such problems as confusing *affect* for *effect* or *their* for *there,* since all these spellings are correct. For help with such word confusion you can use the Glossary of Usage.

The Computer Connection

When you type your composition with a computer or a word processor, you usually have an efficient way to eliminate spelling and typing errors. Most word-processing programs have built-in spell checkers, which will check the spelling throughout an entire document or of just a single word. The computer can check hundreds of words so quickly that you won't have time to get up for a short break before it provides results.

Suggestions for Using a Computer Spell Checker

- Keep a dictionary handy; at times spell checkers suggest alternative spellings that are not useful. For example, one program was not sure that *ruff* was correct in *the queen wore a ruff around her neck.* The suggested replacement words were *buff, cuff, duff,* and *gruff*—all useless. A quick look in a conventional dictionary shows that *ruff* is the correct spelling.
- If your program allows, create a personal dictionary. Proper names, technical terms, and other words that are not in the computer dictionary can be placed in a customized list that will be checked by the program.
- Most spell checkers also check double words like *the the.* Sometimes you must command the checker to ignore double words in contexts where they are appropriate—for example, *they had*

had an accident in 1989 or *he favored the draft, draft exemptions, and an agricultural tax.*

- Computer dictionaries are much less extensive than regular dictionaries and are especially weak on word variations. For example, a list might contain *privateer,* but not *privateering.*
- Most spell checkers will not find words used in the wrong context. One checker noticed nothing wrong in *I appreciate your patients* and *Claude dies his hair.*
- WARNING: Do not depend totally on spell checkers for proofreading your papers. Although valuable, especially for finding typographical errors, they cannot find some kinds of mistakes and should be used as a backup only.

37f TITLES

Almost every writing project requires a title. Depending on the kind of paper, the title might be simple, catchy, businesslike, or technical. In any case, the title should accurately reflect the purpose of the paper and the nature of the content.

(1) Fit the title to the purpose of the paper.

A title should not mislead the reader about the purpose of a paper. For example, a title such as "The Principles and Health Effects of Vegetarianism in the United States" suggests a serious study and is inappropriate for an informal, entertaining paper on vegetarians. On the other hand, "Confessions of a Sometime Vegetarian" leads the reader to expect an informal, entertaining paper. If you are unsure whether a title gives a false impression, whether its meaning is clear, or whether readers will be amused, use a simple, straightforward title, such as "Three Advantages of Vegetarianism."

For formal papers written to inform or persuade, you might want to use a title containing a colon. If so, give the general topic first, followed by the colon, and then restrict the topic in some way—with a statement of focus, with information about the type of paper, or with an explanation: "Right-Handedness: A Peculiarly Human Preference," "The Importance of Grades: A Survey of Student Opinion," "The Innovators: The Pioneers of Rock 'n' Roll." The colon seems to create a sense of authority and tightens the title s information.

(2) Choose a title speci c enough to be informative.

A title should not be so general that it gives readers no idea about the content of a paper. For example, Train Travel is not very descriptive. More informative are titles like Train Travel: A Superior Mode of Transportation, Trains: Our Neglected Resource, or Vacationing by Train in the West.

(3) Avoid cute titles.

As a general rule, you should avoid cute titles such as A Hare-Raising Tale for a paper about raising rabbits or Everybody Out of the Pool! for a paper about futile attempts at carpooling. For one thing, these titles promise clever papers, which you must then deliver. For another, readers are more likely to be annoyed than amused by strained attempts at cleverness.

37g THE FINISHED PAPER

A few guidelines can help you prepare manuscripts, whether handwritten or produced on a typewriter, computer, or word processor. The guidelines are by no means rules; other conventions and formats are also acceptable. For an assigned paper, the best approach, of course, is to ask what the instructor prefers.

(1) Paper

Handwritten Papers

Use lined white paper, and write on only one side of each sheet. Avoid colored paper, paper with narrowly spaced lines, and paper larger or smaller than $8^{1}{}_{2} \times 11$ inches. Also, do not turn in paper torn from a spiral notebook; the ragged edges not only look messy but also stick together.

Typed or Printed Papers

Use 8½-×-11-inch, good-grade, white paper. If you are typing your paper, avoid erasable paper; it is thin and smears easily. Errors are best changed with correction liquid. If you are preparing your paper on a computer or word processor with a printer that uses connected sheets of computer paper, be sure the sheets tear apart cleanly.

(2) Script

Handwritten papers

Use either dark blue or black ink, and make a conscious effort to write legibly. Avoid any personal handwriting quirks or frills, such as *i*'s dotted with circles, unusual capital letters, or anything that might interfere with clarity.

Typed or Printed Papers

Some typewriters and line printers produce unusual script, such as italic or something simulating handwritten script. But usually these fancy scripts are difficult to read. If you have a choice, choose a conventional script. Also, use a black ribbon new enough to leave a clear impression. And if you are typing on a typewriter, make sure the keys are clean so that they will not produce smudges and black dots for *o*'s.

(3) Margins

The usual rule of thumb is as follows.

FIRST PAGE: Leave 2 to 3 inches at the top of the page, 1 inch at the bottom, 1½ inches at the left side, and approximately 1 inch at the right.

ALL OTHER PAGES: Leave 1½ inches at the top and left sides, 1 inch at the bottom, and approximately 1 inch at the right.

If you plan to put a cover on your paper, leave 2 inches on the left side of each page. The extra space will be taken up by the binding, and the margin will be left intact.

Indent paragraphs five spaces in a typewritten manuscript and about 1 inch in a handwritten manuscript.

(4) Hyphenation

Readers do not expect the right margin of either a typed or handwritten manuscript to be perfectly straight. Therefore, you should hyphenate (divide) a word at the end of a line only when writing it out would make the margin extremely uneven. A somewhat uneven margin is not nearly so distracting as a series of hyphenated words down the right margin. When you must hyphenate, be sure to do so according to the guidelines in 29e.

(5) Spacing

Handwritten Papers

If you choose paper with lines at least ½ inch apart, writing on each line should leave ample space. Do not skip lines unless your instructor tells you to do so.

Typed or Printed Papers

Most instructors prefer that you double-space a typed paper so that they have room to write comments and make corrections. Single spacing is conventional for correspondence, some technical papers, items in an outline, and steps in instructions. If you do single-space the entire paper, remember to double-space between paragraphs.

(6) Pagination

Ordinarily, the first page of a paper is not numbered, but it is counted; so the second page is numbered 2. If instructed to number the first page, place the number at the bottom center of the sheet. Number the rest of the pages in the upper right corner, on the right margin and several spaces from the top of the page. Do not use hyphens, parentheses, or periods with page numbers unless instructed to do so.

(7) Title page

If you include a title page, keep it simple: name, title of paper, date, and possibly the instructor's name and a course number or title. Place this information neatly on the page and resist any urge to "decorate." The example on page 348 is typical.

(8) Proofreading and making corrections

Proofread your final copy to check for any remaining errors. The task is more difficult than it might seem because the content distracts the eye from superficial errors. To make errors more obvious, you can read the paper aloud, concentrating on each word; or you can read it backwards line by line or word by word. You can also use a ruler or straight edge of some sort to isolate each single line of type.

Once you have found the errors, how do you correct them? Of course, if you write with a computer or word processor, you can simply correct your errors on the disk and print a clean copy. If you use a conventional typewriter, you will have to use correction tape or fluid and perhaps photocopy your paper to get a clean copy. And if you hand-write your paper, you can make corrections neatly by using correction fluid to blot out errors and then rewriting. Ideally, you want to make your paper free of visible corrections.

But, of course, there is always that error you spot just before you turn in your paper. Make the correction neatly with ink as near the color of the original as possible. Remember, a reader will be prejudiced in favor of a neat paper and against a messy one.

revise
37g

Shopping by Mail:
Convenience or Nuisance?

Alexandra Brooks

Professor Sheffield
English 101
September 15, 1995

Sample Title Page

The Computer Connection

The last step in the writing process is editing. In this step, you put the paper in its final form—the form your reader will see. If you want to make a good impression, you must produce an attractive document with a well-designed format. Also, you must remove any mechanical or typographical errors; they will distract your reader from the content, no matter how logical the organization or how smooth the prose. You've worked too hard so far to overlook this important step. And fortunately, the computer can do much of the work for you.

Suggestions for Editing

- Use a display feature to format the text, and proofread it as it will appear on the printed page. This process allows you to avoid bad page breaks, to see where headings and titles might be separated from the text that follows, and to make sure that you have indented in all the right places.
- Using the cursor or the scroll function, scroll the text up from the end of your paper to the beginning. It's sometimes easier to catch errors when proofreading text backwards—word by word or line by line.
- Take advantage of the editing software currently available:

  a thesaurus that lists synonyms
  a spell checker that locates and corrects misspelled words
  a grammar checker that analyzes the reading levels of prose and looks for problems such as clichés
  a search-and-replace feature that enables you to correct repeated errors, update statistics, or replace a vocabulary items with a more suitable one. (If, for example, you decided to change the word *fireman* to *firefighter,* you would type the replacement word only once—and the computer would make the change throughout.)

- Don't rely entirely on the machine to correct errors and improve your prose. Computer editing functions are limited. Spell checkers, for example, flag any word that isn't in their memory. Furthermore, most of them don't catch errors such as *too* for *to* or *except* for *accept,* since these are not spelling errors. Grammar checkers don't know where you want to put commas. Nor can they choose words with the right connotations or sentence structures with the best effect. In the end, you are still the editor-in-charge.

CHAPTER

38

COMPOSITION IN PROGRESS

comp
38

In this chapter, a composition is shown in all its stages of development. It represents one student's efforts from an initial freewriting through the generation of ideas, a rough outline, and several drafts. The assignment was to write in one week a 300- to 500-word composition on any subject, addressed to a general reader. Thus, the writer was relieved of making decisions about audience but was faced with finding a subject, a purpose, a voice, and a structure.

Notice that once the writer found a subject, it did not change. Its development from draft to draft, however, changed radically. Also, notice that not until the third draft did a definite purpose, voice, and structure emerge.

The student began this assignment by freewriting these notes in ten minutes.

I don't know what to write about. This better work. I have a Math test to study for. What can I eat tonight that would taste different? I've had it with greasy hamburgers, pizza, and fried chicken from take-out places. I need vegetables. Not those institutional vegetables. Like those green peas that look like shriveled marbles. Maybe if I cleaned this place up, it would help me think. The thing that would really help me think is if that radio down the hall wasn't blasting my ear drums. Why is it that people with loud radios never consider whether everyone in ten blocks wants to hear the same music?

It's going to snow. Snow is nice when it first falls. But when it turns brown and slushy it isn't nice. It isn't romantic. It isn't a Hollywood set. It's just wet and cold.

I think I have "Math anxiety" I keep having that dream about Math class. People say it's common, that dream where you have a Math Test and you haven't been to class in weeks. Or maybe never. And you wander around a strange building looking for your classroom.

Looking back over the freewriting exercise, the writer saw a possible subject in the question *Why is it that people with loud radios never consider whether everyone in ten blocks wants to hear the same music?* This question prompted the writer to think about the subject "background noise." Viewing background noise as a problem, the writer then asked questions associated with problems (see 34g) and roughed out some answers.

What causes it?
    Maybe fear of silence? Radios. Television. Stereos. Canned music.
Whom does it affect?
    Me. Almost everyone in America. Families. Shoppers.
What does it affect?
    Relaxation. Nerves. Stress.
Where does it occur?
    Homes. Grocery stores. Department stores. Telephones.

Restaurants. Elevators. Public recreation areas. Dormitories.

What is a possible solution?

Maybe education about the dangers of too much noise. Maybe health education classes. An individual can get away to the country sometime to escape the noise.

What would life be like without the problem?

We could hear the sounds of nature. The normal sounds of the city. We could relax.

The material generated by the questions and answers led to this working outline.

1. Background noise in the home
   television
   stereos
2. Background noise outside the home
   Muzak (canned music) in stores and businesses
   radios in public areas
3. Life without background noise

Writing rapidly, without concern for grammar, spelling, or mechanics, the writer then produced the following rough draft from the working outline.

First Draft

American society seems to be obcessed with background noise. Most households have at least one television set that plays whether anyone is watching. And many households have several television sets that run constantly. In addition, families with teenagers usually have the burden of loud stereos that compete with the television for your attention.

potential thesis

details supporting obsession with noise

But background noise is not confined to homes. Businesses like grocery stores, department stores, and resterants have piped in Muzak that plays constantly in the background. Also, individuals bring their radio to public recreation areas and play pop music that everyone else must listen to, whether they want to or not. It seems that if a sound system is not provided, people bring their own.

It seems that Americans fear silence. But would life without background music be so bad? Without the constant blaring of local radio stations, we might be able to tune in the sounds of nature and everyday life. We could hear the quiet sounds of the woods, the sounds of the country side, the bustle of the city, the sounds of children at play. We could tune into life instead of radio and television.

potential thesis

potential thesis

This first draft is rather unimpressive. There are three potential theses, and the composition lacks enough concrete details to catch a reader's attention. Nevertheless, the draft was certainly productive. It started the writer thinking about the subject and generating a few controlling ideas.

You will notice that the first draft has errors and misspelled words. At this stage, however, editing for grammar and mechanics would be a waste of time. Instead, the writer set the draft aside, reread it the next day, and made several decisions: (1) to deal only with music, not all background noise; (2) to expand the middle section with concrete details; (3) to expand the first idea in the third paragraph (fear of silence) into an introduction; and (4) to expand the description of the sounds of nature and everyday life. The second draft incorporated these changes.

SECOND DRAFT

Our world is filled with uncertainties and dangers, so many that most people suffer from all kinds of fears. Some people fear cancer; some, nuclear war; some lonliness; some, not succeding in life. What it comes to is that people fear what may lay ahead as an obstacle to a long and happy life. All these fears are legitimate, I think. But there is one fear that has swept over our country that is not only ridiculous but is driving me crazy. The fear of one waking moment without background music.

potential thesis

Call a business and let the receptionist put you on hold; you will be treated to a tune that sounds like a combination of "Moon

River" and Lawrence Welk playing a polka. Go the the track to jog and someone will have brought their radio blaring pop music for your listening pleasure. Stop at a traffic light in the summertime. Some person in the lane next to you will have his car radio on so high that you could not hear an eighteen wheeler bearing down on you from 30 feet away. Go to a swimming pool to relax in the sun. Stereo speakers will blast your brain with music to go crazy by. Babies for a 10-mile radius will wake screaming from their afternoon naps, while mothers of babies will tear their hair. Go out for a solitery lunch during exam week and try to cram in a few last minutes of study over your hamburger. Someone will put dozen coins in the juke box and start a series of country and western tunes that will wail the material you've learned right out of your head. Or a grocery store; the Muzak makes you feel as if you should be skating rather than walking through the aisles.

details—types of background noise

Where did this fear of silence come from? There was a time when people could tell where they were just from the sounds around them. In the woods, birds chirped, crickets sang, frogs croaked, creeks babbled. In the fields, cattle bellowed or tractors chugged. In the suburbs, weed eaters whirred and backyard cooks called to each other from patio to patio. In the city horns honked, taxi drivers swore, subways roared.

details—description of life in the past

But no more. I know the Constitution garantees us freedom of speech. But I don't believe it garantees freedom of noise.

comp 38

Although the second draft is much better than the first, it has a number of problems. The introductory material on fear (which contains a potential thesis) is never developed, only mentioned briefly again at the beginning of the fourth paragraph. Furthermore, the voice in the introduction seems to change from serious to light.

In addition, the concrete details in the second paragraph have no logical organization, and they are made somewhat vague by the use of the indefinite *you.* The conclusion has no tight connection with the rest of the composition. And, generally, the purpose and the structure are not clear.

The writer decided not to edit for grammar and mechanics at this point but to set the composition aside once again. Coming back later to the second draft, the writer made an important decision: to abandon the idea of fear and begin with the idea that in the past, people could hear the sounds of nature and life around them. This decision had several positive effects. It got rid of the weak introduction and the overly serious tone at the beginning. And it provided a "hook" for the conclusion: the last sentence of the next draft hooks back to the first sentence. Most significantly, the decision led the writer to a thesis: *Today, people cannot hear the sounds of life and nature because of constant background music.* The thesis suggested an overall chronological structure for the paper—what was in the past; what is in the present.

Another change vastly improved the composition. The writer condensed all the examples in the body of the paper into an "average day" and used a narrative in the first person (*I*). This change got rid of the vague *you* and gave chronological structure to the disjointed details. It also allowed an extension of the details to include a thwarted hiking trip—something personal and not generalized. The use of the first person allowed the writer to develop the subject in a consistent voice: the narrator is frustrated, but not irate. The purpose and structure are also clear: to inform the reader of the problem, using the "average day" as illustration.

THIRD DRAFT

introductory paragraph on sounds of the past

There was a time when people could tell where they were just from the variety of sounds around them. In the woods, birds chirped, crickets sang, frogs croaked, creeks babbled. In the countryside, cattle bellowed, tractors chugged, roosters crowed. In the suburbs, dogs barked, weed eaters whirred, and backyard cooks called to each other from patio to patio. In the city, horns honked, drivers swore, subways roared. Public parks rang with splashes of kids belly flopping in the pool, the twang of tennis rackets, the creaking of swings and see-saws.

But no longer are our days filled with these sounds. That rich variety of sounds is now masked and our lives are filled with three audio backdrops: Muzak, country and western, and pop music. This came to me during an average day last summer.

statement of thesis

Early in the morning, I went to the track to jog and think peaceful thoughts. Someone had brought a radio blaring pop music for my listening pleasure. I went to the grocery store: the Muzak made me feel as if I should have been skating rather than walking down the aisles. On the way from the grocery store, I stopped at a traffic light. In the lane next to me, a high school boy had his car radio turned up so high that I would have been unable to hear an eighteen wheeler bearing down on me from 30 feet away. I went to a swimming pool to relax in the sun, stereo speakers blasted my brain with music to go crazy by. Babies for a 10-mile radius surely must have waked crying from their afternoon naps, while their mothers groan in frustration. I left the pool and went home to my little brother and his friends glued to a television rock video pulssating noise for several blocks around. I fled to my room and called a local employment office to check on my job applications. The receptionist put me on hold; I was treated to a tune that sounded like Lawrence Welk playing "Moon River." I went out for a hamburger, and the juke box was playing pop music so loud that the waitress had to read lips to take orders.

thesis supported with illustrations

comp 38

That night I determined to find some peace and quiet for at least a few hours. So the next day, I got my hiking gear and took off to the woods to rest my ears. After a few miles, I approached the spot where I used to sit and read to the quiet sounds of nature. But the woods were cleared, and construction workers were building a house, hammering and sawing to the rhythms of a country and western station. Just over the hill, a family in a camper had brought along a radio that could pick up rock stations from Europe. Sadly, I walked back to my car. Wondering whether there was any escape for me in a society full of music addicts.

The mystery I am unable to solve is this: Do the people who insist on providing me with this constant background music think they are doing me a favor? Or do they feel that their own desires take precedence over the desires of others? Or is it simply that they don't want to know where they are?

conclusion "hooking" back to first sentence

Looking over the third draft, the writer found problems with the thesis: "That rich variety of sounds is now masked and our lives are filled with three audio backdrops: Muzak, country and western, and pop music." First, the metaphor is illogical; lives are not filled with backdrops. Second, the thesis suggests a three-pronged organization that is not forthcoming. The writer simplified the thesis to read *That rich variety of sounds is now masked by constant background music.*

Now satisfied that the composition had a clear thesis, an appropriate voice, and a logical structure, the writer revised the paper sentence by sentence—correcting errors and improving style. The following is a final draft, complete with a title.

A Search for Silence

There was a time when people could tell where they were just from the variety of sounds around them. In the woods, birds chirped, crickets sang, frogs croaked, creeks babbled. In the countryside, cattle bellowed, tractors chugged, roosters crowed. In the suburbs, dogs barked, weed eaters whirred, and backyard cooks called to each other from patio to patio. In the city, horns honked, drivers swore, subways roared. Public parks rang with splashes of kids belly-flopping in the pool, the twang of tennis rackets, the creaking of swings and seesaws.

But no more. That rich variety of sounds is now masked by constant background music. This revelation came to me during an average day last summer.

insertion of revelation *clarifies a vague* this *new thesis that more accurately predicts subject matter*

Early in the morning, I went to the track to jog and think peaceful thoughts. Someone had brought a radio blaring pop music for my listening pleasure. I went to the grocery store: the Muzak made me feel as if I should have been skating rather than walking down the aisles. On the way from the grocery store, I stopped at a traffic light. In the lane next to me, a high school boy had his car radio turned up so high that I would have been unable to hear an eighteen-wheeler bearing down on me from 30 feet away. I went to a swimming pool to relax in the sun. Stereo speakers blasted my brain with music to go crazy by. Babies for a 10-mile radius surely must have waked crying from their afternoon naps, while their mothers groaned in frustration. I left the pool and went home to my little brother and his friends glued to a television rock video pulsating noise for several blocks around. I fled to my room and called a local employment office to check on my job applications. The receptionist put me on hold; I was treated to a tune that sounded like Lawrence Welk playing "Moon River." I went out for a hamburger, and the jukebox was playing pop music so loud that the waitress had to read lips to take orders.

comma splice corrected

tense shift corrected

spelling error (pulssating) corrected

comp 38

That night I determined to find some peace and quiet for at least a few hours. So the next day, I got my hiking gear and took off to the woods to rest my ears. After a few miles, I approached the spot where I used to sit and read to the quiet sounds of nature. But the woods were cleared, and construction workers were building a house, hammering and sawing to the rhythms of a country and western station. Just over the hill, a family in a camper had brought along a radio that could pick up rock stations from Europe. Sadly, I walked back to my car, wondering whether there was any escape for me in a society of music addicts.

spelling error (rhythms) corrected

sentence fragment attached to preceding sentence

The mystery I am unable to solve is this: Do people who insist on providing me with this constant background music think they are doing me a favor? Or do they feel that their own desires take precedence over the desires of others? Or is it simply that they don't want to know where they are?

The Computer Connection

Computers alter the process of composing. An obvious difference is the absence of messy drafts. In print, a rough draft typically contains all sorts of erasures, arrows, and cross-outs, but on the computer screen, a rough draft does not look rough; instead, superficially it looks just like a final paper.

Suggestions for the Composition in Progress

- Before you quit working on a paper, read it over many times. You should revise until you are satisfied that your purpose and thesis are clear; that you have excluded everything irrelevant; that each paragraph has unity; that every idea is developed; that the organization is smooth and logical; and that there are no problems in the style, grammar, and punctuation.
- Do not hesitate to make notes to yourself on the computer copy just as you might on a hard copy. Notes will remind you that your computer composition is a work under construction. Mark your notes using some type of highlighting such as comment boxes, symbols, and other signals. You can use bold print or underlining to indicate spots that you know will need more work.
- Before you make changes to a draft, copy it to another file. Then if you wish to return to the earlier version, it will be available. You can also keep printouts of earlier versions; you may want to compare the hard copies.

PART

VI

SPECIAL WRITING PROJECTS

Some papers have special purposes and special audiences. To carry out the purpose of a paper and to satisfy its audience, you must become familiar with the characteristics that make the paper unique. For example, an argument requires a conflict, and its readers expect sound critical thinking. A research paper requires a thesis supported by library sources, and its readers expect documentation according to rigid guidelines. Thus, when writing an argument or research paper, make sure you adhere to the expected conventions.

39 Argument and Critical Thinking
40 Research Papers in Progress
41 Research Papers and Documentation

CHAPTER

39

ARGUMENT AND CRITICAL THINKING

Of all the writing projects you encounter in your academic and professional life, the most common is probably argument. If you propose that the data from a laboratory experiment or the symbols in a poem be interpreted in a certain way, you are arguing. If you recommend that your office purchase one computer rather than another, you are arguing. If you try to motivate people to stop littering, you are arguing. An argument can advance a theory, suggest a solution to a problem, or urge a course of action. Developing an argument can be a very gratifying process, for here you have the opportunity to express your own opinions rather than merely to report the ideas and opinions of other people. For the argument to be effective, however, you must proceed logically and objectively—from investigating the subject and gathering evidence to organizing materials and writing the paper. In other words, you must engage in critical thinking throughout the entire process.

The phrase *critical thinking* does not refer to criticizing in the negative sense. Rather, it refers to a systematic mental scrutiny of ideas and material. When most experienced readers and researchers read or listen to oral presentations, this scrutiny is automatic. First, they keep an open mind—prepared to accept new information and opinions. At the same time, they are cautious—alert to fallacious reasoning and to inaccurate, insufficient, and irrelevant evidence. They analyze the material, dividing it into component parts and separating opinions from facts. Furthermore, they question how the material relates to what they already know and what it means in a larger context. They separate the main ideas from the details and the useful ideas from the trivia. In other words, their thinking is disciplined. By manipulating the material, they control it intellectually.

Inexperienced readers and researchers, on the other hand, tend to take information at face value in its entirety. Often, they either accept the whole or reject it. These readers are not in control and, consequently, the material is not very useful to them.

A simple analogy is that of horse and rider. The critical thinker is like the experienced rider, who uses reins and body movements to control the horse and put it through its paces—seemingly without effort. The inexperienced reader is like the city slicker at a dude ranch. As the old story goes, he gets on the horse, takes one rein in either hand, and waits. When nothing happens, he says to the horse, "Well. Commence."

If you are inexperienced in critical thinking, you do not have to sit there like the man on the horse. Fortunately, there is a procedure to guide you. With practice, you will develop the mental discipline necessary to use information to your advantage. As you work on an argument, follow the steps that guide experienced writers through the process: find a subject, sort out the conflict, frame a thesis, gather evidence, evaluate the evidence, and choose a structure for the material. In addition, make sure you have identified as clearly as possible the audience that will read your paper.

39a SUBJECT

You can write an argument on virtually any subject as long as you know what you are talking about. Nothing fizzles so quickly as an argument put forth by a writer ignorant of the subject. You must choose a subject about which you are informed or can become informed. (See Chapter 34.) Also, your knowledge of the subject must extend beyond your own views to encompass all sides of the issue. You cannot write a successful argument unless you can understand the views of the opposition.

For this reason, it probably is not wise to write on a subject about which you are irrevocably prejudiced and therefore unable to think critically. Developing an effective argument requires that you examine an issue carefully, keep an open mind, and be prepared to change your own stand if the evidence points you in a new direction.

Your first step, then, is to consider subjects that you already know about or that you want to learn about. For example, if you are an experienced hunter, you might want to defend hunting against the critics who denounce it as cruel. On the other hand, if you morally oppose hunting but know little about it, you must be willing to do some preliminary research before you write—read articles that support and oppose the practice, talk to hunters, perhaps even interview a psychologist to find out what motivates hunters.

39b CONFLICT

After you have chosen several possible subjects, explore them as areas of conflict. You want a subject about which you can express an opinion, a judgment. Inherent in the subject must be the possibility of conflicting ideas, interpretations, or behavior.

If you can prove your position beyond any doubt, you do not have an opinion; you have a fact. For example, you cannot argue that teenage pregnancy is on the rise; this fact can be statistically proved or disproved. You could, however, argue about the primary reason for teenage pregnancy: lack of sex education, parental negligence, influence of television and movies on teenage mores, and so on. People will certainly disagree about the causes of the problem.

Likewise, you cannot argue something generally accepted, such as the idea that parental love is important to human beings. Although the idea cannot be statistically established, few people would oppose it. On the other hand, you could argue an unorthodox view—for example, that absence of parental love often results in artistic, creative children. You would have to base your argument on psychological theories and on real-life experiences of artists and other creative people.

One good way to examine a subject for conflict is to ask questions. Consider for a moment the subject of requiring high school students to wear uniforms. Try throwing out random questions: What exactly is a uniform? What would be the effects of wearing uniforms? Who would benefit? How would students react at first? How would they react after a time? Why would someone advocate uniforms? What are the social implications? The political implications? How practical or impractical are uniforms?

You can use questions to explore any conflict. (See 34g.) The subject of athletic programs in college, for example, suggests a number of interesting questions. What is a student athlete? How many athletes are really students? How much time do they spend on academic courses? How many classes do athletes attend on average? How many graduate from college? Which courses are most popular with athletes? Who benefits most from student athletics? Who suffers the most? The players? The coaches? The pro clubs? The college or university? Is the idea of student athletes a myth? Should we abandon the myth and pay the players? Should athletes be held to the same standards and rules as other students? Does an athletic program actually pay for itself? Are athletic programs for women equal to those for men?

You can also identify conflicts by looking for relationships. In the case of high school uniforms, you could explore, for example, the relationships between student dress and student behavior; between clothes and self-esteem; between provocative clothes and promiscuous behavior; between *macho* clothes and aggressive behavior; between clothes and social standing; between clothes and individualism.

In the case of student athletics, you could consider relationships such as those between academic involvement and athletic participation; between the student athlete and other students; between college athletics and professional sports; between coaches and their players; between college coaching and professional coaching; and between the lives of college superstars and average players.

Once you have generated some ideas about your subject, you can see conflicts more clearly. Begin by looking at all sides of the issue. What are the logical positions of each side—the pros and cons? For example, consider the pros and cons of the two subjects we have already explored.

Pro: The case for uniforms

Uniforms would eliminate some of the social disadvantages suffered by students who cannot afford expensive clothes.

Uniforms might discourage aggressive behavior. (People in dress shirts and ties might be less likely to wield knives than those in leather vests.)

Uniform dress might encourage students to concentrate on studies rather than on fashion statements.

Uniforms would save parents money, which they could contribute to such school improvements as laboratory equipment or air conditioning.

Con: The case against uniforms

Uniforms would not flatter some students' appearance and would thus cause loss of self-esteem and self-confidence.

Choosing clothes allows a young person to express individuality.

Uniforms would not eliminate status symbols. Wealthier students would still sport cars, expensive haircuts, and designer shoes and sunglasses.

Parents would not likely contribute the saved money to the general needs of the educational system. The money would probably be spent on dress clothes, stereos, cars, and so forth for their children.

Members of ethnic groups could not express their cultural heritage through their style of dress.

Pro: The case for college athletic programs

Athletic programs provide scholarships and thus education for many students otherwise unable to attend college.

Student athletes can polish skills in an amateur arena and become professionals when they mature.

Athletic programs provide a bond between school and community.

Athletic departments do not ignore education; instead, they provide tutors for students with academic problems.

Student athletes are required to stay in shape; therefore, they are less likely than most students to indulge in drugs and alcohol.

Con: The case against college athletic programs

Student athletes do not actually receive an education because they are given special academic privileges, are steered into easy courses, and are not encouraged to graduate.

Athletic departments seduce athletes with false expectations. For example, student athletes rarely know that many "scholarships" are one-year grants renewable according to athletic performance or that only 1 to 2 percent of student football players go on to the pros.

Many college coaches, ambitious to be hired in a professional league, abuse student athletes with pain killers and unrealistic demands. Therefore, many athletes suffer physical damage.

Athletic departments have no interest in education; at one school, for example, the baseball team played over 60 games (most on the road) in four months—that is, in 80 classroom days.

Giving student athletes special privileges damages their ability to function in the real world.

By exploring conflicts, you learn whether you wish to pursue a subject and whether you need to fill in any gaps with some research. For the subjects of school uniforms and athletic programs, for example, you might want to find some case histories of people with experience. Also, you could look for magazine articles on the subject in the *Readers' Guide to Periodical Literature* or in other indexes. (See 40c.) In addition, you might take an informal survey of students to get their ideas.

39c THESIS

Once you have considered the conflicts inherent in a subject and generated some statements on both sides of the issue, you should be able to formulate a thesis, the opinion you wish to argue. (Read about thesis statements in 35d.)

When formulating your thesis, consider whether a reasonable argument can be made against it and whether you could defend against that argument. Be sure to keep an open mind. You may want to change or modify your original position in order to develop a workable thesis—one that is clear and specific enough to allow intelligent debate. Let's suppose you want to formulate a thesis on the school uniform issue. Your argument will falter with a thesis such as *Requiring uniforms for high school students is a good (or bad) idea.* The words *good* and *bad* are too vague. They give no concrete base for support or defense, and thus the thesis lends no direction to the argument. Besides, examination of the conflict showed that uniforms are neither all bad nor all good.

Look back at the pros and cons on the subject. The pros suggest a tentative thesis such as this one: *Requiring uniforms in high school would eliminate the social discord among students and the financial burdens of parents.* The cons suggest something like this: *Requiring uniforms in high school would prevent students from expressing individuality and ethnic identification.* These statements are more specific but too sweeping. Obviously, uniforms would not eliminate all discord and financial burdens, nor prevent all individuality and identification. Each thesis would benefit from qualification: *Requiring uniforms for high school students would help to ease the social discord among students and the financial burdens of parents* and *Requiring uniforms for high school students would lower student morale by destroying a major avenue for individual and ethnic expression.*

Both theses now state a position and a line of defense. You may, of course, restate a thesis while you are drafting the paper. But you should at least begin drafting with a thesis that gives you a direction.

39d KINDS OF EVIDENCE

In settling on a thesis, you have already explored your subject and possibly even researched it. Now you must select the evidence to support your thesis. There are several different kinds of evidence—ranging from facts to informed opinions to logical reasons. No matter which kinds of evidence you have available, be sure to use a critical approach. Select only the evidence that is reliable and directly related to your thesis.

arg/crit
39d

(1) Facts and observations

Some facts are indisputable or easily verifiable. By consulting a dictionary or encyclopedia, for example, you can quickly identify the seventh vice president of the United States or the date of the Wright brothers' first successful flight at Kitty Hawk. Factual information commonly used as evidence, however, is usually a bit more complex. For example, you might want to use data that you or another researcher has obtained from laboratory experiments or mathematical calculations.

Some factual information is derived from observations—such as your own examination of a polluted beach, an archeologist's description of an excavation site, a biologist's observations on insect damage to a forest, an eyewitness account of a riot, or a sociologist's case studies of child abusers.

A popular kind of factual evidence is information gathered in a survey. In fact, professional pollsters and researchers have so perfected their techniques that many statistics can be cited with confidence. If you do a survey yourself, explain your particular methodology so that readers can assess the reliability of your findings. Also, whether you survey by written questionnaire, telephone, or interviews, phrase each question carefully. The following guidelines will help you get good results.

- Define all necessary terms.
  If you are seeking opinions about the value of studying the humanities, you should define *humanities* to ensure valid responses.

- Ask only one thing at a time.
  Avoid phrasing items so that they ask two questions at once, such as "Did your high school prepare you for college English and college science?" The school could have prepared the respondent for one and not the other. Thus, you should ask two separate questions: "Did your high school prepare you for college English?" "Did your high school prepare you for college science?"

- Avoid leading questions.
  You should not lead your reader to a certain answer by asking a question like, "Do you oppose the city council's preferential treatment of businesses?" Because "preferential treatment" is generally undesirable, the phrase would lead most respondents to answer yes. A fairer question would be "Do you think the city council gives preferential treatment to businesses?"

- Phrase questions in positive terms.
  Negative words unnecessarily complicate a question. Readers would be confused by the negative *dis-* and *not* in this question: "Do you disapprove of not allowing gill nets?" The question would be much clearer in positive terms: "Do you approve of gill nets?"

- Avoid ambiguous questions.
  In the question "Would longer hiking trails be beneficial?" a respondent might well wonder whether *beneficial* means beneficial to the hikers, to the parks, or to the environment. More exact phrasing would eliminate the ambiguity: "Would you like the hiking trails to be longer?"

(2) Informed opinions

The opinions of other people can serve as evidence for an argument. But those opinions should come from informed scholars or experts in the field you are discussing. For example, if you were supporting a claim that Shakespeare created roles especially for the actors in his company, you should cite a respected Shakespearean scholar or an expert in theater history. To locate reliable opinions, you will more than likely use the library. For a discussion of library resources and search techniques, see 40c–e.

When you use the exact words of an informed source, honesty requires that you quote faithfully. If you leave out parts of the quotation to save space or to eliminate the irrelevant, be especially careful not to distort the meaning. Notice the way the following quotations alter the meaning of the original statements.

DISTORTED: "Dwight Eisenhower was one of the outstanding leaders . . . in this century."

ORIGINAL: Dwight Eisenhower was one of the outstanding leaders of the Western world in this century.

DISTORTED: "Scientific news is . . . a random collection of amazing facts."

ORIGINAL: Scientific news is too often presented as a random collection of amazing facts that at best have little, if anything, to do with the real world.

Before you quote sources in your paper, read 27a, 27b, and 27g on quotation marks and ellipses and 40h on avoiding plagiarism.

(3) Logical reasoning

Basically, there are two kinds of logical reasoning: induction and deduction. Inductive reasoning involves using specific instances to arrive at a general principle. If you get sick every time you eat cheese, yogurt, ice cream, or butter, you will eventually induce that you are allergic to dairy products. Conversely, deductive reasoning involves using a general principle to predict a specific instance. If you know that you are allergic to dairy products, you will deduce that Aunt Martha's peach ice cream will make you sick.

We move back and forth between the induction and deduction easily and constantly. Take, for example, the idea that a high-fat diet and lack of exercise contribute to heart disease. Medical researchers studied thousands of individual heart patients (the specifics) to reach this conclusion (the general principle). You might use the general principle as evidence that physical education and nutrition classes are essential to the public schools. And you might deduce that students who attend these classes will live longer and healthier lives.

Although both kinds of logic are quite natural and ordinary, they can mislead you to false conclusions, and you should be cautious when using them to support an argument. To guard against the common pitfalls in induction and deduction, see the discussions of hasty generalization and of non sequitur in the next section, Evaluation of Evidence.

A special kind of logic is the analogy, a comparison between two different things and the suggestion that what is true of one is true of the other—for example, what is true of the computer is also true of the brain; what was true of the Roman Empire is also true today. Obviously, since the two things being compared are not alike, the conclusion is at best a probability. Therefore, you should qualify a conclusion drawn from analogy with a word such as *probably, usually,* or *in some instances.* Notice how the word *usually* in the following statement improves the acceptability of the analogy: *The economy is like a complex piece of machinery; therefore, when something goes wrong, we usually have a difficult time finding the cause.*

39e EVALUATION OF EVIDENCE

As you gather evidence, you must think critically about its quality and question whether to include it in your argument. Through constant skepticism and criticism, you can weed out material that is inaccurate, irrelevant, unclear, or illogical. You can also determine whether the material is sufficient to convince readers to agree with you or to act as you wish.

Thinking critically about your evidence requires thoughtful reading and scrutiny. It requires systematic judgment. Most experienced readers and writers have developed a system that they use naturally and instinctively. Inexperienced readers and writers must consciously and deliberately analyze their evidence. If you are inexperienced or need to ensure the quality of the material you use, learn to question. Questioning truth, accuracy, or value is the essence of intellectual discipline. Five questions typify the habit of thinking critically about what you read and hear. By asking these questions, you can better evaluate your evidence.

(1) Is the evidence accurate?

Inaccurate evidence will quickly undermine an argument. Whether the evidence is primary (direct observation) or secondary (someone else's account), it must be accurate. You know the accuracy of your own observations, but you must assess the accuracy of statements made by others. When you read or listen to others, look for several telling characteristics.

Is the source full of facts or full of opinions? A fact is something that has actually happened or that is really true (verifiable); an opinion is a belief that is potentially right or wrong. For example, that the climate is warming in certain parts of the globe is a fact verifiable by recorded data. Currently, however, scientists differ in their opinions about the reasons for the warming trends. A source long on opinions and short on facts is suspicious. There is little value in opinions unsupported by either facts or a sufficient number of examples or illustrations. Of course, if the source is a proved expert, the opinion is backed up by reputation—a career involved in gathering information. Nevertheless, most real experts are careful to support their opinions with sufficient factual data.

What does the tone of the work tell you? If the tone is more emotional than rational, you should beware of using the source as evidence. Material that seems too angry, too sentimental, or too dogmatic reveals a questionable source. Some display of emotion may be appropriate, yet when it is excessive or not balanced with reason and moderation, it should be viewed with suspicion. Likewise, the tone of your own argument should be rational. For such subjects as abortion, capital punishment, gun control, and religion, emotions must be held in check. When writers feel very strongly about a subject, they naturally tend to dramatize. If you cannot present a rational argument on a strongly held conviction, you probably should avoid writing about it.

A source that includes discriminatory language is usually a poor source of evidence. Slurs against women, particular races, places, and groups indicate a source that lacks objectivity. Often this kind of language takes the form of loaded, abusive language such as *religious fanatic, bleeding-heart liberal, knee-jerk conservative, egghead, male chauvinist pig.* (See 32e.) Prejudice in a source or in your own prose can alienate readers at the very time that the purpose should be to win their confidence.

In determining whether a source is accurate, you should also consider the quality of the research. Is the source well documented? Accurate material is not necessarily documented; however, documentation indicates the origin of the information and may give clues to its accuracy. Sometimes the reputation of the publisher can indicate reliability. What is the date of the publication? Some information—particularly on scientific and technical subjects—ages poorly. New research often makes earlier data obsolete. Questioning the research will not ensure the accuracy of a source but will help you avoid weak evidence.

(2) Is the evidence relevant?

Well-crafted arguments do not shift from the real issue. They do not include irrelevant material to pad an argument and thereby disguise a lack of hard evidence. Nor do they include emotional tricks and diversions, such as appeals to tradition and popularity, irrelevant testimonials, ad hominem attacks, straw man positions, and red herrings. You should be alert to these shifts not only in your sources but also in your own writing.

Appeal to Tradition

Possibly the most common way to shift an issue is to appeal to the cultural conditioning of a group—the traditions, the customs, the common heritage. Suppose, for example, a paper considers whether women in the armed services should be sent into combat. To sway an American audience *against* the idea, a writer might invoke the "wisdom of the Founding Fathers, who did not call to war our mothers, our sisters, and our daughters." This kind of rhetoric paints a picture of wise, white-wigged statesmen guarding the future flowers of the nation's motherhood. To sway an audience *toward* the idea, a writer might discuss the "pioneer woman, fighting side by side with her husband to protect the home and family." This scenario paints a picture of a strong, handsome woman, bonnet askew, aiming a rifle through a cabin window at marauders. Both of these pictures contain honored traditions in our culture and thus evoke powerful emotions. But in reality, neither of these pictures is directly relevant to the issue of whether contemporary women should be sent into combat.

Irrelevant testimonial

Advertisers frequently cite the testimony of a celebrity to support a claim: a football star touts a deodorant soap, an actress starts every day with Brand A coffee, a tennis pro gets her stamina from Brand X cereal, a talk-show host drives only a certain kind of car. The audience is expected to transfer approval of the celebrity to approval of the product. In the manner of advertisers, writers sometimes try to support an argument with quotations from inappropriate people—citing a popular novelist on a point of law, for example. You should reject this evidence and avoid this practice. Use only relevant testimonials: the knowledge and opinions of experts in the field in question.

Appeal to popularity

In advertising, the appeal to popularity is rampant: X is popular; therefore, X is good. Television viewers see cheering crowds rushing deliriously toward a plastic building where beautiful women in cute hats smile, sing, and dispense processed chicken nuggets. Viewers, of course, are supposed to feel that they are missing out unless they join the fun and hurry on down to Chickie Doodle. In politics, the tactic is usually called "the bandwagon." Voters are encouraged to "get on the bandwagon and vote for the people's choice." The implication is that the candidate's popularity indicates his or her merit.

In arguments, the tactic usually results in asserting that many wrongs make a right. For example, one might attempt to justify cheating on income taxes or insurance claims by stating that "everyone does it." History clearly demonstrates that popular ideas are not necessarily good ideas. Alert readers will reject evidence that shifts support from legitimate proof to the numbers of proponents.

Ad Hominem Attack

Avoid evidence containing ad hominem attacks, a personal attack on an individual's character rather than on his or her position. A common form of ad hominem attack is guilt by association. In this ploy, a speaker or writer tries to associate someone with an idea or with another person that the audience finds distasteful. Politicians favor this tactic, identifying their opponents with characters that voters reject. For instance, a gubernatorial candidate might attempt to associate his or her opponent with a member of organized crime. Likewise, a writer might attempt to discredit an argument merely by associating its proponents with an "ultraconservative" political group. Of course, people can be judged to some extent by the company they keep. Nevertheless, you should judge an opponent's position on its own strength and not resort to such smear tactics.

Straw Man Position

Altering the opposing view to make it easier to attack is creating a straw man. Suppose, for instance, a writer is arguing for a flat-rate tax system in which each individual pays 10 percent of total income with no deductions. The writer could set up a straw man position like this one: "A graduated tax system benefits only the rich, since they are the only taxpayers who can take advantage of large deductions." It is easy, of course, to attack a system that benefits only the rich. But the evidence oversimplifies the graduated tax structure. For example, a deduction system can encourage individuals and businesses to make contributions to charities, universities, hospitals, medical research laboratories, and other institutions that benefit the whole society at all economic levels. The straw man (graduated tax = pro-rich) is easy to attack, but the argument is also irrelevant.

Red Herring

An old hunting term, *red herring* refers to dragging a herring across a trail to divert the hounds from their prey. The term refers to a diversionary tactic, a dodge that switches the issue. For example, suppose a writer argues that Medicare has increased the cost of medical examinations and uses as support the claim that medical doctors are wealthy because they overcharge their patients. Even if the writer could prove that claim, it would not prove that Medicare escalates health-care costs. It would merely divert the argument into a vaguely related area.

(3) Is the evidence sufficient?

To support a claim or a belief, a writer must include sufficient evidence. But how much is enough? Unfortunately, there are no clear-cut guidelines for deciding. The subject usually determines the amount of evidence you need. For example, in an argument about the harm that results from wearing walkabout radios and stereos, only two reasons might support the claim—that they damage hearing and make the wearers insensitive to dangers such as cars and trains. These two reasons may be sufficiently convincing if they, in turn, are backed up by expert testimony, illustrations, and examples. On the other hand, if an argument asserts that inbreeding is ruining the health of pedigree dogs, a discussion of the deafness and skin ailments of the Dalmatian is not enough. Many more examples and expert testimony would have to be added.

Hasty Generalization

arg/crit 39e

When a writer bases a claim on too little evidence, the problem is called *hasty generalization*—a result of not thinking critically. Hasty generalizations are easy to recognize in everyday conversation. After the purchase of one lemon, the buyer concludes that all similar cars are bad. On the basis of one victory, fans predict a winning season for the local football team. In written arguments, the hasty generalization is usually a bit less obvious. For example, a writer might conclude that the entire South is rapidly entering the economic mainstream by examining only the economy of Atlanta.

A typical kind of hasty generalization occurs when a writer bases a broad conclusion on a nonrepresentative survey. For instance, after interviewing 25 acquaintances in one dormitory, a writer might claim that American college students favor nongraded courses. But 25 students are not likely to represent the attitudes of all American students—and certainly not 25 of the same sex who all attend the same university and live in the same dormitory. Broad conclusions can be drawn only from surveys that elicit information from a representative sample, one that is a microcosm of the group in question.

If the evidence is limited, but it is all that can be collected, a writer must be honest. For example, from a survey of only 50 people, you may not claim that Americans are dissatisfied with their medical system. A careful writer would simply state that in a limited survey of 50 people, the respondents expressed dissatisfaction with their medical system. Though not as sweeping or forceful as the general claim, the limited claim has credibility.

(4) Is the language clear?

Effective evidence must be written clearly. If the meaning of your sources is not clear to you, do not use them as evidence. Material in such sources as scholarly journals and technical publications is frequently incomprehensible to the average person. If you find your sources difficult, try breaking down long, complex sentences into short segments. Also, use a dictionary to find the meanings of unfamiliar words. If you still cannot understand the information, you must locate material that has been restated for lay people, or you must change the subject of your argument.

In evaluating the quality of evidence, be alert to the problem of imprecise language. The meanings of terms should be clear and consistent. Abstract words pose a particular problem; words like *freedom, justice, success,* and *happiness* mean different things to different people and thus must be defined or avoided.

Also, words should not refer to more than one thing at a time. This problem, called ambiguity or equivocation, is sometimes used deliberately to confuse unwary readers. For example, advertisers often use the expression *natural* to mean both "something in nature" and "something desirable." They make much of natural ingredients, which the audience is supposed to interpret as preferable to unnatural ingredients, whatever that means. In an argument, the "nature = good" theme could be used to argue that human beings have always engaged in warfare; therefore, war is part of human nature; therefore, war is natural; therefore, we should not bother to strive for peace. But not everything in nature is necessarily good—for example, tornadoes, earthquakes, and viruses. And furthermore, everything that happens in society is not necessarily part of the natural course of events. To eliminate such confusion in your arguments, always read carefully and always question the meanings of words.

(5) Is the reasoning logical?

Think critically when you read and when you write. Carefully examine not only your sources but also your papers for any material that contains a logical fallacy—a flaw or slip in the reasoning process. In particular, watch for several common types of logical fallacies: post hoc reasoning, oversimplification of cause, either/or reasoning, false analogy, begging the question, and non sequitur.

Post Hoc Reasoning

Post hoc, ergo propter hoc means "after this, therefore because of this." In the post hoc fallacy, a person reasons that simply because A preceded B, A caused B. For example, after the Civil War, small-scale subsistence farming was doomed. But it would be fallacious to blame the war. Although the war preceded the failure, it was not actually the cause; instead, economic and technological forces doomed subsistence farming.

Sometimes post hoc reasoning neglects a common cause and assumes a cause-and-effect relationship between two events that actually have another cause. In the decade before the stock market crash of 1929, for instance, unemployment ranged from 1½ to 4 million. But unemployment did not cause the crash. Both phenomena were part of a complex economic situation that existed in this country and abroad. The way to avoid this kind of logical fallacy is to learn as much as possible, given the time allowed, about the subject under discussion.

Oversimplification of Cause

People frequently oversimplify cause when they do not fully understand an issue. For instance, inflation is blamed on interest rates, declining literacy on television, a rising divorce rate on the women's movement. In fact, inflation, the quality of public education, and the status of marriage are complex issues. Many factors bear on each, and none can be explained as the result of one simple cause. Discerning readers recognize when a writer does not have a grip on the complexities of a subject.

Either/Or Reasoning

The either/or fallacy presents an argument as though there were only two alternatives. This kind of thinking results in bumper stickers like "America—Love It or Leave It," implying that to live in this country requires unqualified approval of everything that takes place here. Writers can also fall into this trap, oversimplifying an issue to include only two possible choices. For example, universities must either have open-admissions policies or enroll only the children of the rich. Society must sanction either capital punishment or violent crime. In such cases, the either/or fallacy shifts an issue into too narrow a framework. In reality, few issues are so simple.

False Analogy

A false analogy involves an assumption that because two things are alike in one way or in several ways, they are alike in some other regard. For example, just because both government and business have income and expenditures, there is no basis for concluding that government can be run in exactly the same way as a business. For one thing, a government is responsible for its unproductive members; business is not. Also, unlike business, government's purpose is not to make a profit.

A notable false analogy was made by the Ayatollah Khomeini when explaining the Iranian government's execution of prostitutes, homosexuals, and adulterers:

> If your finger suffers from gangrene, what do you do? Let the whole hand and then the body become filled with gangrene, or cut the finger off?

Khomeini wanted the audience to reason thus: "Disease in the body equals moral corruption in society. Thus, a moral society is achieved in the same way as a healthy body." The analogy, however, will not work. For one thing, doctors can identify gangrene with some certainty and agree on the necessity to remove a finger. But people rarely agree on what is immoral. For another thing, a person is not part of society in the same way that a finger is part of a body. A person (unlike a finger) has a mind, a personality, and rights.

Begging the Question

Begging the question is a kind of circular reasoning: a writer or speaker "begs" the audience to grant at the outset that which is actually at stake. This kind of reasoning usually takes the form of a semantic trick. For example, readers might be asked to grant that "the unfair tuition increase should be repealed." Of course, readers will oppose anything unfair. The real issue is whether or not the increase is, in fact, unfair. This kind of circular reasoning often comes from people who are emotionally involved with their subjects and seek to involve their audience in the same way. Rhetoric typical of circular reasoning occurs in statements and questions such as these: "Immoral programs should not be shown on prime-time television."

"How can we allow the murder of these innocent animals at slaughterhouses?" People who use this rhetoric ask their audiences to grant that certain programs are immoral and that the slaughter of domestic food animals is murder—the very issues at stake. A writer may be able to beg the question with an uninformed, emotional audience, particularly an audience that already agrees on the issue. Informed readers, however, will not allow such tricks but instead will demand proof of claims.

Non Sequitur

The term *non sequitur* (Latin for "it does not follow") means that the conclusion does not follow from the argument. Thus, in a sense, any fallacy could be called a *non sequitur.* Usually, however, the term refers to a fallacy in an argument based on deduction—an argument in which a person deduces a conclusion from accepted premises.

Logical Deduction

ACCEPTED PREMISE:	Students who miss more than ten class meetings without written permission from the dean will fail the course.
ACCEPTED PREMISE:	Maureen missed more than ten class meetings without written permission from the dean.
VALID CONCLUSION:	Therefore, Maureen will fail the course.

Non Sequitur

ACCEPTED PREMISE:	Students who miss more than ten class meetings without written permission from the dean will fail the course.
ACCEPTED PREMISE:	Maureen failed the course.
INVALID CONCLUSION:	Therefore, Maureen missed more than ten class meetings without written permission from the dean.

Obviously, Maureen could have failed the course for poor grades, not for missing classes; therefore, the conclusion that she necessarily failed for missing classes does not follow.

Ordinarily in an argument, the premises and the conclusions are not set out formally as just shown. Instead, the non sequitur usually occurs in statements where some of the pieces of the argument are implied, as in the following examples:

NON SEQUITUR: Harry should be in politics because he has a good speaking voice. [A good speaking voice is an advantage to a politician. However, it does not follow that anyone with this characteristic should be in politics.]

NON SEQUITUR: My sister is good in math, so she must be smarter than I am. [The writer falsely assumes that mathematic ability is the best measure of intelligence.]

39f STRUCTURE

When you have tentatively settled on a thesis and chosen some supporting evidence, you can begin to assemble the components of the argument. Begin by writing down the thesis at the top of your paper. You can change the thesis, of course, as you draft your argument; but temporarily, you should use it as a guide to choose materials.

Under the thesis, list the pros (the evidence supporting your position) and cons (the evidence against your position). If the subject allows, you can pair points and counterpoints—pro/con, pro/con, pro/con. You should also list any concessions to the opposition or state any points of agreement. Use whatever system allows you to discover the strength of your argument. Then consider whether you still stand by your thesis. If not, rewrite it to reflect your defense.

With the components assembled, you can consider how best to organize the argument. The most common organizations are the classical structure, the discovery structure, and the Rogerian structure. You can follow one of the structures strictly; or you can use one simply as a guide to help you organize your material.

(1) The classical structure

The most traditional structure for argument is the format used for oratorical debates by classical rhetoricians like Aristotle. Originally, the structure had six parts. The first (*exordium*) served to get the audience's attention and introduce the subject. The second (*narratio*) supplied any necessary facts or background. The third (*partitio*) stated the thesis and prepared the audience for the "partitioning," or organization, of the argument to come. The fourth (*confirmatio*) presented evidence in support of the thesis. The fifth (*refutatio*) attempted to disprove the views of the opposition. And the sixth (*peroratio*) summarized the argument and appealed to the audience for agreement.

Contemporary writers still use this logical and forceful structure with few modifications. The Latin headings, of course, are rarely used now; and the format is usually condensed to five parts. But the basic format remains popular.

Introduction describes the subject and states the thesis, usually at the end of the section.
Statement of Fact presents facts or background the reader needs to know to follow the argument.
Proof presents reasoning and evidence supporting the thesis.
Refutation explains why the opposing view is invalid.
Conclusion summarizes the major points of the argument.

In short papers, you need not include headings separating the sections. You can, nevertheless, use the structure the headings indicate.

If the classical structure does not exactly suit the materials in your argument, you can always modify it. Suppose, for example, you want to argue that the United States should develop community-supported agriculture. The most logical strategy would be to begin with the background since the idea is fairly new to this country.

> The idea for Community Supported Agriculture (CSA) has been implemented in Japan and Western Europe for about thirty years. Because farmland is scarce and food is expensive in these countries, people have long needed to work cooperatively. In a CSA arrangement, consumers from a community buy shares in a farm so that a farmer is guaranteed a market and shareholders are guaranteed fresh food they know is safe. Everyone works together to be self-sufficient.

Then you could present the proof that supports joint agriculture. You might, for example, write a paragraph discussing the benefits to farmers.

Farmers get start-up cash from shareholders and thereby avoid the frustrating step of getting a bank loan that they must repay with interest. Also, the risk that farmers normally bear alone is now shared. In times of emergencies like floods and droughts, farmers can call on shareholders to pitch in and work to keep crops from rotting in the field, weeds from choking plants, or soil from drying out. Through participation, shareholders get a thorough education about farms and farmers. Consequently, farmers are no longer invisible members of the community; they gain standing and a well-deserved reputation for hard and essential work.

Additional sections of the argument could describe the benefits to consumers and the advantages of eliminating shipping and other overhead expenses. A few illustrations of successful CSA projects would also help support the feasibility of this kind of farming.

If you have already listed the cons of the argument, you could check your list for any that seem persuasive. Then you could position the refutation at the end of the paper.

The primary fear of farmers is probably that people will not participate. However, participation should not be a problem if farmers can adequately explain the system. In fact, many people who do not own land feel detached and dependent. They would probably welcome the chance to become a part of the process, to see things grow, to taste fresh food free from unnecessary chemical additives. Thus, the key is explanation. Organizers must present a clear statement that includes details about cost per share and shareholder responsibilities. Also, they must be specific about what will be planted, which chemicals will be used, and how produce will be divided. The agricultural system is not easy to set up, but its rewards are worth the effort.

The classical structure can be fairly easily adapted to any subject. Here, for example, is another version of the format.

Introduction to subject and statement of thesis
Concession of any indisputable points
Evidence supporting the thesis
Counterarguments attacking the opposition's points
Summary of major points

Of course, when your subject warrants it, you can present just the essentials: an *introduction* to your subject and *statement of the thesis,* followed by the *supporting evidence.* Be sure, however, that you do not neglect other classical components if they would strengthen your argument.

(2) The discovery structure

In the discovery structure, you invite the reader to explore a subject with you and finally to "discover" with you the natural, logical conclusions of your argument. Thus, your thesis appears in the middle or near the end of the paper. Although any argument can take this form, the discovery structure is a good choice when your subject is little understood. For example, to address a complicated problem such as disposal of nuclear waste, you could discuss alternatives and lead the reader to discover the most feasible.

Discovery is also a good choice when your position is likely to be unpopular. Suppose, for example, you want to argue this thesis: *Everyone between the ages of 18 and 21, except people in the military, should be required to work one year in community service.* Most people would react adversely to the idea because it suggests government infringement on individual freedom. By delaying the thesis, however, you could persuade an audience to consider, if not accept, the idea.

You could begin by discussing the problems that your proposal would help to solve. Your discussion could include some of the following ideas:

> Because of the military, the country seems fairly secure from outside threats; but our society is disrupted with a number of social problems. Too many of our young people have no family structure or supervision. Consequently, they drop out of school, thus losing any hope of meaningful jobs. Some escape into a world of drugs and crime. For some, gangs provide a substitute for family and the security of a group. Others live on welfare or on the street.
>
> As the population grows, the wear and tear on our physical and social environment increases. Litter proliferates; streets and highways are in disrepair; parks and other green spaces decay; schools and hospitals lack adequate staff and the money to provide it.

> Federal, state and local governments rely for funds on the already overtaxed white- and blue-collar workers, who now support the jobless, the homeless, and the elderly. Furthermore, as the economy slows and workers are laid off, the number of people with taxable income decreases.

You could support the discussion of problems with statistical details as well as demographic trends and predictions. You could also perhaps give case histories or hypothetical scenarios involving people affected by the problems.

Then you could introduce the importance of work to individual self-worth, supporting the claim with testimony from social workers or psychologists. Next, you could introduce the idea of a job corps and its many advantages to the participants.

> Working in meaningful jobs would give young people the supervision, the camaraderie, the self-discipline, and the social structure that many need so desperately. They would experience a sense of community and the pride that comes from accomplishment. Furthermore, participants would acquire skills in fields such as clerical work, carpentry, construction engineering, health care, recreation, forestry, and crime prevention.

You might also show how communities benefit.

> Schools, hospitals, parks, street and highway departments--all sorts of services would benefit from extra hands. Moreover, when people work toward improving the community, they better understand its problems and are less likely to demand instant solutions. Also, they develop community pride, which tends to discourage vandalism and crime.

You could use as supporting evidence the successes of communities and neighborhoods that have banded together to improve their collective lifestyle.

You could then move to your thesis, which the audience might now be prepared to accept or at least to consider. You could conclude by asserting that your proposal would be cost efficient: it would provide job training, reduce crime, and increase the number of productive citizens.

The strength of the discovery technique is that you delay the thesis until you can establish a background for its acceptance.

(3) The Rogerian structure

The Rogerian argument was named for the psychologist Carl Rogers, who developed the strategy as a means of compromise between warring factions. According to Rogers, the purpose of many arguments should be not to win but rather to find the truth or to solve a problem. To use the Rogerian format, you structure your argument in five parts.

Statement of the problem explains the problem that led to the conflict.
Opponent's position gives an objective statement of the opposing view, without attacking it.
Your position gives an objective statement of your view.
Areas of agreement points out where the two sides agree.
Resolution suggests a compromise that solves the problem to the satisfaction of both sides.

arg/crit 39f

Obviously, the strategy in the Rogerian structure is to concentrate on a solution rather than on victory. Thus, the format works well with emotionally charged subjects on which opposing sides can never agree completely—subjects such as abortion, pornography, and environmental issues. You would use a Rogerian argument to move the debate off the battleground of personal opinion and place it in an area of mutual benefit through cooperation.

You can also use the Rogerian structure for less controversial subjects. For example, suppose you wanted to argue that a business major is the best undergraduate degree for lawyers. You could begin by stating the problem: the quality of lawyers today is deteriorating. You could support this assertion with some sort of evidence, such as statements by judges or articles in periodicals. Then, you could state the position of the side you oppose and move on to your thesis.

> Traditionally, law-school students have majored in liberal arts, usually political science, English, or history. However, that pre-law major is no longer relevant. Today, the primary legal problems are taxes, leases, mortgages, bankruptcies, and contracts--all involving knowledge of business. Therefore, the most valuable pre-law education would be in the business school of a university or college.

In the Rogerian structure, the next step is to point out areas of agreement. In this case, you could agree that liberal arts courses are important. Then you could move to the resolution: a compromise between the two pre-law curricula.

> Of course, lawyers deal primarily in words. Therefore, they must be able to write and speak well, and they must be able to comprehend what they read. Also, lawyers must understand politics and political theory. And they must have an overview of historical institutions and movements. Thus, the best pre-law curriculum is a business major with electives carefully chosen from the school of liberal arts, electives that teach the specific skills and knowledge that lawyers need. The reverse would be impractical because a major in liberal arts would leave little time for important business electives.

Whichever structure you choose, you are not bound to it irrevocably. As you work through successive drafts of your paper, you may want to adapt the chosen structure to your particular subject. Or you may want to change to another structure altogether. Your goal is to write an effective argument, not to force your material into a specific format. Remember that the process of writing an argument is like the process of writing anything: one draft will not likely produce a good paper. You should expect to make changes as you develop and refine the argument.

39g SAMPLE ARGUMENT

The student who wrote the argument that follows was appalled by the amount of garbage that accumulated around the dumpster and in the parking lot at his apartment complex. He began asking questions about the subject "garbage" and found the two most important to be "What produces the garbage?" and "What can reduce it?" He then looked for relationships and found several potential conflicts—between lifestyle and garbage reduction, between packaging and garbage reduction, between food preparation and garbage reduction. In the library, the student consulted a few periodicals, including *Technology Review, Consumer Reports,* and *Garbage.* His reading not only turned up ideas and facts for use as evidence but also suggested another conflict that eventually framed his argument: recycling and composting versus reuse. The resulting paper follows the Modern Language Association style for indicating sources. A discussion of this style appears in Chapter 41.

Reuse: The Garbage Solution

Too much of the United States is covered with trash, and the problem is getting worse. In 1990, Americans threw away 196 million tons of trash--twice as much as in 1960 ("More Trash" Journal B1). Trash litters the scene from city streets to country roads, from deserts to forests, from mountains to beaches. Along one 3-mile stretch along the Texas coast, volunteers recently picked up 10 tons of trash (Pike 34). Communities face increasing mounds of trash and spend ever larger sums to build landfills and incinerators to dispose of waste--not always safely. Trains and barges loaded with municipal trash and waste roam the country searching for places to dump their loads. The situation is critical. People must change their attitudes. They must become more conscious of the volume of trash and work to reduce it.

problem establishe[d] in introducti[on]

general solution proposed i[n] thesis

arg/crit 39g

Recycling is often proposed as a solution. But although recycling helps reduce the volume of trash, it is an expensive process. According to one study, recyclables are not valuable enough to pay for the costs of local recycling programs (Franklin 23). Also, recycling can be bothersome, and everyone will not put forth the effort required. Materials must be separated into several containers: one for aluminum, one for paper, one for cans, and one for plastic. Bottles and cans must be rinsed out. Often glass must be separated by color, and paper must be sorted by type. Even after recycling, the 196 million tons of trash thrown away in 1990 was reduced to only 163 million tons ("More Trash" Journal B1).

conflict: th[e] best way to reduce garbage

solution of recycling rejected because of costs and inconven-ience

In addition, the recycling process that works well for glass and aluminum does not work as well for paper, tin cans, and plastic. With each recycling, the quality of paper gets worse, and the process releases pollutants because of the presence of chlorine and toxic ink. The tin must be separated from the steel in tin cans, requiring extra cost. And according to Consumer Reports municipal programs only rarely recycle polypropylene, a thermoplastic resin used in packaging and coatings. The most serious drawback to recycling, however, is that alone it cannot sufficiently reduce the glut of trash that constantly accumulates ("Plastics Decoded" 688).

use of transitional expressions to show relationships between paragraphs

recycling rejected as inefficient

Likewise, composting is not a solution. It can help remove some kinds of garbage. For example, food scraps and yard clippings can be converted into valuable humus for soil replacement or enrichment. But on a large scale, there are serious problems with composting. Materials that are not completely degradable, such as the plastic in many disposable diapers, are not compostable. Also, there is the difficulty of separating organic from inorganic material and uncontaminated from contaminated wastes, and composting can produce bad odors that nearby residents will probably not tolerate. Furthermore, toxic substances such as heavy metals and asbestos are "lurking" in the decaying piles of organic matter (Miller 20-21).

composting rejected as both inefficient and offensive

The only effective solution is to reduce the amount of trash that we generate at ever-accelerating rates. Changing habits and merchandising practices will not be easy, but change is essential.

more specific statement of thesis

First, we must reduce packaging. Too many products come in multiple layers of wrapping. A typical microwavable meal comes on a plastic tray, covered with a plastic wrap, all placed inside a paperboard box. One particular frozen dinner comes wrapped inside five different layers of plastic. Fresh fruits and meats are displayed on unnecessary plastic trays and wrapped with unnecessary plastic wrap. Small objects like cassette tapes generally come in elaborate packaging four times the product's original size. Matchbox cars, which originally came in matchboxes, are now sold in foot-long plastic boxes. Understandably, this kind of packaging helps prevent pilfering; but it also increases cost and waste. In a recent television advertisement, a deodorant company boasts about its environmental attitude by pointing out that its product does not come in a box. Perhaps this attitude will spread. Consumers obviously do not control packaging, but by complaining and boycotting, they can certainly influence manufacturers.

transitions (first, secon[d] *and* third) *t[o] introduce points supporting thesis*

first point o[f] support based on observation of packagin[g]

Second, consumers can stop buying products that can be used only once. Reusable cloth towels or sponges can replace paper towels, and cloth diapers can replace disposable diapers. Reusable glasses, cups, dishes, and cookware can replace throw-away plastic and styrofoam. People faced with the inconvenience of washing and cleaning will not welcome these changes; but if they can be impressed with the seriousness of the trash explosion, they can be persuaded to work a little harder to save the environment.

second poin[t] of support based on logic: reuse reduces tras[h]

Third, there must be widespread use of returnable or refillable bottles. Of course, glass can be successfully recycled; it must, however, be ground up and reprocessed. Reuse would be much cheaper and more energy efficient. For the consumer, the most obvious advantage to reusable bottles is the refund upon return. But another advantage is that the liquid inside these thick bottles stays fresher, gets colder, and tastes better because it undergoes fewer chemical changes than liquid in flimsy disposables. And with a little imagination, we could eliminate the annoying accumulation of bottles: in Germany, for example, shoppers bring refillable milk bottles to the market and fill them with milk from a machine. Manufacturers can be persuaded to make the necessary changes if throwaways were taxed. Some states have already successfully levied taxes on wasteful containers. More states and the federal government should follow suit.

third point of support based on logic: consumers will benefit

Through a concerted effort, we can and must reduce the amount of trash that is overwhelming our environment. Consumers must change their purchasing habits and throwaway behavior to reduce the amount of trash they produce. They must view reduction as more important than either recycling or composting. Business and industry must recognize the wastefulness of excessive packaging and throwaway products. Finally, community, state, and federal governments must promote awareness and effectively enforce a clean environment.

conclusion with three parts: (a.) strong statement of general thesis; (b.) summary of argument (c.) extension of responsibility to business, industry, and government

WORKS CITED

Franklin, Marjorie. The Role of Recycling in Integrated Solid Waste Management to the Year 2000. Prairie City, Kansas: Franklin Associates, 1994.

Miller, Susan Katz. "Compost and Its Discontents." Technology Review Jan. 1993: 20-21.

"More Trash Recycles, but Volume Still Grows." Wall Street Journal 24 Aug. 1992: B1.

Pike, Doug. "Hook, Line, and Thinker." Tide Nov./Dec. 1994: 34.

"Plastics Decoded." Consumer Reports Oct. 1991: 688.

The Computer Connection

The main advantage of writing an argument on a computer is generally the same as for writing any kind of composition. The computer allows you to make changes quickly and thus helps you improve a paper's quality. For arguments, however, the computer can provide especially valuable practice. Through online connections, you can interact with a real audience on real issues and conflicts.

Suggestions for Writing an Argument

- Observe the arguments presented on computer networks. By assessing the strengths and weaknesses of these arguments, you can learn valuable tactics.
- Enter arguments through networked groups or electronic mail. Such electronic media allow you to test your argument in part or in whole. For example, you might post one of your assertions on the Internet or on a local bulletin board. The responses you receive should prove invaluable.
- Try out your argument with several different audiences to experience their reactions.
- Try out two different sides of an argument to determine which side would make the most effective paper.
- Gather evidence from networks.
- If you are turning in your composition on disk, use the Internet, commercial online services, CD-ROMs, and local bulletin boards. These services can help you to find, download, and import files that might include an audio excerpt from a speech, a photograph, or even a short video clip of an event or subject you might otherwise spend time trying to describe.

CHAPTER

40

RESEARCH PAPERS IN PROGRESS

res 40

The process of writing a research paper is not very different from the process of writing any paper: choosing a suitable subject and a clear purpose, gathering information, organizing, writing, and revising. And like other kinds of papers, research papers do not always develop in a sequence; writers must often retrace steps or sometimes even start over. In other ways, though, writing research papers is different. Instructors who assign these papers expect effective use of the library; successful paraphrasing, summarizing, and quoting of sources; and the accurate use of some system for citations and references.

40a SUBJECT

When undertaking a research paper, choose your subject very carefully. No amount of work can salvage a poor choice. Good subjects come from many kinds of stimuli: an instructor, a textbook, a television program, your own curiosity. If you keep a journal, you might find a suitable subject there. Otherwise, you might try freewriting, brainstorming, or asking questions. (See Chapter 34, The Search for Ideas.)

Another approach is to go to the library and browse through the material. The news stories, articles, editorials, and letters in newspapers and periodicals are often good sources. Encyclopedias, almanacs, and other reference books contain vast amounts of information. Indexes list topics and titles. In fact, you never know where you might find a subject that will fire your enthusiasm.

When you are deciding on a subject, you should make sure that it fits several criteria.

- The subject must suit the audience.

  Although you must satisfy your instructor's expectations, you do not write to the instructor personally. Instead, you usually address a general audience made up of such readers as college students or graduates. Therefore, the subject should be one that would interest intelligent readers.

- The subject must suit the assignment.

  Consider the type of paper assigned, its expected length, and the kind of material available or required. You may be expected to argue a thesis or to accumulate information. You may be expected to write a short paper of about five pages or a longer one of about twenty pages. You may be expected to use a few sources or a comprehensive body of available material. All these considerations can affect the subject you choose.

- The subject must not be too difficult.

  Many writers get in trouble because they tackle topics that interest them, only to discover that reading the available information is too difficult. For example, suppose a nonexpert wants to write a paper on cancer research but finds that most of the sources are technical and sound like this: "Mutation affecting the 12th amino acid of the c-H-ras oncogene product occurs infrequently in human cancer." If you lack the background to understand the material that covers your subject, you will have to find a less technical subject.

- The subject must not require that an excessive number of sources be checked.

  For some subjects like *Buddhism* or *Shakespeare,* you could easily find more than one hundred books listed in a typical library catalog. You know you cannot possibly search the material adequately within a reasonable time. Whenever you find too much material in the library, you know you must limit or change your subject. Instead of beginning with a subject like *crime,* begin with *detectives in literature;* instead of *earthquakes,* begin with *earthquakes and building.*

- A sufficient amount of material on the subject must be available.
  The number of sources you will need depends on your assignment, the amount of usable information in each source, and the expected length of the paper. You should abandon a subject if you fear that insufficient material is available to develop it thoroughly. If you look up a subject like *hijacking yachts* and you find only one source, you could shift to *hijacking airlines,* which is more extensively covered, or change direction completely.

- The subject should have key words associated with it.
  Key words are specific terms associated with a subject. They are the words that researchers look up in catalogs and indexes in order to find material. Subjects without key words are very difficult to research. What words could you look up for the subject *the problem of inefficiency in business?* An excessively general word like *business* leads to sources on a multitude of unrelated subjects, and abstract words like *inefficiency* or *problem* will not even be listed in catalogs and indexes. You get better results with a subject like *the effect of television advertising on the food choices of children.* It suggests key words (*television, advertising,* and possibly *consumers*) that can lead to useful sources of information. You might look in reference books and indexes before you definitely settle on a subject; you will then be sure that the subject has indexed key words that can lead to material.

- The subject must not be excessively broad.
  Sometimes, you do not know at the beginning of a writing project whether a subject is the right choice. Writers frequently envision one paper but later, particularly after outlining, realize the scope is entirely too broad. The writer of the paper on discrimination in Japanese business (see 41e) intended at first to write about all the problems within the Japanese system—inhumane factories, inflexibility, stress, slow promotion, lack of creativity, and discrimination. Then the writer discovered that he had attempted too much. The paper would be longer than the requirement or time would allow. Therefore, he restricted the topic to only discrimination against women.

The Computer Connection

Using a computer to search for a subject for a research paper can be exciting and productive. Since the computer allows you to experience a wide variety of media, you will find your options for a subject broadened. Computer networks and databases contain such stimulating material as print, graphics, sound, video, and photographs. Advanced multimedia technology can often enrich a paper.

Suggestions for Choosing a Subject for a Research Paper

- If possible, use commercial online services in your search. Subscribers who pay a connect charge and monthly fees can receive services from CompuServe, Prodigy, America Online, Genie, Delphi, and others. Online services such as these provide access to such resources as articles, discussion groups, encyclopedias, and files.
- Use Internet, a worldwide collection of computer networks. Once available only to the government and research organizations, Internet is now widely available to individuals. By using it, you can communicate quickly and simply with people all over the world, and you can gain access to books, journals, and other documents. (Your campus computer services department can supply information about Internet's availability.)
- With Internet, use commands that take you to targeted resources.

  GOPHER is a search tool that will find documents with keywords in them. Those documents can then be read online or downloaded to your computer.

  TELNET allows you to log onto a remote computer or network and use the resources there. For example, you can log into the resources of your library or a university library in some distant place.

  FTP (file transfer protocol) can download files from remote sites to your computer.

  ARCHIE can search for file names and parts of file names. Once you learn the location of files, you can use FTP to download them.

  DOMAINS will narrow your searches to the type of facility that supports the material. A few useful domains are *edu* (educational institutions), *gov* (government), and *mil* (military).

- Explore computer bulletin boards or enter conversations through e-mail. Bulletin board systems, commonly called "boards" or "BBS," are usually operated by individuals as a hobby, but they may also be commercial networks.

40b PURPOSE

A subject suitable for research has a clear purpose that will direct and limit the amount of material to be gathered. Without a clear purpose, a paper will probably contain bits and pieces of information that are only loosely tied together. For example, the subject *Meriwether Lewis* lacks purpose. What will be the point of the paper? What material will be included? On the other hand, the question *Was Meriwether Lewis murdered?* gives direction to the paper. The writer can concentrate on answering the question.

A good subject is inextricably linked to the purpose of the research. To stimulate and focus your research, you can look for a question that has not been definitively answered, an issue you feel strongly about, or a literary work that lends itself to interpretation.

(1) Answering a question

One common stimulus for research is an intriguing question or mystery.

Was the *Hindenburg* sabotaged by enemy agents?

Why did the dinosaurs die out?

Can gorillas learn to talk?

Why did the poet Ezra Pound collaborate with the Fascists?

What produces the special sound of Stradivarius violins?

The sample paper on Mark Twain (see 41b) began with this sort of motivation. After reading in the *Oxford Companion to American Literature* that Mark Twain had left the Confederate army during the Civil War, the writer decided to find out why. If the purpose of your paper is to answer a question, you can support one answer or explore several possible answers.

(2) Presenting an argument

Another logical purpose for a research paper is to present an argument. The sample paper in section 41e argues that in the Japanese business world, discrimination exists against most women. Throughout the discussion, the writer tries to convince readers that this opinion is sound.

If you decide to write an argument, first be sure that the subject is debatable. You should not try to argue an established fact or take a position that everyone would agree on. For example, you are not likely to generate much debate if you argue that Byron wrote poetry, that computer literacy is an asset, or that drunken drivers are dangerous. You could argue, however, that despite Byron's denial, the poem "Childe Harold's Pilgrimage" is autobiographical; that computer literacy should be required of all high school graduates; that drunken drivers should be sentenced to perform public service rather than to serve time in jail.

Some subjects, even though arguable, have been overdone to the point that very little interesting or new can be written about them. You are wise to avoid topics like abortion, marijuana, and the death penalty unless you can contribute fresh ideas to these subjects.

(3) Interpreting literature

A common assignment in English classes involves interpreting literature. A research paper of this kind might focus on a single work, such as a novel, short story, play, or poem. But if the entire work is long or complex, the paper will probably cover only one of its elements. You might, for example, explore one mysterious symbol in a poem or interpret a Renaissance play to demonstrate only the sixteenth-century attitude toward war.

Another approach for a literature paper is to examine two or more works. For instance, you might trace a common theme or technique through a group of poems by the same author. You might contrast several works by one author to illustrate a change in attitude over a period of time. Or you might contrast the writing styles of different authors who deal with the same subject. The student writer of the sample paper in 41c contrasts two different versions of "Cinderella." While reading Anne Sexton's poem "Cinderella," the writer was intrigued by the differences between Sexton's version and the traditional romantic story. As a consequence, the writer decided to research Sexton's source.

Before tackling any literary topic, however, you should first be familiar with the characteristics of novels, short stories, plays, and poems. The following questions will help you find and narrow a subject and guide you through your interpretation.

Novels, short stories, plays

- What is the theme of the work?

  The theme is the central idea of the work—a generalization about life. Do not confuse theme with moral; only in very simplistic writing can theme be expressed in a proverb such as "Virtue is rewarded" or "Absence makes the heart grow fonder." Instead, a theme is usually an insight into the nature of human beings and their relationships to themselves, one another, and the universe.

- What are the conflicts in the work?

  The plot usually arises from conflict between the protagonist (the main character) and the antagonist (an opposing force). The antagonist can be another character or characters, society, nature, or even some trait within the protagonist. Thus, the conflict may be a clash of actions, ideas, or emotions.

- What is the point of view?

  The term *point of view* refers to the perspective of the narrator. In general, there are four points of view: omniscient, limited omniscient, first person, and objective. With an omniscient point of view, the narrator is not a character in the story but rather an all-knowing presence who can see into the minds of characters, tell us what they think, and interpret their actions.

  In a limited-omniscient point of view, the narrator has access to the thoughts of only one character. Thus, the narrator observes the actions of the remaining characters from this single perspective.

  In first-person point of view, one of the characters tells the story (using *I*). The narrator—a major or minor character, an active participant, or an observer—cannot enter the minds of other characters but can only speculate about their thoughts and motives.

  Finally, with the objective (or dramatic) point of view, the reader is an observer of the action and has no access to the mind of any character. Instead, the reader draws conclusions from what the characters say and do, not from what they think.

- How are the characters presented?

  An interpretation could evaluate how effectively an author presents the characters. In most serious literature, characters should not be stereotypes—a "bigoted Southern sheriff," "spoiled rich kid," or "domineering mother." Instead, they should be lifelike, with the complexities and contradictions of real people. In addition, the major characters should be dynamic; they should change in some way as a result of their experiences.

- What is the significance of the setting, that is, the time and place in which the story occurs?

  Writers do not choose a setting at random, and you should consider the choice carefully. Try to evaluate what bearing the setting has on the conflict. If a primary conflict lies between the protagonist and society, the setting may be the antagonist, providing both the catalyst for action and the key to motivation. In any case, the setting will likely support the theme of the work, providing an appropriate backdrop for the struggles of the characters.

Poetry

- Who is speaking in the poem?

  The speaker of a poem is not necessarily the poet. Frequently, the speaker represents a type of person—rejected lover, dying woman, soldier, mother, deposed ruler, traveler, patriot, prisoner. Unless you know who is speaking, you will probably not understand the poem or its purpose.

- What is the tone?

  Through the speaker's vocabulary and sentence structure, the poet establishes a particular tone. The established tone may be, for example, scholarly or familiar, arrogant or folksy, playful or serious, bitter or thankful.

- What is the poem's purpose?

  The purpose may be to express an emotion, a mood, or an idea. It may be to reveal human nature, describe a place, tell a story, or achieve some combination of purposes.

- What is the poem's form?

  A poem may be a narrative—a story in verse. Or it may be a lyric—a verse that expresses emotions like grief or joy, creates a mood like foreboding or celebration, or develops an idea like fate's unfairness or the power of friendship. The form may be traditional—a sonnet, blank verse, couplets, quatrains (see the Glossary of Terms for explanations). Or the form may be free, following no set pattern of rhythm and rhyme.

- Do the sound and rhythm contribute to the purpose?

  The sound and rhythm should be compatible with the emotion, mood, or idea of the poem. (See 33e.)

- What are the central images?

  Images appeal to the senses, calling forth the sights, sounds, smells, tastes, and tactile impressions of the physical world: sun-baked, red clay hills; the blare of a dozen trumpets; heavy, cheap perfume; clammy, wet clay. Poets use images not only to create physical experiences but also to establish moods.

- Are there any symbols in the poem?

  A symbol is an image that stands for an idea or a complex of ideas. Symbols are common in everyday life—for example, a flag often represents patriotism; a skull and crossbones, death; a lightbulb, the flash of inspiration.

  Sometimes symbols are central to the meaning of a poem. Take care, however, not to read each image as a symbol. A symbol points to the meaning beneath the surface. Images are details that create realism or a mood but suggest nothing more. To distinguish between the two is not always easy. Some people exaggerate imagery, calling everything a symbol: a closed door symbolizes alienation; a fish, freedom; a star, the mystery that cannot be solved. Unless the image relates to the theme of a work, it is probably not a symbol. Instead, the image may be a literal detail meant only to add to the background.

- Is the language literal or figurative?

  The language of poetry is often figurative rather than literal—that is, suggestive rather than straightforward. For example, instead of using a literal, factual description of fog, T. S. Eliot pictures a cat's languid and pervasive movements through the evening. When the meaning of a figure of speech is not obvious, the reader must interpret the meaning. (See 33d.) If a poem uses figurative language, you might want to comment on whether a figure is fresh or stale, forceful or weak, effective or silly.

- What does the poem mean?

  A poem's meaning derives from its many elements. A paraphrase (a literal rewording of what a poem says) may be an insufficient expression of the meaning. All the other elements—for example, the symbolism, the suggestions, the tone, and the figures of speech—contribute significantly. Therefore, when you try to discover meaning, look at the poem as a whole, not at just an isolated element. And remember that some poems are very puzzling. Do not get discouraged. Even professional critics have difficulty with interpretation, and frequently they strongly disagree. If after multiple readings you cannot figure out the meaning, just say so and explain why.

40c PRELIMINARY LIBRARY RESEARCH

Whether you have a clear purpose or merely a tentative one, you must do preliminary library work to check its suitability, to put it in focus, and to make sure you can unify the diverse bits of information you will collect and assemble. Thus, at this point, you must go to a library and spend time searching, reading, and thinking.

In the library, you need to accumulate a bibliography (a record of the material you find) because later you will want to return to any relevant information. Also at this stage, you may take some preliminary notes on information that you are fairly sure you can use. Never trust your memory; as you move from source to source, you will forget many ideas and where you found them. Nevertheless, you should not mistake the preliminary stages of research with the actual note-taking stage. If you do, two problems may occur. First, you very possibly will end up throwing away notes you have laboriously written. Second, more likely, you may try to use your notes whether they fit or not, and the resulting paper will be a disconnected hodgepodge. To avoid these problems, you should read widely to focus the subject and weed out inappropriate material.

To begin your search of the library, you must understand what is housed there and how to retrieve whatever you need. In other words, you must know what kinds of sources exist and how they are organized.

(1) Primary and secondary sources

Libraries have two types of material—primary and secondary sources. Primary sources are firsthand, original material such as eyewitness accounts, letters, diaries, original investigations, speeches, literary works, and autobiographies. Secondary sources are those that analyze, combine, or comment on other sources.

Each type of material has its advantages. Secondary sources, which interpret and pull together other materials, can simplify your research and expand its breadth. Primary sources, on the other hand, can have greater immediacy and impact. Some subjects are best developed through primary sources; others through secondary; some require both types. Use whatever sources are appropriate and available.

Primary Source	Secondary Source
transcript of a trial	reporter's interpretation of a trial
Constitution	historian's analysis of the Constitution
poem	literary critic's explanation of a poem's meaning
data of a scientific study	textbook's discussion of the significance of a study

(2) Library organization

Although all libraries do not use the same system, they do share characteristics. All libraries have a central desk where you can get information and check out books; all libraries have some sort of reference area, which contains such works as encyclopedias, dictionaries, indexes, almanacs, and other research aids. All libraries have a catalog of holdings and specific areas for books and for periodicals. In addition, all libraries arrange books according to some numbering system, most often the Library of Congress system or Dewey Decimal system. The call number assigned to each book identifies its location and appears in the catalog and on the book. If you are unfamiliar with the library you plan to use, check signs, brochures, and handouts for information about locations. And when necessary, do not hesitate to ask questions of the librarians.

(3) The reference area

Once you know general locations in the library, you then need to find specific resources. The reference area contains material that is absolutely essential in research. This area usually houses two kinds of material. The first includes encyclopedias, dictionaries, almanacs, and other general works that can provide you with an overview of a subject and help you find a supportable thesis. The second kind includes catalogs, indexes, and abstracts. These direct you to other books, articles, and reports that contain the information you will search for useful material.

(4) General works

To find general information about your subject, you search the reference works that contain broad, comprehensive surveys. But first, you must determine which reference works will help you research your particular subject.

If you are new to library research, particularly in an academic or research library, you might find the following scenario helpful. Assume you enter the library and locate the reference area. You see hundreds of books. Which ones should you check? Although reference works are indexed by subject in the catalog, you might thumb through many cards or hunt through many lists unproductively. A better way is to figure out how your library's collection is organized. A library usually posts its numbering system, but if not, ask a librarian for help. The general works, like encyclopedias, are the easiest to find. They are marked with an **A** in a library using the Library of Congress system and with the numbers 000–099 in a library using the Dewey Decimal system. The other reference works also are arranged systematically by call number. For example, American history appears in the 970s in the Dewey system and under **E** or **F** in the Library of Congress system. Knowing the system, you can browse along the rows of books, looking for useful sources.

Another suggestion is to look at some of the following works. These reference works mainly provide an overview of a subject and suggest how to limit it. Sometimes they contain bibliographies that supply the names of pertinent books and articles. Although not exhaustive, the list indicates the kinds of material available in reference collections.

Encyclopedias

General

Encyclopedia Americana
Encyclopaedia Britannica
Collier's Encyclopedia
New Columbia Encyclopedia

Humanities

Encyclopedia of American History
Cassell's Encyclopaedia of World Literature
Encyclopedia of World History
American Political Dictionary
Encyclopedia of Philosophy
Encyclopedia of World Literature in the 20th Century
Worldmark Encyclopedia of the Nations
Readers' Encyclopedia
Encyclopedia of Science Fiction and Fantasy
Encyclopedia of Mystery and Detection

Social Sciences

International Encyclopedia of the Social Sciences
Encyclopedia of Sociology
Encyclopedia of Psychology
Encyclopedia of Social Work
Encyclopedia of Education
Encyclopedia of Advertising

Science and Technology

McGraw-Hill Encyclopedia of Science and Technology
Van Nostrand's Scientific Encyclopedia
Encyclopedia of the Biological Sciences
Encyclopedia of Chemistry
Encyclopedia of Computer Science
Grzimek's Encyclopedia of Ecology

Film and Television

Magill's Survey of Cinema
New York Times Encyclopedia of Film
Complete Encyclopedia of Television Programs, 1947–1979
New York Times Encyclopedia of Television
Focal Encyclopedia of Film and Television Techniques

Sports

Sportsman's Encyclopedia
Encyclopedia of the Olympic Games

Encyclopedia of Football
Official World Encyclopedia of Sports and Games

Art and Music

Encyclopedia of World Art
Britannica Encyclopaedia of American Art
Encyclopedia of Painting
International Cyclopedia of Music and Musicians
World's Encyclopedia of Recorded Music
Encyclopedia of Pop, Rock, and Soul

Biographies

General

Who's Who in America
International Who's Who
Who's Who (British)
Dictionary of American Biography
Dictionary of National Biography (British)
Webster's Biographical Dictionary
Current Biography
New York Times Biographical Service
Biography and Genealogy Master Index

Specialized

Contemporary Authors
Twentieth Century Authors
American Men and Women of Science
Biographical Dictionary of Scientists
Dictionary of Scientific Biography
Who's Who in Rock
Who's Who in Horror and Fantasy Fiction

Handbooks and Manuals

Oxford Companion to English Literature
Oxford Companion to American Literature
Poetry Handbook: Dictionary or Terms
A Handbook to Literature
Crowell's Handbook of Contemporary Drama
Historian's Handbook
Handbook of Chemistry and Physics
Engineering Manual
Occupational Outlook Handbook
United States Government Manual
TV Facts

Filmgoer's Companion
Oxford Companion to Sports and Games

Atlases and Gazeteers

Atlas of the Universe
National Geographic Atlas of the World
Oxford Economic Atlas of the World
Times Atlas of the World
Webster's New Geographical Dictionary

Almanacs and Yearbooks

Facts on File
Statesman's Year-Book
Statistical Abstract of the United States
World Almanac and Book of Facts
Yearbook of the United Nations
Americana Annual
Britannica Book of the Year
Broadcasting Yearbook

(5) Keywords

To find material on a subject, you must check lists of sources—catalogs, indexes, and abstracts. There, you find subjects listed in alphabetical order under headings, called *keywords,* or *descriptors.* Sometimes you must look under not just one keyword but several.

You can find the keywords that may lead you to sources by checking in the volumes titled *Library of Congress: Subject Headings.* For example, to find out what is known about how people taste food the researcher looked up *taste* and found the entry shown in Figure 1. It lists keywords that can be searched manually in the catalogs, indexes, and abstracts. You can also find keywords for computer searches in thesauruses such as the *Thesaurus of ERIC Descriptors.*

(6) Catalogs

Once you know keywords, or subject headings, that could lead to useful sources, you should look in your library's main catalog, a primary aid for locating material. Catalogs vary from library to library.

Taste *(Physiology. QP456: Psychology. BF261)*
sa Barbel (Anatomy)
Flavor
Food—Sensory evaluation
Food preferences
Taste buds
Tobacco—Sensory evaluation
x Gustation
Tasting (Physiology)
xx Chemical senses
Drinking behavior
Food preferences
Senses and sensation
Tongue
— Threshold
xx Threshold (Perception)
Taste (Aesthetics)
See Aesthetics
Taste buds
xx Barbel (Anatomy)
Taste
Tongue
Taste testing of food
See Food—Sensory evaluation
Taste testing of wine
See Wine tasting
Tasting (Physiology)

Figure 1 Keywords relating to *taste*

Some are the traditional files, alphabetically arranged drawers with each item listed on an index card. Increasingly files are computerized or copied on microfilm. Some catalogs contain all the library's holdings; others contain only lists of books, not periodicals.

Whatever its format, a catalog will contain at least three entries for every work—title, author, and subject. Sometimes the entries are separated into different files, with titles in one, authors in another, and subjects in yet another. Other times all entries (title, author, and subject) are arranged alphabetically in one file. At this point, since you are looking for information on a subject, you will look primarily at the subject file for sources. In a traditional card catalog the subject cards contain the information shown in Figure 2. A computerized catalog using the Library of Congress system lists the works available (Figure 3) and then gives more detailed information about selected items (Figure 4).

A "bibliography" notation means that the work contains a list of additional sources on the same subject. A bibliography can save you time since someone else has already gone through the catalogs and indexes compiling sources. One drawback is that you do not always know how thorough the list is. Also, these lists are not always up to date. However, they can supply very useful supplements to your own list of materials. Bibliographies also may be listed in encyclopedias, other reference books, and specialized volumes such as the *Bibliographic Index* (1937–) and the *World Bibliography of Bibliographies* (1939–). *The Subject Guide to Books in Print* (*BIP*) and the *Cumulative Book Index* (*CBI*)—both comprehensive bibliographies of books—may be worth checking for sources on your subject.

If you use other researchers' bibliographies or comprehensive bibliographies of published books, you may find that your library does not own the books you want. In this case, you might consider getting the books on loan from another library, if the service is available. However, before you order a book on interlibrary loan, you might check the *Book Review Digest*, where you can find book reviews describing many publications. The information there will give you a good idea whether a wait for the material is worth the time, especially since the wait may be lengthy.

subject CLEMENS, SAMUEL LANGHORNE, 1835–1910

call number PS
1331 Canby, Henry Seidel, 1878-1961. *author, title, and publication information*
C25 Turn west, turn east: Mark Twain and
Henry James. Boston, Houghton Mifflin, 1861.
xii, 318 p. ports. (on lining papers) 22 cm. *features suc as length an the inclusion of "portraits," or photographs of people*
bibliography notation Bibliography: p. 301-303.

1. Clemens, Samuel Langhorne,
1835-1910. 2. James, Henry, 1843-1916.
I. Title

Figure 2 Subject card

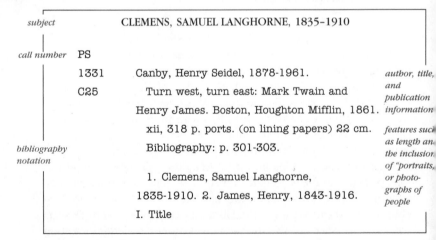

```
FILE:LCCC; TITLE/LINE-SET 3
                                ITEMS 10-15 OF 277
10.  62-19224: Smith, Henry Nash. Mark
       Twain. Cambridge, Belknap Press
       of Harvard University Press,
       1962. ix, 212 p, 25 cm. LC CALL
       NUMBER: PS1331 .S55 1962
11.  63-11599: Smith, Henry Nash. Mark
       Twain. Englewood Cliffs, N.J.,
       Prentice-Hall, 1963. 179 p, 22 cm.
       LC CALL NUMBER: PS1331 .S548 1963
12.  64-21709: Duckett, Margaret. Mark
       Twain and Bret Harte. Norman,
       University of Oklahoma Press,
       1964. xiii, 365 p, illus., ports,
       23 cm. LC CALL NUMBER: PS1333 .D8
13.  65-20437: Salsbury, Edith Colgate.
       Susy and Mark Twain. New York,
       Harper & Row, 1965. xvii, 444 p,
       illus., ports, 25 cm. LC CALL
       NUMBER: PS1332 .S3
14.  66-11966: Cox, James Melville. Mark
       Twain. Princeton, N.J., Princeton
       University Press, 1966. viii, 321
       p, 23 cm. LC CALL NUMBER: PS1331
       .C6
15.  66-17603: Kaplan, Justin. Mr.
       Clemens and Mark Twain. New York,
       Simon and Schuster, 1966. 424 p,
       illus., ports, 24 cm. LC CALL
       NUMBER: PS1331 .K33
READY FOR NEW COMMAND OR NEW ITEM NBR (FOR
NEXT PAGE, XMIT ONLY)
```

Figure 3 Partial printout of works available

```
    66-17603    ITEM 15 OF 277 IN SET 3  (LCCC)

Kaplan, Justin,
  Mr. Clemens and Mark Twain, a
    biography. New York, Simon and
    Schuster, 1966. 424 p. illus., ports,
    24 cm.
LC CALL NUMBER: PS1331 .K33
DEWEY DEC: 817.4 B
SUBJECTS (INDX): Twain, Mark-1835-1910
NOTES:
  Bibliographical references included
    in "Notes" (p. 389-410)
READY FOR NEW COMMAND
```

author, title, and publication information

call numbers

bibliography notation

Figure 4 Detailed information about #15 (Figure 3)

res 40c

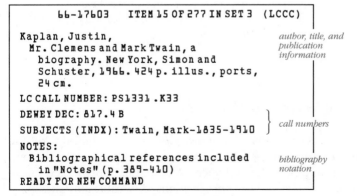

The Computer Connection

Although the electronic, paperless library envisioned by many futurists is not here, you can expect to find more and more libraries with computer systems. Because of the cost, all libraries will not have the newest technology, but several large research libraries have provided online computer searches for about 10 years. The most common online system available today is the catalog of a library's holdings, called an OPAC (online public-access catalog). Searching the catalog with a computer eliminates the tedious job of thumbing through cards stuffed in cramped drawers. In addition to OPAC, you may also find other computerized resources, such as encyclopedias, dictionaries, thesauruses, and lists of quotations.

Suggestions for Using Online and CD-ROM Reference Material

- Use a computer catalog, when available, to save time. The computer will usually print out a list and eliminate the need to copy entries. A big advantage of an online catalog is that with a modem, you can conduct your search on a home computer.
- Take time to acquaint yourself with online and ondisc resources before your composition is due. By the time you need to conduct research under the pressure of a deadline, you should already be able to navigate comfortably through the process.
- Do not overlook reference material on CD-ROMs. A single CD can contain data equal to more than 440 copies of this textbook.
- Be sure to learn the dates covered in any database you use. Frequently, online material will be the most recent. If you are searching for old sources, you may have to use printed material.
- Don't hesitate to ask librarians for assistance; large research libraries employ people trained in online searches.
- Learn about hypertext. In hypertext, several sources are linked, and you can move at will back and forth among them—for example, from a book to an encyclopedia to a dictionary, and even from system to system.

(7) Indexes and abstracts

The library's catalog helps you locate books rather quickly, but the material on many subjects will come mainly from periodicals—journals, magazines, and newspapers. A search of periodicals is essential to ensure that you have not overlooked valuable information.

No matter what subject you are researching, you will probably find it covered in some index. Many indexes provide general coverage; many others are very specialized, covering publications in only one area, such as in ecology, biography, or physics. Some indexes give only publication information; others also provide summaries, or abstracts.

But be forewarned; you cannot rush to the library and complete your work in an hour. Many searches require a time-consuming examination of the printed indexes. Usually you must check several different periodical indexes and many volumes of each index. If you are trying to locate very current information, the issues may not be bound or cumulatively indexed. Consequently, you may have to search a number of unbound monthly issues. Although a search of the periodical indexes takes time, much valuable information could never be located without their help. Even if your library provides computer searches of indexes, you must allow enough time to complete them. You may need an appointment with a librarian to do a thorough search of some databases.

Searches of Printed Indexes and Abstracts

Most students search at least some of the printed indexes shelved in the library. The advantage of such a search is that students have a degree of control. They can pick the indexes that cover material within their level of expertise, and they are free to shift and change the focus of their research as it progresses.

If you are not familiar with the indexes in the library, there are several things you can do. One is to consult *Guide to Reference Works.* This guide lists general and specialized indexes that contain information for the social sciences, the humanities, history, or the pure and applied sciences. You can also ask reference librarians for advice and browse the shelves in appropriate sections.

- General indexes and abstracts

  For material on most topics, people usually start with a search of *Readers' Guide to Periodical Literature.* It indexes articles in popular periodicals such as *Time, Esquire,* and *Psychology Today.* For newspaper articles, most people use the *New York Times Index,* and for government documents, the *Monthly Catalog of United States Government Publications.* If your paper involves a person, you will want to search the *Biography Index.* An excellent starting place for topics related to science and technology is the *General Science Index;* most of the sources indexed there are clear to people without a technical background.

- Specialized indexes and abstracts

  After checking in the general works, you should then turn to more specialized indexes. The following list contains indexes you will find valuable for the humanities, social sciences, and science and technology.

Humanities

International Index (1907–1965)
Social Sciences and Humanities Index (1965–1974)
Humanities Index (1974–)
MLA International Bibliography (1921–)
Essay and General Literature Index (1900–)
Historical Abstracts (1955–)
America: History and Life (1964–)
Music Index (1949–)
Art Index (1929–)
Book Review Index (1905–)

Social Sciences

Social Sciences and Humanities Index (1965–1974)
Social Sciences Index (1974–)
Sociological Abstracts (1953–)
Psychological Abstracts (1927–)
Business Periodicals Index (1958–)
P.A.I.S. (Public Affairs Information Service) (1972–)
Index to Legal Periodicals (1886–)
Criminology and Penology Abstracts (1961–)
Education Index (1929–)
Current Index to Journals in Education (CIJE) (1969–)
American Statistics Index (ASI) (1973–)

Science and Technology

Applied Science and Technology Index (1958–)
Biological Abstracts (1926–)
Biological and Agricultural Index (1947–)
Chemical Abstracts (1907–)
Engineering Index (1906–)
Computer and Control Abstracts (1966–)
Computer Literature Index (1980–)
Index Medicus (1960–)
Hospital Literature Index (1955–)
Technical Book Review Index (1935–)

If you are using an index for the first time, you may need an explanation of its format and any unfamiliar abbreviations. You can find instructions and explanations by consulting the information that usually appears at the front of each issue. Most indexes are not difficult to use; they generally follow a format similar to the one illustrated in Figure 5 from the *Readers' Guide.*

Twain, Mark, 1835-1910
The late Benjamin Franklin. *Saturday Evening Post* 255:18+ Mr '83
Mark Twain on ice-storms. il *Audubon* 85:46-7 Ja '83
about
Mark Twain returns to Hannibal. H. Holzer. il por *Am Hist Illus* 18:26-33 My '83
Twain's barbs for today [one-man performance by W. McLinn] D. A. Hoekema. il por *Christ Century* 100:588-9 Je 8-15 '83
Tweedale, Douglas
A civilian solution? il *Macleans* 96:10+ My 23 '83
Tweeten, Luther
The economics of small farms. bibl f il *Science* 219:1037-41 Mr 4 '83
Twentieth century
The most amazing 60 years in history [Time anniversary issue; with editorial comment by Henry Grunwald] il *Time* 122 Sp Issue:5+, 24-7+ O '83
Twentieth Century-Fox Film Corp.
Hollywood divorce [S. Lansing leaves] por *Fortune* 107:8-9 Ja 24 '83

This article appeared in American History Illustrated, *Volume 18, pp. 26-33, in May 1983. It contains illustrations* (il) *and portraits* (por).

Figure 5 Excerpt from *Readers' Guide*

Computer Searches of Indexes and Abstracts

Many indexes are now listed in databases, which can be searched by computer in a fraction of the time it would take a person to use the paper versions. Some computer searches of indexes are free or inexpensive; researchers with an appropriate computer terminal can conduct a search themselves by following simple instructions. However, many databases are limited in scope—for example, they may include only popular periodicals, and they may cover only a limited number of years. If you conduct an online search, be sure to check the scope of the database.

A computer search of the *Magazine Index* (MI), using the keyword "taste research," turned up ten sources. Figure 6 shows three of these sources. Notice that the entries from the printout give the name of the periodicals and all the information needed to locate the articles precisely. In addition, the second entry shows that the full text of the article is in the computer's database. If the library does not have the periodical, a student could get the article on a computer printout.

```
5/3/1
2005589 DATABASE: MI File 47
  New tastes for seniors. (loss of sense
    of taste)
  Berton, Paul
  Maclean's 98 P60(1) Dec 16 1985
  CODEN: MCNMB

5/3/2
1919336 DATABASE: MI File 47 *Use Format
  9 for FULL TEXT*
  A question of taste in space.
  Savold, David
  Science '85 v6 p86(2) March 1985
  illustration; photograph
  AVAILABILITY: FULL TEXT Online
  LINE COUNT: 00054

5/3/3
1905946 DATABASE: MI File 47
  Space taste. (loss of sense of taste
    during space flight)
  Engler, Nick
  Omni v7 p31(1) May 1985
  CODEN: OMNIDQ
  COLLECTION 28E4318
  illustration; photograph
  AVAILABILITY: COLLECTION 28E4318
```


Figure 6 Printout from computer search

Some libraries provide searches of commercial databases, but a search can be expensive, depending on the amount of information printed out. In many cases, the printouts are so thorough that the sources listed are unavailable in the average library. For specialists, who must thoroughly search the literature, the procedure can be invaluable; for undergraduates, however, a search of commercial files is not always advisable.

The Computer Connection

Consider the time it takes to search through yearly lists of periodical articles published in various indexes. Simply looking through the *Readers' Guide* alone is time consuming, and probably you must look through several additional indexes in compiling a bibliography for a single research project. Computer searches can save you an enormous amount of time. Most libraries are constantly enlarging their capacity for online searches, so whenever possible, take advantage of computers for doing research. Not only is the computer search faster, but the computer will usually print out a list and save you copying time.

Suggestions for Using Online or CD-ROM Indexes

- For your search, carefully select keywords, often called *descriptors.* It's better to check in a thesaurus, such as *Thesaurus of ERIC Descriptors* and *Thesaurus of Psychological Index Terms* to make sure a word is listed in the database. Without the best keyword, a researcher risks overlooking valuable sources or paying for useless lists.
- Locate newspaper articles by using such databases as the Information Bank (index to the *New York Times,* and many other important papers, including the *Washington Post* and *Los Angeles Times*), the Dow Jones News/Retrieval Service (index to the *Wall Street Journal* and *United Press International*), and NEWSEARCH (daily index of more than 2,000 news stories, information articles, and book reviews).
- Search for popular magazine articles in the *Magazine Index* (MI) or the *Readers' Guide* (RG), if these are available on computer.
- Search for information in specialized fields by using such databases as ERIC (education), MLA Bibliography (language and literature), PsycINFO (psychology), PAIS (public affairs), Chemical Abstracts (chemistry), and BIOSIS (biology).
- Of special value are the databases that contain, in addition to the bibliographic entry, either summaries or full text, which you can get printed out. ERIC can print long digests, and the Information Bank contains the complete articles from the *New York Times.*

40d WORKING BIBLIOGRAPHY

As you locate promising sources in the catalogs, indexes, and printouts, you should write down information such as author, title, publication, call number, volume, date, page number, the place where you found the citation—anything that will help you find the sources in the library. This information should be checked for accuracy when you use the work itself. You can also add any other information you need for documenting sources according to the style assigned by your instructor. In this way you can prevent having to go back to look up such details later on.

The traditional method for preparing a working bibliography is to put the information about each source on a separate index card like the one in Figure 7.

Figure 7 Bibliography card

The advantage of using cards is that when you find a source unavailable or irrelevant, you can throw the card away; the stack that is left becomes your "working" bibliography—the sources you will examine closely for possible inclusion in your research paper. Also, you can shuffle the cards into alphabetical order so that you can easily type the reference page in your final paper.

40e LOCATING MATERIAL

You do not have to accumulate a complete bibliography before you begin to locate the books, articles, and reports you have listed. In other words, if you notice a title that sounds interesting, find the source and read it. By reading widely as your paper takes shape, you will have options. The more you know about your subject, the better you will be able to control it: to narrow it, broaden it, shift the focus, or even abandon it altogether. And the sooner, the better.

To locate the sources you have listed, you must be familiar with the layout of your library and the system it uses. In some libraries, the shelves of books are open to users. In that case, you locate books by call numbers. If your library's books are in an area closed to general use, you write out call numbers, authors, and titles on slips of paper. Then a library employee gets the books for you. Special locations—such as specialized reading rooms and departmental libraries—will be noted in the catalogs, usually under call numbers. Be sure to write down these locations and, if necessary, use a library map to find the material.

Your library probably has a separate catalog—called a periodical file—that lists the available periodicals and their locations. The periodicals may be in a closed area, but often they are in bound volumes on shelves you can search. Unbound periodicals (current issues) are usually available in a reading area. Increasingly, periodicals are on microfilm or microfiche and must be read on special machines in a special room. In addition, a few databases contain not only lists of titles but also summaries or entire articles and reports.

40f WORKING OUTLINE

Once you have a working bibliography, you need to become increasingly selective about the materials you collect. At this point, you need to plan your paper, tentatively at least, with a working outline. (See 35f.) Then you can assess your subject and focus it more precisely. If you discover an overabundance of material, you will have to limit your subject further. If your sources cover entirely different points, unconnected to any central purpose, you must shift to the most interesting of the points or the point that holds the greatest promise of leading to a unified paper. And of course, if your outline looks short and incomplete, you will have to expand your subject or change it.

Even for a short paper, the working outline permits you to juggle several pieces of information, fitting them together in various combinations to achieve the best arrangement. New information that you gather can be added wherever it fits best. For information on traditional organizations, consult Chapter 35.

For some papers a working outline might be just a list of major points with the sources lined up underneath. As other sources are accumulated, they can easily be added at the appropriate points. The student writer of the sample paper in section 41b began with this working outline.

```
Mark Twain: Civil War Deserter?
1. coward
2. humor
       Twain
3. childishness
       Van Wyck Brooks
```

4. guilt
   Kaplan
   Mattson
5. family
   Webster

For other papers, the working outline might be a fairly elaborate list, including precise divisions and subdivisions along with some of the sources for developing several different ideas. An early outline of the student research paper that appears in section 41e started out with these divisions.

WOMEN'S ROLE IN JAPANESE BUSINESS

1. Discrimination
   A. In education
      Forbis, Bowman
   B. In the business world
      Ouchi, Dillon, Osako
   C. In the family structure
      Cook, Edwards, Whitehill, Dillon
2. The Equal Employment Opportunity law
   A. Origin
      Lansing & Ready
   B. Language
      Cordilla & Ohta
3. Effects
   A. Positive
      Cannings & Lazonick, Whitehill, Lehner & Graven
   B. Negative
      Whitehill, Cook, Lansing & Ready

When you write a working outline, let it remain flexible. Papers frequently take shape gradually, and new reading or thinking may make changes necessary. You may need to explore new directions even though your original outline does not provide for them. A new direction may turn out to be the key that will unify and improve your paper. Also, if one section of an outline grows disproportionately to the others, you might consider a paper devoted just to that point. For example, the sample paper on Japanese business discrimination (section 41e) originally covered the broader subject of Japanese business problems, but the material on discrimination against women grew so large that it became the primary subject.

40g NOTE-TAKING

Once your paper's direction is established, you are ready to take notes and to decide how best to incorporate your sources into your paper. Note-taking is not an isolated stage in the process of writing a research paper. You can take notes at any point that you find information you want to remember. You will not necessarily use all your notes; but if you do not write down ideas, figures, and statements, you are likely to forget them or to forget where you read them. As you move from one source to another, your interest shifts, and you probably will not remember details about a source several readings back or several days before.

Since good notes can reduce masses of information to a manageable size, you should summarize source material wherever possible. If you are not sure how you will use a source in your paper, though, you can quote it fully or make a notation so that you can easily return to specific pages. One efficient method is to photocopy material and cut and paste it on cards for organizing. Cards are more easily grouped and shifted around than full-length sheets of paper. Whatever technique you prefer, always identify each note. A full reference is not necessary if it is on a card in your working bibliography. The author's name and the page number may be all that are needed for identification. Also, when possible, label the topic the information covers (Figure 8).

If your note does not fit your working outline, make adjustments. Either file the note separately as superfluous or change the

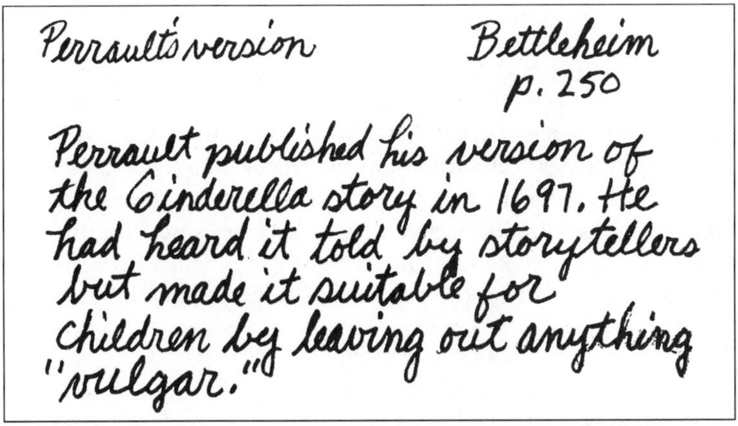

Perrault's version Bettleheim p. 250

Perrault published his version of the Cinderella story in 1697. He had heard it told by storytellers but made it suitable for children by leaving out anything "vulgar."

Figure 8 Note card

outline to include the information on the note. But do not use a note just because you have gone to the trouble to take it. It could destroy the coherence of your paper.

40h PLAGIARISM

Plagiarism is deceiving the reader into thinking that the ideas or words taken from a source are your own. The word *plagiarism* comes from a Latin word that means "kidnapping," and in a sense plagiarism is a kind of kidnapping of material belonging to another. Since plagiarism undermines learning and may even cause failure, why do people plagiarize? The answer varies. Some writers do not understand what plagiarism is; they simply do not know how to present material taken from another source. Other writers cannot effectively rewrite an original sentence or passage because they have not mastered the material. On the other hand, there are writers who deliberately plagiarize because they fear that they cannot produce a satisfactory paper and mistakenly believe that they can camouflage their weaknesses. In addition, poor time management can lead writers to plagiarize. Transforming a source into different words and a different style takes more time than copying. Consequently, writers who rush to produce a last-minute paper may plagiarize sources out of a sense of desperation. The solution is to realize that rewording sources is a time-consuming process and to allow ample time for careful paraphrasing.

(1) Giving credit

Plagiarism can result from not giving credit to the person who thought of an idea, calculated statistics, made a discovery. You cannot pass off as your own another person's work. As these examples taken from the sample research papers indicate, you can easily give credit for ideas by including the name of the person who wrote the original or by referring the reader to a name or source in a list of references.

> Van Wyck Brooks in *The Ordeal of Mark Twain* blames Twain's desertion on an "infantile frame of mind."

According to Ouchi (1981), women are considered temporary employees even though they may work for as long as twenty years at a job.

Later scholars have found more than 500 versions in Europe alone ("Cinderella" 233) and have traced the story's origin to China in the ninth century (Waley 226).

In addition, you must show when you have used someone else's words. Quotation marks around the material let the reader know that a word, phrase, sentence, or short passage appeared in the original source. Long quoted passages are set off from the rest of the paper. (See 40i.)

The only parts of a research paper that do not show credit to someone else are those parts written independently of any sources and those parts containing common knowledge (factual information known widely by educated people). For instance, you would not have to show the source of such information as the fact that Lincoln was president during the Civil War or that Shakespeare wrote *Hamlet.*

(2) Paraphrasing carefully

Make sure that plagiarism does not result from the failure to paraphrase sufficiently, that is, to rewrite a passage in your own words and your own style. To paraphrase well, you must first understand the information in the source. If you do not understand what you are reading, you may need to abandon the subject and find one more general and less technical. Sometimes, though, you cannot abandon the subject. It may be assigned, or you may not have time to start over. If so, you should get help in understanding the material. You cannot accurately paraphrase prose you do not understand.

When you paraphrase, you must be sure that you have changed the prose from the original without any distortion of meaning. Compare the original paragraph that follows with the two unsuccessful attempts at paraphrasing. The plagiarized examples illustrate two extremes—first, a blatant copying of whole sections, and second, the retention of a few significant words and phrases.

ORIGINAL PASSAGE

The "injuries and insolencies" that caused conflict on the frontier were usually rooted in simple trespass either by English cattle or hogs onto the unfenced cornfields of the Indians or by the Indian habit of moving freely over open fields that the English regarded as sacred private property. (Robert M. Utley and Wilcomb E. Washburn, *Indian Wars*)

PLAGIARIZED VERSION 1

Conflict on the frontier between the English and Indians was usually rooted in simple trespass either by English animals onto the unfenced cornfields of the Indians or by the Indian habit of moving freely over open fields that the English considered to be their own private property.

In the plagiarized version, the writer changed the opening words of the original but then with the exception of substituting "animals" for "cattle or hogs" and "considered" for "regarded" copied the rest of the passage almost word for word.

PLAGIARIZED VERSION 2

Conflict on the frontier between the English and the Indians was usually rooted in a lack of respect for property. The English cattle and hogs were permitted to trespass on the unfenced cornfields of the Indians. The Indians trespassed freely on private property that the English regarded as sacred.

The second version is a better attempt, but its writer could still face accusations of plagiarism. The expressions "rooted in," "unfenced cornfields of the Indians," and "regarded as sacred" should have been changed. Neither example gives credit for the information. The next example is a more successful paraphrase that acknowledges the source in the rewording.

SUCCESSFULLY PARAPHRASED VERSION

Utley and Washburn maintain that the frontier conflict between the English and the Indians often had a simple cause--trespassing on the other's property. The English permitted their animals to wander on cornfields that the Indians refused to fence. The Indians, with little notion of private property, wandered freely over English fields.

Successful paraphrasing preserves the meaning of the original but changes its expression. If you find it difficult to change someone else's language, try this technique: read the source; then write down its meaning in your own words as if you are explaining to someone what you just read. Avoid looking back at the source. If you get confused, reread the material but write the paraphrase from memory. After the material has been paraphrased, check to see that it has these characteristics.

- The paraphrase accurately restates the meaning of the original.
- The sentence structure differs from that of the original.
- The paraphrase contains only the ordinary words or phrases appearing in the original.
- Any unique or distinctive expressions are changed or placed in quotation marks.

To paraphrase well, then, you must be able to understand the content, manipulate sentence structure, and distinguish between the words and phrases you can use and those you cannot. Words like articles, prepositions, conjunctions, and pronouns are obviously necessary, and you can use them without fear of plagiarism. You can use the source's nouns, verbs, and adjectives when they have simple denotations and no equivalent synonyms. Words such as *computer, tree, read, see,* and *green* have no ordinary substitutions. But words like *scintillating, bolster,* and *magnum opus* do.

Phrases that appear in an original source are usually distinctive and must be either rewritten or placed inside quotation marks. To protect yourself, always avoid duplicating phrases, except for common ones like *in school, blue sky, nuclear test site.* You certainly could not use phrases like the following without quotation marks.

a particularly sobering illustration
a transfer of coping skills
overly ambitious curriculum
the most pernicious of illusions
to cast in sharp relief

Remember that each person's writing style is distinctive, and a reader can detect a shift. A paper that begins simply and suddenly shifts into sophisticated prose is immediately suspect. In the following passage, the style of the first paragraph is that of the average writer. The second paragraph shifts to a professional style.

> Political campaigns have become more and more like entertainment. To get elected, politicians advertise themselves like commercial products. The commercials do not say much. Instead, they have pictures, music, and slogans.
>
> What is happening is that the use of extended and complex language is being rapidly replaced by the gestures, images, and formats of the arts of show business, toward which most of the news media, especially television, are powerfully disposed. The result is that in the political domain, as well as in other arenas of public discourse--religion and commerce, for example--Americans no longer talk to each other; they entertain each other.

40i USING SOURCES

res
40i

To use an idea in a paper, you have several options. The one you choose is sometimes arbitrary and sometimes dependent on matters such as the style, content, and importance of the source. Whether you choose to quote, paraphrase, or summarize your source, you must always identify the author or title in your sentence or place the identification in parentheses. The information you include and its position depend on the style of documentation you are following. See Chapter 41, Research Papers and Documentation, for details on two commonly used styles—the MLA and the APA.

(1) Quoting a passage

Be cautious about using too many direct quotations. You do not want your entire paper to be a series of quotations interspersed with short passages of your own prose. Instead, quote material when you want to emphasize it or when it is so well stated that a restatement would diminish its effect. There is no point in quoting material with ordinary content and style. Also, never quote directly simply to avoid the trouble of paraphrasing.

Short quoted passages are enclosed in quotation marks. (You can find guidelines in Chapter 27.)

> As Moorman observes, "[Logue] cannot, or has not yet at any rate been able to, even suggest the long agonizing deterioration and subsequent redemption of Achilles after his fateful quarrel with Agamemnon" (15).

Long quotations, more than four typed lines, are usually blocked, that is, indented on the left side and set off from the rest of the paper. Quotation marks are omitted unless they appear in the original.

> Charles Moorman admires Logue's Iliad, even though it is not a literal translation:
>
>> Logue's work does not take the place of a complete translation of the Iliad. He cannot, or has not yet at any rate been able to, even suggest the long agonizing deterioration and subsequent redemption of Achilles after his fateful quarrel with Agamemnon. What he can do, though, is to catch beautifully the tremendous excitement, the vigor and majesty of Homer, and to suggest at least the conflict between corporate and individual values that lies at the heart of the book. (15)

(2) Mixing a quotation and a paraphrase

res 40i

This technique is useful for passages that cannot be completely restated and for retaining any effective style in the original. Notice the way the following example quotes two phrases and paraphrases the rest.

> Logue does not provide a complete translation of Homer's Iliad. He has not yet, for example, attempted to retell the dramatic story of Achilles' "deterioration and subsequent redemption." Nevertheless, he dramatizes the Iliad's splendor and suggests "the conflict between the corporate and individual values that lies at the heart of the book" (Moorman 15).

(3) Paraphrasing a passage

Technically a paraphrase is about the same length as the original and is most useful for a passage full of relevant information. The following retains most of the original's details.

> According to Moorman, Logue's Iliad cannot substitute for a complete translation. The unfinished work does not cover all the events in Homer's epic; Logue has not yet, for example, reproduced the long story of Achilles' decline and eventual heroism. Nevertheless, Logue captures the drama, the energy, and

> the splendor of Homer; and he suggests the book's central conflict between the clashing values of the individual and society (15).

(4) Summarizing the passage

Summaries permit a writer to emphasize important ideas by deleting details. For example, the following version reduces the 81-word passage to 27 words. Furthermore, condensed material is less likely to be plagiarized. In the process of reducing the number of words, a writer is more likely to revise the sentence structure and vocabulary of the original.

> Logue's Iliad is not yet complete. What does exist, however, captures the energy and splendor of Homer's story and the central conflict between the individual and society (Moorman 15).

40j DRAFTING THE PAPER

The way you write the first draft depends on the time you have spent organizing and taking notes. If your notes are carefully composed and systematically arranged, much of the writing has already been done. If you have merely decided on the overall pattern and gathered together some of the material you will use in each section, you must move back and forth from your sources to your own composition. Most writers fall between the two extremes. The note-taking for some sections will be complete; for other sections, it will be unfinished, particularly if the writer is unable to visualize how the source might eventually be used.

Regardless of the stage at which you start to draft your paper, you must at this point focus your attention on the overall scheme—the organization of the whole, the introduction, the synthesis of the parts, the paragraph structures, and the conclusion.

(1) Make sure your overall organization works effectively.

It is not too late to delete, add, or switch sections around. If you have not found the sources needed to back up a section of your plan, you can delete it. Of course, if the section is crucial, you can leave a gap to be filled after further investigation. Interesting material that you have located can be added to the working outline, but only if it really fits. Do not insert a source, no matter how interesting, if it does not support your overall purpose. As you begin to write, you sometimes discover that sections are not in the right order and must be moved to another place. In general, the drafting stage is not too late for changes in the organization.

(2) Write an introduction that makes your purpose clear.

If, at this point, you have lost sight of a clear purpose, you should rethink the whole paper. Are you answering a question? Arguing a thesis? Interpreting literature? Once the purpose is clear to you, you must make it clear to your readers. Some strategies for introductions are discussed in 36b, Introductory Paragraphs. You will also find in the discussion examples illustrating each strategy. Remember that the introduction establishes your reader's first impression of your skills and your subject. A poor first impression is unfortunately hard to change. Therefore, treat the introduction seriously. It does not matter when you write the introduction, but when you do, put into it your best effort.

(3) Make sure your paper has coherence.

Make sure that you lead your reader smoothly not only from paragraph to paragraph but through each paragraph as well. In a typical paragraph you will have a topic sentence stating the point, and then you will use your sources to develop or substantiate that sentence. (For discussion and examples of paragraph organization, see 36a, Body Paragraphs.) The following three note cards were combined to create a single paragraph that explains the "traditional role that women play in Japanese society." (See Figure 9.)

goal: marrige and motherhood — Dillon p. 22

Role influenced by society's belief that "marriage and motherhood" are the ultimate goal of women. Because of arranged marriages, anyone can get married. Extremely high marriage rate.

Care of children — Dillon p. 23

Mothers are given the responsibility of child care. Most women stay home and don't seek jobs. New role: "education mothers"– help educate sons. Ed. very important to male's future. "Mothers play an important role (and live vicariously) through the career development of their sons."

Care of sons and husband — Osako pp 17-18

Collective achievement more important than individual. "Therefore, a woman is considered more virtuous if she devotes herself to the advancement of other family members (notably sons and husbands) rather than pursuing her own career." [p. 18]

Another reason for employment discrimination is the traditional role that women play in Japanese society. Their goals are "marriage and motherhood" (Dillon, 1983). The marriage rate is extremely high, and the care of children is the exclusive job of women. Consequently, women rarely seek employment. Instead, they remain at home and promote the education of their sons, since male children, if successful in school, may someday be successful in business. According to Dillon, "Mothers play an important role (and live vicariously) through the career development of their sons" (p. 23). Osako (1978) writes, "A woman is considered more virtuous if she devotes herself to the advancement of other family members (notably sons and husbands) rather than pursuing her own career" (p. 18).

Figure 9 Three notes combined into paragraph

(4) Use lead-ins to introduce sources.

When you incorporate quotations or paraphrased material into your paper, you usually introduce them so the reader knows where the borrowing begins. Some of the established lead-ins that signal the beginning of a source are these.

Vogel points out that . . .
According to Brooks . . .
Stuart Berg Flexner agrees that . . .
John Wain wrote that . . .

The verb tense of a lead-in depends on whether the statement or work is associated with the past or with the present. Work in science, technology, and the social sciences is frequently related to the time in which it occurred. Therefore, lead-ins are usually in the past tense or present perfect tense.

Darwin discovered . . .
The researchers have studied . . .

But some past events are considered a constant reality and are written about in the present tense. This "historical present" signifies that literary works or other documents are preserved and remain presently available or that a truth is unaffected by time.

Chaucer writes . . .
The Constitution guarantees . . .

Sometimes present and past tenses are mixed, as for example, in a passage about both Shakespeare the man and Shakespeare's drama.

Shakespeare left [past tense] his wife only his "second-best bed"; nevertheless, in his dramas, he shows [present tense] a great deal of respect for women.

Similarly, in a report of a specific or technical investigation, the data might be presented in the past tense and the conclusion in the present.

In the study the salinity measured [past tense] 3.5 percent. The results show [present tense] that the salinity of the bay increased [past tense] during the two years studied.

(5) Write a suitable conclusion.

Several different strategies for conclusions can effectively end a research paper: a return to the thesis, a summary of the major points, a recommendation, or a call for further study. For a more complete list of strategies and for descriptions and examples, see 36c.

CHAPTER

41

RESEARCH PAPERS AND DOCUMENTATION

doc 41

At one time, writers regularly documented papers by placing a superscript (raised) number after each paraphrase, summary, and quotation taken from a source. Then they identified the source in a note at the bottom of the page or the end of the paper. Also they added a bibliography, a list of all the sources used throughout. Thus, the paper was heavily documented. In fact, each source was really listed twice—once in a note and once in the bibliography. Even though this style is still used in some disciplines, the duplication and the problems with typing and printing costs have brought about some changes. Most publications now use a simplified style in which the sources are listed only once, at the end. Either the content of the paper or a notation in parentheses indicates which source from the list has been cited.

You can find an appropriate documentation style in several ways. First, there are style guides published for a number of disciplines. Among the most popular are these.

MLA Handbook for Writers of Research Papers
Publication Manual of the American Psychological Association (APA)
CBE Style Manual: A Guide for Authors, Editors, and Publishers in the Biological Sciences
Handbook for Authors of Papers in American Chemical Society Publications
Chicago Manual of Style

Second, you can follow the style of documentation used by a scholarly journal. Third, you are sometimes required to use guides supplied by instructors, businesses, or agencies. Unless you have special instructions or unusual problems, however, you can find the information needed for documentation in the following explanation of the two most common styles: the MLA style and the APA style. Use whichever style you are assigned or prefer.

41a MLA DOCUMENTATION

The popular MLA style of documentation is detailed in the *MLA Handbook for Writers of Research Papers.* The following description presents the most common uses of sources and the most commonly used forms. Whenever you need special information not covered here, consult the *MLA Handbook.* The style is illustrated in "Reuse: The Garbage Solution" (39g), "Mark Twain: Civil War Deserter?" (41b), and "Anne Sexton's 'Cinderella': A Modern Fairy Tale" (41c).

(1) MLA documentation inside the paper

In the text of a paper, you must show exactly where borrowed material came from—no matter whether it is a paraphrase, summary, or quotation. In the MLA style, the name of the author of the source and usually the page number indicate where the material came from. The *MLA Handbook* specifies the placement and conventions of the documentation.

1. The author's last name and page or pages can appear in parentheses. Note that no comma separates the two and that the parentheses are inside the sentence.

When Orion left for Nevada, Twain went with him (Mack 47-49).

For two or three authors, give the last name of all authors—(Murray and Boston 124) or (Dunn, Frye, and Franklin 74). For more than three authors, give only the first author's last name and the abbreviation for "and others," *et al.*—(Sargent et al. 39).

2. When the author's name appears in the sentence, the page numbers go in parentheses.

Thus, to Kaplan the story is intended to help remove the burden of guilt (322-25).

3. When there is no author, the source (for example, the name of an article) appears in its place.

Later scholars have found more than 500 versions in Europe alone ("Cinderella" 233).

4. When the material ends with a quotation, the parentheses go after the quotation mark but before the period.

He also writes that the war had not yet turned the "green recruits" from "rabbits into soldiers" (265).

5. A secondhand quotation, one taken from a secondary not a primary source, is indicated this way.

Mark Twain called John Wanamaker "that unco-pious butter-mouthed Sunday school-slobbering sneak-thief" (qtd. in Kaplan 319).

6. A reference to an entire work (no specific page) requires no page number.

In 1893, Marian Roalfe Cox cataloged the similarities and differences among 345 variants she discovered in such countries as Greece, Denmark, Russia, Italy, and England.

(2) MLA documentation at the end of the paper

At the end of a paper, in "Works Cited," you list in alphabetical order all the sources you have cited. The components of your citations—their arrangement, capitalization, punctuation, and mechanics—must follow the specifications of the MLA style guide.

The forms for printed sources are fairly standardized. You name the author and title and describe the publication information as illustrated in the following charts. Increasingly, however, the "Works Cited" section of papers also contains material from electronic sources such as online databases, CD-ROMs, diskettes, and magnetic tapes.

The forms for documenting electronic sources in bibliographies are more complex than those for printed sources. Uniformity in the citations is not always possible; too many variations exist among the media and their contents. The most efficient way to follow the MLA style for electronic sources is to follow the citations in "Additional MLA Citation Forms." You can locate the form that most closely resembles your source and model your citation on it.

Remember that if an electronic source also has a printed version, you include first the information in the following chart, which illustrates the major components. Then you add a description of the electronic publication information. Also remember that if your source lacks some of the details in the examples of the electronic citations, you should still cite enough information to help a reader locate the source you have used.

In formatting the major components, you also must pay attention to the spacing. When typing "Works Cited," double-space every line. Indent the second and subsequent lines of a reference five spaces. MLA references have one space after every mark of punctuation. The following chart of basic forms illustrates complete entries and their proper spacing.

The Major Components of MLA Citations for Printed Sources	
Author	One author • Reverse names (last name first). • Place a period at the end. Example: `Boswell, James.`

	Two or three authors • Reverse names of first author only. • Separate names with comma or commas. • Place an *and* before last name. • Place a period at the end. Example: Hunt, Ray C., and Bernard Norling. Example: Watts, Frank, Edward Norton, and Charles Lexington. More than three authors • Name first author only. • Follow with a comma and *et al.* ("and others"). Example: Bates, Richard M., et al.
Title	Book • Underline with a solid line. • Place a period at the end. Example: <u>A Combat Artist in World War II</u>. Periodical article • Place in quotation marks. • Place a period at the end (before the quotation mark). Example: "Reactionary Rhetoric." Periodical • Underline with a solid line. • Place no period at the end. Example: <u>American Journal of Science</u>
Publication Information	Book • Give the city, a brief form of the publisher's name, and year of publication. • Place a colon after the city, a comma after the publisher, and a period at the end. Example: New York: Knopf, 1996. Journal • Give the volume number (arabic numeral), year of publication, and inclusive page numbers. • Place the year in parentheses. • Place a colon after the last parenthesis. • Place a period at the end. Example: 52 (1981): 75-9.

Magazine and newspaper

- Omit the volume number.
- Give date (day/abbreviated month/year) and inclusive page numbers.
- For pages that are not consecutive, give first page number and a plus sign (21+).
- Place a colon after the year.
- Place a period at the end.

Example: 20 Mar. 1994: 4-9.
Example: 9 June 1995: 12+.

Basic Forms in MLA Style for Printed Sources	
Book	Ryan, Cornelius. A Bridge Too Far. New York: Simon, 1974.
	Nie, Norman, et al. Statistical Package for the Social Sciences. New York: McGraw, 1975.
Journal	Sewall, Richard B. "The Tragic Form." Essays in Criticism 4 (1954): 345-58.
	Higgs, E. S., and J. P. White. "Autumn Killing." Antiquity 37 (1963): 282-89.
Magazine	Edwards, Mike. "Kabul." National Geographic Apr. 1985: 494-505.
	Landau, Jon. "In Praise of Elvis Presley." Rolling Stone 23 Dec. 1971: 72.
Newspaper	Cooke, Robert. "A Circus in Old Carthage: Curses and Chariots." Atlanta Constitution 4 June 1985: A4.

In addition to the basic forms used most of the time, there are some variations used occasionally. The following list includes variations of the basic forms and also special forms for such sources as encyclopedia articles, government documents, radio and television programs, films and videotapes, interviews and lectures, online material, and CD-ROMs.

Additional MLA Citation Forms

EDITED BOOK

Hofstadter, Richard, ed. Great Issues in American History. New York: Vintage, 1958.

Michaels, Leonard, and Christopher Ricks, eds. The State of Language. Berkeley: U of California P, 1980.

Prinz, Martin, et al., eds. Guide to Rocks and Minerals. New York: Simon, 1978.

CHAPTER, STORY, OR OTHER PART OF A BOOK

Malory, Sir Thomas. "Isolde the Fair." The Works of Sir Thomas Malory. Ed. Eugene Vinaver. London: Oxford UP, 1954. 276-331.

Stafford, Jean. "The Echo and the Nemesis." The Collected Stories. New York: Farrar, 1970. 35-53.

FOREWORD AND PREFACE

Gardner, John. Foreword. Becoming a Writer. By Dorothea Brande. 1934. Los Angeles: Tarcher, 1981. 11-18.

Tannahill, Reay. Preface. Food in History. By Tannahill. New York: Stein, 1973. 7-9.

MULTIVOLUME WORK

Brown, T. Allston. A History of the New York Stage. 3 vols. New York: Blom, 1903.

In the citation in the text, the volume is followed by a colon, then the page number, as in (3:136).

MULTIVOLUME WORK WITH A SEPARATE TITLE FOR EACH VOLUME

Malone, Dumas. The Sage of Monticello. Vol. 6 of Jefferson and His Time. 6 vols. Boston: Little, 1981.

ONE VOLUME OF A MULTIVOLUME WORK

Foote, Shelby. The Civil War: A Narrative. Vol. 2. New York: Random House, 1963.

REPUBLISHED WORK SUCH AS A PAPERBACK EDITION

Faulkner, William. Absalom, Absalom. 1936. New York: Vintage, 1972.

TRANSLATION

Euripides. Alcestis. Trans. William Arrowsmith. New York: Oxford UP, 1974.

LATER EDITION

Gould, James A., ed. Classic Philosophical Questions. 2nd ed. Columbus: Bobbs, 1975.

BOOK WITH A TITLE WITHIN THE TITLE

Martin, Jay, ed. A Collection of Critical Essays on "The Waste Land." Englewood Cliffs: Prentice, 1968.

Paul, Henry N. The Royal Play of Macbeth. New York: Macmillan, 1950.

WORK WITH CORPORATE AUTHOR

Lunar & Planetary Institute, Houston. Basaltic Volcanism on Terrestrial Plants. Elmsford: Pergamon, 1982.

PAMPHLET

A Brief Guide to Tea. Upton, MA: Upton Tea Imports, 1990.

ARTICLE FROM A FAMILIAR ENCYCLOPEDIA

Bay, Christian. "Civil Disobedience." International Encylopedia of the Social Sciences. 1968 ed.

"Perkins, Maxwell Evarts." Encyclopedia Americana. 1985 ed.

For an article from a less familiar encyclopedia, use the form for a part of a book.

GOVERNMENT DOCUMENT

Cong. Rec. 25 Jan. 1940: 698-99.

United States. Historical Section, Army War College. Order of Battle of the United States Land Forces in the World War (1917-19). Washington: GPO, 1931.

United States. Cong. Staff Investigative Group to the Committee on Foreign Affairs. The Assassination of Representative Leo J. Ryan and the Jonestown, Guyana Tragedy. 96th Cong., 1st sess. H. Doc. 223. Washington: GPO, 1979.

ARTICLE IN A SCHOLARLY JOURNAL

Frye, Northrop. "Varieties of Literary Utopia." Daedalus 94 (1965): 323-47.

When the journal's page numbers run consecutively throughout the year, only the volume number, the year, and the page numbers are listed.

Hytier, Adrienne. "The Battle in Eighteenth-Century French Fiction." Eighteenth Century Life 8.3 (1983): 1-13.

When each issue of the journal begins with page 1, the volume and also the issue must be listed. A period separates the volume number from the issue number.

ARTICLE IN A MAGAZINE OR NEWSPAPER

Drucker, Peter F. "The Age of Social Transformation." Atlantic Monthly Nov. 1994: 53-80.

"Pan Am Charts a Course for Europe, 1939." Wall Street Journal 26 May 1989: B1.

EDITORIAL AND LETTER

Fowler, Elaine W. Letter. Washington Post 1 Mar. 1975: A19.

"Manuage." Editorial. New York Times 2 June 1985: E22.

BOOK REVIEW

Costello, Bonnie. "The Fine Art of Remembrance." Rev. of The Collected Prose, by Elizabeth Bishop. Partisan Review 52.2 (1985): 153-57.

Abstract

Morgan, William Michael. "Strategic Factors in Hawaiian Annexation." Diss. Claremont Graduate School, 1980. DAI 40 (1980): 3129B.

Romney, Jill. "The Effect of Grade Inflation on Student Performance." Research in Higher Education 32 (1991): 521-43. Abstract. Current Index to Journals in Education 24 (1992): item EJ13495.

If the abstract collection contains the word *abstract* in the title as in *DAI* (*Dissertation Abstracts International*), you need not include the word in the citation.

Radio and Television Program

"Japanese Views of World War II." Narr. Julie McCarthy. All Things Considered. Natl. Public Radio. WNYC, New York. 18 Mar. 1995.

"The Sleeping Sharks of Yucatan." The Undersea World of Jacques Cousteau. Dir. Philippe Cousteau. Prod. Andy White. A Marshall Flaum Production in Association with the Cousteau Society and MPC-Metromedia Producers Corporation and ABC News. WFAA, Dallas. 4 June 1975.

Film and Videotape

2001: A Space Odyssey. Dir. Stanley Kubrick. MGM, 1968.

Introduction to Chimpanzee Behavior. Videocassette. National Geographic Society, 1977.

Interview or Lecture

Edwards, Sylvia. Personal interview. 8 Dec. 1986.

Moorman, Charles. Lecture. London. 21 July 1985.

Schoenecke, Michael. "Political and Social Ideology in Jack London's Science Fiction." The 23rd Annual Northern Great Plains History Conference. Eveleth, MN, 23 Sep. 1988.

CARTOON

Roberts, Victoria. Cartoon. New Yorker 10 Oct. 1994: 66.

BOOK ON CD-ROM (WITH PRINTED VERSION)

Linton, W. J. "King Alfred." Claribel and Other Poems. London: Simpkin, Marshall, 1865. 53-60. English Poetry Full-Text Database. CD-ROM. Cambridge, Eng.: Chadwyck-Healey, 1992.

Notice that the title of the database is underlined. Use this same form for a diskette or magnetic tape but substitute *Diskette* or *Magnetic tape* for *CD-ROM.*

ONLINE BOOK (WITH PRINTED VERSION)

Hardy, Thomas. Far from the Madding Crowd. Ed. Ronald Blyth. Harmondsworth: Penguin, 1978. Online. Oxford Text Archive. Internet. 10 May 1995. Available FTP: ota.ox.ac.uk/pub/ota/public/english/Hardy/madcrowd.1802

According to the MLA style, you place a period at the end of the availability statement (for example, in this citation, after "1802"). The closing period is, however, better omitted. If included, it could be mistaken for part of the address. Notice that online sources contain the date of access.

ONLINE BOOK (WITH NO PRINTED VERSION)

Zakour, John M. The Doomsday Brunette. 1994. Online. Internet. 15 May 1995. Available HTTP: zeb.nysaes.cornell.edu/ddb.cgi/go/cl

WORK IN MORE THAN ONE MEDIUM

"Delphi, Treasury of the Athenians." Perseus 1.0: Interactive Sources and Studies on Ancient Greece. Ed. Gregory Crane. CD-ROM, videodisc. New Haven: Yale UP, 1992.

NEWSPAPER OR MAGAZINE ARTICLE ON CD-ROM (WITH PRINTED VERSION)

Vranizan, Michelle. "World Library Turns Page." Sun-Sentinel 16 Feb. 1995: 3D. Business Newsbank. CD-ROM. 10 April 1995.

Thompson, Kevin D. and Alexis DeVeux. "The Third Degree: Black Women Scholars Storming the Ivory Tower." Essence April 1995: 68-70+. CD-ROM. ProQuest. May 1995.

Notice the two dates in each citation. The first is the publication date of the printed version; the second, the publication date of the electronic version.

ONLINE JOURNAL ARTICLE (WITH PRINTED VERSION)

Nichols, Stephen G. "Picture, Image, and Subjectivity in Medieval Culture." MLN: Modern Language Notes 108:4 (1993): 617-37. Online. Internet. 11 Oct. 1994. Available HTTP: muse.mse.jhu.edu/tocs.journals/mln/108.4nichols.html

ONLINE JOURNAL ARTICLE (WITH NO PRINTED VERSION)

Fox, David L. "The Fiction of Reason." Architronic: The Electronic Journal of Architecture 2.3 (1993): 24 pars. Online. Internet. 4 Apr. 1995. Available GOPHER: arcrs4.saed.kent.edu

For articles without numbered pages, give the number of pages or paragraphs or write *n. pag.* (no pagination).

ONLINE NEWSPAPER OR MAGAZINE ARTICLE (NO PRINTED SOURCE)

"Prez.: Shut Pa. Ave by White House." Headline News 20 May 1995: 7 pp. Online. Prodigy. 20 May 1995.

"Let's Go to the Movies." American Heritage n.d.: n. pag. Online. Prodigy. 18 May 1995.

ELECTRONIC DICTIONARY OR ENCYCLOPEDIA

"Bodkin." The Oxford English Dictionary. 2nd ed. CD-ROM. Oxford: Oxford UP, 1992.

"Whitman, Walt." Academic American Encyclopedia. Online. CompuServe. 14 June 1994.

"Absurdity." Roget's Thesaurus of English Words and Phrases. 1911. Roget's Thesaurus. Online. Internet. 26 Apr. 1995. Available HTTP: www.notredame.ac.jp/Roget/data/497.html

ELECTRONIC ABSTRACT

Psaki, Francies Regina. "The Medieval Lyric-Narrative Hybrid." DAI 50 (1989): 682. Cornell U, 1989. Dissertation Abstracts Ondisc. CD-ROM. ProQuest. Mar. 1995.

Hill, John M. Chaucerian Belief. New Haven: Yale UP, 1991. Abstract. Online Chaucer Bibliography. Online. U of Texas, San Antonio Library. Internet. 3 March 1995. Available TELNET: utsaibm.utsa.edu [type "library", "local", "chau"]

E-MAIL

Sweet, Joelle. "Nabokov's Poetry." E-mail to Ralph Williams. 30 Nov. 1994.

Kreutzman, Mark. "Re: Death of King Arthur." E-mail to author. 1 Dec. 1994.

doc 41a

Typing with MLA Style

- Use good quality paper, 8½ × 11 inches, and standard type.
- If your instructor requests a final outline, it should precede the paper. The outline page should not be numbered.
- Use no title page. Instead type identification information at the top left corner of the first page. Center the title.
- Use 1-inch margins on all sides.
- Double-space the entire paper including the list of references at the end.
- On the right margin, ½-inch from the top of the page, type your last name and the page number.
- Do not hyphenate words at the ends of lines.
- Block long quotations of more than four typed lines. They

should be double-spaced and indented ten spaces from the left margin and none from the right.

- Type the references in alphabetical order on a separate page. Title the page "Works Cited." Type the first line of each reference against the left margin. Indent other lines five spaces. If you have more than one entry by the same author, do not repeat the author's name. Use instead three hyphens.

Mangelsdorf, P. C. "The Domestication of Corn." Science 143 (1969),

538-45.

---. Plants and Human Affairs. Bloomington: Indiana UP, 1952.

Olivia Guest

Professor Dugan

ENG 102

April 30, 1992

1" from top of page

Mark Twain: Civil War Deserter?

I. Introduction--Shannon's accusations about Twain's cowardice during the Civil War

II. Explanation in the autobiography

III. Descriptions in "History"

   A. Humorous description

   B. Indictment of war

IV. Accusations of childishness

   A. Van Wyck Brooks

   B. <u>New York Times</u>

   C. Support from "History"

V. Antiwar explanation

   A. Support of explanation

      1. Justin Kaplan

      2. J. Stanley Mattson

   B. Refutation of explanation--Maxwell Geismar

VI. Divided sympathies

   A. Twain's divided sympathy

      1. Connection to the South

      2. Connection to the North

   B. Missouri's divided sympathy

      1. Minimal interest in the war

2. Opposition to secession

3. Confusion illustrated in "History"

VII. Other influences

A. Interest in the continent

B. Orion's influence

VIII. Desertion as a common occurrence

A. Bell Wiley's statistics

B. Twain's description of camp life

Guest 1

½" from top of page

Mark Twain: Civil War Deserter?

centered title

On January 25, 1940, Representative Shannon of Missouri insisted that his state did not want any of the recently issued stamps commemorating Mark Twain. According to Shannon, Twain had disgraced Missouri during the Civil War. Soon after Twain had joined the Confederate forces under a Colonel Jack Burbridge and had been made a lieutenant, Twain deserted. In Shannon's version of what had happened, "A Minie ball came whizzing past his ears, and [Twain] started running. He ran; and, oh, how fast he did run. He never stopped until he got to Keokuk, Iowa. Colonel Burbridge fought 4 years in the Southern Army; Mark Twain about 4 minutes." Shannon concluded his criticism by quoting Captain Billy Ely, who had been company commander of the Burbridge Brigade, "I can say to my fellow Missourians that we had but one coward in our whole group, and his name was Samuel L. Clemens" (Cong. Rec. 698-99).

background established

brackets to indicate insertion

Shannon's version of Mark Twain's military career is not completely accurate, but it does bring up some interesting questions. What was Twain's position during the Civil War? Why did he desert? When we look to Twain himself, we get very little reliable information. In his autobiography we learn that the war interrupted his career as a river pilot. Then he devotes only two sentences to the whole war episode:

purpose: to find out why Twain deserted

> In June I joined the Confederates in Ralls County, Missouri, as a second Lieutenant under General Tom Harris and came near having the distinction of being captured by Colonel Ulysses S. Grant. I resigned

quotation of more than 4 lines indented 10 spaces from left margin

doc 41b

Guest 2 *name and page number on every page*

after two weeks' service in the field, explaining that I was "incapacitated by fatigue" through persistent retreating. (102)

page number after period and 2 spaces

Another version of his career as a soldier appeared first in 1884 in Century Magazine as "The Private History of a Campaign That Failed." However colorful and interesting this account, it is probably more fictional than factual. According to William J. Kimball, "Exactly what happened in the summer of 1861 is probably beyond recovery, but the 'History' is obviously not an accurate account" (382). In the tale Twain tells of kids who join together to play soldier in a real war. They spend their time for the most part avoiding the Union forces they are supposed to be locating. The story contains several very humorous descriptions: the pretentious Dunlap, who changed his name to d'Un Lap; the uncooperative mules and horses, which constantly threw and bit their riders; the men, who rolled down hills in mud, slept in a corn crib, and were captured by dogs ("the most mortifying spectacle of the Civil War"). No one would cook, and no one would take orders.

quotation marks around a short quotation

In addition to the humor, the story also contains a very moving and dark episode in which Sam Clemens thinks that he has shot an innocent stranger. He writes:

> And it seemed an epitome of war; that all war must be just that--the killing of strangers against whom you feel no personal animosity; strangers whom, in other circumstances, you would help if you found them in trouble, and who would help you if you needed it. (263)

Guest 3

Several people have tried to explain Mark Twain's war experiences with less prejudice than Representative Shannon. In fact, together they help to sort out the confusion we feel about Twain's actions.

transitional paragraph

Van Wyck Brooks in The Ordeal of Mark Twain blames Twain's desertion on an "infantile frame of mind." Brooks maintains that Twain's independence from his mother's "leading strings" was so ill developed that he "slipped back into the boy he had been before." Brooks writes that we can see in the "History"

combination of three sources by paraphrasing and quoting

> a singular childishness, a sort of infantility, in fact that is very hard to reconcile with the character of any man of twenty-six and especially one who, a few weeks before, had been a river "sovereign," the master of a great steamboat, a worshipper of energy and purpose. (74-75)

In the New York Times a response to Representative Shannon's attack also points out that although at the time of his desertion Twain was 26, "mentally he was not yet 21" ("Ranger of Hannibal"). In "History," one of Twain's remarks supports this view. After he has become disillusioned with war, Twain comments, "It seemed to me that I was not rightly equipped for this awful business; that war was intended for men, and I for a child's nurse" (263). He also writes that the war had not yet turned the "green recruits" from "rabbits into soldiers" (265).

title used when author unknown

Justin Kaplan in his biography Mr. Clemens and Mark Twain writes that the episode of the killing of the stranger in "History" gave Twain a justification to desert. Now because of

two conflicting sources

doc 41b

Guest 4

the nightmarish killing, even though fictional, Twain was able to condemn war as dreadful. Thus, to Kaplan the story is intended to help remove the burden of guilt (322-25). J. Stanley Mattson also supports the view that the story is antiwar and that Twain is a pacifist. He writes, "It directs an arsenal of grape-shot at the entire concept of the glory of war" (794). Maxwell Geismar in Mark Twain: An American Prophet argues that although the story brings out the horror of war, its overall intention is to be humorous--"humor, yes. Guilt, no!" And Mark Twain left service with about half of the company simply because the "war was a disappointment" (129-30).

parentheses inside the periods

Perhaps more plausible than desertion because of exhaustion, childishness, or the inhumanity of war are explanations based on considerations of family, friends, and locality. Twain's sympathies leaned toward the South; he had recently spent time in Louisiana. When he returned to Missouri, he hid out for a while fearing he would be forced to pilot a Union gunboat. Twain's aunt wrote that when a friend suggested a Confederate company, Twain "accepted at once" (Webster 60). However, his brother Orion, to whom Twain was very close, favored the Union side. Showing how divided Mark Twain was, his aunt wrote:

transitional sentence

author's name in parentheses when not in text

> He loved his country's flag and all that it symbolized. . . . I know he would gladly have given his life for his country, but he was a Southerner, his friends were all Southern, his sympathies were with the South. It was the same problem that Robert E. Lee and thousands faced. (Webster 62)

doc 41b

Guest 5

The divided sympathies and possible indifference of Twain were typical of the feeling in Missouri as a whole. The interest in the war was minimal; "most Missourians probably would gladly have watched the war from the sidelines, waiting to study the meaning of its outcome" (Nagel 128). Voters (70 percent) favored compromise. Lincoln received only 10 percent of the votes. In a special 1861 convention, only 30,000 votes out of 140,000 cast favored secession. Despite the opposition, Missouri entered the war favoring the Union; three-fourths of the soldiers fought for the Union (Nagel 128-29). At the beginning of the "History" Twain writes of "a good deal of confusion in men's minds" and "a good deal of unsettledness, of leading first this way, then that, then the other way" (243). He tells that his pilot-mate and he were "strong for the Union." Then they both became rebels. Later the friend switched again and was piloting a federal gunboat (244).

Henry Seidel Canby expresses Twain's dilemma this way: Twain was "Southern in manners and Northern in mind." But Canby offers another dimension to the problem. Twain was really not interested in North or South, but it was "the continent that excited and persuaded him" (26). About this same time, Twain's brother Orion, a lawyer who had campaigned to get Lincoln elected President, got appointed Secretary of the Nevada Territory. When Orion left for Nevada, Twain went with him (Mack 47-49). Delancey Ferguson reports that "Orion wanted to stop his brother's dallying with the Southern cause" (65).

Guest 6

To people today, desertion seems a terrible crime and cowardly act. But during the Civil War, it was very common. Bell Wiley in The Common Soldier of the Civil War points out that many soldiers unlawfully left camp. He estimates deserters at 100,000 for the Confederate forces and 200,000 for the Federals. Wiley attributes the large numbers of desertions to the monotony of camp life (63). Twain writes in "History":

> We stayed several days at Mason's; and after all these years the memory of the dulness [sic], the stillness, and lifelessness of that slumberous farm-house still oppresses my spirit as with a sense of the presence of death and mourning. There was nothing to do, nothing to think about; there was no interest in life (257).

sic in brackets to indicate spelling error in the original

From a historical perspective, Twain's desertion was not unusual. Because of Twain's closeness to Orion, the decision to leave for Nevada was not surprising. No one should hastily condemn Twain without considering the complexity of the desertion.

conclusion—reasons for Twain's desertion were complex

doc 41b

Guest 7

Works Cited

Brooks, Van Wyck. The Ordeal of Mark Twain. New York: Dutton, 1933.

Canby, Henry Seidel. Turn West, Turn East: Mark Twain and Henry James. Boston: Houghton, 1951.

Clemens, Samuel L. The Autobiography of Mark Twain. Ed. Charles Neider. New York: Harper, 1959.

---. "The Private History of a Campaign That Failed." The American Claimant and Other Stories and Sketches. New York: Harper, 1897.

Cong. Rec. 25 Jan. 1940: 698-99.

Ferguson, Delancey. Mark Twain: Man and Legend. Indianapolis: Bobbs, 1943.

Geismar, Maxwell. Mark Twain: An American Prophet. Boston: Houghton, 1970.

Kaplan, Justin. Mr. Clemens and Mark Twain. 1966. New York: Pocket, 1968.

Kimball, William J. "Samuel Clemens as a Confederate Soldier: Some Observations about 'The Private History of a Campaign That Failed.'" Studies in Short Fiction 5 (1968): 382-84.

Mack, Effie Mona. Mark Twain in Nevada. New York: Scribner's, 1947.

Mattson, J. Stanley. "Mark Twain on War and Peace: The Missouri Rebel and 'The Campaign That Failed.'" American Quarterly 20 (1968): 785-94.

Nagel, Paul C. Missouri: A Bicentennial History. New York: Norton, 1977.

all material double-spaced

hyphens to indicate same author as above

volume, year, pages

doc 41b

Guest 8

author unknown; work alphabetized by title

"Ranger of Hannibal." New York Times 7 Feb. 1940: 20.

Webster, Samuel Charles, ed. Mark Twain, Business Man. Boston: Little, 1946.

Wiley, Bell. The Common Soldier of the Civil War. New York: Scribner's, 1975.

41c SAMPLE RESEARCH PAPER USING MLA STYLE—INTERPRETING LITERATURE

CINDERELLA
BY ANNE SEXTON

You always read about it:
the plumber with twelve children
who wins the Irish Sweepstakes.
From toilets to riches.
That story.

Or the nursemaid,
some luscious sweet from Denmark
who captures the oldest son's heart.
From diapers to Dior.
That story.

Or a milkman who serves the wealthy,
eggs, cream, butter, yogurt, milk,
the white truck like an ambulance
who goes into real estate
and makes a pile.
From homogenized to martinis at lunch.

Or the charwoman
who is on the bus when it cracks up
and collects enough from the insurance.
From mops to Bonwit Teller.
That story.

Once
the wife of a rich man was on her deathbed
and she said to her daughter Cinderella:
Be devout. Be good. Then I will smile
down from heaven in the seam of a cloud.
The man took another wife who had
two daughters, pretty enough
but with hearts like blackjacks.
Cinderella was their maid.
She slept on the sooty hearth each night

and walked around looking like Al Jolson.
Her father brought presents home from town,
jewels and gowns for the other women
but the twig of a tree for Cinderella.
She planted that twig on her mother's grave
and it grew to a tree where a white dove sat.
Whenever she wished for anything the dove
would drop it like an egg upon the ground.
The bird is important, my dears, so heed him.

Next came the ball, as you all know.
It was a marriage market.
The prince was looking for a wife.
All but Cinderella were preparing
and gussying up for the big event.
Cinderella begged to go too.
Her stepmother threw a dish of lentils
into the cinders and said: Pick them
up in an hour and you shall go.
The white dove brought all his friends;
all the warm wings of the fatherland came,
and picked up the lentils in a jiffy.
No, Cinderella, said the stepmother,
you have no clothes and cannot dance.
That's the way with stepmothers.

Cinderella went to the tree at the grave
and cried forth like a gospel singer:
Mama! Mama! My turtledove,
send me to the prince's ball!
The bird dropped down a golden dress
and delicate little gold slippers.
Rather a large package for a simple bird.
So she went. Which is no surprise.
Her stepmother and sisters didn't
recognize her without her cinder face
and the prince took her hand on the spot
and danced with no other the whole day.

As nightfall came she thought she'd better
get home. The prince walked her home
and she disappeared into the pigeon house

and although the prince took an axe and broke
it open she was gone. Back to her cinders.
These events repeated themselves for three days.
However on the third day the prince
covered the palace steps with cobbler's wax
and Cinderella's gold shoe stuck upon it.

Now he would find whom the shoe fit
and find his strange dancing girl for keeps.
He went to their house and the two sisters
were delighted because they had lovely feet.
The eldest went into a room to try the slipper on
but her big toe got in the way so she simply
sliced it off and put on the slipper.
The prince rode away with her until the white dove
told him to look at the blood pouring forth.
That is the way with amputations.
They don't just heal up like a wish.
The other sister cut off her heel
but the blood told as blood will.
The prince was getting tired.
He began to feel like a shoe salesman.
But he gave it one last try.
This time Cinderella fit into the shoe
like a love letter into its envelope.

At the wedding ceremony
the two sisters came to curry favor
and the white dove pecked their eyes out.
Two hollow spots were left
like soup spoons.

Cinderella and the prince
lived, they say, happily ever after,
like two dolls in a museum case
never bothered by diapers or dust,
never arguing over the timing of an egg,
never telling the same story twice,
never getting a middle-aged spread,
their darling smiles pasted on for eternity.
Regular Bobbsey Twins.
That story.

Lee Nordan

Professor Lasser

ENG 102

December 10, 1995

1" from top of page

Anne Sexton's "Cinderella": A Modern Fairy Tale

I. Background of the Cinderella story
   A. A variety of versions
   B. The two most popular versions
II. Sexton's use of the Grimms' plot
III. Sexton's ridicule of the folktale
   A. Modern and unromantic language
   B. Flippant tone
   C. Mockery of happy ending
      1. The happy endings in the first four stanzas
      2. The end of Sexton's version
   D. Rejection of sexist message
      1. The Grimms' view of male as savior
      2. Sexton's rejection

Nordan 1

1/2" from top of page

Anne Sexton's "Cinderella": A Modern Fairy Tale

centered title

In the popular story about Cinderella, a humble, virtuous maiden escapes drudgery and cruelty by marrying a prince and living happily ever after. For centuries, this tale has been known throughout the Orient, Indonesia, Europe, South Africa, and North and South America ("Cinderella" 233). As early as 1893, Marian Roalfe Cox cataloged the similarities and differences among 345 variants she discovered in such countries as Greece, Denmark, Russia, Italy, and England. Later scholars have found more than 500 versions in Europe alone ("Cinderella" 233) and have traced the story's origin to China in the ninth century (Waley 226).

background: history of story

citation—no author

citation—author and page number

Among the numerous versions, two have gained the greatest popularity. The first is a French story by Charles Perrault, originally published in 1697. Perrault took the story from oral tradition but adapted it for children by leaving out all the elements he considered "vulgar" (Bettelheim 250). The second is a German story, recorded by Jakob and Wilhelm Grimm in 1812. This version, titled "Aschenputtel," appeared in the Grimms' collection of old folktales, not written to entertain children but to preserve German language and folklore for posterity. As the Grimms described their purpose, "Our first care was faithfulness to the truth. We strove to penetrate into the wild forests of our ancestors, listening to their noble language, watching their pure customs, recognizing their ancient freedom and hearty faith" (Kready 67). In addition, the Grimms were pleased that morals of the tales could influence children to be "proper" (Brackert xvii, xx, xxvi).

background: the two most popular versions

Nordan 2

In 1971, Anne Sexton updated the celebrated story in Transformations. Sexton's poem "Cinderella" surprises modern American readers familiar with the romantic Walt Disney film, which was based on the Perrault version. As her source, Sexton used instead the Grimms' tale, which Kurt Vonnegut calls "a darker, queerer vision" (ix). According to Gail Pool, the Grimms' fairy tale "existed in the realm of the eerie, the grotesque," where Sexton "had always been her sharpest" (4).

purpose: to compare Sexton's poem with the Grimms tale

citation—page number (author's name in sentence)

Although there are significant differences between the versions of Sexton and the Grimms, the plots are similar. After four introductory stanzas that update the moral of the tale, Sexton, like the Grimms, begins the story with the death of Cinderella's mother and her father's marriage to a woman with two pretty but cruel daughters. In both stories, Cinderella's father brings gifts: gowns and jewels to the stepsisters and the twig of a tree to Cinderella. When Cinderella plants the twig on her mother's grave, it grows into a tree visited by a white dove that grants her wishes.

similarities in the plots

In time, the king of the realm plans a ball so that his son can pick a bride. The stepmother promises that if Cinderella can pick up a dish full of lentils thrown into the ashes, she can go to the ball. The dove, joined by its bird friends, picks up the lentils and drops from its tree a beautiful dress and golden slippers.

Neither Sexton nor the Grimms mention the fairy godmother who appears in some sources. Cinderella does, however, go to the ball; the prince falls in love with her; Cinderella escapes and returns to the kitchen ashes. The festivities are repeated for three

Nordan 3

days until Cinderella's slipper sticks in cobbler's wax (Sexton) or in pitch (Grimms).

Then begins the search for the maiden who can wear the golden slipper. In a gruesome scene, each sister cuts off part of her foot to make it fit the slipper, but the resultant blood and the dove's message give the tricks away. As we know, the slipper fits Cinderella's tiny foot, she marries the prince, and they live happily ever after. But not the sisters. In the romantic world of Perrault and Disney, the sisters are forgiven and married off to noblemen. In the plots of Sexton and Grimm, however, the dove pecks out the sisters' eyes.

Although Sexton uses the Grimms' plot, she treats the tale, as Janet Adam Smith points out, "with a bluntness and brutality that might well have startled the good brothers" (21). Sexton's purpose is to ridicule the value system set forth in the story. To accomplish this purpose, she transforms the tale dramatically. In strikingly modern and unromantic language, she mocks the story's serious tone, its unrealistic ending, and its male-dominated culture.

specific statement of thesis

Sexton begins her poem with four introductory stanzas, each telling a rags-to-riches story. A plumber wins the Irish Sweepstakes and gets out of "toilets"; a "luscious sweet" of a nursemaid marries her employer's son and gets into Dior fashions; a milkman makes "a pile" in real estate; and a charwoman "on the bus when it cracks up" collects a fortune from insurance.

examples of the poem's language

With the same kind of blunt language, Sexton retells the tale of Cinderella. The ash-covered heroine looks "like Al Jolson" and

Nordan 4

cries "like a gospel singer." Searching for the owner of the golden slipper, the prince begins to feel "like a shoe salesman." Scattered throughout the poem are such colloquial phrases as "gussying up," "in a jiffy," and "getting a middle-aged spread."

Sexton's flippant ton

The language underscores Sexton's distinctive tone, which critics have described in various ways. William Pitt Root calls it "witty" and says that "one could hardly fail to notice the spice she dashes into it" (50). J. D. McClatchy writes of her "irreverently zippy style" (22). Diana Hume George refers to Sexton's "tongue-in-cheek tone" (39). In the forword to The Complete Poems, Maxine Kumin disapproves of the "malevolently flippant tone" in a draft of one of Sexton's poems (xxvii). Defending this tone, Helen Vendler writes, "Sexton's aesthetically most realized tone is precisely a malevolently flippant one, however distasteful it might seem to others" (33). In fact, it is this flippant tone that makes Sexton's mockery of the story's values so obvious.

Sexton's mockery of the happy ending

One of the targets for Sexton's mockery is the ever-present happy ending, no matter how much fear and evil have preceded it. As in many other fairy tales, the message of "Cinderella" is that the poor, the deprived, the mistreated, and the unloved need only to wait, to endure the cruelties of life. Eventually, the "beautiful dream" will come true (Brackert xxvii). Sexton's four-stanza introduction stresses the rarity of such happy endings as the plumber's good fortune at the track, the nursemaid's lucrative marriage, the milkman's wealth from real estate, and the charwoman's lucky accident. The mockery is emphasized with the repetitive refrain: "From toilets to riches,"

Nordan 5

"From diapers to Dior," "From homogenized to martinis at lunch," and "From mops to Bonwit Teller."

The parallel between these success stories and the Cinderella story is emphasized by the repetition of "That story," which follows each improbable event. Rise B. Axelrod comments on the hollowness of the "happy" endings in the poem: "In Sexton's vision, neither the ending of the fairy tale nor the American Dream which the ending represents indicates happiness. Rather, the maturation signaled in the culmination of courtship, the institution of marriage, is really a deathly stasis" (11). The details describing the marriage of Cinderella and the prince with their "darling smiles pasted on for eternity" make one think not only of the problem-free Bobbsey twins, popular in early twentieth-century children's books, but also of a plastic bride and groom on the top of a wedding cake or the marriage of Barbie and Ken--definitely lacking reality.

Sexton's rejection of the sexist message

Another target of Sexton's mockery is the Cinderella notion that a helpless female defines success by marriage to a successful and wealthy male; thus, she depends not on her own resources but on magical intervention. The Grimms' version emphasizes this view. In it, according to Jack Zipes, the prince's role is "to bring about salvation of the female and the eventual marriage." Zipes sees this message even more strongly emphasized in the Disney film, "The ultimate message . . . is that, if you are industrious, pure of heart, and keep your faith in a male god, you will be rewarded. He will find you and carry you off to the good kingdom that is not threatened by the wiles of female duplicity" (24-25).

Nordan 6

Sexton removes the romance from the Cinderella story. At the ball that she calls a "marriage market," the prince chooses among a parade of eligible females. The scene evokes the image of a buyer looking over livestock at a cattle auction. Christopher Lehmann-Haupt notes that Sexton creates throughout the poem "similes that deflate romance" (33). Maxine Kumin writes that Sexton's poetry in general attacks women's "roles as goddesses of hearth and bedroom" (xxxiii). Diane Middlebrook observes that Sexton is one of several poets who have resisted stereotyping women's lives and have shown "the middle-class American woman beginning to seek liberation from confinement in domestic roles" (314). And one can see this tendency clearly at the end of the poem. In the last stanza, Sexton reminds readers that the romantic dream ignores the inevitable problems of "diapers or dust," arguments about "the timing of an egg," and "a middle-aged spread."

Although the source of Anne Sexton's "Cinderella" is clearly the version of the brothers Grimm, her purpose is quite different from theirs. The Grimms set out to preserve the German language and the heritage of the old folktales. Additionally, they hoped the morals of the tales might influence children for the good. Sexton, on the other hand, sets out to ridicule the story of Cinderella and its sexist view of marriage as a woman's reward for virtuous behavior. Her sarcastic humor and unromantic language give readers a new look at the old tale.

conclusion: restatement of the differences between Sexton's poem and the Grimms' tale

Nordan 7

Works Cited

Axelrod, Rise B. "The Transforming Art of Anne Sexton." Concerning Poetry 7.1 (1974):6-13.

Bettelheim, Bruno. The Uses of Enchantment: The Meaning and Importance of Fairy Tales. New York: Vintage, 1977.

Brackert, Helmut. Introduction. German Fairy Tales. By Jakob and Wilhelm Grimm. New York: Continuum, 1985. xvii-xxix.

"Cinderella." Funk & Wagnalls Standard Dictionary of Folklore, Mythology, and Legend. New York: Funk & Wagnalls, 1949.

Cox, Marian Roalfe. Cinderella: Three Hundred and Forty-Five Variants. London: David Nutt, 1893.

George, Diana Hume. Oedipus Anne: The Poetry of Anne Sexton. Urbana: U of Illinois P, 1987.

Grimm, Jakob and Wilhelm. "Cinderella." German Fairy Tales. Ed. Helmut Brackert and Volkmar Sander. New York: Continuum, 1985.

---. "Aschenputtel." Kinder und Haus-Marchen. Zurich: Conzett & Huber, 1946.

Kready, Laura F. A Study of Fairy Tales. Boston: Houghton Mifflin, 1916.

Kumin, Maxine. "How It Was." The Complete Poems. By Anne Sexton. Boston: Houghton Mifflin, 1981. xix-xxxiv.

journal issue number along with volume number

part of a book

author of encyclopedia article unknown; work alphabetized by title

edited work

hyphens to indicate same author as above

doc 41c

Nordan 8

Lehmann-Haupt, Christopher. "Grimms' Fairy Tales Retold." New York Times 27 Sept. 1971: A33.

newspaper article

McClatchy, J. D. "Anne Sexton: Somehow to Endure." The Centennial Review 19 (1975): 1-36.

Middlebrook, Diane. "Poets of Weird Abundance." Parnassus: Poetry in Review 12/13.1/2 (1985): 293-315.

Perrault, Charles. "Cinderilla or, the Little Glass Slipper." The Classic Fairy Tales. Ed. Iona Opie and Peter Opie. New York: Oxford UP, 1974.

Pool, Gail. "Anne Sexton: Poetry and Witchcraft." New Boston Review. 23 (Spring 1978): 3-4.

Root, William Pitt. "Anything But Over." Poetry. 123 (Oct. 1973): 50.

Sexton, Anne. Transformations. Boston: Houghton Mifflin, 1971.

Smith, Janet Adam. "The Great God Wish." New York Review of Books 2 Dec. 1971: 21.

Vendler, Helen. "Malevolent Flippancy." The New Republic 185.19 (1981): 33-6.

Vonnegut, Kurt. Foreword. Transformations. Boston: Houghton Mifflin, 1971.

Waley, Arthur. "The Chinese Cinderella Story." Folklore 58 (1947): 226-38.

Zipes, Jack. The Brothers Grim: From Enchanted Forests to the Modern World. New York: Routledge, 1988.

41d APA DOCUMENTATION

Many disciplines follow the APA style of documentation developed by the American Psychological Association. This style appears in publications in such fields as psychology, education, sociology, political science, and geography. Also, many other disciplines in science, technology, and business use the same system with minor variations. The style is commonly known as the name-year system because each citation includes the author's name and the year of publication, a most important bit of information to researchers in these fields.

(1) APA documentation inside the paper

In this system there are several ways to acknowledge sources within the paper's text.

1. The author's last name and the year of publication appear in parentheses. The parentheses are placed inside the sentence; a comma follows the author's name.

    In fact, the Women's Bureau of the Ministry of Labor was given inspector duties but no enforcement powers (Cook, 1987).

    Sometimes you must place in the parentheses more than one author's name. For two authors, insert both last names, separated by an ampersand (&)—(Baron & Hall, 1980). For three to five authors, give all authors in the first reference (Wilson, Allen, Lakoff, & James, 1979); and in subsequent references, give the first author followed by *et al.*—(Wilson et al., 1979). For six or more authors, always give only the first author and *et al.*—(Linn et al., 1989).

2. The author's name is in the sentence, and the year goes in parentheses.

    Dillon (1983) describes the jobs available to women as low-paying, boring, repetitive, and unskilled.

3. Both author's name and the year appear in the sentence.

    In 1975, Forbis gave these statistics.

4. For a quotation, a page number appears in addition to name and year. The parentheses containing the identifying information should be placed immediately after the quotation marks. Any punctuation that the sentence requires (period, comma, etc.) follows the parenthesis.

> Because of information about Japanese success, the United States has come to realize that "Japanese productivity has successfully challenged, even humiliated, America in world competition" (Bowman, 1984, p. 197).

> As Rehder (1983) points out, "Here women receive low wages, little job security, and less opportunity for training or educational development" (p. 43).

The page number for a blocked quotation also appears in parentheses but follows the period that ends the last sentence. See the example:

> . . . many are temporary workers, part-time workers, and workers in small companies. (p. 210)

(2) APA documentation at the end of the paper

In the APA style, you list the cited sources at the end of the paper in a section titled "References." As the list at the close of this paper illustrates, the sources are alphabetized. When you use the APA style, you must arrange the major components of each entry according to specifications. The following charts illustrate the formats of the citations for the most commonly used printed sources—books and periodicals.

Frequently, a source appears in both printed and electronic form (online material, CD-ROMs). In this case, the simplest policy is to cite the printed version, which is often more available to readers. You can then arrange your information according to the specifications in the charts.

If an electronic source has no printed version or a different printed version, you first use the format shown in the charts for author, date, and title. Then, in place of the publication information for a printed source, you include an availability statement, which contains the path or address. This statement will allow a reader to retrieve the source. In addition, you can follow the forms illustrated in "Additional APA Citation Forms."

The Major Components of APA Citations for Printed Sources	
Author	One author • Give last name first. • Use initials instead of full first and middle names. Example: Clark, M. V. Two or more authors • Give last name and initials of all authors, no matter how many. • Separate names with commas. • Place an ampersand (&) before the last author. Example: Romer, M. A., & Shapiro, C. B. Example: Bond, G. T., Gardner, H. L., Hart, F. C., & Magee, T.
Date	Book and journal • Place the year of publication (in parentheses) after the author's name. • Place a period at the end. Example: (1954). Magazine and newspaper • For monthly publications, give the year and month (in parentheses) after the author's name. • For weekly publications, give the year, month, and day (in parentheses) after the author's name. • Place a comma after the year. • Place a period at the end. Example: (1978, January). Example: (1986, August 15).
Title	Book • Capitalize only first word (title and subtitle) and proper nouns. • Place a period at the end. • Underline title and period with a solid line. Example: <u>Centuries of childhood: A social history of family life.</u>

	Periodical article • Use no quotation marks or underlining. • Capitalize only first word (title and subtitle) and proper nouns. • Place a period at the end. Example: The problem of perfection.
	Periodical • Capitalize conventionally (see 31e). • Place a comma after the title. • Underline title and comma with a solid line. Example: Natural History Magazine,
Publication Information	Book • After the title, give the city and a brief form of the publisher's name. • Place a colon after the city and a period at the end. Example: New York: Macmillan.
	Periodical with volume number • Place the underlined volume number (arabic numeral) and a comma after the title. • Give inclusive page numbers. • Place a period at the end. Example: Nature, 298, 197-209.
	Periodical with no volume number • Give inclusive page numbers. • Place p. before one page number and pp. before more than one. • Place a period at the end. Example: p. B1. Example: pp. 12-24.

In documenting references, you need to remember a few specifications about spacing. For student papers, APA allows single spacing in an entry but requires double spacing between entries. You should space twice after a period and once after other marks of punctuation. The first line is indented five spaces; other lines are against the margin. The full forms of the most commonly used kinds of sources appear below.

Basic Forms in APA Style for Printed Sources	
Book	Grotjohn, M. (1957). Beyond laughter. New York: McGraw-Hill.
	Tiger, L., & Fox, R. (1971). The imperial animal. New York: Holt.
Periodical	Bond, D. (1985). Ocean incineration of hazardous wastes: An update. Environmental Science and Technology, 19, 487-497.
	Lockard, J. S., McDonald, L. L., Clifford, D., & Martinez, R. (1976). Panhandling: Sharing of resources. Science, 191, 406-408.
	Paul, C. K. (1979, October). Satellites and world food resources. Technology Today, pp. 18-29.
Newspaper	Witcher, G. (1989, May 22). Smart cars, smart highways. The Wall Street Journal, p. B1.

In the *Publication Manual of the American Psychological Association,* there are numerous variations of these basic forms, most of which are reproduced below. If your source does not fit any of these categories, consult the manual.

Additional APA Citation Forms

EDITED BOOK

Kleinmuntz, B. (Ed.). (1970). Concepts and the structure of memory. New York: Wiley.

Maccoby, E. E., Newcomb, T. M., & Hartley, E. L. (Eds.). (1985). Readings in social psychology. New York: Holt, Rinehart and Winston.

PART OF A BOOK

Lewin, K., Dembo, T., Festinger, L., & Sears, P. S. (1944). Level of aspiration. In J. McV. Hunt (Ed.), Personality and the behavior disorders (pp. 333-378). New York: Ronald.

Part of a Multivolume Work

Gibb, C. A. (1969). Leadership. In G. Linzey & E. Aronson (Eds.), Handbook of social psychology (Vol. 4, pp. 205-282). Reading, MA: Addison-Wesley.

Later Edition

Boshes, L. D., & Gibbs, F. A. (1972). Epilepsy handbook (2nd ed.). Springfield, IL: Thomas.

Work with Corporate Author

League of Women Voters of the United States. (1969). Local league handbook. Washington, DC: Author.

doc 41d

Encyclopedia Article

Grateful dead (1949). In Funk & Wagnalls standard dictionary of folklore, mythology, and legend (vol. 1, pp. 463-464). New York: Crowell.

Hodge, R. W., & Siegel, P. M. (1968). The measurement of social class. In International encyclopedia of the social sciences (Vol. 15, pp. 316-324). New York: Macmillan.

Government Document

Bormuth, J. R. (1969). Development of readability analyses (Univ. of Chicago Final Report No. 7-0052). Washington, DC: U. S. Office of Education.

President's Committee on Mental Retardation. (1976). Mental retardation: The known and the unknown. Washington, DC: U. S. Government Printing Office.

Article in a Periodical with Volume Number

Wright, P. (1960). Two studies of the depth hypothesis. British Journal of Psychology, 60, 63-69.

The volume number, not the issue number, is used when the journal is numbered continuously through the year.

Kaplan, B. M. (1985). Zapping--the real issue is communication. Journal of Advertising Research, 25(2), 9-12.

The volume number and the issue number are given when each issue begins with page 1.

ARTICLE IN A MAGAZINE OR NEWSPAPER, NO AUTHOR, NO VOLUME NUMBER

Tale of the tape. (1989, May 29). Sports Illustrated, p. 14.

Pan Am charts a course for Europe, 1939. (1989, May 26). The Wall Street Journal, p. B1.

EDITORIAL AND LETTER

South Africa: Whites vs. apartheid. (1979, January 5). The Christian Science Monitor, p. 15.

Weinberg, G. L. (1985, June 18). Hitler remark on Armenians reported in '39 [Letter to the editor]. New York Times, p. A26.

BOOK REVIEW

Robinson, P. (1985, April). Freud's willful secretary [Review of Acts of will: The life and work of Otto Rank]. Psychology Today, 19, pp. 69-71.

ABSTRACT

Pippard, J., & Ellam, L. (1981). Electroconvulsive treatment in Great Britain. British Journal of Psychiatry, 139, 563-568. (From Psychological Abstracts, 1982, 68, Abstract No. 1567).

ONLINE DATABASE

Hattiesburg. United States Geographic Name Server [Online]. Available Internet: HTTP: GOPHER: gopher.stanford.edu

After a path statement, you do not use a period. A period, if typed, would not lead to the source.

ONLINE PERIODICAL

Green, T. F. (1994, February 6). Public speech: DeGarmo lecture for 1993 [45 paragraphs]. The Education Policy Analysis Archives [Online], 2(5). Available Internet: HTTP: info.afu.edu/asu—cwis/epaa/v2n5.html

Porteous, S. (1995, May 30). Why Bedford just doesn't want to go [11 paragraphs]. The Daily News Online [Halifax, Nova Scotia]. Available Internet: HTTP: www.cfn.cs.dal.ca/GreenPages/DailyNews.html

ONLINE ABSTRACT

Mihos, J. C. (1995). Morphology of galaxy mergers at intermediate redshift [Online]. Astrophysical Journal, 438, L75-78. NASA Astrophysics Data System: ADS Abstract Service. Abstract from Internet: HTTP: adswww.harvard.edu/

ABSTRACT ON CD-ROM

Lerner, B. (1995). Aim higher [CD-ROM]. National Review, 47, 56-60. Abstract from ProQuest: Access No.: 02270120

FILM

Kramer, S. (Producer), & Benedek, L. (Director). (1951). Death of a salesman [Film].

TELEVISION PROGRAM

Chalow, T. (Producer). (1983, May 5). Fat chance in a thin world. Boston: WGBH.

INTERVIEW

Anderson, A., & Southern, T. (1958). [Interview with Nelson Algren]. In M. Cowley (Ed.), Writers at work (pp. 231-249). New York: Viking.

If the interview is not published, it does not appear in "References." Instead, the text of the paper should clarify the interview's nature and date.

Typing with APA Style

- Use standard-sized (8½-X-11-inch) bond paper and standard type.
- Use a title page.
- Use 1- or 1½-inch margins on every page. The top margin of the first page of text may be wider.
- Double-space the paper. Student papers may have single-spaced references but with double spaces between them.
- Do not hyphenate words at the end of lines.
- Start numbering with the title page (page 1) and number the remaining pages consecutively.
- Block long quotations of more than 40 words. Indent the left margin five spaces. In student papers, the entire block may be single-spaced.
- Type references on a separate page in alphabetical order. Title the reference page "References." Either indent the first line of references 5 to 7 spaces, or use the hanging indent style (second and subsequent lines are indented). APA specifies the first style for papers meant for publication. For more than one entry by the same author, repeat the author's name.

41e SAMPLE RESEARCH PAPER USING APA STYLE—PRESENTING AN ARGUMENT

Tradition versus Change 1

short title and page number on every page

Tradition versus Change: Women in the Japanese Work Force

Stewart R. Morgan

Danforth College

Outline

I. Traditional discrimination against women

A. Educational limitations

B. Traditional male business environment

1. Importance of "group"

2. Importance of a homogeneous system

3. Importance of fraternizing

C. Traditional role of women

1. Marriage and motherhood

2. Choosing a career or a traditional role

3. Traditional jobs

II. Passage of the Equal Employment Opportunity law

A. Origin

B. Weak language

III. Impact of the Equal Employment Opportunity law

A. Improvements

1. Employee attitude

2. Increasing numbers of women in the work force

3. Successful women

B. Obstacles

1. Continuing discrimination

2. Women's attitudes

Tradition versus Change:
Women in the Japanese Work Force

title repeated

Although Japan has made impressive achievements in business, working conditions in Japan have not always been advantageous for women. Traditionally, the Japanese woman's role in society has been as housewife and mother. If employed at all, women have usually been farm laborers or "office flowers." In 1981, Ouchi said bluntly, "Probably no form of organization is more sexist . . . than the Japanese corporation" (p. 92). In 1985, Japan passed an equal opportunity law prohibiting discrimination by sex. If successfully implemented, this law could help break down the barriers to women employees; nevertheless, Japan's strong male-centered and family-centered society is likely to slow any change toward equal treatment.

page number for a direct quotation

statement of thesis

doc 41e

Several factors have made women's advancement in the business world difficult. One obstacle is the competitive and stressful Japanese system of education. Although both men and women go to college, women usually attend two-year colleges while men attend four-year universities (Forbis, 1975). After graduation the top male graduates of the best schools get the best jobs and form an "elite corps" (Bowman, 1984, p. 201). According to Rehder (1983), "Women graduates, regardless of their talent or level of academic achievement, remain outside the mainstream of corporate or government career opportunities" (p. 43). Lansing and Ready (1993) agree that women graduates are commonly turned away from meaningful employment: "In 1985, 23.8

educational system described using 4 sources

author's name in parentheses when omitted from text

year in parentheses when author's name in text

Tradition versus Change 4

percent of all women graduates were without a job" (p. 257).

Bowman (1984) points out that in Japan "the basic social unit . . . is the group rather than the individual" and that in industry a major objective is to develop an "organizational cohesiveness" (p. 199). Ouchi (1981) believes that it is this attitude, rather than a belief in male superiority, that excludes women from employment. He maintains that Japanese organizations are "homogeneous social systems" and reject women because they are "different" (p. 92). He gives as an example a case in which an employer must choose between two equally qualified people--one male, one female. The employer, because of inexperience in evaluating females, would naturally choose the male; "no one in his right mind will choose an uncertainty over a certainty" (pp. 91-92). Osako (1978) observes that a woman is rarely part of a group unless she goes to bars with her male colleagues. Few women in Japan fit into this kind of setting.

traditional business environment described using 3 sources

Another reason for employment discrimination is the traditional role that women play in Japanese society. Their goals are "marriage and motherhood" (Dillon, 1983). The marriage rate is extremely high, and the care of children is the exclusive job of women. Consequently, women rarely seek employment. Instead they remain at home and promote the education of their sons, since male children, if successful in school, may someday be successful in business. According to Dillon, "Mothers play an important role (and live vicariously) through the career development of their sons" (p. 23). Osako (1978) writes, "A woman is considered more virtuous if she devotes herself to the advancement of other family members (notably sons and husbands) rather than pursuing her own career" (p. 18).

women's traditional role described using 2 sources

career vs. traditional role described using 3 sources

The importance of marriage and motherhood places ambitious women in a dilemma. Businesses assume that women employees will retire when they either marry or have their first child (Cook, 1987; Edwards, 1988). When women seek to return to work after their children have left home, they almost never get mainstream jobs or full benefits (Whitehill, 1991). According to Edwards (1988), "When women re-enter the labor force, they are no longer eligible for the 'career' jobs . . . because they are too old. Firms are even reluctant to hire older women for non-career jobs." Therefore, women must often choose between meaningful work and the traditional role of wife and mother.

2 sources cited for same information

doc 41e

Dillon (1983) describes the jobs available to women as low-paying, boring, repetitive, and unskilled. As Cordilia and Ohta (1992) point out:

> Although the overall work force participation of Japanese women is high, Japanese women are far from having equality in the types of work they do. Compared with men, they are underrepresented in management and the professions and overrepresented in clerical positions. Disproportionately few women are in career-track jobs in large companies, whereas disproportionately many are temporary workers, part-time workers, and workers in small companies. (p. 210)

Margaret Shapiro (1988) observes that women in Japanese businesses have the lowest salaries and the worst jobs--"often wearing office uniforms with aprons to run errands and pour tea" (p. A1).

traditional jobs of women described using 3 sources

in student papers quotation of more than 40 words single-spaced and indented 5 spaces

In May 1985, the Japanese government passed the Equal Employment Opportunity Law. The law, which went into effect in April 1986, was intended to eliminate discrimination against women in the workplace; as a solution, however, it has had limited success.

transitional paragraph restating thesis

Tradition versus Change 6

The equal opportunity law in Japan was weak from the start. First, it was not initiated by the Japanese government or by any Japanese women's movement (Cannings & Lazonick, 1994). Instead, the United Nations in 1975 called for all governments to end gender discrimination. Japan wanted to follow other countries in developing legislation to support this initiative (Lansing & Ready, 1993). Second, the law contains weak language. According to Cordilia and Ohta (1992), the law does not forbid discrimination; instead, it asks employers merely to "try" not to discriminate against women in recruiting, hiring, making job assignments, and promoting employees. And third, it contains no enforcement measures or penalties. In fact, the Women's Bureau of the Ministry of Labor was given inspector duties but no enforcement powers (Cook, 1987).

equal opportunity law described using 4 sources

The equal opportunity law will most probably have some impact on the traditional Japanese business environment. Since its passage in 1985, changes have been noted. Cannings and Lazonick (1994) point out that some employers are more willing to hire women, and more female university graduates are entering employment. While these changes may be partly caused by shortages of technical specialists, Cannings and Lazonick believe that the impact of the law is "significant" (p. 60).

improvements from the law covered in 2 paragraphs using 3 sources

In addition, there are notable exceptions to unequal treatment in the workplace. Some women have reached executive positions in such companies as Takashimaya Department Store and Japan Air Lines (Whitehill, 1991). In 1989, an article in the Wall Street Journal profiled three women with full-time employment in the "vanguard of a quiet revolution that is changing the way Japanese live and work" (Lehner & Graven, p. A1). Nevertheless, these cases may not be typical. As Whitehill (1991) points out, "The plain truth is that women continue to find only limited opportunities to share in Japan's prosperous business environment" (p. 139).

obstacles covered in paragraph using 6 sources

The equal opportunity law must overcome strong obstacles. One year after the passage of the law, a survey revealed that most people thought equality was unlikely. According to the responses, women should only do "women's work" in "suitable fields" (Whitehill, 1991, p. 139). As recently as 1989, four years after passage of the law, newspaper employment advertisements still included the gender of applicants eligible for a job. Moreover, most women were employed in part-time work (Cordilia & Ohta, 1992).

doc 41e

One of the strongest obstacles to equality in the workplace is women's attitudes. Japanese women have not taken a strong position on equal rights. According to Cook (1987), the women's movement in Japan is "miniscule" (p. 366). Most Japanese women are "skeptical or indifferent" about change (Lansing & Ready, 1993, p. 256). In fact, as Lehner and Graven point out, "Many Japanese women themselves remain profoundly conservative, unimpressed by Western feminism and content with the well-defined roles that separate them from men" (p. A12). To change, women will have to place the importance of their careers over home and family. As Edwards (1988) writes, "To take advantage of these new opportunities, women will have to be willing to remain in the labor force during the childrearing years--or to forgo having children altogether" (p. 248). It is far from certain that the majority of Japanese women will make this choice.

conclusion: restatement of thesis

The equal opportunity law will certainly affect the Japanese business environment, but the greatest obstacle is the tradition of women staying home to care for their husbands and children. Change will possibly come, but it will be slow. Social traditions are very strong in Japan, and the majority of women may not be willing to choose the stress and long working hours of a career over the duties of wife and mother.

Tradition versus Change 8

References

Bowman, J. S. (1984). Japanese management: Personnel policies in the public sector. Public Personnel Management, 13, 197-247.

Cannings, K., & Lazonick, W. (1994, January). Equal employment opportunity and the "managerial woman" in Japan. Industrial Relations, 33, 44-69.

Cook, A. H. (1987). International comparisons: Problems and research in the industrialized world. In K. S. Koziara, M. H. Moskow, & L. D. Tanner (Eds.), Working women: Past, present, future (pp. 332-373). Washington, DC: Bureau of National Affairs.

Cordilia, A., & Ohta, K. (1992). Central in the family and marginal in the work force: Women's place in Japanese society. In H. Kahne & J. Z. Giele (Eds.), Women's work and women's lives (pp. 187-223). Boulder: Westview.

Dillon, L. (1983). Career development in Japan: Its relation to Japanese productivity. Journal of Career Education, 10, 22-26.

Edwards, N. E. (1988). Equal Employment Opportunity in Japan: A view from the West. Industrial and Labor Relations Review, 41, 240-250.

last names and initials of authors used;

dates in parentheses following names

capitals in names of periodicals

names of periodicals and volume numbers underlined

Forbis, W. H. (1975). Japan today: People, places, power. New York: Harper.

Lansing, P., & Ready, K. (1993). Hiring women managers in Japan: An alternative for foreign employers. In S. Durlabhji & N. E. Marks (Eds.), Japanese business: Cultural perspectives (pp. 253-270). Albany: State University of New York.

Lehner, U., & Graven, K. (1989, September 6). Japanese women rise in their workplaces, challenging tradition. The Wall Street Journal, pp. A1, A12.

Osako, M. M. (1978). Dilemmas of Japanese professional women. Social Problems, 26, 15-25.

Ouchi, W. G. (1981). Theory Z: How Americans can meet the Japanese challenge. Reading, MA: Addison-Wesley.

Rehder, R. R. (1983). Education and training: Have the Japanese beaten us again? Personnel Journal, 62, 42-47.

Shapiro, M. (1988, February 9). In Japan, the sun still rises: Woman's main role remains housewife. The Washington Post, pp. A1, A16.

Whitehill, A. M. (1991). Japanese management: Tradition and transition. London: Routledge.

part of boo[k] cited

no capitals except for proper names and first word of titles and subtitles of articles and books

doc 41e

APPENDIX

A

SPELLING

The English spelling system is often criticized for its "inconsistencies," that is, for its failure to reflect pronunciation accurately. For example, the pronunciation of the word *answer* does not include a /w/ sound, and the pronunciation of the word *night* does not include either a /g/ or an /h/ sound. The sound "ah" can be spelled with an *a* (as in *father*) or an *o* (as in *not*). A *d* sometimes represents the sound /d/ (as in *bagged*) and sometimes the sound /t/ (as in *jumped*). In other words, many English words are not pronounced as their spellings might indicate.

One reason for the inconsistencies is the tendency of English to borrow words from other languages. These words, such as the French *naive* or the Dutch *yacht,* reflect the spelling systems of those languages rather than of our own. But receptiveness to foreign words is one of the strengths of English, making it flexible, adaptable, able to survive. Spelling peculiarities seem a small price to pay for that strength.

Another reason for inconsistencies in the English spelling system is the large number of regional dialects, which frequently have differing pronunciations of the same words. Thus, English spelling often seems to contradict phonetics. But it must. If our spelling were phonetic, English speakers from different regions would have to spell words differently. Consequently, a New Yorker would have to struggle to read an Atlanta newspaper, and written communication between an American and an Australian would require translation.

In addition, the pronunciation of English has changed throughout history. To reflect pronunciation accurately, spelling would have to change over the years, and these changes would create a very inefficient writing system. The written records of the past would too quickly become obscure: knowledge of law, history, and literature, for instance, would be available only to those who knew the old tongues.

Obviously, the primary requirement of a spelling system is not that it be logical but that it be as stable as possible from dialect to dialect and from era to era. Furthermore, it is imperative that you observe the system, no matter how illogical it seems. To most readers in the worlds of business, commerce, and scholarship, spelling is a mark of a person's education, sense of responsibility, and even intelligence. Therefore, you cannot afford to take a casual attitude toward spelling; it is to your professional advantage to take spelling seriously.

SPa TIPS FOR IMPROVING SPELLING

Some people seem to have a natural talent for spelling, an ability that allows them to visualize words correctly. These people can simply look at commonly used words and know immediately if the spelling is correct. Thus, natural spellers rely on dictionaries to spell only unusual or technical words. But many people do not have this talent and instead must always be alert to the possibility of misspelled words in everything they write. If you fall into this second category of spellers, you may want to adopt some or all of the following five techniques for improving spelling.

(1) Use the dictionary.

The best way to solve spelling problems is to use a dictionary. Poor spellers often counter this suggestion with "If I don't know how to spell a word, I can't find it in the dictionary." This assumption usually is not true. With a few exceptions (such as *kn, ph, sc*), an initial consonant is almost always predictable. And initial vowels are almost as easy to predict as consonants—a word like *envision* may begin with either an *i* or an *e,* but it certainly is not likely to begin with an *a,* an *o,* or a *u.* Thus, finding the right section of the dictionary requires little effort. At that point, the word can be located rather quickly.

Suppose, for example, you want to look up the correct spelling of a common word like *concept.* From its sound, you can guess that the first letter is going to be *c* or *k.* The first vowel, if not *a,* is likely to be *o.* It is certain that an *n* will follow that vowel. Next comes an /s/ sound, rarely spelled any way except *s* or *c.* After that comes a sound usually represented by an *e.* Finally, the *p* and *t* are almost completely predictable. In summary, if *concept* is not in the *k*'s, it will certainly be in the *c*'s. And from that point, it should take only a few minutes to track the word down.

(2) Practice pronunciation.

Once you have found a word in the dictionary, be sure you know exactly how to pronounce it. To fix the pronunciation in your mind, say the word aloud several times, pausing between syllables. Then say the word aloud a number of times without pausing. If you have difficulty understanding the pronunciation symbols of dictionaries, you might try the *Oxford American,* which uses an Americanized pronunciation key much simpler than those of most other dictionaries.

(3) Practice writing the word.

After you are sure of the pronunciation, write the word a dozen times or so. This practice not only will help fix the word in your motor memory but also will let you see how it looks in your own handwriting. If possible, also type the word a number of times to help you recognize it in print. When you know a word in sound, script, and type, you are not likely to forget how to spell it.

(4) Keep a word list.

You might find it helpful to keep a list of words that you tend to misspell. You can include those words that instructors have marked on your papers as well as words you must frequently look up in the dictionary. Studying your list and using it when you edit papers will help you master the words you find particularly troublesome.

You can also consult lists of commonly misspelled words, such as those at the end of this chapter. You can single out the words you do not spell with confidence and add them to your individual list.

(5) Study spelling patterns.

Get familiar with spelling patterns, also called "spelling rules." Remember, however, that a rule in spelling is an observation—a description of a pattern that recurs in the language, not an iron-clad law never violated.

SPb SPELLING PATTERNS

Inconsistencies do exist between the spelling system and the sound system. And bizarre spellings do occur, although usually with scientific terms, esoteric words, and proper names. But on the whole, patterns predominate.

(1) Silent *e* with long vowels

Many words end with an unpronounced letter *e*—commonly called "silent *e*." Actually, the silent *e* is a key to pronunciation, as the following pairs of words illustrate.

van/vane	lop/elope
gap/gape	dot/dote
spit/spite	occur/cure
forbid/abide	sum/consume

The word pairs show that silent *e* follows a stressed (accented) syllable with a long vowel, a vowel that requires the muscles in the mouth to tense during pronunciation.

ee in *theme*	*ay* in *mate*
oo in *rude*	*iy* in *bite*
oh in *hope*	

The *e* may attach to a single-syllable word or to a word stressed on the last syllable.

The absence of the *e* on a stressed (accented) syllable indicates a short vowel. Short vowels like the following allow the muscles in the mouth to remain lax during pronunciation.

ih in *fit*	*aw* in *bought*
eh in *bet*	*ah* in *spa*
uh in *cup*	*aeh* in *mat*

The pattern is as follows:

- stressed syllable with long vowel: silent *e* (*tape, ride*)
- stressed syllable with short vowel: no *e* (*tap, rid*)

The rule does not apply when the stressed final syllable has

- more than one vowel in a row (*boom, appear*)
- more than one consonant in a row (*comb, dodge*)

(2) Silent *e* with suffixes

SPb

When a suffix is added to a word that ends in silent *e,* the *e* drops if the suffix begins with a vowel and remains if the suffix begins with a consonant.

Base	Suffix with Vowel, Drop the *E*	Suffix with Consonant, Retain the *E*
arrange	arranging	arrangement
like	likable	likely
sincere	sincerity	sincerely
name	naming	nameless
intense	intensify	intensely
tone	tonal	toneless
waste	wasting	wasteful
excite	exciting	excitement
love	lovable	lovely

EXCEPTION: Three common exceptions to this pattern are *truly, argument,* and *judgment.*

EXCEPTION: The letter *c* may represent the hard sound /kuh/ as in *cup* or the soft sound /s/ as in *circle.* The letter *g* may represent the hard sound /guh/ as in *gum* or the soft sound /juh/ as in *gentle.* With the suffixes *-able* and *-ous,* silent *e* is retained in two situations:

- After soft *c:* service/serviceable
  notice/noticeable
- After soft *g:* outrage/outrageous
  advantage/advantageous

(3) Doubled consonants with verbs

With regular verbs, the past tense and past participle are made by adding *-d* or *-ed* to the base form. (See 4a.) The spelling pattern is as follows.

- When the verb ends in a stressed syllable and a single consonant, the consonant is doubled and *-ed* is added *(pin/pinned, uncap/uncapped).*
- When the verb ends in a stressed syllable and a silent *e,* a *-d* is added to the base *(dine/dined, escape/escaped).*

SPb

Base Form	Past Form and Past Participle
bar	barred
bare	bared
refer	referred
interfere	interfered
grip	gripped
gripe	griped
occur	occurred
cure	cured
mat	matted
mate	mated

The present participle is made by adding *-ing* to the base form of the verb. The spelling pattern is as follows.

- When the verb ends in a stressed syllable and a single consonant, the consonant is doubled and *-ing* is added (*pin/pinning, uncap/uncapping*).
- When the verb ends in a stressed syllable and a silent *e,* the *e* is dropped and *-ing* is added (*dine/dining, escape/escaping*).

Base Form	Present Participle
bar	barring
bare	baring
refer	referring
interfere	interfering
grip	gripping
gripe	griping
occur	occurring
cure	curing
mat	matting
mate	mating

(4) Doubled consonants with prefixes, suffixes, and compounds

When a prefix ends with the same consonant that the base begins with, both consonants are retained.

dis + satisfied	dissatisfied
over + rate	overrate
un + necessary	unnecessary

When a suffix begins with the same consonant that the base ends with, both consonants are retained.

mental + ly	mentally
stubborn + ness	stubbornness
heel + less	heelless

When the first part of a compound word ends with the same consonant that the second part begins with, both consonants are retained.

book + keeper	bookkeeper
beach + head	beachhead
room + mate	roommate

(5) *I* before *e*

Almost everyone knows the "i before e" school rhyme:

> *"I* before *e* except after *c*
> or when sounding like *a* as in *neighbor* and *weigh."*

The rule in this rhyme works with many *ie* words.

achieve	relief
believe	thief
friend	view

It also works with many *c* plus *ei* words.

SPb

ceiling	deceive
conceit	perceive
conceive	receive

And *ei* does appear in words that sound like *weigh.*

eight	neighbor
feign	sleigh
freight	veil

But many words without the *c* or the *weigh* sound are spelled with *ei.*

either	neither
foreign	seize
height	weird

The rhyme does cover words like *believe* and *receive,* but it is not completely reliable. The best solution to the *ie/ei* problem is the dictionary.

(6) *-Cede, -ceed,* and *-sede*

Since *-sede, -ceed,* and *-cede* are pronounced identically, writers sometimes confuse them, spelling *proceed,* for example, as *procede.* Mastering the "cede" words, however, is a simple matter of memorizing the spelling of four words: *supersede, exceed, proceed,* and *succeed.*

> *Supersede* ends in *-sede.*
> *Exceed, proceed,* and *succeed* end in *-ceed.*
> All the rest end in *-cede: recede, secede, concede,* and so on.

SPc LISTS OF FREQUENTLY MISSPELLED WORDS

Several lists of frequently misspelled words are grouped according to the characteristics that cause problems.

Easily Confused Words

accept/except
advice/advise
affect/effect
all ready/already
all together/altogether
allusion/illusion
ally/alley
aloud/allowed
altar/alter
analysis/analyze
ascent/assent
assistance/assistants
board/bored
breath/breathe
bridal/bridle
capital/capitol
censor/censure
choose/chose
cite/site/sight
cloths/clothes
coarse/course
dairy/diary
descent/dissent
device/devise
die/dye
ensure/insure
envelop/envelope
formally/formerly
forth/fourth
foul/fowl
hear/here
heard/herd
idol/idle
incidence/incidents
its/it's
know/no
later/latter
lead/led
lessen/lesson
lightning/lightening
loan/lone
loose/lose

complement/compliment
conscience/conscious
council/counsel
currant/current
passed/past
peace/piece
personal/personnel
presence/presents
principal/principle
prophecy/prophesy
quiet/quit/quite
right/write
road/rode
sail/sale
shone/shown
stationary/stationery
statue/stature
maybe/may be
moral/morale
muscle/mussel
naval/navel
straight/strait
than/then
their/there/they're
through/threw
to/too/two
vain/vein
waist/waste
wait/weight
weather/whether
were/we're/where
which/witch
who's/whose
your/you're

SPc

Words with *s, ss, c,* and *sc*

absence
accessible
adolescent
ascend
assassinate
assistance
associate
conscience
conscious
decision
necessary
nuisance
occasion
permissible
persistence
physical
possession
reminisce
resistance
descend
discussion
ecstasy
embarrass
expense
fascinate
insistent
license
mischievous
muscle
scarcity
sincerely
source
succeed
succession
suspicious
unconscious
unnecessary
vicious

Words with *-able* or *-ible*

acceptable
admissible
incredible
irresistible

advisable	irritable
believable	likeable
changeable	movable
collapsible	noticeable
comfortable	peaceable
compatible	permissible
credible	possible
dependable	probable
edible	profitable
eligible	resistible
flammable	responsible
flexible	separable
gullible	visible
impossible	

Words with *-ence* or *-ance*

abhorrence	dependence
abundance	difference
acquaintance	endurance
appearance	existence
appliance	guidance
assistance	independence
attendance	inference
conference	insistence
deference	intelligence
defiance	interference
magnificence	prominence
maintenance	providence
nuisance	reference
occurrence	resemblance
patience	significance
permanence	surveillance
persistence	temperance
preference	tolerance
prevalence	vengeance

APPENDIX

B

ENGLISH AS A SECOND LANGUAGE

Children acquire language very easily. Any languages children hear often, they learn to speak; and any languages children read often, they learn to write. Furthermore, children can learn language without any formal study because they internalize the grammatical rules as they hear and see individual sentences.

ESL

But for most adults, language is not so simply acquired. Although hearing and seeing a language is essential, most adults also need at least some formal study of grammar. In other words, they need information about the underlying system of a language.

This appendix is designed to help non-native speakers understand the most basic elements underlying English grammar: the components of the noun phrase and the verb phrase. In addition, the appendix includes methods for recognizing complete sentences and for forming questions and negatives. The appendix is best used along with Parts I and II of this textbook, which explain and illustrate grammatical principles. Therefore, you should pay attention to the cross references that point to other sections of the book, and you should review material from Parts I and II whenever you need additional information.

ESLa THE NOUN PHRASE

The term **noun phrase** refers to a single word or a group of words that can function in a noun position—such as subject of a verb, object of a verb, object of a preposition, and so forth. A noun phrase may contain a single noun or a series of modifiers plus a noun. (See Chapter 1.)

information
much information
not much useable information

houses
the houses
the first three red brick houses on Baker Street

announcer
the radio announcer
the same tiresome radio announcer

milk
twice the milk
twice the milk in the recipe

memories
Jane's memories
some of Jane's most pleasant childhood memories

As the examples show, the noun phrase can be expanded from a single word to a rather long string of words. The order of the words, however, is not random but fairly fixed. If you think of a noun phrase as a series of positions, you can more easily discover the proper order. Sections ESLb through ESLf explain the positions and the kinds of items that may appear in those positions.

ESLb HEAD NOUNS

A **head noun** is the obligatory position in a noun phrase (ESLa). All other words in the noun phrase depend upon it grammatically; that is, they "modify" the head noun. Furthermore, the modifiers depend to some extent on whether the head noun is a count noun or a non-count noun.

(1) Count Nouns

A **count noun** names something that can be counted: *one desk, two desks, three desks,* and so forth. Therefore, a count noun usually has a singular and a plural form. In the singular form, a count noun requires a determiner: *a desk, my desk* (ESLc). In the plural form, however, a count noun can appear with or without a determiner: *desks, the desks.* Remember that count nouns can be preceded by *many* but not by *much.*

POSSIBLE: her many accomplishments

IMPOSSIBLE: her much accomplishments

(2) Non-count nouns

A **non-count noun** names something that cannot be counted: *news, information, furniture, butter, milk, homework.* Non-count nouns have no plurals, but you can refer to their parts or amounts by using a phrase that indicates measurement: *half of the butter, some of the information, two pieces of furniture.* Remember that non-count nouns can be preceded by *much* but not by *many.*

POSSIBLE: much good luck

IMPOSSIBLE: many good luck

ESLc

ESLc DETERMINERS

A **determiner** indicates that a noun will appear. The noun may not immediately follow the determiner, but it will appear at some point. Determiners can be classified as articles, demonstrative pronouns, and possessives.

(1) The indefinite article

The **indefinite article** is *a/an.* The *a* form precedes words that begin with a consonant sound (not necessarily a written consonant): *a* *tree, a book, a unicorn* [pronounced *yew-nuh-corn*]. The *an* form precedes words that begin with a vowel sound (not necessarily a written vowel): *an apple, an uncle, an herb* [pronounced *erb*].

Since *a/an* means roughly "one," it accompanies singular count nouns (ESLb.1); it is not appropriate with non-count nouns. Use *a/an* when you introduce a singular count noun into the discourse. Do not use *a/an* with a noun you have already mentioned or with a synonym of that noun. Otherwise, you mislead the reader to think that the noun is new and has not been previously mentioned.

POSSIBLE: Senator Perez is sponsoring a bill [first mention] for reforming the income tax system. If passed, the bill [the same bill] would establish a "flat tax," with everyone paying the same rate regardless of income. Because the proposal [synonym for the same bill] is quite sensible, it is sure to be defeated.

IMPOSSIBLE AND MISLEADING: Senator Perez is sponsoring a bill for reforming the income tax system. If passed, a bill would establish a "flat tax," with everyone paying the same rate regardless of income. Because a proposal is quite sensible, it is sure to be defeated.

(2) The definite article

ESLc

The **definite article** is *the.* This article can precede both count and non-count nouns and both singular and plural nouns. Most of its numerous uses are explained below.

- Use *the* with a common noun (see 1a) that has been previously mentioned in the discourse. You use *the* regardless of whether the noun appears in the same form or as a synonym.

  Low-maintenance landscaping is easy if you stick to ground cover and shrubs. The ground cover provides a neat appearance and discourages weeds, while the shrubs provide design and create interest.

  Gold is one of the oldest marks of wealth. From the earliest times, possession of the bright yellow metal [synonym] indicated prestige.

- Use *the* with a common noun when a modifier after the noun makes it specific.

The car in the garage belongs to Andrew.

The people downstairs moved into the apartment yesterday.

The package that we received on Thursday was left in the rain.

- Use *the* with a common noun that names something universally known or familiar in everyday life.

At most parties, everyone gravitates toward the kitchen.

The siesta is my favorite Mexican custom.

- Use *the* with an ordinal number (*first, second,* etc.).

I took the first empty seat on the plane.

He was the third applicant on the list.

- Use *the* with the superlative degree of an adjective (*best, biggest,* etc.).

She got an award for the best science project.

Geography is the most interesting of all my courses.

- Use *the* with a plural proper name.

The first guests to arrive were the Powells.

The Gleesons opened a bed-and-breakfast inn.

- Use *the* with a public institution.

My group toured the Library of Congress.

The Smithsonian Institute issues a sale catalogue.

- Use *the* with a unique phenomenon or unique individual—in other words, when there can be only one.

Some early astronomers thought the sun revolved around the earth.

While in Rome, he sought an audience with the Pope.

How is the Israeli prime minister chosen?

Some cultures trace ancestry through the mother.

(3) Demonstrative pronouns

The **demonstrative pronouns** are *this, these, that,* and *those.* (See 2b.) They are used primarily to refer to nouns previously mentioned in the discourse or as a kind of summary substitute for material that has preceded. In general, use *this* and *these* with present and future time and *that* and *those* with past time.

> Leaf-cutter ants cultivate a fungus in large underground gardens. When a queen ant moves on to start a new colony, she takes a pellet of this fungus with her.
>
> When hiking, do not neglect to pack food, water, matches, and a first-aid kit. These items can save your life.
>
> As Napoleon approached Moscow, the Russians retreated and destroyed everything in their path—leaving the French without food or shelter from the freezing winds. That disaster was the beginning of the end for Napoleon.
>
> A car key and a house key were found at the crime scene, but police did not know whether those keys belonged to the victim or to the murderer.

(4) Possessives

As determiners, **possessives** may be pronouns or proper nouns.

ESLc

PERSONAL PRONOUNS:	*my, your, his, her, its, our, their*
INDEFINITE PRONOUNS:	*one's, anyone's, nobody's, somebody's,* etc.
PROPER NAMES:	*Tan's, George's, Asia's, Panama's,* etc.

> All players must turn in their score cards.
>
> Medical records should not be open to everyone's scrutiny.
>
> Thailand's Buddhist temples are brilliantly colored.

Possessive common nouns do not ordinarily appear first in a noun phrase but instead are preceded by a determiner.

> The university's funding was cut back.

My church's congregation is very young.

The weather controls a farmer's life.

A few possessive common nouns, however, can appear first in a noun phrase. These possessives usually indicate time.

Have you heard today's news?

They always left the mountains at summer's end.

ESLd PRE-DETERMINERS

When a **pre-determiner** appears in the noun phrase, it comes first—regardless of whether the phrase includes a determiner. Usually, pre-determiners indicate a quantity, and most of them are phrases. Some pre-determiners precede count nouns only, some precede non-count nouns only, and some can precede either. The lists below include the most common pre-determiners.

Preceding count nouns only: *both, both of, either of, neither of, few of, a few of, each, each of, several of, many of, not many of,* etc.

Either of the books will be acceptable.

Both the proposals were excellent.

Each table was set for four guests.

Not many of his ideas were usable.

Preceding non-count nouns only: *a great deal of, much of, not much of, a little of,* etc.

The project will take only a little of your time.

Much of the wood was cherry.

A great deal of the jewelry was stolen.

Preceding both count and non-count nouns: *all, all of, any of, some of, a lot of, half of, a quart of, a bowl of, twice, two (three, four) times,* etc.

They expect twice the number [count] of runners as participated last year.

The agency received twice the money [non-count] requested.

Some of his answers [count] were hilarious.

Some of the information [non-count] was misleading.

We ate a quart of strawberries [count].

We drank a quart of milk [non-count].

NOTE: Pre-determiners that include the phrase *part of* can precede either count or non-count nouns, as long as the nouns are singular.

One part of the paper [count] was missing.

Part of the fabric [non-count] was faded.

A part of the problem is morale [non-count].

ESLe PRE-NOUN MODIFIERS

In between the determiner and the head noun, various other positions are possible in a noun phrase. The items in these positions are usually called **pre-noun** (or **pre-nominal**) **modifiers** because they come before the noun and modify or describe it. Occasionally, the order of the positions might vary slightly. But by and large, variation is rare, and the order is fixed.

Of course, you are not likely to find a noun phrase with all positions filled. It would be too long, too cumbersome, and probably too silly. Nevertheless, all the positions described below are grammatically possible as long as they are filled in the order listed.

1. **Specifiers:** *same, other, chief, main, principal, primary,* etc.

   the other subjects

   both of the principal contributors

2. **Ordinal numbers:** *first, second, third,* etc.
   (Note: *Next* may substitute for an item in the middle of the series and *final* or *last* may substitute for the item at the end.)

   our second meeting

   the last game

3. **Cardinal numbers:** *one, two, three,* etc.

   four bracelets

   the first ten applicants

4. **Superlative adjectives:** *best, worst, least, most, tallest, most valuable,* etc.

   the worst ideas

   the five best performances

5. **Adjectives of size:** *big, huge, enormous, little, medium-sized,* etc.

   an enormous mansion

   several of the small boats

6. **Adjectives of shape:** *square, round, circular, rectangular,* etc.

   the rectangular table

   both of the huge circular driveways

7. **Descriptive adjectives:** *friendly, cruel, obnoxious, extraordinary, thoughtful, kind, beautiful, peculiar, reckless, cautious, peaceful, serene, lazy, clever, stupid, happy, outrageous,* etc.

   a peaceful setting

   their three tiny playful dogs

8. **Adjectives of age:** *old, young, middle-aged, ancient,* etc.

   Luis's reckless young brother

   a lot of lazy old cows

9. **Colors:** *red, green, black, yellow, fuchsia,* etc.

   either of the pink sheets

   all four oblong yellow lanterns

10. **Nationalities:** *German, Honduran, Japanese, Australian,* etc.

    a Portuguese family

    twice the German immigrants

11. **Religions:** *Jewish, Protestant, Hindu, Buddhist,* etc.

    this large Protestant community

    the first Jewish school

12. **Materials:** *gold, silver, wooden, brick, slate,* etc.

    an old silver tray

    several large concrete barriers

13. **Nouns as modifiers:** *kitchen, fence, heart, tennis, radio,* etc.

    my kitchen cabinets

    a crooked wooden fence post

ESLf POST-NOUN MODIFIERS

Post-noun modifiers in the noun phrase follow the head noun (ESLb). These modifiers can be single words, prepositional phrases, or adjective clauses.

- Single-word modifiers

  Generally, the single-word modifiers locate the noun in time or space—for example, *upstairs, outside, inside, yesterday, tomorrow,* etc.

  our first meeting tomorrow

  the black limousine outside

  a reading room upstairs

- Prepositional phrases

  Very often, prepositional phrases also locate the noun in time or space.

  a luncheon around noon

  the carnival before Lent

  a wedding in May

  several layers below the surface

  their lodge in the Rocky Mountains

  the land across the river

Of course, prepositional phrases can also express other relationships besides those of time and space. (See 6a.)

a room with a balcony

all students except three

the fall of Rome

a doll for his daughter

- Adjective clauses

Adjective clauses are introduced by a relative pronoun (such as *who, which, that*) or a relative adverb (such as *when, why, where*). The relative introducer follows and renames the head noun being modified. (See 7c.2, 21c, and 33a.4.)

We need evergreen plants that grow in rocky soil.

Spring is the time when study is the hardest.

I recommend Yan He, who was my laboratory assistant last fall.

ESLg THE ACTIVE-VOICE VERB PHRASE

An **active-voice verb** expresses the action of the subject or links the subject to what follows (4e).

A city employee checks the meters. [*Employee* acts.]

Firefighters rushed to the blaze. [*Firefighters* act.]

Juan is an honor student. [*Juan* linked to *student.*]

The room seems stuffy. [*The room* linked to *stuffy.*]

The **active-voice verb phrase** in English includes four possible verb forms. This section and ESLh–j explain those forms and their proper order. Before reading further, however, you may want to look over Chapter 4, Verbs and Verb Phrases. There you will find information about basic forms, auxiliaries, tense forms, progressive forms, voice, and mood.

Mastering the verb phrase is not difficult if you think of the active-voice verb phrase as four possible positions, in the order shown. Position 4 must be filled; the other three are optional.

1 MODAL AUXILIARY	2 *HAVE* AUXILIARY	3 *BE* AUXILIARY	4 MAIN VERB

Six rules, with no exceptions, govern the phrase.

1. The modal auxiliary must be followed by a base form (*call, bring, go,* etc.)
2. The auxiliary *have* must be followed by a past participle (*called, brought, gone,* etc.).
3. The auxiliary *be* must be followed by a present participle (*calling, bringing, going,* etc.).
4. The main verb, which carries the meaning, must be present.
5. If the modal auxiliary is present, the verb phrase does not show tense.
6. If the modal auxiliary is not present, the first verb in the phrase shows tense.

The following examples show verb phrases in the proper order and form.

- main verb with tense

  Helmuth told the truth.

- modal auxiliary + base form of main verb

  Helmuth should tell the truth.

- *have* with tense + past participle of main verb

  Helmuth has told the truth.

- *be* with tense + present participle of main verb

  Helmuth is telling the truth.

- *have* with tense + past participle of *be* + present participle of main verb

  Helmuth had been telling the truth.

- modal auxiliary + base form of *have* + past participle of *be* + present participle of main verb

  Helmuth may have been telling the truth.

Sections ESLi through ESLj discuss in turn the components of the active-voice verb phrase.

ESLh TENSE

English has special verb forms only for the present and past tenses. (See 4c for a complete discussion of verb tense.)

- A **present tense** verb is marked by an *-s* ending when its subject is any singular noun or any singular pronoun except *I* and *you.*

  Abdul writes his family every Monday.

  She wants to photograph the lions.

  It sits in the corner of my grandmother's living room.

  Everyone likes the new student union.

- A **present tense** verb requires the base form when its subject is *I, you,* any plural noun, or any plural pronoun.

  The sisters make all their own clothes.

  I hope you will visit soon.

  You pay at the end of each month.

  We eat at the cafeteria on weekdays.

  Both of them play the piano.

- A regular verb in the **past tense** is marked by *-d* or *-ed* ending regardless of the subject.

  We moved to a new apartment during semester break.

  Antonia helped organize the conference.

  I hiked through Tibet one summer.

- The **past tense** of an irregular verb is not predictable and must be learned. (See *Irregular Verb* in the Glossary of Terms.)

  Thomas forgot to turn off the oven.

  The sun shone so brightly that we could not see.

  The bell in the steeple fell during the hurricane.

ESLi MODAL AUXILIARIES

Modal auxiliaries express concepts such as ability, advisability, and probability. When modals appear in the verb phrase, they come first and do not permit tense. The examples below suggest the uses of modals. Notice that the verb immediately following the modal is always in the base form.

- Ability: *can, could*

  Maria can help you with your algebra.

  The maintenance department could have replaced the carpet.

- Advisability: *should, would, ought to*

  We should leave for the airport an hour before boarding time.

  If I were you, I would stop smoking.

  The school ought to adopt a dress code.

- Necessity: *must*

  The dean must sign your withdrawal slip.

  All data must be analyzed by next week.

- Possibility: *may, might*

  It may snow before nightfall.

  Our professor said that he might drop our lowest grade.

- Prediction: *will*

  The party will be over before we get there.

  You will learn the accounting program in a few days.

- Fact: *will*

  Oil will float on water.

  The recipe will serve eight people.

- Invitation: *shall*

  Shall we go to dinner?

ESLj AUXILIARIES *HAVE* AND *BE*

The **auxiliaries *have*** and ***be*** may appear alone, in combination, or after a modal.

- *have* auxiliary

  Any form of the *have* auxiliary is always followed by a past participle (*seen, hoped, given,* etc.).

  Her family has lived in Tokyo since 1980.

  The crowd had dwindled since late afternoon.

- *be* auxiliary

  In the active voice, any form of the *be* auxiliary is always followed by a present participle (*seeing, hoping, giving,* etc.).

  Susan is taking German this semester.

  The street vendors were selling handmade pottery.

- *have* and *be* auxiliaries in combination

  When *have* and *be* auxiliaries appear together, *have* comes first, followed by *been.*

  Susan has been taking German this semester.

  The street vendors had been selling handmade pottery.

- *have* and *be* auxiliaries after a modal

  After a modal, *have* and *be* appear in the base form.

  Her family may be living in Tokyo.

  The crowd must have dwindled.

ESLk PASSIVE-VOICE VERB PHRASE

The **passive voice** is used to indicate that the subject does not act but instead receives action. (See 4e, 17d, and ESLg.)

Kyle was given a scholarship. [*Kyle* receives action.]

The car was badly damaged. [*Car* receives action.]

There are four possible positions in the **passive-voice verb phrase** in the order shown. Positions 3 and 4 must be filled; the other two are optional.

1	2	3	4
MODAL AUXILIARY	*HAVE* AUXILIARY	*BE* AUXILIARY	MAIN VERB

Six rules, with no exceptions, govern the phrase. Compare these rules with those governing the active-voice verb phrase (ESLg).

1. The modal auxiliary must be followed by the base form *have* or the base form *be.*
2. The auxiliary *have* must be followed by the past participle *been.*
3. The auxiliary *be* must appear and must be followed by a past participle (*seen, planned, made, bought,* etc.).
4. The main verb, which carries the meaning, must be present.
5. If the modal auxiliary is present, the verb phrase does not show tense.
6. If the modal auxiliary is not present, the first verb in the phrase shows tense.

The following examples show verb phrases in the proper order and form.

- *be* with tense + past participle of main verb

  The art work was displayed in the park.

- modal auxiliary + *be* + past participle of main verb

  The art work will be displayed in the park.

- *have* with tense + *been* + past participle of main verb

  The art work had been displayed in the park.

- modal auxiliary + base form of *have* + *been* + past participle of main verb

  The art work should have been displayed in the park.

ESL1 *DO* AUXILIARY

The **do auxiliary** is unique. Its three forms (*do, does, did*) appear only with the base form of the main verb, and they cannot combine with other auxiliaries or with modals. Most commonly, the *do* auxiliary is used to form questions and negative sentences (ESLn–p).

STATEMENT: The committee approved the proposal.

QUESTION: Did the committee approve the proposal?

NEGATIVE: The committee did not approve the proposal.

In addition, *do* can convey emphatic contrast when no other auxiliary or modal is present in the sentence. In conversation, this emphatic contrast often expresses a protest, and the major stress of the sentence is always on the form of *do.*

FIRST SPEAKER: He doesn't play soccer.

SECOND SPEAKER: Yes, he does play.

The emphatic contrast also appears in written sentences. If read aloud, these sentences would place major stress on the *do* auxiliary.

The Aztecs had no alphabet; they did, however, develop rebus writing.

We do not prepare budgets, but we do provide financial consultants.

ESLm

ESLm CHAINS OF VERBS

Some main verbs in English are often followed either by an infinitive (the *to* form of the verb) or by a present participle (the *-ing* form of the verb). Thus are formed **chains of verbs.**

Alicia intended to study medicine.

We regret losing your order of last week.

My counselor encouraged me to stay in school.

She promised to stop pretending.

Verb chains can be divided into categories according to the patterns they produce. The lists below are not complete, but they do indicate the large number of verbs that chain. Note that some verbs appear in more than one category.

- verb + infinitive

agree decide fail forget hesitate hope intend neglect offer plan prefer pretend promise refuse remember try	to go

- verb + actor + infinitive

allow ask convince encourage force hire instruct invite permit persuade remind teach tell want	me to write

- verb + actor + infinitive without *to* (base form)

have let make	him apply

ESLm

Verbs that express perception or observation often follow this pattern.

feel hear notice observe see watch	it fall

- verb + participle

appreciate avoid consider deny enjoy finish keep on postpone practice recall regret remember risk stop suggest	working

ESLm

- verb + actor + participle

feel hear notice observe see watch	it burning

The patterns frequently combine to form longer chains. In such cases, the strings of verbs can include infinitives as well as participles.

The labor union refused even to begin to negotiate.

Should we consider trying to replace old equipment?

A doctor convinced my father to start eating properly.

The judges decided to let her finish skating.

If the chains get too long, however, the sentences become awkward.

AWKWARD: Do you remember promising to remind me to finish practicing?

AWKWARD: I wanted to offer to hire someone to teach her to ski.

ESLn QUESTIONS

Any of the following verb forms can produce a **question** by shifting to the front of the sentence: the main verb *be,* a modal, the *have* auxiliary, or the *be* auxiliary.

She is bilingual. → Is she bilingual?

The sign will blink. → Will the sign blink?

Our pizza has arrived. → Has our pizza arrived?

Kites were invented in China. → Were kites invented in China?

If the verb phrase does not contain a form of *be,* a modal, or *have* auxiliary, you make the question with the *do* auxiliary: *do/does/did* + subject of sentence + base form of main verb. The appropriate form of *do* depends on the subject of the sentence and the tense of the verb.

- For a present tense verb that ends in *-s,* use *does.*

  Mint grows well in sandy soil. → Does mint grow well in sandy soil?

- For a present tense verb that does not end in *-s,* use *do.*

  Wild tigers live in Asia. → Do wild tigers live in Asia?

- For any past tense verb, use *did.*

  Mr. Sato owned the factory. → Did Mr. Sato own the factory?

  Mr. Sato's daughters bought the factory. → Did Mr. Sato's daughters buy the factory?

ESLo NEGATIVE SENTENCES

To make a sentence **negative**, you must alter the positive version of the verb phrase. Basically, there are three possibilities.

1. If verb phrase contains more than one word, insert *not* after the first word or use a negative contraction of the first word.

   My cat will eat lettuce. →

   My cat will not eat lettuce.

   My cat won't eat lettuce.

   The church has been remodeled since its construction. →

   The church has not been remodeled since its construction.

   The church hasn't been remodeled since its construction.

2. If the only verb is a form of *be*, insert *not* after the verb or use a negative contraction of the verb.

   My music professor is a good pianist. →

   My music professor is not a good pianist.

   My music professor isn't a good pianist.

   The beaches are public. →

   The beaches are not public.

   The beaches aren't public.

3. If the only verb is anything except *be*, insert the *do* auxiliary. Use *do/does/did* + *not* + base form of verb, or use a negative contraction of *do/does/did* + base form of verb.

   She makes her pottery on a wheel. →

   She does not make her pottery on a wheel.

   She doesn't make her pottery on a wheel.

   The robins eat the holly berries. →

   The robins do not eat the holly berries.

   The robins don't eat the holly berries.

The movie got good reviews. →

The movie did not get good reviews.

The movie didn't get good reviews.

ESLp TAG QUESTIONS TO IDENTIFY SENTENCES

One way you can identify a complete sentence is to add a **tag question** at the end. This "tagged on" question asks for a *yes/no* answer.

This class is dull, isn't it?

The lawn hasn't been mowed, has it?

You used my racquet, didn't you?

A tag question begins with one of the following:

- a past or present tense form of the main verb *be* or auxiliary *be: am, is, are, was, were*
- a present or past tense form of the auxiliary *have: have, has, had*
- a present or past tense form of the auxiliary *do: do, does, did*
- a modal auxiliary: *can, will, shall, may, must, might, should, could, would*

The tag-question test is easy to apply. Consider, for example, these six word groups.

She is clever.

The car has been repaired.

Non-voters should not complain.

Meeting the deadline will not be possible.

Some oak trees lose their leaves.

You returned the book.

1. Begin the tag question with the main-verb form of *be* or the first auxiliary in the main-verb phrase. If neither exists, supply *do/does* for present time and *did* for past time.

She is clever, is. . . .

The car has been repaired, has. . . .

Non-voters should not complain, should. . . .

Meeting the deadline will not be possible, will. . . .

Some oak trees lose [present time] their leaves, do. . . .

You returned [past time] the book, did. . . .

2. If the sentence is positive, make the tag question negative. If the sentence is negative, make the tag question positive.

She is [positive] clever, isn't [negative]. . . .

The car has [positive] been repaired, hasn't [negative]. . . .

Non-voters should not [negative] complain, should [positive]. . . .

Meeting the deadline will not [negative] be possible, will [positive]. . . .

Some oak trees lose [positive] their leaves, don't [negative]. . . .

You returned [positive] the book, didn't [negative]. . . .

3. Supply a pronoun to match the subject of the sentence.

She is clever, isn't she?

The car has been repaired, hasn't it?

Non-voters should not complain, should they?

Meeting the deadline will not be possible, will it?

Some oak trees lose their leaves, don't they?

You returned the book, didn't you?

ESLp

All six word groups pass the tag-question test; therefore, all are complete sentences. In contrast, sentence fragments (see Chapter 8) cannot pass the test. Some, like the next two examples, do not have a subject and main verb phrase to make the question.

FRAGMENT: Standing on the corner under his leaky umbrella.

IMPOSSIBLE: Standing on the corner under his leaky umbrella, isn't he?

FRAGMENT: The coffee overflowing into the saucer.

IMPOSSIBLE: The coffee overflowing into the saucer, isn't it?

Although dependent clause fragments (8a) do have a subject and verb, they still do not allow tag questions. The introductory subordinate conjunction (7c) prevents the clause from making a statement. Therefore, the tag question cannot ask for confirmation in the form of a *yes/no* answer.

FRAGMENT: When Maria goes out in the rain.

IMPOSSIBLE: When Maria goes out in the rain, doesn't she?

FRAGMENT: Because he thought he didn't deserve it.

IMPOSSIBLE: Because he thought he didn't deserve it, did he?

GLOSSARY OF USAGE

This glossary provides a brief guide for commonly confused words and phrases, such as *illusion, delusion; ensure, insure; differ from, differ with.* In addition, the glossary serves as a guide for usage, that is, the acceptable use of words and phrases. Usage is sometimes determined by clarity and logic but other times merely by the preferences of influential writers and language experts. Thus, usage is subject to controversy and to change. The advice here is based on information found in current dictionaries and usage guides. However, you should bear in mind that some readers—your instructor, for example—may occasionally have other preferences.

A, An

usage

Use *a* before words with an initial consonant sound; use *an* before words with an initial vowel sound. Remember that the sound, not the letter, controls your choice: *a thought, an idea; a heel, an honor; a unicorn, an uncle; a "k," an "s."*

Accept, Except

Accept is a verb that generally means "to receive something or someone willingly" or "to believe": *We accept your terms. Jefferson accepted the ideas of deism. Except* is usually a preposition meaning "with the exclusion of" or a conjunction (often coupled with *that*) meaning "if it were not for the fact that": *The walls of every room except the kitchen were decorated with silk screens. He is fairly well qualified for the position except that he has no experience in public relations.*

Adverse, Averse

Adverse usually describes some position or thing that is hostile or antagonistic: *adverse criticism, adverse reaction, adverse publicity, adverse report. Adverse* can also refer to something unfavorable or harmful: *The pioneers struggled against the adverse conditions of the Rocky Mountain winter. Antibiotics kill infection but can have an adverse effect on the digestive system.*

Averse is part of the idiom *averse to,* which describes someone who dislikes or opposes something: *The Mormons are averse to any kind of artificial stimulant. The editorial board, averse to all Democratic candidates, used the magazine as a Republican forum.*

Advice, Advise

Advice is a noun, with the *c* pronounced as an /s/ sound: *Your advice is welcome. Advise* is a verb, with the *s* pronounced as a /z/ sound: *We advise beginning students to take BASIC.*

Affect, Effect

Affect is usually a verb that means "to influence" or "to bring about a change": *The weather often affects our emotions.* Sometimes *affect* is a verb meaning "to pretend": *Although he was actually from Wisconsin, Gibbs affected a British accent.* The use of *affect* as a noun is confined to psychology, where it refers to a feeling or an emotion as opposed to a thought or action: *He denied feeling guilty, but his affect was revealed in his blushing and stammering.*

Effect is usually a noun that means "a result": *The prolonged cold spell had a devastating effect on the citrus crop.* As a noun, *effect* is also used in idioms like *take effect* and *come into effect: The drug should take effect within two hours. When will the new regulations come into effect?* But *effect* occasionally is used as a verb meaning "to bring about": *Her efforts effected a change.*

Aggravate, Irritate

In formal English, the verb *aggravate* means "to make worse," "to make more troublesome or more serious": *Unusually heavy traffic aggravated the deterioration of the bridge pilings. The star's frequent lateness aggravated the tension among the cast members. Irritate* means "to annoy," "to exasperate," "to provoke": *Khrushchev's behavior at the UN irritated the Western delegates.*

Informally, some people use *aggravate* for *irritate: The dog's constant barking aggravated the neighbors.* This usage, however, is not acceptable to many readers and should be avoided in formal writing.

Agree to, Agree with, Agree on *or* about

Used with *to, agree* means "to give consent": *The board agreed to hear the evidence on Friday.*

Agree with usually indicates accord: *He agreed with the philosophy of the transcendentalists. Agree with* can also refer to health or constitution: *Mexican food doesn't agree with many people. The desert air agrees with me.*

With *on* or *about, agree* indicates a coming to terms: *We agreed on a meeting in May. The judges could not agree about the criteria for evaluating the contestants.*

All, All of

Before noun phrases, especially in written English, *all* is appropriate: *All the circuits were busy. In all the excitement, I forgot where I parked the car.* However, *all of* is also acceptable: *All of the circuits . . . In all of the excitement . . .*

Before pronouns or proper nouns, *all of* is required: *All of us were embarrassed. In all of Europe, the plague raged.*

In the subject position, *all* takes a singular verb when the meaning is "everything": *All is forgiven. All* takes a plural verb when referring to individuals in a group: *All were refunded their money.*

All Ready, Already

All ready is pronounced with a distinct pause between the two words and means "everything or everyone in a state of readiness": *The floral arrangements were all ready for delivery. The swimmers were all ready to begin the competition.*

The single word *already* means "previously," "by this or that time," "before this or that time": *By the time dinner was served, some of the guests had already left. By January, local hotels are already booked for the summer.*

All Right

All right should always be written as two words, not run together as *alright.*

All That

Do not use *all that* in formal writing to imply comparison: *The movie was not all that bad.* Instead, write something like *The movie was better than we had expected.*

All Together, Altogether

The two-word phrase *all together* means "all at one time," "all in one place," "collectively": *They were standing all together against the menace. The students were housed all together in one run-down barrack.*

The adverb *altogether* means "completely," "in all," or "on the whole": *These statistics are not altogether accurate. The meal cost fifty dollars altogether. Altogether, I wish I had never met the man.*

Allusion, Delusion, Illusion

The noun *allusion* comes from the verb *allude,* which means "to make an indirect reference to something or someone." Thus, *allusion* means "an indirect reference" or "a hint": *Although she was never specific, she made a vague allusion to something sinister in his past.*

Deriving from the verb *delude,* which means "to mislead deliberately and harmfully," *delusion* means "a deception": *Her innocence was a delusion she cultivated cunningly.*

The noun *illusion* has no corresponding verb form. It means "a false perception of reality": *The actor's stature was an illusion; he usually stood on a box to kiss his leading lady.*

Almost, Most

In very informal prose, some people use *most* as an adverb to mean "almost." In formal prose, *almost* is required: *We go to San Francisco almost* [not *most*] *every year. Almost* [not *most*] *all the cement has dried.*

A Lot (of), Lots (of)

These expressions are informal substitutes for such words as *much, many, frequently: You're in a lot of trouble. We went to the movies a lot that summer. He uses lots of Tabasco in his chili. I miss you lots.*

Do not write *a lot* as one word (*alot*).

Among, Between

Many guides dictate the use of *between* only with two items or persons and *among* with more than two: *Rivalry between the two teams was intense. Rivalry among the three teams was intense.*

Nevertheless, the *Oxford English Dictionary,* the most scholarly of word collections in English, states, "In all senses *between* has been, from its earliest appearance, extended to more than two. . . . It is still the only word available to express the relation of a thing to many surrounding things severally and individually; *among* expresses a relation to them collectively and vaguely: we should not say 'the space lying *among* three points,' or 'a treaty *among* three powers,' or 'the choice lies *among* the three candidates in the select list,' or 'to insert a needle among the closed petals of a flower.'"

Between is also used with more than two when it refers to intervals occurring regularly: *Between dances, the boys stood around sweating and*

usage

the girls combed their hair. I cannot stop eating between meals. Certainly *among dances* and *among meals* would make very little sense.

Among is more properly used to suggest a relationship of someone or something to a surrounding group: *She lived among the natives for almost ten years. There is honor among thieves.*

Amount, Number

Amount should be used with nouns that name something that cannot be counted (or made plural), such as *noise, information, linen, mud: Judging from the amount of noise inside, we expected the movie to be outrageous.*

Number should be used with nouns that name things that can be counted (or made plural), such as *shrieks, statistics, handkerchiefs, rocks: Judging from the number of shrieks inside, we expected the movie to be outrageous.*

And Etc.

Etc. is an abbreviation for the Latin phrase *et cetera,* which means "and other (things)." Therefore, the expression *and etc.* is redundant. See also **Et Al., Etc.**

And/Or

Writers sometimes use *and/or* to indicate three options: *Merit is rewarded by promotion and/or salary increase* means that merit is rewarded (1) by promotion or (2) by salary increase or (3) by both. Some readers, however, object to the *and/or* device outside of legal, business, or technical writing. To be on the safe side, you can write out the options.

Ante-, Anti-/Ant-

Ante is Latin for "before" or "in front of." It serves as a prefix in English in such forms as *antebellum* ("before the Civil War") and *antechamber* ("a small room in front of, or entry to, a larger room"). *Anti/ant* comes from Greek, meaning "against" or "opposite," and serves as a prefix in such forms as *antibiotic* ("against bacteria") and antacid ("opposing acid"). A hyphen after *anti-* can clarify reading when the root word begins with a capital letter (*anti-Truman*) or an *i* (*anti-intellectualism*).

usage

Anxious, Eager

In conversation, *anxious* and *eager* are often used interchangeably: *I am eager to move into my new apartment. I am anxious to move into my new apartment.* Nevertheless, in formal situations, most usage experts recommend *anxious* to convey apprehension and *eager* to convey impatient desire: *The pilot was anxious about the high winds. The Senator was anxious to avoid scandal. An eager understudy waited in the wings. The fans were eager for victory.*

Any More, Anymore

The two-word adjective *any more* means "some more" or "additional": *Are any more tests necessary to confirm the presence of radiation? The department has not hired any more clerks since 1994.*

The single-word adverb *anymore* means "presently" or "from now on": *The deer aren't seen in the marshes anymore. Will the shop carry imported cheeses anymore?*

Any One, Anyone

The two-word phrase *any one* refers to any person, place, thing, idea, and so on. It is followed by *of* when it precedes a noun or pronoun: *Any one of the desks will serve our purposes. Any one of you is qualified to serve. Any one* may occur without *of* if its referent has been previously stated: *Four options are available. Choose any one.*

The single word *anyone* means "anybody"; it is never followed by *of* and does not precede nouns and pronouns: *Anyone with drive and a high-energy level can succeed.*

Anyplace, Anywhere

Anyplace is usually restricted to informal situations; *anywhere* is acceptable in both formal and informal English.

Any Way, Anyway, Anyways

The two-word phrase *any way* refers to any course or any direction: *They were trapped any way they turned. Anyway* means "nevertheless" or "regardless of circumstances": *The plot is weak, but the film succeeds anyway. Anyways* is a nonstandard variant of *anyway* and should be avoided.

As, Like

In informal situations, speakers often substitute *like* for the subordinate conjunctions *as, as if, as though* to introduce dependent clauses: *Unfortunately, he dances like he sings. It looks like it's going to rain.* But most usage experts agree that in formal situations *like* should not introduce dependent clauses; the *as* conjunctions are more appropriate: *In a democracy, the government acts as the people dictate. The speaker clutched her throat as if she were gasping for air.*

As To

As to occurs frequently in published prose, particularly in journalism: *The weather service kept residents posted as to the position of the hurricane. The mayor and city council members refused to make any comment as to whether the project would require higher taxes. We consulted an efficiency expert as to how to proceed.* In all cases, *about* may be substituted and probably sounds better.

Averse, Adverse (See Adverse, Averse.)

Awful, Awfully

Awful is an adjective meaning "fearsome," "awesome," or "great"; *awfully* is the adverb form of *awful: The dragon's awful roar shook the knight's confidence. The dragon roared awfully, shaking the knight's confidence.*

Informally, some speakers use *awful* and *awfully* as intensifiers equivalent to *very: The children were awful [awfully] tired.* Such use, however, should be avoided in formal writing or speaking.

A While, Awhile

The two-word phrase *a while,* consisting of an article and a noun, functions as the object of a preposition: *After a while in the city, I began to long for the quiet nights of the country. They stopped for a while in a roadside park.* The single word *awhile,* an adverb, does not occur after a preposition: *The fire will smoke only awhile.*

Bad, Badly

Bad is properly an adjective and thus should modify nouns and pronouns: *We always have bad weather this time of year. This headache is a particularly bad one. Badly* is properly an adverb of manner and should modify verbs and verbals: *She performed the piece badly. The editor soon tired of reading badly written poems.*

Confusion between the two words often occurs after a linking verb in a subject complement position, typically after the verb *feel,* in a sentence such as *I feel badly about not calling my parents.* In this sentence, the position after *feel* is a subject complement position and should be filled with an adjective modifying *I,* not an adverb modifying *feel.* Thus, the correct usage is *I feel bad about not writing my parents often enough.*

usage

Sports announcers frequently use *bad* for *badly* in such expressions as *He's playing bad today* and *He just threw the ball bad.* Standard usage is *playing badly* and *threw the ball badly.*

Beside, Besides

The preposition *beside* means "at the side of" (*she was seated beside the guest speaker*) or "compared with" (*my game looked shabby beside his expertise*) or "having nothing to do with" (*in this case, your opinion is beside the point*).

Besides can function as a preposition meaning "other than" (*Jamison had no ambition besides doing a good job*) or as a transitional expression meaning "moreover" (*the restaurant was too expensive; besides, the food was only mediocre*).

Be careful not to substitute *beside* for *besides: Besides* [not *beside*] *being lazy, the new secretary could not type.*

Between, Among (See Among, Between.)

Between You and I, Between You and Me
Because *between* is a preposition, it requires an objective case pronoun. Thus *between you and I* (or *he, she, they*) is incorrect. Use *between you and me* (or *him, her, them*).

Bring, Take
In standard English, both *bring* and *take* mean "to convey." However, *bring* suggests movement toward the speaker or focal point, whereas *take* suggests movement away from the speaker or focal point: *The teacher asked the students to bring a newspaper article to class. The governor took three antique chairs from the mansion when he left office.*

In some dialects, speakers use *bring* to mean "convey away from," as when one speaker says to another in the same location, *I'll bring you to work this morning.* This substitution, however, is not acceptable in formal English.

Bunch
Conversationally, *bunch* is frequently used to mean a group: *A bunch of guys went to the ball game.* In formal English *bunch* should refer only to things growing together in a cluster—like *a bunch of grapes.*

Burst, Bust
The standard verb *burst, burst, burst* usually means "to explode" or "to fly apart suddenly." In formal English, the verb *bust, busted, busted* is inappropriate for these meanings: *The tank burst* [not *busted*] *suddenly.*

But However, But Yet
In informal situations, speakers sometimes combine *but* with contrastive adverbs—possibly for emphasis: *He was practicing medicine, but yet he had never been to medical school.* Such combinations are not acceptable in formal English. Write, *By 1800, the French were satisfied with wounding an opponent, but* [not *but however*] *American dueling practice still demanded death.*

But That, But What
Informally, writers sometimes introduce dependent clauses with *but that* and *but what* (particularly after a negative and the word *doubt*): *No one*

doubted but that [or *what*] *Miss Marple would persevere.* In formal English, the proper connector is *that: No one doubted that Miss Marple would persevere.*

Can, May

Can indicates ability (*we can meet the deadline if we work the whole weekend*) or power (*a dean can overrule a department head*). *May* indicates permission (*you may invite three guests*). Generally, in formal writing, *can* should not replace *may.* In negative contractions, however, most usage experts accept *can't* for permission, since *mayn't* seems stilted and archaic: *You can't* [not *mayn't*] *be excused from the graduation exercises except in dire emergencies.* Also, many experts accept *cannot* for permission in negatives: *May I have this dance? No, you cannot.*

Can't Help But

Can't help but, a rather common idiom, is appropriate only in informal situations: *I can't help but wish I had kept my old Volkswagen bug.* The idiom can be deleted with no change of meaning.

Capital, Capitol

Capital usually means "head," "very serious," "principal": *capital city, capital error.* It also refers to crimes involving the death sentence: *capital offense, capital punishment.* And in finance, *capital* refers to money or property, particularly that used for investment: *capital for the venture, capital gain, capital goods. Capitol* refers to the building in which a legislature meets.

Censor, Censure

The verb *censor* means "to examine material for immoral or harmful content" or "to ban material" for those reasons: *Some state school boards appoint committees to censor textbooks.* The verb *censure* means "to criticize, blame, or rebuke": *Admiral Stanley was censured for unnecessarily endangering the lives of his men.*

Center Around

Most usage experts prefer *revolve around* to *center around: The controversy revolves* [not *centers*] *around misappropriation of funds.* This notion rests on the argument that one thing cannot logically "center around" something else; thus *centers* is more properly followed by *on* or *in: The controversy centers on* [or *in*] *misappropriation of funds.* Nevertheless, language does not follow the logic of mathematics, and *center around* is widely used by many respectable writers.

Climatic, Climactic

Confusion of *climatic* and *climactic* is not a matter of usage but rather a matter of meaning. The adjective *climatic* refers to climate, to weather: *Fluctuations in the earth's orbit probably affect climatic conditions.* The adjective *climactic* refers to climax, to a turning point or high point: *My childhood was so uneventful that the climactic moment occurred when I was chosen a bus-patrol boy.*

Complected, Complexioned

Complected is a regional variation of *complexioned.* In formal situations, use *complexioned: She was so fair complexioned* [not *complected*] *that she used a number forty-four sunscreen.*

Complement, Compliment

Complement derives from *complete;* thus the verb *complement* usually means "something that completes or perfects": *The oriental garden complemented the architecture of the house.* The verb *compliment* means "to praise or congratulate": *She complimented the photographer on his ability to capture mood.*

Comprise, Compose

Strictly, the whole comprises the parts; the parts compose the whole: *The bureau comprises five departments. Five departments compose the bureau.* The passive expression *is comprised of* is often used to mean "is composed of": *The bureau is comprised of five departments.* Even though *Webster's Collegiate* points out that this usage has been in existence since the eighteenth century, some readers still find it objectionable. To be safe, you should probably avoid *is comprised of* altogether and use instead *is composed of* or *is made up of.*

Conscience, Conscious

The noun *conscience* means "moral sensibility," "recognition of right and wrong": *How could you in good conscience use my money to pay your debts?* The adjective *conscious* means "aware" or "deliberate": *She was suddenly conscious of a shadowy figure ahead. I am certainly not guilty of a conscious insult.*

Consensus

Consensus comes from Latin *con* (*"together"*) and *sentire* (*"to think"* or *"to feel"*). Thus, *consensus of opinion* is considered by many to be redundant. In any case, the phrase has become a cliché and should be avoided. *Consensus* is sufficient.

Continual, Continuous

Careful writers distinguish between the two adjectives *continual* and *continuous.* Strictly speaking, *continual* indicates recurring actions, repeated regularly and frequently; *continuous* indicates something unceasing, occurring without interruption: *Continual irrigation of crops is dangerously lowering the water table. The continuous motion of the sea lulled me to sleep.*

Theodore Bernstein offers a mnemonic device for remembering the difference: "*Continuous* ends in *o u s,* which stands for *o*ne *u*ninterrupted *s*equence."

Convince, Persuade

Most people do not distinguish between *convince* and *persuade;* however, careful writers associate *convince* with belief, and *persuade* with action: *He convinced me of his sincerity. The recruiting officer persuaded her to enlist.* One difference between the two words is that *persuade,* but not *convince,* is best followed with an infinitive: *They persuaded me* [not *convinced me*] *to get back on the horse.*

Could have, Could of

Could of is a misrepresentation of the way *could have* sounds in running speech. Write *I could have* [not *could of*] *left.*

Credible, Creditable, Credulous

Credible means "believable," "plausible": *Her account of the day's events was too amusing to be credible. Creditable* usually means "deserving commendation": *Only one of the divers gave a creditable performance. Credulous* means "believing too readily," "gullible": *Lisa was too credulous to be a probation officer.* (See also **Incredible, Incredulous.**)

usage

Data

Data is the plural of the Latin noun *datum,* which means "fact." Rarely do writers use the singular *datum;* instead they use a more familiar word, such as *fact, result, statistic.* But *data* is very commonly used, traditionally with a plural verb: *The data show that most voters in this area vote for the candidate rather than the party. The data are in question; therefore, we cannot accept the conclusions of the study.*

Increasingly, however, in technical writing, *data* is considered a noncountable noun like *information* and is used with a singular verb: *Our data proves that the oyster beds beyond 2 miles should not be harvested. The data is inconclusive.* Outside of technical writing, the safe route is to use a plural verb with *data.*

Device, Devise

Confusion between these two words is usually a matter of spelling. *Device,* the noun, is pronounced /dih viyce/ and means "something constructed for a specific purpose": *We need a device for holding the jack in place. Devise,* the verb, is pronounced /dih viyze/ and means "to construct something for a specific purpose": *She devised a scheme for undermining her partner's credibility.*

Differ From, Differ With

The phrases are closely related, but *differ from* usually means "to be dissimilar," and *differ with* means "to disagree": *The two dialects differ from each other mainly in the pronunciation of vowels. Most experts differed with Jones's hypothesis.*

Different From, Different Than

Although some usage experts insist that *different* be followed by *from,* not by *than,* the rule is oversimplified. Because *from* is a preposition, *different from* should always have a noun or pronoun object—either stated or implied: *Moseley's batting stance is different from Griffin's [batting stance]. Different than* is preferable when a clause (usually an elliptical clause) follows: *James worked on a different assignment than we did.* To use *different from* in this example, you would have to insert an object for *from: James worked on a different assignment from the one we did.*

Discreet, Discrete

Discreet means "cautious," "unobtrusive," "tactful": *The Secret Service made discreet inquiries into Mark's background. Discrete* means "separate," "distinct": *The language institute and the university were two discrete entities.* To help avoid confusion, you can remember that the noun forms of the two adjectives are different: *discreet, discretion; discrete, discreteness.*

Disinterested, Uninterested

Correct usage of *disinterested* and *uninterested* has long been disputed. Apparently, the word *disinterested* originally meant "not interested" but later took on the additional meanings of "free from self-interest" and "altruistic." *Uninterested* originally meant "impartial" but later came to mean "not interested." The best solution to the current problem of usage is to follow conservative guides. Use *disinterested* to mean "impartial," "uninfluenced by thoughts of personal gain" and *uninterested* to mean "not interested": *Some couples have a disinterested party to negotiate prenuptial financial agreements. Acting uninterested in class is likely to irritate the instructor.*

Due To

Due to introduces adjective phrases and either immediately follows a noun or appears as a subject complement: *Many cases of depression due to chemical deficiencies go undetected. Many cases of depression are due to chemical deficiencies.* Because many people object to the substitution of *due to* for *because of* in adverbials, you are probably wise to avoid a construction such as *Due to advanced technology, contemporary ball players cannot realistically be compared to those of the past.* Write instead, *Because of advanced technology. . . .*

Due to the Fact That

Due to the fact that is an unnecessarily wordy bureaucratic phrase; *because* is the better choice.

Each and Every

Each and every is one of the favorite clichés of politicians and hucksters. Use simply *each* or *every* but not both.

Eager, Anxious (See Anxious, Eager.)

Effect (See Affect, Effect.)

Emigrate, Immigrate

Emigrate means "to leave a country"; *immigrate* means "to enter." One *emigrates* from a place, but *immigrates* to it.

Ensure, Insure

Ensure means "to guarantee" or "to make safe": *Organic gardening will ensure that produce is safe to eat. Safety goggles will ensure the worker against eye injury. Insure* means "to provide insurance against loss, damage, injury, etc.": *Our company will insure your home against loss due to flood, fire, and nuclear attacks.*

Enthused

Enthused has not been fully accepted, although it is often substituted for *enthusiastic.* Avoid *enthused* in formal prose: *Everyone on the staff was enthusiastic* [not *enthused*] *about the new personal shopper service.*

Et Al., Etc.

Et al. is the abbreviation for the Latin *et alii* or *et aliae,* meaning "and other people." This abbreviation is used in some documentation systems for citing books with more than two authors: *Yanella, D., et al.*

Etc. is the abbreviation for *et cetera,* meaning "and other things." *Etc.* is common in business memos and some technical documents but not in formal or literary writing. To punctuate *etc.,* put a comma before it when more than one item precedes but not when only one item precedes: *Use only the title and the last name—Ms. Jones, Mr. Jones, Dr. Jones, etc. Dress out completely with pads etc.* (See also **And Etc.**)

Every Day, Everyday

The two-word phrase *every day* means "each day": *Mrs. Sommes went to the gym every day.* The single word *everyday* means "common" or "used on ordinary days." *He came to the dinner party in everyday work clothes.*

Every One, Everyone

The two-word phrase *every one* refers to every person, place, thing, idea, and so on. It is followed by *of* when it precedes a noun or pronoun: *Every one of the candidates has an image problem. Every one of these ancient civilizations had vanished by 500 B.C. Every one* can occur without *of* if its referent has been previously stated: *Four proposals were submitted, and every one called for a budget of over $500,000.*

The single word *everyone* means "everybody"; it is never followed by *of* and does not precede nouns and pronouns: *Everyone in the audience stood and cheered Ms. Gordon for over fifteen minutes.*

Except, Accept (See Accept, Except.)

Except for the Fact That

Shorten this long, bureaucratic phrase to *except that.*

Explicit, Implicit

Explicit means "not implied or suggested but stated outright": *The job description was so explicit that it even prescribed height and weight requirements. Implicit* means just the opposite, "implied or suggested, not stated outright": *Implicit in the advertisement was the notion that waxing floors is a joyful experience.*

Farther, Further

Farther usually refers to distance; *further* usually means "in addition" or "additionally": *The mountains are farther away than they appear. Regular exercise promotes weight loss, and further, increases the energy level.* Also, as a verb, *further* means "to help to progress": *Derrick would use any means available to further his career in Hollywood.*

Fewer, Less

Fewer is used with nouns that can be counted and made plural: *fewer files, fewer paintings, fewer letters. Less* is used with nouns that cannot be counted or made plural: *less software, less art, less mail.*

Further, Farther (See Farther, Further.)

Good, Well

In formal English, *good* is always an adjective, appearing either before a noun or after a linking verb like *be, seem, look, feel, sound, smell, taste: The good food lifted our flagging spirits. The newly mowed grass smelled good. That hat looks good on you.*

Well functions as an adverb when it refers to the manner in which an action is performed: *She spoke German well. He hits the ball well but his concentration is not good. Well* functions as an adjective only when it refers to health. *Don't you feel well? Get well soon.*

Had Better

Had better means "ought to." In running speech, the *had* sometimes disappears but should never be omitted in writing, except in dialogue. Write *The cabinet had better* [not *better*] *be more responsive to foreign affairs and less to partisan politics.*

Had Ought To

Had ought to is nonstandard; instead, use *ought to: We ought to* [not *had ought to*] *send a housewarming gift.*

Half

You may write *a half* or *half a,* but most usage guides do not approve *a half a: The distance of the cabin from the lake was only a half mile* [or *only half a mile;* not *only a half a mile*].

Hanged, Hung

In every sense but one, the correct forms of the verb *hang* are *hang, hung, hung.* However, in the sense of execution, the verb is *hang, hanged, hanged: The picture was hung. The traitor was hanged.*

Hardly

Because *hardly* has a negative meaning ("insufficiency"), it should not be used with another negative—particularly, with *can't* or *couldn't.* Instead of *can't hardly* or *couldn't hardly,* write *can hardly* or *could hardly.* Also, when *hardly* means "barely," a completing clause begins with *when,* not *than: Hardly had the class started when* [not *than*] *the alarm sounded.*

Healthy, Healthful

Healthy describes people, animals, plants, and economies in a state of good health. *Healthful* describes such things as climate and food that contribute to good health. Increasingly, writers use *healthy* for both senses, but a distinction between the terms often adds clarity.

Hisself

Never use *hisself,* a nonstandard variation of *himself.*

Historic, Historical

Historic narrowly means "making history"; *historical* means "relating to history." *Uncle Tom's Cabin* is a "historic" novel, which affected history. *Gone with the Wind* is a "historical" novel, which uses history as the setting.

Hopefully

Hopefully is a generally accepted adverb meaning "full of hope": *We watched hopefully for a change in the weather.* Many people, however, object to its use as a sentence modifier meaning "it is hoped": *Hopefully, the weather will change.* Logically this second use of *hopefully* makes as much sense as *fortunately, happily, regrettably,* or *certainly,* and according to *Webster's Collegiate Dictionary,* has been in well-established use since 1932. But as the *American Heritage Dictionary* wisely points out, "This usage is by now such a bugbear to traditionalists that it is best avoided on grounds of civility, if not logic."

If, Whether

In some sentences, *if* and *whether* are equally acceptable and clear: *I do not know if* [or *whether*] *the plan is feasible.* But in some sentences *if* is ambiguous, expressing either an alternative or a condition: *Tell me if they are late.* An alternative is more clearly expressed with *whether: Tell me whether they are late.* A condition is more clearly expressed when the *if* clause is moved to the front of the sentence: *If they are late, tell me.*

Illusion, Allusion, Delusion (See Allusion, Delusion, Illusion.)

Immigrate, Emigrate (See Emigrate, Immigrate.)

Implicit, Explicit (See Explicit, Implicit.)

Imply, Infer

Imply means "to suggest"; *infer* means "to arrive at a conclusion." Words and actions can imply meaning. From them, readers, listeners, and observers can infer meaning. *The toss of her head implied a defensive attitude. From the toss of her head, he inferred a defensive attitude.*

In, Into
Into rather than *in* more clearly shows movement from outside to inside: *The fumes seeped into the room.*

Incredible, Incredulous
Incredible describes something that is hard to believe: *The circus act was incredible. Incredulous* describes someone who is skeptical: *She was incredulous despite their assurances.*

Infer, Imply (See Imply, Infer.)

In Regards to
To mean "in reference to," write *in regard to, with regard to, regarding,* or *as regards*—never *in regards to.*

Insure, Ensure (See Ensure, Insure.)

Into, In to
Into, written as one word, is a preposition: *into the water, into the room, into the matter.* Sometimes *in* is a part of a phrasal verb and is followed by the word *to.* Then, *in* and *to* are not joined: *She went in to check the temperature. Turn your papers in to me.*

Irregardless, Regardless
Never write *irregardless* to mean *regardless: I am going regardless* [not *irregardless*] *of the weather.*

usage

Irritate, Aggravate (See Aggravate, Irritate.)

Is When, Is Where
When refers to time, and *where* refers to place. The words are misleading in contexts that do not have these meanings. For example, do not write *A hologram is when people use a laser to create a three-dimensional photograph.* Instead write *A hologram is a three-dimensional photograph produced by a laser.* Also, do not write *A quarterback sneak is where the quarterback, with the ball, plunges into the line.* Instead write *A quarterback sneak is a play in which the quarterback, with the ball, plunges into the line.*

It's, Its

The apostrophe in *it's* shows that the word is a contraction meaning "it is" or "it has." *Its,* like the other possessive personal pronouns that end in *s* (*hers, his, yours, ours, theirs*), contains no apostrophe. The form *its'* does not exist.

Kind of, Sort of

The expressions *kind of* and *sort of* to mean "somewhat" or "rather" are informal. Avoid them in formal writing: *The work was somewhat* [not *kind of*] *tedious.*

Kind of (a), Type of (a), Sort of (a)

The *a* should not appear in expressions such as *this kind of a book, this sort of a plan, this type of a day.*

Later, Latter

Later (pronounced /layt r/) refers to time; *latter* (pronounced /lat r/) means "the second of two."

Lay, Lie

The forms of these two verbs are

	To Lay (To Put or Place)	*To Lie (To Rest or Recline)*
Present	lay	lie
Past	laid	lay
Participles	laid, lying	lain, lying

When *lay* (present tense of *lay*) means "put" or "place," it has an object: *Lay the cards on the table.* When *lay* (past tense of *lie*) means 'reclined," it has no object and either has or could have the word *down* after it: *The dog lay [down] in the mud.* Write *The valuable diamond lies* [not *lays*] *in a case unprotected. He lay* [not *laid*] *in bed all day. I was lying* [not *laying*] *on the beach.* When there is no object and when the meaning is "recline," the proper verb is *lie* (*lay, lain, lying*).

usage

Lend, Loan

Some people prefer the verb *lend* (*lent, lent*) and scorn the verb *loan* (*loaned, loaned*) even though *loan* has a long history, especially in America. The verb *loan* is common in financial contexts: *The bank loaned the money.*

Less, Fewer (See Fewer, Less.)

Lie, Lay (See Lay, Lie.)

Like, As (See As, Like.)

Lose, Loose

Lose is pronounced /looz/ and means "misplace" or "get rid of." *Loose* is pronounced /loos/ and means "not tight." *If you lose your receipts, you can't be reimbursed. To hide his weight gain, he wore only loose-fitting clothes.*

May, Can (See Can, May.)

May Be, Maybe

The verb *may be* is two words. The adverb *maybe* (meaning "perhaps") is one word. *We may be late. Maybe we are late.*

Might Have, Might of

Might of is a misinterpretation of the way *might have* sounds in running speech. *I might have* [not *might of*] *picked the winning numbers.*

Moral, Morale

Moral (meaning "ethical" or "ethical lesson") is pronounced with the stress on the first syllable /mor′ al/: *The moral of the fable is "haste makes waste." Morale* (meaning "spirit") is pronounced with the stress on the second syllable /mo ral′/: *The defeat destroyed the team's morale.*

Most, Almost (See Almost, Most.)

Must Have, Must of

usage

Must of is a misinterpretation of the way *must have* sounds in running speech. *They must have* [not *must of*] *left the play during the third act.*

Myself, Me or I

Confusion about whether to use *me* or *I* in compound constructions probably leads to the incorrect use of *myself*: *The staff and myself thank you. Myself* must refer to a previous *I* or *me* in the same sentence: *I saw the incident myself. I wrote myself a note. They told me to answer the letter myself.*

Noplace, Nowhere

Use *nowhere,* not *noplace,* in formal prose.

Number, Amount (See Amount, Number.)

Of

In formal writing

- Do not use *of* after words such as *large* and *good: That is too large* [not *too large of*] *a meal.*
- Do not use *of* after *off: The cat jumped off* [not *off of*] *the ledge.*
- Do not omit *of* after *type: What type of* [not *type*] *car did you buy?*

O.K.

O.K., also spelled *OK* and *okay,* is informal. In formal writing use instead an expression such as *acceptable, satisfactory,* or *correct.*

Oral, Verbal

The distinction between *oral* and *verbal* can be useful, even though the two meanings are very close. Whereas *verbal* refers to either spoken or written words, *oral* refers specifically to spoken words.

Orient, Orientate

As verbs, both *orient* and *orientate* can mean "to get properly adjusted or aligned." In American English, *orient* is more common: *Orient yourself to the map before you start through the unfamiliar area.*

People, Persons

Persons implies a small and specific group: *The elevator will hold only six persons. People* is more versatile and can refer to any group.

Percent, Per Cent, Percentage

When you do not specify an amount, *percentage* is preferred in formal writing: *A large percentage* [not *percent*] *of the text was destroyed.* When you do specify an amount, use *percent* or *per cent: Employees get a 20 percent discount.*

Persuade, Convince (See Convince, Persuade.)

Playwrite, Playwright

Even though a playwright writes plays, he or she is not called a "playwrite." The correct term is *playwright. Wright* (as in *wheelwright* and *shipwright*) means "one who makes or constructs something" and has no relation to *write.*

Plenty

In writing, avoid *plenty* as an intensifier. Instead, use words such as *very* and *quite: Legal action was quite* [not *plenty*] *appropriate.*

Plus

In formal writing, do not use *plus* to mean *and: They couldn't find summer jobs, and* [not *plus*] *they owed the school tuition.*

Practicable, Practical

Practicable means that something is possible; *practical* means that something is sensible: *A new bridge is practicable but not practical because of the cost.*

Precede, Proceed

The root *cede/ceed* means "go." The prefix *pre-* means "before," and the prefix *pro-* means "forward"; therefore, *precede* means "go before," and *proceed* means "go forward."

Principal, Principle

Because *principal* and *principle* sound alike, they are frequently confused. *Principle* is an abstract noun meaning a "truth," "law," "rule," "code": *He advocates the principle of separation of church and state. Principal* can be both a noun and an adjective. As a noun it generally means "chief official," "main participant"; and as an adjective it means "most important," "chief": *The principal of the school insisted on a dress code. The principal role in the drama is that of the son.*

Proceed, Precede (See Precede, Proceed.)

usage

Prosecute, Persecute

Prosecute usually means "to start legal action." *Persecute* means "to treat oppressively." *The Allies prosecuted those who had persecuted the Jews.*

Quote, Quotation

The use of the verb *quote* for the noun *quotation* is informal. In formal prose, use *The speaker began with a quotation* [not *quote*] *from Emerson.*

Raise, Rise

Raise (*raised, raised*) usually means "to lift" and always has an object: *They raised the Confederate ship from the muddy bottom of the Mississippi. Rise* (*rose, risen*) usually means "to go up" and has no object: *The sun rose before we could get good photographs of the eclipse.*

Real, Really

The use of *real* as an adverb to mean "very" is informal. Instead of *real angry,* write *really angry* or *very angry.*

Rear, Raise

One of the meanings of *rear* is "to nurture a child," although many people now use *raise* in this same sense. According to Theodore Bernstein, this meaning of *raise* is established. He comments: "At one time . . . the battle cry was, 'You raise pigs, but you rear children.' However, in this country at least . . . we raise both pigs and children, and some parents will testify that you can't always tell the difference."

Reason Is Because, Reason Is That

Instead of *reason is because,* write *reason is that: The reason for the lack of job openings is that* [not *because*] *people are retiring at the age of seventy, not sixty-five.*

Regardless, Irregardless (See Irregardless, Regardless.)

Respectfully, Respectively

Respectfully means "showing respect": *She respectfully responded to the request. Respectively* means "in a specific order": *The record and the tape cost $8.99 and $9.99, respectively.*

Right

Right as a modifier is vague; it can mean "somewhat" or "to a large degree": *right confusing, right ridiculous, right dumb.* Consequently, it should be avoided in writing.

Same

Same is a substitute for *it* or *them* in legal documents but in no other writings: *After you have written the letter, submit it* [not *same*] for approval.

Scarcely

In a negative construction, *scarcely* is nonstandard. Do not write *Without scarcely a notice, they moved.* Instead write *With scarcely a notice, they moved.* Do not write *I couldn't scarcely breathe.* Instead write *I could scarcely breathe.*

Scarcely When, Scarcely Than

Scarcely when is preferred over *scarcely than: Scarcely had the announcement been written, when* [not *than*] *the reporters arrived.*

Seldom, Seldom Ever

Ever is unnecessary in the phrase *seldom ever.* Do not write *We seldom ever attend movies.* Instead, write *We seldom attend movies. Ever* is acceptable in the phrase *seldom if ever: We seldom if ever attend movies.*

Set, Sit

The verb *sit, sat, sat* does not have an object: *Sit in row H.* The verb *set, set, set,* meaning "to position or place," must have an object: *Set your glass on the coaster.* A few special meanings of *set,* however, require no object: *The sun sets. The hen sets on her nest.*

Shall, Will

In the past, grammars dictated that *shall* be used with the subjects *I* and *we, will* with other subjects. These grammars also prescribed that for emphasis, promise, determination, or command, the pattern be reversed: *will* with *I* and *we, shall* with other subjects.

Attention to actual usage shows that even in formal prose, people have never used *shall* and *will* consistently in this fashion. Instead, *will* appears commonly with *I* and *we* and also with other subjects in emphatic statements: *I will visit China. They repeated that they will strike if their demands are not met. Shall* seldom appears except in a question with *I* or *we* as the subject: *Shall we reject the offer? Where shall I look?* Frequently, the question is an invitation: *Shall we have lunch? Shall we dance?* In other contexts, *shall* seems extremely formal—almost stuffy.

Should, Would

usage

Following the pattern of *shall* and *will,* many early grammars prescribed the use of *should* with the subjects *I* and *we, would* with all other subjects. (See **Shall, Will**.) The prescription, however, is seldom followed. *Should* is used with all subjects to indicate obligation or expectation: *The public should support the bill. He should be here shortly.* With all subjects *would* can indicate promise: *I swore that I would work out two hours every day.* Furthermore, with all subjects *would* can express a hypothetical situation: *If the schedule were more realistic, more people would fly the shuttle.* Finally, either *should* or *would* is acceptable in certain idioms expressing desire or preference: *I would [should] like to direct your attention to paragraph 3. We would [should] prefer to delay discussion until the next meeting. Would* is more common than *should* in American English.

Should Have, Should of

Should of is a misinterpretation of the way *should have* sounds in running speech: *I should have written* [not *should of written*].

Sit, Set (See Set, Sit.)

Situation

Do not unnecessarily add the word *situation* to a sentence: *If you are in an accident* [not *accident situation*], *you may need legal advice. The questions were too vague to be used on tests* [not *in a testing situation*].

Slow, Slowly

Both *slow* and *slowly* have long been used as adverbs but in special ways. *Slow* occurs only after the verb and usually in short commands: *Drive slow. Slow* also occurs frequently with the verb *run: The clock runs slow. The trains were running slow.* If the rhythm and sense are satisfied, *slowly* can occur either before or after the verb: *The cat slowly stalked the robin across the yard* or *The cat stalked the robin slowly across the yard.*

When the adverb follows a verb describing a process, either *slow* or *slowly* is acceptable, particularly with a compound adverb: *The boat drifted slow [slowly] and steady [steadily] toward the reef.*

Only *slowly* can occur as a sentence adverb. In such cases, it usually appears at the beginning of the structure: *Slowly, Earp rose to his feet, laid four aces on the table, and drew his gun.*

So, So That

So that makes the sentence structure clearer and the tone more formal than *so: Keep a record of your blood pressure so that* [not *so*] *your doctor can make an accurate interpretation.*

So, Very

In writing, do not use *so* to mean "very": *The film was very* [not *so*] *maudlin.*

Some

In formal writing, do not use *some* to mean "somewhat": *The way we speak may differ somewhat* [not *some*] *in the locker room and at a cocktail party.*

Someplace, Somewhere

Someplace is more informal than *somewhere.* In formal prose, write *Supposedly, there is a symbol somewhere* [not *someplace*] *in the poem.*

Sometime, Sometimes

Sometime means "at some unspecified time": *I plan to read the complete works of Shakespeare sometime. Sometimes* means "now and then": *Stray radio signals sometimes open garage doors.*

Sort of

Sort of is more informal than *somewhat* or *to some extent.* In formal prose, write *They are somewhat* [not *sort of*] *confused by the instructions.*

Stationary, Stationery

Stationary means "fixed"; *stationery* means "writing paper." Remember that stationERy is made of papER.

Such a

In formal writing, do not use *such a* to mean "very": *It was a very* [not *such a*] *witty play. Such a* should be used only when it is followed with a *that* clause stating a result: *It was such a witty play that I would like to see it again.*

Suppose to, Supposed to

Do not write *suppose to* for *supposed to.* Although the d sound often is not pronounced in running speech, it should always be written: *We were supposed to* [not *suppose to*] *attend the conference.*

Sure

Sure as an adverb is more informal than *surely* or *certainly* and should be written only in friendly correspondence and dialogue. In formal prose, write *The book surely* [not *sure*] *is radical.*

Sure to, Sure and

Use *sure to,* not *sure and,* in a construction like *Be sure to* [not *sure and*] *go.*

Take, Bring (See Bring, Take.)

usage

Than, Then

Than, a conjunction, completes a comparison; *then* indicates time: *We then learned that the matter was more serious than we had thought.*

That, Which

Although the distinction is not always observed, to be unquestionably correct, you should use *that* to introduce restrictive clauses (no commas) and *which* to introduce nonrestrictive clauses (commas): Flashman *is a book that makes a shameless cad entertaining.* Flashman, *which makes a shameless cad entertaining, is worth reading.*

Their, There, They're

Their, which shows possession, appears only before a noun: *their work, their music, their beliefs. There* indicates location (*go there*) or introduces an inverted sentence (*there are three possible answers*). *They're* means *they are* (*they're late*).

Theirselves, Themselves

Never write *theirselves* instead of *themselves: They declared themselves* [not *theirselves*] *bankrupt.*

Them, Those

A phrase such as *them people* or *them pencils* is considered illiterate. Instead, always write *those people* or *those pencils.*

Then, Than (See Than, Then.)

This Here, That There

This here and *that there* are not standard English. Omit the *here* and *there: This* [not *this here*] *attempt was unsuccessful. He did not hear that* [not *that there*] *warning.*

This Kind of, These Kinds of

Use the singular *this* with *kind of* and the plural *these* with *kinds of: this kind of food, these kinds of food.*

Thusly

An *-ly* added to *thus* is unnecessary; *thus* is already an adverb. *We will thus* [not *thusly*] *cancel plans.*

Till, Until

Till and *until* are both correct and interchangeable. The spelling *'til* is incorrect.

To, Too

To can be a preposition (*to them, to school*) or an infinitive marker (*to go, to win*). *Too* is an adverb meaning "excessively" (*too tired, too much*) or "also" (*we too left*).

Toward, Towards

Toward and *towards* have the same meaning; however, the sound of *toward* is usually preferable: *The camera faced toward* [or *towards*] *the crowd.*

Try to, Try and

Write *try to,* not *try and: You should try to* [not *try and*] *understand.*

-type
The suffix *-type* can be used to create adjectives: *A-type personality, European-type clothes, a* Playboy-*type publication.* If you use an adjective with a *-type* suffix, be sure that the suffix creates the right meaning. *A Bogart hero* refers to one of the characters Humphrey Bogart made famous. *A Bogart-type hero* only resembles those characters. In some constructions the addition of *-type* is unnecessary: *compact car* (not *compact-type car*), *spy novel* (not *spy-type novel*), *suspension bridge* (not *suspension-type bridge*).

Type, Type of
Do not omit the *of* after the noun *type: It is the type of* [not *type*] *computer they recommend.*

Uninterested, Disinterested (See Disinterested, Uninterested.)

Unique
Some people object to phrases like *more unique, somewhat unique, almost unique,* or *very unique.* They argue that *unique* is absolute and thus cannot be compared, modified, or intensified. According to *Webster's Collegiate Dictionary, unique* is absolute when meaning "without like or equal"; but when meaning "distinctively characteristic" or "unusual," *unique* can properly appear in phrases such as *a very unique region* and *a somewhat unique school.*

Until, Till (See Till, Until.)

Up
Omit *up* in verb phrases where it adds no meaning, as in *join up, check up, end up, fold up, call up, divide up, lift up.*

usage

Use, Utilize
The verb *use* means "to put to use." *Utilize* means "to find a special purpose for something." Although these verbs are sometimes thought of as synonyms, *utilize* actually has a narrower meaning than *use: They used the detergent for washing clothes. They utilized the detergent as an insecticide.*

Use to, Used to
Do not leave the *d* out of *used to: The family used to* [not *use to*] *believe in flying saucers.*

Verbal, Oral (See Oral, Verbal.)

Wait for, Wait on

Some people say *wait on* to mean "await." But the expression is not standard English; write instead *wait for: He waited for me* [not *on me*] *under the clock at Holmes'.*

Way, Ways

Write *They have a long way* [not *ways*] *to drive.*

Well, Good (See Good, Well.)

Whether, If (See If, Whether.)

Which, That (See That, Which.)

Which, Who

Do not use *which* to introduce a relative clause modifying a person or people: *They reprimanded the doctor who* [not *which*] *prescribed the drug.* Do not use *who* with animals and things: *The plate pictured an eagle, which* [not *who*] *clutched an olive branch.*

Who's, Whose

Do not confuse *who's* and *whose. Who's,* which is somewhat informal, means *who is: Who's going? Whose* is the possessive form of *who: Whose responsibility is the statistical analysis?*

Will, Shall (See Shall, Will.)

Would, Should (See Should, Would.)

Would Have

In *if* clauses, use *had,* not *would have: If they had* [not *would have*] *checked the engine, the accident would not have occurred.*

usage

Would Have, Would of

Would of is a misinterpretation of the way *would have* sounds in running speech: *Except for the Vietnam War, in 1968 Lyndon Johnson would have* [not *would of*] *run for President.*

Your, You're

Your is the possessive form of *you: your idea, your order, your assignment. You're,* which is somewhat informal, is a contraction of *you are: You're indecisive. You're trapped.*

GLOSSARY OF TERMS

This glossary provides a quick reference to terms—some useful and some essential for writers to know. Many definitions provide all the necessary information. Other definitions may require supplementary information from the text.

Absolute Phrase

An absolute phrase—usually a participial or infinitive phrase—modifies the whole sentence to which it is connected: *Speaking of problems, have you seen our new assignment? To be blunt, Jones has no sense of rhythm.* An absolute phrase that begins with a subject is sometimes called a nominative absolute: *The reservation confirmed, we called a cab. The climbers struggled up the mountain, their lungs aching.* (Section 5d)

terms

Abstract Noun

An abstract noun names something with no physical existence: *beauty, fury, dishonesty.*

Acronym

An acronym is a word formed from the initial letters or syllables of the words in a phrase: *awol* (absent without leave), *COBOL* (common business-oriented language), *CINCPAC* (Commander in Chief, Pacific), *Fiat* (Fabrica Italiana Automobili, Torino).

Active Voice
A verb is in the active voice when its subject acts or controls the action: *Harry bet on the winner. The jury convicted him.* (See also **Passive Voice.**) (Section 4e)

Ad Hominem Attack
An argument that involves an attack on an individual's character rather than on ideas and positions is called an ad hominem attack. (Section 39e.2)

Adjective
An adjective is a word that describes, limits, or qualifies a noun or a noun equivalent: *a tart apple, a foolish remark, a successful opening.* (Section 3a)

Adjective Clause
An adjective clause modifies a noun or pronoun. These clauses are introduced by relative pronouns (*who/whom/whose, which, that*) or relative adverbs (*when, where, why*): *The game, which will be televised, is a sellout. I returned to Pocatello, where I had spent my first ten years.* (Section 7c.2)

Adverb
An adverb modifies an adjective (*fairly complex*), adverb (*very carefully*), verb (*moved backward*), or whole sentence (*Certainly, we want to go*). (Section 3b)

Adverb Clause
An adverb clause modifies a verb, adjective, adverb, or whole sentence. Adverb clauses are introduced by subordinate conjunctions (*when, until, because, since, if, unless, although,* etc.): *After they left Vermont, they moved to Quebec. He thought he was a woodsman because he bought clothes at L.L. Bean.* (Section 7c.1)

terms

Adverbial Conjunction (See Conjunctive Adverb.)

Agreement
The term *agreement* refers to the correspondence of both verbs with subjects and pronouns with antecedents. A verb must agree in number with its subject, and a pronoun must agree in number with its antecedent (singular verb with singular subject, singular pronoun with singular antecedent; plural verb with plural subject, plural pronoun with plural antecedent): *The raccoon washes its food.* [*Raccoon, washes,* and *its* are all singular.]

Raccoons wash their food. [*Raccoons, wash,* and *their* are all plural.] (Chapters 10 and 13)

Alliteration
Alliteration is the repetition of the initial sounds of words to create a musical effect: "sunless sea," "the weary, way-worn wanderer," "the hunter home from the hill," "dusty death."

Analogy
An analogy compares two dissimilar things to show that what is true of one is also true of the other. For example, language is analogous to a river; both have branches, and both constantly change. A false analogy distorts the points of similarity and arrives at an invalid conclusion.

Analysis
In an analysis, a subject is broken into parts or segments in order to clarify the whole. (Section 35e.8 and 36a.2)

Antagonist
In a literary work the antagonist is the force that opposes the main character; the antagonist can be another character or characters, society, nature, or even some trait within the main character. (See also **Protagonist.**)

Antecedent
An antecedent is the noun or noun phrase that a pronoun refers to: *In the 1960s Bob Dylan was at the height of his success.* [*Bob Dylan* is the antecedent of *his.*] *Mosquitoes filled the air; they ruined the entire picnic.* [*Mosquitoes* is the antecedent of *they.*]

Antithesis
In rhetoric, an antithesis is an opposing idea—an idea contrary to the thesis. A writer may state the antithesis to an argument in order to attack it.

Appositive
An appositive renames, restates, or explains the word or words it refers to: *She bought an expensive car, a BMW luxury model.* (Section 33a.6)

Argument
Argument is one of the purposes of writing. In an argument, a writer tries to move readers to act or to agree. (Chapter 39)

Article
An article is a word (*a, an, the*) that signals the presence of a noun. (Section ESLc.1–2)

Audience
In rhetoric, the audience is the anticipated reader or readers of a composition. (Section 35b)

Auxiliary Verb
An auxiliary verb combines with a main verb to form a verb phrase: *is burning, did stand, has been grown, could have watched.* (See also **Helping Verb.**) (Sections 4b and ESLi–j, l)

Balanced Sentence
A balanced sentence has a noticeable symmetry of structure and often vocabulary. This kind of sentence heightens comparison or contrast: *What is true about losing weight is not magic, and what is magic about losing weight is not true.* (Section 33b.4)

Begging the Question
Begging the question is a logical fallacy in which a writer argues in a circle. The writer "begs" the audience to accept as true the very point at issue. (Section 39e.5)

Bibliography
A bibliography is a list of sources on a particular subject. A bibliography most often appears at the end of a research paper as a record of the sources referred to in the text. Annotated bibliographies list and also describe writings relating to a subject.

terms

Blank Verse
Blank verse is poetry written in unrhymed iambic pentameter (a line pattern of five units, each composed of an unstressed and a stressed syllable). Milton's *Paradise Lost* is one example of blank verse.

Brainstorming
In rhetoric, brainstorming involves jotting down anything that comes to mind in order to stimulate ideas. Brainstorming should be unstructured and spontaneous so that blocked ideas can come into consciousness. (Section 34c)

Case

Case refers to the special forms of nouns and pronouns that indicate their function.

Some pronouns have three cases:
Subjective (or nominative) case—used for subjects and subject complements: *I, we, he, she, they, who*
Objective case—used for objects: *me, us, him, her, them, whom*
Possessive (or genitive) case—used to show ownership, authorship, source, and description: *my/mine, our/ours, his, her/hers, their/theirs, whose*

Nouns and all other pronouns have two cases:
Common case—used for all functions except possession: *Linda, everyone, friends, actors*
Possessive (or genitive) case—used for the same functions as the possessive pronouns and formed by adding *'s* to singular forms and *'* to most plural forms: *Linda's, everyone's, friends', actors'*. (Chapter 14)

Cause/Effect

Writers can structure a composition or a paragraph by explaining to readers the cause of a particular effect or the effect of a particular cause. (Sections 35e.10 and 36a.2)

Characterization

Characterization refers to the way an author depicts characters. Characters may be "flat," not developed in any depth; or they may be "round," developed with lifelike complexity. Also, characters may be "static" (unchanged by experiences) or "developing" (changed by experiences).

Chronological Order

The actions narrated in a composition are in chronological order when arranged according to the same time sequence in which they occurred, do occur, or should occur. (Section 36a.3)

Classical Topics

The classical topics, formulated by Greek rhetoricians and orators, reflect typical ways of thinking (definition, comparison, relationship, circumstance, and testimony). Writers can use these "topics" to find and develop a subject for a composition. (Section 34h)

Classification

When a composition is structured according to classification, a general category is divided into smaller groups on the basis of some selected principle. (Sections 35e.5 and 36a.2)

Clause

A clause is a grammatical construction with both a subject and predicate. Independent (main) clauses may stand by themselves as sentences: *My car had a flat.* Dependent (subordinate) clauses must be attached to independent clauses: *I was late because my car had a flat.* (Chapter 7)

Cleft Sentence

A cleft sentence is a construction that emphasizes an element that follows a form of *be*. The construction occurs when an ordinary sentence with a subject-verb-object pattern is changed to one with this pattern: *it* plus a form of *be* plus the element to be emphasized plus a *who, which,* or *that* clause. The term *cleft* refers to the fact that the ordinary sentence is cleft, or cut, into parts. The ordinary sentence *The pitcher hit the home run* can be changed to these cleft sentences: *It was the pitcher who hit the home run. It was a home run that the pitcher hit.*

Cliché

A cliché is an expression made stale and boring by overuse: *quick as a wink, last but not least, hour of need.* (Section 32c.1)

Climactic Order

The parts of a composition may be arranged in climactic order, from the less important to the more important or from the small to the large. (Section 36a.3)

Climactic Sentence

The ideas in a climactic sentence move up a scale from less important to more important, from less intense to more intense, or from ordinary to extraordinary: *Once, in the early days before the buffalo herds had dwindled, Grinnel saw a Cheyenne Indian noiselessly ride his horse close to the side of a huge bull, and springing gracefully on his back, ride the beast for some distance, and then, with his knife, give it its death stroke.* (Section 33b.3)

terms

Coherence

Coherence literally means "the quality of sticking together." A composition whose parts fit together logically is said to have coherence. Coherence can be achieved by logical sequences, transitional devices, pronouns, connecting words, and repetitions. (Section 37c)

Collective Noun

A collective noun refers to a group that forms a unit: *family, team, army, audience.* (Sections 10h and 13e)

Comedy

Comedy is usually lighthearted entertainment. In drama, comedies end happily or at least with justice done.

Comma Splice

A comma splice, a punctuation error, occurs when two independent clauses are connected, or spliced together, with only a comma: *Alcohol enhances confidence, at the same time, it impairs judgment.* Two independent clauses must be joined with a comma and a coordinating conjunction or with a semicolon: *Alcohol enhances confidence, but at the same time, it impairs judgment. Alcohol enhances confidence; at the same time, it impairs judgment.* (Chapter 9)

Comparative Conjunction

A comparative conjunction is a subordinate conjunction with two parts: *as . . . as, so . . . that, such . . . that,* a comparative modifier . . . *than,* a superlative modifier . . . *that.* These conjunctions express comparisons: *He laughed so loud that we got embarrassed. The train was more comfortable than we had expected. She was the hardest teacher that I ever had.* (Section 6b.4)

Comparative Degree

The form of an adjective and adverb used to compare two items is called the "comparative degree." An *-er* ending and the words *more* or *less* usually indicate the comparative degree: *May was wetter than June. Cod is more plentiful than flounder. This paper is less expensive.* (See also **Superlative Degree.**) (Section 3c)

Comparison/Contrast

In rhetoric, a comparison/contrast structure examines the similarities and differences between people, ideas, and things. (Sections 35e.4 and 36a.2)

Complement

In a clause, a complement "completes" the meaning of the predicate. A complement may be

- The object of a transitive verb: *They ate pizza.*
- The indirect object of a transitive verb: *He told me a lie.*
- The object complement of a transitive verb: *They called the storm Frederic.*
- The subject complement following *be* or a linking verb: *The book is a challenge. The water felt hot.*

Complex Sentence

A complex sentence contains one independent clause (ind.) and at least one dependent clause (dep.): *The bus filled* [ind.] *until even the aisle was jammed with people* [dep.]. *When the bell rang* [dep.], *the students raced from the room* [ind.]. (Section 7e.3)

Compound-Complex Sentence

A compound-complex sentence contains two or more independent clauses (ind.) and at least one dependent clause (dep.): *In New England earthworms are called nightwalkers* [ind.]; *in the Midwest, where they are best known as bait* [dep.], *they are called fishing worms* [ind.]. (Section 7e.4)

Compound Sentence

A compound sentence contains two or more independent clauses (ind.): *English has a phonetic alphabet* [ind.]; *Chinese has a pictographic system* [ind.]. (Section 7e.2)

Computer Terms

Understanding computer terms can simplify computer-aided writing (CAW).

Backup—a second copy of a file or a disk, usually on a floppy disk. For security, backups should be created for important material.

BBS—an abbreviation for Bulletin Board System, a message database where people can log in and leave messages related to specific topics

BITNET—an acronym for Because It's Time Network, a collection of connected IBM mainframe computers located primarily at universities

Block—a command to mark off a specific section of the material on the screen so that the section can be moved to another place or deleted

Bug—an error, defect, or problem in software or hardware

CD-ROM—an acronym for Compact Disk, Read Only Memory, a data disk similar in appearance to an audio compact disk capable of storing 600 million bytes of data. A computer user cannot save data on a CD-ROM.

Copy—to copy files from one disk to another

Database—a collection of information stored in a computer's memory. A database can be entered, sorted, searched, displayed, changed, and printed.

Download—to transfer a file or other data from a remote system to a local system

e-mail—electronic mail

Fidonet—worldwide network of personal computers for the exchange of e-mail

Filename—a name under which information is stored on a computer disk. On MS-DOS computers, filenames may be eight characters, a period, and three more characters; on Macintosh computers, filenames may be 31 characters.

Floppy disk—a magnetized plastic disk, inserted into a computer's disk drive, that stores the information typed on the keyboard

Fonts—various type styles and sizes available on computers and printers

Format—to structure new floppy disks so that they can store data. The formatting process divides concentric tracts on the disk into sectors for data storage and retrieval.

FTP—abbreviation for File Transfer Protocol, a means of transferring files between systems on the Internet

Hard disk—a device, permanently installed in most computers, that can store or save more information than a removable floppy disk

Headers—short titles printed automatically at the top of each page

Internet—a worldwide network of more than twenty thousand computers at educational, corporate, governmental, and military sites

Justified margin—a straight right margin of a typed document made by automatically adjusting the letters and spaces across a line. Justification can be turned on or off.

Menu—a list that appears on the screen so that a user can choose a program or a command

Merge—to copy material from one file into another or to print combined files

Modem—a device used to transmit computer data over telephone lines

Net—a network of computers operating as a system

Post—to send a message on a public bulletin board system to a mailing list or a newsgroup

RAM—an acronym for *random access memory*, referring to the storage space in a computer. The storage is temporary unless the information is saved on a hard or floppy disk.

Save—to make a permanent copy of material on a floppy or hard disk. If not saved, material will be lost when the computer is turned off.

Scroll—to move the text of a file up or down on a computer screen

Search and Replace—to command a computer to find a particular word, expression, or character on a page or in an entire document and to substitute another expression throughout—for example, to substitute *cannot* for *can't* throughout

Server—a computer that performs a service for other computers, such as file storage or distribution of e-mail

Sort—to command a computer to shift data into an alphabetical or numerical arrangement

Upload—to transfer a file or other data from a local system to a remote system

Windows—computer screen devices that display two or more documents or two or more parts of the same document simultaneously. Users can then easily compare and edit the information.

Word wrap—the way a computer program automatically carries a word to the next line when the word will not fit inside the right margin

Concrete Noun

A concrete noun names a material object that can be seen, touched, heard, tasted, or smelled: *rock, hamburger, wallet.*

Conflict

In literature, a conflict involves a clash of forces. The usual plot pits the main character against an opposing force—another character or characters, society, nature, or some personal trait.

Conjugation

A conjugation is a list of all the forms of a particular verb—its tenses (present, past, future, present perfect, past perfect, and future perfect), its voices (active and passive), its moods (indicative, imperative, and subjunctive), its persons (first, second, and third), and its numbers (singular and plural).

Conjugation of *Choose, Chose, Chosen*

INDICATIVE MOOD

PRESENT TENSE

ACTIVE VOICE: I/You/We/They choose.
He/She/It chooses.

PASSIVE VOICE: I am chosen.
He/She/It is chosen.
You/We/They are chosen.

PAST TENSE	
ACTIVE VOICE:	I/You/He/She/It/We/They chose.
PASSIVE VOICE:	I/He/She/It was chosen. You/We/They are chosen.
FUTURE TENSE	
ACTIVE VOICE:	I/You/He/She/It/We/They will choose.
PASSIVE VOICE:	I/You/He/She/It/We/They will be chosen.
PRESENT PERFECT TENSE	
ACTIVE VOICE:	I/You/We/They have chosen. He/She/It has chosen.
PASSIVE VOICE:	I/You/We/They have been chosen. He/She/It has been chosen.
PAST PERFECT TENSE	
ACTIVE VOICE:	I/You/He/She/It/We/They had chosen.
PASSIVE VOICE:	I/You/He/She/It/We/They had been chosen.
FUTURE PERFECT TENSE	
ACTIVE VOICE:	I/You/He/She/It/We/They will have chosen.
PASSIVE VOICE:	I/You/He/She/It/We/They will have been chosen.

SUBJUNCTIVE MOOD

PRESENT TENSE	
ACTIVE VOICE:	I/You/He/She/It/We/They choose.
PASSIVE VOICE:	I/You/He/She/It/We/They be chosen.
PAST TENSE	
ACTIVE VOICE:	(same as indicative mood)
PASSIVE VOICE:	I/You/He/She/It/We/They were chosen.
PRESENT PERFECT TENSE	
ACTIVE VOICE:	I/You/He/She/It/We/They have chosen.
PASSIVE VOICE:	I/You/He/She/It/We/They have been chosen.

PAST PERFECT TENSE
ACTIVE AND PASSIVE VOICE: (same as indicative mood)

IMPERATIVE MOOD

PRESENT TENSE
ACTIVE VOICE: Choose.
PASSIVE VOICE: Be chosen.

(See also **Progressive Forms.**)

Conjunction

A conjunction is a grammatical connector that links sentence elements—words, phrases, or clauses. (See also **Coordinating Conjunction, Correlative Conjunction,** and **Subordinating Conjunction.**) (Section 6b)

Conjunctive Adverb (Adverbial Conjunction)

A conjunctive adverb serves as a transitional expression to link ideas: *however, therefore, thus, in addition, on the other hand,* and so on. (See also **Transitional Expression.**)

Connotation

Connotation refers to the feelings and memories evoked by a word. (See also **Denotation.**) (Section 32b.1)

Controlling Idea

The controlling idea, or thesis, of a composition is central to the meaning to be conveyed. Everything included should contribute to the development of this idea. (Section 35d)

terms

Coordinating Conjunction

Coordinating conjunctions (*and, but, or, nor, for, so, yet*) connect grammatically equal structures—words, phrases, clauses. (Section 6b.1)

Coordination

Coordination is the process of combining two or more grammatically equal structures—for example, two or more nouns, verbs, predicates, prepositional phrases, dependent clauses, or independent clauses. For techniques that use coordination, see Sections 33a.1–33a.2.

Correlative Conjunction

A correlative conjunction is a coordinating conjunction that consists of a pair of words or phrases: *both . . . and, not . . . but, not only . . . but also, either . . . or, neither . . . nor.* (Section 6b.2)

Count Noun

A count noun names something that can be counted. Thus, count nouns have plural forms. *Desk* and *bracelet* are count nouns with the plural forms *desks* and *bracelets. Furniture* and *jewelry* with no plural forms are not count nouns. (See also **Mass Noun** and **Non-Count Noun.**)

Couplet

A couplet is two lines of poetry ending with the same rhyme as in

For sweetest things turn sourest by their deeds:
Lilies that fester smell far worse than weeds.

Critical Thinking

Critical thinking is a systematic analysis of material for the purpose of judging its accuracy, relevance, and logic. (Chapter 39)

Cumulative Sentence

A cumulative sentence begins with an independent clause and then piles up—or accumulates—structures at the end in order to create a dramatic effect: *Last night I had very discomforting dreams—full of evil creatures, plunges down precipices, and prolonged re-creations of embarrassing moments from my past.* (Section 33b.2)

Dangling Modifier

A modifier with nothing nearby to modify is called "dangling." A dangling modifier is usually a verbal or an elliptical clause that appears at the beginning of a sentence: *Despising the habit, a resolution was made to quit smoking tomorrow.* The word modified should appear close to the modifier and should be the agent of the action expressed by the verb or verbal in the modifier: *Despising the habit, she resolved to quit smoking tomorrow.* (Section 16a)

terms

Deduction

Deduction is a method of logical reasoning whereby a conclusion follows accepted premises. In a classic example, the two premises "All men are mortal" and "Socrates is a man" are joined to produce the conclusion "Therefore, Socrates is mortal." A conclusion that does not follow logically is called a *non sequitur.*

Definition
The definition of a word can be a synonym or a formal explanation that puts the word in a general class and then differentiates it from other members of that class. In rhetoric, definition can be extended to a paragraph or a whole composition. A writer can explore the meaning of a word by a variety of methods: description, classification, comparison, illustration. (Sections 35e.7 and 36a.2)

Demonstrative Pronoun
The demonstrative pronouns are *this* and *that,* along with their corresponding plurals, *these* and *those.* These demonstratives fill a noun position or precede a noun and function as a determiner: *this pen, that tape, these marks, those noises.* (Sections 2b and ESLe.3)

Denotation
The denotation of a word is its literal and explicit meaning independent of any emotional association. (See also **Connotation.**) (Section 32b.1)

Dependent Clause
A dependent clause (also called a *subordinate clause*) has a subject and predicate but must be tied to an independent clause as a modifier or noun element: *When I noticed the menu's eight-dollar hamburger, I quickly left. They insisted that I say for the weekend.* (Section 7c)

Description
In description, a writer uses concrete details to create a representation of what something is or appears to be. (Sections 35e.1 and 36a.2)

Determiner
A determiner is a word like *a, the, our, this,* or *Susan's* that signals the presence of a noun. (Section 6c)

terms

Direct Address
Words in direct address (set off from the rest of the sentence with commas) name whoever or whatever is being spoken to: *This time, Ed, I'll pay. Get in the car, old dog.* (Section 21g)

Direct Object
A direct object is a word, phrase, or clause that receives or is affected by the verb's action: *Jessica likes historical romances. He said that he felt dizzy.*

Direct Quotation

A direct quotation, enclosed in quotation marks, duplicates the exact words of a speaker or writer: *"The first rule for taxi drivers," Mr. Geno said, "is to be sure the passenger is in the car."* The Times *called it "the latest American humbug."* (See also **Indirect Quotation.**) (Section 27a)

Double Negative

No, not, nothing, hardly, scarcely, and barely are considered negatives in English. Use only one of these words to create a negative statement: *I have no cash. They have hardly begun.* A double negative is redundant and incorrect: *I don't have no cash. They haven't hardly begun.*

Elliptical Construction

In an elliptical construction, a word or several words are omitted, but their sense is clearly understood: *The bus takes an hour; a taxi, only thirty minutes.* [*Takes* is omitted in the second clause.] (Section 7d)

Emphatic Pronoun

An emphatic pronoun (also called an *intensive pronoun*) ends with *-self* or *-selves* and emphasizes a noun or another pronoun: *The Constitution itself says so. We were reprimanded by the conductor himself.* (See also **Reflexive Pronoun.**) (Section 2a)

Enumeration

Enumeration is a structural pattern for a paragraph or an entire composition. Details are listed to support the central idea. (Sections 35e.3 and 36a.2)

Equivocation

In logic, *equivocation* refers to the use of an expression to mean more than one thing in a single context.

terms

Essay

An essay is a short nonfiction composition written from a personal point of view.

Etymology

The etymology of a word is its origin and development.

Euphemism

A euphemism, an expression such as *revenue enhancers* for *taxes* or *passed away* for *died,* is used for evading or glorifying reality. (Section 32c.2)

Evidence

Evidence is the material used to support an opinion. Effective kinds of evidence are facts, details, and expert testimony. (Section 39d)

Expletive

An expletive is a meaningless word (*there* or *it*) that fills out a sentence's structure and allows its subject to be delayed: *There is a fly in the room. It is hard to translate the story.* (Section 6d)

Exposition

The purpose of exposition is to explain by supplying information. The main techniques used in exposition are description, narration, enumeration, comparison/contrast, classification, illustration, definition, analysis, and cause/effect. (Section 35e)

Fallacy

A fallacy in logic is any kind of faulty reasoning—primarily making an error in the reasoning process. (Section 39e)

Figures of Speech

Figures of speech communicate through comparisons and associations. Common figures of speech are the metaphor, simile, personification, and hyperbole. (Section 33d)

Finite Verb

A finite verb serves as the main verb of a clause or sentence. Unlike nonfinite verbs (infinitives, participles, and gerunds), finite verbs do not serve as modifiers and nominals.

Fragment

A fragment is an incomplete sentence punctuated as if it were a complete sentence: *When the team lost eighty-two games.* A fragment can be corrected by incorporation into another sentence: *When the team lost eighty-two games, no one was playing well.* A fragment can also be rewritten as a complete sentence: *The team lost eighty-two games.* (Chapter 8)

Freewriting

Freewriting, writing down whatever thoughts occur, is a technique for stimulating ideas and generating material for a composition. (Section 34e)

Function Word

Function words (prepositions, conjunctions, determiners, or expletives) create structure. (Chapter 6)

Fused Sentence

A fused sentence (sometimes called a *run-on sentence*) contains two independent clauses not separated by a conjunction or proper punctuation: *The students take regular classes however, all the subjects are taught in French.* The clauses must be separated: *The students take regular classes; however, all the subjects are taught in French.* For other ways of correcting fused sentences, see Chapter 9.

Gender

In English, *gender* refers to the sex represented by third-person singular pronouns: masculine (*he, him, his*), feminine (*she, her, hers*), and neuter (*it, its*). A few nouns reflect gender: masculine (*actor*) and feminine (*actress*).

General-Particular Order

In general-particular order, an entire composition or a paragraph begins with a general statement and moves to explain or develop that statement with particular details. (Section 36a.3)

General/Specific Words

General words refer broadly to categories: *food, book, person.* Specific words refer more narrowly to a member or members of a category: *burrito, telephone directories, Joe.* (Section 32b.2)

Genitive Case

Genitive case is a term for possessive case or for an *of* phrase showing possession: *the coach's rule, the rule of the coach.* (See also **Possessive Case.**)

Genre

Genre refers to a category of literature such as fiction, poetry, and drama.

Gerund

A gerund is a verb form (the present participle, or *-ing* form) functioning in a sentence as a noun. A gerund phrase is a gerund plus another element—an object, subject, or modifier: *Writing well can be important in getting a good job.* [*Writing* is a gerund subject; *getting* is a gerund object of preposition. *Writing well* and *getting a good job* are both gerund phrases.] (Section 5c)

Gobbledygook

Gobbledygook (also called *bureaucratic language, double-talk, officialese,* and *doublespeak*) is the abstract and confusing language used by officials who think simple, direct prose will not impress readers. (Section 32d.1)

Hasty Generalization

A hasty generalization is a logical fallacy that involves jumping to a conclusion on the basis of too little evidence. (Section 39e.3)

Helping Verb

Helping verb is a name sometimes given to an auxiliary verb. (See also **Auxiliary Verb.**)

Hyperbole

A hyperbole is a figure of speech that uses exaggeration rather than a literal statement to make a point: *We must have walked a thousand miles on this shopping trip.* (Section 33d)

Idiom

An idiom is an expression peculiar to a language or dialect. The meaning of idiomatic speech is not always clear from the meaning of each word: *put up with his foolishness, carry on about the problem, makes off with the loot.*

Illustration

In a paragraph or a composition developed by illustration, an idea is supported with one or more examples. (Sections 35e.6 and 36a.2)

Image

An image is a vivid description that appeals to the senses of sight, sound, smell, taste, or touch.

Imperative Mood

Verbs in the imperative mood are those used to give commands. *You* is always the understood subject: *Look out! Answer the roll. Delete the conjunction.* (Section 4f.2)

Indefinite Pronoun

An indefinite pronoun (*anyone, everybody, each, either, both,* etc.) does not require an antecedent and need not refer to a specific person or thing. (Section 2e)

Independent Clause

An independent clause, sometimes called a *main clause,* is a structure with a subject and predicate. It need not be connected to any other structure: *We drove to Atlantic City.* (Section 7b)

Indicative Mood

Verbs in the indicative mood make statements and questions: *I saw the movie. Was the movie good?* (Section 4f.1)

Indirect Object

An indirect object, usually a noun or pronoun, appears between a transitive verb and a direct object. The indirect object may be converted to a prepositional phrase with *to, for,* or *of* and moved after the direct object: *They gave the school an award. [They gave an award to the school.]*

Indirect Quotation

In an indirect quotation, the exact words of a source are paraphrased. No quotation marks surround an indirect quotation: *Soren explained that he was curious about their everyday life.* (See also **Direct Quotation.**) (Section 27a)

Induction

Induction is a method of logical reasoning whereby a conclusion follows the study of a representative group. For example, if every tap water sample contains chlorine, one can conclude that the source of the water also contains chlorine. (Section 39d.3)

Infinitive

terms

An infinitive is a verbal made of *to* plus a verb: *to live, to listen, to appear.* An infinitive may function as a noun or as a modifier; it may appear alone or as part of an infinitive phrase: *To finish was his dream.* [*To finish* is an infinitive noun subject.] *She had the determination to finish the assignment.* [*To finish the assignment* is an infinitive phrase used as a modifier.] Though *to* is called the "sign" of the infinitive, it may be omitted after a few verbs like *let, make,* and *hear.* (Section 5a)

Inflection

An inflection is a change in the form of a word that signals a change in meaning or in grammatical relation to another word. The parts of speech, or word classes, that have inflection are nouns (*bird, birds, bird's, birds'*), verbs (*go goes, went, gone, going*), pronouns (*it, its*), adjectives (*tall taller, tallest*), and adverbs (*badly, worse, worst*).

Intensifier

An intensifier is a modifier that adds emphasis: *very ill, extremely successful, really hopeful.* (See also **Qualifier.**)

Intensive Pronoun (See Emphatic Pronoun.)

Interjection

An interjection is an expression of emotion or exclamation (such as *oh, well,* or *wow*) structurally unconnected to a sentence: *Well! it's about time. Oh, I forgot the key.* (Sections 21g and 25g)

Interrogative Pronoun

An interrogative pronoun (*who, whom, whose, which,* or *what*) introduces a question that asks for information. *Whose, which,* and *what* can function as a pronoun or as a determiner: *Whose is this? Which job is available?* (Section 2d)

Intransitive Verb

An intransitive verb expresses action but has no object: *The substance vanished. The package arrived quickly.*

Irregular Verb

The past tense and past participial forms of irregular verbs do not follow the predictable pattern of adding *-d* or *-ed.* Following is a list of most of the irregular verbs in English and their principal parts.

Base	*Past*	*Past Participle*
arise	arose	arisen
awake	awoke, awaked	awakened
be	was	been
bear	bore	borne
beat	beat	beaten
become	became	become
befall	befell	befallen
begin	began	begun
behold	beheld	beheld
bend	bent	bent
bet	bet, betted	bet, betted
bid*	bade, bid	bidden, bid
bind	bound	bound

*When the verb refers to offering a price, *bid* is appropriate for both the past and past participle. Otherwise, either *bade* or *bid* is appropriate for the past; either *bidden* or *bid* is appropriate for the past participle.

Base	*Past*	*Past Participle*
bite	bit	bitten, bit
bleed	bled	bled
blow	blew	blown
break	broke	broken
breed	bred	bred
bring	brought	brought
build	built	built
burn	burnt, burned	burnt, burned
burst	burst	burst
buy	bought	bought
cast	cast	cast
catch	caught	caught
choose	chose	chosen
cling	clung	clung
clothe	clothed, clad	clothed, clad
come	came	come
cost	cost	cost
creep	crept	crept
cut	cut	cut
deal	dealt	dealt
dig	dug	dug
dive	dived, dove	dived
do	did	done
draw	drew	drawn
drink	drank	drunk
drive	drove	driven
eat	ate	eaten
fall	fell	fallen
feed	fed	fed
feel	felt	felt
fight	fought	fought
find	found	found
flee	fled	fled
fling	flung	flung
fly	flew	flown
forbid	forbade, forbad	forbidden
forecast	forecast, forecasted	forecast, forecasted
forget	forgot	forgotten
forgive	forgave	forgiven
freeze	froze	frozen
get	got	got, gotten
give	gave	given
go	went	gone
grind	ground	ground
grow	grew	grown

Base	*Past*	*Past Participle*
hang	hung, hanged*	hung, hanged*
have	had	had
hear	heard	heard
hide	hid	hidden
hit	hit	hit
hold	held	held
hurt	hurt	hurt
inlay	inlaid	inlaid
keep	kept	kept
kneel	knelt	knelt
knit	knitted, knit	knitted, knit
know	knew	known
lay	laid	laid
lead	led	led
leap	leaped, leapt	leaped, leapt
learn	learned, learnt	learned, learnt
leave	left	left
lend	lent	lent
let	let	let
lie	lay	lain
light	lit, lighted	lit, lighted
lose	lost	lost
make	made	made
mean	meant	meant
meet	met	met
melt	melted	melted, molten
mistake	mistook	mistaken
mow	mowed	mowed, mown
pay	paid	paid
prove	proved	proved, proven
put	put	put
quit	quit	quit
read	read	read
rid	rid, ridded	rid, ridded
ride	rode	ridden
ring	rang	rung
rise	rose	risen
run	ran	run
saw	sawed	sawed, sawn
say	said	said
see	saw	seen
seek	sought	sought
sell	sold	sold

*When the verb refers to execution, *hanged* is preferred for both past and past participle. Otherwise, *hung* is preferred.

Base	*Past*	*Past Participle*
send	sent	sent
set	set	set
sew	sewed	sewn, sewed
shake	shook	shaken
shave	shaved	shaved, shaven
shear	sheared	sheared, shorn
shed	shed	shed
shine	shone	shone
shoe	shod	shod
shoot	shot	shot
show	showed	shown, showed
shrink	shrank, shrunk	shrunk, shrunken
shut	shut	shut
sing	sang	sung
sink	sank	sunk, sunken
sit	sat	sat
slay	slew	slain
sleep	slept	slept
slide	slid	slid
sling	slung	slung
slink	slunk	slunk
slit	slit	slit
sow	sowed	sown, sowed
speak	spoke	spoken
speed	sped, speeded	sped, speeded
spell	spelled, spelt	spelled, spelt
spend	spent	spent
spill	spilled, spilt	spilled, spilt
spin	spun	spun
spit	spat	spat
split	split	split
spread	spread	spread
spring	sprang	sprung
stand	stood	stood
steal	stole	stolen
stick	stuck	stuck
sting	stung	stung
stink	stank, stunk	stunk
stride	strode	stridden
strike	struck	struck, stricken*
string	strung	strung
strive	strove	striven
swear	swore	sworn
sweep	swept	swept

**Stricken* is normally used to mean "afflicted," as with disease: *"She was stricken with polio."*

Base	*Past*	*Past Participle*
swell	swelled	swollen, swelled
swim	swam	swum
swing	swung	swung
take	took	taken
teach	taught	taught
tear	tore	torn
tell	told	told
think	thought	thought
throw	threw	thrown
thrust	thrust	thrust
understand	understood	understood
upset	upset	upset
wake	woke, waked	woken, waked
wear	wore	worn
weave	wove	woven
weep	wept	wept
win	won	won
wind	wound	wound
withdraw	withdrew	withdrawn
withhold	withheld	withheld
withstand	withstood	withstood
wring	wrung	wrung
write	wrote	written

Jargon

Jargon is the specialized vocabulary of a group such as lawyers, sociologists, and linguists. Jargon should be avoided when it obscures meaning or over-burdens style. (Section 32d.1)

Journalistic Questions

The journalistic questions, which can generate ideas about a subject, are *who? what? when? where? why?* and *how?*

terms

Linking Verb

A linking verb requires a subject complement to complete its meaning. An adjective complement modifies and a noun complement renames the subject of the clause. Common linking verbs are *be, become, seem, look, feel: The discussion was painful. The supplies grew scarce.*

Loose Sentence

A loose sentence begins with the main idea and then adds modifiers: *Computer chess programs allow stronger play because new methods of searching have improved the evaluation of positions and moves.* (See also **Periodic Sentence.**) (Section 33b.1)

Lyric
A lyric is a relatively short musical poem expressing a personal emotion such as sorrow, love, or admiration.

Main Clause (See Independent Clause.)

Mass Noun
A mass noun, also called a *non-count noun,* names something that cannot be counted. Thus, mass nouns have no plural form. In their normal senses, *clothing, money, water, garbage,* and *equipment* are examples of mass nouns. (See also **Count Noun.**)

Metaphor
A metaphor is a figure of speech that conveys information in a nonliteral way by stating or implying that two things are similar: *The book is a passport into exotic, untrodden lands.* (Section 33d)

Metonymy
Metonymy is a figure of speech in which an associated word is substituted for the intended meaning. Instead of *the president,* the writer substitutes *the White House: The White House supports the tax bill.*

Misplaced Modifier
A misplaced modifier seems to relate to the wrong element in a sentence: *The delivery service brought the package to the house in a van.* [seems to modify *house*] Modifiers should be positioned so that they clearly modify the intended word: *In a van, the delivery service brought the package to the house.* [clearly modifies *brought*] (Section 16b)

terms

Mixed Metaphor
Sometimes several metaphors are strung together to form a mixed metaphor, an expression that begins with one overused metaphor and shifts into another or several: *We were out on a limb; but since we knew we were playing with fire and had all our eggs in one basket, we continued the struggle.*

Modal Auxiliary
A verb auxiliary that cannot undergo conjugation is called a modal auxiliary: *can, could, shall, should, will, would, may, might,* and *must.* Modals ex-

press such ideas as ability, advisability, necessity, and possibility. (Section 4B.3 and ESLi)

Modifier

A modifier is a word, phrase, or clause that describes, limits, or qualifies some other word, phrase, or clause. Adjectives and adverbs (and words functioning as such) are modifiers: *The tribe had no written language. Without warning, the horse stumbled. I got a unicycle, which I could never learn to ride.*

Mood

The mood of a verb is shown by form and meaning. The indicative mood expresses a fact or a question: *I attended. Was the problem solved?* The imperative mood expresses a command: *Buy bonds. Get help.* The subjunctive mood expresses desire or possibility: *I wish I were there.* (See also **Indicative Mood, Imperative Mood,** and **Subjunctive Mood.**) (Section 4f)

Narration

Narration tells a story, recounts events, or outlines the stages of a process. (Sections 35e.2 and 36a.2)

Nominalization

A nominalization is an expression of action in noun form: *contribution, development, failure, inclusion.* Unnecessary nominalizations can sometimes be changed to more forceful verb equivalents: *contribute, develop, fail, include.* (Section 33c.1)

Nominative Absolute (See Absolute Phrase.)

Nominative Case (See Case.)

Non-count Noun

A non-count noun, also called a *mass noun,* names something that cannot be counted. Thus, non-count nouns have no plural form. In their normal senses, *water, sand, furniture,* and *wealth* are examples of non-count nouns. (See also **Count Noun.**) (Section ESLb.2)

Nonfinite Verb (See Finite Verb.)

Nonrestrictive Element

A nonrestrictive element does not restrict or limit the word or phrase it modifies. Commas should surround a nonrestrictive element to indicate its loose connection with a sentence: *I heard someone called a "dork," which can't refer to anything complimentary. The research has led to the CD GUIDE, a successful software product.* (Section 21c)

Non Sequitur

A non sequitur is a logical fallacy in which the conclusion does not follow from the evidence: *If one pill is good, then two must be twice as good.* (Section 39e.5)

Noun

A noun names things in the physical and nonphysical worlds: *Jim, sister, novel, field, generosity, grief,* and so on. (Chapter 1 and Section ESLa–b)

Noun Clause

A noun clause is a dependent clause that functions in the same ways that all nouns do—as subjects, objects, and complements: *What you should do is quit. I know that* cheval *means "horse." The winner will be whoever spends the most money.* (Section 7c.3)

Number

Number refers to the form of a noun, pronoun, or verb that shows singularity (one) or plurality (more than one): singular—*car, it, sings;* plural—*cars, they, sing.* (Section 1b)

Object (See Direct Object, Indirect Object, and Object of Preposition.)

Object Complement

An object complement, either an adjective or a noun, completes a clause's structure by modifying or renaming the direct object: *The drought made water scarce. She named her dog Josh.*

terms

Objective Case (See Case.)

Object of Preposition

An object of a preposition, usually a noun, noun phrase, or pronoun, combines with a preposition to form a prepositional phrase: *at school, after washing the car, in front of them.* (Section 6a)

Paradox

A paradox is the linking of seemingly contradictory ideas or feelings to express a truth: *arming for peace, spending money to make money, listening to silence.*

Paragraph
A paragraph in a composition is a unit of thought or information set off by an indentation of the first line. Most paragraphs develop a topic sentence, stated or implied. (Chapter 36)

Parallelism
In grammar, *parallelism* refers to the use of the same grammatical structure for items in a compound structure, a series, a list, or an outline. (Chapter 20)

Paraphrase
A paraphrase is a rewording of a passage without changing its meaning. (Section 40h.2)

Parenthetical Element
A parenthetical element in a sentence is set off with commas, dashes, or parentheses to show its loose, interruptive, or nonessential nature: *A robot, at least to most people, is a manlike creature. The production—how can I put it politely?—lacks interest. In the story, Zeus had a child by Pluto (not to be confused with the god of the underworld).* (Sections 21f.1, 24d, 24e)

Participle
A participle is a verb form used as an adjective. Participles have two basic forms—the present participle (*-ing* verb form) and past participle (the form that follows *have* in a verb phrase). A participial phrase is a participle plus another element—an object, subject, or modifier: *Remembering, Eugene started over. Meat cut very thin is called scallopini.* [*Remembering* and *cut* are both participles modifying the subjects of both sentences. *Cut very thin* is a participial phrase.] (See also **Absolute Phrase.**) (Section 5b and 5d)

terms

Particular-General Order
In particular-general order, an entire composition or a paragraph begins with specifics and moves to a general statement—the topic sentence or thesis. (Section 36a.3)

Part of Speech
Part of speech refers to the grammatical classification of a word based on its form, function, or meaning. Traditionally, a word is classified as a noun verb, adjective, adverb, pronoun, preposition, conjunction, or interjection.

Passive Voice
A verb is in the passive voice when its subject receives the action. The verb consists of a form of *be* plus a past participle: *The purse was stolen. Your account has been credited.* (See also **Active Voice.**) (Sections 4e and ESLk)

Past Participle
The past participle is the form of a verb that normally follows *have.* The past participle of regular verbs adds *-d* or *-ed* to the base form: *called, increased, pitched, assumed.* Irregular verbs do not have predictable past participles. The forms for the past participles of irregular verbs can be found in dictionaries and in appropriate lists. (See also **Irregular Verb.**)

Perfect Tenses
The perfect tenses are formed by combining *has/have/had* or a modal and *have* with the past participle: *has escaped, had rebuilt, will have withdrawn, could have read.* (Sections 4c and 4d)

Periodic Sentence
In a periodic sentence the main idea is postponed until the end: *Just at the height of his power when he could have become an American monarch, Washington went home to farm.* (See also **Loose Sentence.**) (Section 33b.1)

Person
For pronouns, the term *person* refers to the form that indicates whether a reference is to the speaker or spokesperson (first person: *I, we*), to the person(s) spoken to (second person: *you*), or to the person(s) or thing(s) spoken about (third person: *he, she, it, they*). All other pronouns and nouns are in the third person. For verbs, the term refers to the form that goes with each of the three persons.

Persona
Persona, a term that first meant "mask worn by an actor," refers to the voice an author uses to address the audience. The voice should sound natural whether it is or not.

Personal Pronoun
A personal pronoun refers to a specific person or people (*I, you, she, they,* etc.) or to a specific thing or things (*it, them,* etc.). (For a complete list of the personal pronouns, see Section 2a.)

Personification

Personification is a figure of speech in which something nonhuman is given a human characteristic: *The printer ate the paper. The unplugged TV stared blankly.* (Section 33d)

Phrase

A phrase is a group of related words that together have a single function (as a noun, verb, or modifier). Unlike a clause, a phrase has no subject and finite verb: *a heavy eater, has been applied, in a rural town, tending to be jealous, to close the letter, the meal over.*

Plot

Plot refers to the sequence of events that occurs in a work of literature.

Point of View

Point of view refers to the way the narrator relates the action of a work of literature. The point of a view may be omniscient (the narrator knows everything), limited omniscient (the narrator knows the thoughts of one character), first person (the narrator speaks as *I*), or objective (the narrator describes only what is seen and heard).

Positive Degree

Positive degree refers to the simple, uncompared form of adjectives and adverbs: *crazy, evenly, complex, quick, angrily.* (See also **Comparative Degree** and **Superlative Degree.**) (Section 3c)

Possessive Case

The possessive case is the form of a noun or pronoun that indicates ownership (*Sue's job, their vacation*), authorship (*Poe's story, her essay*), source (*paper's headline, teacher's assignment*), measurement (*a mile's distance*), and description (*a child's bike*). (See also **Case.**) (Chapter 14)

Post Hoc Fallacy

In a post hoc fallacy, one reasons that whatever immediately preceded an outcome also caused it. For example, if a landing on the moon preceded bad weather, one cannot assume correctly that the landing caused the problem. (Section 39e.5)

Predicate

The predicate joins with the subject to form a clause. A predicate consists of at least one finite verb and may also include modifiers and completing words: *The dress was cut low in the front and lower in the back. He sent his grandmother a poinsettia for Christmas.*

Predicate Adjective

A predicate adjective, also called a *subject complement*, follows *be, seem, appear, become, grow, remain, taste, look, smell, sound,* or *feel* and modifies the subject: *The topic was boring. He remained angry.*

Predicate Noun

A predicate noun or nominative, also called a *subject complement*, follows *be, become, remain, seem,* and *appear* and names or refers to the subject: *The topic was euthanasia. He remained an enemy.*

Prefix

A prefix is a syllable that attaches to the beginning of a root to add or alter meaning: *pre-* in *preview* means "before"; *de-* in *devalue* means "reduce"; *mal-* in *malfunction* means "badly."

Preposition

A preposition is a function word like *in, to, from, by,* and *through* that connects its object to the rest of the sentence. The preposition plus its object is called a prepositional phrase: *Over the past year, the school in our neighborhood has deteriorated to the point of needing extensive repairs.* (Section 6a)

Present Participle

The present participle is the form of a verb that ends in *-ing: surviving, making, breathing, lying.* (See also **Participle, Gerund,** and **Progressive Forms.**)

terms

Principal Parts

The principal parts of verbs are the base form (*see, step*), the past form (*saw, stepped*), and the past participle form (*seen, stepped*). (Section 4a)

Problem/Solution

In problem/solution, a writer identifies the problem and then presents a solution. (Sections 35e.9 and 36a.2)

Process Analysis

A process analysis is a composition that traces, usually in chronological order, the steps of an event or an operation.

Progressive Forms

The progressive forms of a verb indicate actions in progress. These forms appear in all six tenses and are made with a form of *be* plus the present participle (*-ing* form): *is looking, was looking, will be looking, has been looking, had been looking, will have been looking.* (Section 4d)

Pronoun

Pronouns are words that appear in the same positions as nouns. A pronoun usually substitutes for a previously stated noun or noun phrase, called its *antecedent: The language was easy to learn because it had many words similar to Latin. Pigs were used in the research; they were fed large amounts of sugar.* (See also **Personal Pronoun, Interrogative Pronoun, Relative Pronoun, Demonstrative Pronoun, Indefinite Pronoun, Reciprocal Pronoun, Reflexive Pronoun,** and **Emphatic Pronoun.**) (Chapter 2)

Proper Noun and Adjective

Proper nouns and adjectives are specific names that begin with a capital letter: *Churchill, Xerox, Crimean War, Natchez Trace, Florida vacation, Easter service, October weather.* (Section 31b)

Protagonist

In literary works, the protagonist is the main character. (See also **Antagonist.**)

Purpose

Purpose is the writer's intention—to entertain, to explain, to argue, to move the audience to action. (Section 35a)

Qualifier

A qualifier is an adverb that serves to intensify or restrict an adjective or adverb: *very tired, highly motivated, somewhat bitter, rather large.*

terms

Quatrain

A quatrain is a poetic unit of four lines. Coleridge's *Rime of the Ancient Mariner* is made up of quatrains.

Question/Answer

In question/answer, the writer begins with a question and moves to an answer. (Section 36a.2)

Quotation (See Direct Quotation and Indirect Quotation.)

Reciprocal Pronoun

The reciprocal pronouns, *each other* and *one another,* are only used as objects: *The two always give each other help. The noise was so loud we could not hear one another.* (Section 2e)

Red Herring

A red herring is a logical fallacy in which a writer diverts the reader from the issue by switching to another, vaguely related subject. (Section 39e.2)

Reflexive Pronoun

A reflexive pronoun, ending in *-self* or *-selves,* is always an object that refers to or "reflects" the subject of the clause: *I wrote myself a note. They couldn't imagine themselves as losers.* (See also **Emphatic Pronoun.**) (Section 2a)

Regular Verb

A regular verb adds *-d* or *-ed* to the base to form the past tense and the past participle: *use, used, used; warn, warned, warned.*

Relative Pronoun

A relative pronoun (*who, whom, whose, whoever, which, whichever, what, whatever,* and *that*) introduces a dependent clause: *No one was injured by the tank that exploded. You can't trust whoever looks honest.* (Section 2c)

Restrictive Element

A restrictive element restricts, limits, or identifies the word or phrase it modifies. A restrictive element is not set off by commas: *The coach created an offense that used a variety of sets.* (See also **Nonrestrictive Element.**) (Section 21c)

terms

Rhetoric

Rhetoric is the effective use of language.

Root

The root of a word provides its base, or primary, meaning. For example, the root of *telegraphy* is *graph,* which means "write"; the root of *amorphous* is *morph,* which means "shape."

Run-on Sentence (See Fused Sentence.)

Satire

Through satire, an author ridicules a subject and exposes weaknesses and vices.

Sentence

A sentence is an independent statement, question, or command beginning with a capital letter and ending with some terminal punctuation. Except for exclamations like "Oh!" and idioms like "The more, the merrier," sentences contain a subject and predicate, usually with modifiers and complements: *A man wearing sweaty, seedy clothes pushed his way in. Why did he enter a race that he was sure to lose?*

Sentence Fragment (See Fragment.)

Sentence Modifier

A sentence modifier is an adverbial element that has an independent or parenthetical meaning. Sentence modifiers, sometimes called *absolutes,* relate to whole sentences rather than to particular words or phrases: *Obviously, she would like a job. Without a doubt, I will be there. She is fasting, although I don't know why.*

Setting

The setting of a work of literature is the time and place in which the story occurs.

Shift

A shift is an unnecessary change from one kind of construction to another. Shifts can occur in tense, voice, number, person, and structure. (Chapter 17)

Simile

A simile is a figure of speech in which two dissimilar things are said to be alike. The words *like* or *as* distinguish a simile from a metaphor: *problems sprouting like weeds, the moon round like a Concord grape, a plot as complicated as an acrostic puzzle.* (Section 33d)

Simple Sentence

A simple sentence has one independent clause (main clause) and no dependent clause (subordinate clause): *The smell of the food reminded me of my childhood.* (Section 7e.1)

Slang
Slang is a kind of informal language that develops when people invent new expressions or change the meaning of existing expressions to create an individual and unique way of speaking: *pinkie* for *little finger, whirlybird* for *helicopter, cop out* for *refusal to commit oneself, yak* for *chat.* (Section 32a)

Sonnet
A sonnet is a poem of 14 lines. The Italian, or Petrarchan, sonnet has an octave (8 lines) rhyming *abba abba* and a sestet (6 lines) usually rhyming *cde cde.* The Elizabethan, or Shakespearean, sonnet has three quatrains (4 lines each) rhyming *abab cdcd efef* and a couplet (2 lines) rhyming *gg.*

Spatial Order
In descriptions with a spatial order, details are arranged so that readers can follow the eye's path. (Section 36a.3)

Split Infinitive
A split infinitive has a modifier between the *to* and the base form of the verb: *to slowly stroll, to desperately yell, to at the last second fall.* In most split infinitives, the modifier should be moved: *to stroll slowly, to yell desperately, to fall at the last second.* (Section 18d)

Squinting Modifier
A squinting modifier appears between two words, both of which it might modify: *The woman he called reluctantly made an appointment.* [*Reluctantly* could modify *called* or *made.*] Squinting modifiers must be repositioned: *The woman he called made an appointment reluctantly.* (Section 16b.4)

Straw Man
In an argument, a straw man is an opponent whose position is distorted or invented to make it easier to attack. (Section 39e.2)

Subject
The subject joins with the predicate to form a clause. A subject consists of a noun (or a noun substitute) plus any modifiers. A simple subject is the subject minus its modifiers. *The interior of the car lit up.* [The subject is *the interior of the car;* the simple subject is *interior.*]

Subject Complement
A subject complement follows *be* or another linking verb and renames or modifies the subject of the clause: *He was a scrawny kid.* [*Kid* renames *he*

and can be called a *predicate noun* or *nominative*.] *The conversation became serious.* [*Serious* modifies *conversation* and can be called a *predicate adjective*.] (See also **Linking Verb.**)

Subjective Case (See Case.)

Subjunctive Mood
The subjunctive mood primarily indicates that something is not a fact or that something should happen: *If I were qualified, I would apply for the job. The doctor insisted that Jack get a second opinion.* Unlike the indicative mood (*I was qualified* and *he gets*), the subjunctive mood has only one form for each tense and person. (Section 4f.3)

Subordinate Clause (See Dependent Clause.)

Subordinating Conjunction
A subordinating conjunction introduces a dependent clause and expresses relationships such as cause, contrast, condition, manner, place, and time. Common subordinating conjunctions are *because, although, if, as if,* and *when.* (Section 6b.3) For a more complete list, see 7c.1. (See also **Adverb Clause.**)

Subordination
Through subordination, writers show that one idea is dependent on another. Subordination can be achieved through dependent clauses, verbals, and appositives. For techniques that use subordination, see 33a.3–33a.6. (See also **Adverb Clause, Adjective Clause, Noun Clause, Infinitive, Participle, Gerund,** and **Appositive.**)

Suffix
A suffix is a syllable or sound that attaches to the end of a word to alter the word's meaning, to change the word from one class to another, or to change the word's form. The suffix *-itis* ("inflamed") added to the root *appendix* creates the word *appendicitis.* The suffix *-ly* changes the adjective *sad* to the adverb *sadly.* The suffix *-ed* changes the present tense verb *call* to the past tense *called.*

Superlative Degree
The form of an adjective and adverb used to make a comparison among three or more items is called the *superlative degree.* An *-est* ending and the words *most* and *least* indicate the superlative degree: *This is the largest hotel in the city. The video you selected is the one most frequently pur-*

chased. This brand of yogurt is the least fattening of all. (See also **Comparative Degree.**) (Section 3c)

Symbol

A symbol is an image that stands for an idea or a complex of ideas. A vulture might symbolize death; spring might symbolize a new beginning; a closed door might symbolize lost opportunity.

Synonym

A synonym is a word with approximately the same meaning as another—for example, *accord* is a synonym for *agreement; stagnation* for *inaction; derision* for *ridicule.*

Syntax

Syntax refers to the arrangement of words to form structures—phrases, clauses, and sentences.

Tag Question

A tag question appears at the end of a statement and asks for verification. It is composed of an auxiliary verb and a pronoun: *The car has been repaired, hasn't it? You read the book, didn't you?* (Section 21g and ESLp)

Tense

Tense is the feature of verbs that indicates a meaning related to time. English is said to have three simple tenses (present, past, and future) and three perfect tenses (present perfect, past perfect, and future perfect). (Sections 4c and ESLh)

Theme

A theme is the central idea of a work, primarily a work of literature.

Thesis

The thesis is the central, or controlling, idea of a nonliterary composition. The content of the composition should support and develop the thesis. (Section 35d)

Topic Sentence

The topic sentence of a paragraph is the main idea developed. If a paragraph has no stated topic sentence, one should be clearly implied. (Section 36a.1)

Tragedy

A tragedy does not end happily. In the plot of a dramatic tragedy, the main character suffers a "fall," the loss of something dear, as the result of events and human weakness.

Tragic Flaw

In drama, a tragic flaw is the human weakness that combines with circumstances to ruin the main character.

Transitional Expression

A transitional expression indicates the relationship between ideas: for example, *however* indicates contrast; *as a result* indicates cause/effect; *furthermore* indicates addition. Sometimes called *conjunctive adverbs* or *conjuncts*, transitional words and phrases serve to link independent clause to independent clause, sentence to sentence, and paragraph to paragraph. The following list includes the most common transitional expressions. (Section 37c.3)

Relationship	*Appropriate Expressions*
Contrast	however, on the other hand, on the contrary, in contrast, still, nevertheless, regardless, instead
Cause/effect	therefore, thus, consequently, for this reason, as a result, otherwise, thus, then, accordingly
Time sequence	first, second, third, next, last, finally, afterward, now, then, again, soon, formerly, eventually, subsequently
Restatement	in other words, in short, in summary, that is, again
Emphasis	in fact, indeed, of course, certainly, after all, surely, actually
Addition	furthermore, moreover, likewise, also, in addition, besides
Summary	in conclusion, on the whole, all in all, in summary
Example	for example, for instance, specifically

terms

Transitive Verb

A transitive verb expresses action and requires an object: *She wrote the letter. Mr. Williams speaks Japanese fluently.*

Verb

A verb is a word that indicates action (*swim*), occurrence (*happen*), or existence (*be*). (Chapter 4)

Verbal

A verbal is one of three verb forms functioning in a sentence as a noun or a modifier: infinitive (*to write*), present participle (*writing*), past participle (*written*). A verbal alone never functions in a clause as a finite verb. A verbal with a subject, object, complement, or modifier is called a *verbal phrase*. (See also **Infinitive, Participle,** and **Gerund.**) (Chapter 5)

Verb Phrase

A verb phrase is a verb made up of more than one word: *is calling, will consider, have been reading.*

Voice

The voice of a verb indicates whether the subject acts (active voice) or receives the action (passive voice). (See also **Active Voice** and **Passive Voice.**) (Section 4e)

Index

Boldface indicates sections.

A, an, as indefinite article, 500–502, **ESLc;** G-522
Abbreviations
of academic degrees and certifications, 194, **30a**
of acronyms, 195, **30a**
in addresses, 195–196, **30a**
capitalization in, 196–197, **30b;** 207, **31f**
of dates, 194–195, **30a**
and full words, 193–196, **30a**
of geographical locations, 195, **30a**
of initials, 195, **30a**
of Latin expressions, 195, **30a**
punctuation with, 162, **25c;** 196–197, **30b**
of reference notations, 195, **30a**
of state names, 195–196, **30a;** 197, **30b**
of time designations, 194–195, **30a**
titles and ranks of people, 193–194, **30a**
-able, -ible, spelling and, 496–497, **SPc**
Absolute phrase, GT-550
defined, 30, **5d**
verbal, 30–31, **5d**
Absolutes, 93, **15b**
Abstract noun, GT-550
Abstracts
APA documentation for online, 476, **41d**
APA documentation style for, 475, **41d**
computer searches of, 415–417, **40c**
MLA documentation for, 441, **41a;** 442, **41a**
printed, 413–414, **40c**
specialized, 414–415, **40c**
Abstract words, 377, **39e**
Academic degrees and certifications
abbreviating, 194, **30a**
capitalization of, 205–206, **31d**
Accept, except, G-522
Accuracy, of evidence, 372–373, **39e**
Acronym, GT-550
abbreviating, 195, **30a;** 196, **30b**
Active sentence, weak passives vs., 247–249, **33c;** GT-551
Active voice, verb phrase in, 508–509, **ESLg**
Addresses, commas in, 140–141, **21h**
Ad hominem attack, 374–375, **39e;** GT-551
Adjective, 12–13, **3a;** GT-551
as absolutes, 93, **15b**
of age, 506, **ESLe**
commas used in series of, 143, **21j**
confusion with adverbs, 91–92, **15a**
coordinate, 136–137, **21d**
defined, 12, **3**
degrees of, 15–16, **3c**
descriptive, 506, **ESLe**
inappropriate comparative and superlative forms, 92–94, **15b**
inappropriate demonstratives, 94, **15c**
nonstandard forms of, 91–94, **15**
predicate, GT-580
proper, 202–204, **31b;** GT-581
of shape, 506, **ESLe**
of size, 506, **ESLe**
as subject complement, 43, **7a**
superlative, 506, **ESLe**
verbals as, 29, **5a**
Adjective clause, 47–48, **7c;** 239, **33a;** GT-551. *See also* Relative pronoun
as post-noun modifier, 508, **ESLf**
Adverb, 13–15, **3b;** GT-551
confusion with adjectives, 91–92, **15a**
conjunctive, 14, **3b;** GT-561
defined, 12, **3**
degrees of, 15–16, **3c**
inappropriate demonstratives, 94, **15c**

as interrogatives, 15, **3c**
nonstandard forms of, 91–94, **15**
position of, 13–14, **3b**
prepositions as, 14, **3b**
qualifier, GT-581
verbals as, 29, **5a**
Adverb clause, 46–47, **7c;** 238, **33a;** GT-551
commas and, 131–134, **21b**
Adverbial conjunction. *See* Conjunctive adverb
Adverse, averse, G-523
Advice, advise, 73, **11c;** G-523
Affect, effect, 73, **11c;** G-523
Age, adjectives of, 506, **ESLe**
Aggravate, irritate, 73, **11c;** G-523
Agreement, GT-551–552
pronoun-antecedent, 80–84, **13**
subject-verb, 62–70, **10**
Agree to, agree with, agree on or **about,** G-524
Albums, italics for titles, 182, **28a**
All, all of, G-524
Alliteration, GT-552
All ready, already, G-524
All right, G-524
All that, G-524
All together, altogether, G-524–525
Allusion, delusion, illusion, G-525
Almanacs, 408, **40c**
Almost, most, G-525
A lot (of), lots (of), G-525
Ambiguity, 377, **39e**
Ambiguous pronoun reference, 77, **12d**
American Psychological Association. *See* APA (American Psychological Association) style
Among, between, G-525–526
Amount, number, G-526
Amounts, as subjects, 68–69, **10h**
Analogy, 371, **39d;** GT-552
false, 379, **39e**
Analysis, GT-552. *See also* Critical thinking
function of, 289–290, **35e**
paragraphs of, 302–303, **36a**
And
antecedents joined by, 81, **13a**
subjects joined by, 64, **10b**
And, or, G-526
And etc., G-526
Anecdotes, in introductory paragraphs, 313–314, **36b**
Animals, capitalization of names, 203, **31b**
Antagonist, GT-552. *See also* Protagonist
Ante-, anti/ant-, G-526
Antecedent, 5, **2;** GT-552
collective nouns as, 83–84, **13e**
joined by *and,* 81, **13a**
joined by *or/nor,* 81–82, **13b**
of pronoun, 74–75, **12a**
pronoun agreement with, 80–84, **13**
titles and headings as, 78–79, **12g**
Antithesis, GT-552
in introductory paragraphs, 312–313, **36b**
Anxious, eager, G-526
Any more, anymore, G-527
Any one, anyone, G-527
Anyplace, anywhere, G-527
APA (American Psychological Association) style, 469–477, **41d**
documentation at end of paper, 470–477, **41d**
documentation inside paper, 469–470, **41d**
sample paper in, 478–486, **41e**
typing with, 477, **41e**
Apostrophe
contractions and, 168, **26b**
inappropriate, 169–170, **26d**
for plurals of letters and words used as words, 168–169, **26c**
for possession, 5, **1c;** 166–168, **26a**
Applications, showing in composition, 320, **36c**
Appositive, GT-552
pronoun case in compound, 87, **14a**
set off by dashes, 155–156, **24a**
subordinating with, 240–242, **33a**
Areas of study, and inappropriate capitalization, 207–208, **31h**
Argument, 361–362, **39;** GT-552
antithesis and, 312–313, **36b**
APA style for paper on, 478–486, **41e**
classical structure of, 381–384, **39f**

computer and, 393, **39g**
conflict in, 364–367, **39b**
discovery structure of, 384–385, **39f**
evidence to support, 368–381, **39d**
informed opinions in, 369–370, **39d**
logical reasoning in, 370–371, **39d**
pros and cons in, 365–366, **39b;** 383, **39f**
as purpose for research paper, 398–399, **40b**
as purpose for writing, 273–274, **35a**
Rogerian structure of, 386–387, **39f**
sample of, 387–392, **39g**
structure of, 381–387, **39f**
subject of, 363–364, **39a**
thesis of, 367–368, **39b;** 381, **39f**
Article (part of speech), 37, **6c;** GT-553
definite, 501–502, **ESLc**
indefinite, 500–501, **ESLc;** 501–502, **ESLc**
Articles (in publications), 37, **6c**
APA documentation style for, 474–475, **41d**
MLA documentation style for, 435, **41a;** 441, **41a;** 443–444, **41a**
Artistic works, capitalization of titles, 206–207, **31e**
As, like, G-527
As to, G-527
Atlases, 408, **40c**
Attention line, colons after, 153, **23f**
Audience, GT-553
analysis of, 274–276, **35b**
for essay examinations, 276, **35b**
teacher as, 275–276, **35b**
Audience surprise, and introductory paragraphs, 311–312, **36b**
Author
in APA citations, 469–470, **41d**
in MLA citations, 440, **41a**
Author entry, in library catalog, 409, **40c**
Auxiliary verb, 18–20, **4b;** GT-533
be as, 19, **4b;** 509, **ESLg;** 512, **ESLj**
do as, 20, **4b;** 513–514, **ESLl**
have, 19, **4b;** 509, **ESLg;** 512, **ESLj**
modal, 19–20, **4b;** 102, **17a;** 511, **ESLi;** GT-574–575
Award names, capitalization of, 203, **31b**
Awful, awfully, G-528
A while, awhile, G-528

Background, in introductory paragraphs, 310–311, **36b**
Backup (computers), GT-557
Bad, badly, G-528
Balanced sentence, 245–246, **33b;** GT-553
Ballets, italics for titles, 182, **28a**
Base form, 71, **11a.** *See also* Root
prefix separation from, 190, **29d**
of present tense verb, 510, **ESLh**
BBS (computers), GT-557
Be
and active-voice verb phrase, 509, **ESLg**
as auxiliary, 19, **4b**
forms of, 18, **4a**
imperative of, 25, **4f**
as linking verb, 43, **7a**
as modal auxiliary, 512, **ESLj**
and passive-voice verb phrase, 513, **ESLk**
pronoun case of, 87–88, **14b**
subject-verb agreement and, 63, **10**
subjunctive verbs and, 25–26, **4f**
ungrammatical shifts and, 110–111, **17h**
voice and, 24, **4e**
Become, subject complement and, 44, **7a**
Begging the question, GT-553
reasoning and, 379–380, **39e**
Beside, besides, G-528–529
Between, among, G-525–526
Between you and I, between you and me, G-529
Bias, discriminatory language and, 226–229, **32e**
Bibliographies, 403, **40c;** 409–410, **40c;** 411, **40c;** GT-553. *See also* Documentation; References section
APA style of, 469–477, **41d;** 477–486, **41e**
cards for, 417–418, **40d**

MLA style of, 434–468, **41a, 41b, 41c**
working, 417–418, **40d**
Bibliography card. *See* Bibliographies; Index cards; Note cards
Biographies, 407, **40c**
Biological terms, capitalization of, 203, **31b**
BITNET (computers), GT-557
Blank verse, GT-553
Block (computers), GT-557
Body paragraphs, 297–308, **36a**
Book review, MLA documentation for, 441, **41a**
Books
APA documentation style for, 473, **41d**
italics for titles, 181, **28a**
MLA documentation for, 437, **41a;** 439, **41a;** 440, **41a**
Brackets
defined, 155, **24**
around insertions in direct quotations, 158–159, **24g**
for parentheses inside parentheses, 159, **24h**
Brainstorming, 262–263, **34b;** GT-553. *See also* Critical thinking; Induction
Brevity, revision and, 327–328, **37b**
Bring, take, 73, **11c;** G-529
Broad pronoun reference, 75–76, **12b**
Bug (computers), GT-557
Bunch, G-529
Bureaucratic language, 221, **32d**
Burst, bust, 73, **11c;** G-529
But however, but yet, G-529
But that, but what, G-529–530

Calendar terms, capitalization of, 203, **31b**
Can, could, 103–104, **17a**
Can, may, G-530
Can't help but, G-530
Capital, capitol, G-530
Capitalization
and abbreviations, 196–197, **30b;** 207, **31f**
of academic and professional degrees, 205–206, **31d**
of complimentary close, 201, **31a**
of elliptical questions, 202, **31a**
of first words, 200–202, **31a**
of formal statement after colon, 202, **31a**
of *I* and *O,* 207, **31g**
inappropriate use of, 207–209, **31h**
of interrupter, 158, **24e**
of items in list, 202, **31a**
optional, 202, **31a**
in outlines, 201, **31a**
in poetry, 201, **31a**
of proper adjectives, 202–204, **31b**
of proper nouns, 202–204, **31b**
of quotations, 201, **30a**
of rank, 204–205, **31c**
of salutation, 201, **31a**
in sentences, 200–201, **30a**
of titles of honor, 204–205, **31c**
in titles of written material and artistic works, 206–207, **31e**
Card catalogs, 409, **40c;** 410, **40c.** *See also* Dewey Decimal system; Library of Congress system
Cardinal numbers, 38, **6c,** 506, **ESLe**
Cards. *See* Index cards; Note cards
Cartoons, MLA documentation for, 443, **41a**
Case, GT-554
after *be,* 87–88, **14b**
in compound constructions, 86–87, **14a**
in elliptical clauses, 89, **14d**
genitive, GT-566
of nouns and pronouns, 85–90, **14**
personal pronouns and, 8, **2a**
possessive, GT-579
possessive, with gerunds, 89–90, **14d**
with *who/whom* and *whoever/whomever,* 88–89, **14c**
Catalogs (library), 408–412, **40c**
author entry, 409, **40c**
bibliography notation and, 409–410, **40c**
card, 409, **40c;** 410, **40c**
keywords, 409, **40c**
locating material in, 418–419, **40e**
subject entry, 409, **40c**
title entry, 409, **40c**

Catalogs (mail-order), italics and, 183, **28a**
Cause, oversimplification in reasoning, 378, **39e**
Cause/effect, GT-554
and clauses, 233, **33a**
function of, 290–291, **35e**
paragraphs of, 304, **36a**
CD-ROM, GT-557
APA documentation for sources, 476, **41d**
MLA documentation for sources, 443, **41a**
-cede, -ceed, and *-sede,* 495, **SPb**
Censor, censure, 73, **11c;** G-530
Center around, G-530
Certifications, abbreviating, 194, **30a**
Chains of verbs, 514–517, **ESLm**
Chapters
MLA documentation for, 439, **41a**
parentheses for references to, 158, **24f**
Characterization, GT-554
as research paper purpose, 401, **40b**
Chemical abbreviations, 196, **30b**
capitalization of, 204, **31b**
Choppy prose, 230–231, **33a**
Chronological order, GT-554
of details, 306, **36a**
Circular reasoning, 379–380, **39e**
Circumstances, and topics for writing, 269, **34h**
Citations. *See* Bibliographies; Documentation; Sources
Civil titles, abbreviating, 194, **30a**
Clarification, with commas, 142, **21i**
Classical structure of argument, 381–387, **39f**
conclusion, 382, **39f**
introduction, 382, **39f**
proof, 382, **39f**
refutation, 382, **39f;** 383, **39f**
statement of fact, 382, **39f**
Classical topics, 269–270, **34h;** GT-554
circumstances, 269, **34h**
comparisons, 269, **34h**
definitions, 269, **34h**
relationships, 269, **34h**
testimonies, 269, **34h**
Classification, GT-555
function of, 288, **35e**
paragraphs of, 301, **36a**
Clause, GT-555. *See also* Adjective clause; Adverb clause; Dependent (subordinate) clause; Elliptical clause; Independent (main) clause; Nonrestrictive element; Noun clause
adjective, 47–48, **7c;** 239, **33a;** 508, **ESLf;** GT-551
adverb, 46–47, **7c;** 131–134, **21b;** 238, **33a;** GT-551
case in elliptical, 89, **14d**
cause/effect relationship and, 233, **33a**
contrasting, 233–234, **33a**
dangling elliptical, 98, **16a**
defined, 40, **7**
dependent, 45–49, **7c;** 55–56, **8a;** 60–61, **9e;** GT-563
elliptical, 50, **7d**
independent, 45, **7b;** 151–152, **23c;** 232–236, **33a;** GT-568
after introductory adverb clauses, 131–132, **21b**
after introductory noun clauses, 132, **21b**
after introductory verbals and verbal phrases, 130–131, **21b**
misplaced, 100, **16b**
noun, 48–49, **7c;** GT-576
patterns of, 40–44, **7a;** 230, **33a**
subject of, 38, **6d**
subjunctive in, 26, **4f**
that in, 26–27, **4f**
unnecessary, 249, **33b**
Cleft sentence, GT-555
Clich, 218–220, **32c;** GT-555
Climactic order, GT-555
of details, 307, **36a**
Climactic sentence, 244–245, **33b;** GT-555
Climatic, climactic, G-531
Coherence, GT-555–556
of research paper, 429–430, **40j**
revision for, 328–336, **37c**
Collective noun, GT-556
as antecedents, 83–84, **13e**

subject-verb agreement and, 68–69, **10h**
Colon
before appositives that end sentences, 151, **23b**
comma splices and fused sentences revised with, 60, **9c**
in correspondence, 152–153, **23f**
before grammatically independent quotations, 152, **23d**
inappropriate, 153–154, **23h**
between independent clauses, 151–152, **23c**
for joining independent clauses, 235, **33a**
before lists, 150–151, **23a**
with numerical elements, 153, **23g**
quotation marks with, 173–174, **27b**
between titles and subtitles, 152, **23e**
Colors, pre-noun modifiers and, 506, **ESLe**
Combined patterns, paragraphs of, 305, **36a**
Comedy, GT-556
Commands. *See* Imperative mood
Comma
adjective clause and, 48, **7c**
in appositives, 155–156, **24a**
in clause cause/effect relationship, 233, **33a**
clause connection with, 232–233, **33a**
comma splices and fused sentences revised with, 58, **9a**
contrastive elements set off with, 139, **21g**
between coordinate adjectives, 136–137, **21d**
in dates, places, addresses, 140–141, **21h**
in direct quotations, 141–142, **21h**
inappropriate use of, 142–144, **21j**
and independent clauses, 128–129, **21a;** 151, **23c**
interjections set off with, 139, **21g**
after introductory prepositional phrases, 129–130, **21b**
and items in series, 135–136, **21d**
nonrestrictive elements set off with, 132–135, **21c**
in nonrestrictive modifiers, 156, **24b**
with numbers expressing amounts, 141, **21h**
parenthetical elements set off with, 138, **21f**
in place of omitted words, 137, **21e**
quotation marks with, 173, **27b**
reading clarified with, 142, **21i**
semicolons and, 147–148, **22c**
tag questions set off with, 140, **21g**
with titles of individuals, 141, **21h**
transitional expressions set off with, 138–139, **21f**
words in direct address set off with, 140, **21g**
Comma splice, 57, **9;** GT-556. *See also* Comma
Common noun
defined, 3, **1a**
and inappropriate capitals, 207, **31h**
Comparative conjunction, GT-556
Comparative adjective, 15–16, **3c**
Comparative adverb, 15–16, **3c**
Comparative conjunction, 36–37, **6b**
Comparative degree, GT-556
inappropriate forms and, 92–94, **15b**
Comparison. *See also* Comparative degree
analogy as, 371, **39d**
double, 93, **15b;** 118, **19c**
incomplete, 118–119, **19c**
and topics for writing, 269, **34h**
Comparison/contrast, GT-556
function of, 286–288, **35e**
paragraphs of, 301, **36a**
Complected, complexioned, G-531
Complement, GT-556–557
indirect object, 42, **7a**
object, 42–43, **7a;** GT-576
in split constructions, 113, **18b**
Complement, compliment, 73, **11c;** G-531
Complete subject, 40, **7**
Complex sentence, 51, **7e;** GT-557

Complimentary close, capitalization in, 201, **31a**
Composition. *See also* APA style; Ideas for writing; MLA style; Paragraphs; Thesis
analysis structure, 289–290, **35e**
cause/effect structure, 290–291, **35e**
classification structure, 288, **35e**
comparison/contrast structure, 286–288, **35e**
computers and, 321, **36c;** 359, **38;** 393, **39g**
concluding paragraphs in, 315–321, **36c**
definition structure, 289, **35e**
description structure, 285, **35e**
drafting process, 296–297, **36**
enumeration structure, 286, **35e**
finished, 344–349, **37g**
illustration structure, 289, **35e**
introductory paragraphs in, 308–315, **36b**
narration structure, 285–286, **35e**
outline of, 291–295, **35f**
patterns for, 284–291, **35e**
problem/solution structure, 290, **35e**
revision of, 322–349, **37**
rough draft of, 281, **35d**
showing applications in, 320, **36c**
stages of development, 350–359, **38**
writing stage of, 296, **36**
Composition title
italics and, 184, **28a**
purpose of, 343–344, **37e**
Compound-complex sentence, 51–52, **7e;** GT-557
Compound construction
case in, 86–87, **14a**
with connecting words, 122–123, **20a**
with coordinating conjunctions, 121, **20a**
with correlative conjunctions, 121–122, **20a**
omissions in, 117, **19a**
parallelism in, 121–123, **20a**
Compound modifiers, hyphens in, 188–189, **29b**
Compound noun, 5, **1c**
hyphens in, 187–188, **29a**
Compound sentence, 51, **7e;** GT-557
independent clauses and, 45, **7b**
Compound words. *See* Doubled consonants
Comprise, compose, 73, **11c;** G-531
Computers. *See also* CD-ROM; Electronic citations; Online sources
and argument structure, 393, **39g**
citations for CD-ROM books, 443, **41a**
citations for on-line books, 443, **41a**
composition process and, 359, **38**
decision making and, 283–284, **35d**
drafting paragraphs and, 321, **36c**
and editing, 349, **37g**
and ideas for writing, 272, **34i**
in libraries, 412, **40c**
and outlines, 295, **35f**
and revision, 323, **37;** 338, **37d**
searches of indexes and abstracts, 415–417, **40c**
spelling and, 342–343, **37e**
subject of research paper and, 397, **40a**
terms for, GT-557–559
Concluding paragraphs, 315–321, **36c.** *See also* Conclusions
Conclusions. *See also* Concluding paragraphs
of argument, 382, **39f**
call for further study in, 319–320, **36c**
logic in argument and, 371, **39d**
for research paper, 432, **40j**
Concrete noun, GT-559. *See also* Noun
Conflict, GT-559
in argument, 364–365, **39b**
in introductory paragraphs, 310, **36b**
questions and, 364–365, **39b**
relationships and, 365, **39b**
Conjugation, GT-559–561

Conjunction, 33–37, **6b;** GT-561. *See also* Comparative conjunction; Coordinating conjunction; Correlative conjunction; Semicolon; Subordinating conjunction
- clauses introduced by, 26, **4f**
- commas and coordinating, 128–129, **21a**
- compounding with coordinating, 121, **20a**
- compounding with correlative, 121–122, **20a**
- comparative, GT-556
- coordinating, GT-561
- correlative, GT-562
- for joining independent clauses, 235, **33a**
- relationships and, 332, **37c**
- subordinating, GT-585

Conjunctive adverb, 14, **3b;** GT-561

Connecting words
- compounding with, 122–123, **20a**
- conjunctions as, 33, **6b**

Connections
- between sentences and paragraphs, 332–336, **37c**
- between subject and verb, 251–253, **33c**

Connotation, 215, **32b;** GT-561. *See also* Denotation

Conscience, conscious, G-531

Consensus, G-531

Consistency, of voice, 278–279, **35c**

Consonants. *See* Doubled consonants

Constructions
- defined, 112, **18**
- incomplete, 116–119, **19**
- omissions in compound constructions, 117, **19a**
- split infinitives, 114–115, **18d**
- split subjects and verbs, 112–113, **18a**
- split verbs, 113–114, **18c**
- split verbs and complements, 113, **18b**

Context, in introductory paragraphs, 310, **36b**

Continual, continuous, G-532

Contractions, apostrophes and, 168, **26b**

Contrastive elements, set off with commas, 139, **21g**

Controlling idea, GT-561

Convince, persuade, G-532

Coordinate adjective, commas between, 136–137, **21d**

Coordinating conjunction, 34–35, **6b;** GT-561
- clauses and, 233, **33a**
- commas and, 128–129, **21a**
- in comma splices and fused sentences, 58, **9a;** 59, **9b**
- in compound structures, 121, **20a**
- inappropriate use of commas with, 143–144, **21j**
- relationship and, 332, **37c**
- semicolon and, 146, **22b;** 147–148, **22c**

Coordination, GT-561
- combining ideas and structures through, 232, **33a**
- combining shared elements through, 236–238, **33a**
- of independent clauses, 232–236, **33a**

Copy (computers), GT-558

Corporate author
- APA documentation style for, 473, **41d**
- MLA documentation style for, 440, **41a**

Corrections, 347, **37g**

Correlative conjunction, 35, **6b;** GT-562
- compound constructions with, 121–122, **20a**
- inappropriate use of commas with, 143, **21j**

Correlative coordinators, 236–238, **33a**

Correspondence, colons in, 152–153, **23f**

Could have, could of, G-532

Count noun, 500, **ESLb;** GT-562. *See also* Non-count noun
- pre-determiners preceding, 504–505, **ESLd**

Couplet, GT-562
Credible, creditable, credulous, G-532
Critical thinking, 362–363, **39;** GT-562
 about evidence, 371–381, **39e**
Cumulative sentence, 243–244, **33b;** GT-562
Current usage, discriminatory language and, 226, **32e**

Dangling modifier, 96–98, **16a;** GT-562
 defined, 95, **16**
 elliptical clauses, 98, **16a**
 verbal phrases as, 96–98, **16a**
Dash
 defined, 155, **24**
 to emphasize sentence elements, 156–157, **24c**
 with interrupters, 157, **24d**
 for joining independent clauses, 235, **33a**
 quotation marks with, 174, **27b**
 to set off appositives containing commas, 155–156, **24a**
 to set off nonrestrictive modifiers containing commas, 156, **24b**
Data, G-532
Database (computers), GT-558
Dates, commas in, 140–141, **21h**
Decimal system, in outlines, 294–295, **35f**
Decision making, 283–284, **35d**
Deduction, 370, **39d;** GT-562
Definite article, 501–502, **ESLc**
Definition, GT-563. *See also* Denotation
 function of, 289, **35e**
 in introductory paragraphs, 313, **36b**
 paragraphs of, 302, **36a**
 and topics for writing, 269, **34h**
Degrees (academic and professional). *See* Academic degrees and certifications
Degrees of comparison, 15–16, **3c**
 comparative degree, GT-556
 superlative degree, GT-585–586
Delusion, illusion, allusion, G-525
Demonstrative pronoun, 8–9, **2b;** 503, **ESLc;** GT-563
 for connections, 334, **37c**
 inappropriate, 94, **15c**
Denotation, 215, **32b;** GT-563. *See also* Connotation
Dependent (subordinate) clause, 40, **7;** 45–49, **7c;** GT-563
 as broad reference, 76
 comma splice or fused sentence revised by, 60–61, **9e**
 as fragments, 55–56, **8a**
Dependent phrase, comma splice or fused sentence revised by, 60–61, **9e**
Description, GT-563
 function of, 285, **35e**
 paragraphs of, 299, **36a**
Descriptive adjectives, 506, **ESLe**
Details
 arrangement in paragraphs, 305–308, **36a**
 revision and, 327, **37b**
Determiner, 37–38, **6c;** 500–504, **ESLc;** GT-563. *See also* Indefinite pronoun; Pre-determiners
 definite article, 501–502, **ESLc**
 demonstrative pronouns as, 503, **ESLc**
 indefinite article, 500–502, **ESLc**
 possessives, 503–504, **ESLc**
Development, revision for, 326–328, **37b**
Device, devise, 73, **11c;** G-533
Dewey Decimal system, 405, **40c**
Dialects, 487, **SP**
Dialogue
 ellipsis marks in, 180, **27h**
 exclamation points in, 164, **25f**
 quotation marks in, 175, **27c**
 sentence fragments in, 55, **8**
Dictionary, 488–489, **SPa**
 italics and, 183, **28a**
Differ from, differ with, G-533
Direct address, GT-563
 words set off with commas, 140, **21g**
Directions (compass)
 abbreviating, 197, **30b**

capitalizing, 208, **31h**
Direct object, 41, **7a;** GT-563
noun clauses as, 49, **7c**
Directories, italics and, 183, **28a**
Direct questions, question marks and, 163, **25d;** 163, **25e**
Direct quotation, GT-564
brackets around insertions in, 158-159, **24g**
commas with, 141-142, **21h**
quotation marks for, 171-172, **27a**
Discourse, shifts between direct and indirect, 109, **17g**
Discovery structure of argument, 384-385, **39f**
Discreet, discrete, G-533
Discriminatory language, 226-229, **32e;** 372, **39e**
objectivity and, 229, **32e**
Disinterested, uninterested, G-533
Do, as auxiliary, 20, **4c;** 513-514, **ESLl**
Documentation, 433-486, **41**
APA style at end of paper, 470-477, **41d**
APA style for paper presenting argument, 478-486, **41e**
APA style inside paper, 469-470, **41d**
MLA style for paper answering questions, 447-456, **41b**
MLA style for paper interpreting literature, 457-468, **41c**
MLA style inside paper, 434-446, **41a**
plagiarism and, 422-426, **40h**
Double comparisons, 93, **15b;** 118, **19c**
Doubled consonants
with prefixes, suffixes, and compounds, 493-494, **SPb**
with verbs, 492-493, **SPb**
Double negative, GT-564
Doublespeak, 221, **32d**
Double-talk, 221, **32d**
Download (computers), GT-558
Drafting, 352-359, **38.** *See also* Composition; Revision
computers and, 323, **37**
of paragraphs, 297-308, **36a**
of research paper, 428-432, **40j**
Drama, interpreting, 400-401, **40b**
Dramatic point of view, 400, **40b**
Dropped verb endings, 72-73, **11a**
Due to the fact that, G-534

e, silent. *See* Silent *e*
Each and every, G-534
Eager, anxious, G-526
Editing, on computers, 349, **37g.** *See also* Manuscript preparation; Revision
Editions
APA documentation style for, 473, **41d**
MLA documentation for, 440, **41a**
Editorials
APA documentation style for, 475, **41d**
MLA documentation for, 441, **41a**
Educational names, capitalization of, 203, **31b**
Effect, affect, G-523
Effect/cause, GT-554
Either/or reasoning, 378-379, **39e**
Electronic citations
APA documentation style for, 470, **41d;** 475-476, **41d**
MLA documentation style for, 444-445, **41a**
Ellipsis marks
at end of sentence, 178, **27g**
for interruption in dialogue, 180, **27h**
lines of poetry, 179-180, **27g**
for omissions, 177-180, **27g**
in quotations, 370, **39d**
single-sentence omissions and, 177-178, **27g**
whole sentence or several sentences omissions and, 178-179, **27g**
Elliptical clause, 50, **7d**
case in, 89, **14d**
dangling, 98, **16a**
Elliptical construction, GT-564
Elliptical questions
capitalization in, 202, **31a**
question marks after, 163, **25d**

E-mail, GT-558
MLA documentation for, 445, **41a**
Emigrate, immigrate, 73, **11c;** G-534
Emphasis
and balanced sentences, 245–246, **33b**
and climactic sentences, 244–245, **33b**
and cumulative sentences, 243–244, **33b**
exclamation points for, 164–165, **25h**
italics (underlining) for, 186, **28f**
and periodic sentences, 242–243, **33b**
Emphatic pronoun, 8, **2a;** 86, **14a;** GT-564
Empty verbs, 246–247, **33c**
-ence, ance, 497, **SPc**
Encyclopedias, 406–407, **40c**
italics and, 183, **28a**
MLA documentation style for, 440, **41a**
End punctuation. *See also* Period; Punctuation
periods as, 161, **25a**
question marks as, 162–163, **25d**
English, nonstandard, 72, **11a**
English as a Second Language, 498, **ESL**
active-voice verb phrase, 508–509, **ESLg**
auxiliaries *have* and *be,* 512, **ESLj**
chains of verbs, 514–517, **ESLm**
count noun and, 500, **ESLb**
definite article, 501–502, **ESLc**
demonstrative pronouns, 503, **ESLc**
determiners and, 500–501, **ESLc**
do auxiliary, 513–514, **ESLl**
head noun and, 499, **ESLa**
modal auxiliaries, 511, **ESLi**
negative sentences, 518–519, **ESLo**
non-count noun, 500, **ESLb**
passive-voice verb phrase, 512–513, **ESLk**
possessives, 503–504, **ESLc**
post-noun modifiers, 507–508, **ESLf**
pre-determiners, 504–505, **ESLd**
pre-noun modifiers, 505–507, **ESLe**
questions, 517, **ESLn**
tag questions to identify sentences, 519–521, **ESLp**
tense, 510, **ESLh**
Ensure, insure, 73, **11c;** G-534
Entertainment, as purpose for writing, 273–274, **35a**
Enthused, G-534
Enumeration, GT-564
function of, 286, **35e**
paragraphs of, 300, **36a**
Equivocation, 377, **39e;** GT-564
ERIC, 408, **40c**
ESL. *See* English as a Second Language
Essay, GT-564
Essay examinations, 276, **35b**
Et al., etc., G-534
Ethnic terms, capitalization of, 203, **31b**
Etymology, GT-564
Euphemisms, 220–221, **32c;** GT-564
Every day, everyday, G-535
Every one, everyone, G-535
Evidence, GT-565
accuracy of, 372–373, **39e**
for argument, 368–371, **39d;** 371–381, **39e**
clarity of language and, 377, **39e**
evaluation of, 371–381, **39e**
facts and observations as, 368–369, **39d**
hasty generalization as, 376, **39e**
informed opinions as, 369–370, **39d**
logical reasoning and, 370–371, **39d;** 377–381, **39e**
questions about, 371–381, **39e**
relevance of, 373–375, **39e**
sufficient, 375–376, **39e**
supporting, 385, **39f**
Ex-, as prefix, 189, **29c**
Exaggeration
of cumulative sentences, 243–244, **33b**
of periodic sentence, 243, **33b**
Except for the fact that, G-535
Exclamation points
defined, 160, **25**
in dialogue, 164, **25f**
for emphasis, 164–165, **25h**

with interjections, 164, **25g**
quotation marks with, 174, **27b**
Expletives, 38–39, **6d;** GT-565
Explicit, implicit, G-535
Exposition, GT-565

Fact(s)
evidence and, 372, **39e**
as evidence in argument, 368–369, **39d**
statement in argument, 382, **39f**
Fallacy, GT-565
either/or, 378–379, **39e**
post hoc, GT-579
in reasoning, 377–378, **39e**
False analogy, 379, **39e**
Farther, further, G-535
Faulty predications, 109–111, **17h**
Federalese, 221, **32d**
Females. *See* Gender
Fewer, less, G-536
Fiction, figures of speech in, 255, **33d**
Fidonet (computers), GT-558
Figurative language, in poetry, **40b**
Figures, parentheses for references to, 158, **24f**
Figures of speech, 254–255; GT-565
analogy, GT-552
hyperbole, GT-567
metaphor, 254, **33d;** GT-574
metonymy, GT-574
personification, GT-579
simile, GT-583
Filename, GT-558
Filler words. *See* Expletives
Films
APA documentation style for, 476, **41d**
italics for titles, 182, **28a**
MLA documentation style for, 442, **41a**
Final draft, 357–359, **38.** *See also* Drafting
Finite verb, GT-565
First draft, 352–353, **38.** *See also* Drafting
First person, formality of voice, 213, **32a**
First-person point of view, 400, **40b**
Floppy disk, GT-558
Fonts, GT-558
Forecasting, in concluding paragraphs, 319, **36c**
Foreign languages
abbreviating words, 195, **30a**
capitalization of names, 208, **31h**
italicizing words, 185, **28d**
nouns as subjects, 69, **10j**
Foreword, MLA documentation for, 439, **41a**
Form, of poem, 401–402, **40b**
Formal voice, word choice and, 212–214, **32a**
Format (computers), GT-558
Fractions, slashes in, 192, **29i**
Fragment, GT-565. *See also* Sentence fragments
Freewriting, 264–265, **34e;** 350–352, **38;** GT-565
FTP, GT-558
Function word, 32–39, **6;** GT-566
Further, farther, G-535
Fused sentence, GT-566
defined, 57, **9**
revising, 57–61, **9**
Future tense
perfect, 22, **4c**
perfect progressive, 23, **4e**
progressive, 22, **4d**

Gazetteers, 408, **40c**
Gender, GT-566. *See also* Sexist language
personal pronouns and, 8, **2a**
sexism and, 227–229, **32e**
Generalization, hasty, 376, **39e**
General-particular order, of details, 307, **36a;** GT-566
General/specific words, GT-566
Generic nouns, and sexist language, 83, **13d**
Genitive case, GT-566
Genre, GT-566. *See also* Fiction; Poetry
Geographical locations, abbreviations of, 195, **30a**

Gerund, 30, **5c;** GT-566
as dangling verbals, 96–98, **16a**
possessive case with, 89–90, **14e**
Gerund phrase, 30, **5c**
Gobbledygook, 221–223, **32d;** GT-567
Good, well, G-536
Government documents
APA documentation style for, 474, **41d**
MLA documentation style for, 441, **41a**
Grammar, revision for, 339–341, **34e**

Had better, G-536
Had ought to, G-536
Half, G-536
Handbooks, 407–408, **40c**
Handwriting, final manuscript, 344, **37g;** 346, **37g**
Hanged, hung, 73, **11c;** G-536
Hard disk, GT-558
Hardly, G-536
Hasty generalization, GT-567
as evidence, 376, **39e**
Have, as auxiliary, 19, **4b**
and active-voice verb phrase, 509, **ESLg**
as modal auxiliary, 512, **ESLj**
and passive-voice verb phrase, 513, **ESLk**
Headers (computers), GT-558
Headings
as antecedents, 78–79, **12g**
colons in memoranda, 153, **23f**
Head noun, 499–500, **ESLb**
Healthy, healthful, G-537
Helping verb, GT-567. *See also* Auxiliary verb
Hisself, G-537
Historic, historical, G-537
Historical names, capitalization of, 203, **31b**
Historical present tense, 105, **17a**
Honor titles, capitalization of, 204–205, **31c**
Hopefully, G-537
Hung, hanged, G-536

Hyperbole, 254, 255, **33d;** GT-567
Hyphens and hyphenation, 345–346, **37g**
in compound modifiers, 188–189, **29b**
in compound nouns, 187–188, **29a**
in compound verbs, 187–188, **29a**
in dense noun phrases, 225, **32d**
in numbers (numerals), 190–191, **29d;** 198, **30c**
with prefixes, 189–190, **29c**
typing, 446, **41a;** 477, **41e**
for word division at end of line, 191, **29e**

I
capitalization of, 207, **31g**
formality of, 213, **32a**
I, myself, or me, G-540
i before *e,* 494, **SPb**
Ideas for writing
brainstorming and, 262–263, **34c**
classical topics and, 269–270, **34h**
clustering and, 263, **34d**
combining 232–242, **33a**
computers and, 272, **34i**
freewriting and, 264–265, **34e**
journals and, 260–261, **34a**
ladders and, 265–266, **34f**
meditation and, 261–262, **34b**
questions and, 266–269, **34g**
Idiom, 55, **8;** GT-567
If, whether, G-537
Illusion, delusion, allusion, G-525
Illustration, GT-567
paragraphs of, 301–302, **36a**
Image, GT-567
of poem, 402, **40b**
Immigrate, emigrate, G-534
Imperative mood, 25, **4f;** GT-567
Implicit, explicit, G-535
Implied pronoun reference, 74–75, **12a**
Imply/infer, 73, **11c;** G-537–538
Imprecise language, 377, **39e**
Impression, as purpose for writing, 273–274, **35a**
In, into, G-538

Incomplete comparisons, 118–119, **19c**
Incomplete constructions, 116–119, **19**
Incredible, incredulous, G-538
Indefinite article, 500–501, **ESLc**
Indefinite pronoun, 10–11, **2e;** 37–38, **6c;** GT-567
  and sexist language, 82–83, **13c**
  as subjects, 65–67, **10d**
  you, they, it, 76, **12c**
Independent (main) clause, 40, **7;** 45, **7b;** GT-568
  appositives with, 241, **33a**
  colons between, 151–152, **23c**
  comma splices and fused sentences and, 61, **9e**
  commas with, 128–129, **21a**
  coordination of, 232–236, **33a**
  semicolons between, 145–146, **22a;** 146–147, **22b;** 147–148, **22c**
Index cards
  for bibliographies, 417–418, **40d**
  for note-taking. 421–422, **40g**
Indexes, 410, **40c**
  computer searches of, 415–417, **40c**
  printed, 413–414, **40c**
  specialized, 414–415, **40c**
Indicative mood, 24–25, **4f;** GT-568
Indirect object, 42, **7a;** GT-568
Indirect quotation, GT-568
  inappropriate use of comma after, 144, **21j**
  quotation marks and, 172, **27a**
Induction, 370, **39d;** GT-568. *See also* Deduction
Infinitive, 28–29, **5a;** 71, **11a;** GT-568
  chains of verbs and, 514–517, **ESLm**
  as dangling verbals, 96–98, **16a**
  shifts in, 105, 106, **17b**
  split, 114–115, **18d;** GT-584
Inflection, GT-568
Information, as purpose for writing, 273–274, **35a**
Information sources. *See* Sources
Informed opinions, 369–370, **39d**
-ing, 17, **4a**
  possessive case with gerunds and, 89–90, **14e**
Initials, abbreviating, 195, **30a**
In regards to, G-538
Insure, ensure, G-534
Intensifier, 119, **19c;** GT-569
Intensive pronoun. *See* Emphatic pronoun
Interest, sources in paragraphs, 312, **36b**
Interjection, 55, **8;** GT-569
  exclamation points with, 164, **25g**
  punctuation for, 161, **25a**
  set off with commas, 139, **21g**
Interlibrary loan, 410, **40c**
Internet, GT-558
Interpreting literature
  as purpose for research paper, 399–403, **40b**
  sample paper in MLA style, 457–468
Interrogative pronoun, 10, **2d;** 38, **6c;** GT-569
Interrogatives, adverbs as, 15, **3b**
Interrupters
  dashes with, 157, **24d**
  parentheses to enclose, 157–158, **24e**
Interviews, MLA documentation for, 442, **41a**
Into, in to, G-538
Intransitive verb, 41, **7a;** GT-569
Interviews, APA documentation style for, 476–477, **41d**
Introduction
  to argument, 382, **39f**
  to research paper, 429, **40j**
Introductory paragraphs, 308–315, **36b**
  anecdotes in, 313–314, **36b**
  antithesis in, 312–313, **36b**
  audience surprise in, 311–312, **36b**
  background in, 310–311, **36b**
  combination of strategies in, 315, **36b**
  conflict in, 310, **36b**
  context in, 310, **36b**
  overview in, 311, **36b**
  problem description in, 309, **36b**

questions in, 314, **36b**
quotations in, 314, **36b**
source of interest in, 312, **36b**
terms in, 313, **36b**
thesis in, 308–309, **36b**
Investigation, composition detailing, 320, **36c**
Irony, in prose, 164, **25h**
Irregardless, regardless, G-538
Irregular verb, 510, **ESL;** GT-569-573
nonstandard use of, 71–72, **11a**
past tense of, 510, **ESLh**
principal parts of, 17, 18, **4a**
Irrelevancy, discriminatory language and, 226, **32e**
Irritate, aggravate, G-523
Is when, is where, G-538
It
indefinite, 76, **12c**
mixed uses of, 77–78, **12e**
It's, as possessive, 170, **26d**
It's, its, G-539
Italics (underlining)
defined, 181, **28**
for emphasis, 159, **24g;** 186, **28f**
for foreign words, 185, **28d**
for letters as letters, 184, **28b**
for numbers, 184, **28b**
punctuation and, 183, **28a**
for sounds, 185, **28c**
for titles, 175–176, **27d;** 181–184, **28a**
for vehicles designated by proper names, 185, **28e**
for words as words, 184, **28b**

Jargon, 221, **32d;** GT-573
Journalistic questions, GT-573
Journals
ideas for writing, 260–261, **34a**
italics for titles, 182, **28a**
MLA documentation for, 437, **41a;** 441, **41a**
Justified margin, GT-558

Keywords, in library research, 408, **40c**
Kind of, sort of, G-539
Kind of (a), type of (a), sort of (a), G-539

Ladders, 265–266, **34f**
Language. *See also* Words
bureaucratic, 221, **32d**
capitalization of foreign, 208, **31h**
clarity of, 377, **39e**
discriminatory, 226–229, **32e;** 372, **39e**
Plain English movement, 222–223, **32d**
of poetry, 402, **40b**
Later, latter, G-539
Latin expressions, abbreviating, 195, **30a**
Lay, lie, G-539
Lead-ins, for research paper, 431–432, **40j**
Lectures, MLA documentation for, 442, **41a**
Lend, loan, 73, **11c;** G-539
Less, fewer, G-536
Letters (alphabet)
capitals, 200–209, **31**
hyphens with repeated, 190, **29d**
plurals of, 168–169, **26c**
Letters (correspondence)
address abbreviations in, 195–196, **30a**
APA documentation style for, 475, **41d**
capitalization in, 201, **31a**
MLA documentation for, 441, **41a**
Library
abstracts, 412–416, **40c**
almanacs and yearbooks in, 408, **40c**
atlases and gazetteers in, 408, **40c**
biographies in, 407, **40c**
catalogs in, 408–412, **40c**
computers and, 412, **40c;** 416–417, **40c**
encyclopedias in, 406–407, **40c**
general works in, 405, **40c**
handbooks and manuals in, 407–408, **40c**

indexes and abstracts in, 412–417, **40c**
interlibrary loan, 410, **40c**
keyword use in, 408, **40c**
locating bibliography material in, 418–419, **40e**
numbering system in, 405, **40c**
organization of, 404, **40c**
reference area in, 405, **40c**
research work in, 403–417, **40c**
Library of Congress system, 405, 408, 409, **40c**
Lie, lay, 73, **11c;** G-539
Like, as, G-527
Limited-omniscient point of view, 400, **40b**
Linking verb, GT-573
Linking words and phrases, 332–336, **37c.** *See also* Connections
for independent clauses, 234–235, **33a**
subjects of verbs, 67, **10f**
verbs, 43–44, **7a**
Listening, writing topics found through, 270–271, **34i**
Lists
capitalization of first word in, 202, **31a**
colons before, 150–151, **23a**
parallelism in, 123–125, **20b**
periods in, 161, 162, **25b**
Literal language, in poetry, 402, **40b.** *See also* Poetry
Literature
interpreting as research paper purpose, 399–403, **40b**
novels, short stories, and plays in, 400–401, **40b**
sample MLA-style paper on, 457–468
Locations. *See* Geographical locations
Logical reasoning, 377–381, **39e.** *See also* Critical thinking
begging the question and, 379–380, **39e**
either/or reasoning and, 378–379, **39e**
as evidence, 370–371, **39d**
fallacy in, 377–378, **39e**
false analogy and, 379, **39e**
non sequitur and, 380–381, **39e**
oversimplification of cause and, 378, **39e**
post hoc reasoning and, 378, **39e**
Loose sentences, 242–244, **33b;** GT-573–574
Lose, loose, 73, **11c;** G-540
Lyric, GT-574

Magazines
APA documentation style for, 475, **41d**
italics for titles, 182, **28a.** *See also* Italics
MLA documentation style for, 438, **41a;** 441, **41a;** 443–444, **41a**
Main clause. *See* Independent (main) clause
Main verb, 18, **4b**
Males. *See* Gender
Manuals, 407–408, **40c**
Manuscript preparation, 344–349, **37g**
corrections, 347, **37g**
hyphenation, 346, **37g**
margins, 345–346, **37g**
pagination, 346, **37g**
paper, 344–345, **37g**
proofreading, 347, **37g**
spacing, 346, **37g**
title page, 347, **37g**
Margins, 345–346, **37g**
justified, GT-558
Masculine nouns. *See* Gender; Noun
Masculine pronoun. *See* Sexist language
Mask, of writer, 278, **35c**
Mass noun, GT-574. *See also* Non-count noun
Materials, pre-noun modifiers and, 507, **ESLe**
May, can, G-530
May be, maybe, G-540
Meaning, in poetry, 403, **40b.** *See also* Function words
Mechanics, revision for, 341–343, **37e**
Meditation, 261–262, **34b**

Memoranda, colons in headings of, 153, **23f**
Menu (computers), GT-558
Merge (computers), GT-558
Metaphor, 254, **33d;** GT-574
mixed, GT-574
Metonymy, GT-574
Might have, might of, G-540
Might/must, 103, **17a**
Military
terms, abbreviating, 196, **30b**
titles, abbreviating, 194, **30a**
Misplaced modifier, 96-97, **16;** 99-101, **16b;** GT-574
clauses, 100, **16b**
prepositional phrases, 99-100, **16b**
squinting, 100-101, **16b**
words, 99, **16b**
Mixed constructions, 109-111, **17h**
Mixed metaphor, GT-574
MLA (Modern Language Association) style
capitalization styles and, 206, **31e**
at end of paper, 436-438, **41a**
inside paper, 434-446, **41a**
sample paper answering questions, 447-456, **41b**
sample paper interpreting literature, 457-468, **41c**
for sources, 387-392, **39g**
typing with, 445-446, **41a**
Modal auxiliaries, 19-20, **4b;** 103-105, **17a;** 511, **ESLi;** GT-574-575
Modem, GT-558
Modern Language Association. *See* MLA style
Modifier, GT-575. *See also* Adjective; Adjective clause; Adverb
adjective clause as, 508, **ESLf**
adjectives as, 12, **3**
adverbs as, 12, **3**
dangling, 95, **16;** GT-562
hyphens in compound, 188-189, **29b**
incomplete comparisons and, 119, **19c**
misplaced, 95-97, **16;** 99-101, **16b;** GT-574
nouns as, 507
post-noun, 507-508, **ESLf**
pre-noun, 505-507, **ESLe**
prepositional phrase as, 33, **6a;** 507, **ESLf**
sentence, GT-583
single-word, 507, **ESLf**
squinting, GT-584
Monotonous prose, 230-232, **33a**
Mood, GT-575
imperative, 25, **4f;** GT-567
indicative, 24-25, **4f;** GT-568
shifts in, 107, **17c**
subjunctive, 25-26, **4f;** GT-585
verb, 19, **4b;** 24-27, **4f**
Moral, morale, G-540
Most, almost, G-525
Movies. *See* Films
Multivolume works
APA documentation style for, 473, **41d**
MLA documentation style for, 439-440, **41a**
Must have, must of, G-540
Myself, me, or I, G-540

Names, capitalization of, 202-204, **31b.** *See also* Noun, proper; State names
Narration, GT-575
function of, 285-286, **35e**
paragraphs of, 299-300, **36a**
Nationalities, pre-noun modifiers and, 506, **ESLe**
Negative
double, GT-564
sentences, 518-519, **ESLo**
Net (computers), GT-558
Neutral nouns and pronouns, 227-228, **32e**
Newspaper
APA documentation style for, 475, **41d**
italics for titles, 182, **28a**
MLA documentation style for, 438, **41a;** 441, **41a**
MLA documentation style for CD-ROM, 443, **41a**

Nicknames
capitalization of, 204, **31b**
quotation marks and, 177, **27g**
Nominalization, 246-247, **33c;** GT-575
Nominative absolute, 30, **5d**
Noncountable noun, 66, **10d**
Non-count noun, 500, **ESLb;** GT-575. *See also* Count noun; Mass noun
pre-determiners preceding, 504-505, **ESLd**
None, subject-verb agreement and, 66-67, **10d**
Nonfiction, figures of speech in, 255, **33d**
Nonrestrictive element, GT-575-576
and appositives, 134-135, **21c**
clauses, 132-133, **21c**
and introductory words, 133, **21c**
and proper nouns, 133-134, **21c**
Nonrestrictive modifier, set off by dashes, 156, **24b**
Non sequitur, 380-381, **39e;** GT-576
Nonstandard English, 72, **11a**
Nonstandard forms
of adjectives and adverbs, 91-94, **15**
verbs, 71-73, **11**
Noplace, nowhere, G-540
Note cards, 421-422, **40g**
Note-taking, 421-422, **40g**
Noun, GT-576. *See also* Adjective clause; Adjective; Determiner
abstract, GT-550
case of, 85-90, **14;** GT-554
collective, GT-556
common, 3, **1a;** 207, **31h**
compound, 5, **1c;** 167, **26a**
compound modifier placement and, 188-189, **29b**
concrete, GT-559
count, 500, **ESLb;** GT-562
defined, 2, **1**
as determiners, 37, **6c**
foreign, 69, **10j**
generic and sexist language, 83, **13d**
head, 499-500, **ESLb**
hyphens in compound, 187-188, **29a**
mass, 500, **ESLb;** GT-574
as modifier, 507, **ESLe**
neutral, 227-228, **32e**
non-count, 500, **ESLb;** GT-575
noncountable, 66, **10d**
plural, 4, **1b**
plural possessive, 167, **26a**
possessive, 5, **1c**
predicate, GT-580
proper, 3, **1a;** 167, **26a;** 202-204, **31b;** GT-581
simple, 4, **1b**
singular, 4, **1b**
verbals as, 29, **5a**
Noun clause, 48-49, **7c;** GT-576. *See also* Relative pronoun
as direct objects, 49, **7c**
as objects of prepositions, 49, **7c**
as subject complements, 49, **7c**
as subjects, 48-49, **7c**
that omitted from, 117-118, **19b**
Noun phrase, 499, **ESLa**
dense, 225, **32d**
subject complement as, 44, **7a**
Novels, interpreting, 400-401, **40b**
Number, GT-576
personal pronouns and, 7, **2a**
shifts in, 108, **17e**
and subject-verb agreement, 62, **10**
Number, amount, G-526
Numbering system, for outlines, 293-295, **35f**
Numbers (numerals)
apostrophes and, 169, **26d**
cardinal, 38, **6c;** 506, **ESLe**
expressed in numerals, 197-198, **30c**
expressed in words, 198-199, **30d**
hyphens in, 190-191, **29d;** 198, **30c**
mixed numerals and words, 199, **30e**
ordinal, 505, **ESLe**
sentences beginning with, 199, **30d**
and words, 199, **30e**
Numerals. *See* Numbers (numerals)
Numerical elements, colons with, 153, **23g**

O, capitalization of, 207, **31g**
Object
direct, GT-563. *See also* Transitive verb

indirect, GT-568
Object complement, 42-43, **7a;** GT-576
Objective case, after verb *be,* 88, **14b**
Objective forms, as objects and with infinitives, 85-86, **14**
Objective (dramatic) point of view, 400, **40b**
Objectivity, discriminatory language and, 372, **39e**
Object of preposition, GT-576
case in, 87, **14a**
noun clauses as, 49, **7c**
Observation, verbs expressing, 516, **ESLm**
Observations, as evidence in argument, 368-369, **39d**
Of, in formal writing, G-541
Officialese, 221, **32d**
O.K., G-541
Online sources
APA documentation style for, 475-476, **41d;** 475-476, **41d**
MLA documentation style for, 443, **41a;** 444, **41a**
Operas, italics for titles, 182, **28a**
Opinions
and evidence, 372, **39e**
informed, 369-370, **39d**
Or, and, G-526
Or/nor
antecedents joined by, 81-82, **13b**
subjects joined by, 65, **10c**
Oral, verbal, G-541
Order
chronological, GT-554
climactic, GT-555
general-particular, GT-566
particular-general, GT-577
spatial, GT-584
Order of details, 305-308, **36a**
Ordinal numbers, 505, **ESLe**
Organization
of research paper, 428-429, **40j**
revision for, 328-331, **37c;** 332, **37c**
Organizations, capitalization of, 203, **31b**
Orient, orientate, 73, **11c;** G-541
Outlines, 291-295, **35f**
capitalization in, 201, **31a**
decimal system, 294-295, **35f**
numbering systems, 293-295, **35f**
parallelism in, 123-125, **20b**
periods in, 161-162, **25b**
rough, 292-293, **35f**
sentence, 293, **35f**
structured, 293-295, **35f**
topic, 293, **35f**
traditional numbering system, 293-294, **35f**
for unity in composition, 323-324, **37a**
working, 419-420, **40f**
Oversimplification of cause, 378, **39e**
Overview, in introductory paragraphs, 311, **36b**

Pages, parentheses for references to, 158, **24f**
Pagination, 346, **37g**
Paintings, italics for titles, 183, **28a**
Pamphlets
italics for titles, 182, **28a**
MLA documentation style for, 440, **41a**
Papers. *See* Composition; Manuscript preparation
Paradox, GT-576
Paragraphs, 296-297, **36;** GT-577. *See also* Composition; Revision
of analysis, 302-303, **36a**
body, 297-308, **36a**
of cause/effect, 304, **36a**
of classification, 301, **36a**
of combined patterns, 304-305, **36a**
of comparison/contrast, 300-301, **36a**
computers and, 321, **36c**
concluding, 315-321, **36c**
connections with sentences, 332-336, **37c**
of definition, 302, **36a**
of description, 299, **36a**
details arranged in, 305-308, **36a**
development of, 327-328, **37b**
of enumeration, 300, **36a**
of illustration, 301-302, **36a**
introductory, 308-315, **36b**

of narration, 299–300, **36a**
outline for, 293, **35f**
of problem/solution, 303, **36a**
of question/answer, 303–304, **36a**
revision of, 325–326, **37a;** 327–328, **37b**
topic sentences, 297–298, **36a**
unity and, 324, **37a;** 325–326, **37a**
Parallelism, GT-577
in compound structures, 121–123, **20a**
defined, 120, **20**
numbers (numerals) in, 199, **30b**
in series, lists, and outlines, 123–125, **20b**
Paraphrase, 423–426, **40h;** GT-577
of passages, 427–428, **40i**
quotation marks and, 172, **27a**
quotations and, 427, **40i**
Parentheses
defined, 155, **24**
to enclose interrupters, 157–158, **24e**
within parentheses, 159, **24h**
quotation marks and, 173, **27b**
for references to pages, figures, tables, and chapters, 158, **24f**
Parenthetical elements, GT-577
commas with, 138, **21f**
Participial phrase, 29–30, **5b**
Participle, 29–30, **5b;** 105, 106–107, **17b;** GT-577
in absolute verbal phrase, 30, **5d**
as dangling verbals, 96–98, **16a**
past, GT-578
present, GT-580
Particular-to-general order of details, 307–308, **36a;** GT-577
Part of speech, GT-577
Passages
paraphrasing, 427–428, **40i**
summarizing, 428, **40i**
Passives, weak, 247–249, **33c**
Passive voice, 23–24, **4e;** 42, **7a;** 107, **17d;** GT-578
verb phrase in, 512–513, **ESLk**
Past participle, 17, **4a;** 106, **17b;** GT-578
of irregular verbs, 71–72, **11a**
past perfect tense and, 103, **17a**
Past perfect tense. *See* Past participle, past perfect tense
Past tense, 21, **4c**
be and, 63, **10**
form of, 71, **11a**
of irregular verbs, 71, **11a;** 510, **ESLh**
perfect, 22, **4c**
perfect progressive, 23, **4d**
progressive, 22, **4d**
simple, 103, **17a**
Patterns. *See also* Composition; Paragraphs
of paragraphs, 299–305, **36a**
spelling, 490–495, **SPb**
PC. *See* Political correctness
People, capitalization of names, 203, **31b**
People, persons, G-541
Percent, per cent, percentage, G-541
Perfect participle, 106, **17b**
Perfect progressive forms, 23, **4d**
Perfect tenses, 21–22, **4c;** 103, **17a;** GT-578
Period
defined, 160, **25**
as end punctuation, 161, **25a**
inappropriate, 162, **25c**
in outlines and displayed lists, 161–162, **25b**
quotation marks with, 173, **27b**
Periodicals
APA documentation style for, 473, 474–475, **41d;** 476, **41d**
MLA documentation style for, 437, **41a**
Periodic sentence, 242–243, **33b;** GT-578
Person, GT-578
compound constructions and, 87, **14a**
formality of voice, 213, **32a**
personal pronouns and, 7–8, **2a**
shifts in, 108–109, **17f**
and subject-verb agreement, 62, **10**
Persona, of writer, 278, **35c;** GT-578
Personal pronoun, 7–8, **2a;** GT-578
apostrophes and, 169, **26d**

Personification, 254, 255, **33d;** GT-579
Persuade, convince, G-532
Phonetics, 487, **SP**
Phrasal prepositions, 32–33, **6a**
Phrasal rhythms, 256, **33e**
Phrase, GT-579. *See also* Dependent phrase; Prepositional phrase; Verbal phrase; Verb phrase
  absolute, GT-550
  absolute verbal, 30–31, **5d**
  dense noun, 225, **32d**
  gerund, 30, **5c**
  indefinite pronouns as subjects and, 66, **10d**
  noun, 499, **ESLa**
  participial, 29–30, **5b**
  prepositional, 32–33, **6a**
  verb, 17, **4;** GT-588
  verbal, 239–240, **33a**
Phrase fragments, 56, **8b**
Place names, capitalization of, 203, **31b**
Places, commas in, 140–141, **21h**
Plagiarism, 422–426, **40h**
  paraphrasing and, 423–426, **40h**
  quotations and, 370, **39d;** 422–423, **40h**
Plain English movement, 222–223, **32d**
Planetary system, capitalization and, 209, **31h**
Plays
  interpreting, 400–401, **40b**
  italics for titles, 182, **28a**
Playwrite, playwright, G-541
Plenty, G-542
Plot, GT-579
Plural nouns, 4, **1b;** 108, **17e**
  compound, 5, **1c**
Plurals
  of letters, 168–169, **26c**
  of words used as words, 168–169, **26c**
Plus, G-542
Poetry. *See also* Lyric
  blank verse, GT-553
  capitalization in, 201, **31a**
  couplet and, GT-562
  figures of speech in, 255, **33e**
  form of, 401–402, **40b**
  images in, 402, **40b**
  interpreting, 401–403, **40b**
  italics for book-length, 181, **28a**
  language in, 402, **40b**
  meaning of, 403, **40b**
  purpose of, 401, **40b**
  quatrain, GT-581
  slashes in, 192, **29h**
  sonnet, GT-584
  sound and rhythm of, 402, **40b**
  speaker in, 401, **40b**
  symbols in, 402, **40b**
  tone of, 401, **40b**
Point of view, GT-579
  first-person, 400, **40b**
  limited-omniscient, 400, **40b**
  in novels, short stories, plays, 400, **40b**
  objective (dramatic), 400, **40b**
Political correctness, 229, **32e**
Position, of dangling modifiers, 96–98, **16a.** *See also* Adverb
Positive adjectives, 15–16, **3c**
Positive adverbs, 15–16, **3c**
Positive degree, 15–16, **3c**
Possession
  apostrophes to indicate, 166–168, **26a**
  joint, 167–168, **26a**
Possessive, 503–504, **ESLc**
Possessive case, GT-579. *See also* Genitive case
  with gerunds, 89–90, **14e**
Possessive nouns, apostrophes with, 5, **1c;** 166–168, **26a**
Possessive pronouns, 37, **6c**
Post (computers), GT-558
Postal Service abbreviations, 197, **30b**
Post hoc fallacy, GT-579
Post hoc reasoning, 378, **39e**
Post-noun modifiers, 507–508, **ESLf.** *See also* Modifier
Practicable, practical, G-542
Practice, of spelling, 489, **SPa**
Precede, proceed, 73, **11c;** G-542
Pre-determiners, 504–505, **ESLd**

Predicate, 40, **7;** GT-579-580
in dependent clauses, 45, **7c**
faulty, 109-111, **17h**
shared, 236, **33a**
Predicate adjective, GT-580
Predicate nominative, 43, **7a;** 85, **14**
Predicate noun, GT-580
Preface, MLA documentation style for, 439, **41a**
Prefix, GT-580. *See also* Doubled consonants
hyphens with, 189-190, **29c**
Prejudice, and discriminatory language, 372, **39e**
Pre-noun (pre-nominal) modifiers, 505-507, **ESLe**
Preposition, 32-33, **6a;** GT-580. *See also* Object of preposition
as adverbs, 14, **3b**
phrasal, 32-33, **6a**
object of, GT-576
Prepositional phrase, 32-33, **6a**
commas with, 129-130, **21b**
indirect object and, 42, **7a**
misplaced, 99-100, **16b**
as post-noun modifier, 507-508, **ESLf**
Present participle, 17, **4a;** GT-580
chains of verbs and, 514-517, **ESLm**
nonstandard use of, 71, **11a**
Present perfect tense, 63, **10**
be and, 63, **10**
Present tense, 21, **4c;** 62, **10;** 510, **ESLh**
be and, 63, **10**
historical, 105, **17a**
perfect, 22, **4c;** 63, **10**
perfect progressive, 23, **4d**
progressive, 22, **4d**
simple, 102-103, **17a**
Primary sources, 404, **40c**
Principal, principle, G-542
Principal parts, GT-580
defined, 17-18, **4a**
nonstandard, 71-72, **11a**
Printed abstracts, 413-415, **40c**
Printed indexes, 413-415, **40c**
Printed sources. *See also* Bibliographies; Documentation; Sources
APA documentation style for, 471-472, **41d**
basic MLA forms for, 438, **41a**
Printing, final manuscript, 345, **37g;** 346, **37g**
function of, 290, **35e**
paragraphs of, 303, **36a**
Problem description, 309, **36b**
Problem/solution, GT-580
Process analysis, GT-580
Product names, capitalization of, 203, **31b**
Professional degrees. *See* Academic degrees and certifications
Progressive tenses, 22-23, **4d;** GT-581
simple past, 103, **17a**
simple present, 102-103, **17a**
Pronoun, GT-581. *See also* Adjective clause
case of, 85-90, **14;** GT-554
compound, 167, **26a**
in compound constructions, 86-87, **14a**
defined, 6-7, **2**
demonstrative, 8-9, **2b;** 334, **37c;** 503, **ESLc;** GT-563
as determiners, 37, **6c**
emphatic, GT-564
indefinite, 10-11, **2e;** 37-38, **6c;** GT-567
interrogative, 10, **2d;** 38, **6c;** GT-569
neutral, 227-228, **32e**
personal, 7-8, **2a;** GT-578
possessive, 37, **6c**
reciprocal, 11, **2e;** GT-582
reflexive, GT-582
relative, 9-10, **2c;** 67, **10e;** GT-582
with suffixes, 86, **14**
Pronoun-antecedent agreement
antecedents joined by *and,* 81, **13a**
antecedents joined by *or/nor,* 81-82, **13b**
collective nouns as antecedents, 83-84, **13e**
generic nouns and sexist language, 83, **13d**
indefinite pronouns and sexist language, 82-83, **13c**

Pronoun reference
ambiguous, 77, **12d**
broad, 75-76, **12b**
implied, 74-75, **12a**
indefinite *you, they, it,* 76, **12c**
mixed uses of *it,* 77-78, **12e**
remote, 78, **12f**
titles and headings as antecedents, 78-79, **12g**
Pronunciation, 488, **SP;** 489, **SPa**
Proof, of argument, 382, **39f**
Proofreading, 323, **37;** 347, **37g**
Proper adjective, GT-581
Proper name, *the* with, 502, **ESLc**
Proper noun, GT-581
capitalization of, 202-204, **31b**
capitalization of substitutes, 204, **31b**
defined, 3, **1a**
possessives of, 167, **26a**
Pros and cons, in argument, 365-366, **39b;** 383, **39f**
Prose
choppy, 230-231, **33a**
cluttered, 221-225, **32d**
exclamation points in, 164, **25h**
monotonous, 230-232, **33a**
precise, 214-217, **32b**
prejudicial language in, 372, **39e**
streamlining, 246-253, **33c**
vigorous, 217-221, **32c**
Prosecute, persecute, G-542
Protagonist, GT-581
Punctuation. *See also* Apostrophe; Brackets; Colon; Comma; Dash; Ellipsis marks; Exclamation point; Hyphen and hyphenation; Parentheses; Period; Question mark; Quotation marks; Semicolon; Slash
abbreviations and, 196-197, **30b**
following titles (works), 183, **28a**
of interrupter, 158, **24e**
revision for, 341-343, **37e**
Purpose, 273-274, **35a**
argument, 273-274, **35a**
entertainment, 273-274, **35a**
impression, 273-274, **35a**
information, 273-274, **35a**
of novels, short stories, plays, 400-401, **40b**
of poetry, 401-403, **40b**
for research papers, 398-403, **40b**
of writer, GT-581

Qualifier, GT-581
as misplaced words, 99, **16b**
Quatrain, GT-581
Question. *See also* Tag questions
capitalization in elliptical, 202, **31a**
and conflict, 364-365, **39b**
verb forms and, 517, **ESLn**
direct, 163, **25d**
elliptical, 163, **25d**
about evidence, 371-381, **39e**
to gather evidence in argument, 368-369, **39d**
and ideas for writing, 266-269, **34g**
in introductory paragraphs, 314, **36b**
journalistic, GT-573
as purpose for research paper, 398, **40b**
tag, 519-521, **ESLp;** GT-586
verb forms and, 517, **ESLn**
Question/answer, GT-581
in paragraph development, 303-304, **36a**
Question mark
defined, 160, **25**
as end punctuation, 162-163, **25d**
quotation marks with, 174, **27b**
within sentences, 163, **25e**
Quotation. *See* also Ellipsis marks
brackets around insertions in direct, 158-159, **124g**
capitalization in, 201, **31a**
colons with, 152, **23d**
commas with, 141-142, **21h;** 144, **21j**
crediting, 422-423, **40h**
direct, 171-172, **27a;** GT-564
ending composition with, 318, **36c**
indirect, 172, **27a;** GT-568
in introductory paragraphs, 314, **36b**
and paraphrases, 427, **40i**
secondhand, 435, **41a**

Quotation marks
with colon, 173-174, **27b**
with dash, 174, **27b**
in dialogue, 175, **27c**
to enclose direct quotations, 171-172, **27a**
evidence and, 370, **39d**
with exclamation point, 174, **27b**
inappropriate use of, 176-177, **27f**
with period and comma, 173, **27b**
with question marks, 174, **27b**
with semicolon, 173-174, **27b**
single, 172, **27a;** 174, **27b**
for sources, 426-427, **40i**
for titles, 175-176, **27d;** 181, **28a**
for words as words, 184, **28b**
around words used in special ways, 176, **27e**
Quote, quotation, G-542

Race, discriminatory language and, 372, **39e**
Radio programs
italics for titles in series, 182, **28a**
MLA documentation for, 442, **41a**
Raise, rise, 73, **11c;** G-542
RAM, GT-558
Ranks (of persons)
abbreviations of, 193-194, **30a**
capitalization of, 204-205, **31c**
Reading, writing topics found through, 270-271, **34i**
Real, really, G-543
Rear, raise, G-543
Reasoning. *See* Logical reasoning
Reason is because, reason is that, G-543
Reciprocal pronoun, 11, **2e;** GT-582
Recommendations, in concluding paragraphs, 316-317, **36c**
Red herring, GT-582
relevance of, 375, **39e**
Redundancies, 224-225, **32d**
Reference area (library)
almanacs and yearbooks in, 408, **40c**
atlases and gazetteers in, 408, **40c**
biographies in, 407, **40c**
catalogs in, 408-412, **40c**
computers and, 412, **40c;** 416-417, **40c**
encyclopedias in, 406-407, **40c**
general works in, 405, **40c**
handbooks and manuals in, 407-408, **40c**
indexes and abstracts in, 412-417, **40c**
Reference notations, abbreviations of, 195, **30a**
References, parentheses for, 158, **24f**
References section, APA documentation for, 470. *See also* Documentation
Reflexive pronoun, 8, **2a;** 86, **14;** GT-582. *See also* Emphatic pronoun
Refutation, of argument, 382, **39f**
Regular verb, 510, **ESLh;** GT-582
forms of, 17, 18, **4a**
Relationships
and conflict, 365, **39b**
and topics for writing, 269, **34h**
Relative pronoun, 9-10, **2c;** GT-582
in elliptical clauses, 50, **7d**
as subjects, 67, **10e**
Relevance
ad hominem attacks and, 374-375, **39e**
of appeal to popularity, 374, **39e**
of evidence, 373-375, **39e**
red herring and, 375, **39e**
straw man position and, 375, **39e**
of testimonial, 374, **39e**
Religions, pre-noun modifiers and, 507, **ESLe**
Religious books, italics and, 183, **28a**
Religious terms, capitalization of, 203, **31b**
Religious titles, abbreviating, 194, **30a**
Remote pronoun reference, 78, **12f**
Repetition, sound and rhythm, 257, **33e**
Reports, italics for titles, 182, **28a**
Republished works, MLA documentation for, 440, **41a**
Research, quality of, 373, **39e**
Research paper
APA documentation for, 469-477, **41d;** 477-486, **41e**
bibliography for, 403, **40c**
coherence of, 429-430, **40j**

conclusion for, 432, **40j**
documentation and, 433–486, **41**
drafting of, 428–432, **40j**
introduction for, 429, **40j**
lead-ins to introduce sources, 431–432, **40j**
library work for, 403–417, **40c**
locating material for, 418–419, **40e**
MLA documentation style for, 434–468, **41a, 41b, 41c**
note-taking for, 421–422, **40g**
organization of, 428–429, **40j**
plagiarism in, 422–426, **40h**
purpose of, 398–403, **40b**
sample in APA style, 478–486, **41e**
sample in MLA style, 447–456, **41b**
sources used in, 404, **40c**
subject of, 394–397, **40a**
typing, 445–446, **41a;** 477, **41d**
using sources for, 426–428, **40i**
working bibliography for, 417–418, **40d**
working outline for, 419–422, **40f**
Respectfully, respectively, G-543
Restrictive element, GT-582
and appositives, 134–135, **21c**
and proper nouns, 133–134, **21c**
clauses, 132–133, **21c**
and introductory words, 133, **21c**
Revision. *See also* Drafting; Sentence revision
for coherence, 328–336, **37c**
computers and, 323, **37;** 338, **37d**
for development, 326–328, **37b**
for grammar, 339–341, **34e**
manuscript preparation, 344–347, **37g**
for mechanics, 341–343, **37e**
of paragraphs, 297, **36a**
process of, 322–323, **37**
proofreading, 347, **37g**
for punctuation, 341–343, **37e**
for spelling, 342–343, **37e**
for style, 336–338, **37d**
for thesis, 325, **37a;** 326–327, **37b**
of titles, 343–344, **37f**
for unity, 323–326, **37a**
Rhetoric, GT-582
Rhythm, of poem, 402, **40b.** *See also* Sound and rhythm
Right, G-543
Rogerian structure of argument, 386–387, **39f**
areas of agreement in, 386–387, **39f**
opponent's position in, 386, **39f**
resolution in, 387, **39f**
statement of problem in, 386, **39f**
writer's position in, 386, **39f**
Role, of writer, 278, **35c**
Root, GT-582. *See also* Base word
Rough draft, thesis and, 281, **35d.** *See also* Drafting
Rough outline, 292–293, **35f**
Run-on (run-together) sentence. *See* Fused sentences

-s form, 17, **4a**
Salutations
capitalization in, 201, **31a**
colons after, 153, **23f**
Same, G-543
Satire, GT-583
Save (computers), GT-558
Scarcely, G-543
Scarcely when, scarcely than, G-543
Scholarly journal, MLA documentation for, 441, **41a**
Script, 345, **37g**
Scroll (computers), GT-558
Sculpture, italics for titles, 183, **28a**
Search and replace, GT-559
Seasons, capitalization and, 208, **31h**
Secondary sources, 404, **40c**
Second draft, 353–355, **38.** *See also* Drafting; Revision
Second person
formality of voice, 213, **32a**
as voice, 277–278, **35h**
-sede, -ceed, and -cede[r], 495, **SPb**
Seldom, seldom ever, G-544
Self-, as prefix, 189, **29c**
-self, -selves, 8, **2a**
Semicolon
clause connection with, 232–233, **33a**
comma splices or fused sentences revised with, 58–60, **9b**
for equality of ideas, 232–233, **33a**
inappropriate, 149, **22e**

between independent clauses joined by coordinating conjunctions, 147–148, **22c**
between independent clauses not joined by coordinating conjunctions, 145–146, **22a**
between independent clauses joined by transitional expressions, 146–147, **22b**
between items in series with internal punctuation, 148–149, **22d**
for joining independent clauses, 235, **33a**
quotation marks with, 173–174, **27b**
Sentence, GT-583. *See also* Compound sentences; Interrupters; Sentence revision; Sentence style
active vs. passive, 247–249, **33c**
balanced, 245–246, **33b;** GT-553
capitalization in, 200–201, **31a**
cleft, GT-555
climactic, 244–245, **33b;** GT-555
colons before appositives in, 151, **23b**
colons introducing lists in, 150–151, **23a**
comma splices and fused sentences revised by two, 60, **9d**
complex, 51, **7e;** GT-557
compound, 51, **7e;** GT-557
compound-complex, 51–52, **7e;** GT-557
connection with paragraphs, 332–336, **37c**
cumulative, 243–244, **33b;** GT-562
dashes to emphasize elements, 156–157, **24c**
defined, 40, **7**
fragments of, 54, **8**
fused, 57–61, **9;** GT-566
inappropriate commas in, 142–143, **21j**
kind of, 50–52, **7e**
as links, 334–335, **37c**
loose, 242–243, **33b;** GT-573–574
negative, 518–519, **ESLo**
pattern of, 40–44, **7a;** 230, **33a**
periodic, 242–243, **33b;** GT-578
question marks within, 163, **25e**
shared elements of, 236–238, **33a**
simple, 50–51, **7e;** GT-583
structure of, 337–338, **37d**
tag questions for, 519–521, **ESLp**
topic, 297–298, **36a;** 327, **37b;** GT-586
Sentence modifier, GT-583
Sentence outline, 293, **35f**
Sentence revision. *See also* Revision
case of nouns and pronouns, 85–90, **14**
comma splices, 57–61, **9**
dangling modifiers, 95, 96–98, **16**
fused sentences, 57–61, **9**
grammar errors and, 339–340, **37e**
incomplete constructions, 116–119, **19**
misplaced modifiers, 95–96, 99–101, **16**
nonstandard adjective and adverb forms, 91–94, **15**
nonstandard verb forms, 71–73, **11**
parallelism, 120–125, **20**
pronoun-antecedent agreement, 80–84, **13**
pronoun reference, 74–79, **12**
and revision, 337–338, **37d**
sentence fragments, 54–56, **8**
shifts, 102–111, **17**
split construction, 112–115, **18**
subject-verb agreement, 62–70, **10**
Sentence structure. *See also* Sentence
faulty predictions, 109–111, **17h**
mixed constructions, 109–111, **17h**
reason or definition, 109, **17h**
and revision, 337–338, **37d;** 339–340, **37e**
shifts in, 109–111, **17h**
Sentence style
emphasis in, 242–246, **33b**
figures of speech and, 254–255, **33d**
sound and rhythm and, 255–258, **33e**
streamlining in, 246–253, **33c**
variety, 230–242, **33a**

Series
  commas between items in, 135–136, **21d**
  elliptical questions in, 163, **25d**
  parallelism in, 123–125, **20b**
  semicolons in, 148–149, **22d**
Server (computers), GT-559
Set, sit, 73, **11c;** G-544
Setting, 401, **40b;** GT-583
Sexism, 227, **32e**
Sexist language, 227–229, **32e**
  generic nouns and, 83, **13d**
  indefinite pronouns and, 82–83, **13c**
Shall, will, G-544
Shape, adjectives of, 506, **ESLe**
Shift, GT-583
  with *can/could* or *will/would,* 102–103, **17a**
  defined, 102, **17**
  between direct and indirect discourse, 109, **17g**
  in infinitives and participles, 105–107, **17b**
  in mood, 107, **17c**
  in number, 108, **17e**
  in person, 108–109, **17f**
  in sentence structure, 109–111, **17h**
  in verb tenses, 102–105, **17a**
  in voice, 107–108, **17d**
Short stories, interpreting, 400–401, **40b**
Should, would, G-544
Should have, should of, G-544
Silent *e*
  with long vowels, 490–491, **SPb**
  with suffixes, 491–492, **SPb**
Simile, 254, **33d;** GT-583
Simple nouns, 4, **1b**
Simple sentence, 50–51, **7e;** GT-583
Simple subject, 40, **7**
Simple tenses, shifts in sequence of, 102–103, **17a**
Singular nouns, 4, **1b;** 108, **17e**
Singular verbs, indefinite pronouns and, 65, **10d**
Situation, G-545
Size, adjectives of, 506, **ESLe**
Slang, 279, **35c;** GT-584
  informality of, 213, **32a**
  quotation marks and, 177, **27g**
Slash
  between alternatives, 191–192, **29f**
  for combinations, 192, **29g**
  for fractions, 192, **29i**
  between lines of poetry, 192, **29h**
Slow, slowly, G-545
So, so that, G-545
So, very, G-545
Software programs. *See* Computers
Some, G-545
Someplace, somewhere, G-545
Sometime, sometimes, G-545
Sonnet, GT-584
Sort (computers), GT-559
Sort of, G-546
Sound and rhythm
  of poem, 402, **40b**
  style and, 255–258, **33e**
Sounds, italics for, 185, **28e**
Source of interest, in introductory paragraphs, 312, **36b**
Sources. *See also* Electronic citations; Online sources; Quotation marks
  APA documentation style, 469–477, **41d;** 478–486, **41e**
  crediting, 422–426, **40h**
  lead-ins to introduce, 431–432, **40j**
  in library, 404, **40c**
  MLA documentation style, 387–392, **39g;** 434–446, **41a**
  quoting, 370, **39d**
  using, 426–428, **40i**
  working bibliography and, 417–418, **40d**
Spacing, 346–347, **37g**
Spatial order of details, 306, **36a;** GT-584
Speaker, in poem, 401, **40b**
Specifiers, 505, **ESLe**
Spelling
  -cede, -ceed[r], and -sede[r], 495, **SPb**
  computers and, 342–343, **37e**
  dictionary and, 488–489, **SPa**
  doubled consonants with verbs, 492–493, **SPb**
  errors in, 342–343, **37e**

frequently misspelled words, 495–498, **SPc**
i before *e,* 494, **SPb**
improving, 488–490, **SPa**
inconsistencies of English, 487–488, **SP**
practicing, 489, **SPa**
pronunciation and, 488, **SP;** 489, **SPa**
silent *e* with long vowels, 490–491, **SPb**
silent *e* with suffixes, 491–492, **SPb**
word list for, 489–490, **SPa**
Split constructions, 112–115, **18**
Split infinitive, 114–115, **18d;** GT-584
Squinting modifiers, 100–101, **16b;** GT-584
Stance, of writer, 278, **35c**
Statement of fact, in argument, 382, **39f**
State names
abbreviations of, 195–196, **30a**
Postal Service abbreviations, 197, **30b**
Stationary, stationery, G-546
Stereotypes, 226–227, **32e**
Stories, MLA documentation for, 439, **41a**
Strategies, combination in introductory paragraphs, 315, **36b**
Straw man, GT-584
relevance of evidence and, 375, **39e**
Streamlining prose
clear subject-verb connection, 251–253, **33c**
empty verbs and nominalizations, 246–247, **33c**
excessive verb forms, 250–251, **33c**
unnecessary *that, who,* and *which* clauses, 249, **33c**
weak passives, 247–249, **33c**
Structure, of argument, 381–387, **39f**
Structured outline, 293–295, **35f**
Style. *See also* APA (American Psychological Association) style; MLA (Modern Language Association) style
cluttered prose, 221–225, **32d**
discriminatory language, 226–229, **32e**
levels of formality, 212–214, **32a**
precise prose, 214–217, **32b**
revision for, 336–338, **37d**
sentence, 230–258, **33**
vigorous prose, 218–221, **32c**
word choice and, 212–229, **32;** 336–337, **37d**
Subject, GT-584. *See also* Subject-verb agreement
complete, 40, **7**
connection with verb, 251–253, **33c**
in dependent clauses, 45, **7c**
ending in *-ics,* 69–70, **10k**
indefinite pronouns as, 65–67, **10d**
joined by *and,* 64, **10b**
joined by *or/nor,* 65, **10c**
of linking verbs, 67, **10f**
noun clauses as, 48–49, **7c**
relative pronouns as, 67, **10e**
shared, 236, **33a**
simple, 40, **7**
in split constructions, 112–113, **18a**
words as, 70, **10l**
Subject complement, GT-584–585
linking verb and, 43, **7a**
noun clauses as, 49, **7c**
Subject entry, 409, **40c**
Subjective case, after verb *be,* 88, **14b**
Subject line, colons after, 153, **23f**
Subject of research paper. *See also* Topics
assignment and, 395, **40a**
and audience, 395, **40a**
computers and, 397, **40b**
difficulty of, 395, **40a**
excessively broad, 396, **40a**
key words for, 396, **40a**
material available on, 396, **40a**
sources for finding, 395–396, **40a**
Subject-verb agreement
with collective nouns and amounts as subjects, 68–69, **10h**
defined, 62, **10**
with foreign nouns as subjects, 69; **10j**
with indefinite pronouns as subjects, 65–67, **10d**
with intervening words between subject and verb, 64, **10a**

with relative pronouns as subjects, 67, **10e**
with subjects ending in *-ics,* 69–70, **10k**
with subjects joined by *and,* 64–65, **10b**
with subjects joined by *or/nor,* 65, **10c**
with subjects of linking verbs, 67, **10f**
with subjects that follow verbs, 67–68, **10g**
with titles as subjects, 69, **10i**
with "words" as subjects, 70, **10l**
Subjunctive mood, 25–26, **4f;** GT-585
Subordinate clause. *See* Dependent clause; Subordination
Subordinating conjunction, 35–36, **6b;** GT-585
inappropriate use of commas with, 143–144, **21j**
relationships and, 332, **37c**
Subordinating word, 55, **8a**
Subordination, GT-585. *See also* Dependent (subordinate) clause
adjective clauses, 239, **33a**
with adverb clauses, 238, **33a**
with appositives, 240–242, **33a**
for combining ideas and structures, 232, **33a**
verbal phrases, 239–240, **33a**
Subtitles, colons to separate from titles, 152, **23e**
Such a, G-546
Suffixes, adverbs and, 14, **3b;** GT-585. *See also* Doubled consonants
Summarizing and summary
in concluding paragraphs, 317, **36c**
of passage, 428, **40i**
words for, 217, **32b**
Superlative adjectives, 15–16, **3c;** 506, **ESLe**
Superlative adverbs, 15–16, **3c**
Superlative degree, GT-585–586. *See also* Comparative degree
inappropriate, 92–94, **15b**
Suppose to, supposed to, G-546
Sure, G-546
Sure to, sure and, G-546
Surplus words. *See* Redundancies
Survey, and evidence, 368–369, **39d**
Symbol, GT-586
in poem, 402, **40b**
Symmetry. *See* Balanced sentence
Symphonies, italics for titles, 182, **28a**
Synonym, 278, **35c;** GT-586
Syntax, GT-586

Tables, parentheses for references to, 158, **24f**
Tag questions, 519–521, **ESLp;** GT-586
question marks after, 163, **25d**
set off with commas, 140, **21g**
Take, bring, G-529
Teacher, as audience, 275–276, **35b**
Technical writing, numbers to begin sentences in, 199, **30e**
Television programs
APA documentation style for, 476, **41d**
italics for series titles, 182, **28a**
MLA documentation for, 442, **41a**
Tense, 20–22, **4c;** 510, **ESLh;** GT-586. *See also* Conjugation; Shift
future, 21, **4c**
future perfect, 22, **4d**
future progressive, 22, **4d**
past, 21, **4c**
past perfect, 22, **4d**
past progressive, 22, **4d**
perfect, 21–22, **4c;** 103, **17a;** GT-578
perfect progressive forms, 23, **4d**
present, 21, **4c**
present perfect, 22, **4d**
present progressive, 22, **4d**
simple, 21, **4c;** 102–103, **17a**
and subject-verb agreement, 62–63, **10**
Terms, computer, GT-557–559
Territories, abbreviations of, 195–196, **30a**
Testimonial, irrelevant, 374, **39e**
Testimonies, and topics for writing, 269, **34h**
Than, then, G-546
That
in clauses, 26–27, **4f**
omitted, 117–118, **19b**

unnecessary clauses with, 249, **33c**
That, which, G-546
That there, this here, G-547
The, as definite article, 501–502, **ESLc**
Their, there, they're, G-546
Theirselves, themselves, G-547
Them, those, G-547
Theme, GT-586
Thesaurus, computer searches and, 408, **40c**
These kinds of, this kind of, G-547
Thesis, GT-586. *See also* Topics
of argument, 367–368, **39c;** 381, **39f**
clarity of, 280, **35d**
as complete idea, 279, **35d**
in concluding paragraphs, 316, **36c**
development of, 326–327, **37b**
discovery structure of argument and, 384–385, **39f**
in introductory paragraph, 308–309, **36b**
and length of composition, 280–281, **35d**
and purpose, 280, **35d**
revision of, 325, **37a;** 326–327, **37b**
supportability of, 281–283, **35d**
topic sentences and, 297–298, **36a**
unity of, 325, **37a**
They, indefinite, 76, **12c**
Thinking skills. *See* Brainstorming; Critical thinking; Deduction; Induction
Third draft, 355–357, **38.** *See also* Drafting
Third person
formality of voice, 213, **32a**
as voice, 277, **35c**
This here, that there, G-547
This kind of, these kinds of, G-547
Thusly, G-547
Till, until, G-547
Time. *See* Tense
Title entry, 409, **40c**
Title page, 347, 348, **37g**
Titles (of persons), 141, **21h**
abbreviations of, 193–194, **30a**
capitalization of, 204–205, **31c**
civil and military abbreviations, 194, **30a**
of honor, capitalization of, 204–205, **31c**
religious, 194, **30a**
Titles (of works)
as antecedents, 78–79, **12g**
APA documentation style for, 471–472, 473–477, **41d**
colons to separate from subtitles, 152, **23e**
italics (underlining) for, 175–176, **27d;** 181–184, **28a**
MLA documentation style for, 438, 439–446, **41a**
punctuation following, 183, **28a**
quotation marks in, 175–176, **27d**
revision of, 343–344, **37e**
as subjects, 69, **10i**
underlining, 175, **27d**
To, too, G-547
Tone, in poem, 401, **40b**
Topic outline, 293, **35f**
Topics. *See also* Classical topics; Ideas for writing; Subject of research paper
for argument, 363–364, **39a**
classical, GT-554
Topic sentence, 297–298, **36a;** GT-586
at beginning of paragraph, 298, **36a**
at end of paragraphs, 298, **36a**
revision and, 327, **37b**
unstated, 298, **36a**
Toward, towards, G-547
Tradition, relevance of evidence and, 373, **39e**
Tragedy, GT-587
Tragic flaw, GT-587
Transitional expression, 59–60, **9b;** 233–234, **33a;** GT-587
relationships and, 332–336, **37c**
semicolons with, 146–147, **22b**
set off with commas, 138–139, **21f**
Transitive verb, 41–43, **7a;** GT-587
indirect object and, 42, **7a**
Translations, MLA documentation for, 440, **41a**
Trite expressions, quotation marks and, 177, **27g.** *See also* Clichs
Try to, try and, G-547

-type, G-548
Type, type of, G-548
Typing
with APA style, 477, **41e**
final manuscript, 345, **37g;** 346, **37g**
with MLA style, 445-446, **41a**

Underlining. *See* Italics (underlining)
Uninterested, disinterested, G-534
Unique, G-548
Unisex language. *See* Sexist language
Unity, revision for, 323-326, **37a**
Unstated topic sentences, 298, **36a**
Until, till, G-547
Up, G-548
Upload (computers), GT-559
Use, utilize, 73, **11c;** G-548
Use to, used to, G-548

Variety, in sentence style, 230-232, **33a**
Vehicles, italics for, 185, **28e**
Verb, GT-587. *See also* Adverb; Constructions; Subject-verb agreement; Verbal; Verb phrase
active-voice, 508, **ESLg**
actor, infinitive, and, 515, **ESLm**
auxiliary, GT-533
basic forms of, 17-18, **4a;** 71, **11a**
chains of, 514-517, **ESLm**
confused with similar words, 73, **11c**
connection with subject, 251-253, **33c**
defined, 17, **4**
empty, 246-247, **33c**
excessive forms of, 250-251, **33c**
finite, GT-565
gerund as, GT-566
helping, GT-567. *See also* Auxiliary verb
hyphens in compound, 187-188, **29a**
indefinite pronouns as subjects and plural, 66, **10d**
and infinitive, 515, **ESLm**
intransitive, 41, **7a;** GT-569
irregular, 17, 18, **4a;** 71-72, **11a;** GT-569-573
linking, 43-44, **7a;** GT-573
main, 18, **4b**
mood of, 19, **4b;** 24-27, **4f**
nonstandard forms, 71-73, **11**
past tense, 510, **ESLh**
in predicate nominative, 43, **7a**
present tense, 510, **ESLh**
principal parts of, 17-18, **4a;** GT-580
progressive forms of, GT-581
questions and, 517, **ESLn**
regular, 17, 18, **4a;** GT-582
shifts in tenses of, 102-105, **17a**
spelling and, 492-493, **SPb**
subjects of linking, 67, **10f**
tense of, 20-22, **4c**
transitive, 41-43, **7a;** GT-587
voice of, 23-24, **4e**
Verbal, 105-106, **17b;** GT-588. *See also* Verb
as adjectives, 29, **5a**
as adverbs, 29, **5a**
commas with, 130-131, **21b**
defined, 28, **5**
gerunds, 30, **5c**
infinitives, 28-29, **5a**
as nouns, 29, **5a**
participles, 29-30, **5b**
Verbal, oral, G-541
Verbal phrase, 239-240, **33a**
absolute, 30-31, **5d**
commas with, 130-131, **21b**
dangling, 96-98, **16a**
defined, 28, **5**
gerund phrases, 30, **5c**
participial phrases, 29-30, **5a**
Verb endings, 72-73, **11b**
Verb phrase, 113-114, **18c;** GT-588
active-voice, 508-509, **ESLg**
auxiliaries and, 18-20, **4b**
defined, 17, **4**
passive-voice, 512-513, **ESLk**
principal parts of, 17-18, **4a**
Very, so, G-545
Videotapes, MLA documentation for, 442, **41a**
Vocabulary
denotation and connotation of, 215, **32b**
word choice and, 212-213, **31a**

Voice, 23–24, **4e;** GT-588; 276–279, **35c.** *See also* Conjugation
active, 23, **4e**
consistency of, 214, **32a;** 278–279, **35c**
for formal paper, 277, **35c;** GT-551
formal or informal, 212–214, **32a**
for informal paper, 277–278, **35c**
passive, 23–24, **4e;** 42, **7a;** GT-578
shifts in, 107–108, **17d**
synonyms and, 278, **35c**

Wait for, wait on, G-549
Warning, in concluding paragraphs, 318–319, **36c**
Way, ways, G-549
Weak passives, 247–249, **33c**
Well, good, G-536
Whether, if, G-537
Which, unnecessary clauses with, 249, **33c**
Which, that, G-546
Which, who, G-549
Who
possessive form of, 169, **26d**
unnecessary clauses with, 249, **33c**
Who's, as possessive, 170, **26d**
Who's, whose, G-549
Whoever/whomever, case and, 88–89, **14c**
Who/whom, case and, 88–89, **14c**
Will, shall, G-544
Will/would, 103–104, **17a**
Windows (computers), GT-559
Women, discriminatory language and, 372, **39e**
Word division, hyphens for, 191, **29e**
Word list, for spelling, 489–490, **SPa**
Word processor. *See* Computers
Words. *See also* Foreign languages
abbreviation vs. full, 193–196, **30a**
abstract, 217, **32b**
choice of, 212–229, **32;** 336–337, **37d**
combinations, 192, **29g**
commas in place of omitted, 137, **21e**
compound, 5, **1b;** 167, **26a;** 187–188, **29a**
concrete, 217, **32b**
dense noun phrases, 225, **32d**
discriminatory language, 226–229, **32e**
euphemisms, 220–221, **32c**
formal, 212–214, **32a**
forms of, 340–341, **37e**
frequently misspelled, 495–497, **SPc**
general, 215–217, **32b**
general/specific, GT-566
gobbledygook, 221–223, **32d**
hyphens for identical, 190, **29d**
misplaced, 99, **16b**
mixed numerals and, 199, **30e**
numbers (numerals) expressed in, 198–199, **30d**
specific, 215–217, **32b**
as subjects, 70, **10l**
surplus (redundancies), 224–225, **32d**
used as words, 168–169, **26c**
used in special ways, 176, **27e**
Word wrap (computers), GT-559
Working outline, 419–420, **40f**
Works Cited lists, MLA documentation for, 436–446, **41a.** *See also* Bibliographies; Documentation; Sources
Would, should, G-544
Would have, G-549
Would have, would of, G-549
Writing, decisions about, 273–294, **35.** *See also* Ideas for writing; Revision; Sentence style; Technical writing; Vocabulary; Words
Written material, capitalization of titles, 206–207, **31e**

Yearbooks, 408, **40c**
You
formality of voice and, 213, **32a**
indefinite, 76, **12c**
Your, you're, G-549

Zip codes, commas in, 141, **21h**

Guide to the Plan of the Book

PART I Review of the Basics

1 **Nouns** noun 2
- 1a Proper and Common Nouns 3
- 1b Singular and Plural Nouns 4
- 1c Possessive Nouns 5

2 **Pronouns** pron 6
- 2a Personal Pronouns 7
- 2b Demonstrative Pronouns 8
- 2c Relative Pronouns 9
- 2d Interrogative Pronouns 10
- 2e Indefinite Pronouns 10

3 **Adjectives and Adverbs** adj/adv 12
- 3a Adjectives 12
- 3b Adverbs 13
- 3c Adjective and Adverb Forms 15

4 **Verbs and Verb Phrases** vb 17
- 4a Basic Forms 17
- 4b Auxiliaries and Verb Phrases 18
- 4c Tense 20
- 4d Progressive Forms 22
- 4e Voice 23
- 4f Mood 24

5 **Verbals and Verbal Phrases** vbl 28
- 5a Infinitives and Infinitive Phrases 28
- 5b Participles and Participial Phrases 29
- 5c Gerunds and Gerund Phrases 30
- 5d Absolute Verbal Phrases 30

6 **Function Words** func 32
- 6a Prepositions and Prepositional Phrases 32
- 6b Conjunctions 33
- 6c Determiners 37
- 6d Expletives 38

7 **Clauses and Sentences** sent 40
- 7a Clause Patterns 40
- 7b Independent Clauses 45
- 7c Dependent Clauses 45
- 7d Elliptical Clauses 50
- 7e Kinds of Sentences 50

ART II Structural and Grammatical Problems

8 **Sentence Fragments** frag 54
- 8a Dependent Clause Fragments 55
- 8b Phrase Fragments 56

Comma Splices and Fused Sentences cs/fs 57
- 9a Revision with a Comma and a Coordinating Conjunction 58
- 9b Revision with a Semicolon 58
- 9c Revision with a Colon 60
- 9d Revision by Creating Two Sentences 60
- 9e Revision with a Dependent Clause or Phrase 60

10 **Subject-Verb Agreement** s–v agr 62
- 10a Intervening Words between Subject and Verb 64
- 10b Subjects Joined by *And* 64
- 10c Subjects Joined by *Or/Nor* 65
- 10d Indefinite Pronouns as Subjects 65
- 10e Relative Pronouns as Subjects 67
- 10f Subjects of Linking Verbs 67
- 10g Subjects That Follow Verbs 67
- 10h Collective Nouns and Amounts as Subjects 68
- 10i Titles as Subjects 69
- 10j Foreign Nouns as Subjects 69
- 10k Subjects Ending in *-ics* 69
- 10l "Words" as Subjects 70

11 **Nonstandard Verb Forms** vb form 71
- 11a Nonstandard Principal Parts 71
- 11b Dropped *-s/-es* and *-d/-ed* Verb Endings 72
- 11c Verbs Confused with Similar Words 73

12 **Pronoun Reference** ref 74
- 12a Implied Reference 74
- 12b Broad Reference 75
- 12c Indefinite *You, They*, and *It* 76
- 12d Ambiguous Reference 77
- 12e Mixed Uses of *It* 77
- 12f Remote Reference 78
- 12g Titles and Headings as Antecedents 78

13 **Pronoun–Antecedent Agreement** pn agr 80
- 13a Antecedents Joined by *And* 81
- 13b Antecedents Joined by *Or/Nor* 81
- 13c Indefinite Pronouns and Sexist Language 82
- 13d Generic Nouns and Sexist Language 83

13e Collective Nouns As Antecedents 83

14 Case of Nouns and Pronouns case 85

14a Case in Compound Construction 86

14b Pronoun Case after *Be* 87

14c *Who/Whom* and *Whoever/Whomever* 88

14d Case in Elliptical Clauses 89

14e Possessive Case with Gerunds 89

15 Nonstandard Adjective and Adverb Forms adj/adv forms 91

15a Confusion of Adjectives and Adverbs 91

15b Inappropriate Comparative and Superlative Forms 92

15c Inappropriate Demonstratives 94

16 Dangling and Misplaced Modifiers dm/mm 95

16a Dangling Modifiers 96

16b Misplaced Modifiers 99

17 Shifts shft 102

17a Shifts in Tense Sequence 102

17b Shifts in Infinitives and Participles 105

17c Shifts in Mood 107

17d Shifts in Voice 107

17e Shifts in Number 108

17f Shifts in Person 108

17g Shifts between Direct and Indirect Disclosure 109

17h Mixed Constructions or Faulty Predications 109

18 Split Constructions split 112

18a Split Subjects and Verbs 112

18b Split Verbs and Complements 113

18c Split Verbs 113

18d Split Infinitives 114

19 Incomplete Constructions inc 116

19a Omissions in Compound Constructions 117

19b Omitted *That* 117

19c Incomplete Comparisons 118

20 Parallelism // 120

20a Parallelism in Compound Structures 121

20b Parallelism in Series, Lists, and Outlines 123

PART III Punctuation and Mechanics

21 Commas , 128

21a Commas between Independent Clauses Joined by Coordinating Conjunctions 128

21b Commas after Introductory Prepositional Phrases, Verbals, and Dependent Clauses 129

21c Commas to Set Off Nonrestrictive Elements 132

21d Commas between Items in a Series and between Coordinate Adjectives 135

21e Commas in Place of Omitted Words 137

21f Commas to Set Off Parenthetical, Transitional, and Contrastive Elements 137

21g Commas to Set Off Interjections, Words in Direct Address, and Tag Questions 139

21h Commas in Special Contexts: in Dates, Places, Addresses; in Numbers; with Titles of Individuals; with Quotation Marks 140

21i Commas to Ensure Intended Reading 142

21j Inappropriate Commas 142

22 Semicolons ; 145

22a Semicolons between Independent Clauses Not Joined by Coordinating Conjunctions 145

22b Semicolons between Independent Clauses Joined by Transitional Expressions 146

22c Semicolons between Independent Clauses Joined by Coordinating Conjunctions 147

22d Semicolons between Items in a Series with Internal Punctuation 148

22e Inappropriate Semicolons 149

23 Colons : 150

23a Colons before Lists 150

23b Colons before Appositives That End Sentences 151

23c Colons between Independent Clauses 151

23d Colons before Grammatically Independent Quotations 152
23e Colons between Titles and Subtitles 152
23f Colons in Correspondence 152
23g Colons with Numerical Elements 153
23h Inappropriate Colons 153

24 Dashes, Parentheses, and Brackets 155

Dashes — 155

24a Dashes to Set Off Appositives Containing Commas 155
24b Dashes to Set Off Nonrestrictive Modifiers Containing Commas 156
24c Dashes to Emphasize Sentence Elements 156
24d Dashes with Interrupters 157

Parentheses ( ) 157

24e Parentheses to Enclose Interrupters 157
24f Parentheses for References to Pages, Figures, Tables, and Chapters 158

Brackets [ ] 158

24g Brackets around Insertions in Direct Quotations 158
24h Brackets for Parentheses inside Parentheses 159

25 Periods, Question Marks, and Exclamation Points 160

Periods . 161

25a Periods as End Punctuation 161
25b Periods in Outlines and Displayed Lists 161
25c Inappropriate Periods 162

Question Marks ? 162

25d Question Marks as End Punctuation 162
25e Question Marks within Sentences 163

Exclamation Points ! 164

25f Exclamation Points in Dialogue 164
25g Exclamation Points with Interjections 164
25h Exclamation Points for Emphasis 164

26 Apostrophes ' 166

26a Apostrophes to Indicate Possession 166
26b Apostrophes to Create Contractions 168
26c Apostrophes to Indicate Plurals of Letters and Words Used as Words 168
26d Inappropriate Apostrophes 169

27 Quotation Marks and Ellipsis Marks 171

Quotation Marks " " 171

27a Quotation Marks to Enclose Direct Quotations 171
27b Quotation Marks with Other Punctuation Marks 173
27c Quotation Marks in Dialogue 175
27d Quotation Marks in Titles 175
27e Quotation Marks around Words Used in Special Ways 176
27f Inappropriate Quotation Marks 176

Ellipsis Marks . . . 177

27g Ellipsis Marks to Show Omissions 177
27h Ellipsis Marks to Show Interruption in Dialogue 180

28 Italics/Underlining ital 181

28a Italics/Underlining in Titles 181
28b Italics/Underlining for Words, Numbers, and Letters Used as Such 184
28c Italics/Underlining for Sounds 185
28d Italics/Underlining for Foreign Words 185
28e Italics/Underlining for Vehicles Designated by Proper Names 185
28f Italics/Underlining for Emphasis 186

29 Hyphens and Slashes 187

Hyphens - 187

29a Hyphens in Compound Nouns and Verbs 187
29b Hyphens in Compound Modifiers 188
29c Hyphens with Some Prefixes 189
29d Hyphens in Numbers 190

Guide to the Plan of the Book

29e Hyphens for Word Divisions at the Ends of Lines 191
Slashes / 191
29f Slashes between Alternatives 191
29g Slashes for Making Combinations 192
29h Slashes between Lines of Poetry 192
29i Slashes for Fractions 192
30 Abbreviations and Numbers 193
Abbreviations abbr 193
30a Abbreviations vs. Full Words 193
30b Punctuation and Capitalization in Abbreviations 196
Numbers num 197
30c Numbers Expressed in Numerals 197
30d Numbers Expressed in Words 198
30e Mixed Numerals and Words 199
31 Capital Letters cap 200
31a Capitalization of First Words 200
31b Capitalization of Proper Names and Proper Adjectives 202
31c Capitalization of Titles of Honor or Rank 204
31d Capitalization of Academic and Professional Degrees 205
31e Capitalization in Titles of Written Material and Artistic Works 206
31f Capitalization in Some Abbreviations 207
31g Capitalization of *I* and *O* 207
31h Inappropriate Capitals 207
PART IV Style
32 Word Choice wd style 212
32a Levels of Formality 212
32b Precise Prose 214
32c Vigorous Prose 217
32d Cluttered Prose 221
32e Discriminatory Language 226
33 Sentence Style sent style 230
33a Variety 230
33b Emphasis 242
33c Streamlining 246
33d Figures of Speech 254
33e Sound and Rhythm 255
PART V The Writing Process
34 The Search for Ideas search 260
34a Journals 260
34b Meditation 261
34c Brainstorming 262
34d Clustering 263
34e Freewriting 264
34f Ladders 265
34g Questions 266
34h Classical Topics 269
34i Reading and Listening 270
35 Decisions decide 273
35a Purpose 273
35b Audience 274
35c Voice 276
35d Thesis 279
35e Patterns 284
35f Outlines 291
36 Paragraphs draft 296
36a Body Paragraphs 297
36b Introductory Paragraphs 308
36c Concluding Paragraphs 315
37 Revision revise 322
37a Unity 323
37b Development 326
37c Coherence 328
37d Style 336
37e Grammar, Punctuation, and Mechanics 339
37f Titles 343
37g The Finished Paper 344
38 Composition in Progress comp 350
PART VI Special Writing Projects
39 Argument and Critical Thinking arg/crit 362
39a Subject 363
39b Conflict 364
39c Thesis 367
39d Kinds of Evidence 368
39e Evaluation of Evidence 371
39f Structure 381
39g Sample Argument 387
40 Research Papers in Progress res 394
40a Subject 394
40b Purpose 398
40c Preliminary Library Research 4[illegible]
40d Working Bibliography 417

Guide to the Plan of the Book

40e Locating Material 418
40f Working Outline 419
40g Note-taking 421
40h Plagiarism 422
40i Using Sources 426
40j Drafting the Paper 428

41 Research Papers and Documentation doc 433

41a MLA documentation 434
41b Sample Research Paper Using MLA Style—Answering a Question 447
41c Sample Research Paper Using MLA Style—Interpreting Literature 457
41d APA Documentation 469
41e Sample Research Using APA Style—Presenting an Argument 478

Appendix A **Spelling** sp 487

Appendix B: **English as a Second Language ESL 498**

Glossary of Usage usage 522

Glossary of Terms terms 550